FINANCIAL STATEMENT ANALYSIS

CFA® Program Curriculum
2023 • LEVEL 2 • VOLUME 2

WILEY

©2022 by CFA Institute. All rights reserved. This copyright covers material written expressly for this volume by the editor/s as well as the compilation itself. It does not cover the individual selections herein that first appeared elsewhere. Permission to reprint these has been obtained by CFA Institute for this edition only. Further reproductions by any means, electronic or mechanical, including photocopying and recording, or by any information storage or retrieval systems, must be arranged with the individual copyright holders noted.

CFA®, Chartered Financial Analyst®, AIMR-PPS®, and GIPS® are just a few of the trademarks owned by CFA Institute. To view a list of CFA Institute trademarks and the Guide for Use of CFA Institute Marks, please visit our website at www.cfainstitute.org.

This publication is designed to provide accurate and authoritative information in regard to the subject matter covered. It is sold with the understanding that the publisher is not engaged in rendering legal, accounting, or other professional service. If legal advice or other expert assistance is required, the services of a competent professional should be sought.

All trademarks, service marks, registered trademarks, and registered service marks are the property of their respective owners and are used herein for identification purposes only.

ISBN 978-1-953337-05-4 (paper)
ISBN 978-1-953337-30-6 (ebook)

2022

Please visit our website at
www.WileyGlobalFinance.com.

CONTENTS

How to Use the CFA Program Curriculum ix
    Errata ix
    Designing Your Personal Study Program ix
    CFA Institute Learning Ecosystem (LES) x
    Feedback x

Financial Statement Analysis

Learning Module 1   **Intercorporate Investments**   3
    Introduction 3
    Basic Corporate Investment Categories 4
    Investments In Financial Assets: IFRS 9 6
        Classification and Measurement 7
        Reclassification of Investments 9
    Investments In Associates And Joint Ventures 10
        Equity Method of Accounting: Basic Principles 11
    Amortization of Excess Purchase Price, Fair Value Option, and Impairment 14
        Amortization of Excess Purchase Price 16
        Fair Value Option 18
        Impairment 18
    Transactions with Associates and Disclosure 19
        Disclosure 22
        Issues for Analysts 23
    Acquisition Method 23
        Acquisition Method 25
        Impact of the Acquisition Method on Financial Statements, Post-Acquisition 27
    The Consolidation Process 30
        Business Combination with Less than 100% Acquisition 30
        Non-controlling (Minority) Interests: Balance Sheet 30
        Non-controlling (Minority) Interests: Income Statement 33
        Goodwill Impairment 34
    Financial Statement Presentation 36
    Variable Interest and Special Purpose Entities 39
        Securitization of Assets 41
    Additional Issues in Business Combinations That impair Comparability 43
        Contingent Assets and Liabilities 43
        Contingent Consideration 43
        In-Process R&D 44
        Restructuring Costs 44
    Summary 44
    Practice Problems 46
    Solutions 58

◎ indicates an optional segment

Learning Module 2	**Employee Compensation: Post-Employment and Share-Based**	**63**
	Introduction	64
	Pensions and Other Post-Employment Benefits	64
	Types of Post-Employment Benefit Plans	65
	Measuring a Defined Benefit Pension Plan's Obligations	67
	Financial Statement Reporting: Defined Contribution Pension Plans	69
	Defined Contribution Pension Plans	69
	Financial Statement Reporting of Pension Plans: Balance Sheet Reporting for Defined Benefit Pension Plans	69
	Balance Sheet Presentation	69
	Financial Statement Reporting: Periodic Pension Costs	70
	Effect of Assumptions and Actuarial Gain and Losses on Pensions	73
	Calculation of Defined Benefit Pension Obligation and Current Service Costs	75
	Disclosure of Assumptions	81
	Assumptions	82
	Disclosures: Net Pension Liability (or Asset) and Periodic Pension Costs	87
	Total Periodic Pension Costs	87
	Periodic Pension Costs Recognised in P&L vs. OCI	88
	Classification of Periodic Pension Costs Recognised in P&L	88
	Disclosures: Cash Flow Information	90
	Share-Based Compensation	92
	Stock Grants	95
	Stock Options	95
	Other Types of Share-Based Compensation	98
	Summary	*99*
	References	*101*
	Practice Problems	*102*
	Solutions	*113*
Learning Module 3	**Multinational Operations**	**119**
	Introduction	120
	Foreign Currency Transactions	121
	Disclosures Related to Foreign Currency Transaction Gains and Losses	128
	Translation of Foreign Currency Financial Statements	134
	Translation Conceptual Issues	134
	Translation Methods	138
	Foreign Currency Is the Functional Currency	140
	Parent's Presentation Currency Is the Functional Currency	141
	Translation of Retained Earnings	143
	Highly Inflationary Economies	145
	Illustration of Translation Methods	148
	Translation Analytical Issues	151
	Translation in an Hyperinflationary Economy	162
	Using Both Translation Methods	167
	Disclosures Related to Translation Methods	168
	Multinational Operations and a Company's Effective Tax Rate	174
	Additional Disclosures on the Effects of Foreign Currency	176
	Disclosures Related to Sales Growth	176
	Disclosures Related to Major Sources of Foreign Exchange Risk	179

◘ indicates an optional segment

Contents

	Summary	*181*
	Practice Problems	*184*
	Solutions	*197*
Learning Module 4	**Analysis of Financial Institutions**	**205**
	Introduction	205
	What Makes Financial Institutions Different?	206
	Global Organizations	209
	Individual Jurisdictions' Regulatory Authorities	212
	Analyzing a Bank: the CAMELS Approach	212
	The CAMELS Approach	213
	Analyzing a Bank: non-CAMELS Factors	230
	Banking-Specific Analytical Considerations Not Addressed by CAMELS	230
	Analytical Considerations Not Addressed by CAMELS That Are Also Relevant for Any Company	232
	Analyzing a Bank: Example of CAMELS Approach	234
	Capital Adequacy	235
	Asset Quality	237
	Management Capabilities	244
	Earnings	245
	Liquidity Position	251
	Sensitivity to Market Risk	253
	Overall CAMELS Assessment	255
	Analyzing Property and Casualty Insurance Companies	256
	Property and Casualty Insurance Companies	257
	Analyzing Life and Health Insurance Companies	265
	Life and Health Insurance Companies	266
	Summary	*272*
	Practice Problems	*274*
	Solutions	*282*
Learning Module 5	**Evaluating Quality of Financial Reports**	**289**
	Introduction	289
	Conceptual Framework	291
	Conceptual Framework for Assessing the Quality of Financial Reports	291
	Potential Problems	293
	Reported Amounts and Timing of Recognition	294
	Classification	296
	M&A Issues and Divergence from Economic Reality	300
	Financial Reporting that Diverges from Economic Reality Despite Compliance with Accounting Rules	302
	General Steps of Evaluation	305
	General Steps to Evaluate the Quality of Financial Reports	306
	Quantitative Tools to Assess the Likelihood of Misreporting	307
	Beneish Model	307
	Other Quantitative Models	310
	Limitations of Quantitative Models	310
	Earnings Quality Indicators	310

○ indicates an optional segment

	Indicators of Earnings Quality	311
	Earnings Persistence and Related Measures of Accruals	314
	Mean Reversion in Earnings	318
	Beating Benchmarks	320
	External Indicators of Poor-Quality Earnings	320
	Revenue Recognition Case: Sunbeam Corporation	320
	Revenue Recognition Case: Sunbeam Corporation	321
	Revenue Recognition Case: MicroStrategy, Inc.	325
	Multiple-Element Contracts	325
	Cost Capitalization Case: WorldCom Corp.	329
	Property/Capital Expenditures Analysis	329
	Bankruptcy Prediction Models	332
	Altman Model	332
	Developments in Bankruptcy Prediction Models	333
	Cash Flow Quality	334
	Indicators of Cash Flow Quality	334
	Evaluating Cash Flow Quality	335
	Balance Sheet Quality	343
	Sources of Information about Risk	347
	Limited Usefulness of Auditor's Opinion as a Source of Information about Risk	347
	Risk-Related Disclosures in the Notes	351
	Management Commentary, Other Required Disclosures, and the Financial Press	355
	Other Required Disclosures	358
	Financial Press as a Source of Information about Risk	359
	Summary	*359*
	References	*361*
	Practice Problems	*363*
	Solutions	*369*
Learning Module 6	**Integration of Financial Statement Analysis Techniques**	**373**
	Introduction	374
	Case Study 1	375
	Phase 1: Define a Purpose for the Analysis	376
	Phase 2: Collect Input Data	376
	Phases 3 and 4: DuPont Analysis	376
	Phase 3: Process Data and Phase 4: Analyze/Interpret the Processed Data	377
	Phases 3 and 4: DuPont Decomposition	382
	Phases 3 and 4: Adjusting for unusual charges	385
	Phases 3 and 4: Asset Base Composition	388
	Asset Base Composition	388
	Phases 3 and 4: Capital Structure Analysis	389
	Capital Structure Analysis	389
	Phases 3 and 4: Earnings and Capital	391
	Segment Analysis and Capital Allocation	391
	Phases 3 and 4: Cash Flow and Capital	393
	Phases 3 & 4: Segment Analysis by Product Group	397

◘ indicates an optional segment

Phases 3 & 4: Accruals and Earnings Quality	400
Phases 3 & 4: Cash Flow Relationships	402
Phases 3 & 4: Decomposition and Analysis of the Company's Valuation	405
Phases 5 and 6: Conclusions and Follow-up	407
Phase 5: Develop and Communicate Conclusions and Recommendations (e.g., with an Analysis Report)	407
Phase 6: Follow-up	408
Summary	*409*
Practice Problems	*410*
Solutions	*413*

Glossary G-1

The Financial Statement Modeling learning module should also appear in the Financial Statement Analysis topic area, not in the Corporate Issuers topic area. We regret the error in its placement in the print curriculum. It has been placed correctly in the candidate learning ecosystem online.

How to Use the CFA Program Curriculum

The CFA® Program exams measure your mastery of the core knowledge, skills, and abilities required to succeed as an investment professional. These core competencies are the basis for the Candidate Body of Knowledge (CBOK™). The CBOK consists of four components:

- A broad outline that lists the major CFA Program topic areas (www.cfainstitute.org/programs/cfa/curriculum/cbok)
- Topic area weights that indicate the relative exam weightings of the top-level topic areas (www.cfainstitute.org/programs/cfa/curriculum)
- Learning outcome statements (LOS) that advise candidates about the specific knowledge, skills, and abilities they should acquire from curriculum content covering a topic area: LOS are provided in candidate study sessions and at the beginning of each block of related content and the specific lesson that covers them. We encourage you to review the information about the LOS on our website (www.cfainstitute.org/programs/cfa/curriculum/study-sessions), including the descriptions of LOS "command words" on the candidate resources page at www.cfainstitute.org.
- The CFA Program curriculum that candidates receive upon exam registration

Therefore, the key to your success on the CFA exams is studying and understanding the CBOK. You can learn more about the CBOK on our website: www.cfainstitute.org/programs/cfa/curriculum/cbok.

The entire curriculum, including the practice questions, is the basis for all exam questions and is selected or developed specifically to teach the knowledge, skills, and abilities reflected in the CBOK.

ERRATA

The curriculum development process is rigorous and includes multiple rounds of reviews by content experts. Despite our efforts to produce a curriculum that is free of errors, there are instances where we must make corrections. Curriculum errata are periodically updated and posted by exam level and test date online on the Curriculum Errata webpage (www.cfainstitute.org/en/programs/submit-errata). If you believe you have found an error in the curriculum, you can submit your concerns through our curriculum errata reporting process found at the bottom of the Curriculum Errata webpage.

DESIGNING YOUR PERSONAL STUDY PROGRAM

An orderly, systematic approach to exam preparation is critical. You should dedicate a consistent block of time every week to reading and studying. Review the LOS both before and after you study curriculum content to ensure that you have mastered the applicable content and can demonstrate the knowledge, skills, and abilities described by the LOS and the assigned reading. Use the LOS self-check to track your progress and highlight areas of weakness for later review.

Successful candidates report an average of more than 300 hours preparing for each exam. Your preparation time will vary based on your prior education and experience, and you will likely spend more time on some study sessions than on others.

CFA INSTITUTE LEARNING ECOSYSTEM (LES)

Your exam registration fee includes access to the CFA Program Learning Ecosystem (LES). This digital learning platform provides access, even offline, to all of the curriculum content and practice questions and is organized as a series of short online lessons with associated practice questions. This tool is your one-stop location for all study materials, including practice questions and mock exams, and the primary method by which CFA Institute delivers your curriculum experience. The LES offers candidates additional practice questions to test their knowledge, and some questions in the LES provide a unique interactive experience.

FEEDBACK

Please send any comments or feedback to info@cfainstitute.org, and we will review your suggestions carefully.

Financial Statement Analysis

LEARNING MODULE 1

Intercorporate Investments

by Susan Perry Williams, CPA, CMA, PhD.

Susan Perry Williams, CPA, CMA, PhD, is Professor Emeritus at the McIntire School of Commerce, University of Virginia (USA).

LEARNING OUTCOMES	
Mastery	The candidate should be able to:
☐	describe the classification, measurement, and disclosure under International Financial Reporting Standards (IFRS) for 1) investments in financial assets, 2) investments in associates, 3) joint ventures, 4) business combinations, and 5) special purpose and variable interest entities
☐	compare and contrast IFRS and US GAAP in their classification, measurement, and disclosure of investments in financial assets, investments in associates, joint ventures, business combinations, and special purpose and variable interest entities
☐	analyze how different methods used to account for intercorporate investments affect financial statements and ratios

INTRODUCTION

Intercorporate investments (investments in other companies) can have a significant impact on an investing company's financial performance and position. Companies invest in the debt and equity securities of other companies to diversify their asset base, enter new markets, obtain competitive advantages, deploy excess cash, and achieve additional profitability. Debt securities include commercial paper, corporate and government bonds and notes, redeemable preferred stock, and asset-backed securities. Equity securities include common stock and non-redeemable preferred stock. The percentage of equity ownership a company acquires in an investee depends on the resources available, the ability to acquire the shares, and the desired level of influence or control.

The International Accounting Standards Board (IASB) and the US Financial Accounting Standards Board (FASB) worked to reduce differences in accounting standards that apply to the classification, measurement, and disclosure of intercorporate investments. The resulting standards have improved the relevance, transparency, and comparability of information provided in financial statements.

Complete convergence between IFRS accounting standards and US GAAP did not occur for accounting for financial instruments, and some differences still exist. The terminology used in this reading is IFRS-oriented. US GAAP may not use identical terminology, but in most cases the terminology is similar.

This reading is organized as follows: Section 2 explains the basic categorization of corporate investments. Section 3 describes reporting under IFRS 9, the IASB standard for financial instruments. Section 4 describes equity method reporting for investments in associates where significant influence can exist including the reporting for joint ventures, a type of investment where control is shared. Section 5 describes reporting for business combinations, the parent/subsidiary relationship, and variable interest and special purpose entities. A summary concludes the reading.

2. BASIC CORPORATE INVESTMENT CATEGORIES

- [ ] describe the classification, measurement, and disclosure under International Financial Reporting Standards (IFRS) for 1) investments in financial assets, 2) investments in associates, 3) joint ventures, 4) business combinations, and 5) special purpose and variable interest entities
- [ ] compare and contrast IFRS and US GAAP in their classification, measurement, and disclosure of investments in financial assets, investments in associates, joint ventures, business combinations, and special purpose and variable interest entities

In general, investments in marketable debt and equity securities can be categorized as 1) investments in financial assets in which the investor has no significant influence or control over the operations of the investee, 2) investments in associates in which the investor can exert significant influence (but not control) over the investee, 3) joint ventures where control is shared by two or more entities, and 4) business combinations, including investments in subsidiaries, in which the investor obtains a controlling interest over the investee. The distinction between investments in financial assets, investments in associates, and business combinations is based on the degree of influence or control rather than purely on the percent holding. However, lack of influence is generally presumed when the investor holds less than a 20% equity interest, significant influence is generally presumed between 20% and 50%, and control is presumed when the percentage of ownership exceeds 50%.

The following excerpt from Note 2 to the Financial Statements in the 2017 Annual Report of GlaxoSmithKline, a British pharmaceutical and healthcare company, illustrates the categorization and disclosure in practice:

> Entities over which the Group has the power to direct the relevant activities so as to affect the returns to the Group, generally through control over the financial and operating policies, are accounted for as subsidiaries.
>
> Where the Group has the ability to exercise joint control over, and rights to the net assets of, entities, the entities are accounted for as joint ventures. Where the Group has the ability to exercise joint control over an arrangement, but has rights to specified assets and obligations for specified liabilities of the arrangement, the arrangement is accounted for as a joint operation. Where the Group has the ability to exercise significant influence over entities, they are accounted for as associates. The results and assets

Basic Corporate Investment Categories

and liabilities of associates and joint ventures are incorporated into the consolidated financial statements using the equity method of accounting. The Group's rights to assets, liabilities, revenue and expenses of joint operations are included in the consolidated financial statements in accordance with those rights and obligations.

A summary of the financial reporting and relevant standards for various types of corporate investment is presented in Exhibit 1 (the headings in Exhibit 1 use the terminology of IFRS; US GAAP categorizes intercorporate investments similarly but not identically). The reader should be alert to the fact that value measurement and/or the treatment of changes in value can vary depending on the classification and whether IFRS or US GAAP is used. The alternative treatments are discussed in greater depth later in this reading.

Exhibit 1: Summary of Accounting Treatments for Investments

	In Financial Assets	In Associates	Business Combinations	In Joint Ventures
Influence	Not significant	Significant	Controlling	Shared control
Typical percentage interest	Usually < 20%	Usually 20% to 50%	Usually > 50% or other indications of control	
US GAAP [b]	FASB ASC Topic 320	FASB ASC Topic 323	FASB ASC Topics 805 and 810	FASB ASC Topic 323
Financial Reporting	Classified as: • Fair value through profit or loss • Fair value through other comprehensive income • Amortized cost	Equity method	Consolidation	IFRS: Equity method
Applicable IFRS [a]	IFRS 9	IAS 28	IAS 27 IFRS 3 IFRS 10	IFRS 11 IFRS 12 IAS 28
US GAAP [b]	FASB ASC Topic 320	FASB ASC Topic 323	FASB ASC Topics 805 and 810	FASB ASC Topic 323

[a] *IFRS 9 Financial Instruments; IAS 28 Investments in Associates; IAS 27 Separate Financial Statements; IFRS 3 Business Combinations; IFRS 10 Consolidated Financial Statements; IFRS 11 Joint Arrangements; IFRS 12, Disclosure of Interests in Other Entities.*
[b] *FASB ASC Topic 320 [Investments–Debt and Equity Securities]; FASB ASC Topic 323 [Investments–Equity Method and Joint Ventures]; FASB ASC Topics 805 [Business Combinations] and 810 [Consolidations].*

3. INVESTMENTS IN FINANCIAL ASSETS: IFRS 9

☐ describe the classification, measurement, and disclosure under International Financial Reporting Standards (IFRS) for 1) investments in financial assets, 2) investments in associates, 3) joint ventures, 4) business combinations, and 5) special purpose and variable interest entities

☐ compare and contrast IFRS and US GAAP in their classification, measurement, and disclosure of investments in financial assets, investments in associates, joint ventures, business combinations, and special purpose and variable interest entities

Both IASB and FASB developed revised standards for financial investments. The IASB issued the first phase of their project dealing with classification and measurement of financial instruments by including relevant chapters in IFRS 9, *Financial Instruments*. IFRS 9, which replaces IAS 39, became effective for annual periods on 1 January 2018. The FASB's guidance relating to the accounting for investments in financial instruments is contained in ASC 825, *Financial Instruments*, which has been updated several times, with the standard being effective for periods after 15 December 2017. The resulting US GAAP guidance has many consistencies with IFRS requirements, but there are also some differences.

IFRS 9 is based on an approach that considers the contractual characteristics of cash flows as well as the management of the financial assets. The portfolio approach of the previous standard (i.e., designation of held for trading, available-for-sale, and held-to-maturity) is no longer appropriate, and the terms *available-for-sale* and *held-to-maturity* no longer appear in IFRS 9. Another key change in IFRS 9, compared with IAS 39, relates to the approach to loan impairment. In particular, companies are required to migrate from an incurred loss model to an expected credit loss model. This results in companies evaluating not only historical and current information about loan performance, but also forward-looking information.[1]

The criteria for using amortized cost are similar to those of the IAS 39 "management intent to hold-to-maturity" classification. Specifically, to be measured at amortized cost, financial assets must meet two criteria:[2]

1. A business model test:[3] The financial assets are being held to collect contractual cash flows; and
2. A cash flow characteristic test: The contractual cash flows are solely payments of principal and interest on principal.

---

[1] Under US GAAP, requirements for assessing credit impairment are included in ASC 326, which is effective for most public companies beginning January 1, 2020.
[2] IFRS 9, paragraph 4.1.2.
[3] A business model refers to how an entity manages its financial assets in order to generate cash flows – by collecting contractual cash flows, selling financial assets or both. (IFRS 9 Financial Instruments, Project Summary, July 2014)

Classification and Measurement

IFRS 9 divides all financial assets into two classifications—those measured at amortized cost and those measured at fair value. Under this approach, there are three different categories of measurement:

- Amortised cost
- Fair value through profit or loss (FVPL) or
- Fair Value through Other comprehensive income (FVOCI).

All financial assets are measured at fair value when initially acquired (which will generally be equal to the cost basis on the date of acquisition). Subsequently, financial assets are measured at either fair value or amortized cost. Financial assets that meet the two criteria above are generally measured at amortized cost. If the financial asset meets the criteria above but may be sold, a "hold-to-collect and sell" business model, it may be measured at fair value through other comprehensive income (FVOCI). However, management may choose the "fair value through profit or loss" (FVPL) option to avoid an accounting mismatch.[4] An "accounting mismatch" refers to an inconsistency resulting from different measurement bases for assets and liabilities, i.e., some are measured at amortized cost and some at fair value. Debt instruments are measured at amortized cost, fair value through other comprehensive income (FVOCI), or fair value through profit or loss (FVPL) depending upon the business model.

Equity instruments are measured at FVPL or at FVOCI; they are not eligible for measurement at amortized cost. Equity investments held-for-trading must be measured at FVPL. Other equity investments can be measured at FVPL or FVOCI; however, the choice is irrevocable. If the entity uses the FVOCI option, only the dividend income is recognized in profit or loss. Furthermore, the requirements for reclassifying gains or losses recognized in other comprehensive income are different for debt and equity instruments.

---

[4] IFRS 9, paragraph 4.1.5.

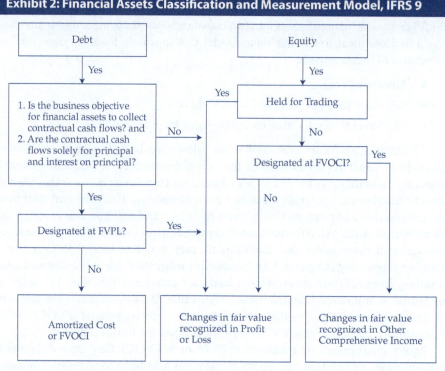

Exhibit 2: Financial Assets Classification and Measurement Model, IFRS 9

Financial assets that are derivatives are measured at fair value through profit or loss (except for hedging instruments). Embedded derivatives are not separated from the hybrid contract if the asset falls within the scope of this standard and the asset as a whole is measured at FVPL.

Exhibit 3 contains an excerpt from the 2017 Deutsche Bank financial statements that describes how financial assets and financial liabilities are determined, measured, and recognized on its financial statements.

Exhibit 3: Excerpt from Deutsche Bank's 2017 Financial Statements

Financial Assets

IFRS 9 requires that an entity's business model and a financial instrument's contractual cash flows will determine its classification and measurement in the financial statements. Upon initial recognition each financial asset will be classified as either fair value through profit or loss ('FVTPL'), amortized cost, or fair value through Other Comprehensive Income ('FVOCI'). As the requirements under IFRS 9 are different than the assessments under the existing IAS 39 rules, there will be some differences from the classification and measurement of financial assets under IAS 39, including whether to elect the fair value option on certain assets. The classification and measurement of financial liabilities remain largely unchanged under IFRS 9 from current requirements.

In 2015, the Group made an initial determination of business models and assessed the contractual cash flow characteristics of the financial assets within such business models to determine the potential classification and measurement changes as a result of IFRS 9. As a result of the initial analysis performed, in 2016 the Group identified a population of financial assets which are to be measured at either amortized cost or fair value through other comprehensive income, which will be subject to the IFRS 9 impairment rules. In 2017, the Group updated its business model assessments and completed outstanding classification decisions. On initial recognition of an equity investment not held for trading, the Group may on an investment-by-investment basis, irrevocably elect to present subsequent fair value changes in OCI. The Group has not made any such elections. Where issued debt liabilities are designated at fair value, the fair value movements attributable to an entity's own credit risk will be recognized in Other Comprehensive Income rather than in the Statement of Income. The standard also allows the Group the option to elect to apply early the presentation of fair value movements of an entity's credit risk in Other Comprehensive Income prior to adopting IFRS 9 in full. The Group did not early adopt this requirement

Reclassification of Investments

Under IFRS 9, the reclassification of equity instruments is not permitted because an entity's initial classification of FVPL and FVOCI is irrevocable. Reclassification of debt instruments is only permitted if the business model for the financial assets (objective for holding the financial assets) has changed in a way that significantly affects operations. Changes to the business model will require judgment and are expected to be very infrequent.

When reclassification is deemed appropriate, there is no restatement of prior periods at the reclassification date. For example, if the financial asset is reclassified from amortized cost to FVPL, the asset is then measured at fair value with any gain or loss immediately recognized in profit or loss. If the financial asset is reclassified from FVPL to amortized cost, the fair value at the reclassification date becomes the carrying amount.

In summary, the major changes made by IFRS 9 are:

- A business model approach to classification of debt instruments.
- Three classifications for financial assets:
  - Fair value through profit or loss (FVPL),
  - fair value through other comprehensive income (FVOCI), and
  - amortized cost.
- Reclassifications of debt instruments are permitted only when the business model changes. The choice to measure equity investments at FVOCI or FVPL is irrevocable.
- A redesign of the provisioning models for financial assets, financial guarantees, loan commitments, and lease receivables. The new standard moves the recognition criteria from an "incurred loss" model to an "expected loss" model. Under the new criteria, there is an earlier recognition of impairment—12 month expected losses for performing assets and lifetime expected losses for non-performing assets, to be captured upfront.[5]

Analysts typically evaluate performance separately for operating and investing activities. Analysis of operating performance should exclude items related to investing activities such as interest income, dividends, and realized and unrealized gains and losses. For comparative purposes, analysts should exclude non-operating assets in the determination of return on net operating assets. IFRS and US GAAP[6] require

---

5 IFRS 9, paragraphs 5.5.4, 5.5.5, 5.5.15, 5.5.16.
6 IFRS 7 Financial Instruments: Disclosures and FASB ASC Section 320-10-50 [Investments–Debt and Equity Securities–Overall–Disclosure].

4. INVESTMENTS IN ASSOCIATES AND JOINT VENTURES

- [ ] describe the classification, measurement, and disclosure under International Financial Reporting Standards (IFRS) for 1) investments in financial assets, 2) investments in associates, 3) joint ventures, 4) business combinations, and 5) special purpose and variable interest entities
- [ ] compare and contrast IFRS and US GAAP in their classification, measurement, and disclosure of investments in financial assets, investments in associates, joint ventures, business combinations, and special purpose and variable interest entities
- [ ] analyze how different methods used to account for intercorporate investments affect financial statements and ratios

Under both IFRS and US GAAP, when a company (investor) holds 20 to 50% of the voting rights of an associate (investee), either directly or indirectly (i.e., through subsidiaries), it is presumed that the company has (or can exercise) significant influence, but not control, over the investee's business activities.[7] Conversely, if the investor holds, directly or indirectly, less than 20% of the voting power of the associate (investee), it is presumed that the investor cannot exercise significant influence, unless such influence can be demonstrated. IAS 28 (IFRS) and FASB ASC Topic 323 (US GAAP) apply to most investments in which an investor has significant influence; they also provide guidance on accounting for investments in associates using the equity method.[8] These standards note that significant influence may be evidenced by

- representation on the board of directors;
- participation in the policy-making process;
- material transactions between the investor and the investee;
- interchange of managerial personnel; or
- technological dependency.

The ability to exert significant influence means that the financial and operating performance of the investee is partly influenced by management decisions and operational skills of the investor. The equity method of accounting for the investment reflects the economic reality of this relationship and provides a more objective basis for reporting investment income.

---

[7] The determination of significant influence under IFRS also includes currently exercisable or convertible warrants, call options, or convertible securities that the investor owns, which give it additional voting power or reduce another party's voting power over the financial and operating policies of the investee. Under US GAAP, the determination of an investor's voting stock interest is based only on the voting shares outstanding at the time of the purchase. The existence and effect of securities with potential voting rights are not considered.

[8] IAS 28 Investments in Associates and Joint Ventures and FASB ASC Topic 323 [Investments–Equity Method and Joint Ventures].

Investments In Associates And Joint Ventures

Joint ventures—ventures undertaken and controlled by two or more parties—can be a convenient way to enter foreign markets, conduct specialized activities, and engage in risky projects. They can be organized in a variety of different forms and structures. Some joint ventures are primarily contractual relationships, whereas others have common ownership of assets. They can be partnerships, limited liability companies (corporations), or other legal forms (unincorporated associations, for example). IFRS identify the following common characteristics of joint ventures: 1) A contractual arrangement exists between two or more venturers, and 2) the contractual arrangement establishes joint control. Both IFRS and US GAAP[9] require the equity method of accounting for joint ventures.[10]

Only under rare circumstances will joint ventures be allowed to use proportionate consolidation under IFRS and US GAAP. On the venturer's financial statements, proportionate consolidation requires the venturer's share of the assets, liabilities, income, and expenses of the joint venture to be combined or shown on a line-by-line basis with similar items under its sole control. In contrast, the equity method results in a single line item (equity in income of the joint venture) on the income statement and a single line item (investment in joint venture) on the balance sheet.

Because the single line item on the income statement under the equity method reflects the net effect of the sales and expenses of the joint venture, the total income recognized is identical under the two methods. In addition, because the single line item on the balance sheet item (investment in joint venture) under the equity method reflects the investors' share of the net assets of the joint venture, the total net assets of the investor is identical under both methods. There can be significant differences, however, in ratio analysis between the two methods because of the differential effects on values for total assets, liabilities, sales, expenses, etc.

Equity Method of Accounting: Basic Principles

Under the equity method of accounting, the equity investment is initially recorded on the investor's balance sheet at cost. In subsequent periods, the carrying amount of the investment is adjusted to recognize the investor's proportionate share of the investee's earnings or losses, and these earnings or losses are reported in income. Dividends or other distributions received from the investee are treated as a return of capital and reduce the carrying amount of the investment and are not reported in the investor's profit or loss. The equity method is often referred to as "one-line consolidation" because the investor's proportionate ownership interest in the assets and liabilities of the investee is disclosed as a single line item (net assets) on its balance sheet, and the investor's share of the revenues and expenses of the investee is disclosed as a single line item on its income statement. (Contrast these disclosures with the disclosures on consolidated statements in Section 6.) Equity method investments are classified as non-current assets on the balance sheet. The investor's share of the profit or loss of equity method investments, and the carrying amount of those investments, must be separately disclosed on the income statement and balance sheet.

---

9 Under US GAAP, ASC 323-10 provides guidance on the application of the equity method of accounting.
10 IFRS 11, Joint Arrangements classifies joint arrangements as either a joint operation or a joint venture. Joint ventures are arrangements wherein parties with joint control have rights to the net assets of the arrangement. Joint ventures are required to use equity method under IAS 28.

EXAMPLE 1

Equity Method: Balance in Investment Account

1. Branch (a fictitious company) purchases a 20% interest in Williams (a fictitious company) for €200,000 on 1 January 2016. Williams reports income and dividends as follows:

	Income	Dividends
2016	€200,000	€50,000
2017	300,000	100,000
2018	400,000	200,000
	€900,000	€350,000

Calculate the investment in Williams that appears on Branch's balance sheet as of the end of 2018.

Solution:

Investment in Williams at 31 December 2018:

Initial cost	€200,000	
Equity income 2016	€40,000	= (20% of €200,000 Income)
Dividends received 2016	(€10,000)	= (20% of €50,000 Dividends)
Equity income 2017	€60,000	= (20% of €300,000 Income)
Dividends received 2017	(€20,000)	= (20% of €100,000 Dividends)
Equity income 2018	€80,000	= (20% of €400,000 Income)
Dividends received 2018	(€40,000)	= (20% of €200,000 Dividends)
Balance-Equity Investment	€310,000	= [€200,000 + 20% × (€900,000 − €350,000)]

This simple example implicitly assumes that the purchase price equals the purchased equity (20%) in the book value of Williams' net assets.

Using the equity method, the investor includes its share of the investee's profit and losses on the income statement. The equity investment is carried at cost, plus its share of post-acquisition income, less dividends received. The recorded investment value can decline as a result of investee losses or a permanent decline in the investee's market value. If the investment value is reduced to zero, the investor usually discontinues the equity method and does not record further losses. If the investee subsequently reports profits, the equity method is resumed after the investor's share of the profits equals the share of losses not recognized during the suspension of the equity method. Exhibit 4 contains excerpts from Deutsche Bank's 2017 annual report that describes its accounting treatment for investments in associates.

Investments In Associates And Joint Ventures

> **Exhibit 4: Excerpt from Deutsche Bank 2017 Annual Report**

[From Note 01] ASSOCIATES

An associate is an entity in which the Group has significant influence, but not a controlling interest, over the operating and financial management policy decisions of the entity. Significant influence is generally presumed when the Group holds between 20 % and 50 % of the voting rights. The existence and effect of potential voting rights that are currently exercisable or convertible are considered in assessing whether the Group has significant influence. Among the other factors that are considered in determining whether the Group has significant influence are representation on the board of directors (supervisory board in the case of German stock corporations) and material intercompany transactions. The existence of these factors could require the application of the equity method of accounting for a particular investment even though the Group's investment is less than 20 % of the voting stock.

Investments in associates are accounted for under the equity method of accounting. The Group's share of the results of associates is adjusted to conform to the accounting policies of the Group and is reported in the Consolidated Statement of Income as Net income (loss) from equity method investments. The Group's share in the associate's profits and losses resulting from intercompany sales is eliminated on consolidation.

If the Group previously held an equity interest in an entity (for example, as available for sale) and subsequently gained significant influence, the previously held equity interest is remeasured to fair value and any gain or loss is recognized in the Consolidated Statement of Income. Any amounts previously recognized in other comprehensive income associated with the equity interest would be reclassified to the Consolidated Statement of Income at the date the Group gains significant influence, as if the Group had disposed of the previously held equity interest.

Under the equity method of accounting, the Group's investments in associates and jointly controlled entities are initially recorded at cost including any directly related transaction costs incurred in acquiring the associate, and subsequently increased (or decreased) to reflect both the Group's pro-rata share of the post-acquisition net income (or loss) of the associate or jointly controlled entity and other movements included directly in the equity of the associate or jointly controlled entity. Goodwill arising on the acquisition of an associate or a jointly controlled entity is included in the carrying value of the investment (net of any accumulated impairment loss). As goodwill is not reported separately it is not specifically tested for impairment. Rather, the entire equity method investment is tested for impairment at each balance sheet date.

If there is objective evidence of impairment, an impairment test is performed by comparing the investment's recoverable amount, which is the higher of its value in use and fair value less costs to sell, with its carrying amount. An impairment loss recognized in prior periods is only reversed if there has been a change in the estimates used to determine the in-vestment's recoverable amount since the last impairment loss was recognized. If this is the case the carrying amount of the investment is increased to its higher recoverable amount. The increased carrying amount of the investment in associate attributable to a reversal of an impairment loss shall not exceed the carrying amount that would have been determined had no impairment loss been recognized for the investment in prior years.

At the date that the Group ceases to have significant influence over the associate or jointly controlled entity the Group recognizes a gain or loss on the disposal of the equity method investment equal to the difference between the sum of the fair value of any retained investment and the proceeds from disposing of the associate and the carrying amount of the investment. Amounts recognized in prior periods in other comprehensive income in relation to the associate are accounted for on the same basis as would have been required if the investee had directly disposed of the related assets or liabilities.

[From Note 17] EQUITY METHOD INVESTMENTS

Investments in associates and jointly controlled entities are accounted for using the equity method of accounting.

The Group holds interests in 77 (2016: 92) associates and 13 (2016: 14) jointly controlled entities. There are no individually material investments in associates and joint ventures.

Aggregated financial information on the Group's share in associates and joint ventures that are individually immaterial (in €m)	Dec 31, 2017	Dec 31, 2016
Carrying amount of all associated that are individually immaterial to the Group	866	1,027
Aggregated amount of the Group's share of profit (loss) from continuing operations	141	183
Aggregated amount of the Group's share of post-tax profit (loss) from discontinued operations	0	0
Aggregated amount of the Group's share of other comprehensive income	(36)	11
Aggregated amount of the Group's share of total comprehensive income	105	194

It is interesting to note the explanations for the treatment of associates when the ownership percentage is less than 20% or is greater than 50%. The equity method reflects the strength of the relationship between the investor and its associates. In the instances where the percentage ownership is less than 20%, Deutsche Bank uses the equity method because it has significant influence over these associates' operating and financial policies either through its representation on their boards of directors and/or other measures. The equity method provides a more objective basis for reporting investment income than the accounting treatment for investments in financial assets because the investor can potentially influence the timing of dividend distributions.

5. AMORTIZATION OF EXCESS PURCHASE PRICE, FAIR VALUE OPTION, AND IMPAIRMENT

☐ describe the classification, measurement, and disclosure under International Financial Reporting Standards (IFRS) for 1) investments in financial assets, 2) investments in associates, 3) joint ventures, 4) business combinations, and 5) special purpose and variable interest entities

☐ compare and contrast IFRS and US GAAP in their classification, measurement, and disclosure of investments in financial assets, investments in associates, joint ventures, business combinations, and special purpose and variable interest entities

Amortization of Excess Purchase Price, Fair Value Option, and Impairment

The cost (purchase price) to acquire shares of an investee is often greater than the book value of those shares. This is because, among other things, many of the investee's assets and liabilities reflect historical cost rather than fair value. IFRS allow a company to measure its property, plant, and equipment using either historical cost or fair value (less accumulated depreciation).[11] US GAAP, however, require the use of historical cost (less accumulated depreciation) to measure property, plant, and equipment.[12]

When the cost of the investment exceeds the investor's proportionate share of the book value of the investee's (associate's) net identifiable tangible and intangible assets (e.g., inventory, property, plant and equipment, trademarks, patents), the difference is first allocated to specific assets (or categories of assets) using fair values. These differences are then amortized to the investor's proportionate share of the investee's profit or loss over the economic lives of the assets whose fair values exceeded book values. It should be noted that the allocation is not recorded formally; what appears initially in the investment account on the balance sheet of the investor is the cost. Over time, as the differences are amortized, the balance in the investment account will come closer to representing the ownership percentage of the book value of the net assets of the associate.

IFRS and US GAAP both treat the difference between the cost of the acquisition and investor's share of the fair value of the net identifiable assets as goodwill. Therefore, any remaining difference between the acquisition cost and the fair value of net identifiable assets that cannot be allocated to specific assets is treated as goodwill and is not amortized. Instead, it is reviewed for impairment on a regular basis, and written down for any identified impairment. Goodwill, however, is included in the carrying amount of the investment, because investment is reported as a single line item on the investor's balance sheet.[13]

EXAMPLE 2

Equity Method Investment in Excess of Book Value

1. Blake Co. and Brown Co. are two hypothetical companies. Assume that Blake Co. acquires 30% of the outstanding shares of Brown Co. At the acquisition date, book values and fair values of Brown's recorded assets and liabilities are as follows:

	Book Value	Fair Value
Current assets	€10,000	€10,000
Plant and equipment	190,000	220,000
Land	120,000	140,000
	€320,000	€370,000
Liabilities	100,000	100,000

---

11 After initial recognition, an entity can choose to use either a cost model or a revaluation model to measure its property, plant, and equipment. Under the revaluation model, property, plant, and equipment whose fair value can be measured reliably can be carried at a revalued amount. This revalued amount is its fair value at the date of the revaluation less any subsequent accumulated depreciation

12 Successful companies should be able to generate, through the productive use of assets, economic value in excess of the resale value of the assets themselves. Therefore, investors may be willing to pay a premium in anticipation of future benefits. These benefits could be a result of general market conditions, the investor's ability to exert significant influence on the investee, or other synergies.

13 If the investor's share of the fair value of the associate's net assets (identifiable assets, liabilities, and contingent liabilities) is greater than the cost of the investment, the difference is excluded from the carrying amount of the investment and instead included as income in the determination of the investor's share of the associate's profit or loss in the period in which the investment is acquired.

	Book Value	Fair Value
Net assets	€220,000	€270,000

Blake Co. believes the value of Brown Co. is higher than the book value of its identifiable net assets. They offer €100,000 for a 30% interest in Brown, which represents a €34,000 excess purchase price. The difference between the fair value and book value of the net identifiable assets is €50,000 (€270,000 – 220,000). Based on Blake Co.'s 30% ownership, €15,000 of the excess purchase price is attributable to the net identifiable assets, and the residual is attributable to goodwill. Calculate goodwill.

Solution:

Purchase price	€100,000
30% of book value of Brown (30% × €220,000)	66,000
Excess purchase price	€34,000
Attributable to net assets	
Plant and equipment (30% × €30,000)	€9,000
Land (30% × €20,000)	6,000
Goodwill (residual)	19,000
	€34,000

As illustrated above, goodwill is the residual excess not allocated to identifiable assets or liabilities. The investment is carried as a non-current asset on the Blake's book as a single line item (Investment in Brown, €100,000) on the acquisition date.

Amortization of Excess Purchase Price

The excess purchase price allocated to the assets and liabilities is accounted for in a manner that is consistent with the accounting treatment for the specific asset or liability to which it is assigned. Amounts allocated to assets and liabilities that are expensed (such as inventory) or periodically depreciated or amortized (plant, property, and intangible assets) must be treated in a similar manner. These allocated amounts are not reflected on the financial statements of the investee (associate), and the investee's income statement will not reflect the necessary periodic adjustments. Therefore, the investor must directly record these adjustment effects by reducing the carrying amount of the investment on its balance sheet and by reducing the investee's profit recognized on its income statement. Amounts allocated to assets or liabilities that are not systematically amortized (e.g., land) will continue to be reported at their fair value as of the date the investment was acquired. As stated above, goodwill is included in the carrying amount of the investment instead of being separately recognized. It is not amortized because it is considered to have an indefinite life.

Using the example above and assuming a 10-year useful life for plant, property, and equipment and using straight-line depreciation, the annual amortization is as follows:

Amortization of Excess Purchase Price, Fair Value Option, and Impairment

Account	Excess Price (€)	Useful Life	Amortization/Year (€)
Plant and equipment	9,000	10 years	900
Land	6,000	Indefinite	0
Goodwill	19,000	Indefinite	0

Annual amortization would reduce the investor's share of the investee's reported income (equity income) and the balance in the investment account by €900 for each year over the 10-year period.

EXAMPLE 3

Equity Method Investments with Goodwill

On 1 January 2018, Parker Company acquired 30% of Prince Inc. common shares for the cash price of €500,000 (both companies are fictitious). It is determined that Parker has the ability to exert significant influence on Prince's financial and operating decisions. The following information concerning Prince's assets and liabilities on 1 January 2018 is provided:

	Prince, Inc.		
	Book Value	Fair Value	Difference
Current assets	€100,000	€100,000	€0
Plant and equipment	1,900,000	2,200,000	300,000
	€2,000,000	€2,300,000	€300,000
Liabilities	800,000	800,000	0
Net assets	€1,200,000	€1,500,000	€300,000

The plant and equipment are depreciated on a straight-line basis and have 10 years of remaining life. Prince reports net income for 2018 of €100,000 and pays dividends of €50,000. Calculate the following:

1. Goodwill included in the purchase price.

Solution:

Purchase price	€500,000
Acquired equity in book value of Prince's net assets (30% × €1,200,000)	360,000
Excess purchase price	€140,000
Attributable to plant and equipment (30% × €300,000)	(90,000)
Goodwill (residual)	€50,000

2. Investment in associate (Prince) at the end of 2018.

Solution:

Investment in associate

Purchase price	€500,000

Parker's share of Prince's net income (30% × €100,000)	30,000
Dividends received (30% of €50,000)	(15,000)
Amortization of excess purchase price attributable to plant and equipment (€90,000 ÷ 10 years)	(9,000)
31 December 2018 balance in investment in Prince	€506,000

An alternate way to look at the balance in the investment account is that it reflects the basic valuation principle of the equity method. At any point in time, the investment account balance equals the investor's (Parker) proportionate share of the net equity (net assets at book value) of the investee (Prince) plus the unamortized balance of the original excess purchase price. Applying this principle to this example:

2018 Beginning net assets =	€1,200,000
Plus: Net income	100,000
Less: Dividends	(50,000)
2018 Ending net assets	€1,250,000
Parker's proportionate share of Prince's recorded net assets (30% × €1,250,000)	€375,000
Unamortized excess purchase price (€140,000 − 9,000)	131,000
Investment in Prince	€506,000

Note that the unamortized excess purchase price is a cost incurred by Parker, not Prince. Therefore, the total amount is included in the investment account balance.

Fair Value Option

Both IFRS and US GAAP give the investor the option to account for their equity method investment at fair value.[14] Under US GAAP, this option is available to all entities; however, under IFRS, its use is restricted to venture capital organizations, mutual funds, unit trusts, and similar entities, including investment-linked insurance funds.

Both standards require that the election to use the fair value option occur at the time of initial recognition and is irrevocable. Subsequent to initial recognition, the investment is reported at fair value with unrealized gains and losses arising from changes in fair value as well as any interest and dividends received included in the investor's profit or loss (income). Under the fair value method, the investment account on the investor's balance sheet does not reflect the investor's proportionate share of the investee's profit or loss, dividends, or other distributions. In addition, the excess of cost over the fair value of the investee's identifiable net assets is not amortized, nor is goodwill created.

Impairment

Both IFRS and US GAAP require periodic reviews of equity method investments for impairment. If the fair value of the investment is below its carrying value and this decline is deemed to be other than temporary, an impairment loss must be recognized.

---

14 IFRS 9 Financial Instruments. FASB ASC Section 825-10-25 [Financial Instruments–Overall–Recognition].

Under IFRS, there must be objective evidence of impairment as a result of one or more (loss) events that occurred after the initial recognition of the investment, and that loss event has an impact on the investment's future cash flows, which can be reliably estimated. Because goodwill is included in the carrying amount of the investment and is not separately recognized, it is not separately tested for impairment. Instead, the entire carrying amount of the investment is tested for impairment by comparing its recoverable amount with its carrying amount.[15] The impairment loss is recognized on the income statement, and the carrying amount of the investment on the balance sheet is either reduced directly or through the use of an allowance account.

US GAAP takes a different approach. If the fair value of the investment declines below its carrying value *and* the decline is determined to be permanent, US GAAP[16] requires an impairment loss to be recognized on the income statement and the carrying value of the investment on the balance sheet is reduced to its fair value.

Both IFRS and US GAAP prohibit the reversal of impairment losses even if the fair value later increases.

Section 6 of this reading discusses impairment tests for the goodwill attributed to a controlling investment (consolidated subsidiary). Note the distinction between the disaggregated goodwill impairment test for consolidated statements and the impairment test of the total fair value of equity method investments.

6. TRANSACTIONS WITH ASSOCIATES AND DISCLOSURE

- [ ] describe the classification, measurement, and disclosure under International Financial Reporting Standards (IFRS) for 1) investments in financial assets, 2) investments in associates, 3) joint ventures, 4) business combinations, and 5) special purpose and variable interest entities
- [ ] compare and contrast IFRS and US GAAP in their classification, measurement, and disclosure of investments in financial assets, investments in associates, joint ventures, business combinations, and special purpose and variable interest entities

Because an investor company can influence the terms and timing of transactions with its associates, profits from such transactions cannot be realized until confirmed through use or sale to third parties. Accordingly, the investor company's share of any unrealized profit must be deferred by reducing the amount recorded under the equity method. In the subsequent period(s) when this deferred profit is considered confirmed, it is added to the equity income. At that time, the equity income is again based on the recorded values in the associate's accounts.

Transactions between the two affiliates may be **upstream** (associate to investor) or **downstream** (investor to associate). In an upstream sale, the profit on the intercompany transaction is recorded on the associate's income (profit or loss) statement. The investor's share of the unrealized profit is thus included in equity income on the investor's income statement. In a downstream sale, the profit is recorded on the

---

15 Recoverable amount is the higher of "value in use" or net selling price. Value in use is equal to the present value of estimated future cash flows expected to arise from the continuing use of an asset and from its disposal at the end of its useful life. Net selling price is equal to fair value less cost to sell.
16 FASB ASC Section 323-10-35 [Investments–Equity Method and Joint Ventures–Overall–Subsequent Measurement].

investor's income statement. Both IFRS and US GAAP require that the unearned profits be eliminated to the extent of the investor's interest in the associate.[17] The result is an adjustment to equity income on the investor's income statement.

> **EXAMPLE 4**
>
> ### Equity Method with Sale of Inventory: Upstream Sale
>
> On 1 January 2018, Wicker Company acquired a 25% interest in Foxworth Company (both companies are fictitious) for €1,000,000 and used the equity method to account for its investment. The book value of Foxworth's net assets on that date was €3,800,000. An analysis of fair values revealed that all fair values of assets and liabilities were equal to book values except for a building. The building was undervalued by €40,000 and has a 20-year remaining life. The company used straight-line depreciation for the building. Foxworth paid €3,200 in dividends in 2018. During 2018, Foxworth reported net income of €20,000. During the year, Foxworth sold inventory to Wicker. At the end of the year, there was €8,000 profit from the upstream sale in Foxworth's net income. The inventory sold to Wicker by Foxworth had not been sold to an outside party.
>
> 1. Calculate the equity income to be reported as a line item on Wicker's 2018 income statement.
>
> **Solution:**
>
> Equity Income
>
> | | |
> |---|---:|
> | Wicker's share of Foxworth's reported income (25% × €20,000) | €5,000 |
> | Amortization of excess purchase price attributable to building, (€10,000 ÷ 20) | (500) |
> | Unrealized profit (25% × €8,000) | (2,000) |
> | Equity income 2018 | €2,500 |
>
> 2. Calculate the balance in the investment in Foxworth to be reported on the 31 December 2018 balance sheet.
>
> | | |
> |---|---:|
> | Purchase price | €1,000,000 |
> | Acquired equity in book value of Foxworth's net assets (25% × €3,800,000) | 950,000 |
> | Excess purchase price | €50,000 |
> | Attributable to: | |
> | Building (25% × €40,000) | €10,000 |
> | Goodwill (residual) | 40,000 |
> | | €50,000 |

---

17 IAS 28 Investments in Associates and Joint Ventures; FASB ASC Topic 323 [Investments–Equity Method and Joint Ventures].

Transactions with Associates and Disclosure

Solution:

Investment in Foxworth:

Purchase price	€1,000,000
Equity income 2018	2,500
Dividends received (25% × €3,200)	(800)
Investment in Foxworth, 31 Dec 2018	€1,001,700
Composition of investment account:	
Wicker's proportionate share of Foxworth's net equity (net assets at book value) [25% × (€3,800,000 + (20,000 − 8,000) − 3,200)]	€952,200
Unamortized excess purchase price (€50,000 − 500)	49,500
	€1,001,700

EXAMPLE 5

Equity Method with Sale of Inventory: Downstream Sale

Jones Company owns 25% of Jason Company (both fictitious companies) and appropriately applies the equity method of accounting. Amortization of excess purchase price, related to undervalued assets at the time of the investment, is €8,000 per year. During 2017 Jones sold €96,000 of inventory to Jason for €160,000. Jason resold €120,000 of this inventory during 2017. The remainder was sold in 2018. Jason reports income from its operations of €800,000 in 2017 and €820,000 in 2018.

1. Calculate the equity income to be reported as a line item on Jones's 2017 income statement.

Solution:

Equity Income 2017

Jones's share of Jason's reported income (25% × €800,000)	€200,000
Amortization of excess purchase price	(8,000)
Unrealized profit (25% × €16,000)	(4,000)
Equity income 2017	€188,000

Jones's profit on the sale to Jason = €160,000 − 96,000 = €64,000

Jason sells 75% (€120,000/160,000) of the goods purchased from Jones; 25% is unsold.

Total unrealized profit = €64,000 × 25% = €16,000

Jones's share of the unrealized profit = €16,000 × 25% = €4,000

Alternative approach:

Jones's profit margin on sale to Jason: 40% (€64,000/€160,000)

Jason's inventory of Jones's goods at 31 Dec 2017: €40,000

> Jones's profit margin on this was 40% × 40,000 = €16,000
>
> Jones's share of profit on unsold goods = €16,000 × 25% = €4,000
>
> 2. Calculate the equity income to be reported as a line item on Jones's 2018 income statement.
>
> ## Solution:
>
> Equity Income 2018
>
> | | |
> |---|---:|
> | Jones's share of Jason's reported income (25% × €820,000) | €205,000 |
> | Amortization of excess purchase price | (8,000) |
> | Realized profit (25% × €16,000) | 4,000 |
> | Equity income 2018 | €201,000 |
>
> Jason sells the remaining 25% of the goods purchased from Jones.

Disclosure

The notes to the financial statements are an integral part of the information necessary for investors. Both IFRS and US GAAP require disclosure about the assets, liabilities, and results of equity method investments. For example, in their 2017 annual report, within its note titled "Principles of Consolidation," Deutsche Bank reports that:

> Investments in associates are accounted for under the equity method of accounting. The Group's share of the results of associates is adjusted to conform to the accounting policies of the Group and is reported in the Consolidated Statement of Income as Net income (loss) from equity method investments. The Group's share in the associate's profits and losses resulting from intercompany sales is eliminated on consolidation.
>
> If the Group previously held an equity interest in an entity (for example, as available for sale) and subsequently gained significant influence, the previously held equity interest is remeasured to fair value and any gain or loss is recognized in the Consolidated Statement of Income. Any amounts previously recognized in other comprehensive income associated with the equity interest would be reclassified to the Consolidated Statement of Income at the date the Group gains significant influence, as if the Group had disposed of the previously held equity interest.
>
> Under the equity method of accounting, the Group's investments in associates and jointly controlled entities are initially recorded at cost including any directly related transaction costs incurred in acquiring the associate, and subsequently increased (or decreased) to reflect both the Group's pro-rata share of the post-acquisition net income (or loss) of the associate or jointly controlled entity and other movements included directly in the equity of the associate or jointly controlled entity. Goodwill arising on the acquisition of an associate or a jointly controlled entity is included in the carrying value of the investment (net of any accumulated impairment loss). As goodwill is not reported separately it is not specifically tested for impairment. Rather, the entire equity method investment is tested for impairment at each balance sheet date.

For practical reasons, associated companies' results are sometimes included in the investor's accounts with a certain time lag, normally not more than one quarter. Dividends from associated companies are not included in investor income because it would be a double counting. Applying the equity method recognizes the investor's full share of the associate's income. Dividends received involve exchanging a portion of equity interest for cash. In the consolidated balance sheet, the book value of shareholdings in associated companies is increased by the investor's share of the company's net income and reduced by amortization of surplus values and the amount of dividends received.

Issues for Analysts

Equity method accounting presents several challenges for analysis. First, analysts should question whether the equity method is appropriate. For example, an investor holding 19% of an associate may in fact exert significant influence but may attempt to avoid using the equity method to avoid reporting associate losses. On the other hand, an investor holding 25% of an associate may be unable to exert significant influence and may be unable to access cash flows, and yet may prefer the equity method to capture associate income.

Second, the investment account represents the investor's percentage ownership in the net assets of the investee company through "one-line consolidation." There can be significant assets and liabilities of the investee that are not reflected on the investor's balance sheet, which will significantly affect debt ratios. Net margin ratios could be overstated because income for the associate is included in investor net income but is not specifically included in sales. An investor may actually control the investee with less than 50% ownership but prefer the financial results using the equity method. Careful analysis can reveal financial performance driven by accounting structure.

Finally, the analyst must consider the quality of the equity method earnings. The equity method assumes that a percentage of each dollar earned by the investee company is earned by the investor (i.e., a fraction of the dollar equal to the fraction of the company owned), even if cash is not received. Analysts should, therefore, consider potential restrictions on dividend cash flows (the statement of cash flows).

ACQUISITION METHOD 7

- [ ] describe the classification, measurement, and disclosure under International Financial Reporting Standards (IFRS) for 1) investments in financial assets, 2) investments in associates, 3) joint ventures, 4) business combinations, and 5) special purpose and variable interest entities
- [ ] compare and contrast IFRS and US GAAP in their classification, measurement, and disclosure of investments in financial assets, investments in associates, joint ventures, business combinations, and special purpose and variable interest entities
- [ ] analyze how different methods used to account for intercorporate investments affect financial statements and ratios

Business combinations (controlling interest investments) involve the combination of two or more entities into a larger economic entity. Business combinations are typically motivated by expectations of added value through synergies, including potential for increased revenues, elimination of duplicate costs, tax advantages, coordination of the production process, and efficiency gains in the management of assets.[18]

Under IFRS, there is no distinction among business combinations based on the resulting structure of the larger economic entity. For all business combinations, one of the parties to the business combination is identified as the acquirer. Under US GAAP, an acquirer is identified, but the business combinations are categorized as merger, acquisition, or consolidation based on the legal structure after the combination. Each of these types of business combinations has distinctive characteristics that are described in Exhibit 5. Features of variable interest and special purpose entities are also described in Exhibit 5 because these are additional instances where control is exerted by another entity. Under both IFRS and US GAAP, business combinations are accounted for using the *acquisition method*.

Exhibit 5: Types of Business Combinations

Merger

The distinctive feature of a merger is that only one of the entities remains in existence. One hundred percent of the target is absorbed into the acquiring company. Company A may issue common stock, preferred stock, bonds, or pay cash to acquire the net assets. The net assets of Company B are transferred to Company A. Company B ceases to exist and Company A is the only entity that remains.

Company A + Company B = Company A

Acquisition

The distinctive feature of an acquisition is the legal continuity of the entities. Each entity continues operations but is connected through a parent–subsidiary relationship. Each entity is an individual that maintains separate financial records, but the parent (the acquirer) provides consolidated financial statements in each reporting period. Unlike a merger or consolidation, the acquiring company does not need to acquire 100% of the target. In fact, in some cases, it may acquire less than 50% and still exert control. If the acquiring company acquires less than 100%, non-controlling (minority) shareholders' interests are reported on the consolidated financial statements.

Company A + Company B = (Company A + Company B)

Consolidation

The distinctive feature of a consolidation is that a new legal entity is formed and none of the predecessor entities remain in existence. A new entity is created to take over the net assets of Company A and Company B. Company A and Company B cease to exist and Company C is the only entity that remains.

Company A + Company B = Company C

---

18 IFRS 3, *Business Combinations*, revised in 2008 and FASB ASC Topic 805 [*Business Combinations*] provide guidance on business combinations.

Special Purpose or Variable Interest Entities

The distinctive feature of a special purpose (variable interest) entity is that control is not usually based on voting control, because equity investors do not have a sufficient amount at risk for the entity to finance its activities without additional subordinated financial support. Furthermore, the equity investors may lack a controlling financial interest. The sponsoring company usually creates a special purpose entity (SPE) for a narrowly defined purpose. IFRS require consolidation if the substance of the relationship indicates control by the sponsor.

Under IFRS 10, *Consolidated Financial Statements* and SIC-12, *Consolidation-Special Purpose Entities*, the definition of control extends to a broad range of activities. The control concept requires judgment and evaluation of relevant factors to determine whether control exists. Control is present when 1) the investor has the ability to exert influence on the financial and operating policy of the entity; and 2) is exposed, or has rights, to variable returns from its involvement with the investee. Consolidation criteria apply to all entities that meet the definition of control.

US GAAP uses a two-component consolidation model that includes both a variable interest component and a voting interest (control) component. Under the variable interest component, US GAAP[19] requires the primary beneficiary of a variable interest entity (VIE) to consolidate the VIE regardless of its voting interests (if any) in the VIE or its decision-making authority. The primary beneficiary is defined as the party that will absorb the majority of the VIE's expected losses, receive the majority of the VIE's expected residual returns, or both.

In the past, business combinations could be accounted for either as a purchase transaction or as a uniting (or pooling) of interests. However, the use of the pooling accounting method for acquisitions is no longer permitted, and IFRS and US GAAP now require that all business combinations be accounted for in a similar manner. The *acquisition method* developed by the IASB and the FASB replaces the purchase method, and substantially reduces any differences between IFRS and US GAAP for business combinations.[20]

Acquisition Method

IFRS and US GAAP require the acquisition method of accounting for business combinations, although both have a few specific exemptions.

Under this approach, the fair value of the consideration given by the acquiring company is the appropriate measurement for acquisitions and also includes the acquisition-date fair value of any contingent consideration. Direct costs of the business combination, such as professional and legal fees, valuation experts, and consultants, are expensed as incurred.

The acquisition method (which replaced the purchase method) addresses three major accounting issues that often arise in business combinations and the preparation of consolidated (combined) financial statements:

- The recognition and measurement of the assets and liabilities of the combined entity;
- The initial recognition and subsequent accounting for goodwill; and
- The recognition and measurement of any non-controlling interest.

---

19 FASB ASC Topic 810 [Consolidation].
20 IFRS 10, Consolidated Financial Statements; IFRS 3, Business Combinations; FASB ASC Topic 805 [Business Combinations]; FASB ASC Topic 810 [Consolidations].

Recognition and Measurement of Identifiable Assets and Liabilities

IFRS and US GAAP require that the acquirer measure the identifiable tangible and intangible assets and liabilities of the acquiree (acquired entity) at fair value as of the date of the acquisition. The acquirer must also recognize any assets and liabilities that the acquiree had not previously recognized as assets and liabilities in its financial statements. For example, identifiable intangible assets (for example, brand names, patents, technology) that the acquiree developed internally would be recognized by the acquirer.

Recognition and Measurement of Contingent Liabilities[21]

On the acquisition date, the acquirer must recognize any contingent liability assumed in the acquisition if 1) it is a present obligation that arises from past events, and 2) it can be measured reliably. Costs that the acquirer expects (but is not obliged) to incur, however, are not recognized as liabilities as of the acquisition date. Instead, the acquirer recognizes these costs in future periods as they are incurred. For example, expected restructuring costs arising from exiting an acquiree's business will be recognized in the period in which they are incurred.

There is a difference between IFRS and US GAAP with regard to treatment of contingent liabilities. IFRS include contingent liabilities if their fair values can be reliably measured. US GAAP includes only those contingent liabilities that are probable and can be reasonably estimated.

Recognition and Measurement of Indemnification Assets

On the acquisition date, the acquirer must recognize an indemnification asset if the seller (acquiree) contractually indemnifies the acquirer for the outcome of a contingency or an uncertainty related to all or part of a specific asset or liability of the acquiree. The seller may also indemnify the acquirer against losses above a specified amount on a liability arising from a particular contingency. For example, the seller guarantees that an acquired contingent liability will not exceed a specified amount. In this situation, the acquirer recognizes an indemnification asset at the same time it recognizes the indemnified liability, with both measured on the same basis. If the indemnification relates to an asset or a liability that is recognized at the acquisition date and measured at its acquisition date fair value, the acquirer will also recognize the indemnification asset at the acquisition date at its acquisition date fair value.

Recognition and Measurement of Financial Assets and Liabilities

At the acquisition date, identifiable assets and liabilities acquired are classified in accordance with IFRS (or US GAAP) standards. The acquirer reclassifies the financial assets and liabilities of the acquiree based on the contractual terms, economic conditions, and the acquirer's operating or accounting policies, as they exist at the acquisition date.

Recognition and Measurement of Goodwill

IFRS allows two options for recognizing goodwill at the transaction date. The goodwill option is on a transaction-by-transaction basis. "Partial goodwill" is measured as the fair value of the acquisition (fair value of consideration given) less the acquirer's share of the fair value of all identifiable tangible and intangible assets, liabilities, and contingent liabilities acquired. "Full goodwill" is measured as the fair value of the

---

21 A contingent liability must be recognized even if it is not probable that an outflow of resources or economic benefits will be used to settle the obligation.

Acquisition Method

entity as a whole less the fair value of all identifiable tangible and intangible assets, liabilities, and contingent liabilities. US GAAP views the entity as a whole and requires full goodwill.[22]

Because goodwill is considered to have an indefinite life, it is not amortized. Instead, it is tested for impairment annually or more frequently if events or circumstances indicate that goodwill might be impaired.

EXAMPLE 6

Recognition and Measurement of Goodwill

Acquirer contributes $800,000 for an 80% interest in Acquiree. The identifiable net assets have a fair value of $900,000. The fair value of the entire entity is determined to be $1 million.

	IFRS Partial Goodwill
Fair value of consideration	$800,000
80% of Fair value of identifiable net assets	720,000
Goodwill recognized	$80,000

	IFRS and US GAAP Full Goodwill
Fair value of entity	$1,000,000
Fair value of identifiable assets	900,000
Goodwill recognized	$100,000

Recognition and Measurement when Acquisition Price Is Less than Fair Value

Occasionally, a company faces adverse circumstances such that its market value drops below the fair value of its net assets. In an acquisition of such a company, where the purchase price is less than the fair value of the target's (acquiree's) net assets, the acquisition is considered to be a "bargain purchase" acquisition. IFRS and US GAAP require the difference between the fair value of the acquired net assets and the purchase price to be recognized immediately as a gain in profit or loss. Any contingent consideration must be measured and recognized at fair value at the time of the business combination. Any subsequent changes in value of the contingent consideration are recognized in profit or loss.

Impact of the Acquisition Method on Financial Statements, Post-Acquisition

Example 7 shows the consolidated balance sheet of an acquiring company after the acquisition.

---

22 FASB ASC Topic 805 [Business Combinations].

> **EXAMPLE 7**
>
> ## Acquisition Method Post-Combination Balance Sheet
>
> 1. Franklin Company, a hypothetical company, acquired 100% of the outstanding shares of Jefferson, Inc. (another fictitious company) by issuing 1,000,000 shares of its €1 par common stock (€15 market value). Immediately before the transaction, the two companies compiled the following information:
>
> | | Franklin Book Value (000) | Jefferson Book Value (000) | Jefferson Fair Value (000) |
> |---|---|---|---|
> | Cash and receivables | €10,000 | €300 | €300 |
> | Inventory | 12,000 | 1,700 | 3,000 |
> | PP&E (net) | 27,000 | 2,500 | 4,500 |
> | | €49,000 | €4,500 | €7,800 |
> | Current payables | 8,000 | 600 | 600 |
> | Long-term debt | 16,000 | 2,000 | 1,800 |
> | | 24,000 | 2,600 | 2,400 |
> | Net assets | €25,000 | €1,900 | €5,400 |
> | Shareholders' equity: | | | |
> | Capital stock (€1 par) | €5,000 | €400 | |
> | Additional paid in capital | 6,000 | 700 | |
> | Retained earnings | €14,000 | €800 | |
>
> Jefferson has no identifiable intangible assets. Show the balances in the post-combination balance sheet using the acquisition method.
>
> ## Solution:
>
> Under the acquisition method, the purchase price allocation would be as follows:
>
> | | |
> |---|---|
> | Fair value of the stock issued | |
> | (1,000,000 shares at market value of €15) | €15,000,000 |
> | Book value of Jefferson's net assets | 1,900,000 |
> | Excess purchase price | €13,100,000 |
> | Fair value of the stock issued | €15,000,000 |
> | Fair value allocated to identifiable net assets | 5,400,000 |
> | Goodwill | €9,600,000 |
>
> Allocation of excess purchase price (based on the differences between fair values and book values):
>
> | | |
> |---|---|
> | Inventory | €1,300,000 |
> | PP&E (net) | 2,000,000 |
> | Long-term debt | 200,000 |
> | Goodwill | 9,600,000 |
> | | €13,100,000 |

Acquisition Method

Both IFRS and US GAAP record the fair value of the acquisition at the market value of the stock issued, or €15,000,000. In this case, the purchase price exceeds the book value of Jefferson's net assets by €13,100,000. Inventory, PP&E (net), and long-term debt are adjusted to fair values. The excess of the purchase price over the fair value of identifiable net assets results in goodwill recognition of €9,600,000.

The post-combination balance sheet of the combined entity would appear as follows:

Franklin Consolidated Balance Sheet (Acquisition Method) (000)	
Cash and receivables	€10,300
Inventory	15,000
PP&E (net)	31,500
Goodwill	9,600
Total assets	€66,400
Current payables	€8,600
Long-term debt	17,800
Total liabilities	€26,400
Capital stock (€1 par)	€6,000
Additional paid in capital	20,000
Retained earnings	14,000
Total stockholders' equity	€40,000
Total liabilities and stockholders' equity	€66,400

Assets and liabilities are combined using book values of Franklin plus fair values for the assets and liabilities acquired from Jefferson. For example, the book value of Franklin's inventory (€12,000,000) is added to the fair value of inventory acquired from Jefferson (€3,000,000) for a combined inventory of €15,000,000. Long-term debt has a book value of €16,000,000 on Franklin's pre-acquisition statements, and Jefferson's fair value of debt is €1,800,000. The combined long-term debt is recorded as €17,800,000.

Franklin's post-merger financial statement reflects in stockholders' equity the stock issued by Franklin to acquire Jefferson. Franklin issues stock with a par value of €1,000,000; however, the stock is measured at fair value under both IFRS and US GAAP. Therefore, the consideration exchanged is 1,000,000 shares at market value of €15, or €15,000,000. Prior to the transaction, Franklin had 5,000,000 shares of €1 par stock outstanding (€5,000,000). The combined entity reflects the Franklin capital stock outstanding of €6,000,000 (€5,000,000 plus the additional 1,000,000 shares of €1 par stock issued to effect the transaction). Franklin's additional paid in capital of €6,000,000 is increased by the €14,000,000 additional paid in capital from the issuance of the 1,000,000 shares (€15,000,000 less par value of €1,000,000) for a total of €20,000,000. At the acquisition date, only the acquirer's retained earnings are carried to the combined entity. Earnings of the target are included on the consolidated income statement and retained earnings only in post-acquisition periods.

In the periods subsequent to the business combination, the financial statements continue to be affected by the acquisition method. Net income reflects the performance of the combined entity. Under the acquisition method, amortization/depreciation is based on historical cost of Franklin's assets and the fair value of Jefferson's assets. Using Example 7, as Jefferson's acquired inventory is sold, the cost of goods sold would be €1,300,000 higher and depreciation on PP&E would be €2,000,000 higher over the life of the asset than if the companies had not combined.

8. THE CONSOLIDATION PROCESS

☐ describe the classification, measurement, and disclosure under International Financial Reporting Standards (IFRS) for 1) investments in financial assets, 2) investments in associates, 3) joint ventures, 4) business combinations, and 5) special purpose and variable interest entities

☐ compare and contrast IFRS and US GAAP in their classification, measurement, and disclosure of investments in financial assets, investments in associates, joint ventures, business combinations, and special purpose and variable interest entities

Consolidated financial statements combine the separate financial statements for distinct legal entities, the parent and its subsidiaries, as if they were one economic unit. Consolidation combines the assets, liabilities, revenues, and expenses of subsidiaries with the parent company. Transactions between the parent and subsidiary (intercompany transactions) are eliminated to avoid double counting and premature income recognition. Consolidated statements are presumed to be more meaningful in terms of representational faithfulness. It is important for the analyst to consider the differences in IFRS and US GAAP, valuation bases, and other factors that could impair the validity of comparative analyses.

Business Combination with Less than 100% Acquisition

The acquirer purchases 100% of the equity of the target company in a transaction structured as a merger or consolidation. For a transaction structured as an acquisition, however, the acquirer does not have to purchase 100% of the equity of the target in order to achieve control. The acquiring company may purchase less than 100% of the target because it may be constrained by resources or it may be unable to acquire all the outstanding shares. As a result, both the acquirer and the target remain separate legal entities. Both IFRS and US GAAP presume a company has control if it owns more than 50% of the voting shares of an entity. In this case, the acquiring company is viewed as the parent, and the target company is viewed as the subsidiary. Both the parent and the subsidiary typically prepare their own financial records, but the parent also prepares consolidated financial statements at each reporting period. The consolidated financial statements are the primary source of information for investors and analysts.

Non-controlling (Minority) Interests: Balance Sheet

A non-controlling (minority) interest is the portion of the subsidiary's equity (residual interest) that is held by third parties (i.e., not owned by the parent). Non-controlling interests are created when the parent acquires less than a 100% controlling interest in a subsidiary. IFRS and US GAAP have similar treatment for how non-controlling

The Consolidation Process

interests are classified.[23] Non-controlling interests in consolidated subsidiaries are presented on the consolidated balance sheet as a separate component of stockholders' equity. IFRS and US GAAP differ, however, on the measurement of non-controlling interests. Under IFRS, the parent can measure the non-controlling interest at either its fair value (full goodwill method) or at the non-controlling interest's proportionate share of the acquiree's identifiable net assets (partial goodwill method). Under US GAAP, the parent must use the full goodwill method and measure the non-controlling interest at fair value.

Example 8 illustrates the differences in reporting requirements.

EXAMPLE 8

Non-controlling Asset Valuation

On 1 January 2018, the hypothetical Parent Co. acquired 90% of the outstanding shares of the hypothetical Subsidiary Co. in exchange for shares of Parent Co.'s no par common stock with a fair value of €180,000. The fair market value of the subsidiary's shares on the date of the exchange was €200,000. Below is selected financial information from the two companies immediately prior to the exchange of shares (before the parent recorded the acquisition):

	Parent Book Value	Subsidiary Book Value	Subsidiary Fair Value
Cash and receivables	€40,000	€15,000	€15,000
Inventory	125,000	80,000	80,000
PP&E (net)	235,000	95,000	155,000
	€400,000	€190,000	€250,000
Payables	55,000	20,000	20,000
Long-term debt	120,000	70,000	70,000
	175,000	90,000	90,000
Net assets	€225,000	€100,000	€160,000
Shareholders' equity:			
Capital stock (no par)	€87,000	€34,000	
Retained earnings	€138,000	€66,000	

1. Calculate the value of PP&E (net) on the consolidated balance sheet under both IFRS and US GAAP.

Solution:

Relative to fair value, the PP&E of the subsidiary is understated by €60,000. Under the acquisition method (IFRS and US GAAP), as long as the parent has control over the subsidiary (i.e., regardless of whether the parent had purchased 51% or 100% of the subsidiary's stock), it would include 100% of the subsidiary's assets and liabilities at fair value on the consolidated balance sheet. Therefore, PP&E on the consolidated balance sheet would be valued at €390,000.

---

23 IFRS 10, Consolidated Financial Statements and FASB ASC Topic 810 [Consolidation].

2. Calculate the value of goodwill and the value of the non-controlling interest at the acquisition date under the full goodwill method.

Solution:

Under the full goodwill method (mandatory under US GAAP and optional under IFRS), goodwill on the consolidated balance sheet would be the difference between the total fair value of the subsidiary and the fair value of the subsidiary's identifiable net assets.

Fair value of the subsidiary	€200,000
Fair value of subsidiary's identifiable net assets	160,000
Goodwill	€40,000

The value of the non-controlling interest is equal to the non-controlling interest's proportionate share of the subsidiary's fair value. The non-controlling interest's proportionate share of the subsidiary is 10% and the fair value of the subsidiary is €200,000 on the acquisition date. Under the full goodwill method, the value of the non-controlling interest would be €20,000 (10% × €200,000).

3. Calculate the value of goodwill and the value of the non-controlling interest at the acquisition date under the partial goodwill method.

Solution:

Under the partial goodwill method (IFRS only), goodwill on the parent's consolidated balance sheet would be €36,000, the difference between the purchase price and the parent's proportionate share of the subsidiary's identifiable assets.

Acquisition price	€180,000
90% of fair value	144,000
Goodwill	€36,000

The value of the non-controlling interest is equal to the non-controlling interest's proportionate share of the fair value of the subsidiary's identifiable net assets. The non-controlling interest's proportionate share is 10%, and the fair value of the subsidiary's identifiable net assets on the acquisition date is €160,000. Under the partial goodwill method, the value of the non-controlling interest would be €16,000 (10% × €160,000).

Regardless of which method is used, goodwill is not amortized under either IFRS or US GAAP but it is tested for impairment at least annually.

For comparative purposes, below is the balance sheet at the acquisition date under the full goodwill and partial goodwill methods.

Comparative Consolidated Balance Sheet at Acquisition Date: Acquisition Method

	Full Goodwill	Partial Goodwill
Cash and receivables	€55,000	€55,000
Inventory	205,000	205,000
PP&E (net)	390,000	390,000
Goodwill	40,000	36,000

	Full Goodwill	Partial Goodwill
Total assets	€690,000	€686,000
Payables	€75,000	€75,000
Long-term debt	190,000	190,000
Total liabilities	€265,000	€265,000
Shareholders' equity:		
Noncontrolling interests	€20,000	€16,000
Capital stock (no par)	€267,000	€267,000
Retained earnings	138,000	138,000
Total equity	€425,000	€421,000
Total liabilities and shareholders' equity	€690,000	€686,000

Non-controlling (Minority) Interests: Income Statement

On the income statement, non-controlling (minority) interests are presented as a line item reflecting the allocation of profit or loss for the period. Intercompany transactions, if any, are eliminated in full.

Using assumed data consistent with the facts in Example 8, the amounts included for the subsidiary in the consolidated income statements under IFRS and US GAAP are presented below. Income taxes are ignored in the table. In practice, however, non-controlling interest on the consolidated income statement is the non-controlling interest's share of the subsidiary's after-tax income.

	Full Goodwill	Partial Goodwill
Sales	€250,000	€250,000
Cost of goods sold	137,500	137,500
Interest expense	10,000	10,000
Depreciation expense	39,000	39,000
Income from continuing operations	€63,500	€63,500
Non-controlling interest (10%)	(6,350)	(6,350)
Consolidated net income to parent's shareholders	€57,150	€57,150

Income to the parent's shareholders is €57,150 using either method. This is because the fair value of the PP&E is allocated to non-controlling shareholders as well as to the controlling shareholders under the full goodwill and the partial goodwill methods. Therefore, the non-controlling interests will share in the adjustment for excess depreciation resulting from the €60,000 increase in PP&E. Because depreciation expense is the same under both methods, it results in identical net income to all shareholders, whichever method is used to recognize goodwill and to measure the non-controlling interest.

Although net income to parent's shareholders is the same, the impact on ratios would be different because total assets and stockholders' equity would differ.

Impact on Ratios		
	Full Goodwill (%)	Partial Goodwill (%)
Return on assets	8.28	8.33
Return on equity	13.45	13.57

Over time, the value of the subsidiary will change as a result of net income and changes in equity. As a result, the value of the non-controlling interest on the parent's consolidated balance sheet will also change.

Goodwill Impairment

Although goodwill is not amortized, it must be tested for impairment at least annually or more frequently if events or changes in circumstances indicate that it might be impaired. If it is probable that some or all of the goodwill will not be recovered through the profitable operations of the combined entity, it should be partially or fully written off by charging it to an expense. Once written down, goodwill cannot be later restored.

IFRS and US GAAP differ on the definition of the levels at which goodwill is assigned and how goodwill is tested for impairment.

Under IFRS, at the time of acquisition, the total amount of goodwill recognized is allocated to each of the acquirer's cash-generating units that will benefit from the expected synergies resulting from the combination with the target. A cash-generating unit represents the lowest level within the combined entity at which goodwill is monitored for impairment purposes.[24] Goodwill impairment testing is then conducted under a one-step approach. The recoverable amount of a cash-generating unit is calculated and compared with the carrying value of the cash-generating unit.[25] An impairment loss is recognized if the recoverable amount of the cash-generating unit is less than its carrying value. The impairment loss (the difference between these two amounts) is first applied to the goodwill that has been allocated to the cash-generating unit. Once this has been reduced to zero, the remaining amount of the loss is then allocated to all of the other non-cash assets in the unit on a pro rata basis.

Under US GAAP, at the time of acquisition, the total amount of goodwill recognized is allocated to each of the acquirer's reporting units. A reporting unit is an operating segment or component of an operating segment that is one level below the operating segment as a whole. Goodwill impairment testing is then conducted under a two-step approach: identification of impairment and then measurement of the loss. First, the carrying amount of the reporting unit (including goodwill) is compared to its fair value. If the carrying value of the reporting unit exceeds its fair value, potential impairment has been identified. The second step is then performed to measure the amount of the impairment loss. The amount of the impairment loss is the difference between the implied fair value of the reporting unit's goodwill and its carrying amount. The implied fair value of goodwill is determined in the same manner as in a business combination (it is the difference between the fair value of the reporting unit and the fair value of the reporting unit's assets and liabilities). The impairment loss is applied to the goodwill that has been allocated to the reporting unit. After the goodwill of the

---

24 A cash-generating unit is the smallest identifiable group of assets that generates cash inflows that are largely independent of the cash inflows from other assets or groups of assets.
25 The recoverable amount of a cash-generating unit is the higher of net selling price (i.e., fair value less costs to sell) and its value in use. Value in use is the present value of the future cash flows expected to be derived from the cash-generating unit. The carrying value of a cash-generating unit is equal to the carrying value of the unit's assets and liabilities including the goodwill that has been allocated to that unit.

The Consolidation Process

reporting unit has been eliminated, no other adjustments are made automatically to the carrying values of any of the reporting unit's other assets or liabilities. However, it may be prudent to test other asset values for recoverability and possible impairment.

Under both IFRS and US GAAP, the impairment loss is recorded as a separate line item in the consolidated income statement.

EXAMPLE 9

Goodwill Impairment: IFRS

1. The cash-generating unit of a French company has a carrying value of €1,400,000, which includes €300,000 of allocated goodwill. The recoverable amount of the cash-generating unit is determined to be €1,300,000, and the estimated fair value of its identifiable net assets is €1,200,000. Calculate the impairment loss.

Solution:

Recoverable amount of unit	€1,300,000
Carrying amount of unit	1,400,000
Impairment loss	€100,000

The impairment loss of €100,000 is reported on the income statement, and the goodwill allocated to the cash-generating unit would be reduced by €100,000 to €200,000.

If the recoverable amount of the cash-generating unit had been €800,000 instead of €1,300,000, the impairment loss recognized would be €600,000. This would first be absorbed by the goodwill allocated to the unit (€300,000). Once this has been reduced to zero, the remaining amount of the impairment loss (€300,000) would then be allocated on a pro rata basis to the other non-cash assets within the unit.

EXAMPLE 10

Goodwill Impairment: US GAAP

1. A reporting unit of a US corporation (e.g., a division) has a fair value of $1,300,000 and a carrying value of $1,400,000 that includes recorded goodwill of $300,000. The estimated fair value of the identifiable net assets of the reporting unit at the impairment test date is $1,200,000. Calculate the impairment loss.

Solution:

Step 1 – Determination of an Impairment Loss

Because the fair value of the reporting unit is less than its carrying book value, a potential impairment loss has been identified.

Fair value of unit: $1,300,000 < $1,400,000

Step 2 – Measurement of the Impairment Loss

Fair value of reporting unit	$1,300,000
Less: net assets	1,200,000
Implied goodwill	$100,000
Current carrying value of goodwill	$300,000
Less: implied goodwill	100,000
Impairment loss	$200,000

The impairment loss of $200,000 is reported on the income statement, and the goodwill allocated to the reporting unit would be reduced by $200,000 to $100,000.

If the fair value of the reporting unit was $800,000 (instead of $1,300,000), the implied goodwill would be a negative $400,000. In this case, the maximum amount of the impairment loss recognized would be $300,000, the carrying amount of goodwill.

9. FINANCIAL STATEMENT PRESENTATION

☐ describe the classification, measurement, and disclosure under International Financial Reporting Standards (IFRS) for 1) investments in financial assets, 2) investments in associates, 3) joint ventures, 4) business combinations, and 5) special purpose and variable interest entities

☐ compare and contrast IFRS and US GAAP in their classification, measurement, and disclosure of investments in financial assets, investments in associates, joint ventures, business combinations, and special purpose and variable interest entities

The presentation of consolidated financial statements is similar under IFRS and US GAAP. For example, selected financial statements for GlaxoSmithKline are shown in Exhibit 6 and Exhibit 7. GlaxoSmithKline is a leading pharmaceutical company headquartered in the United Kingdom.

The consolidated balance sheet in Exhibit 6 combines the operations of GlaxoSmithKline and its subsidiaries. The analyst can observe that in 2017 GlaxoSmithKline had investments in financial assets (other investments of £918,000,000 and liquid investments of £78,000,000), and investments in associates and joint ventures of £183,000,000. In 2017 GlaxoSmithKline did not acquire any additional companies, however, it made a number of small business disposals during the year for a net cash consideration of £342,000,000, including contingent consideration receivable of £86,000,000. In addition, during 2017 GlaxoSmithKline made cash investment of £15,000,000 in Associates and disposed of two associated for a cash consideration of £198,000,000.[26] The decrease in goodwill on the balance sheet reflects exchange adjustments recognized by GlaxoSmithKline due to the weakness of the functional

---

26 Note 38: Acquisitions and Disposals, GlaxoSmithKline financial statements 2017

Financial Statement Presentation

currency of the parent (Pound Sterling). Note that GlaxoSmithKline has £6,172,000 in contingent consideration liabilities, which relate to future events such as development milestones or sales performance for acquired companies. Of the £6 billion total contingent liability, £1,076,000 is expected to be paid within one year in respect of the Novartis Vaccines business, which reached its sales milestone. The remaining contingent consideration relates to the acquisition of the Shionogi-ViiV Healthcare joint venture and Novartis Vaccines are expected to be paid over a number of years.[27] The analyst can also note that GlaxoSmithKline is the parent company in a less than 100% acquisition. The minority interest of £3,557,000,000 in the equity section is the portion of the combined entity that accrues to non-controlling shareholders.

Exhibit 6: GlaxoSmithKline Consolidated Balance Sheet at 31 December 2017

	Notes	2017 £m	2016 £m
Non-current assets			
Property, plant and equipment	17	**10,860**	10,808
Goodwill	18	**5,734**	5,965
Other intangible assets	19	**17,562**	18,776
Investments in associates and joint ventures	20	**183**	263
Other investments	21	**918**	985
Deferred tax assets	14	**3,796**	4,374
Derivative financial instruments	42	**8**	—
Other non-current assets	22	**1,413**	1,199
Total non-current assets		**40,474**	42,370
Current assets			
Inventories	23	**5,557**	5,102
Current tax recoverable	14	**258**	226
Trade and other receivables	24	**6,000**	6,026
Derivative financial instruments	42	**68**	156
Liquid investments	31	**78**	89
Cash and cash equivalents	25	**3,833**	4,897
Assets held for sale	26	**113**	215
Total current assets		**15,907**	16,711
Total assets		**56,381**	59,081
Current liabilities			
Short-term borrowings	31	**(2,825)**	(4,129)
Contingent consideration liabilities	39	**(1,076)**	(561)
Trade and other payables	27	**(20,970)**	(11,964)
Derivative financial instruments	42	**(74)**	(194)
Current tax payable	14	**(995)**	(1,305)
Short-term provisions	29	**(629)**	(848)
Total current liabilities		**(26,569)**	(19,001)
Non-current liabilities			

---

[27] The notes state that the amount included in the balance sheet is the present value of the expected contingent consideration payments, which have been discounted using a rate of 8.5%.

	Notes	2017 £m	2016 £m
Long-term borrowings	31	(14,264)	(14,661)
Corporation tax payable	14	(411)	—
Deferred tax liabilities	14	(1,396)	(1,934)
Pensions and other post-employment benefits	28	(3,539)	(4,090)
Other provisions	29	(636)	(652)
Contingent consideration liabilities	39	(5,096)	(5,335)
Other non-current liabilities	30	(981)	(8,445)
Total non-current liabilities		(26,323)	(35,117)
Total liabilities		(52,892)	(54,118)
Net assets		3,489	4,963
Equity			
Share capital	33	1,343	1,342
Share premium account	33	3,019	2,954
Retained earnings	34	(6,477)	(5,392)
Other reserves	34	2,047	2,220
Shareholders' equity		(68)	1,124
Non-controlling interests		3,557	3,839
Total equity		3,489	4,963

The consolidated income statement for GlaxoSmithKline is presented in Exhibit 7. IFRS and US GAAP have similar formats for consolidated income statements. Each line item (e.g., turnover [sales], cost of sales, etc.) includes 100% of the parent and the subsidiary transactions after eliminating any **upstream** (subsidiary sells to parent) or **downstream** (parent sells to subsidiary) intercompany transactions. The portion of income accruing to non-controlling shareholders is presented as a separate line item on the consolidated income statement. Note that net income would be the same under IFRS and US GAAP.[28] The analyst will need to make adjustments for any analysis comparing specific line items that might differ between IFRS and US GAAP.

Exhibit 7: GlaxoSmithKline Consolidated Income Statement for the Year Ended 31 December 2017

	Notes	2017 Total £m	2016 £m	2015 £m
Turnover	6	30,186	27,889	23,923
Cost of sales		(10,342)	(9,290)	(8,853)
Gross profit		19,844	18,599	15,070
Selling, general and administration		(9,672)	(9,366)	(9,232)
Research and development		(4,476)	(3,628)	(3,560)
Royalty income		356	398	329
Other operating income	7	(1,965)	(3,405)	7,715
Operating profit	8	4,087	2,598	10,322

---

28 It is possible, however, for differences to arise through the application of different accounting rules (e.g., valuation of fixed assets).

	Notes	2017 Total £m	2016 £m	2015 £m
Finance income	11	65	72	104
Finance costs	12	(734)	(736)	(757)
Profit on disposal of interests in Associates		95	—	843
Share of after tax profits of associates and joint ventures	13	13	5	14
Profit before taxation		**3,525**	**1,939**	**10,526**
Taxation	14	(1,356)	(877)	(2,154)
Profit after taxation for the year		**2,169**	**1,062**	**8,372**
Profit/(loss) attributable to non-controlling interests		637	150	(50)
Profit attributable to shareholders		1,532	912	8,472
		2,169	1,062	8,372
Basic earnings per share (pence)	15	31.4p	18.8p	174.3p
Diluted earnings per share (pence)	15	31.0p	18.6p	172.3p

VARIABLE INTEREST AND SPECIAL PURPOSE ENTITIES 10

- ☐ describe the classification, measurement, and disclosure under International Financial Reporting Standards (IFRS) for 1) investments in financial assets, 2) investments in associates, 3) joint ventures, 4) business combinations, and 5) special purpose and variable interest entities
- ☐ compare and contrast IFRS and US GAAP in their classification, measurement, and disclosure of investments in financial assets, investments in associates, joint ventures, business combinations, and special purpose and variable interest entities

Special purpose entities (SPEs) are enterprises that are created to accommodate specific needs of the sponsoring entity.[29] The sponsoring entity (on whose behalf the SPE is created) frequently transfers assets to the SPE, obtains the right to use assets held by the SPE, or performs services for the SPE, while other parties (capital providers) provide funding to the SPE. SPEs can be a legitimate financing mechanism for a company to segregate certain activities and thereby reduce risk. SPEs may take the form of a limited liability company (corporation), trust, partnership, or unincorporated entity. They are often created with legal arrangements that impose strict and sometimes permanent limits on the decision-making powers of their governing board or management.

---

[29] The term "special purpose entity" is used by IFRS and "variable interest entity" and "special purpose entity" is used by US GAAP.

Beneficial interest in an SPE may take the form of a debt instrument, an equity instrument, a participation right, or a residual interest in a lease. Some beneficial interests may simply provide the holder with a fixed or stated rate of return, while beneficial interests give the holder the rights or the access to future economic benefits of the SPE's activities. In most cases, the creator/sponsor of the entity retains a significant beneficial interest in the SPE even though it may own little or none of the SPE's voting equity.

In the past, sponsors were able to avoid consolidating SPEs on their financial statements because they did not have "control" (i.e., own a majority of the voting interest) of the SPE. SPEs were structured so that the sponsoring company had financial control over their assets or operating activities, while third parties held the majority of the voting interest in the SPE.

These outside equity participants often funded their investments in the SPE with debt that was either directly or indirectly guaranteed by the sponsoring companies. The sponsoring companies, in turn, were able to avoid the disclosure of many of these guarantees as well as their economic significance. In addition, many sponsoring companies created SPEs to facilitate the transfer of assets and liabilities from their own balance sheets. As a result, they were able to recognize large amounts of revenue and gains, because these transactions were accounted for as sales. By avoiding consolidation, sponsoring companies did not have to report the assets and the liabilities of the SPE; financial performance as measured by the unconsolidated financial statements was potentially misleading. The benefit to the sponsoring company was improved asset turnover, lower operating and financial leverage metrics, and higher profitability.

Enron, for example, used SPEs to obtain off-balance sheet financing and artificially improve its financial performance. Its subsequent collapse was partly attributable to its guarantee of the debt of the SPEs it had created.

To address the accounting issues arising from the misuse and abuse of SPEs, the IASB and the FASB worked to improve the consolidation models to take into account financial arrangements where parties other than the holders of the majority of the voting interests exercise financial control over another entity. IFRS 10, *Consolidated Financial Statements*, revised the definition of control to encompass many special purpose entities. Special purpose entities involved in a structured financial transaction will require an evaluation of the purpose, design, and risks.

In developing new accounting standards to address this consolidation issue, the FASB used the more general term variable interest entity (VIE) to more broadly define an entity that is financially controlled by one or more parties that do not hold a majority voting interest. Therefore, under US GAAP, a VIE includes other entities besides SPEs. FASB ASC Topic 810 [*Consolidation*] provides guidance for US GAAP, which classifies special purpose entities as variable interest entities if:

1. total equity at risk is insufficient to finance activities without financial support from other parties, or

2. equity investors lack any one of the following:

    a. the ability to make decisions;

    b. the obligation to absorb losses; or

    c. the right to receive returns.

Common examples of variable interests are entities created to lease real estate or other property, entities created for the securitization of financial assets, or entities created for research and development activity.

Under FASB ASC Topic 810 [*Consolidation*], the primary beneficiary of a VIE must consolidate it as a subsidiary regardless of how much of an equity investment the beneficiary has in the VIE. The primary beneficiary (which is often the sponsor) is

Variable Interest and Special Purpose Entities

the entity that is expected to absorb the majority of the VIE's expected losses, receive the majority of the VIE's residual returns, or both. If one entity will absorb a majority of the VIE's expected losses and another unrelated entity will receive a majority of the VIE's expected residual returns, the entity absorbing a majority of the losses must consolidate the VIE. If there are non-controlling interests in the VIE, these would also be shown in the consolidated balance sheet and consolidated income statement of the primary beneficiary. ASC Topic 810 also requires entities to disclose information about their relationships with VIEs, even if they are not considered the primary beneficiary.

Securitization of Assets

Example 11 shows the effects of securitizing assets on companies' balance sheets.

EXAMPLE 11

Receivables Securitization

Odena, a (fictional) Italian auto manufacturer, wants to raise €55M in capital by borrowing against its financial receivables. To accomplish this objective, Odena can choose between two alternatives:

Alternative 1   Borrow directly against the receivables; or

Alternative 2   Create a special purpose entity, invest €5M in the SPE, have the SPE borrow €55M, and then use the funds to purchase €60M of receivables from Odena.

Using the financial statement information provided below, describe the effect of each Alternative on Odena, assuming that Odena meets the definition of control and will consolidate the SPE.

Odena Balance Sheet	
Cash	€30,000,000
Accounts receivable	60,000,000
Other assets	40,000,000
Total assets	€130,000,000
Current liabilities	€27,000,000
Noncurrent liabilities	20,000,000
Total liabilities	€47,000,000
Shareholder equity	€83,000,000
Total liabilities and equity	€130,000,000

Alternative 1:

Odena's cash will increase by €55M (to €85M) and its debt will increase by €55M (to €75M). Its sales and net income will not change.

Odena: Alternative 1 Balance Sheet	
Cash	€85,000,000
Accounts receivable	60,000,000
Other assets	40,000,000
Total assets	€185,000,000

Current liabilities	€27,000,000
Noncurrent liabilities	75,000,000
Total liabilities	€102,000,000
Shareholder equity	€83,000,000
Total liabilities and equity	€185,000,000

Alternative 2:

Odena's accounts receivable will decrease by €60M and its cash will increase by €55 (it invests €5M in cash in the SPE). However, if Odena is able to sell the receivables to the SPE for more than their carrying value (for example, €65), it would also report a gain on the sale in its profit and loss. Equally important, the SPE may be able to borrow the funds at a lower rate than Odena, since they are bankruptcy remote from Odena (i.e., out of reach of Odena's creditors), and the lenders to the SPE are the claimants on its assets (i.e., the purchased receivables).

SPE Balance Sheet	
Accounts receivable	€60,000,000
Total assets	€60,000,000
Long-term debt	€55,000,000
Equity	5,000,000
Total liabilities and equity	€60,000,000

Because Odena consolidates the SPE, its financial balance sheet would look like the following:

Odena: Alternative 2 Consolidated Balance Sheet	
Cash	€85,000,000
Accounts receivable	60,000,000
Other assets	40,000,000
Total assets	€185,000,000
Current liabilities	€27,000,000
Noncurrent liabilities	75,000,000
Total liabilities	€102,000,000
Shareholder equity	€83,000,000
Total liabilities and equity	€185,000,000

Therefore, the consolidated balance sheet of Odena would look exactly the same as if it borrowed directly against the receivables. In addition, as a result of the consolidation, the transfer (sale) of the receivables to the SPE would be reversed along with any gain Odena recognized on the sale.

ADDITIONAL ISSUES IN BUSINESS COMBINATIONS THAT IMPAIR COMPARABILITY

☐ describe the classification, measurement, and disclosure under International Financial Reporting Standards (IFRS) for 1) investments in financial assets, 2) investments in associates, 3) joint ventures, 4) business combinations, and 5) special purpose and variable interest entities

☐ compare and contrast IFRS and US GAAP in their classification, measurement, and disclosure of investments in financial assets, investments in associates, joint ventures, business combinations, and special purpose and variable interest entities

Accounting for business combinations is a complex topic. In addition to the basics covered so far in this reading, we briefly mention some of the more common issues that impair comparability between IFRS and US GAAP.

Contingent Assets and Liabilities

Under IFRS, the cost of an acquisition is allocated to the fair value of assets, liabilities, and contingent liabilities. Contingent liabilities are recorded separately as part of the cost allocation process, provided that their fair values can be measured reliably. Subsequently, the contingent liability is measured at the higher of the amount initially recognized or the best estimate of the amount required to settle. As mentioned previously, GlaxoSmithKline had approximately £6 billion in contingent liabilities in relation to a number of purchases for the year ended 31 December 2017, with the notes to the financial statements further stating that the £6 billion was the expected value of the contingent consideration payments, discounted at an appropriate discount rate. Contingent assets are not recognized under IFRS.

Under US GAAP, contractual contingent assets and liabilities are recognized and recorded at their fair values at the time of acquisition. Non-contractual contingent assets and liabilities must also be recognized and recorded only if it is "more likely than not" they meet the definition of an asset or a liability at the acquisition date. Subsequently, a contingent liability is measured at the higher of the amount initially recognized or the best estimate of the amount of the loss. A contingent asset, however, is measured at the lower of the acquisition date fair value or the best estimate of the future settlement amount.

Contingent Consideration

Contingent consideration may be negotiated as part of the acquisition price. For example, the acquiring company (parent) may agree to pay additional money to the acquiree's (subsidiary's) former shareholders if certain agreed upon events occur. These can include achieving specified sales or profit levels for the acquiree and/or the combined entity. Under both IFRS and US GAAP, contingent consideration is initially measured at fair value. IFRS and US GAAP classify contingent consideration as an asset, liability or equity. In subsequent periods, changes in the fair value of liabilities (and assets, in the case of US GAAP) are recognized in the consolidated income statement. Both IFRS and US GAAP do not remeasure equity classified contingent consideration; instead, settlement is accounted for within equity.

In-Process R&D

IFRS and US GAAP recognize in-process research and development acquired in a business combination as a separate intangible asset and measure it at fair value (if it can be measured reliably). In subsequent periods, this research and development is subject to amortization if successfully completed (a marketable product results) or to impairment if no product results or if the product is not technically and/or financially viable.

Restructuring Costs

IFRS and US GAAP do not recognize restructuring costs that are associated with the business combination as part of the cost of the acquisition. Instead, they are recognized as an expense in the periods the restructuring costs are incurred.

SUMMARY

Intercompany investments play a significant role in business activities and create significant challenges for the analyst in assessing company performance. Investments in other companies can take five basic forms: investments in financial assets, investments in associates, joint ventures, business combinations, and investments in special purpose and variable interest entities. Key concepts are as follows:

- Investments in financial assets are those in which the investor has no significant influence. They can be measured and reported as
    - Fair value through profit or loss.
    - Fair value through other comprehensive income.
    - Amortized cost.

    IFRS and US GAAP treat investments in financial assets in a similar manner.
- Investments in associates and joint ventures are those in which the investor has significant influence, but not control, over the investee's business activities. Because the investor can exert significant influence over financial and operating policy decisions, IFRS and US GAAP require the equity method of accounting because it provides a more objective basis for reporting investment income.
    - The equity method requires the investor to recognize income as earned rather than when dividends are received.
    - The equity investment is carried at cost, plus its share of post-acquisition income (after adjustments) less dividends received.
    - The equity investment is reported as a single line item on the balance sheet and on the income statement.
- IFRS and US GAAP accounting standards require the use of the acquisition method to account for business combinations. Fair value of the consideration given is the appropriate measurement for identifiable assets and liabilities acquired in the business combination.
- Goodwill is the difference between the acquisition value and the fair value of the target's identifiable net tangible and intangible assets. Because it is considered to have an indefinite life, it is not amortized. Instead, it is evaluated

Additional Issues in Business Combinations That impair Comparability

at least annually for impairment. Impairment losses are reported on the income statement. IFRS use a one-step approach to determine and measure the impairment loss, whereas US GAAP uses a two-step approach.

- If the acquiring company acquires less than 100%, non-controlling (minority) shareholders' interests are reported on the consolidated financial statements. IFRS allows the non-controlling interest to be measured at either its fair value (full goodwill) or at the non-controlling interest's proportionate share of the acquiree's identifiable net assets (partial goodwill). US GAAP requires the non-controlling interest to be measured at fair value (full goodwill).
- Consolidated financial statements are prepared in each reporting period.
- Special purpose (SPEs) and variable interest entities (VIEs) are required to be consolidated by the entity which is expected to absorb the majority of the expected losses or receive the majority of expected residual benefits.

PRACTICE PROBLEMS

The following information relates to questions 1-6

Burton Howard, CFA, is an equity analyst with Maplewood Securities. Howard is preparing a research report on Confabulated Materials, SA, a publicly traded company based in France that complies with IFRS 9. As part of his analysis, Howard has assembled data gathered from the financial statement footnotes of Confabulated's 2018 Annual Report and from discussions with company management. Howard is concerned about the effect of this information on Confabulated's future earnings.

Information about Confabulated's investment portfolio for the years ended 31 December 2017 and 2018 is presented in Exhibit 1. As part of his research, Howard is considering the possible effect on reported income of Confabulated's accounting classification for fixed income investments.

Exhibit 1: Confabulated's Investment Portfolio (€ Thousands)

Characteristic	Bugle AG	Cathay Corp	Dumas SA
Classification	FVPL	FVOCI	Amortized cost
Cost*	€25,000	€40,000	€50,000
Market value, 31 December 2017	29,000	38,000	54,000
Market value, 31 December 2018	28,000	37,000	55,000

All securities were acquired at par value.

In addition, Confabulated's annual report discusses a transaction under which receivables were securitized through a special purpose entity (SPE) for Confabulated's benefit.

1. The balance sheet carrying value of Confabulated's investment portfolio (in € thousands) at 31 December 2018 is *closest* to:

    A. 112,000.

    B. 115,000.

    C. 118,000.

2. The balance sheet carrying value of Confabulated's investment portfolio at 31 December 2018 would have been higher if which of the securities had been reclassified as FVPL security?

    A. Bugle.

    B. Cathay.

    C. Dumas.

3. Compared to Confabulated's reported interest income in 2018, if Dumas had

been classified as FVPL, the interest income would have been:

   A. lower.

   B. the same.

   C. higher.

4. Compared to Confabulated's reported earnings before taxes in 2018, if Dumas had been classified as a FVPL security, the earnings before taxes (in € thousands) would have been:

   A. the same.

   B. €1,000 lower.

   C. €1,000 higher.

5. Confabulated's reported interest income would be lower if the cost was the same but the par value (in € thousands) of:

   A. Bugle was €28,000.

   B. Cathay was €37,000.

   C. Dumas was €55,000.

6. Confabulated's special purpose entity is *most likely* to be:

   A. held off-balance sheet.

   B. consolidated on Confabulated's financial statements.

   C. consolidated on Confabulated's financial statements only if it is a "qualifying SPE."

The following information relates to questions 7-11

Cinnamon, Inc. is a diversified manufacturing company headquartered in the United Kingdom. It complies with IFRS. In 2017, Cinnamon held a 19 percent passive equity ownership interest in Cambridge Processing. In December 2017, Cinnamon announced that it would be increasing its ownership interest to 50 percent effective 1 January 2018 through a cash purchase. Cinnamon and Cambridge have no intercompany transactions.

Peter Lubbock, an analyst following both Cinnamon and Cambridge, is curious how the increased stake will affect Cinnamon's consolidated financial statements. He asks Cinnamon's CFO how the company will account for the investment, and is told that the decision has not yet been made. Lubbock decides to use his existing forecasts for both companies' financial statements to compare the outcomes of alternative accounting treatments.

Lubbock assembles abbreviated financial statement data for Cinnamon (Exhibit 1) and Cambridge (Exhibit 2) for this purpose.

Exhibit 1: Selected Financial Statement Information for Cinnamon, Inc. (£ Millions)

Year ending 31 December	2017	2018*
Revenue	1,400	1,575
Operating income	126	142
Net income	62	69
31 December	**2017**	**2018***
Total assets	1,170	1,317
Shareholders' equity	616	685

Estimates made prior to announcement of increased stake in Cambridge.

Exhibit 2: Selected Financial Statement Information for Cambridge Processing (£ Millions)

Year ending 31 December	2017	2018*
Revenue	1,000	1,100
Operating income	80	88
Net income	40	44
Dividends paid	20	22
31 December	**2017**	**2018***
Total assets	800	836
Shareholders' equity	440	462

Estimates made prior to announcement of increased stake by Cinnamon.

7. In 2018, if Cinnamon is deemed to have control over Cambridge, it will *most likely* account for its investment in Cambridge using:

   A. the equity method.

   B. the acquisition method.

   C. proportionate consolidation.

8. At 31 December 2018, Cinnamon's total shareholders' equity on its balance sheet would *most likely* be:

   A. highest if Cinnamon is deemed to have control of Cambridge.

   B. independent of the accounting method used for the investment in Cambridge.

   C. highest if Cinnamon is deemed to have significant influence over Cambridge.

9. In 2018, Cinnamon's net profit margin would be *highest* if:

   A. it is deemed to have control of Cambridge.

   B. it had not increased its stake in Cambridge.

Practice Problems

    C. it is deemed to have significant influence over Cambridge.

10. At 31 December 2018, assuming control and recognition of goodwill, Cinnamon's reported debt to equity ratio will *most likely* be highest if it accounts for its investment in Cambridge using the:

    A. equity method.

    B. full goodwill method.

    C. partial goodwill method.

11. Compared to Cinnamon's operating margin in 2017, if it is deemed to have control of Cambridge, its operating margin in 2018 will *most likely* be:

    A. lower.

    B. higher.

    C. the same.

The following information relates to questions 12–16

Zimt, AG is a consumer products manufacturer headquartered in Austria. It complies with IFRS. In 2017, Zimt held a 10 percent passive stake in Oxbow Limited. In December 2017, Zimt announced that it would be increasing its ownership to 50 percent effective 1 January 2018.

Franz Gelblum, an analyst following both Zimt and Oxbow, is curious how the increased stake will affect Zimt's consolidated financial statements. Because Gelblum is uncertain how the company will account for the increased stake, he uses his existing forecasts for both companies' financial statements to compare various alternative outcomes.

Gelblum gathers abbreviated financial statement data for Zimt (Exhibit 1) and Oxbow (Exhibit 2) for this purpose.

Exhibit 1: Selected Financial Statement Estimates for Zimt AG (€ Millions)

Year ending 31 December	2017	2018*
Revenue	1,500	1,700
Operating income	135	153
Net income	66	75
31 December	**2017**	**2018***
Total assets	1,254	1,421
Shareholders' equity	660	735

Estimates made prior to announcement of increased stake in Oxbow.

Exhibit 2: Selected Financial Statement Estimates for Oxbow Limited (€ Millions)

Year ending 31 December	2017	2018*
Revenue	1,200	1,350
Operating income	120	135
Net income	60	68
Dividends paid	20	22
31 December	**2017**	**2018***
Total assets	1,200	1,283
Shareholders' equity	660	706

Estimates made prior to announcement of increased stake by Zimt.

12. At 31 December 2018, Zimt's total assets balance would *most likely* be:

    A. highest if Zimt is deemed to have control of Oxbow.

    B. highest if Zimt is deemed to have significant influence over Oxbow.

    C. unaffected by the accounting method used for the investment in Oxbow.

13. Based on Gelblum's estimates, if Zimt is deemed to have significant influence over Oxbow, its 2018 net income (in € millions) would be *closest* to:

    A. €75.

    B. €109.

    C. €143.

14. Based on Gelblum's estimates, if Zimt is deemed to have joint control of Oxbow, and Zimt uses the proportionate consolidation method, its 31 December 2018 total liabilities (in € millions) will *most likely* be *closest* to:

    A. €686.

    B. €975.

    C. €1,263.

15. Based on Gelblum's estimates, if Zimt is deemed to have control over Oxbow, its 2018 consolidated sales (in € millions) will be *closest* to:

    A. €1,700.

    B. €2,375.

    C. €3,050.

16. Based on Gelblum's estimates, and holding the size of Zimt's ownership stake in Oxbow constant, Zimt's net income in 2018 will *most likely* be:

    A. highest if Zimt is deemed to have control of Oxbow.

    B. highest if Zimt is deemed to have significant influence over Oxbow.

    C. independent of the accounting method used for the investment in Oxbow.

Practice Problems

The following information relates to questions 17–22

BetterCare Hospitals, Inc. operates a chain of hospitals throughout the United States. The company has been expanding by acquiring local hospitals. Its largest acquisition, that of Statewide Medical, was made in 2001 under the pooling of interests method. BetterCare complies with US GAAP.

BetterCare is currently forming a 50/50 joint venture with Supreme Healthcare under which the companies will share control of several hospitals. BetterCare plans to use the equity method to account for the joint venture. Supreme Healthcare complies with IFRS and will use the proportionate consolidation method to account for the joint venture.

Erik Ohalin is an equity analyst who covers both companies. He has estimated the joint venture's financial information for 2018 in order to prepare his estimates of each company's earnings and financial performance. This information is presented in Exhibit 1.

Exhibit 1: Selected Financial Statement Forecasts for Joint Venture ($ Millions)

Year ending 31 December	2018
Revenue	1,430
Operating income	128
Net income	62
31 December	**2018**
Total assets	1,500
Shareholders' equity	740

Supreme Healthcare recently announced it had formed a special purpose entity through which it plans to sell up to $100 million of its accounts receivable. Supreme Healthcare has no voting interest in the SPE, but it is expected to absorb any losses that it may incur. Ohalin wants to estimate the impact this will have on Supreme Healthcare's consolidated financial statements.

17. Compared to accounting principles currently in use, the pooling method BetterCare used for its Statewide Medical acquisition has *most likely* caused its reported:

    A. revenue to be higher.

    B. total equity to be lower.

    C. total assets to be higher.

18. Based on Ohalin's estimates, the amount of joint venture revenue (in $ millions) included on BetterCare's consolidated 2018 financial statements should be *closest* to:

    A. $0.

    B. $715.

    C. $1,430.

19. Based on Ohalin's estimates, the amount of joint venture net income included on the consolidated financial statements of each venturer will *most likely* be:
    A. higher for BetterCare.
    B. higher for Supreme Healthcare.
    C. the same for both BetterCare and Supreme Healthcare.

20. Based on Ohalin's estimates, the amount of the joint venture's 31 December 2018 total assets (in $ millions) that will be included on Supreme Healthcare's consolidated financial statements will be *closest* to:
    A. $0.
    B. $750.
    C. $1,500.

21. Based on Ohalin's estimates, the amount of joint venture shareholders' equity at 31 December 2018 included on the consolidated financial statements of each venturer will *most likely* be:
    A. higher for BetterCare.
    B. higher for Supreme Healthcare.
    C. the same for both BetterCare and Supreme Healthcare.

22. If Supreme Healthcare sells its receivables to the SPE, its consolidated financial results will *least likely* show:
    A. a higher revenue for 2018.
    B. the same cash balance at 31 December 2018.
    C. the same accounts receivable balance at 31 December 2018.

The following information relates to questions 23-29

John Thronen is an analyst in the research department of an international securities firm. Thronen is preparing a research report on Topmaker, Inc., a publicly-traded company that complies with IFRS. Thronen reviews two of Topmaker's recent transactions relating to investments in Blanco Co. and Rainer Co.

Investment in Blanca Co.

On 1 January 2016, Topmaker invested $11 million in Blanca Co. debt securities (with a 5.0% stated coupon rate on par value, payable each 31 December). The par value of the securities is $10 million, and the market interest rate in effect when the bonds were purchased was 4.0%. Topmaker designates the investment as held-to-maturity. On 31 December 2016, the fair value of the securities was $12 million.

Blanca Co. plans to raise $40 million in capital by borrowing against its financial receivables. Blanca plans to create a special purpose entity (SPE), invest $10 million in the SPE, have the SPE borrow $40 million, and then use the total funds to purchase $50 million of receivables from Blanca. Blanca meets the definition

Practice Problems

of control and plans to consolidate the SPE. Blanca's current balance sheet is presented in Exhibit 1.

Exhibit 1: Blanca Co. Balance Sheet at 31 December 2016 ($ millions)

Cash	20	Current liabilities	25
Accounts receivable	50	Noncurrent liabilities	30
Other assets	30	Shareholders' equity	45
Total assets	**100**	**Total liabilities and equity**	**100**

Investment in Rainer Co.

On 1 January 2016, Topmaker acquired a 15% equity interest with voting power in Rainer Co. for $300 million. Exhibit 2 presents selected financial information for Rainer on the acquisition date. Thronen notes that the plant and equipment are depreciated on a straight-line basis and have 10 years of remaining life. Topmaker has representation on Rainer's board of directors and participates in the associate's policy-making process.

Exhibit 2: Selected Financial Data for Rainer Co., 1 January 2018 (Acquisition Date) ($ millions)

	Book Value	Fair Value
Current assets	270	270
Plant and equipment	2,900	3,160
Total assets	3,170	3,430
Liabilities	1,830	1,830
Net assets	1,340	1,600

Thronen notes that, for fiscal year 2018, Rainer reported total revenue of $1,740 million and net income of $360 million, and paid dividends of $220 million.

Thronen is concerned about possible goodwill impairment for Topmaker due to expected changes in the industry effective at the end of 2017. He calculates the impairment loss based on selected data from the projected consolidated balance sheet data presented in Exhibit 3, assuming that the cash-generating unit and reporting unit of Topmaker are the same.

Exhibit 3: Selected Financial Data for Topmaker, Inc., Estimated Year Ending 31 December 2017 ($ millions)

Carrying value of cash-generating unit/reporting unit	15,200
Recoverable amount of cash-generating unit/reporting unit	14,900
Fair value of reporting unit	14,800
Identifiable net assets	14,400
Goodwill	520

Finally, Topmaker announces its plan to increase its ownership interest in Rainer to 80% effective 1 January 2018 and will account for the investment in Rainer using the partial goodwill method. Thronen estimates that the fair market value of the Rainer's shares on the expected date of exchange is $2 billion with the identifiable assets valued at $1.5 billion.

23. The carrying value of Topmaker's investment in Blanca's debt securities reported on the balance sheet at 31 December 2016 is:

    A. $10.94 million.

    B. $11.00 million.

    C. $12.00 million.

24. Based on Exhibit 1 and Blanca's plans to borrow against its financial receivables, the new consolidated balance sheet will show total assets of:

    A. $50 million.

    B. $140 million.

    C. $150 million.

25. Based on Exhibit 2, Topmaker's investment in Rainer resulted in goodwill of:

    A. $21 million.

    B. $60 million.

    C. $99 million.

26. Topmaker's influence on Rainer's business activities can be *best* described as:

    A. significant.

    B. controlling.

    C. shared control.

27. Using only the information from Exhibit 2, the carrying value of Topmaker's investment in Rainer at the end of 2016 is *closest* to:

    A. $282 million.

    B. $317 million.

    C. $321 million.

28. Based on Exhibit 3, Topmaker's impairment loss under IFRS is:

    A. $120 million.

    B. $300 million.

    C. $400 million.

29. Based on Thronen's value estimates on the acquisition date of 1 January 2018, the estimated value of the minority interest related to Rainer will be:

    A. $300 million.

    B. $400 million.

    C. $500 million.

Practice Problems

The following information relates to questions 30-35

Percy Byron, CFA, is an equity analyst with a UK-based investment firm. One firm Byron follows is NinMount PLC, a UK-based company. On 31 December 2018, NinMount paid £320 million to purchase a 50 percent stake in Boswell Company. The excess of the purchase price over the fair value of Boswell's net assets was attributable to previously unrecorded licenses. These licenses were estimated to have an economic life of six years. The fair value of Boswell's assets and liabilities other than licenses was equal to their recorded book values. NinMount and Boswell both use the pound sterling as their reporting currency and prepare their financial statements in accordance with IFRS.

Byron is concerned whether the investment should affect his "buy" rating on NinMount common stock. He knows NinMount could choose one of several accounting methods to report the results of its investment, but NinMount has not announced which method it will use. Byron forecasts that both companies' 2019 financial results (excluding any merger accounting adjustments) will be identical to those of 2018.

NinMount's and Boswell's condensed income statements for the year ended 31 December 2018, and condensed balance sheets at 31 December 2018, are presented in Exhibits 1 and 2, respectively.

Exhibit 1: NinMount PLC and Boswell Company Income Statements for the Year Ended 31 December 2018 (£ millions)

	NinMount	Boswell
Net sales	950	510
Cost of goods sold	(495)	(305)
Selling expenses	(50)	(15)
Administrative expenses	(136)	(49)
Depreciation & amortization expense	(102)	(92)
Interest expense	(42)	(32)
Income before taxes	125	17
Income tax expense	(50)	(7)
Net income	75	10

Exhibit 2: NinMount PLC and Boswell Company Balance Sheets at 31 December 2018 (£ millions)

	NinMount	Boswell
Cash	50	20
Receivables—net	70	45
Inventory	130	75
Total current assets	250	140
Property, plant, & equipment—net	1,570	930
Investment in Boswell	320	—

	NinMount	Boswell
Total assets	2,140	1,070
Current liabilities	110	90
Long-term debt	600	400
Total liabilities	710	490
Common stock	850	535
Retained earnings	580	45
Total equity	1,430	580
Total liabilities and equity	2,140	1,070

Note: Balance sheets reflect the purchase price paid by NinMount, but do not yet consider the impact of the accounting method choice.

30. NinMount's current ratio on 31 December 2018 *most likely* will be highest if the results of the acquisition are reported using:

    A. the equity method.

    B. consolidation with full goodwill.

    C. consolidation with partial goodwill.

31. NinMount's long-term debt to equity ratio on 31 December 2018 *most likely* will be lowest if the results of the acquisition are reported using:

    A. the equity method.

    B. consolidation with full goodwill.

    C. consolidation with partial goodwill.

32. Based on Byron's forecast, if NinMount deems it has acquired control of Boswell, NinMount's consolidated 2019 depreciation and amortization expense (in £ millions) will be *closest* to:

    A. 102.

    B. 148.

    C. 204.

33. Based on Byron's forecast, NinMount's net profit margin for 2019 *most likely* will be highest if the results of the acquisition are reported using:

    A. the equity method.

    B. consolidation with full goodwill.

    C. consolidation with partial goodwill.

34. Based on Byron's forecast, NinMount's 2019 return on beginning equity *most likely* will be the same under:

    A. either of the consolidations, but different under the equity method.

    B. the equity method, consolidation with full goodwill, and consolidation with partial goodwill.

Practice Problems

C. none of the equity method, consolidation with full goodwill, or consolidation with partial goodwill.

35. Based on Byron's forecast, NinMount's 2019 total asset turnover ratio on beginning assets under the equity method is *most likely*:

    A. lower than if the results are reported using consolidation.

    B. the same as if the results are reported using consolidation.

    C. higher than if the results are reported using consolidation.

SOLUTIONS

1. B is correct. Under IFRS 9, FVPL and FVOCI securities are carried at market value, whereas amortized cost securities are carried at historical cost. €28,000 + 37,000 + 50,000 = €115,000.

2. C is correct. If Dumas had been classified as a FVPL security, its carrying value would have been the €55,000 fair value rather than the €50,000 historical cost.

3. B is correct. The coupon payment is recorded as interest income whether securities are amortized cost or FVPL. No adjustment is required for amortization since the bonds were bought at par.

4. C is correct. Unrealized gains and losses are included in income when securities are classified as FVPL. During 2018 there was an unrealized gain of €1,000.

5. B is correct. The difference between historical cost and par value must be amortized under the effective interest method. If the par value is less than the initial cost (stated interest rate is greater than the effective rate), the interest income would be lower than the interest received because of amortization of the premium.

6. B is correct. Under IFRS, SPEs must be consolidated if they are conducted for the benefit of the sponsoring entity. Further, under IFRS, SPEs cannot be classified as qualifying. Under US GAAP, qualifying SPEs (a classification which has been eliminated) do not have to be consolidated.

7. B is correct. If Cinnamon is deemed to have control over Cambridge, it would use the acquisition method to account for Cambridge and prepare consolidated financial statements. Proportionate consolidation is used for joint ventures; the equity method is used for some joint ventures and when there is significant influence but not control.

8. A is correct. If Cinnamon is deemed to have control over Cambridge, consolidated financial statements would be prepared and Cinnamon's total shareholders' equity would increase and include the amount of the noncontrolling interest. If Cinnamon is deemed to have significant influence, the equity method would be used and there would be no change in the total shareholders' equity of Cinnamon.

9. C is correct. If Cinnamon is deemed to have significant influence, it would report half of Cambridge's net income as a line item on its income statement, but no additional revenue is shown. Its profit margin is thus higher than if it consolidated Cambridge's results, which would impact revenue and income, or if it only reported 19 percent of Cambridge's dividends (no change in ownership).

10. C is correct. The full and partial goodwill method will have the same amount of debt; however, shareholders' equity will be higher under full goodwill (and the debt to equity ratio will be lower). Therefore, the debt to equity will be higher under partial goodwill. If control is assumed, Cinnamon cannot use the equity method.

11. A is correct. Cambridge has a lower operating margin (88/1,100 = 8.0%) than Cinnamon (142/1,575 = 9.0%). If Cambridge's results are consolidated with Cinnamon's, the consolidated operating margin will reflect that of the combined company, or 230/2,675 = 8.6%.

Solutions

12. A is correct. When a company is deemed to have control of another entity, it records all of the other entity's assets on its own consolidated balance sheet.

13. B is correct. If Zimt is deemed to have significant influence, it would use the equity method to record its ownership. Under the equity method, Zimt's share of Oxbow's net income would be recorded as a single line item. Net income of Zimt = 75 + 0.5(68) = 109.

14. B is correct. Under the proportionate consolidation method, Zimt's balance sheet would show its own total liabilities of €1,421 − 735 = €686 plus half of Oxbow's liabilities of €1,283 − 706 = €577. €686 + (0.5 × 577) = €974.5.

15. C is correct. Under the assumption of control, Zimt would record its own sales plus 100 percent of Oxbow's. €1,700 + 1,350 = €3,050.

16. C is correct. Net income is not affected by the accounting method used to account for active investments in other companies. "One-line consolidation" and consolidation result in the same impact on net income; it is the disclosure that differs.

17. B is correct. Statewide Medical was accounted for under the pooling of interest method, which causes all of Statewide's assets and liabilities to be reported at historical book value. The excess of assets over liabilities generally is lower using the historical book value method than using the fair value method (this latter method must be used under currently required acquisition accounting). It would have no effect on revenue.

18. A is correct. Under the equity method, BetterCare would record its interest in the joint venture's net profit as a single line item, but would show no line-by-line contribution to revenues or expenses.

19. C is correct. Net income will be the same under the equity method and proportional consolidation. However, sales, cost of sales, and expenses are different because under the equity method the net effect of sales, cost of sales, and expenses is reflected in a single line.

20. B is correct. Under the proportionate consolidation method, Supreme Healthcare's consolidated financial statements will include its 50 percent share of the joint venture's total assets.

21. C is correct. The choice of equity method or proportionate consolidation does not affect reported shareholders' equity.

22. A is correct. Revenue will not be higher for 2018 because Supreme Healthcare controls the SPE and thus eliminates intra-entity transactions and balances in consolidation. Consolidated revenue will thus present the results as if this transaction did not occur.

23. A is correct. Since the investment is designated as held-to-maturity, it is reported at amortized cost at 31 December 2016 using the effective interest method where the amortization is calculated as the difference between the amount received and the interest income.

    The interest payment each period is $500,000, which is calculated as the product of the par value of $10 million and the stated 5% coupon rate. The interest income of $440,000 is the product of the 4.0% market rate in effect when the bonds were purchased and the initial fair value of $11 million. The difference between the interest payment of $500,000 and the interest income of $440,000, equal to $60,000, is the amortization amount for 2016.

So, the initial fair value of $11 million is reduced by the amortization amount of $60,000, resulting in an amortized cost of $10.94 million at 31 December 2016.

24. B is correct. The SPE balance sheet will show accounts receivable of $50 million, long-term debt of $40 million and equity of $10 million. When the balance sheets of Blanca and the SPE are consolidated, Blanca's cash will increase by $40 million due to the sale of the receivables to the SPE (net of its $10 million cash investment in the SPE). Long-term debt (non-current liabilities) will also increase by $40 million. So, the consolidated balance sheet will show total assets of $140 million and will look the same as if Blanca borrowed directly against the receivables.

Blanca Co. Current Balance Sheet (before consolidation)

Cash	20	Current liabilities	25
Accounts receivable	50	Noncurrent liabilities	30
Other assets	30	Shareholders' equity	45
Total assets	**100**	**Total liabilities and equity**	**100**

SPE Balance Sheet ($ Millions)

		Long-term debt	$40
Accounts receivable	$50	Equity	$10
Total assets	**$50**	**Total liabilities and equity**	**$50**

Blanca Co. Consolidated Balance Sheet ($ Millions)

Cash	$60	Current liabilities	$25
Accounts receivable	$50	Noncurrent liabilities	$70
Other assets	$30	Shareholder's equity	$45
Total assets	**$140**	**Total liabilities and equity**	**$140**

25. B is correct. The goodwill in Topmaker's $300 million purchase of Rainer's common shares using the equity method is $60 million, calculated as:

	$ Millions
Purchase price	$300
Less: 15% of book value of Rainer: (15% x $1,340)	201
Excess purchase price	99
Attributable to net assets	39
Plant and equipment (15% x ($3,160 − $2,900))	
Goodwill (residual)	60
	99

26. A is correct. Topmaker's representation on the Rainer board of directors and participation in Rainer's policymaking process indicate significant influence. Signif-

Solutions

icant influence is generally assumed when the percentage of ownership interest is between 20% and 50%. Topmaker's representation on the board of directors and participation in the policymaking process, however, demonstrate significant influence despite its 15% equity interest.

27. B is correct. The carrying value of Topmaker's investment in Rainer using the equity method is $317 million and is calculated as:

	$ Millions
Purchase price	$300
Plus: Topmaker's share of Rainer's net income (15% x $360)	54
Less: Dividends received (15% x $220)	33
Less: Amortization of excess purchase price attributable to plant and equipment (15% x ($3,160 – $2,900))) / 10 years	3.9
Investment in associate (Rainer) at the end of 2016	$317.1

28. B is correct. The goodwill impairment loss under IFRS is $300 million, calculated as the difference between the recoverable amount of a cash-generating unit and the carrying value of the cash-generating unit. Topmaker's recoverable amount of the cash-generating unit is $14,900 million, which is less than the carrying value of the cash-generating unit of $15,200 million. This results in an impairment loss of $300 million ($14,900 – $15,200).

29. A is correct. According to IFRS, under the partial goodwill method, the value of the minority interest is equal to the non-controlling interest's proportionate share of the subsidiary's identifiable net assets. Rainer's proportionate share is 20% and the value of its identifiable assets on the acquisition date is $1.5 billion. The value of the minority interest is $300 million (20% x $1.5 billion).

30. A is correct. The current ratio using the equity method of accounting is Current assets/Current liabilities = £250/£110 = 2.27. Using consolidation (either full or partial goodwill), the current ratio = £390/£200 = 1.95. Therefore, the current ratio is highest using the equity method.

31. A is correct. Using the equity method, long-term debt to equity = £600/£1,430 = 0.42. Using the consolidation method, long-term debt to equity = long-term debt/equity = £1,000/£1,750 = 0.57. Equity includes the £320 noncontrolling interest under either consolidation. It does not matter if the full or partial goodwill method is used since there is no goodwill.

32. C is correct. The projected depreciation and amortization expense will include NinMount's reported depreciation and amortization (£102), Boswell's reported depreciation and amortization (£92), and amortization of Boswell's licenses (£10 million). The licenses have a fair value of £60 million. £320 purchase price indicates a fair value of £640 for the net assets of Boswell. The net book (fair) value of the recorded assets is £580. The previously unrecorded licenses have a fair value of £60 million. The licenses have a remaining life of six years; the amortization adjustment for 2018 will be £10 million. Therefore, Projected depreciation and amortization = £102 + £92 + £10 = £204 million.

33. A is correct. Net income is the same using any of the methods but under the equity method, net sales are only £950; Boswell's sales are not included in the net sales figure. Therefore, net profit margin is highest using the equity method.

34. A is correct. Net income is the same using any of the choices. Beginning equity under the equity method is £1,430. Under either of the consolidations, beginning equity is £1,750 since it includes the £320 noncontrolling interest. Return on beginning equity is highest under the equity method.

35. A is correct. Using the equity method, Total asset turnover = Net sales/Beginning total assets = £950/£2,140 = 0.444. Total asset turnover on beginning assets using consolidation = £1,460/£2,950 = 0.495. Under consolidation, Assets = £2,140 − 320 + 1,070 + 60 = £2,950. Therefore, total asset turnover is lowest using the equity method.

ID MODULE

LEARNING MODULE
2

Employee Compensation: Post-Employment and Share-Based

by Elaine Henry, PhD, CFA, and Elizabeth A. Gordon, PhD, MBA, CPA.

Elaine Henry, PhD, CFA, is at Stevens Institute of Technology (USA). Elizabeth A. Gordon, PhD, MBA, CPA, is at Temple University (USA).

LEARNING OUTCOMES	
Mastery	The candidate should be able to:
☐	describe the types of post-employment benefit plans and implications for financial reports
☐	explain and calculate measures of a defined benefit pension obligation (i.e., present value of the defined benefit obligation and projected benefit obligation) and net pension liability (or asset)
☐	describe the components of a company's defined benefit pension costs
☐	explain and calculate the effect of a defined benefit plan's assumptions on the defined benefit obligation and periodic pension cost
☐	explain and calculate how adjusting for items of pension and other post-employment benefits that are reported in the notes to the financial statements affects financial statements and ratios
☐	interpret pension plan note disclosures including cash flow related information
☐	explain issues associated with accounting for share-based compensation
☐	explain how accounting for stock grants and stock options affects financial statements, and the importance of companies' assumptions in valuing these grants and options

1. INTRODUCTION

This reading covers two complex aspects of employee compensation: post-employment (retirement) benefits and share-based compensation. Retirement benefits include pensions and other post-employment benefits, such as health insurance. Examples of share-based compensation are stock options and stock grants.

A common issue underlying both of these aspects of employee compensation is the difficulty in measuring the value of the compensation. One factor contributing to the difficulty is that employees earn the benefits in the periods that they provide service but typically receive the benefits in future periods, so measurement requires a significant number of assumptions.

This reading provides an overview of the methods companies use to estimate and measure the benefits they provide to their employees and how this information is reported in financial statements. There has been some convergence between International Financial Reporting Standards (IFRS) and US generally accepted accounting principles (US GAAP) in the measurement and accounting treatment for pensions, other post-employment benefits, and share-based compensation, but some differences remain. Although this reading focuses on IFRS as the basis for discussion, instances where US GAAP significantly differ are discussed.

The reading is organized as follows: Section 2 addresses pensions and other post-employment benefits, and Section 3 covers share-based compensation with a primary focus on the accounting for and analysis of stock options. A summary and practice problems conclude the reading.

2. PENSIONS AND OTHER POST-EMPLOYMENT BENEFITS

☐ describe the types of post-employment benefit plans and implications for financial reports

This section discusses the accounting and reporting of pensions and other post-employment benefits by the companies that provide these benefits (accounting and reporting by pension and other retirement funds are not covered in this reading). Under IFRS, IAS 19, *Employee Benefits*, provides the principal source of guidance in accounting for pensions and other post-employment benefits.[1] Under US GAAP, the guidance is spread across several sections of the FASB Codification.[2]

The discussion begins with an overview of the types of benefits and measurement issues involved, including the accounting treatment for defined contribution plans. It then continues with financial statement reporting of pension plans and other post-employment benefits, including an overview of critical assumptions used to value these benefits. The section concludes with a discussion of evaluating defined benefit pension plan and other post-employment benefit disclosures.

---

1 This reading describes IFRS requirements contained in IAS 19 as updated in June 2011 and effective beginning January 2013.
2 Guidance on pension and other post-employment benefits is included in FASB ASC Topic 712 [Compensation-Nonretirement Postemployment Benefits], FASB ASC Topic 715 [Compensation-Retirement Benefits], FASB ASC Topic 960 [Plan Accounting-Defined Benefit Pension Plans], and FASB ASC Topic 965 [Plan Accounting-Health and Welfare Benefit Plans].

Types of Post-Employment Benefit Plans

Companies may offer various types of benefits to their employees following retirement, including pension plans, health care plans, medical insurance, and life insurance. Some of these benefits involve payments in the current period, but many are promises of future benefits. The objectives of accounting for employee benefits is to measure the cost associated with providing these benefits and to recognise these costs in the sponsoring company's financial statements during the employees' periods of service. Complexity arises because the sponsoring company must make assumptions to estimate the value of future benefits. The assumptions required to estimate and recognise these future benefits can have a significant impact on the company's reported performance and financial position. In addition, differences in assumptions can reduce comparability across companies.

Pension plans, as well as other post-employment benefits, may be either defined contribution plans or defined benefit plans. Under **defined contribution pension plans**, specific (or agreed-upon) contributions are made to an employee's pension plan. The agreed upon amount is the pension expense. Typically, in a defined contribution (DC) pension plan, an individual account is established for each participating employee. The accounts are generally invested through a financial intermediary, such as an investment management company or an insurance company. The employees and the employer may each contribute to the plan. After the employer makes its agreed-upon contribution to the plan on behalf of an employee—generally in the same period in which the employee provides the service—the employer has no obligation to make payments beyond this amount. The future value of the plan's assets depends on the performance of the investments within the plan. Any gains or losses related to those investments accrue to the employee. Therefore, in DC pension plans, the employee bears the risk that plan assets will not be sufficient to meet future needs. The impact on the company's financial statements of DC pension plans is easily assessed because the company has no obligations beyond the required contributions.

In contrast to DC pension plans, **defined benefit pension plans** are essentially promises by the employer to pay a defined amount of pension in the future. As part of total compensation, the employee works in the current period in exchange for a pension to be paid after retirement. In a defined benefit (DB) pension plan, the amount of pension benefit to be provided is defined, usually by reference to age, years of service, compensation, etc. For example, a DB pension plan may provide for the retiree to be paid, annually until death, an amount equal to 1 percent of the final year's salary times the number of years of service. The future pension payments represent a liability or obligation of the employer (i.e., the sponsoring company). To measure this obligation, the employer must make various actuarial assumptions (employee turnover, average retirement age, life expectancy after retirement) and computations. It is important for an analyst to evaluate such assumptions for their reasonableness and to analyse the impact of these assumptions on the financial reports of the company.

Under IFRS and US GAAP, all plans for pensions and other post-employment benefits other than those explicitly structured as DC plans are classified as DB plans.[3] DB plans include both formal plans and those informal arrangements that create a constructive obligation by the employer to its employees.[4] The employer must estimate the total cost of the benefits promised and then allocate these costs to the periods in

---

[3] Multi-employer plans are an exception under IFRS. These are plans to which many different employers contribute on behalf of their employees, such as an industry association pension plan. For multi-employer plans, the employer accounts for its proportionate share of the plan. If, however, the employer does not have sufficient information from the plan administrator to meet the reporting requirement for a defined benefit plan, IFRS allow the employer to account for the plan as if it were a defined contribution plan.

[4] For example, a company has a constructive obligation if the benefits it promises are not linked solely to the amount of its contributions or if it indirectly or directly guarantees a specified return on pension assets.

which the employees provide service. This estimation and allocation further increases the complexity of pension reporting because the timing of cash flows (contributions into the plan and payments from the plan) can differ significantly from the timing of accrual-basis reporting. Accrual-basis reporting is based on when the services are rendered and the benefits are earned.

Most DB pension plans are funded through a separate legal entity, typically a pension trust, and the assets of the trust are used to make the payments to retirees. The sponsoring company is responsible for making contributions to the plan. The company also must ensure that there are sufficient assets in the plan to pay the ultimate benefits promised to plan participants. Regulatory requirements usually specify minimum funding levels for DB pension plans, but those requirements vary by country. The funded status of a pension plan—overfunded or underfunded—refers to whether the amount of assets in the pension trust is greater than or less than the estimated liability. If the amount of assets in the DB pension trust exceeds the present value of the estimated liability, the DB pension plan is said to be overfunded; conversely, if the amount of assets in the pension trust is less than the estimated liability, the plan is said to be underfunded. Because the company has promised a defined amount of benefit to the employees, it is obligated to make those pension payments when they are due regardless of whether the pension plan assets generate sufficient returns to provide the benefits. In other words, the company bears the investment risk. Many companies are reducing the use of DB pension plans because of this risk.

Similar to DB pension plans, **other post-employment benefits** (OPB) are promises by the company to pay benefits in the future, such as life insurance premiums and all or part of health care insurance for its retirees. OPB are typically classified as DB plans, with accounting treatment similar to DB pension plans. However, the complexity in reporting for OPB may be even greater than for DB pension plans because of the need to estimate future increases in costs, such as health care, over a long time horizon. Unlike DB pension plans, however, companies may not be required by regulation to fund an OPB in advance to the same degree as DB pension plans. This is partly because governments, through some means, often insure DB pension plans but not OPB, partly because OPB may represent a much smaller financial liability, and partly because OPB are often easier to eliminate should the costs become burdensome. It is important that an analyst determine what OPB are offered by a company and the obligation they represent.

Types of post-employment benefits offered by employers differ across countries. For instance, in countries where government-sponsored universal health care plans exist (such as Germany, France, Canada, Brazil, Mexico, New Zealand, South Africa, India, Israel, Bhutan, and Singapore), companies are less likely to provide post-retirement health care benefits to employees. The extent to which companies offer DC or DB pension plans also varies by country.

Exhibit 1 summarizes these three types of post-employment benefits.

Exhibit 1: Types of Post-Employment Benefits

Type of Benefit	Amount of Post-Employment Benefit to Employee	Obligation of Sponsoring Company	Sponsoring Company's Pre-funding of its Future Obligation
Defined contribution pension plan	Amount of future benefit is not defined. Actual future benefit will depend on investment performance of plan assets. Investment risk is borne by employee.	Amount of the company's obligation (contribution) is defined in each period. The contribution, if any, is typically made on a periodic basis with no additional future obligation.	Not applicable.
Defined benefit pension plan	Amount of future benefit is defined, based on the plan's formula (often a function of length of service and final year's compensation). Investment risk is borne by company.	Amount of the future obligation, based on the plan's formula, must be estimated in the current period.	Companies typically pre-fund the DB plans by contributing funds to a pension trust. Regulatory requirements to pre-fund vary by country.
Other post-employment benefits (e.g., retirees' health care)	Amount of future benefit depends on plan specifications and type of benefit.	Eventual benefits are specified. The amount of the future obligation must be estimated in the current period.	Companies typically do not pre-fund other post-employment benefit obligations.

3. MEASURING A DEFINED BENEFIT PENSION PLAN'S OBLIGATIONS

☐ explain and calculate measures of a defined benefit pension obligation (i.e., present value of the defined benefit obligation and projected benefit obligation) and net pension liability (or asset)

Both IFRS and US GAAP measure the **pension obligation** as the present value of future benefits earned by employees for service provided to date. The obligation is called the present value of the defined benefit obligation (PVDBO) under IFRS and the projected benefit obligation (PBO) under US GAAP.[5] This measure is defined as "the present value, without deducting any plan assets, of expected future payments required to settle the obligation arising from employee service in the current and prior periods" under IFRS and "the actuarial present value as of a date of all benefits

---

[5] In addition to the projected benefit obligation, US GAAP identify two other measures of the pension liability. The **vested benefit obligation** (VBO) is the "actuarial present value of vested benefits" (FASB ASC Glossary). The **accumulated benefit obligation** (ABO) is "the actuarial present value of benefits (whether vested or non-vested) attributed, generally by the pension benefit formula, to employee service rendered before a specified date and based on employee service and compensation (if applicable) before that date. The accumulated benefit obligation differs from the projected benefit obligation in that it includes no assumption about future compensation levels" (FASB ASC Glossary). Both the vested benefit obligation and the accumulated benefit obligation are based on the amounts promised as a result of an employee's service up to a specific date. Thus, both of these measures will be less than the projected benefit obligation (VBO < ABO < PBO).

attributed by the pension benefit formula to employee service rendered prior to that date" under US GAAP. In the remainder of this reading, the term "pension obligation" will be used to generically refer to PVDBO and PBO.

In determining the pension obligation, a company estimates the future benefits it will pay. To estimate the future benefits, the company must make a number of assumptions[6] such as future compensation increases and levels, discount rates, and expected vesting. For instance, an estimate of future compensation is made if the pension benefit formula is based on future compensation levels (examples include pay-related, final-pay, final-average-pay, or career-average-pay plans). The expected annual increase in compensation over the employee service period can have a significant impact on the defined benefit obligation. The determination of the benefit obligation implicitly assumes that the company will continue to operate in the future (the "going concern assumption") and recognises that benefits will increase with future compensation increases.

Another key assumption is the discount rate—the interest rate used to calculate the present value of the future benefits. This rate is based on current rates of return on high-quality corporate bonds (or government bonds in the absence of a deep market in corporate bonds) with currency and durations consistent with the currency and durations of the benefits.

Under both DB and DC pension plans, the benefits that employees earn may be conditional on remaining with the company for a specified period of time. "Vesting" refers to a provision in pensions plans whereby an employee gains rights to future benefits only after meeting certain criteria, such as a pre-specified number of years of service. If the employee leaves the company before meeting the criteria, he or she may be entitled to none or a portion of the benefits earned up until that point. However, once the employee has met the vesting requirements, he or she is entitled to receive the benefits earned in prior periods (i.e., once the employee has become vested, benefits are not forfeited if the employee leaves the company). In measuring the defined benefit obligation, the company considers the probability that some employees may not satisfy the vesting requirements (i.e., may leave before the vesting period) and uses this probability to calculate the current service cost and the present value of the obligation. Current service cost is the increase in the present value of a defined benefit obligation as a result of employee service in the current period. Current service cost is not the only cause of change in the present value of a defined benefit obligation.

The estimates and assumptions about future salary increases, the discount rate, and the expected vesting can change. Of course, any changes in these estimates and assumptions will change the estimated pension obligation. If the changes increase the obligation, the increase is referred to as an actuarial loss. If the changes decrease the obligation, the change is referred to as an actuarial gain.

---

6 These assumptions are referred to as "actuarial assumptions." Thus, losses or gains due to changes in these assumptions, or due to differences between these assumptions and what actually occurs, are referred to as "actuarial gains or losses."

FINANCIAL STATEMENT REPORTING: DEFINED CONTRIBUTION PENSION PLANS

4

☐ describe the types of post-employment benefit plans and implications for financial reports

Defined Contribution Pension Plans

The accounting treatment for defined contribution pension plans is relatively simple. From a financial statement perspective, the employer's obligation for contributions into the plan, if any, is recorded as an expense on the income statement. Because the employer's obligation is limited to a defined amount that typically equals its contribution, no significant pension-related liability accrues on the balance sheet. An accrual (current liability) is recognised at the end of the reporting period only for any unpaid contributions.

FINANCIAL STATEMENT REPORTING OF PENSION PLANS: BALANCE SHEET REPORTING FOR DEFINED BENEFIT PENSION PLANS

5

☐ explain and calculate measures of a defined benefit pension obligation (i.e., present value of the defined benefit obligation and projected benefit obligation) and net pension liability (or asset)

The accounting treatment for defined benefit pension plans is more complex, primarily because of the complexities of measuring the pension obligation and expense.

Balance Sheet Presentation

Both IFRS and US GAAP require a pension plan's funded status to be reported on the balance sheet. The funded status is determined by netting the pension obligation against the fair value of the pension plan assets. If the pension obligation exceeds the pension plan assets, the plan has a deficit. If the plan assets exceed the pension obligation, the plan has a surplus. Summarizing this information in equation form gives

Funded status = Fair value of the plan assets − PV of the Defined benefit obligation

If the plan has a deficit, an amount equal to the net underfunded pension obligation is reported on the balance sheet as a net pension liability. If the plan has a surplus, an asset equal to the overfunded pension obligation is reported on the balance sheet as a net pension asset (except that the amount of reported assets is subject to a ceiling defined as the present value of future economic benefits, such as refunds from the plan or reductions of future contributions). Disclosures in the notes provide additional information about the net pension liability or asset reported on the balance sheet.

> **EXAMPLE 1**
>
> ### Determination of Amounts to be Reported on the Balance Sheet
>
> 1. The following information pertains to two hypothetical companies' defined benefit pension plans as of 31 December 2010:
>
>   - For company ABC, the present value of the company's defined benefit obligation is €6,723 and the fair value of the pension plan's assets is €4,880.
>   - For company DEF, the present value of the company's defined benefit obligation is €5,485 and the fair value of the pension plan assets is €5,998. In addition, the present value of available future refunds and reductions in future contributions is €326.
>
>   Calculate the amount each company would report as a pension asset or liability on its 2010 balance sheet.
>
> ### Solution:
>
> Company ABC would report the full underfunded status of its pension plan (i.e., the amount by which the present value of the defined benefit obligation exceeds the fair value of plan assets) as a liability. Specifically, the company would report a pension liability of €1,843.
>
> | | |
> |---|---:|
> | Present value of defined benefit obligation | €6,723 |
> | Fair value of plan assets | (4,880) |
> | Net pension liability | €1,843 |
>
> Company DEF's pension plan is overfunded by €513, which is the amount by which the fair value of the plan's assets exceed the defined benefit obligation (€5,998 – €5,485). However, when a company has a surplus in a defined benefit plan, the amount of asset that can be reported is the lower of the surplus and the asset ceiling (the present value of future economic benefits, such as refunds from the plan or reductions of future contributions). In this case, the asset ceiling is given as €326, so the amount of company DEF's reported net pension asset would be limited to €326.

6. FINANCIAL STATEMENT REPORTING: PERIODIC PENSION COSTS

- describe the components of a company's defined benefit pension costs

The periodic cost of a company's DB pension plan is the change in the net pension liability or asset adjusted for the employer's contributions. Each period, the periodic pension cost is recognised in profit or loss (P&L) and/or in other comprehensive income (OCI). (In some cases, amounts of pension costs may qualify for inclusion as part of

Financial Statement Reporting: Periodic Pension Costs

the costs of such assets as inventories and thus be included in P&L as part of cost of goods sold when those inventories are later sold. The focus here is on the amounts not capitalised.) IFRS and US GAAP differ in the way that the periodic pension cost is divided between P&L and OCI.

Under IFRS, the periodic pension cost is viewed as having three components, two of which are recognised in P&L and one of which is recognised in OCI.

1. *Service costs.* The first component of periodic pension cost is service cost. Current service cost is the amount by which a company's pension obligation increases as a result of employees' service in the current period. Past service cost is the amount by which a company's pension obligation relating to employees' service in prior periods changes as a result of plan amendments or a plan curtailment.[7] Under IFRS, service costs (including both current service costs and past service costs) are recognised as an expense in P&L.

2. *Net interest expense/income.* The second component of periodic pension cost is net interest expense or income, which we will refer to as "net interest expense/income." Net interest expense/income is calculated by multiplying the net pension liability or net pension asset by the discount rate used in determining the present value of the pension liability. A net interest expense represents the financing cost of deferring payments related to the plan, and a net interest income represents the financing income from prepaying amounts related to the plan. Under IFRS, the net interest expense/income is recognised in P&L.

3. *Remeasurement.* The third component of periodic pension cost is remeasurement of the net pension liability or asset. Remeasurement includes (a) actuarial gains and losses and (b) any differences between the actual return on plan assets and the amount included in the net interest expense/income calculation. Under IFRS, remeasurement amounts are recognised in OCI. Remeasurement amounts are not subsequently amortised to P&L.

Similar to IFRS, under US GAAP current service cost is recognised in P&L. However, under US GAAP, past service costs are reported in OCI in the period in which the change giving rise to the cost occurs. In subsequent periods, these past service costs are amortised to P&L over the average service lives of the affected employees.

Also similar to IFRS, under US GAAP the periodic pension cost for P&L includes interest expense on pension obligations (which increases the amount of the periodic cost) and returns on the pension plan assets (which reduce the amount of the periodic cost). Unlike IFRS, however, under US GAAP, the two components are not presented net. Also, under US GAAP, returns on plan assets included in the P&L recognition of pension costs (pension expense) use an expected return rather than the actual return. (Under IFRS, returns on plan assets included in the P&L recognition of pension costs (pension expense) use the discount rate as the expected return.) Thus, under US GAAP, differences between the expected return and the actual return on plan assets represent another source of actuarial gains or losses. As noted, actuarial gains and losses can also result from changes in the actuarial assumptions used in determining the benefit obligation. Under US GAAP, all actuarial gains and losses are included in the net pension liability or net pension asset and can be reported either in P&L or in OCI. Typically, companies report actuarial gains and losses in OCI and recognise gains and losses in P&L only when certain conditions are met under a so-called corridor approach.

---

[7] A curtailment occurs when there is a significant reduction by the entity either in the number of employees covered by a plan or in benefits.

Under the corridor approach, the net cumulative unrecognised actuarial gains and losses at the beginning of the reporting period are compared with the defined benefit obligation and the fair value of plan assets at the beginning of the period. If the cumulative amount of unrecognised actuarial gains and losses becomes too large (i.e., exceeds 10 percent of the greater of the defined benefit obligation or the fair value of plan assets), then the excess is amortised over the expected average remaining working lives of the employees participating in the plan and is included as a component of periodic pension cost in P&L. The term "corridor" refers to the 10 percent range, and only amounts in excess of the corridor must be amortised.

To illustrate the corridor approach, assume that the beginning balance of the defined benefit obligation is $5,000,000, the beginning balance of fair value of plan assets is $4,850,000, and the beginning balance of unrecognised actuarial losses is $610,000. The expected average remaining working lives of the plan employees is 10 years. In this scenario, the corridor is $500,000, which is 10 percent of the defined benefit obligation (selected as the greater of the defined benefit obligation or the fair value of plan assets). Because the balance of unrecognised actuarial losses exceeds the $500,000 corridor, amortisation is required. The amount of the amortisation is $11,000, which is the excess of the unrecognised actuarial loss over the corridor divided by the expected average remaining working lives of the plan employees [($610,000 − $500,000) ÷ 10 years]. Actuarial gains or losses can also be amortised more quickly than under the corridor method; companies may use a faster recognition method, provided the company applies the method of amortisation to both gains and losses consistently in all periods presented.

To summarize, under IFRS, the periodic pension costs recognised in P&L include service costs (both current and past) and net interest expense/income. The periodic pension costs recognised in OCI include remeasurements that comprise net return on plan assets and actuarial gains and losses. Under US GAAP, the periodic pension costs recognised in P&L include current service costs, interest expense on plan liabilities, expected returns on plan assets (which is a reduction of the cost), the amortisation of past service costs, and actuarial gains and losses to the extent not reported in OCI. The components of a company's defined benefit periodic pension costs are summarized in Exhibit 2.

Exhibit 2: Components of a Company's Defined Benefit Pension Periodic Costs

IFRS Component	IFRS Recognition	US GAAP Component	US GAAP Recognition
Service costs	Recognised in P&L.	Current service costs	Recognised in P&L.
		Past service costs	Recognised in OCI and subsequently amortised to P&L over the service life of employees.
Net interest income/expense	Recognised in P&L as the following amount: Net pension liability or asset × interest rate[a]	Interest expense on pension obligation	Recognised in P&L.
		Expected return on plan assets	Recognised in P&L as the following amount: Plan assets × expected return.

IFRS Component	IFRS Recognition	US GAAP Component	US GAAP Recognition
Remeasurements: Net return on plan assets and actuarial gains and losses	Recognised in OCI and not subsequently amortised to P&L. - Net return on plan assets = Actual return – (Plan assets × Interest rate). - Actuarial gains and losses = Changes in a company's pension obligation arising from changes in actuarial assumptions.	Actuarial gains and losses including differences between the actual and expected returns on plan assets	Recognised immediately in P&L or, more commonly, recognised in OCI and subsequently amortised to P&L using the corridor or faster recognition method.[b] - Difference between expected and actual return on assets = Actual return – (Plan assets × Expected return). - Actuarial gains and losses = Changes in a company's pension obligation arising from changes in actuarial assumptions.

[a] The interest rate used is equal to the discount rate used to measure the pension liability (the yield on high-quality corporate bonds.)
[b] If the cumulative amount of unrecognised actuarial gains and losses exceeds 10 percent of the greater of the value of the plan assets or of the present value of the DB obligation (under US GAAP, the projected benefit obligation), the difference must be amortised over the service lives of the employees.

Reporting the Periodic Pension Cost.
As noted above, some amounts of pension costs may qualify for capitalisation as part of the costs of self-constructed assets, such as inventories. Pension costs included in inventories would thus be recognised in P&L as part of cost of goods sold when those inventories are sold. For pension costs that are not capitalised, IFRS do not specify where companies present the various components of periodic pension cost beyond differentiating between components included in P&L and in OCI. In contrast, for pension costs that are not capitalised, US GAAP require all components of periodic pension cost that are recognised in P&L to be aggregated and presented as a net amount within the same line item on the income statement. Both IFRS and US GAAP require total periodic pension cost to be disclosed in the notes to the financial statements.

EFFECT OF ASSUMPTIONS AND ACTUARIAL GAIN AND LOSSES ON PENSIONS

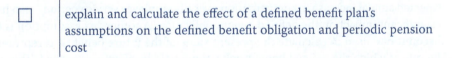

explain and calculate the effect of a defined benefit plan's assumptions on the defined benefit obligation and periodic pension cost

As noted, a company's pension obligation for a DB pension plan is based on many estimates and assumptions. The amount of future pension payments requires assumptions about employee turnover, length of service, and rate of increase in compensation levels. The length of time the pension payments will be made requires assumptions about employees' life expectancy post-employment. Finally, the present value of these future payments requires assumptions about the appropriate discount rate (which is used as the rate at which interest expense or income will subsequently accrue on the net pension liability or asset).

Changes in any of the assumptions will increase or decrease the pension obligation. An increase in pension obligation resulting from changes in actuarial assumptions is considered an actuarial loss, and a decrease is considered an actuarial gain. The estimate of a company's pension liability also affects several components of periodic pension costs, apart from actuarial gains and losses. First, the service cost component of annual pension cost is essentially the amount by which the pension liability increases as a result of the employees' service during the year. Second, the interest expense component of annual pension cost is based on the amount of the liability. Third, the past service cost component of annual pension cost is the amount by which the pension liability increases because of changes to the plan.

Estimates related to plan assets can also affect annual pension cost reported in P&L (pension expense), primarily under US GAAP. Because a company's periodic pension cost reported in P&L under US GAAP includes the *expected* return on pension assets rather than the actual return, the assumptions about the expected return on plan assets can have a significant impact. Also, the expected return on plan assets requires estimating in which future period the benefits will be paid. As noted above, a divergence of actual returns on pension assets from expected returns results in an actuarial gain or loss.

Understanding the effect of assumptions on the estimated pension obligation and on periodic pension costs is important both for interpreting a company's financial statements and for evaluating whether a company's assumptions appear relatively conservative or aggressive.

The projected unit credit method is the IFRS approach to measuring the DB obligation. Under the projected unit credit method, each period of service (e.g., year of employment) gives rise to an additional unit of benefit to which the employee is entitled at retirement. In other words, for each period in which an employee provides service, they earn a portion of the post-employment benefits that the company has promised to pay. An equivalent way of thinking about this is that the amount of eventual benefit increases with each additional year of service. The employer measures each unit of service as it is earned to determine the amount of benefits it is obligated to pay in future reporting periods.

The objective of the projected unit credit method is to allocate the entire expected retirement costs (benefits) for an employee over the employee's service periods. The defined benefit obligation represents the actuarial present value of all units of benefit (credit) to which the employee is entitled (i.e., those that the employee has earned) as a result of prior and current periods of service. This obligation is based on actuarial assumptions about demographic variables, such as employee turnover and life expectancy, and on estimates of financial variables, such as future inflation and the discount rate. If the pension benefit formula is based on employees' future compensation levels, then the unit of benefit earned each period will reflect this estimate.

Under both IFRS and US GAAP, the assumed rate of increase in compensation—the expected annual increase in compensation over the employee service period—can have a significant impact on the defined benefit obligation. Another key assumption is the discount rate used to calculate the present value of the future benefits. It represents the rate at which the defined benefit obligation could be effectively settled. This rate is based on current rates of return on high quality corporate bonds with durations consistent with the durations of the benefit.

CALCULATION OF DEFINED BENEFIT PENSION OBLIGATION AND CURRENT SERVICE COSTS

8

☐ explain and calculate the effect of a defined benefit plan's assumptions on the defined benefit obligation and periodic pension cost

[Margin note: Remeasurement component of periodic Pension cost: actuarial gains and losses + net return on plan assets.]

The following example illustrates the calculation of the defined benefit pension obligation and current service costs, using the projected unit credit method, for an individual employee under four different scenarios. Interest on the opening obligation also increases the obligation and is part of current costs. The fourth scenario is used to demonstrate the impact on a company's pension obligation of changes in certain key estimates. Example 2 and Example 3 focus on the pension obligation. The change in pension obligation over the period is included in the calculation of pension expense (pension cost reported in P&L).

EXAMPLE 2

Calculation of Defined Benefit Pension Obligation for an Individual Employee

The following information applies to each of the four scenarios. Assume that a (hypothetical) company establishes a DB pension plan. The employee has a salary in the coming year of €50,000 and is expected to work five more years before retiring. The assumed discount rate is 6 percent, and the assumed annual compensation increase is 4.75 percent. For simplicity, assume that there are no changes in actuarial assumptions, all compensation increases are awarded on the first day of the service year, and no additional adjustments are made to reflect the possibility that the employee may leave the company at an earlier date.

Current salary	€50,000.00
Years until retirement	5
Annual compensation increases	4.75%
Discount rate	6.00%
Final year's estimated salary[a]	€60,198.56

[a] Final year's estimated salary = Current year's salary × [(1 + Annual compensation increase)$^{\text{Years until retirement} - 1}$].

At the end of Year 1, the final year's estimated salary = €50,000 × [(1 + 0.0475)^4] = €60,198.56, assuming that the employee's salary increases by 4.75 percent each year. With no change in assumption about the rate of increase in compensation or the date of retirement, the estimate of the final year's salary will remain unchanged.

At the end of Year 2, assuming the employee's salary actually increased by 4.75 percent, the final year's estimated salary = €52,375 × [(1 + 0.0475)^3] = €60,198.56.

Scenario 1: Benefit is paid as a lump sum amount upon retirement.

The plan will pay a lump sum pension benefit equal to 1.5 percent of the employee's final salary for each year of service beyond the date of establishment. The lump sum payment to be paid upon retirement = (Final salary × Benefit formula) × Years of service = (€60,198.56 × 0.015) × 5 = €4,514.89.

Annual unit credit (benefit) per service year = Value at retirement/Years of service = €4,514.89/5 = €902.98.

If the discount rate (the interest rate at which the defined benefit obligation could be effectively settled) is assumed to be 0 percent, the amount of annual unit credit per service year is the amount of the company's annual obligation and the closing obligation each year is simply the annual unit credit multiplied by the number of past and current years of service. However, because the assumed discount rate must be based on the yield on high-quality corporate bonds and will thus not equal 0 percent, the future obligation resulting from current and prior service is discounted to determine the value of the obligation at any point in time.

The following table shows how the obligation builds up for this employee.

Year	1	2	3	4	5
Estimated annual salary	€50,000.00	€52,375.00	€54,862.81	€57,468.80	€60,198.56
Benefits attributed to:					
Prior years[a]	€0.00	€902.98	€1,805.96	€2,708.94	€3,611.92
Current year[b]	902.98	902.98	902.98	902.98	902.97*
Total benefits earned	€902.98	€1,805.96	€2,708.94	€3,611.92	€4,514.89
Opening obligation[c]	€0.00	€715.24	€1,516.31	€2,410.94	€3,407.47
Interest cost at 6 percent[d]	0.00	42.91	90.98	144.66	204.45
Current service costs[e]	715.24	758.16	803.65	851.87	902.97
Closing obligation[f]	€715.24	€1,516.31	€2,410.94	€3,407.47	€4,514.89

*Final amounts may differ slightly to compensate for rounding in earlier years.

[a] The benefit attributed to prior years = Annual unit credit × Years of prior service.
 For Year 2, €902.98 × 1 = €902.98.
 For Year 3, €902.98 × 2 = €1,805.96.

[b] The benefit attributed to current year = Annual unit credit based on benefit formula = Final year's estimated salary × Benefit formula = Value at retirement date/Years of service = (€60,198.56 × 1.5%) = €4,514.89/5 = €902.98.

[c] The opening obligation is the closing obligation at the end of the previous year, but can also be viewed as the present value of benefits earned in prior years:
 Benefits earned in prior years/$[(1 + \text{Discount rate})^{\text{Years until retirement}}]$.
 Opening obligation Year 1 = €0.
 Opening obligation Year 2 = €902.98/$[(1 + 0.06)^4]$ = €715.24.
 Opening obligation Year 3 = €1,805.96/$[(1 + 0.06)^3]$ = €1,516.32.

[d] The interest cost is the increase in the present value of the defined benefit obligation due to the passage of time:
 Interest cost = Opening obligation × Discount rate.
 For Year 2 = €715.24 × 0.06 = €42.91.
 For Year 3 = €1,516.32 × 0.06 = €90.98.

[e] Current service costs are the present value of annual unit credits earned in the current period:
 Annual unit credit/$[(1 + \text{Discount rate})^{\text{Years until retirement}}]$.
 For Year 1 = €902.98/$[(1 + 0.06)^4]$ = €715.24.
 For Year 2 = €902.98/$[(1 + 0.06)^3]$ = €758.16.

 Note: Given no change in actuarial assumptions and estimates of financial growth, the current service costs in any year (except the first) are the previous year's current service costs increased by the discount rate; the current service costs increase with the passage of time.

Calculation of Defined Benefit Pension Obligation and Current Service Costs

> [f] *The closing obligation is the opening obligation plus the interest cost and the current service costs but can also be viewed as the present value of benefits earned in prior and current years. There is a slight difference due to rounding.*
> *Total benefits earned/[(1 + Discount rate)$^{\text{Years until retirement}}$].*
> *Closing obligation Year 1 = €902.98/[(1 + 0.06)^4] = €715.24.*
> *Closing obligation Year 2 = €1,805.96/[(1 + 0.06)^3] = €1,516.32.*
> *Closing obligation Year 3 = €2,708.94/[(1 + 0.06)^2] = €2,410.95.*
>   *Note:* Assuming no past service costs or actuarial gains/losses, the closing obligation less the fair value of the plan assets represents both the funded status of the plan and the net pension liability/asset. The change in obligation is the amount of expense for pensions on the income statement.

Scenario 2: Prior years of service, and benefit paid as a lump sum upon retirement.

The plan will pay a lump sum pension benefit equal to 1.5 percent of the employee's final salary for each year of service beyond the date of establishment. In addition, at the time the pension plan is established, the employee is given credit for 10 years of prior service with immediate vesting. The lump sum payment to be paid upon retirement = (Final salary × Benefit formula) × Years of service = (€60,198.56 × 0.015) × 15 = €13,544.68.

Annual unit credit = Value at retirement date/Years of service = €13,544.68/15 = €902.98.

The following table shows how the obligation builds up for this employee.

Year	1	2	3	4	5
Benefits attributed to:					
Prior years[a]	€9,029.78	€9,932.76	€10,835.74	€11,738.72	€12,641.70
Current years	902.98	902.98	902.98	902.98	902.98
Total benefits earned	€9,932.76	€10,835.74	€11,738.72	€12,641.70	€13,544.68
Opening obligation[b]	€6,747.58	€7,867.67	€9,097.89	€10,447.41	€11,926.13
Interest at 6 percent	404.85	472.06	545.87	626.85	715.57
Current service costs	715.24	758.16	803.65	851.87	902.98
Closing obligation	€7,867.67	€9,097.89	€10,447.41	€11,926.13	€13,544.68

> [a] *Benefits attributed to prior years of service = Annual unit credit × Years of prior service. At beginning of Year 1 = (€60,198.56 × 0.015) × 10 = €9,029.78.*
> [b] *Opening obligation is the present value of the benefits attributed to prior years = Benefits attributed to prior years/(1 + Discount rate)$^{\text{Number of years to retirement}}$.*
> *At beginning of Year 1 = €9,029.78/(1.06)^5 = €6,747.58. This is treated as past service costs in Year 1 because there was no previous recognition and there is immediate vesting.*

Scenario 3: Employee to receive benefit payments for 20 years (no prior years of service).

Years of receiving pension = 20.

Estimated annual payment (end of year) for each of the 20 years = (Estimated final salary × Benefit formula) × Years of service = (€60,198.56 × 0.015) × 5 = €4,514.89.

Value at the end of Year 5 (retirement date) of the estimated future payments = PV of €4,514.89 for 20 years at 6 percent = €51,785.46.[8]

---

[8] This is a simplification of the valuation process for illustrative purposes. For example, the actuarial valuation would use mortality rates, not just assumed life expectancy. Additionally, annualizing the present value of an ordinary annuity probably understates the liability because the actual benefit payments are usually made monthly or bi-weekly rather than annually.

Annual unit credit = Value at retirement date/Years of service = €51,785.46/5 = €10,357.09.

Year	1	2	3	4	5
Benefit attributed to:					
Prior years	€0.00	€10,357.09	€20,714.18	€31,071.27	€41,428.36
Current year	10,357.09	10,357.09	10,357.09	10,357.09	10,357.10
Total benefits earned	€10,357.09	€20,714.18	€31,071.27	€41,428.36	€51,785.46
Opening obligation	€0.00	€8,203.79	€17,392.03	€27,653.32	€39,083.36
Interest at 6 percent	0.00	492.23	1,043.52	1,659.20	2,345.00
Current service costs	8,203.79	8,696.01	9,217.77	9,770.84	10,357.10
Closing obligation	€8,203.79	€17,392.03	€27,653.32	€39,083.36	€51,785.46

In this scenario, the pension obligation at the end of Year 3 is €27,653.32 and the portion of pension expense (pension costs reported in P&L) attributable to interest and current service costs for Year 3 is €10,261.29 (= €1,043.52 + €9,217.77). The total pension expense would include other items such as a reduction for return on plan assets.

Scenario 4: Employee to receive benefit payments for 20 years and is given credit for 10 years of prior service with immediate vesting.

Estimated annual payment (end of year) for each of the 20 years = (Estimated final salary × Benefit formula) × Years of service = (€60,198.56 × 0.015) × (10 + 5) = €13,544.68.

Value at the end of Year 5 (retirement date) of the estimated future payments = PV of €13,544.68 for 20 years at 6 percent = €155,356.41.

Annual unit credit = Value at retirement date/Years of service = €155,356.41/15 = €10,357.09.

Year	1	2	3	4	5
Benefit attributed to:					
Prior years	€103,570.94	€113,928.03	€124,285.12	€134,642.21	€144,999.30
Current year	10,357.09	10,357.09	10,357.09	10,357.09	10,357.11
Total benefits earned	€113,928.03	€124,285.12	€134,642.21	€144,999.30	€155,356.41
Opening obligation[a]	€77,394.23	€90,241.67	€104,352.18	€119,831.08	€136,791.79
Interest at 6 percent	4,643.65	5,414.50	6,261.13	7,189.87	8,207.51
Current service costs	8,203.79	8,696.01	9,217.77	9,770.84	10,357.11
Closing obligation	€90,241.67	€104,352.18	€119,831.08	€136,791.79	€155,356.41

[a] *This is treated as past service costs in Year 1 because there was no previous recognition and there is immediate vesting.*

Calculation of Defined Benefit Pension Obligation and Current Service Costs

EXAMPLE 3

The Effect of a Change in Assumptions

Based on Scenario 4 of Example 2 (10 years of prior service and the employee receives benefits for 20 years after retirement):

1. What is the effect on the Year 1 closing pension obligation of a 100 basis point increase in the assumed discount rate—that is, from 6 percent to 7 percent? What is the effect on pension cost in Year 1?

Solution:

The estimated final salary and the estimated annual payments after retirement are unchanged at €60,198.56 and €13,544.68, respectively. However, the value at the retirement date is changed. Value at the end of Year 5 (retirement date) of the estimated future payments = PV of €13,544.68 for 20 years at 7 percent = €143,492.53. Annual unit credit = Value at retirement date/Years of service = €143,492.53/15 = €9,566.17.

Year	1
Benefit attributed to:	
Prior years	€95,661.69
Current year	9,566.17
Total benefits earned	€105,227.86
Opening obligation[a]	€68,205.46
Interest at 7 percent	4,774.38
Current service costs	7,297.99
Closing obligation	€80,277.83

[a] Opening obligation = Benefit attributed to prior years discounted for the remaining time to retirement at the assumed discount rate = $95{,}661.69/(1 + 0.07)^5$.

A 100 basis point increase in the assumed discount rate (from 6 percent to 7 percent) will *decrease* the Year 1 closing pension obligation by €90,241.67 − €80,277.83 = €9,963.84. The Year 1 pension cost declined from €12,847.44 (= 4,643.65 + 8,203.79) to €12,072.37 (= 4,774.38 + 7,297.99). The change in the interest component is a function of the decline in the opening obligation (which will decrease the interest component) and the increased discount rate (which will increase the interest component). In this case, the increase in the discount rate dominated and the interest component increased. The current service costs and the opening obligation both declined because of the increase in the discount rate.

2. What is the effect on the Year 1 closing pension obligation of a 100 basis point increase in the assumed annual compensation increase—that is, from 4.75 percent to 5.75 percent? Assume this is independent of the change in Question 1.

Solution:

The estimated final salary is $[€50{,}000 \times [(1 + 0.0575)^4] = €62{,}530.44$. Estimated annual payment for each of the 20 years = (Estimated final salary × Benefit formula) × Years of service = (€62,530.44 × 0.015) × (10 + 5)

= €14,069.35. Value at the end of Year 5 (retirement date) of the estimated future payments = PV of €14,069.35 for 20 years at 6 percent = €161,374.33. Annual unit credit = Value at retirement date/Years of service = €161,374.33/15 = €10,758.29.

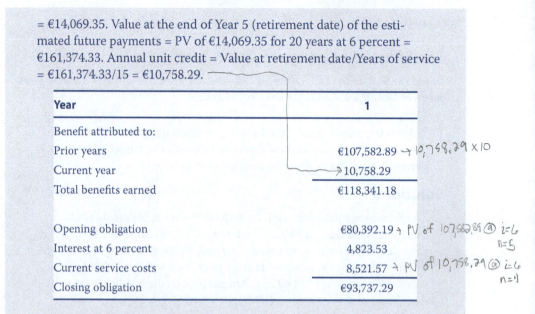

Year	1
Benefit attributed to:	
Prior years	€107,582.89
Current year	10,758.29
Total benefits earned	€118,341.18
Opening obligation	€80,392.19
Interest at 6 percent	4,823.53
Current service costs	8,521.57
Closing obligation	€93,737.29

A 100 basis point increase in the assumed annual compensation increase (from 4.75 percent to 5.75 percent) will *increase* the pension obligation by €93,737.29 − €90,241.67 = €3,495.62.

Example 3 illustrates that an increase in the assumed discount rate will *decrease* a company's pension obligation. In the Solution to 1, there is a slight increase in the interest component of the pension obligation and periodic pension cost (from €4,643.65 in Scenario 4 of Example 2 to €4,774.38 in Example 3). Depending on the pattern and duration of the annual benefits being projected, however, it is possible that the amount of the interest component could decrease because the decrease in the opening obligation may more than offset the effect of the increase in the discount rate.

Example 3 also illustrates that an increase in the assumed rate of annual compensation increase will *increase* a company's pension obligation when the pension formula is based on the final year's salary. In addition, a higher assumed rate of annual compensation increase will increase the service components and the interest component of a company's periodic pension cost because of an increased annual unit credit and the resulting increased obligation. An increase in life expectancy also will increase the pension obligation unless the promised pension payments are independent of life expectancy—for example, paid as a lump sum or over a fixed period.

Finally, under US GAAP, because the expected return on plan assets reduces periodic pension costs reported in P&L, a higher expected return will decrease pension cost reported in P&L (pension expense). Exhibit 3 summarizes the impact of some key estimates on the balance sheet and the periodic pension cost.

Exhibit 3: Impact of Key DB Pension Assumptions on Balance Sheet and Periodic Costs

Assumption	Impact of Assumption on Balance Sheet	Impact of Assumption on Periodic Cost
Higher discount rate.	Lower obligation.	Periodic pension costs will typically be lower because of lower opening obligation and lower service costs.

Disclosure of Assumptions

Assumption	Impact of Assumption on Balance Sheet	Impact of Assumption on Periodic Cost
Higher rate of compensation increase.	Higher obligation.	Higher service costs.
Higher expected return on plan assets.	No effect, because fair value of plan assets is used on balance sheet.	Not applicable for IFRS. Lower periodic pension expense under US GAAP.

Accounting for other post-employment benefits also requires assumptions and estimates. For example, assumed trends in health care costs are an important component of estimating costs of post-employment health care plans. A higher assumed medical expense inflation rate will result in a higher post-employment medical obligation. Companies also estimate various patterns of health care cost trend rates—for example, higher in the near term but becoming lower after some point in time. For post-employment health plans, an increase in the assumed inflationary trends in health care costs or an increase in life expectancy will increase the obligation and associated periodic expense of these plans.

The sections above have explained how the amounts to be reported on the balance sheet are calculated, how the various components of periodic pension cost are reflected in income, and how changes in assumptions can affect pension-related amounts. The next section evaluates disclosures of pension and other post-employment benefits, including disclosures about key assumptions.

DISCLOSURE OF ASSUMPTIONS 9

- ☐ explain and calculate how adjusting for items of pension and other post-employment benefits that are reported in the notes to the financial statements affects financial statements and ratios
- ☐ interpret pension plan note disclosures including cash flow related information

Several aspects of the accounting for pensions and other post-employment benefits described above can affect comparative financial analysis using ratios based on financial statements.

- Differences in key assumptions can affect comparisons across companies.
- Amounts disclosed in the balance sheet are net amounts (plan liabilities minus plan assets). Adjustments to incorporate gross amounts would change certain financial ratios.
- Periodic pension costs recognized in P&L (pension expense) may not be comparable. IFRS and US GAAP differ in their provisions about costs recognised in P&L versus in OCI.
- Reporting of periodic pension costs in P&L may not be comparable. Under US GAAP, all of the components of pension costs in P&L are reported in operating expense on the income statement even though some of the components are of a financial nature (specifically, interest expense and the expected return on assets). However, under IFRS, the components of periodic pension costs in P&L can be included in various line items.

- Cash flow information may not be comparable. Under IFRS, some portion of the amount of contributions might be treated as a financing activity rather than an operating activity; under US GAAP, the contribution is treated as an operating activity.

Information related to pensions can be obtained from various portions of the financial statement note disclosures, and appropriate analytical adjustments can be made. In the following sections, we examine pension plan note disclosures and highlight analytical issues related to each of the points listed above.

Assumptions

Companies disclose their assumptions about discount rates, expected compensation increases, medical expense inflation, and—for US GAAP companies—expected return on plan assets. Comparing these assumptions over time and across companies provides a basis to assess any conservative or aggressive biases. Some companies also disclose the effects of a change in their assumptions.

Exhibit 4 presents the assumed discount rates (Panel A) and assumed annual compensation increases (Panel B) to estimate pension obligations for four companies operating in the automotive and equipment manufacturing sector. Fiat S.p.A. (an Italy-based company) and the Volvo Group[9] (a Sweden-based company) use IFRS. General Motors and Ford Motor Company are US-based companies that use US GAAP. All of these companies have both US and non-US defined benefit pension plans, which facilitates comparison.

Exhibit 4

Panel A. Assumed discount rates used to estimate pension obligations (percent)

	2009	2008	2007	2006	2005
Fiat S.p.A. (Italy)	5.02	5.10	4.70	3.98	3.53
The Volvo Group (Sweden)	4.00	4.50	4.50	4.00	4.00
General Motors (non-US plans)	5.31	6.22	5.72	4.76	4.72
Ford Motor Company (non-US plans)	5.93	5.58	5.58	4.91	4.58
Fiat S.p.A. (US plans)	5.50	5.10	5.80	5.80	5.50
The Volvo Group (US plans)	4.00–5.75	5.75–6.25	5.75–6.25	5.50	5.75
General Motors (US plans)	5.52	6.27	6.35	5.90	5.70
Ford Motor Company (US plans)	6.50	6.25	6.25	5.86	5.61

Panel B. Assumed annual compensation increases used to estimate pension obligations (percent)

	2009	2008	2007	2006	2005
Fiat S.p.A. (Italy)	4.02	4.65	4.60	3.65	2.58
The Volvo Group (Sweden)	3.00	3.50	3.20	3.20	3.20
General Motors (non-US plans)	3.23	3.59	3.60	3.00	3.10
Ford Motor Company (non-US plans)	3.13	3.21	3.21	3.30	3.44

---

9 The Volvo Group primarily manufactures trucks, buses, construction equipment, and engines and engine components for boats, industry, and aircraft. The Volvo car division was sold to Ford Motor Company in 1999, and Ford sold Volvo Car Corporation to the Zhejiang Geely Holding Group in 2010.

Disclosure of Assumptions

Panel B. Assumed annual compensation increases used to estimate pension obligations (percent)

	2009	2008	2007	2006	2005
Fiat S.p.A. (US plans)*	na	na	na	na	na
The Volvo Group (US plans)	3.00	3.50	3.50	3.50	3.50
General Motors (US plans)	3.94	5.00	5.25	5.00	4.90
Ford Motor Company (US plans)	3.80	3.80	3.80	3.80	4.00

In the United States, Fiat has obligations to former employees under DB pension plans but no longer offers DB plans. As a result, annual compensation increases are not applicable (na).

The assumed discount rates used to estimate pension obligations are generally based on the market interest rates of high-quality corporate fixed-income investments with a maturity profile similar to the timing of a company's future pension payments. The trend in discount rates across the companies (in both their non-US plans and US plans) is generally similar. In the non-US plans, discount rates increased from 2005 to 2008 and then decreased in 2009 except for Ford, which increased discount rates in 2009. In the US plans, discount rates increased from 2005 to 2007 and held steady or decreased in 2008. In 2009, Fiat and Ford's discount rates increased while Volvo and GM's discount rates decreased. Ford had the highest assumed discount rates for both its non-US and US plans in 2009. Recall that a higher discount rate assumption results in a lower estimated pension obligation. Therefore, the use of a higher discount rate compared with its peers may indicate a less conservative bias.

Explanations for differences in the level of the assumed discount rates, apart from bias, are differences in the regions/countries involved and differences in the timing of obligations (for example, differences in the percentage of employees covered by the DB pension plan that are at or near retirement). In this example, the difference in regions/countries might explain the difference in rates used for the non-US plans but would not explain the difference in the rates shown for the companies' US plans. The timing of obligations under the companies' DB pension plans likely varies, so the relevant market interest rates selected as the discount rate will vary accordingly. Because the timing of the pension obligations is not disclosed, differences in timing cannot be ruled out as an explanation for differences in discount rates.

An important consideration is whether the assumptions are internally consistent. For example, do the company's assumed discount rates and assumed compensation increases reflect a consistent view of inflation? For Volvo, both the assumed discount rates and the assumed annual compensation increases (for both its non-US and US plans) are lower than those of the other companies, so the assumptions appear internally consistent. The assumptions are consistent with plans located in lower-inflation regions. Recall that a lower rate of compensation increase results in a lower estimated pension obligation.

In Ford's US and non-US pension plans, the assumed discount rate is increasing and the assumed rate of compensation increase is decreasing or holding steady in 2009. Each of these will reduce the pension obligation. Therefore, holding all else equal, Ford's pension liability is decreasing because of the higher assumed discount rate and the reduced assumed rate of compensation increase.

Another relevant assumption—for US GAAP companies but not for IFRS companies—is the expected return on pension plan assets. Under US GAAP, a higher expected return on plan assets lowers the periodic pension cost. (Of course, a higher expected return on plan assets presumably reflects riskier investments, so it would not be advisable for a company to simply invest in riskier investments to reduce periodic pension expense.) Because companies are also required to disclose the target asset allocation for their pension plan assets, analysts can assess reasonableness of those assumptions by comparing companies' assumed expected return on plan assets in the context of the plans' asset allocation. For example, a higher expected return is consistent with a greater proportion of plan assets being allocated to riskier asset classes.

Companies with other post-employment benefits also disclose information about these benefits, including assumptions made to estimate the obligation and expense. For example, companies with post-employment health care plans disclose assumptions about increases in health care costs. The assumptions are typically that the inflation rate in health care costs will taper off to some lower, constant rate at some year in the future. That future inflation rate is known as the ultimate health care trend rate. Holding all else equal, each of the following assumptions would result in a higher benefit obligation and a higher periodic cost:

- A higher assumed near-term increase in health care costs,
- A higher assumed ultimate health care cost trend rate, and
- A later year in which the ultimate health care cost trend rate is assumed to be reached.

Conversely, holding all else equal, each of the following assumptions would result in a lower benefit obligation and a lower periodic cost:

- A lower assumed near-term increase in health care costs,
- A lower assumed ultimate health care cost trend rate, and
- An earlier year in which the ultimate health care cost trend rate is assumed to be reached.

Example 4 examines two companies' assumptions about trends in US health care costs.

> **EXAMPLE 4**
>
> ## Comparison of Assumptions about Trends in US Health Care Costs
>
> In addition to disclosing assumptions about health care costs, companies also disclose information on the sensitivity of the measurements of both the obligation and the periodic cost to changes in those assumptions. Exhibit 5 presents information obtained from the notes to the financial statements for CNH Global N.V. (a Dutch manufacturer of construction and mining equipment) and Caterpillar Inc. (a US manufacturer of construction and mining equipment, engines, and turbines). Each company has US employees for whom they provide post-employment health care benefits.
>
> Panel A shows the companies' assumptions about health care costs and the amounts each reported for post-employment health care benefit plans. For example, CNH assumes that the initial year's (2010) increase in health care costs will be 9 percent, and this rate of increase will decline to 5 percent over the next seven years to 2017. Caterpillar assumes a lower initial-year increase of 7 percent and a decline to the ultimate health care cost trend rate of 5 percent in 2016.
>
> Panel B shows the effect of a 100 basis point increase or decrease in the assumed health care cost trend rates. A 1 percentage point increase in the assumed health care cost trend rates would increase Caterpillar's 2009 service and interest cost component of the other post-employment benefit costs by $23 million and the related obligation by $220 million. A 1 percentage point increase in the assumed health care cost trend rates would increase CNH Global's 2009 service and interest cost component of the other post-employment benefit costs by $8 million and the related obligation by $106 million.

Disclosure of Assumptions

Exhibit 5: Post-Employment Health Care Plan Disclosures

Panel A. Assumptions and Reported Amounts for US Post-Employment Health Care Benefit Plans

	Assumptions about Health Care Costs			Amounts Reported for Other Post-Employment Benefits ($ Millions)	
	Initial Health Care Cost Trend Rate 2010	Ultimate Health Care Cost Trend Rate	Year Ultimate Trend Rate Attained	Accumulated Benefit Obligation Year-End 2009	Periodic Expense for Benefits for 2009
CNH Global N.V.	9.0%	5%	2017	$1,152	$65
Caterpillar Inc.	7.0%	5%	2016	$4,537	$287

Panel B. Effect of 1 Percentage Point Increase (Decrease) in Assumed Health Care Cost Trend Rates on 2009 Total Accumulated Post-Employment Benefit Obligations and Periodic Expense

	1 Percentage Point Increase	1 Percentage Point Decrease
CNH Global N.V.	+$106 million (Obligation) +$8 million (Expense)	−$90 million (Obligation) −$6 million (Expense)
Caterpillar Inc.	+$220 million (Obligation) +$23 million (Expense)	−$186 million (Obligation) −$20 million (Expense)

Sources: Caterpillar information is from the company's Form 10-K filed 19 February 2010, Note 14 (pages A-36 and A-42). CNH Global information is from the company's 2009 Form 20-F, Note 12 (pages F-41, F-43, and F-45).

Based on the information in Exhibit 5, answer the following questions:

1. Which company's assumptions about health care costs appear less conservative?

Solution:

Caterpillar's assumptions about health care costs appear less conservative (the assumptions will result in lower health care costs) than CNH's. Caterpillar's initial assumed health care cost increase of 7 percent is significantly lower than CNH's assumed 9 percent. Further, Caterpillar assumes that the ultimate health care cost trend rate of 5 percent will be reached a year earlier than assumed by CNH.

2. What would be the effect of adjusting the post-employment benefit obligation and the periodic post-employment benefit expense of the less conservative company for a 1 percentage point increase in health care cost trend rates? Does this make the two companies more comparable?

Solution:

The sensitivity disclosures indicate that a 1 percentage point increase in the assumed health care cost trend rate would increase Caterpillar's post-employment benefit obligation by $220 million and its periodic cost by $23 million. However, Caterpillar's initial health care cost trend rate is 2 percentage points lower than CNH's. Therefore, the impact of a 1 percentage point change for Caterpillar multiplied by 2 provides an approximation of the adjustment required for comparability to CNH. Note, however, that the sensitivity of the pension obligation and expense to a change of more than 1 percentage point in the assumed health care cost trend rate cannot be assumed to be exactly linear, so this adjustment is only an approximation. Further, there may be justifiable differences in the assumptions based on the location of their US operations.

3. What would be the change in each company's 2009 ratio of debt to equity assuming a 1 percentage point increase in the health care cost trend rate? Assume the change would have no impact on taxes. Total liabilities and total equity at 31 December 2009 are given below.

At 31 December 2009 (US$ millions)	CNH Global N.V.	Caterpillar Inc.
Total liabilities	$16,398	$50,738
Total equity	$6,810	$8,823

Solution:

A 1 percentage point increase in the health care cost trend rate increases CNH's ratio of debt to equity by about 2 percent, from 2.41 to 2.46. A 1 percentage point increase in the health care cost trend rate increases Caterpillar's ratio of debt to equity by about 3 percent, from 5.75 to 5.92.

CNH Global N.V. ($ millions)	Reported	Adjustment for 1 percentage point increase in health care cost trend rate	Adjusted
Total liabilities	$16,398	+ $106	$16,504
Total equity	$6,810	− $106	$6,704
Ratio of debt to equity	2.41		2.46

Caterpillar Inc. ($ millions)	Reported	Adjustment for 1 percentage point increase in health care cost trend rate	Adjusted
Total liabilities	$50,738	+ $220	$50,958
Total equity	$8,823	− $220	$8,603
Ratio of debt to equity	5.75		5.92

This section has explored the use of pension and other post-employment benefit disclosures to assess a company's assumptions and explore how the assumptions can affect comparisons across companies. The following sections describe the use of disclosures to further analyse a company's pension and other post-employment benefits.

DISCLOSURES: NET PENSION LIABILITY (OR ASSET) AND PERIODIC PENSION COSTS

10

☐ explain and calculate how adjusting for items of pension and other post-employment benefits that are reported in the notes to the financial statements affects financial statements and ratios

☐ interpret pension plan note disclosures including cash flow related information

Under both IFRS and US GAAP standards, the amount disclosed in the balance sheet is a net amount. Analysts can use information from the notes to adjust a company's assets and liabilities for the gross amount of the benefit plan assets and the gross amount of the benefit plan liabilities. An argument for making such adjustments is that they reflect the underlying economic liabilities and assets of a company; however, it should be recognised that actual consolidation is precluded by laws protecting a pension or other benefit plan as a separate legal entity.

At a minimum, an analyst will compare the gross benefit obligation (i.e., the benefit obligation without deducting related plan assets) with the sponsoring company's total assets, including the gross amount of the benefit plan assets, shareholders' equity, and earnings. Although presumably infrequent in practice, if the gross benefit obligation is large relative to these items, a small change in the pension liability can have a significant financial impact on the sponsoring company.

Total Periodic Pension Costs

The total periodic cost of a company's DB pension plan is the change in the net pension liability or asset—excluding the effect of the employer's periodic contribution into the plan. To illustrate this point, assume a company has a completely new DB pension plan. At inception, the net pension liability equals $0 ($0 plan assets minus $0 obligations). In the first period, the plan obligation increases by $500 because of service costs. If the employer makes no contribution to the plan, then the net pension liability would increase to $500 ($0 plan assets minus $500 obligations) and the periodic service costs would be exactly equal to that change. If, however, the employer contributes $500 to the plan in that period, then the net pension liability would remain at $0 ($500 plan assets minus $500 obligations). In this situation, although the change in net pension liability is $0, the periodic pension cost is $500.

Thus, the total periodic pension cost in a given period is calculated by summing the periodic components of cost or, alternatively, by adjusting the change in the net pension liability or asset for the amount of employer contributions. The relationship between the periodic pension cost and the plan's funded status can be expressed as Periodic pension cost = Ending funded status – Employer contributions – Beginning funded status.[10]

Note that, unlike employer contributions into the plan's assets, the payment of cash out of a DB plan to a retiree does not affect the net pension liability or asset. Payment of cash out of a DB plan to a retiree reduces plan assets and plan obligations in an equal amount.

---

10 Note that a net pension liability is treated as a negative funded status in this relationship.

Periodic Pension Costs Recognised in P&L vs. OCI

Each period, the components of periodic pension cost—other than any amounts that qualify for capitalisation as part of the costs of such assets as inventories—are recognised either in P&L (an expense) or in OCI. To understand the total pension cost of the period, an analyst should thus consider the amounts shown both in P&L and in OCI.

IFRS and US GAAP differ in their provisions about which periodic pension costs are recognised in P&L versus in OCI. These differences can be relevant to an analyst in comparing the reported profitability of companies that use different sets of standards. Under IFRS, P&L for the period includes both current and past service costs; in contrast, under US GAAP, P&L for the period includes only current service costs (and any amortisation of past service costs.) Under IFRS, P&L incorporates a return on plan assets set equal to the discount rate used in estimating the pension obligation; in contrast, under US GAAP, P&L incorporates an expected return on plan assets. Under US GAAP, P&L may show the impact of amortising actuarial gains or losses that were recognised in previous periods' OCI. Under IFRS, P&L would not show any similar impact because amortising amounts from OCI into P&L is not permitted.

An analyst comparing an IFRS-reporting company with a US GAAP–reporting company could adjust the reported amounts of P&L to achieve comparability. For example, the analyst could adjust the US GAAP company's P&L to make it similar to an IFRS company by including past service costs arising during the period, excluding amortisation of past service costs arising in previous periods, and including an amount of return on plan assets at the discount rate rather than the expected rate. Alternatively, the analyst could use comprehensive income (net income from P&L plus OCI) as the basis for comparison.

Classification of Periodic Pension Costs Recognised in P&L

Amounts of periodic pension costs recognised in P&L (pension expense) are generally treated as operating expenses. An issue with the reported periodic pension expense is that conceptually the components of this expense could be classified as operating and/or non-operating expenses. It can be argued that only the current service cost component is an operating expense, whereas the interest component and asset returns component are both non-operating. The interest expense component of pension expense is conceptually similar to the interest expense on any of the company's other liabilities. The pension liability is essentially equivalent to borrowing from employees, and the interest expense of that borrowing can be considered a financing cost. Similarly, the return on pension plan assets is conceptually similar to returns on any of the company's other financial assets. These classification issues apply equally to OPB costs.

To better reflect a company's operating performance, an adjustment can be made to operating income by adding back the full amount of pensions costs reported in the P&L (pension expense) and then subtracting only the service costs (or the total of service costs and settlements and curtailments). Note that this adjustment excludes from operating income the amortisation of past service costs and the amortisation of net actuarial gains and losses. This adjustment also eliminates the interest expense component and the return on plan assets component from the company's operating income. The interest expense component would be added to the company's interest expense, and the return on plan assets would be treated as non-operating income.

In addition to adjusting for the classification of different components of pension costs, an adjustment can be made to incorporate the *actual return* on plan assets. Recall that under IFRS, the net interest expense/income calculation effectively includes a return on plan assets calculated using the discount rate used to determine the present value of the pension liability and any difference from the actual return is shown as a

Disclosures: Net Pension Liability (or Asset) and Periodic Pension Costs

component of OCI. Under US GAAP, the *expected* return on plan assets is included as a component of periodic pension cost in P&L and any difference between the actual and expected return is shown as a component of OCI. Under either set of standards, an adjustment can incorporate the actual return. This adjustment changes net income and potentially introduces earnings volatility. The reclassification of interest expense would not change net income. Example 5 illustrates adjustments to operating and non-operating incomes.

EXAMPLE 5

Adjusting Periodic Costs Expensed to P&L and Reclassifying Components between Operating and Non-Operating Income

SABMiller plc is a UK-based company that brews and distributes beer and other beverages. The following information was taken from the company's 2010 Annual Report. Note that in 2010, IFRS required the use of expected return on plan assets, similar to US GAAP. All amounts are in millions of US dollars.

Summary information from the Consolidated Income Statement
For the year ended 31 March 2010

Revenue	$18,020
Net operating expenses	(15,401)
Operating profit	2,619
Interest payable and similar charges*	(879)
Interest receivable and similar income*	316
Share of post-tax results of associates	873
Profit before taxation	$2,929

Note: This is the terminology used in the income statement. The solution to question 2 below uses *interest expense* and *interest and investment income*.

Excerpt from Note 31: Pensions and post-retirement benefits

	Pension	OPB	Total
Current service costs	$(8)	$(3)	$(11)
Interest costs	(29)	(10)	(39)
Expected return on plan assets	14		14
Total	$(23)	$(13)	$(36)
Actual return (loss) on plan assets	$47		

(Components of the amount recognised in net operating expenses for pension and other post-retirement benefits.)

Based on the information above,

1. Adjust pre-tax income for the actual rather than expected return on plan assets.

Solution:

The total amount of periodic pension cost reported in P&L as an expense is $23. If the actual return on plan assets of $47 is used instead of the expected return on plan assets, the total P&L expense (income) will be $(10) [(= 8 + 29 − 47) or (= 23 + 14 − 47)]. Use of the actual rather than expected return on plan assets provides an estimate of the economic expense (income) for the pension. Profit before taxation adjusted for actual rather than expected return on plan assets will be higher by $33 ($47 − $14) and will total $2,962.

2. Adjust the individual line items on the company's income statement to re-classify the components of the pension and other post-retirement benefits expense as operating expense, interest expense, or interest income.

Solution:

All adjustments are summarized below.

	Reported	Adjustments	Adjusted
Revenue	$18,020		$18,020
Net operating expenses	−15,401	+ 36 − 11[a]	−15,376
Operating profit	2,619		2,644
Interest expense	−879	− 39[b]	−918
Interest and investment income	316	+ 47[c]	363
Share of post-tax results of associates	873		873
Profit before taxation	$2,929	$33	$2,962

[a] Operating income is adjusted to include only the current service costs. The $36 total of pension and OPB expenses are excluded from operating expenses, and only the $11 current service cost component is included in operating expenses.
[b] The $39 interest cost component is reclassified as interest expense.
[c] The actual return on plan assets is added as investment income.

11. DISCLOSURES: CASH FLOW INFORMATION

☐ explain and calculate how adjusting for items of pension and other post-employment benefits that are reported in the notes to the financial statements affects financial statements and ratios

☐ interpret pension plan note disclosures including cash flow related information

For a sponsoring company, the cash flow impact of pension and other post-employment benefits is the amount of contributions that the company makes to fund the plan—or for plans without funding requirements, the amount of benefits paid. The amount of contributions a company makes to fund a pension or other post-employment benefit plan is partially determined by the regulations of the countries in which the company operates. In the United States, for example, the amount of contributions to DB pension plans is governed by ERISA (the Employee Retirement and Income Security Act) and depends on the funded status of the plan. Companies may choose to make contributions in excess of those required by regulation.

If a sponsoring company's periodic contributions to a plan exceed the total pension costs of the period, the excess can be viewed from an economic perspective as a reduction of the pension obligation. The contribution covers not only the pension obligation arising in the current period but also the pension obligations of another period. Such a contribution would be similar in concept to making a principal payment on a loan in excess of the scheduled principal payment. Conversely, a periodic contribution that is less than the total pension cost of the period can be viewed as a source of financing. Where the amounts of benefit obligations are material, an analyst may choose to adjust the cash flows that a company presents in its statement of cash flows. Example 6 describes such an adjustment.

EXAMPLE 6

Adjusting Cash Flow

Vassiliki Doukas is analysing the cash flow statement of a hypothetical company, GeoRace plc, as part of a valuation. Doukas suggests to her colleague, Dimitri Krontiras, that the difference between the company's contributions to the pension plan and the total pension costs incurred during a period is similar to a form of borrowing or a repayment of borrowing, depending on the direction of the difference; this affects the company's reported cash from operating activities and cash from financing activities. Based on information from the company's 2009 annual report (currency in £ millions), she determines that the company's total pension cost was £437; however, the company also disclosed that it made a contribution of £504. GeoRace reported cash inflow from operating activities of £6,161 and cash outflow from financing activities of £1,741. The company's effective tax rate was 28.7 percent.

Use the information provided to answer the following questions:

1. How did the company's 2009 contribution to the pension plan compare with the total pension cost for the year?

Solution:

The company's contribution to the pension plan in 2009 was £504, which was £67 more than the total pension cost of £437. The £67 difference is approximately £48 on an after-tax basis, using the effective tax rate of 28.7 percent.

Total pension costs	£437
Company's contribution	£504
Amount by which the sponsoring company's contribution exceeds total pension cost (pre-tax)	£67
Tax rate	28.7%
After-tax amount by which the sponsoring company's contribution exceeds total pension cost	£48 [= £67 × (1 − 0.2870)]

2. How would cash from operating activities and financing activities be adjusted to illustrate Doukas' interpretation of the difference between the company's contribution and the total pension cost?

Solution:

The company's contribution to the pension plan in 2009 was £67 (£48 after tax) greater than the 2009 total pension cost. Interpreting the excess contribution as similar to a repayment of borrowing (financing use of funds) rather than as an operating cash flow would increase the company's cash outflow from financing activities by £48, from £1,741 to £1,789, and increase the cash inflow from operations by £48, from £6,161 to £6,209.

12 SHARE-BASED COMPENSATION

> explain issues associated with accounting for share-based compensation

In this section, we provide an overview of executive compensation other than pension plans and other post-retirement benefits, focusing on share-based compensation. First, we briefly discuss common components of executive compensation packages, their objectives, and advantages and disadvantages of share-based compensation. The discussion of share-based compensation then moves to accounting for and reporting of stock grants and stock options. The explanation includes a discussion of fair value accounting, the choice of valuation models, the assumptions used, common disclosures, and important dates in measuring and reporting compensation expense.

Employee compensation packages are structured to achieve varied objectives, including satisfying employees' needs for liquidity, retaining employees, and motivating employees. Common components of employee compensation packages are salary, bonuses, non-monetary benefits, and share-based compensation.[11] The salary component provides for the liquidity needs of an employee. Bonuses, generally in the form of cash, motivate and reward employees for short- or long-term performance or goal achievement by linking pay to performance. Non-monetary benefits, such as medical care, housing, and cars, may be provided to facilitate employees performing their jobs. Salary, bonuses, and non-monetary benefits are short-term employee benefits.

Share-based compensation is intended to align employees' interests with those of the shareholders and is typically a form of deferred compensation. Both IFRS and US GAAP[12] require a company to disclose in their annual report key elements of management compensation. Regulators may require additional disclosure. The disclosures enable analysts to understand the nature and extent of compensation, including the share-based payment arrangements that existed during the reporting period. Below are examples of descriptions of the components and objectives of executive compensation programs for companies that report under IFRS and under US GAAP. Exhibit 6 shows

---

11 An extensive overview of different employee compensation mechanisms can be found in Lynch and Perry (2003).
12 IAS 24 *Related Party Disclosures*, paragraph 17; FASB ASC Section 718-10-50 [Compensation-Stock Compensation-Overall-Disclosure].

excerpts of the disclosure for the executive compensation program of SABMiller plc; SABMiller plc reports under IFRS and includes a nine-page remuneration report as part of its annual report.

> **Exhibit 6: Excerpts from Remuneration Report of SABMiller plc**
>
> ... On balance, the committee concluded that its policy of agreeing a total remuneration package for each executive director comprising an annual base salary, a short-term incentive in the form of an annual cash bonus, long-term incentives through participation in share incentive plans, pension contributions, other usual security and health benefits, and benefits in kind, continued to be appropriate....
>
> The committee's policy continues to be to ensure that executive directors and members of the executive committee are rewarded for their contribution to the group's operating and financial performance at levels which take account of industry, market and country benchmarks, and that their remuneration is appropriate to their scale of responsibility and performance, and will attract, motivate and retain individuals of the necessary calibre. The committee takes account of the need to be competitive in the different parts of the world in which the company operates....
>
> The committee considers that alignment with shareholders' interests and linkage to SABMiller's long-term strategic goals is best achieved through a twin focus on earnings per share and, from 2010 onwards, additional value created for shareholders, and a blend of absolute and relative performance.
>
> *Source:* SABMiller plc, Annual Report 2010.

In the United States, similar disclosures are required in a company's proxy statement that is filed with the SEC. Exhibit 7 shows the disclosure of American Eagle Outfitters, Inc.'s executive compensation program, including a description of the key elements and objectives.

> **Exhibit 7: Excerpts from Executive Compensation Disclosures of American Eagle Outfitters, Inc.**
>
> ## Compensation Program Elements
>
> Our executive compensation program is designed to place a sizeable amount of pay at risk for all executives and this philosophy is intended to cultivate a pay-for-performance environment. Our executive compensation plan design has six key elements:
>
> - Base Salary
> - Annual Incentive Bonus
> - Long-term Incentive Cash Plan—in place for the Chief Executive Officer and Vice Chairman, Executive Creative Director only
> - Restricted Stock ("RS")—issued as Units ("RSUs") and Awards ("RSAs")
> - Performance Shares ("PS")
> - Non-Qualified Stock Options ("NSOs")
>
> Two of the elements (Annual Incentive Bonus and LTICP) were entirely "at risk" based on the Company's performance in Fiscal 2009 and were subject to forfeiture if the Company did not achieve threshold performance goals. Performance Shares are entirely "at risk" and subject to forfeiture if the Company does not achieve threshold performance goals by the close of Fiscal 2011, as described below. At

threshold performance, the CEO's total annual compensation declines by 46% relative to target performance. The NEO's total annual compensation declines by an average of 33% relative to target performance. Company performance below threshold levels results in forfeiture of all elements of direct compensation other than base salary, RSUs and NSOs. NSOs provide compensation only to the extent that vesting requirements are satisfied and our share price appreciates. We strategically allocate compensation between short-term and long-term components and between cash and equity in order to maximize executive performance and retention. Long-term compensation and equity awards comprise an increasingly larger proportion of total compensation as position level increases. The portion of total pay attributable to long-term incentive cash and equity compensation increases at successively higher levels of management. This philosophy ensures that executive compensation closely aligns with changes in stockholder value and achievement of performance objectives while also ensuring that executives are held accountable for results relative to position level.

Source: American Eagle Outfitters, Inc. Proxy Statement (Form Def 14A) filed 26 April 2010.

Share-based compensation, in addition to theoretically aligning the interests of employees (management) with shareholders, has the advantage of potentially requiring no cash outlay.[13] Share-based compensation arrangements can take a variety of forms, including those that are equity-settled and those that are cash-settled. However, share-based compensation is treated as an expense and thus as a reduction of earnings even when no cash changes hands. In addition to decreasing earnings through compensation expense, stock options have the potential to dilute earnings per share.

Although share-based compensation is generally viewed as motivating employees and aligning managers' interests with those of the shareholders, there are several disadvantages of share-based compensation. One disadvantage is that the recipient of the share-based compensation may have limited influence over the company's market value (consider the scenario of overall market decline), so share-based compensation does not necessarily provide the desired incentives. Another disadvantage is that the increased ownership may lead managers to be risk averse. In other words, fearing a large market value decline (and loss in individual wealth), managers may seek less risky (and less profitable) projects. An opposite effect, excessive risk taking, can also occur with the awarding of options. Because options have skewed payouts that reward excessive risk taking, managers may seek more risky projects. Finally, when share-based compensation is granted to employees, existing shareholders' ownership is diluted.

For financial reporting, a company reports compensation expense during the period in which employees earn that compensation. Accounting for cash salary payments and cash bonuses is relatively straightforward. When the employee has earned the salary or bonus, an expense is recorded. Typically, compensation expense for managers is reported in sales, general, and administrative expenses on the income statement.

Share-based compensation is more varied and includes such items as stock, stock options, stock appreciation rights, and phantom shares. By granting shares or share options in addition to other compensation, companies are paying additional compensation for services rendered by employees. Under both IFRS and US GAAP, companies use the fair value of the share-based compensation granted to measure the value of the employees' services for purposes of reporting compensation expense. However, the specifics of the accounting depend on the type of share-based compensation given to the employee. Under both IFRS and US GAAP, the usual disclosures required for share-based compensation include (1) the nature and extent of share-based

---

13 Although issuing employee stock options requires no initial cash outlay, the company implicitly forgoes issuing new shares of stock at the then-current market price (and receiving cash) when the options are exercised.

compensation arrangements during the period, (2) how the fair value of a share-based compensation arrangement was determined, and (3) the effect of share-based compensation on the company's income for the period and on its financial position.

Two common forms of equity-settled share-based compensation, stock grants and stock options, are discussed below.

STOCK GRANTS 13

☐ explain how accounting for stock grants and stock options affects financial statements, and the importance of companies' assumptions in valuing these grants and options

A company can grant stock to employees outright, with restrictions, or contingent on performance. For an outright stock grant, compensation expense is reported on the basis of the fair value of the stock on the grant date—generally the market value at grant date. Compensation expense is allocated over the period benefited by the employee's service, referred to as the service period. The employee service period is presumed to be the current period unless there are some specific requirements, such as three years service in the future, before the employee is vested (has the right to receive the compensation).

Another type of stock award is a restricted stock, which requires the employee to return ownership of those shares to the company if certain conditions are not met. Common restrictions include the requirements that employees remain with the company for a specified period or that certain performance goals are met. Compensation expense for restricted stock grants is measured as the fair value (usually market value) of the shares issued at the grant date. This compensation expense is allocated over the employee service period.

Shares granted contingent on meeting performance goals are called performance shares. The amount of the grant is usually determined by performance measures other than the change in stock price, such as accounting earnings or return on assets. Basing the grant on accounting performance addresses employees' potential concerns that the stock price is beyond their control and thus should not form the basis for compensation. However, performance shares can potentially have the unintended impact of providing incentives to manipulate accounting numbers. Compensation expense is equal to the fair value (usually market value) of the shares issued at the grant date. This compensation expense is allocated over the employee service period.

STOCK OPTIONS 14

☐ explain how accounting for stock grants and stock options affects financial statements, and the importance of companies' assumptions in valuing these grants and options

Like stock grants, compensation expense related to option grants is reported at fair value under both IFRS and US GAAP. Both require that fair value be estimated using an appropriate valuation model.

Whereas the fair value of stock grants is usually based on the market value at the date of the grant, the fair value of option grants must be estimated. Companies cannot rely on market prices of options to measure the fair value of employee stock options because features of employee stock options typically differ from traded options. To measure the fair value of employee stock options, therefore, companies must use a valuation model. The choice of valuation or option pricing model is one of the critical elements in estimating fair value. Several models are commonly used, such as the Black–Scholes option pricing model or a binomial model. Accounting standards do not prescribe a particular model. Generally, though, the valuation method should (1) be consistent with fair value measurement, (2) be based on established principles of financial economic theory, and (3) reflect all substantive characteristics of the award.

Once a valuation model is selected, a company must determine the inputs to the model, typically including exercise price, stock price volatility, estimated life of each award, estimated number of options that will be forfeited, dividend yield, and the risk-free rate of interest.[14] Some inputs, such as the exercise price, are known at the time of the grant. Other critical inputs are highly subjective—such as stock price volatility or the estimated life of stock options—and can greatly change the estimated fair value and thus compensation expense. Higher volatility, a longer estimated life, and a higher risk-free interest rate increase the estimated fair value, whereas a higher assumed dividend yield decreases the estimated fair value.

Combining different assumptions with alternative valuation models can significantly affect the fair value of employee stock options. Below is an excerpt from GlaxoSmithKline, plc explaining the assumptions and model used in valuing its stock options. (Although not discussed in the disclosure, from 2007 to 2009 the trends of decreasing interest rates, lower share price, and increasing dividend yield would decrease estimated fair values and thus lower option expense. In contrast, the trend of increasing volatility would increase the estimated fair values.)

Exhibit 8: Assumptions Used in Stock Option Pricing Models: Excerpts from Financial Statements of GlaxoSmithKline, plc

Note 42—Employee share schemes *[excerpt]*

Option pricing

For the purposes of valuing options and awards to arrive at the share based payment charge, the Black–Scholes option pricing model has been used. The assumptions used in the model for 2007, 2008 and 2009 are as follows:

	2009	2008	2007
Risk-free interest rate	1.4% – 2.9%	1.3% – 4.8%	4.7% – 5.3%
Dividend yield	5.20%	4.80%	4.00%
Volatility	23% – 29%	19% – 24%	17% – 25%
Expected lives of options granted under:			
Share option schemes	5 years	5 years	5 years
Savings-related share option and share award schemes	3–4 years	3 years	3 years
Weighted average share price for grants in the year:			
Ordinary Shares	£11.72	£11.59	£14.41

---

14 The estimated life of an option award incorporates such assumptions as employee turnover and is usually shorter than the expiration period.

	2009	2008	2007
ADS*	$33.73	$45.02	$57.59

American Depositary Shares

Volatility is determined based on the three and five year share price history where appropriate. The fair value of performance share plan grants take into account market conditions. Expected lives of options were determined based on weighted average historic exercises of options.
Source: GlaxoSmithKline Annual Report 2009.

In accounting for stock options, there are several important dates, including the grant date, the vesting date, the exercise date, and the expiration date. The **grant date** is the day that options are granted to employees. The **service period** is usually the period between the grant date and the vesting date.

The **vesting date** is the date that employees can first exercise the stock options. The vesting can be immediate or over a future period. If the share-based payments vest immediately (i.e., no further period of service is required), then expense is recognised on the grant date. If the share-based awards do not vest until a specified service period is completed, compensation expense is recognised and allocated over the service period. If the share-based awards are conditional upon the achievement of a performance condition or a market condition (i.e., a target share price), then compensation expense is recognised over the estimated service period. The **exercise date** is the date when employees actually exercise the options and convert them to stock. If the options go unexercised, they may expire at some pre-determined future date, commonly 5 or 10 years from the grant date.

The grant date is also usually the date that compensation expense is measured if both the number of shares and the option price are known. If facts affecting the value of options granted depend on events after the grant date, then compensation expense is measured at the exercise date. In the example below, Coca Cola, Inc. reported, in the 2009 Form 10-K, $241 million of compensation expense from option grants.

EXAMPLE 7

Disclosure of Stock Options' Current Compensation Expense, Vesting, and Future Compensation Expense

Using information from Coca Cola, Inc.'s Note 9 to financial statements, given below, determine the following:

Excerpts from Note 9: Stock Compensation Plans in the Notes to Financial Statements of Coca Cola, Inc.

NOTE 9: STOCK COMPENSATION PLANS

Our Company grants stock options and restricted stock awards to certain employees of the Company. Total stock-based compensation expense was approximately $241 million in 2009, $266 million in 2008 and $313 million in 2007 and was included as a component of selling, general and administrative expenses in our consolidated statements of income. The total income tax benefit recognized in our consolidated statements of income for share-based compensation arrangements was approximately $68 million, $72 million and $91 million for 2009, 2008 and 2007, respectively.

As of December 31, 2009, we had approximately $335 million of total unrecognised compensation cost related to nonvested share-based compensation arrangements granted under our plans. This cost is expected to be recognized

> over a weighted-average period of 1.7 years as stock-based compensation expense. This expected cost does not include the impact of any future stock-based compensation awards.
>
> *Source*: Coca Cola, Inc. Form 10-K filed 26 February 2010.

1. Total compensation expense relating to options already granted that will be recognised in future years as options vest.

Solution:

Coca Cola, Inc. discloses that unrecognised compensation expense relating to stock options already granted but not yet vested totals $335 million.

2. Approximate compensation expense in 2010 and 2011 relating to options already granted.

Solution:

The options already granted will vest over the next 1.7 years. Compensation expense related to stock options already granted will be $197 million ($335/1.7 years) in 2010 and $138 million in 2011 ($335 total less $197 expensed in 2010). New options granted in the future will likely raise the total reported compensation expense.

As the option expense is recognised over the relevant vesting period, the impact on the financial statements is to ultimately reduce retained earnings (as with any other expense). The offsetting entry is an increase in paid-in capital. Thus, the recognition of option expense has no net impact on total equity.

15　OTHER TYPES OF SHARE-BASED COMPENSATION

☐ explain issues associated with accounting for share-based compensation

Both stock grants and stock options allow the employee to obtain direct ownership in the company. Other types of share-based compensation, such as stock appreciation rights (SARs) or phantom stock, compensate an employee on the basis of changes in the value of shares without requiring the employee to hold the shares. These are referred to as cash-settled share-based compensation. With SARs, an employee's compensation is based on increases in a company's share price. Like other forms of share-based compensation, SARs serve to motivate employees and align their interests with shareholders. The following are two additional advantages of SARs:

- The potential for risk aversion is limited because employees have limited downside risk and unlimited upside potential similar to employee stock options, and
- Shareholder ownership is not diluted.

Similar to other share-based compensation, SARs are valued at fair value and compensation expense is allocated over the service period of the employee. While phantom share plans are similar to other types of share-based compensation, they differ somewhat because compensation is based on the performance of hypothetical

Other Types of Share-Based Compensation

stock rather than the company's actual stock. Unlike SARs, phantom shares can be used by private companies or business units within a company that are not publicly traded or by highly illiquid companies.

SUMMARY

This reading discussed two different forms of employee compensation: post-employment benefits and share-based compensation. Although different, the two are similar in that they are forms of compensation outside of the standard salary arrangements. They also involve complex valuation, accounting, and reporting issues. Although IFRS and US GAAP are converging on accounting and reporting, it is important to note that differences in a country's social system, laws, and regulations can result in differences in a company's pension and share-based compensation plans that may be reflected in the company's earnings and financial reports.

Key points include the following:

- Defined contribution pension plans specify (define) only the amount of contribution to the plan; the eventual amount of the pension benefit to the employee will depend on the value of an employee's plan assets at the time of retirement.

- Balance sheet reporting is less analytically relevant for defined contribution plans because companies make contributions to defined contribution plans as the expense arises and thus no liabilities accrue for that type of plan.

- Defined benefit pension plans specify (define) the amount of the pension benefit, often determined by a plan formula, under which the eventual amount of the benefit to the employee is a function of length of service and final salary.

- Defined benefit pension plan obligations are funded by the sponsoring company contributing assets to a pension trust, a separate legal entity. Differences exist in countries' regulatory requirements for companies to fund defined benefit pension plan obligations.

- Both IFRS and US GAAP require companies to report on their balance sheet a pension liability or asset equal to the projected benefit obligation minus the fair value of plan assets. The amount of a pension asset that can be reported is subject to a ceiling.

- Under IFRS, the components of periodic pension cost are recognised as follows: Service cost is recognised in P&L, net interest income/expense is recognised in P&L, and remeasurements are recognised in OCI and are not amortised to future P&L.

- Under US GAAP, the components of periodic pension cost recognised in P&L include current service costs, interest expense on the pension obligation, and expected returns on plan assets (which reduces the cost). Other components of periodic pension cost—including past service costs, actuarial gains and losses, and differences between expected and actual returns on plan assets—are recognised in OCI and amortised to future P&L.

- Estimates of the future obligation under defined benefit pension plans and other post-employment benefits are sensitive to numerous assumptions, including discount rates, assumed annual compensation increases, expected return on plan assets, and assumed health care cost inflation.

- Employee compensation packages are structured to fulfill varied objectives, including satisfying employees' needs for liquidity, retaining employees, and providing incentives to employees.
- Common components of employee compensation packages are salary, bonuses, and share-based compensation.
- Share-based compensation serves to align employees' interests with those of the shareholders. It includes stocks and stock options.
- Share-based compensation has the advantage of requiring no current-period cash outlays.
- Share-based compensation expense is reported at fair value under IFRS and US GAAP.
- The valuation technique, or option pricing model, that a company uses is an important choice in determining fair value and is disclosed.
- Key assumptions and input into option pricing models include such items as exercise price, stock price volatility, estimated life of each award, estimated number of options that will be forfeited, dividend yield, and the risk-free rate of interest. Certain assumptions are highly subjective, such as stock price volatility or the expected life of stock options, and can greatly change the estimated fair value and thus compensation expense.

REFERENCES

Lynch, L.J., S.E. Perry. 2003. "An Overview of Management Compensation." Journal of Accounting Education, vol. 21, no. 1 (1st Quarter):43–60. 10.1016/S0748-5751(02)00034-9

PRACTICE PROBLEMS

The following information relates to questions 1-7

The board of directors at Sallie-Kwan Industrials (SKI), a publicly traded company, is meeting with various committees following the release of audited financial statements prepared in accordance with US GAAP. The finance committee (FC) is next on the agenda to review retirement benefits funding and make recommendations to the board.

SKI's three retirement benefit plans are described as follows:

Plan A

- Benefit: Annual payments for life equal to 1% of the employee's final salary for each year of service beyond the date of the plan's establishment
- The employer makes regular contributions to the plan in order to meet the future obligation
- Closed to new participants; benefits accrue for existing participants
- Fair value of assets: €5.98 billion
- Present value of obligation: €4.80 billion
- Present value of reductions in future contributions: €1.50 billion
- Ten-year vesting schedule; 70% of the participants are fully vested

Plan B

- Benefit: Discretionary retirement withdrawals; amounts depend on the plan's investment performance
- Employer makes its agreed-upon contribution to the plan on behalf of the employee in the same period during which the employee provides the service; SKI is current on this obligation
- The employee may also contribute to the plan during employment years
- Available to all employees after one year of service; 80% of the employees are fully vested

Plan C

- Benefit: Medical, prescription drug, and dental coverage for the retiree, spouse, and dependents under age 18
- 80% funded
- Available to all employees on day one of service

The FC chair reviews Plan A's funded status and the amount recorded on the balance sheet with the board, explaining that the current service cost change from last quarter has primarily resulted from a higher percentage of employees that are expected to leave before the full vesting period.

A board member inquires how Plan A's periodic pension costs affect SKI's operating performance. The FC chair reviews the adjustments needed to account for

Practice Problems

individual pension components that are considered operating costs and those considered non-operating costs, when calculating profit before taxation. Note 16 in the income statement lists the following: current service costs of €40 million, interest costs of €263 million, expected return on plan assets of €299 million, and actual return on plan assets of €205 million. Moreover, Note 16 indicates that SKI was required to use expected return on plan assets for the reporting year in question.

Next, the FC chairman presents the following case study data to illustrate SKI's current pension obligation for an average fully vested participant in Plan A with 10 years of prior service:

- Current annual salary: €100,000
- Years to retirement: 17
- Retirement life expectancy: 20 years
- Current plan assumptions:
  - Annual compensation increase: 6%
  - Discount rate: 4%
  - Compensation increases are awarded on the first day of the service year; no adjustments are made to reflect the possibility that the employee may leave the firm at an earlier date.

A discussion ensues regarding the effect on the pension obligation, for an average participant, of changing Plan A's annual compensation increase to 5%.

Lastly, the FC chair recommends that the board consider modifying some key assumptions affecting Plan A in response to recent market trends. The chair also reviews how these changes will alter SKI's plan obligation.

Recommendation 1: Change the assumed discount rate to 5%.

Recommendation 2: Increase the retirement life expectancy assumption by eight years.

Recommendation 3: Reduce investment risk by decreasing the expected return to 3%.

1. The participant bears the greatest amount of investment risk under which plan?
   A. Plan A
   B. Plan B
   C. Plan C

2. The plan for which the amount of SKI's financial obligation is defined in the current period with no obligation for future retirement benefits is:
   A. Plan A.
   B. Plan B.
   C. Plan C.

3. For Plan A, SKI should report a net pension:
   A. asset of €1.50 billion.
   B. asset of €1.18 billion.

C. liability of €1.18 billion.

4. Based on the FC chair's explanation about the current service cost change, the present value of Plan A's obligation:
   A. decreased.
   B. stayed the same.
   C. increased.

5. Based on Note 16, after reclassifying pension components to reflect economic income or expense, the net adjustment to profit before taxation is:
   A. −€205 million.
   B. −€94 million.
   C. +€129 million.

6. Based on the case study illustration and the effect of changing the annual compensation rate, the annual unit credit for the average participant would decrease by an amount *closest* to:
   A. €4,349.
   B. €4,858.
   C. €5,446.

7. All else being equal, which of the following FC recommendations will increase the plan's obligation?
   A. Recommendation 1
   B. Recommendation 2
   C. Recommendation 3

The following information relates to questions 8-13

Natalie Holmstead, a senior portfolio manager, works with Daniel Rickards, a junior analyst. Together they are evaluating the financial statements of Company XYZ (XYZ) with a focus on post-employment benefits. XYZ has a defined benefit pension plan and prepares financial statements according to IFRS requirements.

Rickards calculates the current service cost for a single employee's defined benefit pension obligation using the projected unit credit method. The employee is expected to work for 7 years before retiring and has 15 years of vested service. Rickards assumes a discount rate of 4.00% and a lump sum value of the employee's benefit at retirement of $393,949.

Next, Holmstead and Rickards discuss the present value of the defined benefit obligation (PVDBO). Rickards makes the following statements to clarify his understanding:

Statement 1   An actuarial loss is accompanied by an increase in the PVDBO.

Practice Problems

Statement 2   The PVDBO measures the present value of future benefits earned by plan participants and includes plan assets.

Statement 3   The company should use the expected long-term rate of return on plan assets as the discount rate to calculate the PVDBO.

XYZ's pension plan offers benefits based on the employee's final year's salary. Rickards calculates the PVDBO as of the end of the current period, based on the information presented in Exhibit 1.

Exhibit 1: Select XYZ Defined Benefit Pension Plan Data

	Current Period	Prior Period
Assumed future compensation growth rate	2.5%	3.0%
Plan assets (in $ millions)	3,108	
Net pension liability (in $ millions)	525	
Present value of reductions of future contributions (in $ millions)	48	

Rickards adjusts the balance sheet and cash flow statement information presented in Exhibit 2 to better reflect the economic nature of certain items related to the pension plan.

Exhibit 2: Select XYZ Balance Sheet and Cash Flow Data (in $ millions)

Item	Current Period
Total assets	24,130
Total liabilities	17,560
Total equity	6,570
Total pension cost	96
Pension contribution	66
Financing cash flow	2,323
Operating cash flow	−1,087
Effective tax rate	30%

Finally, Rickards examines the data in Exhibit 3 and calculates the effect of a 100-basis-point increase in health care inflation on XYZ's debt-to-equity ratio.

Exhibit 3: Sensitivity of Accumulated Post-Employment Benefit Obligations to Changes in Assumed Health Care Inflation (in $ millions)

Item	100-bp Increase	100-bp Decrease
Benefit obligation change	$93	−$76

Item	100-bp Increase	100-bp Decrease
Change in benefit expense reported in P&L	$12	−$10

8. The current service cost is *closest* to:

    A. $14,152.

    B. $15,758.

    C. $17,907.

9. Which of Rickards's statements about the PVDBO is correct?

    A. Statement 1

    B. Statement 2

    C. Statement 3

10. Based on Exhibit 1, the PVDBO is *closest* to:

    A. $3,585 million.

    B. $3,633 million.

    C. $3,681 million.

11. Based on Exhibit 1 and the method XYZ uses to link pension benefits to salaries, the change in the compensation growth rate compared with the prior period will *most likely* result in:

    A. lower periodic pension cost.

    B. no change in the periodic pension cost.

    C. higher periodic pension cost.

12. Based on Exhibit 2, Rickards should adjust the operating and financing cash flows by:

    A. $21 million.

    B. $30 million.

    C. $96 million.

13. Based on Exhibits 2 and 3, as well as Holmstead's assumption about future health care inflation, the debt-to-equity ratio calculated by Rickards for XYZ should be *closest* to:

    A. 2.69.

    B. 2.71.

    C. 2.73.

Practice Problems

The following information relates to questions 14–20

Kensington plc, a hypothetical company based in the United Kingdom, offers its employees a defined benefit pension plan. Kensington complies with IFRS. The assumed discount rate that the company used in estimating the present value of its pension obligations was 5.48 percent. Information on Kensington's retirement plans is presented in Exhibit 1.

Exhibit 1: Kensington plc Defined Benefit Pension Plan

(in millions)	2010
Components of periodic benefit cost	
Service cost	£228
Net interest (income) expense	273
Remeasurements	–18
Periodic pension cost	£483
Change in benefit obligation	
Benefit obligations at beginning of year	£28,416
Service cost	228
Interest cost	1,557
Benefits paid	–1,322
Actuarial gain or loss	0
Benefit obligations at end of year	£28,879
Change in plan assets	
Fair value of plan assets at beginning of year	£23,432
Actual return on plan assets	1,302
Employer contributions	693
Benefits paid	–1,322
Fair value of plan assets at end of year	£24,105
Funded status at beginning of year	–£4,984
Funded status at end of year	–£4,774

14. At year-end 2010, £28,879 million represents:
    A. the funded status of the plan.
    B. the defined benefit obligation.
    C. the fair value of the plan's assets.

15. For the year 2010, the net interest expense of £273 represents the interest cost on

the:

A. ending benefit obligation.

B. beginning benefit obligation.

C. beginning net pension obligation.

16. For the year 2010, the remeasurement component of Kensington's periodic pension cost represents:

A. the change in the net pension obligation.

B. actuarial gains and losses on the pension obligation.

C. actual return on plan assets minus the amount of return on plan assets included in the net interest expense.

17. Which of the following is *closest* to the actual rate of return on beginning plan assets and the rate of return on beginning plan assets that is included in the interest income/expense calculation?

A. The actual rate of return was 5.56 percent, and the rate included in interest income/expense was 5.48 percent.

B. The actual rate of return was 1.17 percent, and the rate included in interest income/expense was 5.48 percent.

C. Both the actual rate of return and the rate included in interest income/expense were 5.48 percent.

18. Which component of Kensington's periodic pension cost would be shown in OCI rather than P&L?

A. Service cost

B. Net interest (income) expense

C. Remeasurements

19. The relationship between the periodic pension cost and the plan's funded status is *best* expressed in which of the following?

A. Periodic pension cost of −£483 = Ending funded status of −£4,774 − Employer contributions of £693 − Beginning funded status of −£4,984.

B. Periodic pension cost of £1,322 = Benefits paid of £1,322.

C. Periodic pension cost of £210 = Ending funded status of −£4,774 − Beginning funded status of −£4,984.

20. An adjustment to Kensington's statement of cash flows to reclassify the company's excess contribution for 2010 would *most likely* entail reclassifying £210 million (excluding income tax effects) as an outflow related to:

A. investing activities rather than operating activities.

B. financing activities rather than operating activities.

C. operating activities rather than financing activities.

Practice Problems

The following information relates to questions 21–25

XYZ SA, a hypothetical company, offers its employees a defined benefit pension plan. Information on XYZ's retirement plans is presented in Exhibit 1. It also grants stock options to executives. Exhibit 2 contains information on the volatility assumptions used to value stock options.

Exhibit 1: XYZ SA Retirement Plan Information 2009

Employer contributions	1,000
Current service costs	200
Past service costs	120
Discount rate used to estimate plan liabilities at beginning of year	7.00%
Benefit obligation at beginning of year	42,000
Benefit obligation at end of year	41,720
Actuarial loss due to increase in plan obligation	460
Plan assets at beginning of year	39,000
Plan assets at end of year	38,700
Actual return on plan assets	2,700
Expected rate of return on plan assets	8.00%

Exhibit 2: XYZ SA Volatility Assumptions Used to Value Stock Option Grants

Grant Year	Weighted Average Expected Volatility
2009 valuation assumptions	
2005–2009	21.50%
2008 valuation assumptions	
2004–2008	23.00%

21. The total periodic pension cost is *closest* to:

    A. 320.

    B. 1,020.

    C. 1,320.

22. The amount of periodic pension cost that would be reported in P&L under IFRS is *closest* to:

    A. 28.

    B. 538.

    C. 1,020.

23. Assuming the company chooses not to immediately recognise the actuarial loss and assuming there is no amortisation of past service costs or actuarial gains and

losses, the amount of periodic pension cost that would be reported in P&L under US GAAP is *closest* to:

A. 28.

B. 59.

C. 530.

24. Under IFRS, the amount of periodic pension cost that would be reported in OCI is *closest* to:

A. 20.

B. 490.

C. 1,020.

25. Compared to 2009 net income as reported, if XYZ had used the same volatility assumption for its 2009 option grants that it had used in 2008, its 2009 net income would have been:

A. lower.

B. higher.

C. the same.

The following information relates to questions 26-31

Stereo Warehouse is a US retailer that offers employees a defined benefit pension plan and stock options as part of its compensation package. Stereo Warehouse prepares its financial statements in accordance with US GAAP.

Peter Friedland, CFA, is an equity analyst concerned with earnings quality. He is particularly interested in whether the discretionary assumptions the company is making regarding compensation plans are contributing to the recent earnings growth at Stereo Warehouse. He gathers information from the company's regulatory filings regarding the pension plan assumptions in Exhibit 1 and the assumptions related to option valuation in Exhibit 2.

Exhibit 1: Assumptions Used for Stereo Warehouse Defined Benefit Plan

	2009	2008	2007
Expected long-term rate of return on plan assets	6.06%	6.14%	6.79%
Discount rate used to estimate PBO at beginning of year	4.85	4.94	5.38
Estimated future salary increases	4.00	4.44	4.25

Practice Problems

	2009	2008	2007
Inflation	3.00	2.72	2.45

Exhibit 2: Option Valuation Assumptions

	2009	2008	2007
Risk-free rate	4.6%	3.8%	2.4%
Expected life	5.0 yrs	4.5 yrs	5.0 yrs
Dividend yield	1.0%	0.0%	0.0%
Expected volatility	29%	31%	35%

26. Compared to the 2009 reported financial statements, if Stereo Warehouse had used the same expected long-term rate of return on plan assets assumption in 2009 as it used in 2007, its year-end 2009 pension obligation would *most likely* have been:

    A. lower.

    B. higher.

    C. the same.

27. Compared to the reported 2009 financial statements, if Stereo Warehouse had used the same discount rate as it used in 2007, it would have *most likely* reported lower:

    A. net income.

    B. total liabilities.

    C. cash flow from operating activities.

28. Compared to the assumptions Stereo Warehouse used to compute its periodic pension cost in 2008, earnings in 2009 were *most favorably* affected by the change in the:

    A. discount rate.

    B. estimated future salary increases.

    C. expected long-term rate of return on plan assets.

29. Compared to the pension assumptions Stereo Warehouse used in 2008, which of the following pairs of assumptions used in 2009 is *most likely* internally inconsistent?

    A. Estimated future salary increases, inflation

    B. Discount rate, estimated future salary increases

    C. Expected long-term rate of return on plan assets, discount rate

30. Compared to the reported 2009 financial statements, if Stereo Warehouse had used the 2007 volatility assumption to value its employee stock options, it would

have *most likely* reported higher:

A. net income.

B. compensation expense.

C. deferred compensation liability.

31. Compared to the assumptions Stereo Warehouse used to value stock options in 2008, earnings in 2009 were most favorably affected by the change in the:

A. expected life.

B. risk-free rate.

C. dividend yield.

SOLUTIONS

1. B is correct. Plan B is a defined contribution (DC) pension plan because the amount of future benefit is not defined and SKI has an obligation to make only agreed-upon contributions. The actual future benefits depend on the investment performance of the individual's plan assets, and the employee bears the investment risk.

   A is incorrect because Plan A is a defined benefit (DB) pension plan. In a DB plan, the amount of future benefit is defined based on the plan's formula (i.e., 1% of the employee's final salary for each year of service). With a DB pension plan, SKI bears the investment risk.

   C is incorrect because Plan C is a health care plan and is classified as a DB plan. Under IFRS and US GAAP, all plans for pensions and other post-employment benefits (OPB) other than those explicitly structured as DC plans are classified as DB plans. The amount of future benefit depends on plan specifications and type of benefit, and it represents a promise by the firm to pay benefits in the future. SKI, not the employee, is responsible for estimating future increases in costs, such as health care, over a long time horizon.

2. B is correct. Plan B is a DC pension plan. SKI's financial obligation is defined in each period, and the employer makes its agreed-upon contribution to the plan on behalf of the employee in the same period during which the employee provides the service. SKI is current on this obligation and has no additional financial obligation for the current period.

3. B is correct. SKI's DB pension plan is overfunded by €1.18 billion, the amount by which the fair value of the pension plan assets exceeds the defined benefit obligation (€5.98 billion − €4.80 billion). When a company has a surplus in a DB pension plan, the amount of assets that can be reported is the lower of the surplus or the asset ceiling (the present value of future economic benefits, such as refunds from the plan or reductions in future contributions). In this case, the asset ceiling is given as €1.50 billion, so the amount of SKI's reported net pension asset is the amount of the surplus, because this amount is lower than the asset ceiling.

4. A is correct. A higher percentage of employees is expected to leave before the full 10-year vesting period, which would decrease the present value of the DB obligation. If the employee leaves the company before meeting the 10-year vesting requirement, she may be entitled to none or a portion of the benefits earned up until that point. In measuring the DB obligation, the company considers the probability that some employees may not satisfy the vesting requirements (i.e., may leave before the vesting period) and use this probability to calculate the current service cost and the present value of the obligation.

5. B is correct. Operating income is adjusted to include only the current service costs, the interest cost component is reclassified as interest expense, and the actual return on plan assets is added as investment income. Profit before taxation adjusted for actual rather than expected return on plan assets will decrease by €94 million (205 − 299).

	Total (€ millions)
Current service costs	− €40
Interest costs	− €263
Expected return on plan assets	+ €299

	Total (€ millions)
Total of pension and OPB expenses	– €4 million
Actual return (loss) on plan assets	€205 million

Because the actual return on plan assets is less than the expected return on plan assets, operating income will be adjusted downward by 299 – 205 = 94. Alternatively, the adjustments to the individual pension cost components are as follows:

Line Items to Adjust	Adjustments (€ millions)
Revenue	—
Net operating expenses	+4 – 40 = –36
Operating profit	—
Interest expense	–263
Interest and investment income	+205
Share of post-tax results of associates	—
Adjustment to profit before taxation	–€94 million

6. B is correct. The final year's estimated earnings at the end of Year 1 for the average participant would decrease by approximately €35,747.71.

	Current Assumptions	Case Study Assumptions
Current salary	€100,000	€100,000
Years until retirement	17	17
Years of service (includes prior 10)	27	27
Retirement life expectancy	20	20
Annual compensation increases	6%	5%
Discount rate	4%	4%
Final year's estimated earnings	€254,035.17	€218,287.46
Estimated annual payment for each of the 20 years	€68,589.50	€58,937.61
Value at the end of year 17 (retirement date) of the estimated future payments	€932,153.69	€800,981.35
Annual unit credit	€34,524.21	€29,665.98

Because there are now 17 years until retirement, there are 16 years until retirement from the end of Year 1. The final year's estimated earnings, estimated at the end of Year 1, are as follows:

Current year's salary × [(1 + Annual compensation increase)$^{\text{Years until retirement}}$]

Annual compensation increase of 6%: €100,000 × [(1.06)^{16}] = €254,035.17

Annual compensation increase of 5%: €100,000 × [(1.05)^{16}] = €218,287.46

The estimated annual payment for each of the 20 years (retirement life expectancy) is

(Estimated final salary × Benefit formula) × Years of service

Solutions

Annual compensation increase of 6%: (€254,035.17 × 0.01) × (10 + 17)

= €68,589.50

Annual compensation increase of 5%: (€218,287.46 × 0.01) × (10 + 17)

= €58,937.61

The value at the end of Year 17 (retirement date) of the estimated future payments is the PV of the estimated annual payment for each of the 20 years at the discount rate of 4%:

Annual compensation increase of 6%: PV of €68,589.50 for 20 years at 4%

= €932,153.69

Annual compensation increase of 5%: PV of €58,937.61 for 20 years at 4%

= €800,981.35

The annual unit credit = Value at retirement/Years of service:

Annual compensation increase of 6%: €932,153.69/27 = €34,524.21

Annual compensation increase of 5%: €800,981.35/27 = €29,665.98

The annual unit credit for the average participant would decrease by €34,524.21 − €29,665.98 = €4,858.23.

7. B is correct. An increase in the retirement life expectancy (from 20 to 28 years) will increase the DB pension obligation, because Plan A pays annual payments for life.

8. A is correct. Current service cost is the present value of annual unit credit earned in the current period.

    Annual unit credit (benefit) per service year

    = Value at retirement / Years of service.

    Years of service = 15 (vested years of past service) + 7 (expected years until retirement)

    = 22.

    Annual unit credit = $393,949 / 22 = $17,906.77.

    Current service cost (for 1 year)

    = Annual unit credit/$(1 + \text{Discount rate})^{\text{Years until retirement at the end of Year 1}}$

    = $17,906.77/(1 + 0.04)^6$ = $14,151.98.

9. A is correct. To estimate the PVDBO, the company must make a number of assumptions, such as future compensation increases, discount rates, and expected vesting. If changes in assumptions increase the obligation, the increase is referred to as an actuarial loss.

    B is incorrect because the PVDBO does not include the value of plan assets in the calculation.

    C is incorrect because the expected long-term rate of return on plan assets is not used to calculate the PVDBO. The interest rate used to calculate the PVDBO is based on current rates of return on high-quality corporate bonds (or government bonds, in the absence of a deep market in corporate bonds) with currency and durations consistent with the currency and durations of the benefits.

10. B is correct. The funded status of a pension plan is calculated as follows:

    Funded status = Fair value of the plan assets − PVDBO

    Based on the information provided in Exhibit 1, the PVDBO is calculated as follows:

    PVDBO = Funded status (Net pension liability) + Plan assets

    $525 + $3,108 = $3,633 million

11. A is correct. A decrease in the assumed future compensation growth rate will decrease a company's pension obligation when the pension formula is based on the final year's salary. Lowering the assumed future compensation growth rate decreases the service and interest components of periodic pension costs because of a decreased annual unit credit.

12. A is correct. Rickards' task is to adjust the balance sheet and cash flow statement information to better reflect the economic nature of certain items related to the pension plan. When a company's periodic contribution to a plan is lower than the total pension cost of the period, it can be viewed as a source of financing. To reflect this event, the deficit amount is adjusted by the effective tax rate and should be reclassified from an operating cash flow to a financing cash flow. The company's contribution to the pension plan was $66 million, which is $30 million less than the pension cost of $96 million. The $30 million difference is $21 million on an after-tax basis, using the effective tax rate of 30%. Therefore, $21 million should be classified as an operating cash outflow (negative value) and a financing cash inflow (positive value).

13. C is correct. To calculate the debt-to-equity ratio, both liabilities and total equity need to be adjusted for the estimated impact of a 100-bp increase in health care costs. The proposed increase in health care costs will increase total liabilities and decrease equity by the same amount. Consequently, the debt-to-equity ratio changes as follows:

    Sensitivity of benefit obligation to 100-bp increase = $93

    Adjusted liabilities = $17,560 + $93 = $17,653

    Adjusted equity = $6,570 − $93 = $6,477

    Adjusted debt-to-equity ratio = $17,653/$6,477 = 2.7255 ≈ 2.73

    Consequently, a 100-bp increase in health care costs increases the debt-to-equity ratio to approximately 2.73.

14. B is correct. The £28,879 million year-end benefit obligation represents the defined benefit obligation.

15. C is correct. The net interest expense of £273 million represents the interest cost on the beginning net pension obligation (beginning funded status) using the discount rate that the company uses in estimating the present value of its pension obligations. This is calculated as −£4,984 million times 5.48 percent = −£273 million; this represents an interest expense on the amount that the company essentially owes the pension plan.

16. C is correct. The remeasurement component of periodic pension cost includes both actuarial gains and losses on the pension obligation and net return on plan assets. Because Kensington does not have any actuarial gains and losses on the pension obligation, the remeasurement component includes only net return on plan assets. In practice, actuarial gains and losses are rarely equal to zero. The net

return on plan assets is equal to actual returns minus beginning plan assets times the discount rate, or £1,302 million − (£23,432 million × 0.0548) = £18 million.

17. A is correct. The actual return on plan assets was 1,302/23,432 = 0.0556, or 5.56 percent. The rate of return included in the interest income/expense is the discount rate, which is given in this example as 5.48 percent.

    The rate of 1.17 percent, calculated as the net interest income divided by beginning plan assets, is not used in pension cost calculations.

18. C is correct. Under IFRS, the component of periodic pension cost that is shown in OCI rather than P&L is remeasurments.

19. A is correct. The relation between the periodic pension cost and the plan's funded status can be expressed as Periodic pension cost = Ending funded status − Employer contributions − Beginning funded status.

20. B is correct. Kensington's periodic pension cost was £483. The company's contributions to the plan were £693. The £210 difference between these two numbers can be viewed as a reduction of the overall pension obligation. To adjust the statement of cash flows to reflect this view, an analyst would reclassify the £210 million (excluding income tax effects) as an outflow related to financing activities rather than operating activities.

21. B is correct. The total periodic pension cost is the change in the net pension liability adjusted for the employer's contribution into the plan. The net pension liability increased from 3,000 to 3,020, and the employer's contribution was 1,000. The total periodic pension cost is 1,020. This will be allocated between P&L and OCI.

22. B is correct. Under IFRS, the components of periodic pension cost that would be reported in P&L are the service cost (composed of current service and past service costs) and the net interest expense or income, calculated by multiplying the net pension liability or net pension asset by the discount rate used to measure the pension liability. Here, the service costs are 320 (= 200 + 120) and the net interest expense is 210 [= (42,000 + 120 − 39,000) × 7%]. Thus, the total periodic pension cost is equal to 538.

23. A is correct. Under US GAAP—assuming the company chooses not to immediately recognise the actuarial loss and assuming there is no amortisation of past service costs or actuarial gains and losses—the components of periodic pension cost that would be reported in P&L include the current service cost of 200, the interest expense on the pension obligation at the beginning of the period of 2,940 (= 7.0% × 42,000), and the expected return on plan assets, which is a reduction of the cost of 3,120 (= 8.0% × 39,000). Summing these three components gives 20.

24. B is correct. The component of periodic pension cost that would be reported in OCI is the remeasurements component. It consists of actuarial gains and losses on the pension obligation and net return on plan assets. Here, the actuarial loss was 460. In addition, the actual return on plan assets was 2,700, which was 30 lower than the return of 2,730 (= 39,000 × 0.07) incorporated in the net interest income/expense. Therefore, the total remeasurements are 490.

25. A is correct. In 2009, XYZ used a lower volatility assumption than it did in 2008. Lower volatility reduces the fair value of an option and thus the reported expense. Using the 2008 volatility estimate would have resulted in higher expense and thus lower net income.

26. C is correct. The assumed long-term rate of return on plan assets is not a com-

ponent that is used in calculating the pension obligation, so there would be no change.

27. B is correct. A higher discount rate (5.38 percent instead of 4.85 percent) will reduce the present value of the pension obligation (liability). In most cases, a higher discount rate will decrease the interest cost component of the net periodic cost because the decrease in the obligation will more than offset the increase in the discount rate (except if the pension obligation is of short duration). Therefore, periodic pension cost would have been lower and reported net income higher. Cash flow from operating activities should not be affected by the change.

28. B is correct. In 2009, the three relevant assumptions were lower than in 2008. Lower expected salary increases reduce the service cost component of the periodic pension cost. A lower discount rate will increase the defined benefit obligation and increase the interest cost component of the periodic pension cost (the increase in the obligation will, in most cases, more than offset the decrease in the discount rate). Reducing the expected return on plan assets typically increases the periodic pension cost.

29. A is correct. The company's inflation estimate rose from 2008 to 2009. However, it lowered its estimate of future salary increases. Normally, salary increases will be positively related to inflation.

30. B is correct. A higher volatility assumption increases the value of the stock option and thus the compensation expense, which, in turn, reduces net income. There is no associated liability for stock options.

31. C is correct. A higher dividend yield reduces the value of the option and thus option expense. The lower expense results in higher earnings. Higher risk-free rates and expected lives result in higher call option values.

LEARNING MODULE

3

Multinational Operations

by Timothy S. Doupnik, PhD, and Elaine Henry, PhD, CFA.

Timothy S. Doupnik, PhD (USA). Elaine Henry, PhD, CFA, is at Stevens Institute of Technology (USA).

LEARNING OUTCOMES

Mastery	The candidate should be able to:
☐	compare and contrast presentation in (reporting) currency, functional currency, and local currency
☐	describe foreign currency transaction exposure, including accounting for and disclosures about foreign currency transaction gains and losses
☐	analyze how changes in exchange rates affect the translated sales of the subsidiary and parent company
☐	compare the current rate method and the temporal method, evaluate how each affects the parent company's balance sheet and income statement, and determine which method is appropriate in various scenarios
☐	calculate the translation effects and evaluate the translation of a subsidiary's balance sheet and income statement into the parent company's presentation currency
☐	analyze how the current rate method and the temporal method affect financial statements and ratios
☐	analyze how alternative translation methods for subsidiaries operating in hyperinflationary economies affect financial statements and ratios
☐	describe how multinational operations affect a company's effective tax rate
☐	explain how changes in the components of sales affect the sustainability of sales growth
☐	analyze how currency fluctuations potentially affect financial results, given a company's countries of operation

1 INTRODUCTION

☐ compare and contrast presentation in (reporting) currency, functional currency, and local currency

☐ describe foreign currency transaction exposure, including accounting for and disclosures about foreign currency transaction gains and losses

According to the World Trade Organization, merchandise exports worldwide were nearly US$15 trillion in 2010.[1] The amount of worldwide merchandise exports in 2010 was more than twice the amount in 2003 (US$7.4 trillion) and more than four times the amount in 1993 (US$3.7 trillion). The top five exporting countries in 2010, in order, were China, the United States, Germany, Japan, and the Netherlands. In the United States alone, 293,131 companies were identified as exporters in 2010, but only 2.2% of those companies were large (more than 500 employees).[2] The vast majority of US companies with export activity were small or medium-sized entities.

The point illustrated by these statistics is that many companies engage in transactions that cross national borders. The parties to these transactions must agree on the currency in which to settle the transaction. Generally, this will be the currency of either the buyer or the seller. Exporters that receive payment in foreign currency and allow the purchaser time to pay must carry a foreign currency receivable on their books. Conversely, importers that agree to pay in foreign currency will have a foreign currency account payable. To be able to include them in the total amount of accounts receivable (payable) reported on the balance sheet, these foreign currency denominated accounts receivable (payable) must be translated into the currency in which the exporter (importer) keeps its books and presents financial statements.

The prices at which foreign currencies can be purchased or sold are called foreign exchange rates. Because foreign exchange rates fluctuate over time, the value of foreign currency payables and receivables also fluctuates. The major accounting issue related to foreign currency transactions is how to reflect the changes in value for foreign currency payables and receivables in the financial statements.

Many companies have operations located in foreign countries. For example, the Swiss food products company Nestlé SA reports that it has factories in 83 countries and a presence in almost every country in the world. US-based Procter & Gamble's annual filing discloses more than 400 subsidiaries located in more than 80 countries around the world. Foreign subsidiaries are generally required to keep accounting records in the currency of the country in which they are located. To prepare consolidated financial statements, the parent company must translate the foreign currency financial statements of its foreign subsidiaries into its own currency. Nestlé, for example, must translate the assets and liabilities its various foreign subsidiaries carry in foreign currency into Swiss francs to be able to consolidate those amounts with the Swiss franc assets and liabilities located in Switzerland.

A multinational company like Nestlé is likely to have two types of foreign currency activities that require special accounting treatment. Most multinationals (1) engage in transactions that are denominated in a foreign currency and (2) invest in foreign subsidiaries that keep their books in a foreign currency. To prepare consolidated

---

1 World Trade Organization, *International Trade Statistics 2011*, Table I4, page 21.
2 US Census Bureau, Department of Commerce. *A Profile of US Importing and Exporting Companies, 2009–2010.* Released 12 April 2012.

Introduction

financial statements, a multinational company must translate the foreign currency amounts related to both types of international activities into the currency in which the company presents its financial statements.

This reading presents the accounting for foreign currency transactions and the translation of foreign currency financial statements. The conceptual issues related to these accounting topics are discussed, and the specific rules embodied in International Financial Reporting Standards (IFRS) and US GAAP are demonstrated through examples. Fortunately, differences between IFRS and US GAAP with respect to foreign currency translation issues are minimal.

Analysts need to understand the effects of foreign exchange rate fluctuations on the financial statements of a multinational company and how a company's financial statements reflect foreign currency gains and losses, whether realized or not.

Foreign Currency Transactions

When companies from different countries agree to conduct business with one another, they must decide which currency will be used. For example, if a Mexican electronic components manufacturer agrees to sell goods to a customer in Finland, the two parties must agree whether the Finnish company will pay for the goods in Mexican pesos, euro, or perhaps even a third currency such as the US dollar. If the transaction is denominated in Mexican pesos, the Finnish company has a foreign currency transaction but the Mexican company does not. To account for the inventory being purchased and the account payable in Mexican pesos, the Finnish company must translate the Mexican peso amounts into euro using appropriate exchange rates. Although the Mexican company also has entered into an international transaction (an export sale), it does not have a foreign currency transaction and no translation is necessary. It simply records the sales revenue and account receivable in Mexican pesos, which is the currency in which it keeps its books and prepares financial statements.

The currency in which financial statement amounts are presented is known as the **presentation currency**. In most cases, a company's presentation currency will be the currency of the country where the company is located. Finnish companies are required to keep accounting records and present financial results in euro, US companies in US dollars, Chinese companies in Chinese yuan, and so on.

Another important concept in accounting for foreign currency activities is the **functional currency**, which is the currency of the primary economic environment in which an entity operates. Normally, the functional currency is the currency in which an entity primarily generates and expends cash. In most cases, an organization's functional currency will be the same as its presentation currency. And, because most companies primarily generate and expend cash in the currency of the country where they are located, the functional and presentation currencies are most often the same as the **local currency** where the company operates.

Because the local currency generally is an entity's functional currency, a multinational corporation with subsidiaries in a variety of different countries is likely to have a variety of different functional currencies. The Thai subsidiary of a Japanese parent company, for example, is likely to have the Thai baht as its functional currency, whereas the Japanese parent's functional currency is the Japanese yen. But in some cases, the foreign subsidiary could have the parent's functional currency as its own. For example, prior to its 2011 acquisition of McAfee, Intel Corporation had determined that the US dollar was the functional currency for all of its significant foreign subsidiaries. However, subsequent to the acquisition of McAfee, as stated in Intel Corporation's 2011 Annual Report, Note 1: Basis of Presentation, "Certain of the operations acquired from McAfee have a functional currency other than the US dollar."

By definition, for accounting purposes, a foreign currency is any currency other than a company's functional currency, and **foreign currency transactions** are those denominated in a currency other than the company's functional currency. Foreign currency transactions occur when a company (1) makes an import purchase or an export sale that is denominated in a foreign currency or (2) borrows or lends funds where the amount to be repaid or received is denominated in a foreign currency. In each of these cases, the company has an asset or a liability denominated in a foreign currency.

Foreign Currency Transaction Exposure to Foreign Exchange Risk

Assume that FinnCo, a Finland-based company, imports goods from Mexico in January under 45-day credit terms, and the purchase is denominated in Mexican pesos. By deferring payment until April, FinnCo runs the risk that from the date the purchase is made until the date of payment, the value of the Mexican peso might increase relative to the euro. FinnCo would then need to spend more euro to settle its Mexican peso account payable. In this case, FinnCo is said to have an **exposure to foreign exchange risk**. Specifically, FinnCo has a foreign currency **transaction exposure**. Transaction exposure related to imports and exports can be summarized as follows:

- *Import purchase.* A transaction exposure arises when the importer is obligated to pay in foreign currency and is allowed to defer payment until sometime after the purchase date. The importer is exposed to the risk that from the purchase date until the payment date the foreign currency might increase in value, thereby increasing the amount of functional currency that must be spent to acquire enough foreign currency to settle the account payable.

- *Export sale.* A transaction exposure arises when the exporter agrees to be paid in foreign currency and allows payment to be made sometime after the purchase date. The exporter is exposed to the risk that from the purchase date until the payment date, the foreign currency might decrease in value, thereby decreasing the amount of functional currency into which the foreign currency can be converted when it is received.

The major issue in accounting for foreign currency transactions is how to account for the foreign currency risk—that is, how to reflect in the financial statements the change in value of the foreign currency asset or liability. Both IFRS and US GAAP require the change in the value of the foreign currency asset or liability resulting from a foreign currency transaction to be treated as a gain or loss reported on the income statement.[3]

Accounting for Foreign Currency Transactions with Settlement before Balance Sheet Date

Example 1 demonstrates FinnCo's accounting, assuming that it purchased goods on account from a Mexican supplier that required payment in Mexican pesos, and that it made payment before the balance sheet date. The basic principle is that all transactions are recorded at the spot rate on the date of the transaction. The foreign currency risk on *transactions*, therefore, arises only when the transaction date and the payment date are different.

---

[3] International standards are presented in International Accounting Standard (IAS) 21, "The Effects of Changes in Foreign Exchange Rates," and US GAAP standards are presented in FASB ASC Topic 830, "Foreign Currency Matters."

Introduction

> **EXAMPLE 1**
>
> ## Accounting for Foreign Currency Transactions with Settlement before the Balance Sheet Date
>
> 1. FinnCo purchases goods from its Mexican supplier on 1 November 20X1; the purchase price is 100,000 Mexican pesos. Credit terms allow payment in 45 days, and FinnCo makes payment of 100,000 pesos on 15 December 20X1. FinnCo's functional and presentation currency is the euro. Spot exchange rates between the euro (EUR) and Mexican peso (MXN) are as follows:
>
> | | |
> |---|---|
> | 1 November 20X1 | MXN1 = EUR0.0684 |
> | 15 December 20X1 | MXN1 = EUR0.0703 |
>
>   FinnCo's fiscal year end is 31 December. How will FinnCo account for this foreign currency transaction, and what effect will it have on the 20X1 financial statements?
>
> ## Solution:
>
> The euro value of the Mexican peso account payable on 1 November 20X1 was EUR6,840 (MXN100,000 × EUR0.0684). FinnCo could have paid for its inventory on 1 November by converting 6,840 euro into 100,000 Mexican pesos. Instead, the company purchases 100,000 Mexican pesos on 15 December 20X1, when the value of the peso has increased to EUR0.0703. Thus, FinnCo pays 7,030 euro to purchase 100,000 Mexican pesos. The net result is a loss of 190 euro (EUR7,030 − EUR6,840).
>
> Although the cash outflow to acquire the inventory is EUR7,030, the cost included in the inventory account is only EUR6,840. This cost represents the amount that FinnCo could have paid if it had not waited 45 days to settle its account. By deferring payment, and because the Mexican peso increased in value between the transaction date and settlement date, FinnCo has to pay an additional 190 euro. ==The company will report a foreign exchange loss of EUR190 in its net income in 20X1.== This is a realized loss because FinnCo actually spent an additional 190 euro to purchase its inventory. The net effect on the financial statements, in EUR, can be seen as follows:
>
> | Balance Sheet | | | | Income Statement | |
> |---|---|---|---|---|---|
> | **Assets** | | **= Liabilities +** | **Stockholders' Equity** | **Revenues and Gains** | **Expenses and Losses** |
> | Cash | −7,030 | | Retained | | Foreign |
> | Inventory | +6,840 | | earnings −190 | | exchange loss −190 |
> | | −190 | | | | |

Accounting for Foreign Currency Transactions with Intervening Balance Sheet Dates
Another important issue related to the accounting for foreign currency transactions is what, if anything, should be done if a balance sheet date falls between the initial transaction date and the settlement date. For foreign currency transactions whose

settlement dates fall in subsequent accounting periods, both IFRS and US GAAP require adjustments to reflect intervening changes in currency exchange rates. Foreign currency transaction gains and losses are reported on the income statement, creating one of the few situations in which accounting rules allow, indeed require, companies to include (recognize) a gain or loss in income before it has been realized.

Subsequent foreign currency transaction gains and losses are recognized from the balance sheet date through the date the transaction is settled. Adding together foreign currency transaction gains and losses for both accounting periods (transaction initiation to balance sheet date and balance sheet date to transaction settlement) produces an amount equal to the actual realized gain or loss on the foreign currency transaction.

EXAMPLE 2

Accounting for Foreign Currency Transaction with Intervening Balance Sheet Date

1. FinnCo sells goods to a customer in the United Kingdom for £10,000 on 15 November 20X1, with payment to be received in British pounds on 15 January 20X2. FinnCo's functional and presentation currency is the euro. Spot exchange rates between the euro (€) and British pound (£) are as follows:

    | 15 November 20X1 | £1 = €1.460 |
    | 31 December 20X1 | £1 = €1.480 |
    | 15 January 20X2 | £1 = €1.475 |

FinnCo's fiscal year end is 31 December. How will FinnCo account for this foreign currency transaction, and what effect will it have on the 20X1 and 20X2 financial statements?

Solution:

The euro value of the British pound account receivable at each of the three relevant dates is determined as follows:

		Account Receivable (£10,000)	
Date	€/£ Exchange Rate	Euro Value	Change in Euro Value
15 Nov 20X1	€1.460	14,600	N/A
31 Dec 20X1	€1.480	14,800	+ 200
15 Jan 20X2	€1.475	14,750	− 50

A change in the euro value of the British pound receivable from 15 November to 31 December would be recognized as a foreign currency transaction gain or loss on FinnCo's 20X1 income statement. In this case, the increase in the value of the British pound results in a transaction gain of €200 [£10,000 × (€1.48 − €1.46)]. Note that the gain recognized in 20X1 income is unrealized, and remember that this is one of few situations in which companies include an unrealized gain in income.

Any change in the exchange rate between the euro and British pound that occurs from the balance sheet date (31 December 20X1) to the transaction settlement date (15 January 20X2) will also result in a foreign currency transaction gain or loss. In our example, the British pound weakened slightly against the euro during this period, resulting in an exchange rate of €1.475/

Introduction

> £1 on 15 January 20X2. The £10,000 account receivable now has a value of €14,750, which is a decrease of €50 from 31 December 20X1. FinnCo will recognize a foreign currency transaction loss on 15 January 20X2 of €50 that will be included in the company's calculation of net income for the first quarter of 20X2.
>
> From the transaction date to the settlement date, the British pound has increased in value by €0.015 (€1.475 − €1.460), which generates a realized foreign currency transaction gain of €150. A gain of €200 was recognized in 20X1 and a loss of €50 is recognized in 20X2. Over the two-month period, the net gain recognized in the financial statements is equal to the actual realized gain on the foreign currency transaction.

In Example 2, FinnCo's British pound account receivable resulted in a net foreign currency transaction gain because the British pound strengthened (increased) in value between the transaction date and the settlement date. In this case, FinnCo has an asset exposure to foreign exchange risk. This asset exposure benefited the company because the foreign currency strengthened. If FinnCo instead had a British pound account payable, a liability exposure would have existed. The euro value of the British pound account payable would have increased as the British pound strengthened, and FinnCo would have recognized a foreign currency transaction loss as a result.

Whether a change in exchange rate results in a foreign currency transaction gain or loss (measured in local currency) depends on (1) the nature of the exposure to foreign exchange risk (asset or liability) and (2) the direction of change in the value of the foreign currency (strengthens or weakens).

		Foreign Currency	
Transaction	Type of Exposure	Strengthens	Weakens
Export sale	Asset (account receivable)	Gain	Loss
Import purchase	Liability (account payable)	Loss	Gain

A foreign currency receivable arising from an export sale creates an asset exposure to foreign exchange risk. If the foreign currency strengthens, the receivable increases in value in terms of the company's functional currency and a foreign currency transaction gain arises. The company will be able to convert the foreign currency when received into more units of functional currency because the foreign currency has strengthened. Conversely, if the foreign currency weakens, the foreign currency receivable loses value in terms of the functional currency and a loss results.

A foreign currency payable resulting from an import purchase creates a liability exposure to foreign exchange risk. If the foreign currency strengthens, the payable increases in value in terms of the company's functional currency and a foreign currency transaction loss arises. The company must spend more units of functional currency to be able to settle the foreign currency liability because the foreign currency has strengthened. Conversely, if the foreign currency weakens, the foreign currency payable loses value in terms of the functional currency and a gain exists.

Analytical Issues

Both IFRS and US GAAP require foreign currency transaction gains and losses to be reported in net income (even if the gains and losses have not yet been realized), but neither standard indicates where on the income statement these gains and losses should be placed. The two most common treatments are either (1) as a component of other operating income/expense or (2) as a component of non-operating income/

expense, in some cases as a part of net financing cost. The calculation of operating profit margin is affected by where foreign currency transaction gains or losses are placed on the income statement.

> **EXAMPLE 3**
>
> ## Placement of Foreign Currency Transaction Gains/Losses on the Income Statement—Effect on Operating Profit
>
> 1. Assume that FinnCo had the following income statement information in both 20X1 and 20X2, excluding a foreign currency transaction gain of €200 in 20X1 and a transaction loss of €50 in 20X2.
>
> | | 20X1 | 20X2 |
> |---|---|---|
> | Revenues | €20,000 | €20,000 |
> | Cost of goods sold | 12,000 | 12,000 |
> | Other operating expenses, net | 5,000 | 5,000 |
> | Non-operating expenses, net | 1,200 | 1,200 |
>
> FinnCo is deciding between two alternatives for the treatment of foreign currency transaction gains and losses. Alternative 1 calls for the reporting of foreign currency transaction gains/losses as part of "Other operating expenses, net." Under Alternative 2, the company would report this information as part of "Non-operating expenses, net."
>
> FinnCo's fiscal year end is 31 December. How will Alternatives 1 and 2 affect the company's gross profit margin, operating profit margin, and net profit margin for 20X1? For 20X2?
>
> ### Solution:
>
> Remember that a gain would serve to reduce expenses, whereas a loss would increase expenses.
>
> | 20X1—Transaction Gain of €200 | | |
> |---|---|---|
> | | **Alternative 1** | **Alternative 2** |
> | Revenues | €20,000 | €20,000 |
> | Cost of goods sold | (12,000) | (12,000) |
> | Gross profit | 8,000 | 8,000 |
> | Other operating expenses, net | (4,800) incl. gain | (5,000) |
> | Operating profit | 3,200 | 3,000 |
> | Non-operating expenses, net | (1,200) | (1,000) incl. gain |
> | Net profit | €2,000 | €2,000 |
>
> Profit margins in 20X1 under the two alternatives can be calculated as follows:
>
> | | **Alternative 1** | **Alternative 2** |
> |---|---|---|
> | Gross profit margin | €8,000/€20,000 = 40.0% | €8,000/€20,000 = 40.0% |

Introduction

	Alternative 1	Alternative 2
Operating profit margin	3,200/20,000 = 16.0%	3,000/20,000 = 15.0%
Net profit margin	2,000/20,000 = 10.0%	2,000/20,000 = 10.0%

20X2—Transaction Loss of €50

	Alternative 1		Alternative 2	
Revenues	€20,000		€20,000	
Cost of goods sold	(12,000)		(12,000)	
Gross profit	8,000		8,000	
Other operating expenses, net	(5,050)	incl. loss	(5,000)	
Operating profit	2,950		3,000	
Non-operating expenses, net	(1,200)		(1,250)	incl. loss
Net profit	€1,750		€1,750	

Profit margins in 20X2 under the two alternatives can be calculated as follows:

	Alternative 1	Alternative 2
Gross profit margin	€8,000/€20,000 = 40.0%	€8,000/€20,000 = 40.0%
Operating profit margin	2,950/20,000 = 14.75%	3,000/20,000 = 15.0%
Net profit margin	1,750/20,000 = 8.75%	1,750/20,000 = 8.75%

Gross profit and net profit are unaffected, but operating profit differs under the two alternatives. In 20X1, the operating profit margin is larger under Alternative 1, which includes the transaction gain as part of "Other operating expenses, net." In 20X2, Alternative 1 results in a smaller operating profit margin than Alternative 2. Alternative 2 has the same operating profit margin in both periods. Because exchange rates do not fluctuate by the same amount or in the same direction from one accounting period to the next, Alternative 1 will cause greater volatility in operating profit and operating profit margin over time.

Because accounting standards do not provide guidance on the placement of foreign currency transaction gains and losses on the income statement, companies are free to choose among the alternatives. Two companies in the same industry could choose different alternatives, which would distort the direct comparison of operating profit and operating profit margins between those companies.

A second issue that should be of interest to analysts relates to the fact that unrealized foreign currency transaction gains and losses are included in net income when the balance sheet date falls between the transaction and settlement dates. The implicit assumption underlying this accounting requirement is that the unrealized gain or loss as of the balance sheet date reflects the company's ultimate net gain or loss. In reality, though, the ultimate net gain or loss may vary dramatically because of the possibility for changes in trend and volatility of currency prices.

This effect was seen in the previous hypothetical Example 2 with FinnCo. Using given currency exchange rate data shows that the real-world effect can also be quite dramatic. Assume that a French company purchased goods from a Canadian supplier on 1 December 20X1, with payment of 100,000 Canadian dollars (C$) to be made on

15 May 20X2. Actual exchange rates between the Canadian dollar and euro (€) during the period 1 December 20X1 and 15 May 20X2, the euro value of the Canadian dollar account payable, and the foreign currency transaction gain or loss are shown below:

		Account Payable (C$100,000)	
	€/C$	€ Value	Change in € Value (Gain/Loss)
1 Dec X1	0.7285	72,850	N/A
31 Dec X1	0.7571	75,710	2,860 loss
31 Mar X2	0.7517	75,170	540 gain
15 May X2	0.7753	77,530	2,360 loss

As the Canadian dollar strengthened against the euro in late 20X1, the French company would have recorded a foreign currency transaction loss of €2,860 in the fourth quarter of 20X1. The Canadian dollar reversed course by weakening over the first three months of 20X2, resulting in a transaction gain of €540 in the first quarter, and then strengthened against the euro in the second quarter of 20X2, resulting in a transaction loss of €2,360. At the time payment is made on 15 May 20X2, the French company realizes a net foreign currency transaction loss of €4,680 (€77,530 − €72,850).

2. DISCLOSURES RELATED TO FOREIGN CURRENCY TRANSACTION GAINS AND LOSSES

☐ describe foreign currency transaction exposure, including accounting for and disclosures about foreign currency transaction gains and losses

Because accounting rules allow companies to choose where they present foreign currency transaction gains and losses on the income statement, it is useful for companies to disclose both the amount of transaction gain or loss that is included in income and the presentation alternative they have selected. IFRS require disclosure of "the amount of exchange differences recognized in profit or loss," and US GAAP require disclosure of "the aggregate transaction gain or loss included in determining net income for the period," but neither standard specifically requires disclosure of the line item in which these gains and losses are located.

Exhibit 1 provides disclosures from BASF AG's 2011 annual report that the German company made related to foreign currency transaction gains and losses. Exhibit 2 presents similar disclosures found in the Netherlands-based Heineken NV's 2011 Annual Report. Both companies use IFRS to prepare their consolidated financial statements.

BASF's income statement in Exhibit 1 does not include a separate line item for foreign currency gains and losses. From Note 6 in Exhibit 1, an analyst can determine that BASF has chosen to include "Income from foreign currency and hedging transactions" in "Other operating income." Of the total amount of €2,008 million reported as "Other operating income" in 2011, €170 million is attributable to foreign currency and hedging transaction income. It is not possible to determine from BASF's financial statements whether or not these gains were realized in 2011, and any unrealized gain reported in 2011 income might or might not be realized in 2012.

Disclosures Related to Foreign Currency Transaction Gains and Losses

Note 7 in Exhibit 1 indicates that "Expenses from foreign currency and hedging transactions as well as market valuation" in 2011 were €399 million, making up 15% of Other operating expenses. Combining foreign currency transaction gains and losses results in a net loss of €229 million, which is equal to 2.55% of BASF's "Income before taxes and minority interests."

Exhibit 1: Excerpts from BASF AG's 2011 Annual Report Related to Foreign Currency Transactions

Consolidated Statements of Income Million €	Explanation in Notes	2011	2010
Sales	(4)	73,497	63,873
Cost of sales		(53,986)	(45,310)
Gross profit on sales		**19,511**	**18,563**
Selling expenses		(7,323)	(6,700)
General and administrative expenses		(1,315)	(1,138)
Research and development expenses		(1,605)	(1,492)
Other operating income	(6)	2,008	1,140
Other operating expenses	(7)	(2,690)	(2,612)
Income from operations	(4)	**8,586**	**7,761**
(detail omitted)			
Financial result	(8)	**384**	**(388)**
Income before taxes and minority interests		**8,970**	**7,373**
Income taxes	(9)	(2,367)	(2,299)
Income before minority interests		**6,603**	**5,074**
Minority interests	(10)	(415)	(517)
Net income		**6,188**	**4,557**

Notes:

1. Summary of Accounting Policies

   Foreign currency transactions: The cost of assets acquired in foreign currencies and revenues from sales in foreign currencies are recorded at the exchange rate on the date of the transaction. Foreign currency receivables and liabilities are valued at the exchange rates on the balance sheet date.

2. Other Operating Income

Million €	2011	2010
Reversal and adjustment of provisions	170	244
Revenue from miscellaneous revenue-generating activities	207	142
Income from foreign currency and hedging transactions	170	136
Income from the translation of financial statements in foreign currencies	42	76
Gains on the disposal of property, plant and equipment and divestitures	666	101
Reversals of impairments of property, plant and equipment	—	40
Gains on the reversal of allowance for doubtful business-related receivables	77	36
Other	676	365
	2,008	1,140

Income from foreign currency and hedging transactions concerned foreign currency transactions, the measurement at fair value of receivables and payables in foreign currencies, as well as currency derivatives and other hedging transactions.

3. Other Operating Expenses

Million €	2011	2010
Restructuring measures	233	276
Environmental protection and safety measures, costs of demolition and removal, and planning expenses related to capital expenditures that are not subject to mandatory capitalization	203	98
Valuation adjustments on tangible and intangible assets	366	247
Costs from miscellaneous revenue-generating activities	220	180
Expenses from foreign currency and hedging transactions as well as market valuation	399	601
Losses from the translation of the financial statements in foreign currencies	56	63
Losses from the disposal of property, plant and equipment and divestitures	40	24
Oil and gas exploration expenses	184	190
Expenses from additions to allowances for business-related receivables	124	107
Expenses from the use of inventories measured at market value and the derecognition of obsolete inventory	233	188
Other	632	638
	2,690	2,612

Expenses from foreign currency and hedging transactions as well as market valuation concern foreign currency translations of receivables and payables as well as changes in the fair value of currency derivatives and other hedging transactions.

In Exhibit 2, Heineken's Note 2, Basis of Preparation, part (c) explicitly states that the euro is the company's functional currency. Note 3(b)(i) indicates that monetary assets and liabilities denominated in foreign currencies at the balance sheet date are translated to the functional currency and that foreign currency differences arising on the translation (i.e., translation gains and losses) are recognized on the income statement. Note 3(r) discloses that foreign currency gains and losses are included on a net basis in the other net finance income and expenses. Note 12, "Net finance income and expense," shows that a net foreign exchange loss of €107 million existed in 2011 and a net gain of €61 million arose in 2010. The net foreign currency transaction gain in 2010 amounted to 3.1% of Heineken's profit before income tax that year, and the net translation loss in 2011 represented 5.3% of the company's profit before income tax in that year. Note 12 also shows gains and losses related to changes in the fair value of derivatives, some of which related to foreign currency derivatives.

Disclosures Related to Foreign Currency Transaction Gains and Losses

Exhibit 2: Excerpts from Heineken NV's 2011 Annual Report Related to Foreign Currency Transactions

Consolidated Income Statement for the Year Ended 31 December in Millions of EUR	Note	2011	2010
Revenue	5	17,123	16,133
Other income	8	64	239
Raw materials, consumables, and services	9	(10,966)	(10,291)
Personnel expenses	10	(2,838)	(2,665)
Amortisation, depreciation, and impairments	11	(1,168)	(1,118)
Total expenses		**(14,972)**	**(14,074)**
Results from operating activities		**2,215**	**2,298**
Interest income	12	70	100
Interest expenses	12	(494)	(590)
Other net finance income/(expenses)	12	(6)	(19)
Net finance expenses		**(430)**	**(509)**
Share of profit of associates and joint ventures and impairments thereof (net of income tax)	16	240	193
Profit before income tax		**2,025**	**1,982**
Income tax expenses	13	(465)	(403)
Profit		**1,560**	**1,579**
Attributable to:			
Equity holders of the Company (net profit)		1,430	1,447
Minority interest		130	132
Profit		**1,560**	**1,579**

Notes:

4. Basis of preparation

   a. Functional and presentation currency

   These consolidated financial statements are presented in euro, which is the Company's functional currency. All financial information presented in euro has been rounded to the nearest million unless stated otherwise.

5. Significant accounting policies

   a. Foreign currency

      i. Foreign currency transactions

         Transactions in foreign currencies are translated to the respective functional currencies of Heineken entities at the exchange rates at the dates of the transactions. Monetary assets and liabilities denominated in foreign currencies at the reporting date are retranslated to the functional currency at the exchange rate at that date.... Foreign currency differences arising on retranslation are recognised in profit or loss, except for differences arising on the retranslation of available-for-sale (equity) investments and foreign currency differences arising on the retranslation of a financial liability designated as a hedge of a net investment, which are recognised in other comprehensive income.[4]

    b. Interest income, interest expenses and other net finance income and expenses

...Foreign currency gains and losses are reported on a net basis in the other net finance income and expenses.

6. Net finance income and expense

Recognised in profit or loss		
In millions of EUR	2011	2010
Interest income	**70**	**100**
Interest expenses	**(494)**	**(590)**
Dividend income on available-for-sale investments	2	1
Dividend income on investments held for trading	11	7
Net gain/(loss) on disposal of available-for-sale investments	1	—
Net change in fair value of derivatives	96	(75)
Net foreign exchange gain/(loss)	(107)	61
Impairment losses on available-for-sale investments	—	(3)
Unwinding discount on provisions	(7)	(7)
Other net financial income/(expenses)	(2)	(3)
Other net finance income/(expenses)	**(6)**	**(19)**
Net finance income/(expenses)	**(430)**	**(509)**

Disclosures related to foreign currency are commonly found both in the Management Discussion & Analysis (MD&A) and the Notes to Financial Statements sections of an annual report. In applying US GAAP to account for its foreign currency transactions, Yahoo! Inc. reported the following in the Quantitative and Qualitative Disclosures about Market Risk section of its 2011 annual report:

> Our exposure to foreign currency transaction gains and losses is the result of assets and liabilities, (including inter-company transactions) that are denominated in currencies other than the relevant entity's functional currency.... We may enter into derivative instruments, such as foreign currency forward contracts or other instruments to minimize the short-term foreign currency fluctuations on such assets and liabilities. The gains and losses on the forward contracts may not offset any or more than a portion of the transaction gains and losses on certain foreign currency receivables, investments and payables recognized in earnings. Transaction gains and losses on these foreign exchange contracts are recognized each period in other income, net included on the consolidated statements of income. During the years ended December 31, 2011, 2010, and 2009, we recorded net realized and unrealized foreign currency transaction gains of $9 million and $13 million, and a transaction loss of $1 million, respectively.

---

4 Note that this excerpt uses "retranslation" in the same way that "translation" is used throughout the rest of this reading. The translation of currency for foreign subsidiaries will be covered in the next section.

Disclosures Related to Foreign Currency Transaction Gains and Losses

Yahoo!'s disclosure clearly explains that both realized and unrealized foreign currency transaction gains and losses are reflected in income, specifically as a part of non-operating activities. The net foreign currency transaction gain in 2011 of $9 million represented only 1.1% of the company's pretax income ($827.5 million) for the year.

Some companies may choose not to disclose either the location or the amount of their foreign currency transaction gains and losses, presumably because the amounts involved are immaterial. There are several reasons why the amount of transaction gains and losses can be immaterial for a company:

1. The company engages in a limited number of foreign currency transactions that involve relatively small amounts of foreign currency.
2. The exchange rates between the company's functional currency and the foreign currencies in which it has transactions tend to be relatively stable.
3. Gains on some foreign currency transactions are naturally offset by losses on other transactions, such that the net gain or loss is immaterial. For example, if a US company sells goods to a customer in Canada with payment in Canadian dollars to be received in 90 days and at the same time purchases goods from a supplier in Canada with payment to be made in Canadian dollars in 90 days, any loss that arises on the Canadian dollar receivable due to a weakening in the value of the Canadian dollar will be exactly offset by a gain of equal amount on the Canadian dollar payable.
4. The company engages in foreign currency hedging activities to offset the foreign exchange gains and losses that arise from foreign currency transactions. Hedging foreign exchange risk is a common practice for many companies engaged in foreign currency transactions.

The two most common types of hedging instruments used to minimize foreign exchange transaction risk are foreign currency forward contracts and foreign currency options. Nokia Corporation describes its foreign exchange risk management approach in its 2011 Form 20-F annual report in Note 34, Risk Management. An excerpt from that note follows:

> Nokia operates globally and is thus exposed to foreign exchange risk arising from various currencies. Foreign currency denominated assets and liabilities together with foreign currency denominated cash flows from highly probable or probable purchases and sales contribute to foreign exchange exposure. These transaction exposures are managed against various local currencies because of Nokia's substantial production and sales outside the Euro zone.
>
> According to the foreign exchange policy guidelines of the Group, which remains the same as in the previous year, material transaction foreign exchange exposures are hedged unless hedging would be uneconomical due to market liquidity and/or hedging cost. Exposures are defined using nominal values of the transactions. Exposures are mainly hedged with derivative financial instruments such as forward foreign exchange contracts and foreign exchange options. The majority of financial instruments hedging foreign exchange risk have duration of less than a year. The Group does not hedge forecasted foreign currency cash flows beyond two years.

Elsewhere in its annual report, Nokia provides additional disclosures about the currencies to which it has exposure and the accounting for different types of hedges. The company also summarizes the effect of material exchange rate movements. For example, the 4.2% appreciation of the US dollar in 2011 had a positive effect on net sales expressed in euro (40% of Nokia's net sales are in US dollars or currencies

3. TRANSLATION OF FOREIGN CURRENCY FINANCIAL STATEMENTS

☐ analyze how changes in exchange rates affect the translated sales of the subsidiary and parent company

Many companies have operations in foreign countries. Most operations located in foreign countries keep their accounting records and prepare financial statements in the local currency. For example, the US subsidiary of German automaker BMW AG keeps its books in US dollars. IFRS and US GAAP require parent companies to prepare consolidated financial statements in which the assets, liabilities, revenues, and expenses of both domestic and foreign subsidiaries are added to those of the parent company. To prepare worldwide consolidated statements, parent companies must translate the foreign currency financial statements of their foreign subsidiaries into the parent company's presentation currency. BMW AG, for example, must translate both the US dollar financial statements of its US subsidiary and the South African rand financial statements of its South African subsidiary into euro to consolidate these foreign operations. If, for example, the US dollar and South African rand appreciate against the euro over the course of a given year, the amount of sales translated into euro will be greater than if the subsidiary's currencies weaken against the euro.

IFRS and US GAAP have similar rules for the translation of foreign currency financial statements. To fully understand the results from applying these rules, however, several conceptual issues must first be examined.

Translation Conceptual Issues

In translating foreign currency financial statements into the parent company's presentation currency, two questions must be addressed:

1. What is the appropriate exchange rate to use in translating each financial statement item?

2. How should the translation adjustment that inherently arises from the translation process be reflected in the consolidated financial statements? In other words, how is the balance sheet brought back into balance?

These issues and the basic concepts underlying the translation of financial statements are demonstrated through the following example.

Spanco is a hypothetical Spain-based company that uses the euro as its presentation currency. Spanco establishes a wholly owned subsidiary, Amerco, in the United States on 31 December 20X1 by investing €10,000 when the exchange rate between the euro and the US dollar is €1 = US$1. The equity investment of €10,000 is physically converted into US$10,000 to begin operations. In addition, Amerco borrows US$5,000 from local banks on 31 December 20X1. Amerco purchases inventory that costs US$12,000 on 31 December 20X1 and retains US$3,000 in cash. Amerco's balance sheet at 31 December 20X1 thus appears as follows:

Amerco Balance Sheet, 31 December 20X1 (in US Dollars)

Cash	$3,000	Notes payable	$5,000
Inventory	12,000	Common stock	10,000
Total	$15,000	Total	$15,000

To prepare a consolidated balance sheet in euro as of 31 December 20X1, Spanco must translate all of the US dollar balances on Amerco's balance sheet at the €1 = US$1 exchange rate. The translation worksheet as of 31 December 20X1 is as follows:

Translation Worksheet for Amerco, 31 December 20X1

	USD	Exchange Rate (€)	EUR
Cash	$3,000	1.00	€3,000
Inventory	12,000	1.00	12,000
Total	$15,000		€15,000
Notes payable	5,000	1.00	5,000
Common stock	10,000	1.00	10,000
Total	$15,000		€15,000

By translating each US dollar balance at the same exchange rate (€1.00), Amerco's translated balance sheet in euro reflects an equal amount of total assets and total liabilities plus equity and remains in balance.

During the first quarter of 20X2, Amerco engages in no transactions. During that period, however, the US dollar weakens against the euro such that the exchange rate on 31 March 20X2 is €0.80 = US$1.

To prepare a consolidated balance sheet at the end of the first quarter of 20X2, Spanco now must choose between the current exchange rate of €0.80 and the historical exchange rate of €1.00 to translate Amerco's balance sheet amounts into euro. The original investment made by Spanco of €10,000 is a historical fact, so the company wants to translate Amerco's common stock in such a way that it continues to reflect this amount. This goal is achieved by translating common stock of US$10,000 into euro using the historical exchange rate of €1 = US$1.

Two approaches for translating the foreign subsidiary's assets and liabilities are as follows:

1. All assets and liabilities are translated at the **current exchange rate** (the spot exchange rate on the balance sheet date).

2. Only **monetary assets and liabilities** are translated at the current exchange rate; **non-monetary assets and liabilities** are translated at **historical exchange rates** (the exchange rates that existed when the assets and liabilities were acquired). Monetary items are cash and receivables (payables) that are to be received (paid) in a fixed number of currency units. Non-monetary assets include inventory, fixed assets, and intangibles, and non-monetary liabilities include deferred revenue.

These two different approaches are demonstrated and the results analyzed in turn.

All Assets and Liabilities Are Translated at the Current Exchange Rate

The translation worksheet on 31 March 20X2, in which all assets and liabilities are translated at the current exchange rate (€0.80), is as follows:

Translation Worksheet for Amerco, 31 March 20X2

	US Dollar	Exchange Rate (€)	Euro	Change in Euro Value since 31 Dec 20X1
Cash	$3,000	0.80 C	€2,400	−€600
Inventory	12,000	0.80 C	9,600	−2,400
Total	$15,000		€12,000	−€3,000
Notes payable	5,000	0.80 C	4,000	−1,000
Common stock	10,000	1.00 H	10,000	0
Subtotal	$15,000		14,000	−1,000
Translation adjustment			(2,000)	−2,000
Total			€12,000	−€3,000

Note: C = current exchange rate; H = historical exchange rate

By translating all assets at the lower current exchange rate, total assets are written down from 31 December 20X1 to 31 March 20X2 in terms of their euro value by €3,000. Liabilities are written down by €1,000. To keep the euro translated balance sheet in balance, a *negative* translation adjustment of €2,000 is created and included in stockholders' equity on the consolidated balance sheet.

Those foreign currency balance sheet accounts that are translated using the current exchange rate are revalued in terms of the parent's functional currency. This process is very similar to the revaluation of foreign currency receivables and payables related to foreign currency transactions. The net translation adjustment that results from translating individual assets and liabilities at the current exchange rate can be viewed as the *net* foreign currency translation gain or loss caused by a change in the exchange rate:

(€600)	loss on cash
(€2,400)	loss on inventory
€1,000	gain on notes payable
(€2,000)	net translation loss

The negative translation adjustment (net translation loss) does not result in a cash outflow of €2,000 for Spanco and thus is unrealized. The loss could be realized, however, if Spanco were to sell Amerco at its book value of US$10,000. The proceeds from the sale would be converted into euro at €0.80 per US$1, resulting in a cash inflow of €8,000. Because Spanco originally invested €10,000 in its US operation, a *realized* loss of €2,000 would result.

The second conceptual issue related to the translation of foreign currency financial statements is whether the unrealized net translation loss should be included in the determination of consolidated net income currently or deferred in the stockholders' equity section of the consolidated balance sheet until the loss is realized through sale of the foreign subsidiary. There is some debate as to which of these two treatments is most appropriate. This issue is discussed in more detail after considering the second approach for translating assets and liabilities.

Only Monetary Assets and Monetary Liabilities Are Translated at the Current Exchange Rate

Now assume only monetary assets and monetary liabilities are translated at the current exchange rate. The worksheet at 31 March 20X2, in which only monetary assets and liabilities are translated at the current exchange rate (€0.80), is as follows:

Translation of Foreign Currency Financial Statements

Translation Worksheet for Amerco, 31 March 20X2

	US Dollar	Exchange Rate (€)	Euro	Change in Euro Value since 31 Dec 20X1
Cash	$3,000	0.80 C	€2,400	–€600
Inventory	12,000	1.00 H	12,000	0
Total	$15,000		€14,400	–€600
Notes payable	5,000	0.80 C	4,000	–1,000
Common stock	10,000	1.00 H	10,000	0
Subtotal	$15,000		14,000	–1,000
Translation adjustment			400	400
Total			€14,400	–€600

Note: C = current exchange rate; H = historical exchange rate

Using this approach, cash is written down by €600 but inventory continues to be carried at its euro historical cost of €12,000. Notes payable is written down by €1,000. To keep the balance sheet in balance, a positive translation adjustment of €400 must be included in stockholders' equity. The translation adjustment reflects the *net* translation gain or loss related to monetary items only:

(€600)	loss on cash
€1,000	gain on notes payable
€400	net translation gain

The positive translation adjustment (net translation gain) also is *unrealized*. The gain could be *realized*, however, if:

1. The subsidiary uses its cash (US$3,000) to pay as much of its liabilities as possible, and
2. The parent sends enough euro to the subsidiary to pay its remaining liabilities (US$5,000 – US$3,000 = US$2,000). As of 31 December 20X1, at the €1.00 per US$1 exchange rate, Spanco will have sent €2,000 to Amerco to pay liabilities of US$2,000. On 31 March 20X2, given the €0.80 per US$1 exchange rate, the parent needs to send only €1,600 to pay US$2,000 of liabilities. As a result, Spanco would enjoy a foreign exchange gain of €400.

The second conceptual issue again arises under this approach. Should the unrealized foreign exchange gain be recognized in current period net income or deferred on the balance sheet as a separate component of stockholders' equity? The answer to this question, as provided by IFRS and US GAAP, is described in Section 3, Translation Methods.

Balance Sheet Exposure

Those assets and liabilities translated at the *current* exchange rate are revalued from balance sheet to balance sheet in terms of the parent company's presentation currency. These items are said to be *exposed* to translation adjustment. Balance sheet items translated at *historical* exchange rates do not change in parent currency value and therefore are not exposed to translation adjustment. Exposure to translation adjustment is referred to as balance sheet translation exposure, or accounting exposure.

A foreign operation will have a **net asset balance sheet exposure** when assets translated at the current exchange rate are greater than liabilities translated at the current exchange rate. A **net liability balance sheet exposure** exists when liabilities translated at the current exchange rate are greater than assets translated at the current exchange rate. Another way to think about the issue is to realize that there is a net asset balance sheet exposure when exposed assets are greater than exposed liabilities and a net liability balance sheet exposure when exposed liabilities are greater than exposed assets. The sign (positive or negative) of the current period's translation adjustment is a function of two factors: (1) the nature of the balance sheet exposure (asset or liability) and (2) the direction of change in the exchange rate (strengthens or weakens). The relationship between exchange rate fluctuations, balance sheet exposure, and the current period's translation adjustment can be summarized as follows:

Balance Sheet Exposure	Foreign Currency (FC)	
	Strengthens	Weakens
Net asset	Positive translation adjustment	Negative translation adjustment
Net liability	Negative translation adjustment	Positive translation adjustment

These relationships are the same as those summarized in Section 2 with respect to foreign currency transaction gains and losses. In reference to the example in Section 3, for instance, the amount of exposed assets (the US$3,000 cash) was less than the amount of exposed liabilities (US$5,000 of notes payable), implying a net liability exposure. Further, in the example the foreign currency (US$) weakened, resulting in a positive translation adjustment.

The combination of balance sheet exposure and direction of exchange rate change determines whether the current period's translation adjustment will be positive or negative. After the initial period of operations, a cumulative translation adjustment is required to keep the translated balance sheet in balance. The cumulative translation adjustment will be the sum of the translation adjustments that arise over successive accounting periods. For example, assume that Spanco translates all of Amerco's assets and liabilities using the current exchange rate (a net asset balance sheet exposure exists), which, because of a weakening US dollar in the first quarter of 20X2, resulted in a negative translation adjustment of €2,000 on 31 March 20X2 (as shown in Section 3). Assume further that in the second quarter of 20X2, the US dollar strengthens against the euro and there still is a net asset balance sheet exposure, which results in a *positive* translation adjustment of €500 for that quarter. Although the current period translation adjustment for the second quarter of 20X2 is positive, the cumulative translation adjustment as of 30 June 20X2 still will be negative, but the amount now will be only €1,500.

4 TRANSLATION METHODS

☐ compare the current rate method and the temporal method, evaluate how each affects the parent company's balance sheet and income statement, and determine which method is appropriate in various scenarios

The two approaches to translating foreign currency financial statements described in the previous section are known as (1) the **current rate method** (all assets and liabilities are translated at the current exchange rate), and (2) the **monetary/non-monetary method** (only monetary assets and liabilities are translated at the current exchange rate). A variation of the monetary/non-monetary method requires not only monetary

Translation Methods

assets and liabilities but also non-monetary assets and liabilities that are measured at their current value on the balance sheet date to be translated at the current exchange rate. This variation of the monetary/non-monetary method sometimes is referred to as the **temporal method**.

The basic idea underlying the temporal method is that assets and liabilities should be translated in such a way that the measurement basis (either current value or historical cost) in the foreign currency is preserved after translating to the parent's presentation currency. To achieve this objective, assets and liabilities carried on the foreign currency balance sheet at a current value should be translated at the current exchange rate, and assets and liabilities carried on the foreign currency balance sheet at historical costs should be translated at historical exchange rates. Although neither the IASB nor the FASB specifically refer to translation methods by name, the procedures specified by IFRS and US GAAP for translating foreign currency financial statements essentially require the use of either the current rate or the temporal method.

Which method is appropriate for an individual foreign entity depends on that entity's functional currency. As noted earlier, the functional currency is the currency of the primary economic environment in which an entity operates. A foreign entity's functional currency can be either the parent's presentation currency or another currency, typically the currency of the country in which the foreign entity is located. Exhibit 3 lists the factors that IFRS indicate should be considered in determining a foreign entity's functional currency. Although not identical, US GAAP provide similar indicators for determining a foreign entity's functional currency.

When the functional currency indicators listed in Exhibit 3 are mixed and the functional currency is not obvious, IFRS indicate that management should use its best judgment in determining the functional currency. In this case, however, indicators 1 and 2 should be given priority over indicators 3 through 9.

> **Exhibit 3: Factors Considered in Determining the Functional Currency**
>
> In accordance with IFRS, the following factors should be considered in determining an entity's functional currency:
>
> 1. The currency that mainly influences sales prices for goods and services.
> 2. The currency of the country whose competitive forces and regulations mainly determine the sales price of its goods and services.
> 3. The currency that mainly influences labour, material, and other costs of providing goods and services.
> 4. The currency in which funds from financing activities are generated.
> 5. The currency in which receipts from operating activities are usually retained.
>
> Additional factors to consider in determining whether the foreign entity's functional currency is the same as the parent's functional currency are
>
> 6. Whether the activities of the foreign operation are an extension of the parent's or are carried out with a significant amount of autonomy.
> 7. Whether transactions with the parent are a large or a small proportion of the foreign entity's activities.
> 8. Whether cash flows generated by the foreign operation directly affect the cash flow of the parent and are available to be remitted to the parent.

9. Whether operating cash flows generated by the foreign operation are sufficient to service existing and normally expected debt or whether the foreign entity will need funds from the parent to service its debt.

The following three steps outline the functional currency approach required by accounting standards in translating foreign currency financial statements into the parent company's presentation currency:

1. Identify the functional currency of the foreign entity.
2. Translate foreign currency balances into the foreign entity's functional currency.
3. Use the current exchange rate to translate the foreign entity's functional currency balances into the parent's presentation currency, if they are different.

To illustrate how this approach is applied, consider a US parent company with a Mexican subsidiary that keeps its accounting records in Mexican pesos. Assume that the vast majority of the subsidiary's transactions are carried out in Mexican pesos, but it also has an account payable in Guatemalan quetzals. In applying the three steps, the US parent company first determines that the Mexican peso is the functional currency of the Mexican subsidiary. Second, the Mexican subsidiary translates its foreign currency balances (i.e., the Guatemalan quetzal account payable), into Mexican pesos using the current exchange rate. In step 3, the Mexican peso financial statements (including the translated account payable) are translated into US dollars using the current rate method.

Now assume, alternatively, that the primary operating currency of the Mexican subsidiary is the US dollar, which thus is identified as the Mexican subsidiary's functional currency. In that case, in addition to the Guatemalan quetzal account payable, all of the subsidiary's accounts that are denominated in Mexican pesos also are considered to be foreign currency balances (because they are not denominated in the subsidiary's functional currency, which is the US dollar). Along with the Guatemalan quetzal balance, each of the Mexican peso balances must be translated into US dollars as if the subsidiary kept its books in US dollars. Assets and liabilities carried at current value in Mexican pesos are translated into US dollars using the current exchange rate, and assets and liabilities carried at historical cost in Mexican pesos are translated into US dollars using historical exchange rates. After completing this step, the Mexican subsidiary's financial statements are stated in terms of US dollars, which is both the subsidiary's functional currency and the parent's presentation currency. As a result, there is no need to apply step 3.

The following two sections describe the procedures to be followed in applying the functional currency approach in more detail.

Foreign Currency Is the Functional Currency

In most cases, a foreign entity will operate primarily in the currency of the country where it is located, which will differ from the currency in which the parent company presents its financial statements. For example, the Japanese subsidiary of a French parent company is likely to have the Japanese yen as its functional currency, whereas the French parent company must prepare consolidated financial statements in euro. When a foreign entity has a functional currency that differs from the parent's presentation currency, the foreign entity's foreign currency financial statements are translated into the parent's presentation currency using the following procedures:

1. All assets and liabilities are translated at the current exchange rate at the balance sheet date.
2. Stockholders' equity accounts are translated at historical exchange rates.

Translation Methods

3. Revenues and expenses are translated at the exchange rate that existed when the transactions took place. For practical reasons, a rate that approximates the exchange rates at the dates of the transactions, such as an average exchange rate, may be used.

These procedures essentially describe the *current rate method*. When the current rate method is used, the cumulative translation adjustment needed to keep the translated balance sheet in balance is reported as a separate component of stockholders' equity.

The basic concept underlying the current rate method is that the entire investment in a foreign entity is exposed to translation gain or loss. Therefore, all assets and all liabilities must be revalued at each successive balance sheet date. The net translation gain or loss that results from this procedure is unrealized, however, and will be realized only when the entity is sold. In the meantime, the unrealized translation gain or loss that accumulates over time is deferred on the balance sheet as a separate component of stockholders' equity. When a specific foreign entity is sold, the cumulative translation adjustment related to that entity is reported as a realized gain or loss in net income.

The current rate method results in a net asset balance sheet exposure (except in the rare case in which an entity has negative stockholders' equity):

Items Translated at Current Exchange Rate

Total assets > Total liabilities → Net asset balance sheet exposure

When the foreign currency increases in value (i.e., strengthens), application of the current rate method results in an increase in the positive cumulative translation adjustment (or a decrease in the negative cumulative translation adjustment) reflected in stockholders' equity. When the foreign currency decreases in value (i.e., weakens), the current rate method results in a decrease in the positive cumulative translation adjustment (or an increase in the negative cumulative translation adjustment) in stockholders' equity.

Parent's Presentation Currency Is the Functional Currency

In some cases, a foreign entity might have the parent's presentation currency as its functional currency. For example, a Germany-based manufacturer might have a 100%-owned distribution subsidiary in Switzerland that primarily uses the euro in its day-to-day operations and thus has the euro as its functional currency. As a Swiss company, however, the subsidiary is required to record its transactions and keep its books in Swiss francs. In that situation, the subsidiary's Swiss franc financial statements must be translated into euro as if the subsidiary's transactions had originally been recorded in euro. US GAAP refer to this process as *remeasurement*. IFRS do not refer to this process as remeasurement but instead describe this situation as "reporting foreign currency transactions in the functional currency." To achieve the objective of translating to the parent's presentation currency as if the subsidiary's transactions had been recorded in that currency, the following procedures are used:

1.
   a. Monetary assets and liabilities are translated at the current exchange rate.
   b. Non-monetary assets and liabilities measured at historical cost are translated at historical exchange rates.

c. Non-monetary assets and liabilities measured at current value are translated at the exchange rate at the date when the current value was determined.

2. Stockholders' equity accounts are translated at historical exchange rates.

3.
   a. Revenues and expenses, other than those expenses related to non-monetary assets (as explained in 3.b. below), are translated at the exchange rate that existed when the transactions took place (for practical reasons, average rates may be used).

   b. Expenses related to non-monetary assets, such as cost of goods sold (inventory), depreciation (fixed assets), and amortization (intangible assets), are translated at the exchange rates used to translate the related assets.

These procedures essentially describe the *temporal method*.

Under the temporal method, companies must keep record of the exchange rates that exist when non-monetary assets (inventory, prepaid expenses, fixed assets, and intangible assets) are acquired, because these assets (normally measured at historical cost) are translated at historical exchange rates. Keeping track of the historical exchange rates for these assets is not necessary under the current rate method. Translating these assets (and their related expenses) at historical exchange rates complicates application of the temporal method.

The historical exchange rates used to translate inventory (and cost of goods sold) under the temporal method will differ depending on the cost flow assumption—first in, first out (FIFO); last in, first out (LIFO); or average cost—used to account for inventory. Ending inventory reported on the balance sheet is translated at the exchange rate that existed when the inventory's acquisition is assumed to have occurred. If FIFO is used, ending inventory is assumed to be composed of the most recently acquired items and thus inventory will be translated at relatively recent exchange rates. If LIFO is used, ending inventory is assumed to consist of older items and thus inventory will be translated at older exchange rates. The weighted-average exchange rate for the year is used when inventory is carried at weighted-average cost. Similarly, cost of goods sold is translated using the exchange rates that existed when the inventory items assumed to have been sold during the year (using FIFO or LIFO) were acquired. If weighted-average cost is used to account for inventory, cost of goods sold will be translated at the weighted-average exchange rate for the year.

Under both international and US accounting standards, when the temporal method is used, the translation adjustment needed to keep the translated balance sheet in balance is reported as a gain or loss in net income. US GAAP refer to these as *remeasurement* gains and losses. The basic assumption underlying the recognition of a translation gain or loss in income relates to timing. Specifically, if the foreign entity primarily uses the parent company's currency in its day-to-day operations, then the foreign entity's monetary items that are denominated in a foreign currency generate translation gains and losses that will be realized in the near future and thus should be reflected in current net income.

The temporal method generates either a net asset or a net liability balance sheet exposure, depending on whether assets translated at the current exchange rate—that is, monetary assets and non-monetary assets measured on the balance sheet date at current value (exposed assets)—are greater than or less than liabilities translated at the current exchange rate—that is, monetary liabilities and non-monetary liabilities measured on the balance sheet date at current value (exposed liabilities):

Items Translated at Current Exchange Rate

Exposed assets > Exposed liabilities → Net asset balance sheet exposure

Exposed assets < Exposed liabilities → Net liability balance sheet exposure

Most liabilities are monetary liabilities. Only cash and receivables are monetary assets, and non-monetary assets generally are measured at their historical cost. As a result, liabilities translated at the current exchange rate (exposed liabilities) often exceed assets translated at the current exchange rate (exposed assets), which results in a net liability balance sheet exposure when the temporal method is applied.

Translation of Retained Earnings

Stockholders' equity accounts are translated at historical exchange rates under both the current rate and the temporal methods. This approach creates somewhat of a problem in translating retained earnings (R/E), which are the accumulation of previous years' income less dividends over the life of the company. At the end of the first year of operations, foreign currency (FC) retained earnings are translated into the parent's currency (PC) as follows:

Net income in FC	[Translated according to the method used to translate the income statement]	=	Net income in PC
− Dividends in FC	× Exchange rate when dividends declared	=	− Dividends in PC
R/E in FC			R/E in PC

Retained earnings in parent currency at the end of the first year become the beginning retained earnings in parent currency for the second year, and the translated retained earnings in the second year (and subsequent years) are then calculated in the following manner:

Beginning R/E in FC	[From last year's translation]	→	Beginning R/E in PC
+ Net income in FC	[Translated according to method used to translate the income statement]	=	+ Net income in PC
− Dividends in FC	× Exchange rate when dividends declared	=	− Dividends in PC
Ending R/E in FC			Ending R/E in PC

Exhibit 4 summarizes the translation rules as discussed in Section 3.

Exhibit 4: Rules for the Translation of a Foreign Subsidiary's Foreign Currency Financial Statements into the Parent's Presentation Currency under IFRS and US GAAP

	Foreign Subsidiary's Functional Currency	
	Foreign Currency	**Parent's Presentation Currency**
Translation method:	Current Rate Method	Temporal Method
Exchange rate at which financial statement items are translated from the foreign subsidiary's bookkeeping currency to the parent's presentation currency:		
Assets		
Monetary, such as cash and receivables	Current rate	Current rate
Non-monetary		
• measured at current value (e.g., marketable securities and inventory measured at market value under the lower of cost or market rule)	Current rate	Current rate
• measured at historical costs, (e.g., inventory measured at cost under the lower of cost or market rule; property, plant & equipment; and intangible assets)	Current rate	Historical rates
Liabilities		
Monetary, such as accounts payable, accrued expenses, long-term debt, and deferred income taxes	Current rate	Current rate
Non-monetary		
• measured at current value	Current rate	Current rate
• not measured at current value, such as deferred revenue	Current rate	Historical rates
Equity		
Other than retained earnings	Historical rates	Historical rates
Retained earnings	Beginning balance plus translated net income less dividends translated at historical rate	Beginning balance plus translated net income less dividends translated at historical rate
Revenues	Average rate	Average rate
Expenses		
Most expenses	Average rate	Average rate
Expenses related to assets translated at historical exchange rate, such as cost of goods sold, depreciation, and amortization	Average rate	Historical rates

	Foreign Subsidiary's Functional Currency	
	Foreign Currency	Parent's Presentation Currency
Translation method:	**Current Rate Method**	**Temporal Method**
Treatment of the translation adjustment in the parent's consolidated financial statements	Accumulated as a separate component of equity	Included as gain or loss in net income

Highly Inflationary Economies

When a foreign entity is located in a highly inflationary economy, the entity's functional currency is irrelevant in determining how to translate its foreign currency financial statements into the parent's presentation currency. IFRS require that the foreign entity's financial statements first be restated for local inflation using the procedures outlined in IAS 29, "Financial Reporting in Hyperinflationary Economies." Then, the inflation-restated foreign currency financial statements are translated into the parent's presentation currency using the current exchange rate.

US GAAP require a very different approach for translating the foreign currency financial statements of foreign entities located in highly inflationary economies. US GAAP do not allow restatement for inflation but instead require the foreign entity's financial statements to be remeasured as if the functional currency were the reporting currency (i.e., the temporal method).

US GAAP define a highly inflationary economy as one in which the cumulative three-year inflation rate exceeds 100% (but note that the definition should be applied with judgment, particularly because the trend of inflation can be as important as the absolute rate). A cumulative three-year inflation rate of 100% equates to an average of approximately 26% per year. IAS 21 does not provide a specific definition of high inflation, but IAS 29 indicates that a cumulative inflation rate approaching or exceeding 100% over three years would be an indicator of hyperinflation. If a country in which a foreign entity is located ceases to be classified as highly inflationary, the functional currency of that entity must be identified to determine the appropriate method for translating the entity's financial statements.

The FASB initially proposed that companies restate for inflation and then translate the financial statements, but this approach met with stiff resistance from US multinational corporations. Requiring the temporal method ensures that companies avoid a "disappearing plant problem" that exists when the current rate method is used in a country with high inflation. In a highly inflationary economy, as the local currency loses purchasing power within the country, it also tends to weaken in value in relation to other currencies. Translating the historical cost of assets such as land and buildings at progressively weaker exchange rates causes these assets to slowly disappear from the parent company's consolidated financial statements. Example 4 demonstrates the effect of three different translation approaches when books are kept in the currency of a highly inflationary economy. Example 4 pertains to Turkey in the period 2000 to 2002, when it was recognized as one of the few highly inflationary countries. Turkey is no longer viewed as having a highly inflationary economy. (In 2010, the International Practices Task Force of the Center for Audit Quality SEC Regulations Committee indicated that Venezuela had met the thresholds for being considered highly inflationary.)

EXAMPLE 4

Foreign Currency Translation in a Highly Inflationary Economy

1. Turkey was one of the few remaining highly inflationary countries at the beginning of the 21st century. Annual inflation rates and selected exchange rates between the Turkish lira (TL) and US dollar during the 2000–2002 period were as follows:

Date	Exchange Rates	Year	Inflation Rate (%)
01 Jan 2000	TL542,700 = US$1		
31 Dec 2000	TL670,800 = US$1	2000	38
31 Dec 2001	TL1,474,525 = US$1	2001	69
31 Dec 2002	TL1,669,000 = US$1	2002	45

Assume that a US-based company established a subsidiary in Turkey on 1 January 2000. The US parent sent the subsidiary US$1,000 on 1 January 2000 to purchase a piece of land at a cost of TL542,700,000 (TL542,700/US$ × US$1,000 = TL542,700,000). Assuming no other assets or liabilities, what are the annual and cumulative translation gains or losses that would be reported under each of three possible translation approaches?

Solution:

Approach 1: Translate Using the Current Rate Method

The historical cost of the land is translated at the current exchange rate, which results in a new translated amount at each balance sheet date.

Date	Carrying Value	Current Exchange Rate	Translated Amount in US$	Annual Translation Gain (Loss)	Cumulative Translation Gain (Loss)
01 Jan 2000	TL542,700,000	542,700	$1,000	N/A	N/A
31 Dec 2000	542,700,000	670,800	809	($191)	($191)
31 Dec 2001	542,700,000	1,474,525	368	(441)	(632)
31 Dec 2002	542,700,000	1,669,000	325	(43)	(675)

At the end of three years, land that was originally purchased with US$1,000 would be reflected on the parent's consolidated balance sheet at US$325 (and remember that land is not a depreciable asset). A cumulative translation loss of US$675 would be reported as a separate component of stockholders' equity on 31 December 2002. Because this method accounts for adjustments in exchange rates but does not account for likely changes in the local currency values of assets, it does a poor job of accurately reflecting the economic reality of situations such as the one in our example. That is the major reason this approach is not acceptable under either IFRS or US GAAP.

Translation Methods

Approach 2: Translate Using the Temporal Method (US GAAP ASC 830)

The historical cost of land is translated using the historical exchange rate, which results in the same translated amount at each balance sheet date.

Date	Carrying Value	Historical Exchange Rate	Translated Amount in US$	Annual Translation Gain (Loss)	Cumulative Translation Gain (Loss)
01 Jan 2000	TL542,700,000	542,700	$1,000	N/A	N/A
31 Dec 2000	542,700,000	542,700	1,000	N/A	N/A
31 Dec 2001	542,700,000	542,700	1,000	N/A	N/A
31 Dec 2002	542,700,000	542,700	1,000	N/A	N/A

Under this approach, land continues to be reported on the parent's consolidated balance sheet at its original cost of US$1,000 each year. There is no translation gain or loss related to balance sheet items translated at historical exchange rates. This approach is required by US GAAP and ensures that non-monetary assets do not disappear from the translated balance sheet.

Approach 3: Restate for Inflation/Translate Using Current Exchange Rate (IAS 21)

The historical cost of the land is restated for inflation, and then the inflation-adjusted historical cost is translated using the current exchange rate.

Date	Inflation Rate (%)	Restated Carrying Value	Current Exchange Rate	Translated Amount in US$	Annual Translation Gain (Loss)	Cumulative Translation Gain (Loss)
01 Jan 00		TL542,700,000	542,700	$1,000	N/A	N/A
31 Dec 00	38	748,926,000	670,800	1,116	$116	$116
31 Dec 01	69	1,265,684,940	1,474,525	858	(258)	(142)
31 Dec 02	45	1,835,243,163	1,669,000	1,100	242	100

Under this approach, land is reported on the parent's 31 December 2002 consolidated balance sheet at US$1,100 with a cumulative, unrealized gain of US$100. Although the cumulative translation gain on 31 December 2002 is unrealized, it could have been realized if (1) the land had appreciated in TL value by the rate of local inflation, (2) the Turkish subsidiary sold the land for TL1,835,243,163, and (3) the sale proceeds were converted into US$1,100 at the current exchange rate on 31 December 2002.

This approach is required by IAS 21. It is the approach that, apart from doing an appraisal, perhaps best represents economic reality, in the sense that it reflects both the likely change in the local currency value of the land as well as the actual change in the exchange rate.

5 ILLUSTRATION OF TRANSLATION METHODS

- [ ] compare the current rate method and the temporal method, evaluate how each affects the parent company's balance sheet and income statement, and determine which method is appropriate in various scenarios
- [ ] calculate the translation effects and evaluate the translation of a subsidiary's balance sheet and income statement into the parent company's presentation currency

To demonstrate the procedures required in translating foreign currency financial statements (excluding hyperinflationary economies), assume that Interco is a Europe-based company that has the euro as its presentation currency. On 1 January 20X1, Interco establishes a wholly owned subsidiary in Canada, Canadaco. In addition to Interco making an equity investment in Canadaco, a long-term note payable to a Canadian bank was negotiated to purchase property and equipment. The subsidiary begins operations with the following balance sheet in Canadian dollars (C$):

Canadaco Balance Sheet, 1 January 20X1

Assets	
Cash	C$1,500,000
Property and equipment	3,000,000
	C$4,500,000
Liabilities and Equity	
Long-term note payable	C$3,000,000
Capital stock	1,500,000
	C$4,500,000

Canadaco purchases and sells inventory in 20X1, generating net income of C$1,180,000, out of which C$350,000 in dividends are paid. The company's income statement and statement of retained earnings for 20X1 and balance sheet at 31 December 20X1 follow:

Canadaco Income Statement and Statement of Retained Earnings, 20X1

Sales	C$12,000,000
Cost of sales	(9,000,000)
Selling expenses	(750,000)
Depreciation expense	(300,000)
Interest expense	(270,000)
Income tax	(500,000)
Net income	C$1,180,000
Less: Dividends, 1 Dec 20X1	(350,000)

Illustration of Translation Methods

Retained earnings, 31 Dec 20X1   C$830,000

Canadaco Balance Sheet, 31 December 20X1

Assets		Liabilities and Equity	
Cash	C$980,000	Accounts payable	C$450,000
Accounts receivable	900,000	Total current liabilities	450,000
Inventory	1,200,000	Long-term notes payable	3,000,000
Total current assets	C$3,080,000	Total liabilities	C$3,450,000
Property and equipment	3,000,000	Capital stock	1,500,000
Less: accumulated depreciation	(300,000)	Retained earnings	830,000
Total	C$5,780,000	Total	C$5,780,000

Inventory is measured at historical cost on a FIFO basis.

To translate Canadaco's Canadian dollar financial statements into euro for consolidation purposes, the following exchange rate information was gathered:

Date	€ per C$
1 January 20X1	0.70
Average, 20X1	0.75
Weighted-average rate when inventory was acquired	0.74
1 December 20X1 when dividends were declared	0.78
31 December 20X1	0.80

During 20X1, the Canadian dollar strengthened steadily against the euro from an exchange rate of €0.70 at the beginning of the year to €0.80 at year-end.

The translation worksheet that follows shows Canadaco's translated financial statements under each of the two translation methods. Assume first that Canadaco's functional currency is the Canadian dollar, and thus the current rate method must be used. The Canadian dollar income statement and statement of retained earnings are translated first. Income statement items for 20X1 are translated at the average exchange rate for 20X1 (€0.75), and dividends are translated at the exchange rate that existed when they were declared (€0.78). The ending balance in retained earnings as of 31 December 20X1 of €612,000 is transferred to the Canadian dollar balance sheet. The remaining balance sheet accounts are then translated. Assets and liabilities are translated at the current exchange rate on the balance sheet date of 31 December 20X1 (€0.80), and the capital stock account is translated at the historical exchange rate (€0.70) that existed on the date that Interco made the capital contribution. A positive translation adjustment of €202,000 is needed as a balancing amount, which is reported in the stockholders' equity section of the balance sheet.

If instead Interco determines that Canadaco's functional currency is the euro (the parent's presentation currency), the temporal method must be applied as shown in the far right columns of the table. The differences in procedure from the current rate method are that inventory, property, and equipment (and accumulated depreciation), as well as their related expenses (cost of goods sold and depreciation), are translated at the historical exchange rates that existed when the assets were acquired: €0.70 in the case of property and equipment, and €0.74 for inventory. The balance sheet is translated first, with €472,000 determined as the amount of retained earnings needed to keep the balance sheet in balance. This amount is transferred to the income statement and statement of retained earnings as the ending balance in retained earnings as of 31 December 20X1. Income statement items then are translated, with cost of goods sold and depreciation expense being translated at historical exchange rates. A negative translation adjustment of €245,000 is determined as the amount needed to arrive at the ending balance in retained earnings of €472,000, and this adjustment is reported as a translation loss on the income statement.

The positive translation adjustment under the current rate method can be explained by the facts that Canadaco has a net asset balance sheet exposure (total assets exceed total liabilities) during 20X1 and the Canadian dollar strengthened against the euro. The negative translation adjustment (translation loss) under the temporal method is explained by the fact that Canadaco has a net liability balance sheet exposure under this method (because the amount of exposed liabilities [accounts payable plus notes payable] exceeds the amount of exposed assets [cash plus receivables]) during 20X1 when the Canadian dollar strengthened against the euro.

Canadaco Income Statement and Statement of Retained Earnings, 20X1

Canadaco's Functional Currency Is:		Local Currency (C$)		Parent's Currency (€)	
		Current Rate		**Temporal**	
	C$	Exch. Rate	€	Exch. Rate	€
Sales	12,000,000	0.75 A	9,000,000	0.75 A	9,000,000
Cost of goods sold	(9,000,000)	0.75 A	(6,750,000)	0.74 H	(6,660,000)
Selling expenses	(750,000)	0.75 A	(562,500)	0.75 A	(562,500)
Depreciation expense	(300,000)	0.75 A	(225,000)	0.70 H	(210,000)
Interest expense	(270,000)	0.75 A	(202,500)	0.75 A	(202,500)
Income tax	(500,000)	0.75 A	(375,000)	0.75 A	(375,000)
Income before trans. gain (loss)	1,180,000		885,000		990,000
Translation gain (loss)	N/A		N/A	to balance	(245,000)
Net income	1,180,000		885,000		745,000
Less: Dividends, 12/1/20X1	(350,000)	0.78 H	(273,000)	0.78 H	(273,000)
Retained earnings, 12/31/20X1	830,000		612,000	from B/S	472,000

Note: C = current exchange rate; A = average-for-the-year exchange rate; H = historical exchange rate

Canadaco Balance Sheet, 31 December 20X1

Canadaco's Functional Currency Is:		Local Currency (C$)		Parent's Currency (€)	
		Current Rate		**Temporal**	
	C$	Exch. Rate	€	Exch. Rate	€

Assets

Translation Analytical Issues

Canadaco's Functional Currency Is:		Local Currency (C$)		Parent's Currency (€)	
		Current Rate		Temporal	
	C$	Exch. Rate	€	Exch. Rate	€
Cash	980,000	0.80 C	784,000	0.80 C	784,000
Accounts receivable	900,000	0.80 C	720,000	0.80 C	720,000
Inventory	1,200,000	0.80 C	960,000	0.74 H	888,000
Total current assets	3,080,000		2,464,000		2,392,000
Property and equipment	3,000,000	0.80 C	2,400,000	0.70 H	2,100,000
Less: accumulated depreciation	(300,000)	0.80 C	(240,000)	0.70 H	(210,000)
Total assets	5,780,000		4,624,000		4,282,000
Liabilities and Equity					
Accounts payable	450,000	0.80 C	360,000	0.80 C	360,000
Total current liabilities	450,000		360,000		360,000
Long-term notes payable	3,000,000	0.80 C	2,400,000	0.80 C	2,400,000
Total liabilities	3,450,000		2,760,000		2,760,000
Capital stock	1,500,000	0.70 H	1,050,000	0.70 H	1,050,000
Retained earnings	830,000	from I/S	612,000	to balance	472,000
Translation adjustment	N/A	to balance	202,000		N/A
Total	5,780,000		4,624,000		4,282,000

Note: C = current exchange rate; A = average-for-the-year exchange rate; H = historical exchange rate

TRANSLATION ANALYTICAL ISSUES

6

☐ analyze how the current rate method and the temporal method affect financial statements and ratios

The two different translation methods used to translate Canadaco's Canadian dollar financial statements into euro result in very different amounts to be included in Interco's consolidated financial statements. The chart below summarizes some of these differences:

Canadaco's Functional Currency Is:	Local Currency (C$)	Parent's Currency (€)	
	Translation Method		
Item	Current Rate (€)	Temporal (€)	Difference (%)
Sales	9,000,000	9,000,000	0.0

Handwritten note: For either FIFO or weighted average cost, the current rate method will give higher gross profit to the parent company if the subsidiary's currency is depreciating

Canadaco's Functional Currency Is:	Local Currency (C$)	Parent's Currency (€)	
	Translation Method		
Item	Current Rate (€)	Temporal (€)	Difference (%)
Net income	885,000	745,000	+18.8
Income before translation gain (loss)	885,000	990,000	−10.6
Total assets	4,624,000	4,282,000	+8.0
Total equity	1,864,000	1,522,000	+22.5

In this particular case, the current rate method results in a significantly larger net income than the temporal method. This result occurs because under the current rate method, the translation adjustment is not included in the calculation of income. If the translation loss were excluded from net income, the temporal method would result in a significantly larger amount of net income. The combination of smaller net income under the temporal method and a positive translation adjustment reported on the balance sheet under the current rate method results in a much larger amount of total equity under the current rate method. Total assets also are larger under the current rate method because all assets are translated at the current exchange rate, which is higher than the historical exchange rates at which inventory and fixed assets are translated under the temporal method.

To examine the effects of translation on the underlying relationships that exist in Canadaco's Canadian dollar financial statements, several significant ratios are calculated from the original Canadian dollar financial statements and the translated (euro) financial statements and presented in the table below.

Canadaco's Functional Currency Is:		Local Currency (C$)	Parent's Currency (€)
	C$	Current Rate (€)	Temporal (€)
Current ratio	6.84	6.84	6.64
Current assets	3,080,000	2,464,000	2,392,000
Current liabilities =	450,000 =	360,000 =	360,000
Debt-to-assets ratio	0.52	0.52	0.56
Total debt	3,000,000	2,400,000	2,400,000
Total assets =	5,780,000 =	4,624,000 =	4,282,000
Debt-to-equity ratio	1.29	1.29	1.58
Total debt	3,000,000	2,400,000	2,400,000
Total equity =	2,330,000 =	1,864,000 =	1,522,000
Interest coverage	7.22	7.22	7.74
EBIT	1,950,000	1,462,500	1,567,500
Interest payments =	270,000 =	202,500 =	202,500
Gross profit margin	0.25	0.25	0.26
Gross profit	3,000,000	2,250,000	2,340,000
Sales =	12,000,000 =	9,000,000 =	9,000,000
Operating profit margin	0.16	0.16	0.17
Operating profit	1,950,000	1,462,500	1,567,500
Sales =	12,000,000 =	9,000,000 =	9,000,000

Translation Analytical Issues

Canadaco's Functional Currency Is:			Local Currency (C$)		Parent's Currency (€)
		C$	Current Rate (€)		Temporal (€)
Net profit margin		0.10	0.10		0.08
Net income		1,180,000	885,000		745,000
Sales	=	12,000,000	= 9,000,000	=	9,000,000
Receivables turnover		13.33	12.50		12.50
Sales		12,000,000	9,000,000		9,000,000
Accounts receivable	=	900,000	= 720,000	=	720,000
Inventory turnover		7.50	7.03		7.50
Cost of goods sold		9,000,000	6,750,000		6,660,000
Inventory	=	1,200,000	= 960,000	=	888,000
Fixed asset turnover		4.44	4.17		4.76
Sales		12,000,000	9,000,000		9,000,000
Property & equipment (net)	=	2,700,000	= 2,160,000	=	1,890,000
Return on assets		0.20	0.19		0.17
Net income		1,180,000	885,000		745,000
Total assets	=	5,780,000	= 4,624,000	=	4,282,000
Return on equity		0.51	0.47		0.49
Net income		1,180,000	885,000		745,000
Total equity	=	2,330,000	= 1,864,000	=	1,522,000

Comparing the current rate method (€) and temporal method (€) columns in the above table shows that financial ratios calculated from Canadaco's translated financial statements (in €) differ significantly depending on which method of translation is used. Of the ratios presented, only receivables turnover is the same under both translation methods. This is the only ratio presented in which there is no difference in the type of exchange rate used to translate the items that comprise the numerator and the denominator. Sales are translated at the average exchange rate and receivables are translated at the current exchange rate under both methods. For each of the other ratios, at least one of the items included in either the numerator or the denominator is translated at a different type of rate (current, average, or historical) under the temporal method than under the current rate method. For example, the current ratio has a different value under the two translation methods because inventory is translated at the current exchange rate under the current rate method and at the historical exchange rate under the temporal method. In this case, because the euro/Canadian dollar exchange rate on 31 December 20X1 (€0.80) is higher than the historical exchange rate when the inventory was acquired (€0.74), the current ratio is larger under the current rate method of translation.

Comparing the ratios in the Canadian dollar and current rate method (euro) columns of the above table shows that many of the underlying relationships that exist in Canadaco's Canadian dollar financial statements are preserved when the current rate method of translation is used (i.e., the ratio calculated from the Canadian dollar and euro translated amounts is the same). The current ratio, the leverage ratios (debt-to-assets and debt-to-equity ratios), the interest coverage ratio, and the profit margins (gross profit margin, operating profit margin, and net profit margin) are the same in the Canadian dollar and current rate method (euro) columns of the above table. This result occurs because each of the ratios is calculated using information from either the balance sheet or the income statement, but not both. Those ratios that compare amounts from the balance sheet with amounts from the income statement (e.g., turnover and return ratios) are different. In this particular case, each of the turnover and return ratios is larger when calculated from the Canadian dollar amounts than when calculated using the current rate (euro) amounts. The underlying Canadian dollar relationships are distorted when translated using the current rate method because the balance sheet amounts are translated using the current exchange rate while revenues and expenses are translated using the average exchange rate. (These distortions would not occur if revenues and expenses also were translated at the current exchange rate.)

Comparing the ratios in the Canadian dollar and temporal method (euro) columns of the table shows that translation using the temporal method distorts all of the underlying relationships that exist in the Canadian dollar financial statements, except inventory turnover. Moreover, it is not possible to generalize the direction of the distortion across ratios. In Canadaco's case, using the temporal method results in a larger gross profit margin and operating profit margin but a smaller net profit margin as compared with the values of these ratios calculated from the original Canadian dollar amounts. Similarly, receivables turnover is smaller, inventory turnover is the same, and fixed asset turnover is larger when calculated from the translated amounts.

In translating Canadaco's Canadian dollar financial statements into euro, the temporal method results in a smaller amount of net income than the current rate method only because IFRS and US GAAP require the resulting translation loss to be included in net income when the temporal method is used. The translation loss arises because the Canadian dollar strengthened against the euro and Canadaco has a larger amount of liabilities translated at the current exchange rate (monetary liabilities) than it has assets translated at the current exchange rate (monetary assets). If Canadaco had a net monetary asset exposure (i.e., if monetary assets exceeded monetary liabilities), a translation gain would arise and net income under the temporal method (including the translation gain) would be greater than under the current rate method. Example 5 demonstrates how different types of balance sheet exposure under the temporal method can affect translated net income.

EXAMPLE 5

Effects of Different Balance Sheet Exposures under the Temporal Method *(Canadaco's functional currency is the parent's functional currency)*

1. Canadaco begins operations on 1 January 20X1, with cash of C$1,500,000 and property and equipment of C$3,000,000. In Case A, Canadaco finances the acquisition of property and equipment with a long-term note payable and begins operations with net monetary liabilities of C$1,500,000 (C$3,000,000 long-term note payable less C$1,500,000 cash). In Case B, Canadaco finances the acquisition of property and equipment with capital stock and begins operations with net monetary assets of C$1,500,000. To isolate the effect that balance sheet exposure has on net income under the temporal method, assume that Canadaco continues to have C$270,000 in interest expense in Case B, even though there is no debt financing. This assumption is inconsistent with reality, but it allows us to more clearly see the effect of balance sheet exposure on net income. The only difference between Case A and Case B is the net monetary asset/liability position of the company, as shown in the following table:

Translation Analytical Issues

Canadaco Balance Sheet, 1 January 20X1

	Case A	Case B
Assets		
Cash	C$1,500,000	C$1,500,000
Property and equipment	3,000,000	3,000,000
	C$4,500,000	C$4,500,000
Liabilities and Equity		
Long-term note payable	C$3,000,000	C$0
Capital stock	1,500,000	4,500,000
	C$4,500,000	C$4,500,000

Canadaco purchases and sells inventory in 20X1, generating net income of C$1,180,000, out of which dividends of C$350,000 are paid. The company has total assets of C$5,780,000 as of 31 December 20X1. Canadaco's functional currency is determined to be the euro (the parent's presentation currency), and the company's Canadian dollar financial statements are translated into euro using the temporal method. Relevant exchange rates are as follows:

Date	€ per C$
1 January 20X1	0.70
Average, 20X1	0.75
Weighted-average rate when inventory was acquired	0.74
1 December 20X1 when dividends were declared	0.78
31 December 20X1	0.80

What effect does the nature of Canadaco's net monetary asset or liability position have on the euro translated amounts?

Solution:

Translation of Canadaco's 31 December 20X1 balance sheet under the temporal method in Case A and Case B is shown in the following table:

Canadaco Balance Sheet on 31 December 20X1 under the Temporal Method

	Case A: Net Monetary Liabilities			Case B: Net Monetary Assets		
	C$	Exch. Rate	€	C$	Exch. Rate	€
Assets						
Cash	980,000	0.80 C	784,000	980,000	0.80 C	784,000
Accounts receivable	900,000	0.80 C	720,000	900,000	0.80 C	720,000
Inventory	1,200,000	0.74 H	888,000	1,200,000	0.74 H	888,000
Total current assets	3,080,000		2,392,000	3,080,000		2,392,000
Property and equipment	3,000,000	0.70 H	2,100,000	3,000,000	0.70 H	2,100,000
Less: accum. deprec.	(300,000)	0.70 H	(210,000)	(300,000)	0.70 H	(210,000)

	Case A: Net Monetary Liabilities			Case B: Net Monetary Assets		
	C$	Exch. Rate	€	C$	Exch. Rate	€
Total assets	5,780,000		4,282,000	5,780,000		4,282,000
Liabilities and Equity						
Accounts payable	450,000	0.80 C	360,000	450,000	0.80 C	360,000
Total current liabilities	450,000		360,000	450,000		360,000
Long-term notes payable	3,000,000	0.80 C	2,400,000	0		0
Total liabilities	3,450,000		2,760,000	450,000		360,000
Capital stock	1,500,000	0.70 H	1,050,000	4,500,000	0.70 H	3,150,000
Retained earnings	830,000		472,000	830,000		772,000
Total	5,780,000		4,282,000	5,780,000		4,282,000

Note: C = current exchange rate; A = average-for-the-year exchange rate; H = historical exchange rate.

To keep the balance sheet in balance, retained earnings must be €472,000 in Case A (net monetary liability exposure) and €772,000 in Case B (net monetary asset exposure). The difference in retained earnings of €300,000 is equal to the translation loss that results from holding a Canadian dollar–denominated note payable during a period in which the Canadian dollar strengthens against the euro. This difference is determined by multiplying the amount of long-term note payable in Case A by the change in exchange rate during the year [C$3,000,000 × (€0.80 − €0.70) = €300,000]. Notes payable are exposed to foreign exchange risk under the temporal method, whereas capital stock is not. Canadaco could avoid the €300,000 translation loss related to long-term debt by financing the acquisition of property and equipment with equity rather than debt.

Translation of Canadaco's 20X1 income statement and statement of retained earnings under the temporal method for Case A and Case B is shown in the following table:

Canadaco Income Statement and Statement of Retained Earnings for 20X1 under the Temporal Method

	Case A: Net Monetary Liabilities			Case B: Net Monetary Assets		
	C$	Exch. Rate	€	C$	Exch. Rate	€
Sales	12,000,000	0.75 A	9,000,000	12,000,000	0.75 A	9,000,000
Cost of goods sold	(9,000,000)	0.74 H	(6,660,000)	(9,000,000)	0.74 H	(6,660,000)
Selling expenses	(750,000)	0.75 A	(562,500)	(750,000)	0.75 A	(562,500)
Depreciation expense	(300,000)	0.70 H	(210,000)	(300,000)	0.70 H	(210,000)
Interest expense	(270,000)	0.75 A	(202,500)	(270,000)	0.75 A	(202,500)
Income tax	(500,000)	0.75 A	(375,000)	(500,000)	0.75 A	(375,000)
Income before translation gain (loss)	1,180,000		990,000	1,180,000		990,000
Translation gain (loss)	N/A		(245,000)	N/A		55,000
Net income	1,180,000		745,000	1,180,000		1,045,000
Less: Dividends on 1 December 20X1	(350,000)	0.78 H	(273,000)	(350,000)	0.78 H	(273,000)

Translation Analytical Issues

	Case A: Net Monetary Liabilities			Case B: Net Monetary Assets		
	C$	Exch. Rate	€	C$	Exch. Rate	€
Retained earnings on 31 December 20X1	830,000		472,000	830,000		772,000

Note: C = current exchange rate; A = average-for-the-year exchange rate; H = historical exchange rate.

Income before translation gain (loss) is the same in both cases. To obtain the amount of retained earnings needed to keep the balance sheet in balance, a translation loss of €245,000 must be subtracted from net income in Case A (net monetary liabilities), whereas a translation gain of €55,000 must be added to net income in Case B (net monetary assets). The difference in net income between the two cases is €300,000, which equals the translation loss related to the long-term note payable.

When using the temporal method, companies can manage their exposure to translation gain (loss) more easily than when using the current rate method. If a company can manage the balance sheet of a foreign subsidiary such that monetary assets equal monetary liabilities, no balance sheet exposure exists. Elimination of balance sheet exposure under the current rate method occurs only when total assets equal total liabilities. This equality is difficult to achieve because it requires the foreign subsidiary to have no stockholders' equity.

For Canadaco, in 20X1, applying the current rate method results in larger euro amounts of total assets and total equity being reported in the consolidated financial statements than would result from applying the temporal method. The direction of these differences between the two translation methods is determined by the direction of change in the exchange rate between the Canadian dollar and the euro. For example, total exposed assets are greater under the current rate method because all assets are translated at the current exchange rate. The current exchange rate at 31 December 20X1 is greater than the exchange rates that existed when the non-monetary assets were acquired, which is the translation rate for these assets under the temporal method. Therefore, the current rate method results in a larger amount of total assets because the Canadian dollar strengthened against the euro. The current rate method would result in a smaller amount of total assets than the temporal method if the Canadian dollar had weakened against the euro.

Applying the current rate method also results in a much larger amount of stockholders' equity than the temporal method. A positive translation adjustment arises under the current rate method, which is included in equity, whereas a translation loss reduces total equity (through retained earnings) under the temporal method.

Example 6 shows the effect that the direction of change in the exchange rate has on the translated amounts. Canadaco's Canadian dollar financial statements are translated into euro, first assuming no change in the exchange rate during 20X1, and then assuming the Canadian dollar strengthens and weakens against the euro. Using the current rate method to translate the foreign currency financial statements into the parent's presentation currency, the foreign currency strengthening increases the revenues, income, assets, liabilities, and total equity reported on the parent company's consolidated financial statements. Likewise, smaller amounts of revenues, income, assets, liabilities, and total equity will be reported if the foreign currency weakens against the parent's presentation currency.

When the temporal method is used to translate foreign currency financial statements, foreign currency strengthening still increases revenues, assets, and liabilities reported in the parent's consolidated financial statements. Net income and stockholders' equity, however, translate into smaller amounts (assuming that the foreign subsidiary has a net monetary liability position) because of the translation loss. The opposite results are obtained when the foreign currency weakens against the parent's presentation currency.

EXAMPLE 6

Effect of Direction of Change in the Exchange Rate on Translated Amounts

Canadaco's Canadian dollar (C$) financial statements are translated into euro (€) under three scenarios: (1) the Canadian dollar remains stable against the euro, (2) the Canadian dollar strengthens against the euro, and (3) the Canadian dollar weakens against the euro. Relevant exchange rates are as follows:

	€ per C$		
Date	Stable	Strengthens	Weakens
1 January 20X1	0.70	0.70	0.70
Average, 20X1	0.70	0.75	0.65
Weighted-average rate when inventory was acquired	0.70	0.74	0.66
Rate when dividends were declared	0.70	0.78	0.62
31 December 20X1	0.70	0.80	0.60

What amounts will be reported on the parent's consolidated financial statements under the three different exchange rate assumptions if Canadaco's Canadian dollar financial statements are translated using the:

1. current rate method?

Solution:

Current Rate Method: Using the current rate method, Canadaco's Canadian dollar financial statements would be translated into euro as follows under the three different exchange rate assumptions:

Canadaco Income Statement and Statement of Retained Earnings for 20X1 under the Current Rate Method

	C$	C$ Stable Exch. Rate	€	C$ Strengthens Exch. Rate	€	C$ Weakens Exch. Rate	€
Sales	12,000,000	0.70	8,400,000	0.75 A	9,000,000	0.65 A	7,800,000
Cost of goods sold	(9,000,000)	0.70	(6,300,000)	0.75 A	(6,750,000)	0.65 A	(5,850,000)
Selling expenses	(750,000)	0.70	(525,000)	0.75 A	(562,500)	0.65 A	(487,500)
Deprec. expense	(300,000)	0.70	(210,000)	0.75 A	(225,000)	0.65 A	(195,000)

Translation Analytical Issues

	C$	\multicolumn{3}{c}{C$ Stable}	\multicolumn{2}{c}{C$ Strengthens}	\multicolumn{2}{c}{C$ Weakens}
	C$	Exch. Rate	€	Exch. Rate	€	Exch. Rate	€
Interest expense	(270,000)	0.70	(189,000)	0.75 A	(202,500)	0.65 A	(175,500)
Income tax	(500,000)	0.70	(350,000)	0.75 A	(375,000)	0.65 A	(325,000)
Net income	1,180,000		826,000		885,000		767,000
Less: Dividends	(350,000)	0.70	(245,000)	0.78 H	(273,000)	0.62 H	(217,000)
Retained earnings	830,000		581,000		612,000		550,000

Note: C = current (period-end) exchange rate; A = average-for-the-year exchange rate; H = historical exchange rate.

Compared with the translated amount of sales and net income under a stable Canadian dollar, a stronger Canadian dollar results in a larger amount of sales and net income being reported in the consolidated income statement. A weaker Canadian dollar results in a smaller amount of sales and net income being reported in consolidated net income.

Canadaco Balance Sheet on 31 December 20X1 under the Current Rate Method

		C$ Stable		C$ Strengthens		C$ Weakens	
	C$	Exch. Rate	€	Exch. Rate	€	Exch. Rate	€
Assets							
Cash	980,000	0.70	686,000	0.80 C	784,000	0.60 C	588,000
Accounts receivable	900,000	0.70	630,000	0.80 C	720,000	0.60 C	540,000
Inventory	1,200,000	0.70	840,000	0.80 C	960,000	0.60 C	720,000
Total current assets	3,080,000		2,156,000		2,464,000		1,848,000
Property and equipment	3,000,000	0.70	2,100,000	0.80 C	2,400,000	0.60 C	1,800,000
Less: accum. deprec.	(300,000)	0.70	(210,000)	0.80 C	(240,000)	0.60 C	(180,000)
Total assets	5,780,000		4,046,000		4,624,000		3,468,000
Liabilities and Equity							
Accounts payable	450,000	0.70	315,000	0.80 C	360,000	0.60 C	270,000
Total current liabilities	450,000		315,000		360,000		270,000
Long-term notes pay	3,000,000	0.70	2,100,000	0.80 C	2,400,000	0.60 C	1,800,000
Total liabilities	3,450,000		2,415,000		2,760,000		2,070,000
Capital stock	1,500,000	0.70	1,050,000	0.70 H	1,050,000	0.70 H	1,050,000
Retained earnings	830,000		581,000		612,000		550,000

	C$	C$ Stable Exch. Rate	€	C$ Strengthens Exch. Rate	€	C$ Weakens Exch. Rate	€
Translation adjustment	N/A		0		202,000		(202,000)
Total equity	2,330,000		1,631,000		1,864,000		1,398,000
Total	5,780,000		4,046,000		4,624,000		3,468,000

Note: C = current (period-end) exchange rate; A = average-for-the-year exchange rate; H = historical exchange rate.

The translation adjustment is zero when the Canadian dollar remains stable for the year; it is positive when the Canadian dollar strengthens and negative when the Canadian dollar weakens. Compared with the amounts that would appear in the euro consolidated balance sheet under a stable Canadian dollar assumption, a stronger Canadian dollar results in a larger amount of assets, liabilities, and equity being reported on the consolidated balance sheet, and a weaker Canadian dollar results in a smaller amount of assets, liabilities, and equity being reported on the consolidated balance sheet.

2. temporal method?

Solution:

Temporal Method: Using the temporal method, Canadaco's financial statements would be translated into euro as follows under the three different exchange rate scenarios:

Canadaco Balance Sheet on 31 December 20X1

Temporal Method

	C$	C$ Stable Exch. Rate	€	C$ Strengthens Exch. Rate	€	C$ Weakens Exch. Rate	€
Assets							
Cash	980,000	0.70	686,000	0.80 C	784,000	0.60 C	588,000
Accounts receivable	900,000	0.70	630,000	0.80 C	720,000	0.60 C	540,000
Inventory	1,200,000	0.70	840,000	0.74 H	888,000	0.66 H	792,000
Total current assets	3,080,000		2,156,000		2,392,000		1,920,000
Property and equipment	3,000,000	0.70	2,100,000	0.70 H	2,100,000	0.70 H	2,100,000
Less: accum. deprec.	(300,000)	0.70	(210,000)	0.70 H	(210,000)	0.70 H	(210,000)
Total assets	5,780,000		4,046,000		4,282,000		3,810,000
Liabilities and Equity							
Accounts payable	450,000	0.70	315,000	0.80 C	360,000	0.60 C	270,000

Translation Analytical Issues

		Temporal Method					
		C$ Stable		C$ Strengthens		C$ Weakens	
	C$	Exch. Rate	€	Exch. Rate	€	Exch. Rate	€
Total current liabilities	450,000		315,000		360,000		270,000
Long-term notes pay	3,000,000	0.70	2,100,000	0.80 C	2,400,000	0.60 C	1,800,000
Total liabilities	3,450,000		2,415,000		2,760,000		2,070,000
Capital stock	1,500,000	0.70	1,050,000	0.70 H	1,050,000	0.70 H	1,050,000
Retained earnings	830,000		581,000		472,000		690,000
Total equity	2,330,000		1,631,000		1,522,000		1,740,000
Total	5,780,000		4,046,000		4,282,000		3,810,000

Note: C = current (period-end) exchange rate; A = average-for-the-year exchange rate; H = historical exchange rate.

Compared with the stable Canadian dollar scenario, a stronger Canadian dollar results in a larger amount of assets and liabilities but a smaller amount of equity reported on the consolidated balance sheet. A weaker Canadian dollar results in a smaller amount of assets and liabilities but a larger amount of equity reported on the consolidated balance sheet.

Canadaco Income Statement and Statement of Retained Earnings for 2008 under the Temporal Method

		C$ Stable		C$ Strengthens		C$ Weakens	
	C$	Exch. Rate	€	Exch. Rate	€	Exch. Rate	€
Sales	12,000,000	0.70	8,400,000	0.75 A	9,000,000	0.65 A	7,800,000
Cost of sales	(9,000,000)	0.70	(6,300,000)	0.74 H	(6,660,000)	0.66 H	(5,940,000)
Selling expenses	(750,000)	0.70	(525,000)	0.75 A	(562,500)	0.65 A	(487,500)
Depreciation expense	(300,000)	0.70	(210,000)	0.70 H	(210,000)	0.70 H	(210,000)
Interest expense	(270,000)	0.70	(189,000)	0.75 A	(202,500)	0.65 A	(175,500)
Income tax	(500,000)	0.70	(350,000)	0.75 A	(375,000)	0.65 A	(325,000)
Income before translation gain (loss)	1,180,000		826,000		990,000		662,000
Translation gain (loss)	N/A		0		(245,000)		245,000
Net income	1,180,000		826,000		745,000		907,000
Less: Dividends	(350,000)	0.70	(245,000)	0.78 H	(273,000)	0.62 H	(217,000)
Retained earnings	830,000		581,000		472,000		690,000

Note: C = current (period-end) exchange rate; A = average-for-the-year exchange rate; H = historical exchange rate.

No translation gain or loss exists when the Canadian dollar remains stable during the year. Because the subsidiary has a net monetary liability expo-

> sure to changes in the exchange rate, a stronger Canadian dollar results in a translation loss and a weaker Canadian dollar results in a translation gain. Compared with a stable Canadian dollar, a stronger Canadian dollar results in a larger amount of sales and a smaller amount of net income reported on the consolidated income statement. This difference in direction results from the translation loss that is included in net income. (As demonstrated in Example 5, a translation gain would have resulted if the subsidiary had a net monetary asset exposure.) A weaker Canadian dollar results in a smaller amount of sales but a larger amount of net income than if the Canadian dollar had remained stable.

Exhibit 5 summarizes the relationships illustrated in Example 5 and Example 6, focusing on the typical effect that a strengthening or weakening of the foreign currency has on financial statement amounts compared with what the amounts would be if the foreign currency were to remain stable.

Exhibit 5: Effect of Currency Exchange Rate Movement on Financial Statements

	Temporal Method, Net Monetary Liability Exposure	Temporal Method, Net Monetary Asset Exposure	Current Rate Method
Foreign currency strengthens relative to parent's presentation currency	↑ Revenues ↑ Assets ↑ Liabilities ↓ Net income ↓ Shareholders' equity Translation loss	↑ Revenues ↑ Assets ↑ Liabilities ↑ Net income ↑ Shareholders' equity Translation gain	↑ Revenues ↑ Assets ↑ Liabilities ↑ Net income ↑ Shareholders' equity Positive translation adjustment
Foreign currency weakens relative to parent's presentation currency	↓ Revenues ↓ Assets ↓ Liabilities ↑ Net income ↑ Shareholders' equity Translation gain	↓ Revenues ↓ Assets ↓ Liabilities ↓ Net income ↓ Shareholders' equity Translation loss	↓ Revenues ↓ Assets ↓ Liabilities ↓ Net income ↓ Shareholders' equity Negative translation adjustment

7 TRANSLATION IN AN HYPERINFLATIONARY ECONOMY

☐ analyze how alternative translation methods for subsidiaries operating in hyperinflationary economies affect financial statements and ratios

As noted earlier, IFRS and US GAAP differ substantially in their approach to translating the foreign currency financial statements of foreign entities operating in the currency of a hyperinflationary economy. US GAAP simply require the foreign currency financial statements of such an entity to be translated as if the parent's currency is

Translation in an Hyperinflationary Economy

the functional currency (i.e., the temporal method must be used with the resulting translation gain or loss reported in net income). IFRS require the foreign currency financial statements first to be restated for inflation using the procedures of IAS 29, and then the inflation-adjusted financial statements are translated using the current exchange rate.

IAS 29 requires the following procedures in adjusting financial statements for inflation:

Balance Sheet

- Monetary assets and monetary liabilities are not restated because they are already expressed in terms of the monetary unit current at the balance sheet date. Monetary items consist of cash, receivables, and payables.

- Non-monetary assets and non-monetary liabilities are restated for changes in the general purchasing power of the monetary unit. Most non-monetary items are carried at historical cost. In these cases, the restated cost is determined by applying to the historical cost the change in the general price index from the date of acquisition to the balance sheet date. Some non-monetary items are carried at revalued amounts; for example, property, plant, and equipment revalued according to the allowed alternative treatment in IAS 16, "Property, Plant and Equipment." These items are restated from the date of revaluation.

- All components of stockholders' equity are restated by applying the change in the general price level from the beginning of the period or, if later, from the date of contribution to the balance sheet date.

Income Statement

- All income statement items are restated by applying the change in the general price index from the dates when the items were originally recorded to the balance sheet date.

- The net gain or loss in purchasing power that arises from holding monetary assets and monetary liabilities during a period of inflation is included in net income.

The procedures for adjusting financial statements for inflation are similar in concept to the procedures followed when using the temporal method for translation. By restating non-monetary assets and liabilities along with stockholders' equity in terms of the general price level at the balance sheet date, these items are carried at their historical amount of purchasing power. Only the monetary items, which are not restated for inflation, are exposed to inflation risk. The effect of that exposure is reflected through the purchasing power gain or loss on the net monetary asset or liability position.

Holding cash and receivables during a period of inflation results in a **purchasing power loss**, whereas holding payables during inflation results in a **purchasing power gain**. This relationship can be demonstrated through the following examples.

Assume that the general price index (GPI) on 1 January 20X1 is 100; that is, a representative basket of goods and services can be purchased on that date for $100. At the end of 20X1, the same basket of goods and services costs $120; thus, the country has experienced an inflation rate of 20% [($120 − $100) ÷ $100]. Cash of $100 can be used to acquire one basket of goods on 1 January 20X1. One year later, however, when the GPI stands at 120, the same $100 in cash can now purchase only 83.3% of a basket of goods and services. At the end of 20X1, it now takes $120 to purchase the same amount as $100 could purchase at the beginning of the year. The difference between the amount of cash needed to purchase one market basket at year end ($120) and the amount actually held ($100) results in a purchasing power loss of $20 from holding cash of $100 during the year.

Borrowing money during a period of inflation increases purchasing power. Assume that a company expects to receive $120 in cash at the end of 20X1. If it waits until the cash is received, the company will be able to purchase exactly 1.0 basket of goods and services when the GPI stands at 120. If instead, the company borrows $120 on 1 January 20X1 when the GPI is 100, it can acquire 1.2 baskets of goods and services. This transaction results in a purchasing power gain of $20. Of course, there is an interest cost associated with the borrowing that offsets a portion of this gain.

A net purchasing power gain will arise when a company holds a greater amount of monetary liabilities than monetary assets, and a net purchasing power loss will result when the opposite situation exists. As such, purchasing power gains and losses are analogous to the translation gains and losses that arise when the currency is weakening in value and the temporal method of translation is applied.

Although the procedures required by IFRS and US GAAP for translating the foreign currency financial statements in high-inflation countries are fundamentally different, the results, in a rare occurrence, can be very similar. Indeed, if the exchange rate between two currencies changes by exactly the same percentage as the change in the general price index in the highly inflationary country, then the two methodologies produce the same results. Example 7 demonstrates this scenario.

EXAMPLE 7

Translation of Foreign Currency Financial Statements of a Foreign Entity Operating in a High Inflation Country

1. ABC Company formed a subsidiary in a foreign country on 1 January 20X1, through a combination of debt and equity financing. The foreign subsidiary acquired land on 1 January 20X1, which it rents to a local farmer. The foreign subsidiary's financial statements for its first year of operations, in foreign currency units (FC), are as follows:

Foreign Subsidiary Income Statement

(in FC)	20X1
Rent revenue	1,000
Interest expense	(250)
Net income	750

Foreign Subsidiary Balance Sheets

(in FC)	1 Jan 20X1	31 Dec 20X1
Cash	1,000	1,750
Land	9,000	9,000
Total	10,000	10,750
Note payable (5%)	5,000	5,000
Capital stock	5,000	5,000
Retained earnings	0	750

Translation in an Hyperinflationary Economy

(in FC)	1 Jan 20X1	31 Dec 20X1
Total	10,000	10,750

The foreign country experienced significant inflation in 20X1, especially in the second half of the year. The general price index during the year was as follows:

1 January 20X1	100
Average, 20X1	125
31 December 20X1	200

The inflation rate in 20X1 was 100%, and the foreign country clearly meets the definition of a highly inflationary economy.

As a result of the high inflation rate in the foreign country, the FC weakened substantially during the year relative to other currencies. Relevant exchange rates between ABC's presentation currency (US dollars) and the FC during 20X1 were as follows:

	US$ per FC
1 January 20X1	1.00
Average, 20X1	0.80
31 December 20X1	0.50

What amounts will ABC Company include in its consolidated financial statements for the year ended 31 December 20X1 related to this foreign subsidiary?

Solution:

Assuming that ABC Company wishes to prepare its consolidated financial statements in accordance with IFRS, the foreign subsidiary's 20X1 financial statements will be restated for local inflation and then translated into ABC's presentation currency using the current exchange rate as follows:

	FC	Restatement Factor	Inflation-Adjusted FC	Exch. Rate	US$
Cash	1,750	200/200	1,750	0.50	875
Land	9,000	200/100	18,000	0.50	9,000
Total	10,750		19,750		9,875
Note payable	5,000	200/200	5,000	0.50	2,500
Capital stock	5,000	200/100	10,000	0.50	5,000
Retained earnings	750		4,750	0.50	2,375
Total	10,750		19,750		9,875
Revenues	1,000	200/125	1,600	0.50	800
Interest expense	(250)	200/125	(400)	0.50	(200)
Subtotal	750		1,200		600

	FC	Restatement Factor	Inflation-Adjusted FC	Exch. Rate	US$
Purchasing power gain/loss			3,550	0.50	1,775
Net income			4,750		2,375

All financial statement items are restated to the GPI at 31 December 20X1. The net purchasing power gain of FC3,550 can be explained as follows:

Gain from holding note payable	FC5,000 × (200 − 100)/100 =	FC5,000
Loss from holding beginning balance in cash	−1,000 × (200 − 100)/100 =	(1,000)
Loss from increase in cash during the year	−750 × (200 − 125)/125 =	(450)
Net purchasing power gain (loss)		FC3,550

Note that all inflation-adjusted FC amounts are translated at the current exchange rate, and thus no translation adjustment is needed.

Now assume alternatively that ABC Company wishes to comply with US GAAP in preparing its consolidated financial statements. In that case, the foreign subsidiary's FC financial statements are translated into US dollars using the temporal method, with the resulting translation gain/loss reported in net income, as follows:

	FC	Exch. Rate	US$
Cash	1,750	0.50 C	875
Land	9,000	1.00 H	9,000
Total	10,750		9,875
Note payable	5,000	0.50 C	2,500
Capital stock	5,000	1.00 H	5,000
Retained earnings	750		2,375
Total	10,750		9,875
Revenues	1,000	0.80 A	800
Interest expense	(250)	0.80 A	(200)
Subtotal	750		600
Translation gain*			1,775
Net income			2,375

* The dividend is US$0 and the increase in retained earnings is US$2,375 (from the balance sheet); so, net income is US$2,375, and thus the translation gain is US$1,775.

Note: C = current (period-end) exchange rate; A = average-for-the-year exchange rate; H = historical exchange rate

Application of the temporal method as required by US GAAP in this situation results in exactly the same US dollar amounts as were obtained under the restate/translate approach required by IFRS. The equivalence of results under the two approaches exists because of the exact one-to-one inverse relationship between the change in the foreign country's GPI and the change in the dollar value of the FC, as predicted by the theory of purchasing power parity. The GPI doubled and the FC lost half its purchasing power, which caused the FC to lose half its value in dollar terms.

To the extent that this relationship does not hold, and it rarely ever does, the two different methodologies will generate different translated amounts. For example, if the 31 December 20X1 exchange rate had adjusted to only US$0.60 per FC1 (rather than US$0.50 per FC1), then translated net income would have been US$2,050 under US GAAP and US$2,850 under IFRS.

USING BOTH TRANSLATION METHODS

☐ analyze how the current rate method and the temporal method affect financial statements and ratios

Under both IFRS and US GAAP, a multinational corporation may need to use both the current rate and the temporal methods of translation at a single point in time. This situation will apply when some foreign subsidiaries have a foreign currency as their functional currency (and therefore are translated using the current rate method) and other foreign subsidiaries have the parent's currency as their functional currency (and therefore are translated using the temporal method). As a result, a multinational corporation's consolidated financial statements can reflect simultaneously both a net translation gain or loss that is included in the determination of net income (from foreign subsidiaries translated using the temporal method) and a separate cumulative translation adjustment reported on the balance sheet in stockholders' equity (from foreign subsidiaries translated using the current rate method).

Exxon Mobil Corporation is an example of a company that has a mixture of foreign currency and parent currency functional currency subsidiaries, as evidenced by the following excerpt from its 2011 annual report, Note 1 Summary of Accounting Policies:

> **Foreign Currency Translation.** The Corporation selects the functional reporting currency for its international subsidiaries based on the currency of the primary economic environment in which each subsidiary operates. Downstream and Chemical operations primarily use the local currency. However, the US dollar is used in countries with a history of high inflation (primarily in Latin America) and Singapore, which predominantly sells into the US dollar export market. Upstream operations which are relatively self-contained and integrated within a particular country, such as Canada, the United Kingdom, Norway and continental Europe, use the local currency. Some upstream operations, primarily in Asia and Africa, use the US dollar because they predominantly sell crude and natural gas production into US dollar–denominated markets. For all operations, gains or losses from remeasuring foreign currency transactions into the functional currency are included in income.

Because of the judgment involved in determining the functional currency of foreign operations, two companies operating in the same industry might apply this judgment differently. For example, although Exxon Mobil has identified the local currency as the functional currency for many of its international subsidiaries, Chevron Corporation has designated the US dollar as the functional currency for substantially all of its overseas operations, as indicated in its 2011 annual report, Note 1 Summary of Significant Accounting Policies:

> **Currency Translation.** The US dollar is the functional currency for substantially all of the company's consolidated operations and those of its equity affiliates. For those operations, all gains and losses from currency

remeasurement are included in current period income. The cumulative translation effects for those few entities, both consolidated and affiliated, using functional currencies other than the US dollar are included in "Currency translation adjustment" on the Consolidated Statement of Equity.

Evaluating net income reported by Exxon Mobil against net income reported by Chevron presents a comparability problem. This problem can be partially resolved by adding the translation adjustments reported in stockholders' equity to net income for both companies. The feasibility of this solution depends on the level of detail disclosed by multinational corporations with respect to the translation of foreign currency financial statements.

Disclosures Related to Translation Methods

Both IFRS and US GAAP require two types of disclosures related to foreign currency translation:

1. the amount of exchange differences recognized in net income, and
2. the amount of cumulative translation adjustment classified in a separate component of equity, along with a reconciliation of the amount of cumulative translation adjustment at the beginning and end of the period.

US GAAP also specifically require disclosure of the amount of translation adjustment transferred from stockholders' equity and included in current net income as a result of the disposal of a foreign entity.

The amount of exchange differences recognized in net income consists of

- foreign currency *transaction* gains and losses, and
- *translation* gains and losses resulting from application of the temporal method.

Neither IFRS nor US GAAP require disclosure of the two separate amounts that constitute the total exchange difference recognized in net income, and most companies do not provide disclosure at that level of detail. However, BASF AG (shown earlier in Exhibit 1) is an exception. Note 6 in BASF's annual report separately discloses gains from foreign currency and hedging transactions and gains from translation of financial statements, both of which are included in the line item "Other Operating Income" on the income statement, as shown below:

6. Other Operating Income		
Million €	2011	2010
Reversal and adjustment of provisions	170	244
Revenue from miscellaneous revenue-generating activities	207	142
Income from foreign currency and hedging transactions	170	136
Income from the translation of financial statements in foreign currencies	42	76
Gains on the disposal of property, plant and equipment and divestitures	666	101
Reversals of impairments of property, plant and equipment	—	40
Gains on the reversal of allowance for doubtful business-related receivables	77	36
Other	676	365

Using Both Translation Methods

Million €	2011	2010
	2,008	1,140

The company provides a similar level of detail in Note 7 related to "Other Operating Expenses."

Disclosures related to foreign currency translation are commonly found in both the MD&A and the Notes to Financial Statements sections of an annual report. Example 8 uses the foreign currency translation–related disclosures made in 2011 by Yahoo! Inc.

EXAMPLE 8

Disclosures Related to Foreign Currency Translation: Yahoo! Inc. 2011 Annual Report

Yahoo! Inc. is a US-based digital media company that reports in US dollars and prepares financial statements in accordance with US GAAP.

The stockholders' equity section of Yahoo!'s consolidated balance sheets includes the following line items:

	31 December	
(in thousands)	2010	2011
Common stock	$1,306	$1,242
Additional paid-in capital	10,109,913	9,825,899
Treasury stock	—	(416,237)
Retained earnings	1,942,656	2,432,294
Accumulated other comprehensive income (loss)	504,254	697,869
Total Yahoo! Inc. stockholders' equity	12,558,129	12,541,067

The consolidated statement of stockholders' equity provides detail on the components comprising "Accumulated other comprehensive income." The relevant portion of that statement appears below:

	Years Ended 31 December		
	2009		2011
Accumulated other comprehensive income			
Balance, beginning of year	120,276	369,236	504,254
Net change in unrealized gains/losses on available-for-sale securities, net of tax	(1,936)	3,813	(16,272)
Foreign currency translation adjustments, net of tax	250,896	131,205	209,887
Balance, end of year	369,236	504,254	697,869

Yahoo! reported the following net income in 2010 and 2011, as shown on the consolidated statement of income:

	2010	2011	% Change
Net income	$1,244,628	$1,062,699	−14.6%

Yahoo!'s disclosures for its three geographic segments are disclosed in a note to the financial statements. Revenue (excluding total acquisition costs) and direct segment operating costs are shown below:

	2009	2010	2011
Revenue ex-TAC by segment:			
Americas	3,656,752	3,467,850	3,142,879
EMEA	390,456	368,884	407,467
Asia Pacific	635,281	751,495	830,482
Total revenue ex-TAC	4,682,489	4,588,229	4,380,828
Direct costs by segment:			
Americas	620,690	568,017	560,016
EMEA	115,778	118,954	135,266
Asia Pacific	138,739	146,657	194,394

In the MD&A section of the 2011 annual report, Yahoo! describes the source of its translation exposure:

Translation Exposure

We are also exposed to foreign exchange rate fluctuations as we convert the financial statements of our foreign subsidiaries and our investments in equity interests into US dollars in consolidation. If there is a change in foreign currency exchange rates, the conversion of the foreign subsidiaries' financial statements into US dollars results in a gain or loss which is recorded as a component of accumulated other comprehensive income which is part of stockholders' equity.

Revenue ex-TAC (total acquisition costs) and related expenses generated from our international subsidiaries are generally denominated in the currencies of the local countries. The statements of income of our international operations are translated into US dollars at exchange rates indicative of market rates during each applicable period. To the extent the US dollar strengthens against foreign currencies, the translation of these foreign currency-denominated transactions results in reduced consolidated revenue and operating expenses. Conversely, our consolidated revenue and operating expenses will increase if the US dollar weakens against foreign currencies. Using the foreign currency exchange rates from the year ended December 31, 2010, revenue ex-TAC for the Americas segment for the year ended December 31, 2011 would have been lower than we reported by $6 million, revenue ex-TAC for the EMEA segment would have been lower than we reported by $16 million, and revenue ex-TAC for the Asia Pacific segment would have been lower than we reported by $59 million. Using the foreign currency exchange rates from the year ended December 31, 2010, direct costs for the Americas segment for the year ended December 31, 2011 would have been lower than we reported by $2 million, direct costs for the EMEA segment would have been lower than we reported by $5 million, and direct costs for the Asia Pacific segment would have been lower than we reported by $15 million.

Using the information above, address the following questions:

1. By how much did accumulated other comprehensive income change during the year ended 31 December 2011? Where can this information be found?

   Accumulated other comprehensive income increased by $193,615 thousand (from $504,254 thousand beginning balance to $697,869 thousand at the end of the year). This information can be found in two places: the stockhold-

Using Both Translation Methods

ers' equity section of the balance sheet and the consolidated statement of stockholders' equity.

2. How much foreign currency translation adjustment was included in other comprehensive income for the year ended 31 December 2011? How does such an adjustment arise?

   The amount of foreign currency translation adjustment included in other comprehensive income for 2011 was $209,887 thousand. The foreign currency translation adjustment arises from applying the current rate method to translate the foreign currency functional currency financial statements of foreign subsidiaries. Assuming that Yahoo!'s foreign subsidiaries have positive net assets, the positive translation adjustment in 2011 results from a strengthening in foreign currencies (weakening in the US dollar).

3. If foreign currency translation adjustment had been included in net income (rather than in other comprehensive income), how would the 2010/2011 change in income have been affected?

   If foreign currency translation adjustment had been included in net income (rather than other comprehensive income), the percentage decrease in reported net income from 2010 to 2011 of 14.6% would have been smaller (7.5%).

	2010	2011	% Change
Net income	$1,244,628	$1,062,699	–14.6%
Foreign currency translation adjustment	131,205	209,887	
	$1,375,833	$1,272,586	–7.5%

4. From what perspective does Yahoo! describe its foreign currency risk?

   Yahoo! describes its foreign currency risk from the perspective of how the US dollar fluctuates against foreign currencies because the dollar is the reporting currency. If the US dollar strengthens, then foreign currencies must weaken, which will result in reduced revenues, expenses, and income from foreign operations.

5. What percentage of total revenue ex-TAC was generated by the Asia-Pacific segment for the year ended 31 December 2011? What would this percentage have been if there had been no change in foreign currency exchange rates during the year?

   The Asia-Pacific segment represented 19.0% of total revenue ex-TAC. Information from the MD&A disclosure can be used to determine that if there had been no change in foreign currency exchange rates during the year, the segment would have represented a slightly lower percentage of total revenue (17.9%).

	2011, as reported			2011, if no change in exchange rates	
Revenue ex-TAC by segment:					
Americas	3,142,879	71.7%	6,000	3,136,879	73.0%

	2011, as reported			2011, if no change in exchange rates	
EMEA	407,467	9.3%	16,000	391,467	9.1%
Asia Pacific	830,482	19.0%	59,000	771,482	17.9%
Total revenue ex-TAC	4,380,828	100.0%		4,299,828	100.0%

As noted in the previous section, because of the judgment involved in determining the functional currency of foreign operations, two companies operating in the same industry might use different predominant translation methods. As a result, income reported by these companies may not be directly comparable. Exxon Mobil Corporation and Chevron Corporation, both operating in the petroleum industry, are an example of two companies for which this is the case. Whereas Chevron has identified the US dollar as the functional currency for substantially all of its foreign subsidiaries, Exxon Mobil indicates that its downstream and chemical operations, as well as some of its upstream operations, primarily use the local currency as the functional currency. As a result, Chevron primarily uses the temporal method with translation gains and losses included in income, while Exxon Mobil uses the current rate method to a much greater extent, with the resulting translation adjustments excluded from income. To make the income of these two companies more comparable, an analyst can use the disclosures related to translation adjustments to include these as gains and losses in determining an adjusted amount of income. Example 9 demonstrates this process for Exxon Mobil and Chevron.

EXAMPLE 9

Comparing Net Income for Exxon Mobil Corporation and Chevron Corporation

1. Exxon Mobil Corporation uses the current rate method to translate the foreign currency financial statements of a substantial number of its foreign subsidiaries and includes the resulting translation adjustments in the "Accumulated other non-owner changes in equity" line item in the stockholders' equity section of the consolidated balance sheet. Detail on the items composing "Accumulated other non-owner changes in equity," including "Foreign exchange translation adjustment," is provided in the consolidated statement of shareholders' equity.

    Chevron Corporation uses the temporal method to translate the foreign currency financial statements of substantially all of its foreign subsidiaries. For those few entities using functional currencies other than the US dollar, however, the current rate method is used and the resulting translation adjustments are included in the "Accumulated other comprehensive loss" component of stockholders' equity. The consolidated statement of stockholders' equity provides detail on the changes in the component of stockholders' equity, including a "Currency translation adjustment."

    Combining net income from the income statement and the change in the cumulative translation adjustment account from the statement of stockholders' equity, an adjusted net income in which translation adjustments are treated as gains and losses can be calculated for each company, as shown in the following table (amounts in millions of US dollars):

Using Both Translation Methods

Exxon Mobil	2011	2010	2009
Reported net income	42,206	31,398	19,658
Translation adjustment	(867)	1,034	3,629
Adjusted net income	41,339	32,432	23,287

Chevron	2011	2010	2009
Reported net income	27,008	19,136	10,563
Translation adjustment	17	6	60
Adjusted net income	27,025	19,142	10,623

The direction, positive or negative, of the translation adjustment is the same for both companies in 2009 and 2010 but not in 2011. Overall, Exxon Mobil has significantly larger translation adjustments than Chevron because Exxon Mobil designates the local currency as functional currency for a substantially larger portion of its foreign operations.

A comparison of the relative amounts of net income generated by the two companies is different depending on whether reported net income or adjusted net income is used. Exxon Mobil's reported net income in 2009 is 1.90 times larger than Chevron's, whereas its adjusted net income is 2.2 times larger, as shown in the following table.

	2011	2010	2009
Exxon Mobil reported net income/ Chevron reported net income	1.6	1.6	1.9
Exxon Mobil adjusted net income/ Chevron adjusted net income	1.5	1.7	2.2

==Including translation adjustments as gains and losses in the measurement of an adjusted net income provides a more comparable basis for evaluating the profitability of two companies that use different predominant translation methods. Bringing the translation adjustments into the calculation of adjusted net income still might not provide truly comparable measures, however, because of the varying effect that the different translation methods have on reported net income.==

Some analysts believe that all non-owner changes in stockholders' equity, such as translation adjustments, should be included in the determination of net income. This approach is referred to as clean-surplus accounting, as opposed to dirty-surplus accounting, in which some income items are reported as part of stockholders' equity rather than as gains and losses on the income statement. One of the dirty-surplus items found in both IFRS and US GAAP financial statements is the translation adjustment that arises when a foreign currency is determined to be the functional currency of a foreign subsidiary. Disclosures made in accordance with IFRS and US GAAP provide analysts with the detail needed to calculate net income on a clean-surplus basis. In fact, both sets of standards now require companies to prepare a statement of comprehensive income in which unrealized gains and losses that have been deferred in stockholders' equity are included in a measure of comprehensive income.

9. MULTINATIONAL OPERATIONS AND A COMPANY'S EFFECTIVE TAX RATE

☐ describe how multinational operations affect a company's effective tax rate

In general, multinational companies incur income taxes in the country in which the profit is earned. Transfer prices, the prices that related companies charge on intercompany transactions, affect the allocation of profit between the companies. An entity with operations in multiple countries with different tax rates could aim to set transfer prices such that a higher portion of its profit is allocated to lower tax rate jurisdictions. Countries have established various laws and practices to prevent aggressive transfer pricing practices. Transfer pricing has been defined as "the system of laws and practices used by countries to ensure that goods, services and intellectual property transferred between related companies are appropriately priced, based on market conditions, such that profits are correctly reflected in each jurisdiction."[5] Also, most countries are party to tax treaties that prevent double-taxation of corporate profits by granting a credit for taxes paid to another country.

Whether and when a company also pays income taxes in its home country depends on the specific tax regime. In the United States, for example, multinational companies are liable only for a residual tax on foreign income, after applying a credit for foreign taxes paid on that same income. The effect of the tax credit is that the multinational company owes taxes on the foreign income only to the extent that the US corporate tax rate exceeds the foreign rate of tax on that income. In addition, much of the foreign income earned by US multinationals is not taxed until it is repatriated.[6]

An analyst can obtain information about the effect of multinational operations from companies' disclosure on effective tax rates. Accounting standards require companies to provide an explanation of the relationship between tax expense and accounting profit. The explanation is presented as a reconciliation between the average effective tax rate (tax expense divided by pretax accounting profits) and the relevant statutory rate. The purpose of this disclosure is to enable users of financial statements to understand whether the relationship between tax expense and accounting profit in a particular fiscal period is unusual and to understand the significant factors—including the effect of foreign taxes—that could affect that relationship in the future.[7] Changes in the effective tax rate impact of foreign taxes could be caused by changes in the applicable tax rates and/or changes in the mix of profits earned in different jurisdictions.

EXAMPLE 10

Below are excerpts from the effective tax rate reconciliation disclosures by two companies: Heineken N.V., a Dutch brewer, and Colgate Palmolive, a US consumer products company. Use the disclosures to answer the following questions:

---

5 TP Analytics. http://www.tpanalytics.com.
6 United States Government Accountability Office (GAO) Report GAO-08-950. *US Multinational Corporations: Effective Tax Rates Are Correlated with Where Income Is Reported.* August 2008.
7 International Accounting Standard 12 *Income Taxes*, ¶84.

Heineken N.V. Annual Report 2011
Notes to the consolidated financial statements
13. Income tax expense (excerpt)

Reconciliation of the effective tax rate

In millions of EUR	2011	2010
Profit before income tax	2,025	1,982
Share of net profit of associates and joint ventures and impairments thereof	(240)	(193)
Profit before income tax excluding share of profit of associates and joint ventures (inclusive impairments thereof)	1,785	1,789

	%	2011	%	2010
Income tax using the Company's domestic tax rate	25.0	446	25.5	456
Effect of tax rates in foreign jurisdictions	3.5	62	1.9	34
Effect of non-deductible expenses	3.2	58	4	72
Effect of tax incentives and exempt income	(6.0)	−107	−8.2	−146
Recognition of previously unrecognised temporary differences	(0.5)	−9	−0.1	−2
Utilisation or recognition of previously unrecognised tax losses	(0.3)	−5	−1.2	−21
Unrecognised current year tax losses	1.0	18	0.8	15
Effect of changes in tax rate	0.1	1	0.2	3
Withholding taxes	1.5	26	1.4	25
Under/(over) provided in prior years	(1.5)	−27	−2.3	−42
Other reconciling items	0.1	2	0.5	9
	26.1	465	22.5	403

COLGATE-PALMOLIVE COMPANY Annual Report 2011
Notes to Consolidated Financial Statements
10. Income Taxes (excerpt)

The difference between the statutory US federal income tax rate and the Company's global effective tax rate as reflected in the Consolidated Statements of Income is as follows:

Percentage of Income before income taxes	2011	2010	2009
Tax at United States statutory rate	35.0%	35.0%	35.0%
State income taxes, net of federal benefit	0.4	1.1	0.5
Earnings taxed at other than United States statutory rate	(1.7)	(4.6)	(2.5)
Venezuela hyperinflationary transition charge	—	2.8	—
Other, net	(1.1)	(1.7)	(0.8)
Effective tax rate	32.6%	32.6%	32.2%

> 1. Which company's home country has a lower statutory tax rate?
>
> **Solution:**
>
> Heineken's home country tax rate (25.0% in 2011) is lower than Colgate Palmolive's home country tax rate (35.0%).
>
> 2. What was the impact of multinational operations on each company's 2011 effective tax rate?
>
> **Solution:**
>
> The line item labeled "Effect of tax rates in foreign jurisdictions" indicates that multinational operations increased Heineken's effective tax rate by 3.5 percentage points. The line item labeled "Earnings taxed at other than United States statutory rate" indicates that multinational operations lowered Colgate Palmolive's effective tax rate by 1.7 percentage points in 2011.
>
> 3. Changes in the tax rate impact of multinational operations can often be explained by changes of profit mix between countries with higher or lower marginal tax rates. What do Heineken's disclosures suggest about the geographic mix of its 2011 profit?
>
> **Solution:**
>
> Multinational operations increased Heineken's effective tax rate by 3.5 percentage points in 2011 but only 1.9 percentage points in 2010. This greater impact in 2011 could indicate that Heineken's profit mix in 2011 shifted to countries with higher marginal tax rates. (The change could also indicate that the marginal tax rates increased in the countries in which Heineken earns profits.)

10. ADDITIONAL DISCLOSURES ON THE EFFECTS OF FOREIGN CURRENCY

☐ explain how changes in the components of sales affect the sustainability of sales growth

☐ analyze how currency fluctuations potentially affect financial results, given a company's countries of operation

We turn now to the question of how an analyst can use multinational companies' disclosures to better understand the effects of foreign currency.

Disclosures Related to Sales Growth

Companies often make important disclosures about foreign currency effect on sales growth in the MD&A. Additional disclosures are also often made in financial presentations to the analyst community.

Additional Disclosures on the Effects of Foreign Currency

For a multinational company, sales growth is driven not only by changes in volume and price but also by changes in the exchange rates between the reporting currency and the currency in which sales are made. Arguably, growth in sales that comes from changes in volume or price is more sustainable than growth in sales that comes from changes in exchange rates. Further, management arguably has greater control over growth in sales resulting from greater volume or higher price than from changes in exchange rates. Thus, an analyst will consider the foreign currency effect on sales growth both for forecasting future performance and for evaluating a management team's historical performance.

Companies often include disclosures about the effect of exchange rates on sales growth in the MD&A. Such disclosures may also appear in other financial reports, such as company presentations to investors or earnings announcements. Exhibit 6 provides an example of disclosure from the MD&A, and Example 11 illustrates even more detailed disclosure from a company's report to analysts.

Exhibit 6

General Mills' 2011 annual report includes the following disclosures about the components of net sales growth in its international segment. The first excerpt is from the MD&A, and the second is from a supplementary schedule reconciling non-GAAP measures. Although the overall effect on international net sales growth was minimal "flat," the geographic detail provided in the supplementary schedule shows that the effects varied widely by region.

Excerpt from MD&A

Components of International Net Sales Growth

	Fiscal 2011 vs. 2010	Fiscal 2010 vs. 2009
Contributions from volume growth[a]	6 pts	Flat
Net price realization and mix	1 pt	3 pts
Foreign currency exchange	Flat	1 pt
Net sales growth	7 pts	4 pts

[a] *Measured in tons based on the stated weight of our product shipments.*

Excerpt from Supplementary Schedule on Non-GAAP Measures

International Segment and Region Sales Growth Rates Excluding Impact of Foreign Exchange

	Fiscal Year 2011		
	Percentage change in Net Sales as Reported	Impact of Foreign Currency Exchange	Percentage change in Net Sales on Constant Currency Basis
Europe	5%	−2%	7%
Canada	8	5	3
Asia/Pacific	14	5	9
Latin America	−5	−16	11

International Segment and Region Sales Growth Rates Excluding Impact of Foreign Exchange

	Fiscal Year 2011		
	Percentage change in Net Sales as Reported	Impact of Foreign Currency Exchange	Percentage change in Net Sales on Constant Currency Basis
Total International segment	7%	Flat	7%

EXAMPLE 11

Use the information disclosed in Procter & Gamble Company's CAGNY [Consumer Analyst Group of New York] conference slides to answer the following questions:

1. Why does the company present "organic sales growth"?
2. On average, for the four quarters beginning October 2008 and ending September 2009, how did changes in foreign exchange rates affect P&G's reported sales growth?

The Procter & Gamble Company

2012 CAGNY CONFERENCE SLIDES

Reg G Reconciliation of Non-GAAP measures

In accordance with the SEC's Regulation G, the following provides definitions of the non-GAAP measures used in the earnings call and slides with the reconciliation to the most closely related GAAP measure.

1. *Organic Sales Growth:*

    Organic sales growth is a non-GAAP measure of sales growth excluding the impacts of acquisitions, divestitures and foreign exchange from year-over-year comparisons. We believe this provides investors with a more complete understanding of underlying sales trends by providing sales growth on a consistent basis. "Organic sales" is also one of the measures used to evaluate senior management and is a factor in determining their at-risk compensation. The reconciliation of reported sales growth to organic sales is as follows:

Total P&G	Net Sales Growth	Foreign Exchange Impact	Acquisition/ Divestiture Impact	Organic Sales Growth
JAS 06	27%	–1%	–20%	6%
OND 06	8%	–3%	0%	5%
JFM07	8%	–2%	0%	6%
AMJ07	8%	–3%	0%	5%
JAS07	8%	–3%	0%	5%
OND07	9%	–5%	1%	5%

Additional Disclosures on the Effects of Foreign Currency

Total P&G	Net Sales Growth	Foreign Exchange Impact	Acquisition/ Divestiture Impact	Organic Sales Growth
JFM08	9%	−5%	1%	5%
AMJ08	10%	−6%	1%	5%
JAS08	9%	−5%	1%	5%
Average–JAS 06–JAS 08	11%	−4%	−2%	5%
OND08	−3%	5%	0%	2%
JFM09	−8%	9%	0%	1%
AMJ09	−11%	9%	1%	−1%
JAS09	−6%	7%	1%	2%
Average–OND 08–JAS 09	−7%	8%	0%	1%
OND09	6%	−2%	1%	5%
JFM010	7%	−3%	0%	4%
AMJ010	5%	−1%	0%	4%
JAS010	2%	3%	−1%	4%
OND010	2%	2%	−1%	3%
JFM011	5%	−1%	0%	4%
AMJ011	10%	−5%	0%	5%
JAS011	9%	−5%	0%	4%
OND011	4%	0%	0%	4%
Average–OND 09–OND 11	5%	−1%	0%	4%
JFM 12 (Estimate)	0% to 2%	3%	0%	3% to 5%
AMJ 12 (Estimate)	−1% to 2%	5% to 4%	0%	4% to 6%

Solution to 1:

According to its disclosures, Procter & Gamble presents "organic sales growth" because the company believes it provides investors with a better understanding of underlying sales trends and because it is one of the measures used for management evaluation and compensation.

Solution to 2:

The average effect of foreign exchange changes during the period was negative: Although organic sales grew by 1%, the company reported net sales growth of −7% as a result of a negative 8% foreign exchange effect In other words, if no foreign exchange effect had occurred, reported sales growth and organic sales growth would have been equal, both at 1%.

Disclosures Related to Major Sources of Foreign Exchange Risk

Disclosures about the effects of currency fluctuations often include sensitivity analyses. For example, a company might describe the major sources of foreign exchange risk given its countries of operations and then disclose the profit impact of a given change in exchange rates.

Exhibit 7 includes two excerpts from the 2011 BMW AG annual report. The first excerpt, from the management report, describes the source of the company's currency risks and its approach to measuring and managing those risks. The second excerpt, from the additional disclosures section of the notes, presents the results of the company's sensitivity analysis.

Exhibit 7

Excerpts from 2011 BMW AG Annual Report

Excerpt from the management report describing the source of the company's currency risks and its approach to measuring and managing those risks:

"The sale of vehicles outside the euro zone gives rise to exchange risks. Three currencies (the Chinese renminbi, the US dollar and the British pound) accounted for approximately two-thirds of the BMW Group's foreign currency exposures in 2011. We employ cash-flow-at-risk models and scenario analyses to measure exchange rate risks. These tools provide information which serves as the basis for decision-making in the area of currency management.

"We manage currency risks both at a strategic (medium and long term) and at an operating level (short and medium term). In the medium and long term, foreign exchange risks are managed by "natural hedging", in other words by increasing the volume of purchases denominated in foreign currency or increasing the volume of local production. In this context, the expansion of the plant in Spartanburg, USA, and the new plant under construction in Tiexi* at the Shenyang site in China are helping to reduce foreign exchange risks in two major sales markets. For operating purposes (short and medium term), currency risks are hedged on the financial markets. Hedging transactions are entered into only with financial partners of good credit standing. Counterparty risk management procedures are carried out continuously to monitor the creditworthiness of those partners."

Excerpt, from the additional disclosures section of the notes, presenting the results of the company's sensitivity analysis risks:

"The BMW Group measures currency risk using a cash-flow-at-risk model. The starting point for analysing currency risk with this model is the identification of forecast foreign currency transactions or "exposures". At the end of the reporting period, the principal exposures for the coming year were as follows:

in € million	31.12.2011	31.12.2010
Euro/Chinese Renminbi	7,114	6,256
Euro/US Dollar	4,281	3,888
Euro/British Pound	3,266	3,056
Euro/Japanese Yen	1,334	1,086

"In the next stage, these exposures are compared to all hedges that are in place. The net cash flow surplus represents an uncovered risk position. The cash-flow-at-risk approach involves allocating the impact of potential exchange rate fluctuations to operating cash flows on the basis of probability distributions. Volatilities and correlations serve as input factors to assess the relevant probability distributions.

"The potential negative impact on earnings for the current period is computed on the basis of current market prices and exposures to a confidence level of 95% and a holding period of up to one year for each currency. Aggregation of these results creates a risk reduction effect due to correlations between the various portfolios.

Additional Disclosures on the Effects of Foreign Currency

"The following table shows the potential negative impact for the BMW Group—measured on the basis of the cash-flow-at-risk approach—attributable at the balance sheet date to unfavourable changes in exchange rates for the principal currencies."

in € million	31.12.2011	31.12.2010
Euro/Chinese Renminbi	180	265
Euro/US Dollar	121	103
Euro/British Pound	182	184
Euro/Japanese Yen	23	30

The level of detail varies in companies' disclosures about sensitivity of earnings to foreign currency fluctuations, with some companies providing information on the range of possible values of foreign exchange rates. An analyst can use sensitivity analysis disclosures in conjunction with his or her own forecast of exchange rates when developing forecasts of profit and cash flow. When detailed disclosures are provided, the analyst can explicitly incorporate foreign exchange impact. Alternatively, in the absence of detailed disclosures, the analyst can incorporate the sensitivity analysis when calibrating the downside risks to base-case profit and cash flow forecasts.

SUMMARY

The translation of foreign currency amounts is an important accounting issue for companies with multinational operations. Foreign exchange rate fluctuations cause the functional currency values of foreign currency assets and liabilities resulting from foreign currency transactions as well as from foreign subsidiaries to change over time. These changes in value give rise to foreign exchange differences that companies' financial statements must reflect. Determining how to measure these foreign exchange differences and whether to include them in the calculation of net income are the major issues in accounting for multinational operations.

- The local currency is the national currency of the country where an entity is located. The functional currency is the currency of the primary economic environment in which an entity operates. Normally, the local currency is an entity's functional currency. For accounting purposes, any currency other than an entity's functional currency is a foreign currency for that entity. The currency in which financial statement amounts are presented is known as the presentation currency. In most cases, the presentation currency will be the same as the local currency.

- When an export sale (import purchase) on an account is denominated in a foreign currency, the sales revenue (inventory) and foreign currency account receivable (account payable) are translated into the seller's (buyer's) functional currency using the exchange rate on the transaction date. Any change in the functional currency value of the foreign currency account receivable (account payable) that occurs between the transaction date and the settlement date is recognized as a foreign currency transaction gain or loss in net income.

- If a balance sheet date falls between the transaction date and the settlement date, the foreign currency account receivable (account payable) is translated at the exchange rate at the balance sheet date. The change in the functional currency value of the foreign currency account receivable (account payable) is recognized as a foreign currency transaction gain or loss in income. Analysts should understand that these gains and losses are unrealized at the time they are recognized and might or might not be realized when the transactions are settled.
- A foreign currency transaction gain arises when an entity has a foreign currency receivable and the foreign currency strengthens or it has a foreign currency payable and the foreign currency weakens. A foreign currency transaction loss arises when an entity has a foreign currency receivable and the foreign currency weakens or it has a foreign currency payable and the foreign currency strengthens.
- Companies must disclose the net foreign currency gain or loss included in income. They may choose to report foreign currency transaction gains and losses as a component of operating income or as a component of non-operating income. If two companies choose to report foreign currency transaction gains and losses differently, operating profit and operating profit margin might not be directly comparable between the two companies.
- To prepare consolidated financial statements, foreign currency financial statements of foreign operations must be translated into the parent company's presentation currency. The major conceptual issues related to this translation process are, What is the appropriate exchange rate for translating each financial statement item, and how should the resulting translation adjustment be reflected in the consolidated financial statements? Two different translation methods are used worldwide.
- Under the current rate method, assets and liabilities are translated at the current exchange rate, equity items are translated at historical exchange rates, and revenues and expenses are translated at the exchange rate that existed when the underlying transaction occurred. For practical reasons, an average exchange rate is often used to translate income items.
- Under the temporal method, monetary assets (and non-monetary assets measured at current value) and monetary liabilities (and non-monetary liabilities measured at current value) are translated at the current exchange rate. Non-monetary assets and liabilities not measured at current value and equity items are translated at historical exchange rates. Revenues and expenses, other than those expenses related to non-monetary assets, are translated at the exchange rate that existed when the underlying transaction occurred. Expenses related to non-monetary assets are translated at the exchange rates used for the related assets.
- Under both IFRS and US GAAP, the functional currency of a foreign operation determines the method to be used in translating its foreign currency financial statements into the parent's presentation currency and whether the resulting translation adjustment is recognized in income or as a separate component of equity.
- The foreign currency financial statements of a foreign operation that has a foreign currency as its functional currency are translated using the current rate method, and the translation adjustment is accumulated as a separate component of equity. The cumulative translation adjustment related to a

Additional Disclosures on the Effects of Foreign Currency

specific foreign entity is transferred to net income when that entity is sold or otherwise disposed of. The balance sheet risk exposure associated with the current rate method is equal to the foreign subsidiary's net asset position.

- The foreign currency financial statements of a foreign operation that has the parent's presentation currency as its functional currency are translated using the temporal method, and the translation adjustment is included as a gain or loss in income. US GAAP refer to this process as remeasurement. The balance sheet exposure associated with the temporal method is equal to the foreign subsidiary's net monetary asset/liability position (adjusted for non-monetary items measured at current value).

- IFRS and US GAAP differ with respect to the translation of foreign currency financial statements of foreign operations located in a highly inflationary country. Under IFRS, the foreign currency statements are first restated for local inflation and then translated using the current exchange rate. Under US GAAP, the foreign currency financial statements are translated using the temporal method, with no restatement for inflation.

- Applying different translation methods for a given foreign operation can result in very different amounts reported in the parent's consolidated financial statements.

- Companies must disclose the total amount of translation gain or loss reported in income and the amount of translation adjustment included in a separate component of stockholders' equity. Companies are not required to separately disclose the component of translation gain or loss arising from foreign currency transactions and the component arising from application of the temporal method.

- Disclosures related to translation adjustments reported in equity can be used to include these as gains and losses in determining an adjusted amount of income following a clean-surplus approach to income measurement.

- Foreign currency translation rules are well established in both IFRS and US GAAP. Fortunately, except for the treatment of foreign operations located in highly inflationary countries, the two sets of standards have no major differences in this area. The ability to understand the impact of foreign currency translation on the financial results of a company using IFRS should apply equally well in the analysis of financial statements prepared in accordance with US GAAP.

- An analyst can obtain information about the tax impact of multinational operations from companies' disclosure on effective tax rates.

- For a multinational company, sales growth is driven not only by changes in volume and price but also by changes in the exchange rates between the reporting currency and the currency in which sales are made. Arguably, growth in sales that comes from changes in volume or price is more sustainable than growth in sales that comes from changes in exchange rates.

PRACTICE PROBLEMS

The following information relates to questions 1-9

Adrienne Yu is an analyst with an international bank. She analyzes Ambleu S.A. ("Ambleu"), a multinational corporation, for a client presentation. Ambleu complies with IFRS, and its presentation currency is the Norvoltian krone (NVK). Ambleu's two subsidiaries, Ngcorp and Cendaró, have different functional currencies: Ngcorp uses the Bindiar franc (FB) and Cendaró uses the Crenland guinea (CRG).

Yu first analyzes the following three transactions to assess foreign currency transaction exposure:

Transaction 1: Cendaró sells goods to a non-domestic customer that pays in dollars on the purchase date.

Transaction 2: Ngcorp obtains a loan in Bindiar francs on 1 June 2016 from a European bank with the Norvoltian krone as its presentation currency.

Transaction 3: Ambleu imports inventory from Bindiar under 45-day credit terms, and the payment is to be denominated in Bindiar francs.

Yu then reviews Transactions 2 and 3. She determines the method that Ambleu would use to translate Transaction 2 into its 31 December 2016 consolidated financial statements. While analyzing Transaction 3, Yu notes that Ambleu purchased inventory on 1 June 2016 for FB27,000/ton. Ambleu pays for the inventory on 15 July 2016. Exhibit 1 presents selected economic data for Bindiar and Crenland.

Exhibit 1: Selected Economic Data for Bindiar and Crenland

Date	Spot FB/NVK Exchange Rate	Bindiar Inflation Rate (%)	Spot CRG/NVK Exchange Rate	Crenland Inflation Rate (%)	Crenland GPI
31 Dec 2015	—	—	5.6780	—	100.0
1 Jun 2016	4.1779	—	—	—	—
15 Jul 2016	4.1790	—	—	—	—
31 Dec 2016	4.2374	3.1	8.6702	40.6	140.6
Average 2016	4.3450	—	—	—	—
31 Dec 2017	4.3729	2.1	14.4810	62.3	228.2
Average 2017	4.3618	—	11.5823	—	186.2

Prior to reviewing the 2016 and 2017 consolidated financial statements of Ambleu, Yu meets with her supervisor, who asks Yu the following two questions:

Question 1 Would a foreign currency translation loss reduce Ambleu's net sales growth?

Practice Problems 185

Question 2   According to IFRS, what disclosures should be included relating to Ambleu's treatment of foreign currency translation for Ngcorp?

To complete her assignment, Yu analyzes selected information and notes from Ambleu's 2016 and 2017 consolidated financial statements, presented in Exhibit 2.

Exhibit 2: Selected Information and Notes from Consolidated Financial Statements of Ambleu S.A. (in NVK millions)

Income Statement	2017	2016	Balance Sheet	2017	2016
Revenue [1]	1,069	1,034	Cash [3]	467	425
Profit before tax	294	269	Intangibles [4]	575	570
Income tax expense [2]	–96	–94	—	—	—
Net profit	198	175	—	—	—

Note 1: Cendaro's revenue for 2017 is CRG125.23 million.
Note 2:

Reconciliation of Income Tax Expense	2017 (in NVK millions)	2016 (in NVK millions)
Income tax at Ambleu's domestic tax rate	102	92
Effect of tax rates on non-domestic jurisdictions	–14	–9
Unrecognized current year tax losses	8	11
Income tax expense	96	94

Note 3: The parent company transferred NVK15 million to Cendaró on 1 January 2016 to purchase a patent from a competitor for CRG85.17 million.
Note 4: The 2016 consolidated balance sheet includes Ngcorp's total intangible assets of NVK3 million, which were added to Ngcorp's balance sheet on 15 July 2016.

1. Which transaction would generate foreign currency transaction exposure for Ambleu?

   A. Transaction 1

   B. Transaction 2

   C. Transaction 3

2. Yu's determination regarding Transaction 2 should be based on the currency of the:

   A. loan.

   B. bank.

   C. borrower.

3. Based on Exhibit 1, what is the foreign exchange gain resulting from Transaction 3 on the 31 December 2016 financial statements?

   A. NVK1.70 per ton

   B. NVK90.75 per ton

C. NVK248.54 per ton

4. What is the *best* response to Question 1?
   A. Yes
   B. No, because it would reduce organic sales growth
   C. No, because it would reduce net price realization and mix

5. Based on Exhibit 1, the *best* response to Question 2 is that Ambleu should disclose:
   A. a restatement for local inflation.
   B. that assets carried at historical cost are translated at historical rates.
   C. the amount of foreign exchange differences included in net income.

6. Based on Exhibit 1 and Note 1 in Exhibit 2, the amount that Ambleu should include in its 31 December 2017 revenue from Cendaró is *closest* to:
   A. NVK10.60 million.
   B. NVK13.25 million.
   C. NVK19.73 million.

7. Based on Exhibit 2 and Note 2, the change in Ambleu's consolidated income tax rate from 2016 to 2017 *most likely* resulted from a:
   A. decrease in Ambleu's domestic tax rate.
   B. more profitable business mix in its subsidiaries.
   C. stronger Norvoltian krone relative to the currencies of its subsidiaries.

8. Based on Exhibit 1 and Note 3 in Exhibit 2, the cumulative translation loss recognized by Ambleu related to the patent purchase on the 31 December 2017 financial statements is *closest* to:
   A. NVK0.39 million.
   B. NVK1.58 million
   C. NVK9.12 million.

9. Based on Exhibit 1 and Note 4 in Exhibit 2, the total intangible assets on Ngcorp's balance sheet as of 31 December 2016 are *closest* to:
   A. FB12.54 million.
   B. FB12.71 million.
   C. FB13.04 million.

Practice Problems

The following information relates to questions 10-16

Triofind, Inc. (Triofind), based in the country of Norvolt, provides wireless services to various countries, including Norvolt, Borliand, Abuelio, and Certait. The company's presentation currency is the Norvolt euro (NER), and Triofind complies with IFRS. Triofind has two wholly owned subsidiaries, located in Borliand and Abuelio. The Borliand subsidiary (Triofind-B) was established on 30 June 2016, by Triofind both investing NER1,000,000, which was converted into Borliand dollars (BRD), and borrowing an additional BRD500,000.

Marie Janssen, a financial analyst in Triofind's Norvolt headquarters office, translates Triofind-B's financial statements using the temporal method. Non-monetary assets are measured at cost under the lower of cost or market rule. Spot BRD/NER exchange rates are presented in Exhibit 1, and the balance sheet for Triofind-B is presented in Exhibit 2.

Exhibit 1: Spot BRD/NER Exchange Rates

Date	BRD per NER
30 June 2016	1.15
Weighted-average rate when inventory was acquired (2016)	1.19
31 December 2016	1.20
Weighted-average rate when inventory was acquired (2017)	1.18
30 June 2017	1.17

Exhibit 2: Triofind-B Balance Sheet for 2016 and 2017 (BRD)

Assets	31 December 2016	30 June 2017	Liabilities and Stockholders' Equity	31 December 2016	30 June 2017
Cash	900,000	1,350,000	Notes payable	500,000	500,000
Inventory	750,000	500,000	Common stock	1,150,000	1,150,000
			Retained earnings		200,000
Total	1,650,000	1,850,000	Total	1,650,000	1,850,000

Janssen next analyzes Triofind's Abuelio subsidiary (Triofind-A), which uses the current rate method to translate its results into Norvolt euros. Triofind-A, which prices its goods in Abuelio pesos (ABP), sells mobile phones to a customer in Certait on 31 May 2017 and receives payment of 1 million Certait rand (CRD) on 31 July 2017.

On 31 May 2017, Triofind-A also received NER50,000 from Triofind and used the funds to purchase a new warehouse in Abuelio. Janssen translates the financial statements of Triofind-A as of 31 July 2017 and must determine the appropriate value for the warehouse in Triofind's presentation currency. She observes that the cumulative Abuelio inflation rate exceeded 100% from 2015 to 2017. Spot exchange rates and inflation data are presented in Exhibit 3.

Exhibit 3: Spot Exchange Rates and Inflation Data for Triofind-A

Date	NER per CRD	NER per ABP	Abuelio Monthly Inflation Rate (%)
31 May 2017	0.2667	0.0496	—
30 June 2017	0.2703	0.0388	25
31 July 2017	0.2632	0.0312	22

Janssen gathers corporate tax rate data and company disclosure information to include in Triofind's annual report. She determines that the corporate tax rates for Abuelio, Norvolt, and Borliand are 35%, 34%, and 0%, respectively, and that Norvolt exempts the non-domestic income of multinationals from taxation. Triofind-B constitutes 25% of Triofind's net income, and Triofind-A constitutes 15%. Janssen also gathers data on components of net sales growth in different countries, presented in Exhibit 4.

Exhibit 4: Components of Net Sales Growth (%) Fiscal Year 2017

Country	Contribution from Volume Growth	Contribution from Price Growth	Foreign Currency Exchange	Net Sales Growth
Abuelio	7	6	−2	11
Borliand	4	5	4	13
Norvolt	7	3	—	10

10. Based on Exhibits 1 and 2 and Janssen's translation method, total assets for Triofind-B translated into Triofind's presentation currency as of 31 December 2016 are *closest* to:

    A. NER1,375,000.

    B. NER1,380,252.

    C. NER1,434,783.

11. Based on Exhibits 1 and 2, the translation adjustment for Triofind-B's liabilities into Triofind's presentation currency for the six months ended 31 December 2016 is:

    A. negative.

    B. zero.

    C. positive.

12. Based on Exhibits 1 and 2 and Janssen's translation method, retained earnings for Triofind-B translated into Triofind's presentation currency as of 30 June 2017 are *closest* to:

    A. NER150,225.

    B. NER170,940.

    C. NER172,414.

Practice Problems

13. The functional currency for Triofind-A's sale of mobile phones to a customer in Certait is the:

    A. Certait real.

    B. Norvolt euro.

    C. Abuelio peso.

14. Based on Exhibit 3, the value of the new warehouse in Abuelio on Triofind's balance sheet as of 31 July 2017 is *closest* to:

    A. NER31,452.

    B. NER47,964.

    C. NER50,000.

15. Relative to its domestic tax rate, Triofind's effective tax rate is *most likely*:

    A. lower.

    B. the same.

    C. higher.

16. Based on Exhibit 4, the country with the highest sustainable sales growth is:

    A. Norvolt.

    B. Abuelio.

    C. Borliand.

The following information relates to questions 17-22

Pedro Ruiz is an analyst for a credit rating agency. One of the companies he follows, Eurexim SA, is based in France and complies with International Financial Reporting Standards (IFRS). Ruiz has learned that Eurexim used EUR220 million of its own cash and borrowed an equal amount to open a subsidiary in Ukraine. The funds were converted into hryvnia (UAH) on 31 December 20X1 at an exchange rate of EUR1.00 = UAH6.70 and used to purchase UAH1,500 million in fixed assets and UAH300 million of inventories.

Ruiz is concerned about the effect that the subsidiary's results might have on Eurexim's consolidated financial statements. He calls Eurexim's Chief Financial Officer, but learns little. Eurexim is not willing to share sales forecasts and has not even made a determination as to the subsidiary's functional currency.

Absent more useful information, Ruiz decides to explore various scenarios to determine the potential impact on Eurexim's consolidated financial statements. Ukraine is not currently in a hyperinflationary environment, but Ruiz is concerned that this situation could change. Ruiz also believes the euro will appreciate against the hryvnia for the foreseeable future.

17. If Ukraine's economy becomes highly inflationary, Eurexim will *most likely* trans-

late inventory by:

A. restating for inflation and using the temporal method.

B. restating for inflation and using the current exchange rate.

C. using the temporal method with no restatement for inflation.

18. Given Ruiz's belief about the direction of exchange rates, Eurexim's gross profit margin would be *highest* if it accounts for the Ukraine subsidiary's inventory using:

A. FIFO and the temporal method.

B. FIFO and the current rate method.

C. weighted-average cost and the temporal method.

19. If the euro is chosen as the Ukraine subsidiary's functional currency, Eurexim will translate its fixed assets using the:

A. average rate for the reporting period.

B. rate in effect when the assets were purchased.

C. rate in effect at the end of the reporting period.

20. If the euro is chosen as the Ukraine subsidiary's functional currency, Eurexim will translate its accounts receivable using the:

A. rate in effect at the transaction date.

B. average rate for the reporting period.

C. rate in effect at the end of the reporting period.

21. If the hryvnia is chosen as the Ukraine subsidiary's functional currency, Eurexim will translate its inventory using the:

A. average rate for the reporting period.

B. rate in effect at the end of the reporting period.

C. rate in effect at the time the inventory was purchased.

22. Based on the information available and Ruiz's expectations regarding exchange rates, if the hryvnia is chosen as the Ukraine subsidiary's functional currency, Eurexim will *most likely* report:

A. an addition to the cumulative translation adjustment.

B. a translation gain or loss as a component of net income.

C. a subtraction from the cumulative translation adjustment.

Practice Problems

The following information relates to questions 23-28

Consolidated Motors is a US-based corporation that sells mechanical engines and components used by electric utilities. Its Canadian subsidiary, Consol-Can, operates solely in Canada. It was created on 31 December 20X1, and Consolidated Motors determined at that time that it should use the US dollar as its functional currency.

Chief Financial Officer Monica Templeton was asked to explain to the board of directors how exchange rates affect the financial statements of both Consol-Can and the consolidated financial statements of Consolidated Motors. For the presentation, Templeton collects Consol-Can's balance sheets for the years ended 20X1 and 20X2 (Exhibit 1), as well as relevant exchange rate information (Exhibit 2).

Exhibit 1: Consol-Can Condensed Balance Sheet for Fiscal Years Ending 31 December (C$ millions)

Account	20X2	20X1
Cash	135	167
Accounts receivable	98	—
Inventory	77	30
Fixed assets	100	100
Accumulated depreciation	(10)	—
Total assets	400	297
Accounts payable	77	22
Long-term debt	175	175
Common stock	100	100
Retained earnings	48	—
Total liabilities and shareholders' equity	400	297

Exhibit 2: Exchange Rate Information

	US$/C$
Rate on 31 December 20X1	0.86
Average rate in 20X2	0.92
Weighted-average rate for inventory purchases	0.92
Rate on 31 December 20X2	0.95

Templeton explains that Consol-Can uses the FIFO inventory accounting method and that purchases of C$300 million and the sell-through of that inventory occurred evenly throughout 20X2. Her presentation includes reporting the translated amounts in US dollars for each item, as well as associated translation-related gains and losses. The board responds with several questions.

- Would there be a reason to change the functional currency to the Canadian dollar?

- Would there be any translation effects for Consolidated Motors if the functional currency for Consol-Can were changed to the Canadian dollar?
- Would a change in the functional currency have any impact on financial statement ratios for the parent company?
- What would be the balance sheet exposure to translation effects if the functional currency were changed?

23. After translating Consol-Can's inventory and long-term debt into the parent company's currency (US$), the amounts reported on Consolidated Motor's financial statements on 31 December 20X2 would be *closest* to (in millions):

    A. $71 for inventory and $161 for long-term debt.

    B. $71 for inventory and $166 for long-term debt.

    C. $73 for inventory and $166 for long-term debt.

24. After translating Consol-Can's 31 December 20X2 balance sheet into the parent company's currency (US$), the translated value of retained earnings will be *closest* to:

    A. $41 million.

    B. $44 million.

    C. $46 million.

25. In response to the board's first question, Templeton would *most likely* reply that such a change would be justified if:

    A. the inflation rate in the United States became hyperinflationary.

    B. management wanted to flow more of the gains through net income.

    C. Consol-Can were making autonomous decisions about operations, investing, and financing.

26. In response to the board's second question, Templeton should reply that if the change is made, the consolidated financial statements for Consolidated Motors would begin to recognize:

    A. realized gains and losses on monetary assets and liabilities.

    B. realized gains and losses on non-monetary assets and liabilities.

    C. unrealized gains and losses on non-monetary assets and liabilities.

27. In response to the board's third question, Templeton should note that the change will *most likely* affect:

    A. the cash ratio.

    B. fixed asset turnover.

    C. receivables turnover.

28. In response to the board's fourth question, the balance sheet exposure (in C$

Practice Problems

millions) would be *closest* to:

A. –19.

B. 148.

C. 400.

The following information relates to questions 29-34

Romulus Corp. is a US-based company that prepares its financial statements in accordance with US GAAP. Romulus Corp. has two European subsidiaries: Julius and Augustus. Anthony Marks, CFA, is an analyst trying to forecast Romulus's 20X2 results. Marks has prepared separate forecasts for both Julius and Augustus, as well as for Romulus's other operations (prior to consolidating the results.) He is now considering the impact of currency translation on the results of both the subsidiaries and the parent company's consolidated financials. His research has provided the following insights:

- The results for Julius will be translated into US dollars using the current rate method.
- The results for Augustus will be translated into US dollars using the temporal method.
- Both Julius and Augustus use the FIFO method to account for inventory.
- Julius had year-end 20X1 inventory of €340 million. Marks believes Julius will report €2,300 in sales and €1,400 in cost of sales in 20X2.

Marks also forecasts the 20X2 year-end balance sheet for Julius (Exhibit 1). Data and forecasts related to euro/dollar exchange rates are presented in Exhibit 2.

Exhibit 1: Forecasted Balance Sheet Data for Julius, 31 December 20X2 (€ millions)	
Cash	50
Accounts receivable	100
Inventory	700
Fixed assets	1,450
Total assets	2,300
Liabilities	700
Common stock	1,500
Retained earnings	100
Total liabilities and shareholder equity	2,300

Exhibit 2: Exchange Rates ($/€)	
31 December 20X1	1.47
31 December 20X2	1.61

20X2 average	1.54
Rate when fixed assets were acquired	1.25
Rate when 20X1 inventory was acquired	1.39
Rate when 20X2 inventory was acquired	1.49

29. Based on the translation method being used for Julius, the subsidiary is *most likely*:

    A. a sales outlet for Romulus's products.

    B. a self-contained, independent operating entity.

    C. using the US dollar as its functional currency.

30. To account for its foreign operations, Romulus has *most likely* designated the euro as the functional currency for:

    A. Julius only.

    B. Augustus only.

    C. both Julius and Augustus.

31. When Romulus consolidates the results of Julius, any unrealized exchange rate holding gains on monetary assets should be:

    A. reported as part of operating income.

    B. reported as a non-operating item on the income statement.

    C. reported directly to equity as part of the cumulative translation adjustment.

32. When Marks translates his forecasted balance sheet for Julius into US dollars, total assets as of 31 December 20X2 (dollars in millions) will be *closest* to:

    A. $1,429.

    B. $2,392.

    C. $3,703.

33. When Marks converts his forecasted income statement data for Julius into US dollars, the 20X2 gross profit margin will be *closest* to:

    A. 39.1%.

    B. 40.9%.

    C. 44.6%.

34. Relative to the gross margins the subsidiaries report in local currency, Romulus's consolidated gross margin *most likely*:

    A. will not be distorted by currency translations.

    B. would be distorted if Augustus were using the same translation method as Julius.

Practice Problems

C. will be distorted because of the translation and inventory accounting methods Augustus is using.

The following information relates to questions 35-40

Redline Products, Inc. is a US-based multinational with subsidiaries around the world. One such subsidiary, Acceletron, operates in Singapore, which has seen mild but not excessive rates of inflation. Acceletron was acquired in 2000 and has never paid a dividend. It records inventory using the FIFO method.

Chief Financial Officer Margot Villiers was asked by Redline's board of directors to explain how the functional currency selection and other accounting choices affect Redline's consolidated financial statements. Villiers gathers Acceletron's financial statements denominated in Singapore dollars (SGD) in Exhibit 1 and the US dollar/Singapore dollar exchange rates in Exhibit 2. She does not intend to identify the functional currency actually in use but rather to use Acceletron as an example of how the choice of functional currency affects the consolidated statements.

Exhibit 1: Selected Financial Data for Acceletron, 31 December 2007 (SGD millions)

Cash	SGD125
Accounts receivable	230
Inventory	500
Fixed assets	1,640
Accumulated depreciation	(205)
Total assets	SGD2,290
Accounts payable	185
Long-term debt	200
Common stock	620
Retained earnings	1,285
Total liabilities and equity	2,290
Total revenues	SGD4,800
Net income	SGD450

Exhibit 2: Exchange Rates Applicable to Acceletron

Exchange Rate in Effect at Specific Times	USD per SGD
Rate when first SGD1 billion of fixed assets were acquired	0.568
Rate when remaining SGD640 million of fixed assets were acquired	0.606
Rate when long-term debt was issued	0.588
31 December 2006	0.649
Weighted-average rate when inventory was acquired	0.654
Average rate in 2007	0.662

Exchange Rate in Effect at Specific Times	USD per SGD
31 December 2007	0.671

35. Compared with using the Singapore dollar as Acceletron's functional currency for 2007, if the US dollar were the functional currency, it is *most likely* that Redline's consolidated:

    A. inventories will be higher.

    B. receivable turnover will be lower.

    C. fixed asset turnover will be higher.

36. If the US dollar were chosen as the functional currency for Acceletron in 2007, Redline could reduce its balance sheet exposure to exchange rates by:

    A. selling SGD30 million of fixed assets for cash.

    B. issuing SGD30 million of long-term debt to buy fixed assets.

    C. issuing SGD30 million in short-term debt to purchase marketable securities.

37. Redline's consolidated gross profit margin for 2007 would be *highest* if Acceletron accounted for inventory using:

    A. FIFO, and its functional currency were the US dollar.

    B. LIFO, and its functional currency were the US dollar.

    C. FIFO, and its functional currency were the Singapore dollar.

38. If the current rate method is used to translate Acceletron's financial statements into US dollars, Redline's consolidated financial statements will *most likely* include Acceletron's:

    A. USD3,178 million in revenues.

    B. USD118 million in long-term debt.

    C. negative translation adjustment to shareholder equity.

39. If Acceletron's financial statements are translated into US dollars using the temporal method, Redline's consolidated financial statements will *most likely* include Acceletron's:

    A. USD336 million in inventory.

    B. USD956 million in fixed assets.

    C. USD152 million in accounts receivable.

40. When translating Acceletron's financial statements into US dollars, Redline is *least likely* to use an exchange rate of USD per SGD:

    A. 0.671.

    B. 0.588.

    C. 0.654.

SOLUTIONS

1. C is correct. In Transaction 3, the payment for the inventory is due in Bindiar francs, a different currency from the Norvoltian krone, which is Ambleu's presentation currency. Because the import purchase (account payable) is under 45-day credit terms, Ambleu has foreign currency transaction exposure. The payment is subject to fluctuations in the FB/NVK exchange rate during the 45-day period between the sale and payment dates. Thus, Ambleu is exposed to potential foreign currency gains if the Bindiar franc weakens against the Norvoltian krone or foreign currency losses if the Bindiar franc strengthens against the Norvoltian krone.

2. C is correct. The currency of Ngcorp as the borrowing foreign subsidiary, relative to that of Ambleu, determines Ambleu's choice of translation method for Transaction 2. Because Ngcorp's functional currency is the Bindiar franc and Ambleu's presentation currency is the Norvoltian krone, the current rate method rather than the temporal method should be used. Regardless of the currency in which the loan is denominated, the loan is first recorded in Ngcorp's financial statements. Then, Ngcorp's financial statements, which include the bank loan, are translated into Ambleu's consolidated financial statements.

3. A is correct. On Ambleu's balance sheet, the cost included in the inventory account is the translation of FB27,000/ton into Norvoltian krone on the purchase date. Ambleu could have paid this amount on the purchase date but chose to wait 45 days to settle the account. The inventory cost is determined using the FB/NVK exchange rate of 4.1779 on the purchase date of 1 June 2016. FB27,000/FB4.1779/NVK = NVK6,462.58/ton

    The cash outflow is the amount exchanged from the Norvoltian krone to the Bindiar franc to pay the FB27,000/ton owed for the inventory 45 days after the transaction date. This payment uses the FB/NVK exchange rate of 4.1790 on the settlement date of 15 July 2016.

    FB 27,000/FB4.1790 per NVK = NVK6,460.88/ton

    Foreign exchange gain = Inventory cost − Cash payment

    = NVK6,462.58 − NVK6,460.88

    = NVK1.70/ton

    Thus, Ambleu's cash outflow is less than the cost included in the inventory account, and NVK1.70/ton is the realized foreign exchange gain relating to this transaction. By deferring payment for 45 days, and because the Bindiar franc decreased in value during this period, Ambleu pays NVK1.70/ton less than the inventory cost on the purchase date of 1 June 2016. Thus, Ambleu will report a foreign exchange gain in its 2016 net income.

4. A is correct. Net sales growth equals organic sales growth plus or minus the effects of acquisitions, divestitures, and foreign exchange. A foreign currency translation loss would reduce net sales growth. Thus the answer to Question 1 is yes.

5. C is correct. IFRS requires that Ambleu disclose "the amount of exchange differences recognized in profit or loss" when determining net income for the period. Because companies may present foreign currency transaction gains and losses in various places on the income statement, it is useful for companies to disclose

both the amount of transaction gain or loss that is included in income as well as the presentation alternative used.

6. A is correct. Crenland experienced hyperinflation from 31 December 2015 to 31 December 2017, as shown by the General Price Index, with cumulative inflation of 128.2% during this period. According to IFRS, Cendaró's financial statements must be restated for local inflation, then translated into Norvoltian kroner using the current exchange rate. The 2017 revenue from Cendaró that should be included in Ambleu's income statement is calculated as follows:

Revenue in CRG × (GPI 31 December 2017/GPI average 2017)

= Inflation-adjusted revenue in CRG

CRG125.23 million × (228.2/186.2) = CRG153.48 million

Inflation-adjusted revenue in CRG/31 December 2017 exchange rate (CRG/NVK)

= Revenue in Norvoltian kroner

CRG153.48 million/14.4810 = NVK10.60 million

7. B is correct. The consolidated income tax rate is calculated as income tax expense divided by profit before tax. Note 2 shows that Ambleu's consolidated income tax rate decreases by 2.29%, from 34.94% (=94/269) in 2016 to 32.65% (=96/294) in 2017. The largest component of the decrease stems from the 1.42% change in the effect of tax rates in non-domestic jurisdictions, which lowers Ambleu's consolidated income tax rate in 2016 by 3.34% (=9/269) and in 2017 by 4.76% (=14/294). The decrease in 2017 could indicate that Ambleu's business mix shifted to countries with lower marginal tax rates, resulting in a lower consolidated income tax rate and more profit. (The change could also indicate that the marginal tax rates decreased in the countries in which Ambleu earns profits.)

8. B is correct. IAS 29 indicates that a cumulative inflation rate approaching or exceeding 100% over three years would be an indicator of hyperinflation. Because the cumulative inflation rate for 2016 and 2017 in Crenland was 128.2%, Cendaró's accounts must first be restated for local inflation. Then, the inflation-restated Crenland guinea financial statements can be translated into Ambleu's presentation currency, the Norvoltian krone, using the current exchange rate.

Using this approach, the cumulative translation loss on 31 December 2017 for the CRG85.17 million patent purchase is –NVK1.58 million, as shown in the following table.

Date	Inflation Rate (%)	Restated Carrying Value (CRG/MM)	Current Exchange Rate (CRG/NVK)	Translated Amount (NVK MM)	Annual Translation Gain/Loss (NVK MM)	Cumulative Translation Gain/Loss (NVK MM)
1 Jan 2016	—	85.17	5.6780	15.00	N/A	N/A
31 Dec 2016	40.6	119.75	8.6702	13.81	–1.19	–1.19
31 Dec 2017	62.3	194.35	14.4810	13.42	–0.39	–1.58

9. B is correct. Because Ngcorp has a functional currency that is different from Ambleu's presentation currency, the intangible assets are translated into Norvoltian kroner using the current rate method. The current FB/NVK exchange rate is 4.2374 as of 31 December 2016. Thus, the intangible assets on Ngcorp's 2016 balance sheet are NVK3 million × FB4.2374/NVK = FB12.71 million.

Solutions

10. B is correct. Using the temporal method, monetary assets (i.e., cash) are translated using the current exchange rate (as of 31 December 2016) of BRD1.20/NER (or NER0.8333/BRD), and non-monetary assets are translated using the historical exchange rate when acquired. Inventory is translated at its 2016 weighted-average rate of BRD1.19/NER (or NER0.8403/BRD). Therefore, the total assets for Triofind-B translated into Norvolt euros (Triofind's presentation currency) as of 31 December 2016 are calculated as follows:

Assets	31 December 2016 (BRD)	Applicable Exchange Rate (NER/BRD)	Rate Used	NER
Cash	900,000	0.8333	Current	750,000
Inventory	750,000	0.8403	Average	630,252
Total	1,650,000			1,380,252

11. A is correct. The monetary balance sheet items for Triofind-B are translated at the current exchange rate, which reflects that the Borliand dollar weakened during the period relative to the Norvolt euro. The rate as of 30 June 2016 was BRD1.15/NER (or NER/BRD0.8696) and as of 31 December 2016 was BRD1.20/NER (or NER/BRD0.8333). Therefore, notes payable translates to NER416,667 (BRD500,000 × NER/BRD0.8333) as of 31 December 2016, compared with NER434,783 (BRD500,000 × NER/BRD0.8696) as of 30 June 2016. Thus, the translation adjustment for liabilities is negative.

12. A is correct. Triofind uses the temporal method to translate the financial statements of Triofind-B. The temporal method uses the current exchange rate for translating monetary assets and liabilities and the historical exchange rate (based on the date when the assets were acquired) for non-monetary assets and liabilities. Monetary assets and liabilities are translated using the current exchange rate (as of 30 June 2017) of NER1 = BRD1.17 (or NER0.8547/BRD), and non-monetary assets and liabilities are translated using the historical exchange rate (as of 30 June 2016) of NER1 = BRD1.15 (or NER0.8696/BRD). Inventory is translated at the 2017 weighted average rate of NER1 = BRD1.18 (or NER0.8475/BRD). The difference required to maintain equality between (a) total assets and (b) total liabilities and shareholder's equity is then recorded as retained earnings. The retained earnings for Triofind-B translated into Norvolt euros (Triofind's presentation currency) as of 30 June 2017 is calculated as follows:

Assets	30 June 2017 (BRD)	Exchange Rate (NER/BRD)	Rate Used	30 June 2017 (NER)	Liabilities and Stockholders' Equity	30 June 2017 (BRD)	Exchange Rate (NER/BRD)	Rate Used	30 June 2017 (NER)
Cash	1,350,000	0.8547	C	1,153,846	Notes Payable	500,000	0.8547	C	427,350
Inventory	500,000	0.8475	H	423,729	Common Stock	1,150,000	0.8696	H	1,000,000
					Retained Earnings	200,000			150,225
	1,850,000			1,577,575	Total	1,850,000			1,577,575

13. C is correct. The functional currency is the currency of the primary economic environment in which an entity operates. Abuelio is Triofind-A's primary economic environment, and its currency is the Abuelio peso (ABP). Another important factor used to determine the functional currency is the currency that mainly influ-

ences sales prices for goods and services. The fact that Triofind-A prices its goods in Abuelio pesos supports the case for the ABP to be the functional currency.

14. B is correct. Triofind complies with IFRS, and Abuelio can be considered a highly inflationary economy because its cumulative inflation rate exceeded 100% from 2015 to 2017. Thus, Triofind-A's financials must be restated to include local inflation rates and then translated using the current exchange rate into Norvolt euros, which is Triofind's presentation currency. This approach reflects both the likely change in the local currency value of the warehouse as well as the actual change in the exchange rate. The original purchase price is ABP1,008,065 (NER50,000/ABP0.0496). The value of the new warehouse in Abuelio as of 31 July 2017 is NER47,964, calculated as follows:

Date	Abuelio Monthly Inflation Rate (%)	Restated Warehouse Value (ABP)	NER/ABP	Warehouse Value (NER)
31 May 2017		1,008,065	0.0496	50,000
30 June 2017	25	1,260,081	0.0388	48,891
31 July 2017	22	1,537,298	0.0312	47,964

15. A is correct. Norvolt exempts the non-domestic income of multinationals from taxation. Because Norvolt has a corporate tax rate of 34%, the 0% tax rate in Borliand and the fact that 25% of Triofind's net income comes from Borliand should result in a lower effective tax rate on Triofind's consolidated financial statements compared with Triofind's domestic tax rate. Abuelio's tax rate of 35% is very close to that of Norvolt, and it constitutes only 15% of Triofind's net income, so its effect is unlikely to be significant.

16. B is correct. Although Borliand shows the highest growth in Norvolt euro terms, this result is partially because of currency fluctuations, which cannot be controlled. Abuelio had the highest change in sales resulting from price and volume at 13% (excluding foreign currency exchange). This growth is more sustainable than net sales growth, which includes currency fluctuations, because Triofind's management has more control over growth in sales resulting from greater volume or higher prices.

17. B is correct. IAS 21 requires that the financial statements of the foreign entity first be restated for local inflation using the procedures outlined in IAS 29, "Financial Reporting in Hyperinflationary Economies." Then, the inflation-restated foreign currency financial statements are translated into the parent's presentation currency using the current exchange rate. Under US GAAP, the temporal method would be used with no restatement.

18. B is correct. Ruiz expects the EUR to appreciate against the UAH and expects some inflation in the Ukraine. In an inflationary environment, FIFO will generate a higher gross profit than weighted-average cost. For either inventory choice, the current rate method will give higher gross profit to the parent company if the subsidiary's currency is depreciating. Thus, using FIFO and translating using the current rate method will generate a higher gross profit for the parent company, Eurexim SA, than any other combination of choices.

19. B is correct. If the parent's currency is chosen as the functional currency, the temporal method must be used. Under the temporal method, fixed assets are translated using the rate in effect at the time the assets were acquired.

Solutions

20. C is correct. Monetary assets and liabilities such as accounts receivable are translated at current (end-of-period) rates regardless of whether the temporal or current rate method is used.

21. B is correct. When the foreign currency is chosen as the functional currency, the current rate method is used. All assets and liabilities are translated at the current (end-of-period) rate.

22. C is correct. When the foreign currency is chosen as the functional currency, the current rate method must be used and all gains or losses from translation are reported as a cumulative translation adjustment to shareholder equity. When the foreign currency decreases in value (weakens), the current rate method results in a negative translation adjustment in stockholders' equity.

23. B is correct. When the parent company's currency is used as the functional currency, the temporal method must be used to translate the subsidiary's accounts. Under the temporal method, monetary assets and liabilities (e.g., debt) are translated at the current (year-end) rate, non-monetary assets and liabilities measured at historical cost (e.g., inventory) are translated at historical exchange rates, and non-monetary assets and liabilities measured at current value are translated at the exchange rate at the date when the current value was determined. Because beginning inventory was sold first and sales and purchases were evenly acquired, the average rate is most appropriate for translating inventory and C$77 million × 0.92 = $71 million. Long-term debt is translated at the year-end rate of 0.95. C$175 million × 0.95 = $166 million.

24. B is correct. Translating the 20X2 balance sheet using the temporal method, as is required in this instance, results in assets of US$369 million. The translated liabilities and common stock are equal to US$325 million, meaning that the value for 20X2 retained earnings is US$369 million – US$325 million = US$44 million.

Temporal Method (20X2)

Account	C$	Rate	US$
Cash	135	0.95	128
Accounts receivable	98	0.95	93
Inventory	77	0.92	71
Fixed assets	100	0.86	86
Accumulated depreciation	(10)	0.86	(9)
Total assets	400		369
Accounts payable	77	0.95	73
Long-term debt	175	0.95	166
Common stock	100	0.86	86
Retained earnings	48	to balance	44
Total liabilities and shareholders' equity	400		369

25. C is correct. The Canadian dollar would be the appropriate reporting currency when substantially all operating, financing, and investing decisions are based on the local currency. The parent country's inflation rate is never relevant. Earnings manipulation is not justified, and at any rate changing the functional currency would take the gains off of the income statement.

26. C is correct. If the functional currency were changed from the parent currency (US dollar) to the local currency (Canadian dollar), the current rate method

would replace the temporal method. The temporal method ignores unrealized gains and losses on non-monetary assets and liabilities, but the current rate method does not.

27. B is correct. If the Canadian dollar is chosen as the functional currency, the current rate method will be used and the current exchange rate will be the rate used to translate all assets and liabilities. Currently, only monetary assets and liabilities are translated at the current rate. Sales are translated at the average rate during the year under either method. Fixed assets are translated using the historical rate under the temporal method but would switch to current rates under the current rate method. Therefore, there will most likely be an effect on sales/fixed assets. Because the cash ratio involves only monetary assets and liabilities, it is unaffected by the translation method. Receivables turnover pairs a monetary asset with sales and is thus also unaffected.

28. B is correct. If the functional currency were changed, then Consol-Can would use the current rate method and the balance sheet exposure would be equal to net assets (total assets − total liabilities). In this case, 400 − 77 − 175 = 148.

29. B is correct. Julius is using the current rate method, which is most appropriate when it is operating with a high degree of autonomy.

30. A is correct. If the current rate method is being used (as it is for Julius), the local currency (euro) is the functional currency. When the temporal method is being used (as it is for Augustus), the parent company's currency (US dollar) is the functional currency.

31. C is correct. When the current rate method is being used, all currency gains and losses are recorded as a cumulative translation adjustment to shareholder equity.

32. C is correct. Under the current rate method, all assets are translated using the year-end 20X2 (current) rate of $1.61/€1.00. €2,300 × 1.61 = $3,703.

33. A is correct. Under the current rate method, both sales and cost of goods sold would be translated at the 20X2 average exchange rate. The ratio would be the same as reported under the euro. €2,300 − €1,400 = €900, €900/€2,300 = 39.1%. Or, $3,542 − $2,156 = $1,386, $1,386/$3,542 = 39.1%.

34. C is correct. Augustus is using the temporal method in conjunction with FIFO inventory accounting. If FIFO is used, ending inventory is assumed to be composed of the most recently acquired items, and thus inventory will be translated at relatively recent exchange rates. To the extent that the average weight used to translate sales differs from the historical rate used to translate inventories, the gross margin will be distorted when translated into US dollars.

35. C is correct. If the US dollar is the functional currency, the temporal method must be used. Revenues and receivables (monetary asset) would be the same under either accounting method. Inventory and fixed assets were purchased when the US dollar was stronger, so at historical rates (temporal method), translated they would be lower. Identical revenues/lower fixed assets would result in higher fixed-asset turnover.

36. A is correct. If the US dollar is the functional currency, the temporal method must be used, and the balance sheet exposure will be the net monetary assets of 125 + 230 − 185 − 200 = −30, or a net monetary liability of SGD30 million. This net monetary liability would be eliminated if fixed assets (non-monetary) were sold to increase cash. Issuing debt, either short-term or long-term, would increase the net monetary liability.

37. A is correct. Because the US dollar has been consistently weakening against the Singapore dollar, cost of sales will be lower and gross profit higher when an earlier exchange rate is used to translate inventory, compared with using current exchange rates. If the Singapore dollar is the functional currency, current rates would be used. Therefore, the combination of the US dollar (temporal method) and FIFO will result in the highest gross profit margin.

38. A is correct. Under the current rate method, revenue is translated at the average rate for the year, SGD4,800 × 0.662 = USD3,178 million. Debt should be translated at the current rate, SGD200 × 0.671 = USD134 million. Under the current rate method, Acceletron would have a net asset balance sheet exposure. Because the Singapore dollar has been strengthening against the US dollar, the translation adjustment would be positive rather than negative.

39. B is correct. Under the temporal method, inventory and fixed assets would be translated using historical rates. Accounts receivable is a monetary asset and would be translated at year-end (current) rates. Fixed assets are found as (1,000 × 0.568) + (640 × 0.606) = USD 956 million.

40. B is correct. USD0.671/SGD is the current exchange rate. That rate would be used regardless of whether Acceletron uses the current rate or temporal method. USD0.654 was the weighted-average rate when inventory was acquired. That rate would be used if the company translated its statements under the temporal method but not the current rate method. USD0.588/SGD was the exchange rate in effect when long-term debt was issued. As a monetary liability, long-term debt is always translated using current exchange rates. Consequently, that rate is not applicable regardless of how Acceletron translates its financial statements.

LEARNING MODULE

4

Analysis of Financial Institutions

by Jack T. Ciesielski, CPA, CFA, and Elaine Henry, PhD, CFA.

Jack T. Ciesielski, CPA, CFA, is at R.G. Associates, Inc., former publisher of The Analyst's Accounting Observer (USA). Elaine Henry, PhD, CFA, is at Stevens Institute of Technology (USA).

LEARNING OUTCOMES

Mastery	The candidate should be able to:
☐	describe how financial institutions differ from other companies
☐	describe key aspects of financial regulations of financial institutions
☐	explain the CAMELS (capital adequacy, asset quality, management, earnings, liquidity, and sensitivity) approach to analyzing a bank, including key ratios and its limitations
☐	analyze a bank based on financial statements and other factors
☐	describe other factors to consider in analyzing a bank
☐	describe key ratios and other factors to consider in analyzing an insurance company

INTRODUCTION 1

☐ describe how financial institutions differ from other companies
☐ describe key aspects of financial regulations of financial institutions

Financial institutions provide a wide range of financial products and services. They serve as intermediaries between providers and recipients of capital, facilitate asset and risk management, and execute transactions involving cash, securities, and other financial assets.

Given the diversity of financial services, it is unsurprising that numerous types of financial institutions exist. Types of financial institutions include deposit-taking, loan-making institutions (referred to as *banks* in this reading), investment banks, credit card companies, brokers, dealers, exchanges, clearing houses, depositories, investment managers, financial advisers, and insurance companies. In many situations, overlap of services exists across types of institutions. For example, banks not only take deposits and make loans but also may undertake investment management and other securities-related activities and may offer such products as derivatives, which are effectively insurance against adverse effects of movements in the interest rate, equity, and foreign currency markets. As another example of overlap, life insurance companies not only provide mortality-related insurance products but also offer savings vehicles. This reading focuses primarily on two types of financial institutions: banks (broadly defined as deposit-taking, loan-making institutions) and insurance companies.

Section 2 explains what makes financial institutions different from other types of companies, such as manufacturers or merchandisers. Section 3 discusses how to analyze a bank. Section 4 focuses on analyzing insurance companies. A summary of key points concludes the reading.

What Makes Financial Institutions Different?

A distinctive feature of financial institutions—in particular, banks—is their systemic importance, which means that their smooth functioning is essential to the overall health of an economy. The most fundamental role of banks is to serve as intermediaries, accepting deposits from capital providers and providing capital via loans to borrowers. Their role as intermediaries between and among providers and recipients of capital creates financial inter-linkages across all types of entities, including households, banks, corporations, and governments. The network of inter-linkages across entities means that the failure of one bank will negatively affect other financial and non-financial entities. The larger the bank and the more widespread its inter-linkages, the greater its potential impact on the entire financial system. If an extremely large bank were to fail, the negative impact of its failure could spread and potentially result in the failure of the entire financial system.

Systemic risk has been defined as "a risk of disruption to financial services that is (i) caused by an impairment of all or parts of the financial system and (ii) has the potential to have serious negative consequences for the economy as a whole. Fundamental to the definition is the notion of contagion across the economy from a disruption or failure in a financial institution, market or instrument. All types of financial intermediaries, markets and infrastructure can potentially be systemically important to some degree."[1] The problem of systemic risk (the risk of failure of the financial system as a result of the failure of a major financial institution) has emerged as an issue in many countries around the world in the aftermath of the 2008 global financial crisis. *Financial contagion* is a situation in which financial shocks spread from their place or sector of origin to other locales or sectors. Globally, a faltering economy may infect other, healthier economies.

Because of their systemic importance, financial institutions' activities are heavily regulated. Regulations attempt to constrain excessive risk taking that could cause an entity to fail. Regulations address various aspects of a financial institution's operations, including the amount of capital that must be maintained, the minimum liquidity, and the riskiness of assets.

The liabilities of most banks are made up primarily of deposits. For example, as of December 2016, deposits constituted over 80% of the total liabilities of domestically chartered commercial banks in the United States.[2] The failure of a bank to honor its

---

[1] "Guidance to Assess the Systemic Importance of Financial Institutions, Markets and Instruments: Initial Considerations," report to the G–20 finance ministers and central bank governors, prepared by the staff of the International Monetary Fund and the Bank for International Settlements and the secretariat of the Financial Stability Board (October 2009): https://www.imf.org/external/np/g20/pdf/100109.pdf.
[2] "Assets and Liabilities of Commercial Banks in the United States - H.8," Federal Reserve statistical release (https://www.federalreserve.gov).

Introduction

deposits could have negative consequences across the economy. Even the expectation that a bank might not be able to honor its deposits could cause depositors to withdraw their money from the bank, and a large sudden withdrawal of deposits (a bank run) could cause an actual failure and financial contagion across the economy. Therefore, deposits are often insured (up to a stated limit) by the government of the country in which the bank operates.

Another distinctive feature of financial institutions is that their assets are predominantly financial assets, such as loans and securities. In contrast, the assets of most non-financial companies are predominantly tangible assets. Financial assets create direct exposure to a different variety of risks, including credit risks, liquidity risks, market risks, and interest rate risks. Unlike many tangible assets, financial assets are often measured at fair market value for financial reporting.

This reading focuses on the financial analysis of banks and insurers (property and casualty insurers and life and health insurers). There are many other types of financial institutions, including different types of depository institutions. Some of these other financial institutions are described briefly in Exhibit 1. Note that the list in Exhibit 1 includes types of entities that an analyst may evaluate for potential investment and, therefore, excludes supra-national organizations. Typically, supra-national entities are formed by member countries to focus on lending activities in support of specific missions. For example, the World Bank—whose mission is to reduce poverty and support development globally—comprises 189 member countries and provides loans and grants through the International Bank for Reconstruction and Development and the International Development Association.[3] Other prominent examples of supra-national entities are the Asian Development and Asian Infrastructure Investment Bank.

Exhibit 1: A Sampling of Financial Institutions

The list that follows is illustrative only and should not be viewed as comprehensive. The list is organized by primary activity, but many service overlaps exist. Additionally, the structure of financial service providers differs across countries, and state ownership of financial institutions is more common in some countries.

Institutions That Provide Basic Banking Services

- **Commercial banks.** This term generally refers to institutions whose business focuses on classic banking services, such as taking deposits, making loans, and facilitating payment transactions. Historically, regulation in some countries, such as the United States and France, created distinctions between commercial banking activities (e.g., deposit taking and loan making), insurance activities, and investment banking activities, such as securities underwriting, trading, and investing. In general, this distinction has been declining. For example, in France, regulations beginning in the mid-1980s eliminated many restrictions on banks' allowable types of activities, and in the United States, a 1999 law granted commercial banks the ability to undertake broad-based securities and insurance activities.[4] Germany's universal banks provide commercial banking, investment banking, insurance, and other financial and non-financial services, and Spain's leading commercial banks are "dominant in cross-selling mutual funds to their retail clients."[5]

---

[3] www.worldbank.org.
[4] Berger, Allen N., Phillip Molyneux, and John O.S. Wilson, *The Oxford Handbook of Banking* (Oxford, UK: Oxford University Press, 2009).
[5] Berger et al., *The Oxford Handbook of Banking*.

Japanese banks are permitted to engage in a range of activities including equity ownership in non-financial corporations (within limits) that strengthens their role in corporate governance beyond that typical of a creditor.[6]

- **Credit unions, cooperative and mutual banks.** These are depository institutions that function like banks and offer many of the same services as banks. They are owned by their members, rather than being publicly traded like many banks. Another difference from commercial banks is that these institutions are organized as non-profits and, therefore, do not pay income taxes.
- **Specialized financial service providers.**
  - **Building societies** and **savings and loan associations** are depository institutions that specialize in financing long-term residential mortgages.
  - **Mortgage banks** originate, sell, and service mortgages and are usually active participants in the securitization markets.
  - **Trust banks (Japan)** are commercial banks, and because their deposits are in the form of "money trusts" (typically with three- to five-year terms and one-year minimums), they can make long-term commercial loans and securities investments. Japan also has city banks (universal banks), regional banks, second regional banks, and Shinkin banks and credit cooperatives (which provide commercial banking services to their members—smaller enterprises and individuals).[7]
  - **Online payment companies**, such as Paypal (United States), Alipay (China), and other non-bank online payment companies, have expanded rapidly and continue to broaden service offerings.

Intermediaries within the Investment Industry

Within this category, services offered by different entities are particularly varied. A few of these are described briefly below.

- *Managers of pooled investment vehicles, such as open-end mutual funds, closed-end funds, and exchange-traded funds.* These financial institutions pool money from investors and buy and sell securities and other assets. The investors share ownership in the investment vehicle. Pooled investment vehicles, as required by regulation, disclose their investment policies, deposit and redemption procedures, fees and expenses, past performance statistics, and other information.
- *Hedge funds.* These funds also pool investors' money and invest it. They tend to follow more complex strategies; be less transparent, less liquid, and less regulated; and have higher fees and higher minimum investment amounts than open-end mutual funds, closed-end funds, and exchange-traded funds.
- *Brokers and dealers.* These firms facilitate trade in securities, earning a commission or spread on the trades.

---

[6] Berger et al., *The Oxford Handbook of Banking*.
[7] Berger et al., *The Oxford Handbook of Banking*.

Insurers

- **Property and casualty (P&C) insurance companies** provide protection against adverse events related to autos, homes, or commercial activities.
- **Life and health (L&H) insurers** provide mortality- and health-related insurance products. Life insurance companies also provide savings products.
- **Reinsurance companies** sell insurance to insurers. Rather than paying policyholder claims directly, they reimburse insurance companies for claims paid.[8]

Global Organizations

With respect to global systemic risk, important differences exist between the banking and insurance sectors.[9] Unlike banks, the overall insurance market has a smaller proportion of cross-border business, although the reinsurance business is largely international. The international aspect of the reinsurance business increases the importance of the insurance sector to the global financial system: Reinsurers may be an international link to financial institutions domiciled in different parts of the world, thereby increasing systemic vulnerability. Another important difference is that insurance companies' foreign branches are generally required to hold assets in a jurisdiction that are adequate to cover the related policy liabilities in that jurisdiction.

Aside from minimizing systemic risk, other reasons for the establishment of global and regional regulatory bodies include the harmonization and globalization of regulatory rules, standards, and oversight. Consistency of standards and regulations helps minimize regulatory arbitrage (whereby multinational companies capitalize on differences in jurisdictions' regulatory systems in order to avoid unfavorable regulation) around the world.

One of the most important global organizations focused on financial stability is the Basel Committee on Banking Supervision, which was established in 1974 and is a standing committee hosted and supported by the Bank for International Settlements. Members of the Basel Committee include central banks and entities responsible for supervising banks. The list of members of the Basel Committee in Exhibit 2 illustrates the range of entities involved with supervising banking activity in different countries and jurisdictions.

Exhibit 2: Members of the Basel Committee as of July 2017

Country/Jurisdiction	Institutional Representative
Argentina	Central Bank of Argentina
Australia	Reserve Bank of Australia
	Australian Prudential Regulation Authority
Belgium	National Bank of Belgium
Brazil	Central Bank of Brazil

---

8 Insurance Information Institute (www.iii.org).
9 "Core Principles: Cross-Sectoral Comparison," report by the Joint Forum (Basel Committee on Banking Supervision, International Organization of Securities Commissions, and International Association of Insurance Supervisors; November 2001): https://www.iaisweb.org/page/supervisory-material/joint-forum//file/34300/core-principles-cross-sectoral-comparison.

Country/Jurisdiction	Institutional Representative
Canada	Bank of Canada Office of the Superintendent of Financial Institutions
Chinese mainland	People's Bank of China China Banking Regulatory Commission
European Union	European Central Bank European Central Bank Single Supervisory Mechanism
France	Bank of France Prudential Supervision and Resolution Authority
Germany	Deutsche Bundesbank (Central Bank of Germany) Federal Financial Supervisory Authority (BaFin)
Hong Kong SAR	Hong Kong Monetary Authority
India	Reserve Bank of India
Indonesia	Bank Indonesia Indonesia Financial Services Authority
Italy	Bank of Italy
Japan	Bank of Japan Financial Services Agency
Korea	Bank of Korea Financial Supervisory Service
Luxembourg	Surveillance Commission for the Financial Sector
Mexico	Bank of Mexico Comisión Nacional Bancaria y de Valores (National Banking and Securities Commission)
Netherlands	Netherlands Bank
Russia	Central Bank of the Russian Federation
Saudi Arabia	Saudi Arabian Monetary Agency
Singapore	Monetary Authority of Singapore
South Africa	South African Reserve Bank
Spain	Bank of Spain
Sweden	Sveriges Riksbank (Central Bank of Sweden) Finansinspektionen (Financial Supervisory Authority)
Switzerland	Swiss National Bank Swiss Financial Market Supervisory Authority FINMA
Turkey	Central Bank of the Republic of Turkey Banking Regulation and Supervision Agency
United Kingdom	Bank of England Prudential Regulation Authority
United States	Board of Governors of the Federal Reserve System Federal Reserve Bank of New York Office of the Comptroller of the Currency Federal Deposit Insurance Corporation

Observers

Country/Jurisdiction	Institutional representative
Chile	Central Bank of Chile Banking and Financial Institutions Supervisory Agency
Malaysia	Central Bank of Malaysia

Introduction

Observers	
Country/Jurisdiction	**Institutional representative**
United Arab Emirates	Central Bank of the United Arab Emirates

Source: www.bis.org.

The Basel Committee developed the international regulatory framework for banks known as Basel III, which is the enhanced framework succeeding Basel I and Basel II. The purposes of the measures contained in Basel III are the following: "to improve the banking sector's ability to absorb shocks arising from financial and economic stress, whatever the source, improve risk management and governance, and strengthen banks' transparency and disclosures."[10]

Three important highlights of Basel III are the minimum capital requirement, minimum liquidity, and stable funding. First, Basel III specifies the minimum percentage of its risk-weighted assets that a bank must fund with equity capital. This minimum capital requirement prevents a bank from assuming so much financial leverage that it is unable to withstand loan losses (asset write-downs). Second, Basel III specifies that a bank must hold enough high-quality liquid assets to cover its liquidity needs in a 30-day liquidity stress scenario. This minimum liquidity requirement ensures that a bank would have enough cash to cover a partial loss of funding sources (e.g., customers' deposits, other borrowings) or a cash outflow resulting from off-balance-sheet funding commitments. Third, Basel III requires a bank to have a minimum amount of stable funding relative to the bank's liquidity needs over a one-year horizon. Stability of funding is based on the tenor of deposits (e.g., longer-term deposits are more stable than shorter-term deposits) and the type of depositor (e.g., funds from consumers' deposits are considered more stable than funds raised in the interbank markets).

As a result of preventing banks from assuming excessive financial leverage, Basel III has prompted banks to focus on asset quality, hold capital against other types of risk (such as operational risk), and develop improved risk assessment processes. Basel III also presents fundamental changes regarding the quality and composition of the capital base of financial institutions. It has improved the ability of their capital base to sustain losses, so these are confined to the financial institutions' capital investors and are not transmitted to depositors, taxpayers, or other institutions in the financial system, thereby reducing risk of contagion.

Having developed the regulatory framework, the Basel Committee monitors the adoption and implementation of Basel III by member jurisdictions.

A number of other important organizations are involved in international cooperation in the area of financial stability. Some of these international organizations are described briefly below.

- The Financial Stability Board includes representatives from supervisory and regulatory authorities for the G–20 members plus Hong Kong SAR, Singapore, Spain, and Switzerland. Its overall goal is to strengthen financial stability. It aims to identify systemic risk in the financial sector and coordinate actions that jurisdictional authorities can take to address the risks.

- The International Association of Deposit Insurers' objective is to "enhance the effectiveness of deposit insurance systems."

- The International Association of Insurance Supervisors (IAIS) includes representatives from insurance regulators and supervisors from most countries around the world. Its overall goal is to promote effective supervision of the insurance industry globally.

---

10 www.bis.org.

- The International Organization of Securities Commissions (IOSCO) includes representatives from the regulators of the securities markets of various countries and jurisdictions. Its overall goals include maintaining fair and efficient securities markets.

The latter two organizations are part of a Joint Forum with the Basel Committee. The Joint Forum comprises representatives from the Basel Committee, IAIS, and IOSCO and works on issues common to the banking, insurance, and securities sectors.

Individual Jurisdictions' Regulatory Authorities

The global organizations described in the previous section aim to foster financial stability by working with individual jurisdictions' regulatory authorities. It is the individual jurisdictions' regulatory bodies that have authority over specific aspects of a financial institution's operations.

Globally, there are many regulators with overlapping and differing responsibilities over financial institutions; the global network of regulators and the resulting regulations are complex. Although there is some overlap between member institutions in the Basel Committee and other global organizations mentioned in the previous section, specific membership varies. For example, the 83 member organizations of the International Association of Deposit Insurers include some institutions that are Basel Committee members, such as the US Federal Deposit Insurance Corporation (FDIC), and some that are not Basel Committee members, such as the Singapore Deposit Insurance Corporation Ltd. and Germany's Bundesverband deutscher Banken (Deposit Protection Fund). In some countries, the same regulatory body oversees both banking and insurance—for example, Japan's Financial Services Agency. And in other countries, there is a separate regulatory body for insurance companies—for example, the US National Association of Insurance Commissioners (NAIC) and the China Insurance Regulatory Commission.

As a financial institution's operations expand globally, compliance requirements increase. One of the most global financial institutions, HSBC Holdings, discloses that their operations are "regulated and supervised by approximately 400 different central banks and other regulatory authorities in those jurisdictions in which we have offices, branches or subsidiaries. These authorities impose a variety of requirements and controls."[11]

2 ANALYZING A BANK: THE CAMELS APPROACH

- [ ] explain the CAMELS (capital adequacy, asset quality, management, earnings, liquidity, and sensitivity) approach to analyzing a bank, including key ratios and its limitations
- [ ] analyze a bank based on financial statements and other factors

---

11 HSBC Holdings Form 20-F (31 December 2016).

Analyzing a Bank: the CAMELS Approach

In this section, the term "bank" is used in its general sense and applies to entities whose primary business activities are taking deposits and making loans. This section first describes an approach widely used as a starting point to analyze a bank, known as CAMELS, and follows with a description of additional factors to consider when analyzing a bank. The section concludes with a case study analysis of a real bank.

The CAMELS Approach

"CAMELS" is an acronym for the six components of a widely used bank rating approach originally developed in the United States.[12] The six components are **C**apital adequacy, **A**sset quality, **M**anagement capabilities, **E**arnings sufficiency, **L**iquidity position, and **S**ensitivity to market risk.

A bank examiner using the CAMELS approach to evaluate a bank conducts an analysis and assigns a numerical rating of 1 through 5 to each component. A rating of 1 represents the best rating, showing the best practices in risk management and performance and generating the least concern for regulators. A rating of 5 is the worst rating, showing the poorest performance and risk management practices and generating the highest degree of regulatory concern.[13] After the components are rated, a composite rating for the entire bank is constructed from the component ratings. This is not a simple arithmetic mean of the six component ratings: Each component is weighted by the examiner performing the study. The examiner's judgment will affect the weighting accorded to each component's rating. Two examiners could evaluate the same bank on a CAMELS basis and even assign the same ratings to each component and yet arrive at different composite ratings for the entire bank.

Although the CAMELS system was developed as a tool for bank examiners, it provides a useful framework for other purposes, such as equity or debt investment analysis of banks. The following sections discuss each component of the rating system.

Capital Adequacy

It is important for a bank (as with any company) to have adequate capital so that potential losses can be absorbed without causing the bank to become financially weak or even insolvent. Losses reduce the amount of a bank's retained earnings, which is one component of capital. Large enough losses could even result in insolvency. A strong capital position lowers the probability of insolvency and bolsters public confidence in the bank.

Capital adequacy for banks is described in terms of the proportion of the bank's assets funded with capital. For purposes of determining capital adequacy, a bank's assets are adjusted based on their risk, with riskier assets requiring a higher weighting. The risk weightings are specified by individual countries' regulators, and these regulators typically take Basel III into consideration. The risk adjustment results in an amount for risk-weighted assets to use when determining the amount of capital required to fund those assets. For example, cash has a risk weighting of zero, so cash is not included in the risk-weighted assets. As a result, no capital is required to fund cash. Corporate loans have a risk weighting of 100%, and certain risky assets, such as loans on high-volatility commercial real estate and loans that are more than 90 days past due, have a weighting greater than 100%. As a simple example, consider a hypothetical bank with three assets: $10 in cash, $1,000 in performing loans, and $10

---

[12] Information on the evolution of risk assessment can be found in "Supervisory Risk Assessment and Early Warning Systems," Ranjana Sahajwala and Paul Van den Bergh, Basel Committee on Banking Supervision Working Paper No. 4 (December 2000). Further information about the CAMELS rating system can be found in the FDIC's description of the Uniform Financial Institutions Rating System at www.fdic.gov.
[13] Sahajwala and Van den Bergh, "Supervisory Risk Assessment and Early Warning Systems."

in non-performing loans. The bank's risk-weighted assets (RWAs) would equal ($10 × 0%) + ($1,000 × 100%) + ($10 × 150%) = $1,015. Also, off-balance-sheet exposures are assigned risk weights and included in the risk-weighted assets.

For purposes of determining a bank's capital and its capital adequacy, a bank's capital is classified into hierarchical tiers. The most important of these tiers is Common Equity Tier 1 Capital. According to the FDIC:

> Basel III capital standards emphasize common equity tier 1 capital as the predominant form of bank capital. Common equity tier 1 capital is widely recognized as the most loss-absorbing form of capital, as it is permanent and places shareholders' funds at risk of loss in the event of insolvency. Moreover, Basel III strengthens minimum capital ratio requirements and risk-weighting definitions, increases Prompt Corrective Action (PCA) thresholds, establishes a capital conservation buffer, and provides a mechanism to mandate counter-cyclical capital buffers.[14]
>
> Common Equity Tier 1 Capital includes common stock, issuance surplus related to common stock, retained earnings, accumulated other comprehensive income, and certain adjustments including the deduction of intangible assets and deferred tax assets. Other Tier 1 Capital includes other types of instruments issued by the bank that meet certain criteria. The criteria require, for example, that the instruments be subordinate to such obligations as deposits and other debt obligations, not have a fixed maturity, and not have any type of payment of dividends or interest that is not totally at the discretion of the bank. Tier 2 Capital includes instruments that are subordinate to depositors and to general creditors of the bank, have an original minimum maturity of five years, and meet certain other requirements.

The minimum capital requirements set forth in Basel III are described here because they are global. However, it is the individual countries' regulators who have authority to establish the minimum capital requirements for institutions within their jurisdiction.

- Common Equity Tier 1 Capital must be at least 4.5% of risk-weighted assets.
- Total Tier 1 Capital must be at least 6.0% of risk-weighted assets.
- Total Capital (Tier 1 Capital plus Tier 2 Capital) must be at least 8.0% of risk-weighted assets.[15]

EXAMPLE 1

Capital Position

Exhibit 3 presents an excerpt from an annual report disclosure by HSBC Holdings plc about its capital position. The excerpt shows the group's capital ratios, amount of capital by tier, and risk-weighted assets by type.

---

14 FDIC, "Risk Management Manual of Examination Policies," Section 2.1 (www.fdic.gov). For a comprehensive description of capital tiers under Basel III, refer to "Basel III: A global regulatory framework for more resilient banks and banking systems" (pp. 13–27), available at www.bis.org.
15 www.bis.org.

Analyzing a Bank: the CAMELS Approach

> **Exhibit 3: Excerpt from Annual Report Disclosure of HSBC Holdings plc**
>
> **Capital Ratios**
>
> | | At 31 Dec. | |
> |---|---|---|
> | | **2016 (%)** | **2015 (%)** |
> | Common equity tier 1 ratio | 13.6 | 11.9 |
> | Tier 1 ratio | 16.1 | 13.9 |
> | Total capital ratio | 20.1 | 17.2 |
>
> **Total Regulatory Capital and Risk-Weighted Assets**
>
> | | At 31 Dec. | |
> |---|---|---|
> | | **2016 ($m)** | **2015 ($m)** |
> | Regulatory Capital | | |
> | Common equity tier 1 capital | 116,552 | 130,863 |
> | Additional tier 1 capital | 21,470 | 22,440 |
> | Tier 2 capital | 34,336 | 36,530 |
> | Total regulatory capital | 172,358 | 189,833 |
> | | | |
> | Risk-weighted assets | 857,181 | 1,102,995 |
>
> **Risk-weighted assets (RWAs) by risk types**
>
> | | RWAs ($bn) | Capital required* ($bn) |
> |---|---|---|
> | Credit risk | 655.7 | 52.5 |
> | Counterparty credit risk | 62.0 | 5.0 |
> | Market risk | 41.5 | 3.3 |
> | Operational risk | 98.0 | 7.8 |
> | At 31 Dec 2016 | 857.2 | 68.6 |
>
> * "Capital required" represents the Pillar 1 capital charge at 8% of RWAs.
>
> *Source:* HSBC Holdings plc Annual Report and Accounts 2016 (p. 127).

1. Based on Exhibit 3, did HSBC's capital ratios strengthen or weaken in 2016?

Solution:

HSBC's capital ratios strengthened in 2016. Its Common Equity Tier 1 ratio increased from 11.9% of RWAs to 13.6% of RWAs. Its Tier 1 ratio also increased from 13.9% to 16.1%, and its Total Capital Ratio increased from 17.2% to 20.1%.

> 2. Based on Exhibit 3, what was the primary reason for the change in HSBC's capital ratios in 2016?
>
> ### Solution:
> The primary reason for the change in HSBC's capital ratios in 2016 was a reduction in the amount of risk-weighted assets. Total risk-weighted assets declined from $1,102,995 million to $857,181 million.

Asset Quality

Asset quality pertains to the amount of existing and potential credit risk associated with a bank's assets, focusing primarily on financial assets. The concept of asset quality extends beyond the composition of a bank's assets and encompasses the strength of the overall risk management processes by which the assets are generated and managed.

Loans typically constitute the largest portion of a bank's assets. Asset quality for loans reported on the balance sheet depends on the creditworthiness of the borrowers and the corresponding adequacy of adjustments for expected loan losses. Loans are measured at amortized cost and are shown on the balance sheet net of allowances for loan losses.

Investments in securities issued by other entities, often another significant portion of a bank's assets, are measured differently, depending on how the security is categorized. Specifically, under International Financial Reporting Standards (IFRS),[16] financial assets are classified in one of three categories, depending on the company's business model for managing the asset and on the contractual cash flows of the asset. The financial asset's category specifies how it is subsequently measured (either amortized cost or fair value) and, for those measured based on fair value, how any changes in value are reported–either through other comprehensive income (OCI) or through profit and loss (PL). The three categories for financial assets are (1) measured at amortized cost, (2) measured at fair value through other comprehensive income (FVOCI), and (3) measured at fair value through profit and loss (FVTPL).

In contrast to IFRS, US GAAP require all equity investments "(except those accounted for under the equity method of accounting or those that result in consolidation of the investee) to be measured at fair value with changes in fair value recognized in net income."[17] Another exception to fair value measurement is that an equity investment without a readily determinable fair value can be measured at cost minus impairment. Thus, under US GAAP, the three categories used to classify and measure investments apply *only to debt securities*: held to maturity (measured at amortized cost), trading (measured at fair value through net income), and available for sale (measured at fair value through other comprehensive income).

The following example addresses asset quality from the perspective of overall asset composition. The example includes the asset portion of a bank's balance sheet. In practice, terminology used by different entities can vary, and an analyst should refer to the footnotes for further detail on a line item. Here, two comments can be helpful in interpreting the line items in the example. First, when determining the total amount of bank loans, two line items are clearly relevant: "Loans and advances to banks" and "Loans and advances to customers." In addition, note that "Reverse repurchase agreements" are a form of collateralized loan made by a bank to a client. In a repurchase agreement, a borrower (i.e., a bank client) sells a financial asset to a lender (i.e., a bank) and commits to repurchase the financial asset for a fixed price

---

16 IFRS 9 *Financial Instruments*, issued July 2014 and effective beginning January 2018.
17 Accounting Standards Update 2016-01 *Financial Instruments—Overall* (Subtopic 825-10) *Recognition and Measurement of Financial Assets and Financial Liabilities*. This Accounting Standards Update was issued in January 2016 and is effective for public business entities for fiscal years beginning after 15 December 2017.

at a future date. The difference between the selling price and the higher repurchase price effectively constitutes interest on the borrowing. The borrower describes the transaction as a "repurchase agreement," and the lender describes the transaction as a "reverse repurchase agreement."[18] Second, the term "assets held for sale" is related to discontinued operations and specifically refers to long-term assets whose value is driven mainly by their intended disposition rather than their continued use.[19] This term should not be confused with the securities-related term "available for sale" (described above).

EXAMPLE 2

Asset Quality: Composition of Assets

Exhibit 4 presents the asset portion of the balance sheet of HSBC Holdings, which is prepared according to IFRS.

Exhibit 4: Excerpt from Consolidated Balance Sheet

HSBC Holdings plc
Consolidated Balance Sheet [Excerpt]
at 31 December

Assets	2016 $m	2015 $m
Cash and balances at central banks	128,009	98,934
Items in the course of collection from other banks	5,003	5,768
Hong Kong Government certificates of indebtedness	31,228	28,410
Trading assets	235,125	224,837
Financial assets designated at fair value	24,756	23,852
Derivatives	290,872	288,476
Loans and advances to banks	88,126	90,401
Loans and advances to customers	861,504	924,454
Reverse repurchase agreements, non-trading	160,974	146,255
Financial investments	436,797	428,955
Assets held for sale	4,389	43,900
Prepayments, accrued income and other assets	59,520	54,398
Current tax assets	1,145	1,221
Interests in associates and joint ventures	20,029	19,139
Goodwill and intangible assets	21,346	24,605
Deferred tax assets	6,163	6,051
Total assets at 31 Dec	2,374,986	2,409,656

Source: HSBC Holdings plc Annual Report and Accounts 2016.

1. The following items are the most liquid: Cash and balances at central banks, Items in the course of collection from other banks, and Hong Kong Government certificates of indebtedness. What proportion of HSBC's total assets

---

[18] The Office of Financial Research (part of the US Department of the Treasury) estimates that the size of the repurchase ("repo") market is $3.5 trillion.
[19] IFRS 5 *Non-Current Assets Held for Sale and Discontinued Operations*.

was invested in these liquid assets in 2015? In 2016? Did HSBC's balance sheet liquidity decrease or increase in 2016?

Solution:

HSBC's balance sheet liquidity increased in 2016.

In 2015, the proportion of HSBC's balance sheet invested in highly liquid assets was 5.5%

[($98,934 + $5,768 + $28,410)/$2,409,656 = 5.5%].

In 2016, the proportion of HSBC's balance sheet invested in highly liquid assets was 6.9%

[($128,009 + $5,003 + $31,228)/$2,374,986 = 6.9%].

2. How did the percentage of investments to total assets change from 2015 to 2016? (Include trading assets, financial assets designated at fair value, and financial investments as investments.)

Solution:

The percentage of investments on HSBC's balance sheet increased in 2016.

In 2015, the percentage of investments to total assets was 28.1%

[($224,837 + $23,852 + $428,955)/$2,409,656 = 28.1%].

In 2016, the percentage of investments to total assets was 29.3%

[($235,125 + $24,756 + $436,797)/$2,374,986 = 29.3%].

3. What proportion of HSBC's assets are loans? (As noted, the banks' loans include "Loans and advances to banks" and "Loans and advances to customers." In addition, "Reverse repurchase agreements" are a form of collateralized loan.)

Solution:

In 2015, loans represented 48.2% [($90,401 + $924,454 + $146,255)/$2,409,656 = 48.2%] of HSBC's total assets, and in 2016, loans represented 46.8% [($88,126 + $861,504 + $160,974)/$2,374,986 = 46.8%] of HSBC's total assets.

The next example addresses asset quality from the perspective of credit quality. Assessment of credit risk is of course fundamental to banks' decisions about loans—the largest category of a banks' assets. As noted, investments in securities often constitute a significant portion of a bank's assets, and those activities also involve credit risk. Further, a bank's trading activities—including off-balance-sheet trading activities—create exposure to counterparty credit risk. Off-balance-sheet obligations such as guarantees, unused committed credit lines, and letters of credit represent potential assets (as well as potential liabilities) to the bank and thus involve credit risk. In addition to credit risk, other factors, such as liquidity, can also affect the value and marketability of a bank's assets. Diversification of credit risk exposure (and avoiding credit concentration) across the entire asset base—loans and investments—and among counterparties is an important aspect of asset quality.

EXAMPLE 3

Credit Quality of Assets

Exhibit 5 presents an excerpt from an annual report disclosure by HSBC Holdings plc about the credit quality of its financial instruments. The exhibit shows the distribution of financial instruments by credit quality.

Financial instruments included in the exhibit correspond to total amounts for some line items of assets listed on the balance sheet and to partial amounts for line items on the balance sheet where only a portion of the asset involves exposure to credit risk. Total amounts are included for the following balance sheet items: Cash and balances at central banks; Items in the course of collection from other banks; Hong Kong Government certificates of indebtedness; Derivatives; Loans and advances to banks; Loans and advances to customers; and Reverse repurchase agreements, non-trading. Partial amounts are included for the following balance sheet items: Trading assets; Financial assets designated at fair value; Financial investments; Assets held for sale; and Prepayments, accrued income and other assets.

Exhibit 5: Excerpt from Annual Report Disclosure of HSBC Holdings plc

		At 31 Dec. 2016 ($m)	At 31 Dec. 2015 ($m)
Neither past due nor impaired	Strong credit quality	$1,579,517	$1,553,830
	Good credit quality	$313,707	$331,141
	Satisfactory credit quality	$263,995	$293,178
	Sub-standard credit quality	$26,094	$26,199
	Past due but not impaired	$9,028	$13,030
	Impaired	$20,510	$28,058
	Total gross amount	$2,212,851	$2,245,436
	Impairment allowances	$(8,100)	$(11,027)
	Total	$2,204,751	$2,234,409

Source: HSBC Holdings plc Annual Report and Accounts 2016 (pp. 88–89).

Solutions Exhibit

		At 31 Dec. 2016	At 31 Dec. 2015	Percentage change in dollar amount
		Percentage of total gross amount	Percentage of total gross amount	
Neither past due nor impaired	Strong credit quality	71.4%	69.2%	1.7%
	Good credit quality	14.2%	14.7%	−5.3%
	Satisfactory credit quality	11.9%	13.1%	−10.0%
	Sub-standard credit quality	1.2%	1.2%	−0.4%
	Past due but not impaired	0.4%	0.6%	−30.7%
	Impaired	0.9%	1.2%	−26.9%
	Total gross amount	100.0%	100.0%	−1.5%
	Impairment allowances	−0.4%	−0.5%	−26.5%

1. Based on Exhibit 5, did the credit quality of HSBC's financial instruments improve or deteriorate in 2016? Specifically, how did the proportion of assets invested in strong credit quality instruments change from year to year?

Solution:

Based on Exhibit 5, the credit quality of HSBC's financial instruments improved in 2016. As shown in the Solutions Exhibit, the percentage of total investment assets invested in strong credit quality instruments rose from 69.2% in 2015 to 71.4% in 2016 [$1,553,830/$2,245,436 = 69.2%; $1,579,517/$2,212,851 = 71.4%].

2. Based on Exhibit 5, does the change in HSBC's impairment allowances in 2016 reflect the change in the credit quality of financial instruments (specifically the amount of impaired assets)?

Solution:

Yes. Based on Exhibit 5, the change in HSBC's impairment allowances in 2016 reflects the change in the credit quality of financial instruments. In general, it is expected that the amount of impairment allowances will be related to the amount of impaired assets. The 26.5% decrease in the amount of HSBC's impairment allowances in 2016 corresponds to the 26.9% decrease in impaired assets. As a corollary, the amount of impairment allowances as a percentage of impaired assets remained roughly constant in both years ($11,027/$28,058 = 39.3% for 2015 and $8,100/$20,510 = 39.5% for 2016).

Management Capabilities

Many of the attributes of effective management of financial institutions are the same as those for other types of entities. Effective management involves successfully identifying and exploiting appropriate profit opportunities while simultaneously managing risk.

For all types of entities, compliance with laws and regulations is essential. A strong governance structure—with an independent board that avoids excessive compensation or self-dealing—is also critically important. Sound internal controls, transparent management communication, and financial reporting quality are indicators of management effectiveness. Across all entities, overall performance is ultimately the most reliable indicator of management effectiveness.

For financial institutions, a particularly important aspect of management capability is the ability to identify and control risk, including credit risk, market risk, operating risk, legal risk, and other risks. Directors of banks set overall guidance on risk exposure levels and appropriate implementation policies and provide oversight of bank management. Banks' senior managers must develop and implement effective procedures for measuring and monitoring risks consistent with that guidance.

Earnings

As with any entity, financial institutions should ideally generate an amount of earnings to provide an adequate return on capital to their capital providers and specifically to reward their stockholders through capital appreciation and/or distribution of the earnings. Further, all companies' earnings should ideally be high quality and trending upward. In general, high-quality earnings mean that accounting estimates are unbiased and the earnings are derived from sustainable rather than non-recurring items.

For banks, one important area involving significant estimates is loan impairment allowances. In estimating losses on the loan portfolio collectively, statistical analysis of historical loan losses can provide a basis for an estimation, but statistical analysis based on past data must be supplemented with management judgement about the potential for deviation in future. In estimating losses on individual loans, assessments are required concerning the likelihood of the borrower's default or bankruptcy and the value of any collateral. HSBC describes the complexity of estimating loan impairment allowances as follows: "The exercise of judgement requires the use of assumptions which are highly subjective and very sensitive to the risk factors, in particular to changes in economic and credit conditions across a large number of geographical areas. Many of the factors have a high degree of interdependency and there is no single factor to which our loan impairment allowances as a whole are sensitive."[20]

Banks also must use estimates in valuing some financial assets and liabilities that must be measured at fair value. When fair value of an investment is based on observable market prices, valuation requires little judgment. However, when fair values cannot be based on observable market prices, judgment is required.

Under both IFRS and US GAAP, fair value measurements of financial assets and liabilities are categorized on the basis of the type of inputs used to establish the fair value. Both sets of standards use the concept of a *fair value hierarchy*.[21] The three "levels" of the fair value hierarchy pertain to the observability of the inputs used to establish the fair value.

- Level 1 inputs are quoted prices for identical financial assets or liabilities in active markets.
- Level 2 inputs are observable but are not the quoted prices for identical financial instruments in active markets. Level 2 inputs include quoted prices for similar financial instruments in active markets, quoted prices for identical financial instruments in markets that are not active, and observable data

---

20 HSBC Holdings plc Annual Report and Accounts 2016, page 199: www.hsbc.com/investor-relations/group-results-and-reporting/annual-report
21 Refer to IFRS 13 *Fair Value Measurement* and Financial Accounting Standards Board ASC 820 *Fair Value Measurement*.

such as interest rates, yield curves, credit spreads, and implied volatility. The inputs are used in a model to determine the fair value of the financial instrument.

- **Level 3 inputs are unobservable.** The fair value of a financial instrument is based on a model (or models) and unobservable inputs. Financial modeling, by its very nature, contains subjective estimates that are unobservable and will differ from one modeler to another. For example, a financial instrument's value might be based on an option-pricing model employing an unobservable and subjective estimate of the instrument's market volatility. Another example is that a financial instrument's value might be based on estimated future cash flows, discounted to a present value. Neither the estimated future cash flows nor the discount rate can be observed objectively, because they depend on the determinations made by the modeler.

In practice, the "Level 1, 2, 3" fair value terminology can also refer to the valuation approach used. A Level 3 valuation technique is one that relies on one or more significant inputs that are unobservable. For example, as noted, a company might value a private equity investment using a model of estimated future cash flows.

Also, in practice, the "Level 1, 2, 3" terminology can refer to the assets or liabilities being valued using a given level of input. For example, investments can be referred to as "Level 1," "Level 2," or "Level 3" investments depending on whether their fair value is determined based on observable market prices for the exact instrument, observable market inputs for similar investments, or unobservable inputs, respectively.

Other areas involving significant estimates are common to non-financial and financial companies. Judging whether goodwill impairment exists requires estimating future cash flows of a business unit. Deciding to recognize a deferred tax asset relies on making assumptions about the probability of future taxes. Determining whether and how much of a liability to recognize in connection with contingencies (e.g., litigation) typically depends on professional expert advice but nonetheless requires some management judgment.

Regarding sustainability of a bank's earnings, it is important to examine the composition of earnings. Banks' earnings typically comprise (a) net interest income (the difference between interest earned on loans minus interest paid on the deposits supporting those loans), (b) service income, and (c) trading income. Of these three general sources, trading income is typically the most volatile. Thus, a greater proportion of net interest income and service income is typically more sustainable than trading income. In addition, lower volatility within net interest income is desirable: Highly volatile net interest income could indicate excessive interest rate risk exposure.

EXAMPLE 4

Composition of Earnings

An analyst has gathered the information in Exhibit 6 to evaluate how important each source of income is to HSBC.

Exhibit 6: Five-Year Summary of HSBC's Total Operating Income

	2016 ($m)	2015 ($m)	2014 ($m)	2013 ($m)	2012 ($m)
Net interest income	$29,813	$32,531	$34,705	$35,539	$37,672
Net fee income	$12,777	$14,705	$15,957	$16,434	$16,430
Net trading income	$9,452	$8,723	$6,760	$8,690	$7,091

Analyzing a Bank: the CAMELS Approach

	2016 ($m)	2015 ($m)	2014 ($m)	2013 ($m)	2012 ($m)
Net income/(expense) from financial instruments designated at fair value	($2,666)	$1,532	$2,473	$768	($2,226)
Gains less losses from financial investments	$1,385	$2,068	$1,335	$2,012	$1,189
Dividend income	$95	$123	$311	$322	$221
Net insurance premium income	$9,951	$10,355	$11,921	$11,940	$13,044
Gains on disposal of US branch network, US cards business, and Ping An Insurance (Group) Company of China, Ltd.	—	—	—	—	$7,024
Other operating income/(expense)	($971)	$1,055	$1,131	$2,632	$2,100
Total operating income	**$59,836**	**$71,092**	**$74,593**	**$78,337**	**$82,545**

Source: HSBC Holdings plc Annual Report and Accounts 2016 (p. 31).

1. Based on Exhibit 6, what is HSBC's primary source of operating income, and what proportion of total operating income was earned from this source in 2016?

Solution:

HSBC's primary source of operating income is net interest income. In 2016, 49.8% ($29,813/$59,836 = 49.8%) of total operating income was earned from net interest income in 2016.

2. Based on Exhibit 6, what proportion of total operating income did HSBC earn from trading income in 2016?

Solution:

In 2016, HSBC earned 15.8% ($9,452/$59,836 = 15.8%) of total operating income from trading activities.

3. Based on Exhibit 6, describe the trend in HSBC's operating income.

Solution:

From 2012 to 2016, HSBC's operating income declined each year. The composition of operating income was fairly constant from 2012 to 2015, with around 46% from net interest income and 21% from fee income.

Exhibit 7: Five-Year Summary of HSBC's Total Operating Income: Common-Size Statement

	2016	2015	2014	2013	2012
	As a Percentage of Total Operating Income					
Net interest income	49.8%	45.8%	46.5%	45.4%	45.6%
Net fee income	21.4%	20.7%	21.4%	21.0%	19.9%
Net trading income	15.8%	12.3%	9.1%	11.1%	8.6%
Net income/(expense) from financial instruments designated at fair value	−4.5%	2.2%	3.3%	1.0%	−2.7%
Gains less losses from financial investments	2.3%	2.9%	1.8%	2.6%	1.4%

	2016	2015	2014	2013	2012
Dividend income	0.2%	0.2%	0.4%	0.4%	0.3%
Net insurance premium income	16.6%	14.6%	16.0%	15.2%	15.8%
Gains on disposal of US branch network, US cards business, and Ping An Insurance (Group) Company of China, Ltd.	—	—	—	—	8.5%
Other operating income/(expense)	−1.6%	1.5%	1.5%	3.4%	2.5%
Total operating income	100.0%	100.0%	100.0%	100.0%	100.0%

Liquidity Position

Adequate liquidity is essential for any type of entity. Banks' systemic importance increases the importance of adequate liquidity. If a non-bank entity's insufficient liquidity prevents it from paying a current liability, the impact would primarily affect the entity's own supply chain. In contrast, because deposits constitute the primary component of a bank's current liabilities, the impact of a bank's failure to honor a current liability could affect an entire economy. Deposits in most banks are insured up to some specified amount by government insurers; thus, liquidity is a key focus of regulators.

The Basel III Regulatory Framework[22] cites the sudden illiquidity accompanying the financial crisis of 2008 as a main motivation for the introduction of a global liquidity standard. Because of the sudden pressures on liquidity at the inception of the financial crisis, some banks experienced difficulties, despite having an adequate capital base. Basel III thus introduced two minimum liquidity standards, both to be phased in over subsequent years.

- The Liquidity Coverage Ratio (LCR) is expressed as the minimum percentage of a bank's expected cash outflows that must be held in highly liquid assets. For this ratio, the expected cash outflows (the denominator) are the bank's anticipated one-month liquidity needs in a stress scenario, and the highly liquid assets (the numerator) include only those that are easily convertible into cash. The standards set a target minimum of 100%.

- The Net Stable Funding Ratio (NSFR) is expressed as the minimum percentage of a bank's *required* stable funding that must be sourced from *available* stable funding. For this ratio, required stable funding (the denominator) is a function of the composition and maturity of a bank's asset base, whereas available stable funding (the numerator) is a function of the composition and maturity of a bank's funding sources (i.e., capital and deposits and other liabilities). Under Basel III, the available stable funding is determined by assigning a bank's capital and liabilities to one of five categories presented in Exhibit 8, shown below. The amount assigned to each category is then multiplied by an available stable funding (ASF) factor, and the total available stable funding is the sum of the weighted amounts.[23]

---

22 Basel Committee on Banking Supervision, "Basel III: A Global Regulatory Framework For More Resilient Banks and Banking System": www.bis.org/publ/bcbs189.pdf.
23 Basel Committee on Banking Supervision, "Basel III: The Net Stable Funding Ratio" (October 2014, p. 3): www.bis.org/bcbs/publ/d295.pdf. Exhibit 8 is adapted from page 6 of this document.

Exhibit 8: Categories of Available Stable Funding

ASF Factor	Components of ASF Category
100%	- Total regulatory capital (excluding Tier 2 instruments with residual maturity of less than one year) - Other capital instruments and liabilities with effective residual maturity of one year or more
95%	- Stable non-maturity (demand) deposits and term deposits with residual maturity of less than one year provided by retail and small business customers
90%	- Less stable non-maturity deposits and term deposits with residual maturity of less than one year provided by retail and small business customers
50%	- Funding with residual maturity of less than one year provided by non-financial corporate customers - Operational deposits - Funding with residual maturity of less than one year from sovereigns, public sector entities, and multilateral and national development banks - Other funding with residual maturity between six months and less than one year not included in the above categories, including funding provided by central banks and financial institutions
0%	- All other liabilities and equity not included in the above categories, including liabilities without a stated maturity (with a specific treatment for deferred tax liabilities and minority interests) - Net Stable Funding Ratio derivative liabilities net of Net Stable Funding Ratio derivative assets if Net Stable Funding Ratio derivative liabilities are greater than Net Stable Funding Ratio derivative assets - "Trade date" payables arising from purchases of financial instruments, foreign currencies, and commodities

The rationale for the Net Stable Funding Ratio is that it relates the liquidity needs of the financial institution's assets to the liquidity provided by the funding sources. With assets, for example, loans with long-dated maturities require stable funding whereas highly liquid assets do not. With funding sources, long-dated deposits and other liabilities are considered more stable than short-dated liabilities, and deposits from retail customers are considered more stable than deposits with the same maturity from other counterparties. The standards set a target minimum of greater than 100%.

Among the several liquidity-monitoring metrics described in Basel III,[24] two are discussed here: concentration of funding and contractual maturity mismatch. Concentration of funding refers to the proportion of funding that is obtained from a single source. Excessive concentration of funding exposes a bank to the risk that a single funding source could be withdrawn.

Contractual maturity mismatch refers to the maturity dates of a bank's assets compared to the maturity dates of a bank's funding sources. In a normal yield curve environment, where long-term interest rates are higher than short-term rates, a bank can maximize its net interest income—all else equal—by borrowing short term and lending long term. In doing so, the bank would minimize the interest paid to its depositors and maximize interest earned on its loan assets. In excess, however, such maturity mismatches expose the bank to liquidity risk if the bank needs to return

---

[24] Basel Committee on Banking Supervision, "Basel III: A Global Regulatory Framework For More Resilient Banks and Banking System": www.bis.org/publ/bcbs189.pdf.

cash on its maturing deposits prior to the time that it receives cash repayment of loans from its borrowers. Monitoring maturity mismatch is thus an important tool in liquidity risk management.

> **EXAMPLE 5**
>
> The following excerpts from HSBC's annual report explain the bank's approach to management of its liquidity and funding risk. The disclosures state that the group's principal operating entities were within the risk tolerance levels established by the board for the Liquidity Coverage Ratio, the Net Stable Funding Ratio, depositor concentration, and term funding maturity concentration.
>
> ### Exhibit 9: Liquidity Disclosure—Excerpts from HSBC's Annual Report
>
> The management of liquidity and funding is primarily undertaken locally (by country) in our operating entities in compliance with the Group's LFRF [liquidity and funding risk management framework], and with practices and limits set by the GMB [Group Management Board] through the RMM [Risk Management Meeting of the Group Management Board] and approved by the Board. Our general policy is that each defined operating entity should be self-sufficient in funding its own activities. Where transactions exist between operating entities, they are reflected symmetrically in both entities.
>
> As part of our asset, liability and capital management structure, we have established asset and liability committees ("ALCO") at Group level, in the regions and in operating entities. . . . The primary responsibility for managing liquidity and funding within the Group's framework and risk appetite resides with the local operating entities' ALCOs, Holdings ALCO and the RMM. . . .
>
> The Liquidity Coverage Ratio ("LCR") aims to ensure that a bank has sufficient unencumbered high-quality liquid assets ("HQLA") to meet its liquidity needs in a 30-calendar-day liquidity stress scenario. HQLA consist of cash or assets that can be converted into cash at little or no loss of value in markets. We reported a Group European Commission ("EC") LCR at 31 December 2016 of 136% (31 December 2015: 116%) to the PRA [UK Prudential Regulation Authority]. . . . At 31 December 2016, all the Group's principal operating entities were within the LCR risk tolerance level established by the Board. . . . The liquidity position of the Group can also be represented by the stand-alone ratios of each of our principal operating entities. . . .
>
> The Net Stable Funding Ratio ("NSFR") requires institutions to maintain sufficient stable funding relative to required stable funding, and reflects a bank's long-term funding profile (funding with a term of more than a year). It is designed to complement the LCR. At 31 December 2016, the Group's principal operating entities were within the NSFR risk tolerance level established by the Board and applicable under the LFRF.
>
> The LCR and NSFR metrics assume a stressed outflow based on a portfolio of depositors within each deposit segment. The validity of these assumptions is challenged if the portfolio of depositors is not large enough to avoid depositor concentration. Operating entities are exposed to term re-financing concentration risk if the current maturity profile results in future maturities being overly concentrated in any defined period. At 31 December 2016, all principal operating entities were within the risk tolerance levels set for depositor concentration and term funding maturity concentration. These risk tolerances were established by the Board. . . .

[The table below displays the following liquidity metrics for HSBC's principal operating entities: individual LCR on an EC LCR basis and NSFR.]

Operating Entities' Liquidity Measures

	LCR		NSFR
	Dec-16 (%)	Dec-15 (%)	Dec-16 (%)
HSBC UK liquidity group	123	107	116
The Hongkong and Shanghai Banking Corporation, Hong Kong Branch	185	150	157
The Hongkong and Shanghai Banking Corporation, Singapore Branch	154	189	112
HSBC Bank USA	130	116	120
HSBC France	122	127	120
Hang Seng Bank	218	199	162
HSBC Canada	142	142	139
HSBC Bank China	253	183	49
HSBC Middle East, UAE Branch	241		141
HSBC Mexico	177		128
HSBC Private Bank	178		155

Source: HSBC Holdings plc Annual Report and Accounts 2016 (pp. 108, 143, and 144).

1. Based on the exhibit, in 2016, which of HSBC's operating entities had the highest level of liquid assets relative to its liquidity needs in a stress scenario?

Solution:

Based on the exhibit, HSBC Bank China had the highest level of liquid assets relative to its liquidity needs in a stress scenario. Its 2016 LCR of 253% is higher than that of any of the other HSBC entities.

2. Based on the exhibit, which of HSBC's operating entities had the most stable funding relative to its required need for stable funding?

Solution:

Based on the exhibit, Hang Seng Bank had the most stable funding relative to its required need for stable funding. Its 2016 NSFR of 162% is higher than that of any of the other HSBC entities.

3. Based on the exhibit, which of HSBC's operating entities is the furthest away from achieving the Basel III target for NSFR?

Solution:

Based on the exhibit, HSBC Bank China is the furthest away from achieving the Basel III standard of NSFR greater than 100%. Its NSFR of 49% is lower than that of any of the other HSBC entities. (It is possible that these metrics result from RMB capital controls in China or jurisdictional issues; however, the example does not provide sufficient information to confirm the reason.)

Sensitivity to Market Risk

Almost every entity has some exposure to changes in interest rates, exchange rates, equity prices, or commodity prices. Every company in the United States, for example, is required to provide quantitative and qualitative disclosures in annual filings about exposure to market risk. The nature of banks' operations generally makes sensitivity of earnings to market risks a particularly important consideration for analysts. Mismatches in the maturity, repricing frequency, reference rates, or currency of banks' loans and deposits create exposure to market movements. Further, exposure to risk arises not only from loans and deposits on a bank's balance sheet but also from off-balance-sheet exposures, including, for example, guarantees or derivatives positions linked to interest rates, exchange rates, equities, or commodities. It is important to understand how an adverse change in any of these markets would affect a bank's earnings. It is also important to evaluate the strength of a bank's ability to manage market risks.

Banks disclose information about the sensitivity of earnings to different market conditions—namely, the earnings impact of a shift up or down in some market. Consider a bank's sensitivity to interest rate risk. Even in a purely hypothetical situation of a bank with assets and liabilities that are identical in terms of interest rates, maturity, and frequency of repricing, an increase in interest rates would cause the bank's net interest income to increase. This would occur simply because banks have more assets than liabilities. In reality, of course, the terms of a bank's assets and liabilities differ. Generally, the yield on a bank's loan assets is presumed to be higher than the rate it must pay its depositors, particularly consumer deposits. With respect to term structure, in a typical yield curve environment, longer-dated assets would have a higher yield *ceteris paribus* than shorter-dated funding sources, but another aspect of interest rate sensitivity is repricing frequency. For example, having assets with greater repricing frequency than liabilities would benefit earnings in a rising interest rate scenario. In sum, many structural factors affect interest rate sensitivity.

The following example includes an interest rate sensitivity disclosure showing the earnings impact of an upward and downward shift in interest rates. Disclosures such as these reflect the existing structure of a bank's assets and liabilities.

EXAMPLE 6

Market Risk

The following excerpts from HSBC's annual report explain the bank's approach to monitoring its market risk and illustrates one of the tools used by the bank: sensitivity analysis.

Exhibit 10: Excerpt from HSBC's Annual Report

Our objective is to manage and control market risk exposures while maintaining a market profile consistent with our risk appetite. We use a range of tools to monitor and limit market risk exposures including sensitivity analysis, value at risk and stress testing.

The following table sets out the assessed impact on our base case projected net interest income ("NII") for 2016 (excluding insurance) of a series of four quarterly parallel shocks of 25 basis points to the current market-implied path of interest rates worldwide at the beginning of each quarter from 1 January 2017. . . .

The sensitivities shown represent our assessment as to the change in expected base case net interest income under the two rate scenarios, assuming that all other non-interest rate risk variables remain constant, and there are no management actions. . . .

We expect NII to rise in the rising rate scenario and fall in the falling rate scenario. This is due to a structural mismatch between our assets and liabilities (on balance we would expect our assets to reprice more quickly, and to a greater extent, than our liabilities).

Net Interest Income Sensitivity (Audited)

	US dollar bloc ($m)	Rest of Americas bloc ($m)	Hong Kong dollar bloc ($m)	Rest of Asia bloc ($m)	Sterling bloc ($m)	Euro bloc ($m)	Total ($m)
Change in 2016 net interest income arising from a shift in yield curves of:							
+25 basis points at the beginning of each quarter	605	47	504	280	61	212	1,709
−25 basis points at the beginning of each quarter	−1,024	−41	−797	−292	−261	9	−2,406

Source: HSBC Holdings plc Annual Report and Accounts 2016 (pp. 78 and 117).

1. Based on the exhibit, by how much would HSBC's planned net interest income decrease if the yield curves shifted downward by 25 basis points at the beginning of each quarter for four quarters?

Solution

HSBC's planned net interest income would decrease by $2,406 million if the yield curves shifted downward by 25 basis points at the beginning of each quarter.

2. If a decrease in interest rates would hurt the earnings of banks such as HSBC, why would central banks lower interest rates so significantly following the financial crisis in order to prop up the financial sector?

Solution

An interest rate sensitivity table such as the one presented by HSBC is a static presentation and thus assumes that the relation between the structure of assets and liabilities in place at the time would remain stationary. Following the financial crisis, the central banks' actions reduced interest rates at which banks could borrow (effectively, to near zero), while the rates that banks were able to charge their loan customers were—while still low—far higher than their borrowing costs. Further, the central banks' actions were not intended solely to prop up banks' earnings but also to provide liquidity and stimulus to the overall economy.

As described in the example, another tool that HSBC uses to measure and monitor market risk is value at risk (VaR). Recall that VaR is a way to estimate the amount of potential loss based on simulations that incorporate historical pricing information. HSBC estimates its VaR using a 99% confidence level, a one-day holding period, and two prior years of pricing data on foreign exchange rates, interest rates, equity prices, commodity prices, and associated volatilities.

3 ANALYZING A BANK: NON-CAMELS FACTORS

☐ describe other factors to consider in analyzing a bank
☐ analyze a bank based on financial statements and other factors

While the CAMELS approach to assessing bank soundness is fairly comprehensive, there are important bank-specific attributes that it does not completely address. There are also important attributes not addressed by the CAMELS approach that apply to both banks and other types of companies.

Banking-Specific Analytical Considerations Not Addressed by CAMELS

The CAMELS acronym is useful as a composite of major factors, but it is neither comprehensive nor comprehensively integrated. Also, the ordering of the factors does not signify importance. For example, strong capital (the "C") and strong liquidity (the "L") are equally important in the Basel III standards.[25]

The following bank attributes are either unaddressed or not fully addressed by a CAMELS analysis:

- **Government support.** Governments do not normally strive to save a company or even an entire industry that may be facing failure. In capitalist societies, failure is the unfortunate occasional by-product of risk taking with capital, and bankruptcy laws and courts serve to administer the results of failed capital allocation. The banking industry is different from other industries, however, regarding government support. It is in a government's interest to have a healthy banking system because a nation's economy is affected by banks' lending activity, and a nation's central bank needs a healthy banking system for the effective transmission of monetary policy. A healthy banking system also facilitates commerce by providing adequate payment processing and instilling depositor confidence in the safekeeping of their deposits.

  Government agencies monitor the health of banks in the entire system and will close banks that might fail or will arrange mergers with healthy ones able to absorb them. This pruning activity addresses issues with banks that might otherwise weaken the banking system if left unattended. Alternatively, governments may directly assist banks to keep them afloat rather than closing them or arranging for mergers with healthier banks. Visible examples of both assisting and pruning activities occurred during the financial crisis of 2008. For example, the US Treasury created the Troubled Asset Relief Program (TARP) to purchase loans held by banks and to provide equity

---

25 Basel Committee on Banking Supervision, "Basel III: A Global Regulatory Framework For More Resilient Banks and Banking System" (December 2010, p. 8, item B.34): www.bis.org/publ/bcbs189.pdf.

injections to the banks. During the same period, the Treasury also arranged numerous mergers among banking giants, leading to even bigger banking giants.

CAMELS analysis will not provide an assessment of government support, but an investor can qualitatively assess whether a bank will enjoy the support of the government in times of economic distress. The following are factors to consider:

- *Size of the bank.* Is the bank large enough to bring damage to a significant part of the economy in the event of its failure? Is it "too big to fail"?
- *Status of the country's banking system.* Is the nation's banking system healthy enough to handle a particular bank's failure? Rather than force the banking system to cope with the failure of a particular bank, would it be a better solution for the government to intervene with taxpayer funds to support it? The global financial crisis of 2008–2009 led the US Federal Reserve to develop the concept of SIFIs: systemically important financial institutions, ones that would pose a significant risk to the economy in the event of a failure. Such institutions have been the target of an increased degree of regulation in the post-crisis era.

- **Government ownership.** Public ownership of banks may include a strong ownership representation by the government of their home country. Government ownership may exist for several reasons. A "development" view of government ownership incorporates a belief that government ownership aids financial development of the banks, leading to broad economic growth. A more pessimistic view is that a nation's banking system is not strong enough to stand on its own and attract large amounts of capital, because of low ethical standards within the industry or a lack of confidence in the banking system among the nation's public at large—an important source of funds for any bank.[26]

Whatever the reason may be for a government's ownership stake in a bank, its presence adds another dimension of security for a bank investor. A government that owns a stake in a bank is likely to intervene on the bank's behalf in the event of economic distress. Conversely, a government that plans to reduce its ownership stake in a bank may directly reduce that dimension of security; however, that may not always be the case. During the global financial crisis of 2008–2009, some governments became reluctant owners of banks, which were ultimately supported by taxpayer funding. When government ownership of such banks was reduced after the crisis ended, markets viewed the reduction as a signal of renewed strength.

- **Mission of banking entity.** Not all banks share the same mission. For example, community banks primarily serve the needs of the immediate community in which they operate. That community's welfare could be driven by an economy based on farming, mining, or oil or could depend on a single large manufacturing entity. The fortunes of the banks and their borrowers and depositors would depend on economic factors that affect the primary industry or employer. Contrast that situation with a global banking entity absorbing deposits from all around the world while investing globally as well. The global bank is more diversified against a single risk than any community bank.

---

26 Rafael La Porta, Florencio Lopez-de-Silanes, and Andrei Shleifer, "Government Ownership of Banks," NBER Working Paper No. 7620 (March 2000).

The mission of the bank and the economics of its constituents will affect the way the bank manages its assets and liabilities. That is a qualitative assessment that the bank investor needs to make, and it is not addressed by a CAMELS analysis.

- **Corporate culture.** A bank's culture may be very risk averse and cautious and make only loans perceived to be low risk, or alternatively, it may be risk seeking and willing to take risk in pursuit of high returns on investment. Or a bank's culture may be somewhere in the middle of those two extremes. An overly cautious culture may be too risk averse to provide adequate returns to shareholders for taking on the risk of ownership. A highly risk-hungry culture may lead to boom and bust results and volatility. Differences in the cultural environment are particularly important for banks operating in multiple countries, where there may be a disconnect between corporate culture and national culture.

    A bank investor can qualitatively assess a bank's cultural environment by considering factors such as these:

    - Has the bank generated recent losses resulting from a narrowly focused investment strategy, such as a large, outsized exposure to a particularly risky country or area of the economy?
    - Has the bank restated its financial statements owing to financial reporting internal control failures?
    - Does the bank award above-average equity-based compensation to its top managers, possibly incentivizing risk-taking behavior and short-termism?
    - What does the bank's experience with loss reserves say about its culture? Has it frequently been slow to provide for losses, only to record large asset write-downs later?

Analytical Considerations Not Addressed by CAMELS That Are Also Relevant for Any Company

There are other factors relevant to the analysis of a bank—and to any kind of company—that are not covered by the CAMELS approach. The following factors merit consideration by debt and equity investors in banks as well as investors in non-banking entities:

- **Competitive environment.** A bank's competitive position, relative to its peers, may affect how it allocates capital and assesses risks; it may also affect the aforementioned cultural mindset. A regional bank may have a near-monopolistic hold on a particular region and not take very many risks beyond maintaining its grip. A global bank may be affected by the actions of other global banks. Managers of a global bank may not be satisfied with following the lead of other banks and may pursue ambitious goals of growing market share at all costs and with little regard for risks, or they may be content with more profitable but slower growth. It depends on how the bank's managers perceive their competitive position and how they will react to the perception.
- **Off-balance-sheet items.** Off-balance-sheet assets and liabilities pose a risk to entities and their investors if they should unexpectedly drain resources. The global financial crisis of 2008–2009 was hastened by the Lehman Brothers bankruptcy, and the opacity of their involvement with such financial instruments as credit derivatives prevented concise pre-crisis analysis of

the risks they shouldered. However difficult to examine, off-balance-sheet exposures need consideration whenever one analyzes a bank or financial institution.

Not all off-balance-sheet items involve exotic or highly engineered financial instruments. Operating leases are a low-risk example of off-balance-sheet liabilities: They are not a recognized liability of a company, yet they provide a creditor with a claim on a company's future cash flows. Fortunately, visibility into such future obligations is easily accessed by investors in the lease footnotes.

A financial institution analyst should be alert to the existence in the financial statements of an accounting construct known as variable interest entities, or VIEs. Variable interest entities are a form of "special-purpose entity" usually formed solely for one purpose: perhaps to hold only certain assets or assets that may be financed with specific debt instruments. Before the accounting for variable interest entities was developed, companies sometimes used outside parties to take a majority ownership stake in the special-purpose entity, ensuring that they would not have to consolidate the special-purpose entity's assets and liabilities. The accounting standard setters developed the VIE model to capture the consolidation of such special-purpose entities. By meeting generalized criteria for consolidation apart from clearly defined equity ownership tests, a company that is the primary beneficiary of a VIE's existence may be required to consolidate the VIE's financial statements with its own, even if it has no equity ownership in it. Yet a variable interest entity may also result in off-balance-sheet assets and liabilities for a bank if the bank has an interest in the VIE but is not required to consolidate it. If the VIE is not consolidated with the bank, its existence and certain financial information must be disclosed. Those non-consolidated VIEs should be of interest to investors: The reasons given for non-consolidation should be examined for reasonableness, and the implications to the bank of various scenarios affecting the VIE should be considered.

Benefit plans are another "off-balance-sheet" item for investors to examine. Although these are not completely off-balance-sheet items because the net benefit plan assets or obligations appear on the balance sheet, the economics that drive them are different from the bank's business. Shortfalls in assets due to market performance can cause rapid increases in required contributions to plans. Interest rate decreases, which drive plan obligations higher, can also cause rapid cash drains for required contributions to plans. Bank investors should examine benefits plan footnotes to determine the degree of risk posed by such plans.

One particular off-balance-sheet item that is found in financial companies only—sometimes in banks—is assets under management (AUM). Banks may have trust departments that generate management fees based on the assets under management. Those assets belong to the clients and are not consolidated with a bank's balance sheet accounts, yet they drive the returns of the bank. If such returns are material to a bank's results, the bank investor should be concerned with the size and growth or decline in assets under management.

- **Segment information.** Banks may be organized in different lines of business. They can be organized according to domestic and foreign markets; they can be organized along consumer or industrial lines of business; they may offer financial services, such as leasing or market making in securities; and they may have related businesses that are not strictly banking driven, such as trust operations. Regardless of the lines of business a bank (or any

- **Currency exposure.** Although it may not be a problem for smaller, regional banks that operate in a single currency, floating currency exchange rates can create problems for global banks. Banks may finance and lend in a variety of currencies, resulting in foreign currency transaction exposure. Large banks may actively trade in foreign currencies and actively hedge using foreign exchange derivatives, leading to unforeseen gains or losses when world events affect currencies unexpectedly; not all banks may be successful currency traders. Global banks face the same balance sheet translation issues that affect other multinational corporations. When a bank's home currency strengthens against the functional currencies of its foreign subsidiaries, the translation of balance sheet accounts at the end of an accounting period may lead to currency translation adjustments that can reduce capital.

- **Risk factors.** Investors should review the risk factors presented in a company's annual filing. Sometimes derided as a mere list of worst-case scenarios created by a company's legal counsel, the risk factors section of a company's filing can also fill gaps in an investor's knowledge about legal and regulatory issues that might not otherwise be uncovered.

- **Basel III disclosures.** The Basel III requirements include extensive disclosures that complement the minimum risk-based capital requirements and other quantitative requirements with the goal of promoting market discipline by providing useful regulatory information to investors and other interested parties on a consistent, comparable basis.[27]

4. ANALYZING A BANK: EXAMPLE OF CAMELS APPROACH

- ☐ explain the CAMELS (capital adequacy, asset quality, management, earnings, liquidity, and sensitivity) approach to analyzing a bank, including key ratios and its limitations
- ☐ analyze a bank based on financial statements and other factors

This section illustrates the CAMELS approach using Citigroup's financial statements as an example. The CAMELS approach is based on the evidence gathered by the analyst in assessing each CAMELS component, and this evidence will vary from investor to investor. Some aspects of the CAMELS approach will matter more to certain investors than others: An equity investor may be far more concerned with earnings and earnings quality than with capital adequacy. A fixed-income investor might be far more concerned with capital adequacy and liquidity than earnings. The interests of each type of investor will determine what kind of analysis they perform to assess each CAMELS component. The following example of Citigroup is not intended to show all possible analyses.

---

[27] Basel Committee on Banking Supervision, "Standards: Revised Pillar 3 Disclosure Requirements" (January 2015, p. 3): https://www.bis.org/bcbs/publ/d309.pdf.

Analyzing a Bank: Example of CAMELS Approach

It should also be understood that although the CAMELS approach entails quantitative aspects, it is not a wholly formulaic approach to analyzing a bank. An analyst's judgment and discretion also matter greatly in the application of the CAMELS approach. Judgment and discretion figure into the kind of testing done by an investor to gather evidence for the various CAMELS components, and judgment and discretion also figure into the rating of the various CAMELS components once the evidence has been reviewed.

The following sections present examples of the relevant information for each component and conclude with a summary assessment. In each case, the summary assessment includes a rating, where a rating of 1 is the highest and a rating of 5 is the lowest.

Capital Adequacy

As noted above, capital adequacy relates to the proportion of a bank's assets funded by capital, with the assets accorded varying risk weightings. Not only are assets stratified into risk classes, but the bank capital funding those assets is also stratified into tiers: Common Equity Tier 1 Capital, Total Tier 1 Capital, and Tier 2 Capital.

Common Equity Tier 1 Capital includes common stock, issuance surplus related to common stock, retained earnings, accumulated other comprehensive income, and certain adjustments, including the deduction of intangible assets and deferred tax assets.

Exhibit 11 shows the calculation of Citigroup's Common Equity Tier 1 Capital, Risk-Weighted Assets, and Common Equity Tier 1 Capital Ratio at the end of 2016 and 2015. Citigroup's ratio is well within the required limits in both years. The ratio declined slightly in 2016, from 14.60% to 14.35%. The decline in the ratio is mostly attributable to the increase in deferred tax assets disallowed in the computation of Common Equity Tier 1 Capital.

Exhibit 11: Components of Citigroup Common Equity Tier 1 Capital under Current Regulatory Standards (Basel III Advanced Approaches with Transition Arrangements)

(In millions of dollars)	31 Dec. 2016	31 Dec. 2015
Citigroup common stockholders' equity	$206,051	$205,286
Add: Qualifying non-controlling interests	259	369
Regulatory capital adjustments and deductions:		
Less: Net unrealized gains (losses) on securities available for sale (AFS), net of tax	(320)	(544)
Less: Defined benefit plan liability adjustment, net of tax	(2,066)	(3,070)
Less: Accumulated net unrealized losses on cash flow hedges, net of tax (4)	(560)	(617)
Less: Cumulative unrealized net gain (loss) related to changes in fair value of financial liabilities attributable to own creditworthiness, net of tax	(37)	176
Less: Intangible assets:		
Goodwill, net of related deferred tax liabilities	20,858	21,980
Identifiable intangible assets other than mortgage servicing rights (MSRs), net of related deferred tax liabilities	2,926	1,434
Less: Defined benefit pension plan net assets	514	318
Less: Deferred tax assets (DTAs) arising from net operating loss, foreign tax credit, and general business credit carry-forwards	12,802	9,464
Less: Excess over 10%/15% limitations for other DTAs, certain common stock investments, and mortgage servicing rights	4,815	2,652

(In millions of dollars)	31 Dec. 2016	31 Dec. 2015
Total Common Equity Tier 1 Capital	$167,378	$173,862
Risk-Weighted Assets under Current Regulatory Standards:		
Credit risk	$773,483	$791,036
Market risk	64,006	74,817
Operational risk	329,275	325,000
Total risk-weighted assets	$1,166,764	$1,190,853
Common Equity Tier 1 Capital Ratio (Tier 1 Capital/Total risk-weighted assets)	**14.35%**	**14.60%**
Stated minimum Common Equity Tier 1 Capital Ratio	4.50%	4.50%

Total Tier 1 Capital includes other instruments issued by the bank that meet certain criteria based on their subordination to deposit and other debt obligations, bear no fixed maturity, and carry no requirement to pay dividends or interest without full discretion of the bank. Preferred stocks can be constructed to meet these criteria.

Exhibit 12 shows the calculation of Citigroup's Total Tier 1 Capital and Total Tier 1 Capital Ratio at the end of 2016 and 2015. Again, Citigroup's ratio is well within the required limits in both years. The ratio improved in 2016, from 14.81% to 15.29%. The increase in this ratio is mostly attributable to additional perpetual preferred stock qualifying for inclusion in 2016 and the decrease in the amount of deferred tax assets disallowed in the computation of Total Tier 1 Capital.

Exhibit 12: Components of Citigroup Total Tier 1 Capital under Current Regulatory Standards (Basel III Advanced Approaches with Transition Arrangements)

(In millions of dollars)	31 Dec. 2016	31 Dec. 2015
Common Equity Tier 1 Capital (from Exhibit 11)	$167,378	$173,862
Additional Tier 1 Capital:		
Qualifying perpetual preferred stock	19,069	16,571
Qualifying trust preferred securities	1,371	1,707
Qualifying non-controlling interests	17	12
Regulatory capital adjustments and deductions:		
Less: Cumulative unrealized net gain (loss) related to changes in fair value of financial liabilities attributable to own creditworthiness, net of tax	(24)	265
Less: Defined benefit pension plan net assets	343	476
Less: DTAs arising from net operating loss, foreign tax credit and general business credit carry-forwards	8,535	14,195
Less: Permitted ownership interests in covered funds	533	567
Less: Minimum regulatory capital requirements of insurance underwriting subsidiaries	61	229
Total additional Tier 1 Capital	$11,009	$2,558
Total Tier 1 Capital (Common Equity Tier 1 Capital + Additional Tier 1 Capital)	$178,387	$176,420
Total risk-weighted assets (from Exhibit 11)	$1,166,764	$1,190,853
Tier 1 Capital Ratio	**15.29%**	**14.81%**

(In millions of dollars)	31 Dec. 2016	31 Dec. 2015
Minimum Tier 1 Capital Ratio	6.00%	6.00%

Tier 2 Capital includes, on a limited basis, portions of the allowance for loan and lease losses and other instruments that are subordinate to depositors and general creditors. Exhibit 13 shows the calculation of Citigroup's Tier 2 Capital and Total Capital Ratio at the end of 2016 and 2015. Consistent with the Common Equity Tier 1 Capital Ratio and the Total Tier 1 Capital Ratio, the 2016 Total Capital Ratio far exceeds the minimum requirement. The Total Capital Ratio improved from the 2015 level, from 16.69% to 17.33%. The improvement was mostly due to the increase in Total Tier 1 Capital and the amount of qualifying subordinated debt.

Exhibit 13: Components of Citigroup Tier 2 Capital under Current Regulatory Standards (Basel III Advanced Approaches with Transition Arrangements)

(In millions of dollars)	31 Dec. 2016	31 Dec. 2015
Total Tier 1 Capital (Common Equity Tier 1 Capital + Additional Tier 1 Capital)	$178,387	$176,420
Qualifying subordinated debt	22,818	21,370
Qualifying trust preferred securities	317	0
Qualifying non-controlling interests	22	17
Excess of eligible credit reserves over expected credit losses	660	1,163
Regulatory capital adjustments and deductions:		
Add: Unrealized gains on AFS equity exposures includable in Tier 2 Capital	3	5
Less: Minimum regulatory capital requirements of insurance underwriting subsidiaries	61	229
Total Tier 2 Capital	$23,759	$22,326
Total Capital (Tier 1 Capital + Tier 2 Capital)	$202,146	$198,746
Total risk-weighted assets	$1,166,764	$1,190,853
Total Capital Ratio	17.33%	16.69%
Minimum Capital Ratio	8.00%	8.00%

In summary, Citigroup's capital adequacy at the end of 2016 appears to be solidly positive. For each of the three chief capital ratios, the company has exceeded the minimum levels required for being considered to be a well-capitalized bank. A rating of 1 could be justified by their ratios, which far exceeded the minimum levels.

Asset Quality

Asset quality matters greatly to a bank. As financial intermediaries in an economy, banks owe their existence to the creation of loans. If a bank's credit policies are unsound, its capital base can be quickly eroded during economic downturns, creating strains on the bank's liquidity and its ability to generate earnings. Creating new loans becomes problematic.

A portion of bank assets are held in highly liquid financial instruments, such as cash, deposits held at other banks, and instruments that may convert into cash in a very short time frame, such as repurchase agreements and some receivables. These are not highly risky assets.

Increasing in riskiness are the investments made by the bank in financial instruments with cash deemed to be in excess of operating needs. Under US GAAP and IFRS, these investments may be classified as available-for-sale investments, which are reported at fair value, or held-to-maturity investments, which are reported at their amortized cost unless an impairment occurs. While these investments are riskier than the liquid securities and reflect an investment decision made by management, their value is quite transparent and their reported value reflects their realizability in cash—although it takes more analytical effort to make that assertion for held-to-maturity securities.

The riskiest, and often the largest, asset classes are the loans underwritten by the bank. Loans embody credit risk and the judgment of management in extending credit to customers. The underwriting risks and the management judgments in assessing them are reflected in the allowance for loan losses. It is here that the analyst faces some of the most difficult assessments in understanding the quality of banking assets and is at a disadvantage, because some information simply is unavailable to an analyst (or investor). Conversely, an examiner for a supervisory regulator has the ability to see the bank from the inside and assess the soundness of loan (and investment) policies and procedures. An examiner may also review the construction and workings of internal control procedures and may be able to examine how exceptions to credit policies are being handled.[28]

Although the analyst is interested in all of those inner workings, he/she can be concerned only with circumstantial evidence that the credit policies are sound and are being maintained. That circumstantial evidence can be found in the financial statements, but it is not completely obvious from merely looking at a balance sheet. There are ways to find evidence of asset quality, as will be shown with Citigroup. Exhibit 14 shows the asset side of Citigroup's balance sheet on a condensed basis at the end of 2016 and 2015.

Exhibit 14: Citigroup Asset Composition, 31 December 2016 and 2015

	31 December 2016		31 December 2015	
(In millions of dollars)	$	% Total Assets	$	% Total Assets
Liquid assets:				
Cash and due from banks	$23,043	1.3%	$20,900	1.2%
Deposits with banks	137,451	7.7%	112,197	6.5%
Federal funds sold and securities borrowed or purchased under resale agreements	236,813	13.2%	219,675	12.7%
Brokerage receivables	28,887	1.6%	27,683	1.6%
Trading account assets	243,925	13.6%	241,215	13.9%
Total liquid assets	670,119	37.4%	621,670	35.9%
Investments:				
Available-for-sale	299,424	16.7%	299,136	17.3%
Held-to-maturity	45,667	2.5%	36,215	2.1%
Non-marketable equity securities	8,213	0.5%	7,604	0.4%
Total investments	353,304	19.7%	342,955	19.8%

---

28 See Section 3.1 of the FDIC's "RMS Manual of Examination Policies," available at https://www.fdic.gov/regulations/safety/manual/section3-1.pdf.

Analyzing a Bank: Example of CAMELS Approach

(In millions of dollars)	31 December 2016 $	% Total Assets	31 December 2015 $	% Total Assets
Loans:				
Consumer	325,366	*18.2%*	325,785	*18.8%*
Corporate	299,003	*16.7%*	291,832	*16.9%*
Loans, net of unearned income	624,369	*34.9%*	617,617	*35.7%*
Allowance for loan losses	(12,060)	*−0.7%*	(12,626)	*−0.7%*
Total loans, net	612,309	*34.2%*	604,991	*35.0%*
Goodwill	21,659	*1.2%*	22,349	*1.3%*
Intangible assets (other than MSRs)	5,114	*0.3%*	3,721	*0.2%*
Mortgage servicing rights (MSRs)	1,564	*0.1%*	1,781	*0.1%*
Other assets	128,008	*7.1%*	133,743	*7.7%*
Total assets	$1,792,077	*100.0%*	$1,731,210	*100.0%*

Observations from the composition of the assets:

- Citigroup's liquid assets are the largest single group of all, at 37.4% in 2016, and slightly greater than the year before, indicating greater liquidity.
- The proportion of investments to total assets of 19.7% is practically unchanged from 2015; the majority of the investments are available-for-sale securities reported at fair value.
- Consumer and corporate loans are the highest-risk assets and in both years amount to more than one-third of all assets. They are the second largest class of assets after the liquid assets.

In assessing asset quality, an analyst would want to focus on the riskiest assets in the mix: the investments and the loans. He or she would want to determine that the investments, while transparent in value, represent sound investment decisions and that the loans result from similarly reasoned underwriting policies. The analyst would want assurance that the stated amount of loans is collectible and that the allowance for loan losses is reasonably stated.

First, take a look at the investments. Exhibit 15 shows Citigroup's available-for-sale securities by class at the end of 2016. Exhibit 15 was extracted from Note 13 of the 2016 10-K, which showed the amortized cost by investment instrument, gross unrealized gains, gross unrealized losses, and fair value as stated in the balance sheet. Added to the table were the gross unrealized gains and losses expressed as a percentage of amortized cost, which is the amount invested.

Exhibit 15: Citigroup Available-for-Sale (AFS) Securities at 31 December 2016

(In millions of dollars)	Amortized Cost	Gross Unrealized Gains	Gross Unrealized Losses	Fair Value	% of Cost: Gross Unrealized Gains	% of Cost: Gross Unrealized Losses
Debt securities AFS						
Mortgage-backed securities:						
US government-sponsored agency guaranteed	$38,663	$248	$506	$38,405	0.6%	1.3%
Prime	2	—	—	2	—	—

		Gross Unrealized			% of Cost: Gross Unrealized	
(In millions of dollars)	Amortized Cost	Gains	Losses	Fair Value	Gains	Losses
Alt-A	43	7	—	50	16.3%	—
Non-US residential	3,852	13	7	3,858	0.3%	0.2%
Commercial	357	2	1	358	0.6%	0.3%
Total mortgage-backed securities	$42,917	$270	$514	$42,673	0.6%	1.2%
US Treasury and federal agency securities						
US Treasury	$113,606	$629	$452	$113,783	0.6%	0.4%
Agency obligations	9,952	21	85	9,888	0.2%	0.9%
Total US Treasury and federal agency securities	$123,558	$650	$537	$123,671	0.5%	0.4%
State and municipal	$10,797	$80	$757	$10,120	0.7%	7.0%
Foreign government	98,112	590	554	98,148	0.6%	0.6%
Corporate	17,195	105	176	17,124	0.6%	1.0%
Asset-backed securities	6,810	6	22	6,794	0.1%	0.3%
Other debt securities	503	—	—	503	0.0%	0.0%
Total debt securities AFS	$299,892	$1,701	$2,560	$299,033	0.6%	0.9%
Marketable equity securities AFS	$377	$20	$6	$391	5.3%	1.6%
Total securities AFS	$300,269	$1,721	$2,566	$299,424	0.6%	0.9%

The fair value ($299,424 million) is less than the amortized cost ($300,269 million) in the aggregate, and the net difference is $845 million; the largest contributor to that loss is the state and municipal obligations, with a $757 million loss. At a 7% loss in value, those were the only securities to generate losses greater than 2%.

Observations from the AFS securities valuation table:

- Although Citigroup has not generated a net winning strategy with its available-for-sale investments, its losses do not suggest reckless abandon.
- In future years, new US GAAP standards will eliminate the AFS classification for marketable equity securities. They will still be measured at fair value, just as they were measured at year end 2016. Starting in 2018, however, the gains and losses resulting from remeasurement will be shown directly in the income statement instead of being recorded in other comprehensive income. As of 31 December 2016, Citigroup's unrealized gains on its AFS equity investments exceeded its unrealized losses. Based on market values at that point in time, the reclassification would benefit the group's income.

A closer look at the gross unrealized losses is possible, because Note 13 also contains a simple aging of the losses: It shows how much of the $2.566 billion of unrealized losses are less than 12 months old and how much of the losses are 12 months old or older, by category. The longer a loss position exists, the greater the possibility that a security is impaired on an "other-than-temporary" basis. It would be unusual for losses to exist for long periods of time and then suddenly reverse.

The aging for the losses in Citigroup's available-for-sale securities is shown in Exhibit 16. Observations from the aging of AFS unrealized losses table:

- A slight majority (54%) of the losses are less than 12 months old, making them of less concern than the rest.

Analyzing a Bank: Example of CAMELS Approach

- Of the $1.172 billion of gross unrealized losses 12 months old or older, 60% ($702 million) are related to state and municipal securities, which raises a concern that the largest class of losses may in fact become realized.

Exhibit 16: Citigroup Aging of Unrealized Losses on Available-for-Sale Securities at 31 December 2016

	Less than 12 months		12 months or longer		Total	
(In millions of dollars)	Fair value	Gross unrealized losses	Fair value	Gross unrealized losses	Fair value	Gross unrealized losses
Mortgage-backed securities						
US government-sponsored agency sponsored	$23,534	$436	$2,236	$70	$25,770	$506
Prime	1	—	—	—	1	—
Non-US residential	486	—	1,276	7	1,762	7
Commercial	75	1	58	—	133	1
Total mortgage-backed securities	$24,096	$437	$3,570	$77	$27,666	$514
US Treasury and federal agency securities						
US Treasury	$44,342	$445	$1,335	$7	$45,677	$452
Agency obligations	6,552	83	250	2	6,802	85
Total US Treasury and federal agency securities	$50,894	$528	$1,585	$9	$52,479	$537
State and municipal	$1,616	$55	$3,116	$702	$4,732	$757
Foreign government	38,226	243	8,973	311	47,199	554
Corporate	7,011	129	1,877	47	8,888	176
Asset-backed securities	411	—	3,213	22	3,624	22
Other debt securities	5	—	—	—	5	—
Marketable equity securities AFS	19	2	24	4	43	6
Total securities AFS	$122,278	$1,394	$22,358	$1,172	$144,636	$2,566

A similar analysis can be done for the held-to-maturity (HTM) securities. Even though they represent a much smaller proportion of total assets, they still provide evidence of the manager's investment acumen. The result of the HTM securities review of the losses and aging of the losses is consistent with the results of the available-for-sale securities review. Though not presented in exhibits because of space limitations, Citigroup's unrealized losses on its HTM securities totaled $457 million, which is 1.3% of the amount invested. Of that $457 million loss in value, 82% ($373 million) stemmed from held-to-maturity securities that were showing losses older than 12 months, of which $180 million related to state and municipal securities.

Observations on the HTM securities:

- The losses on the HTM securities are much less in dollar amount than the losses on the AFS securities, and although they are minor in percentage terms of a loss, they are troubling because of their age. Problem assets do not usually improve with age, and the fact that the bulk of the losses on the HTM securities are older than 12 months may indicate management reluctance to report economic reality.

- Because HTM securities are reported at amortized cost on the balance sheet, the classification obscures the fair value of the securities. The age of the securities generating the losses indicates that there may be more severe impairment than already recognized. The analysis of the HTM securities reinforces the observations noted in the analysis of the available-for-sale securities review.

Investment assets are not as significant in amount or as risky as the loans. The analyst wants to determine that the loans are the result of a sound credit policy and will be realized over their term. This cannot be determined without analyzing the allowance for loan losses. As was seen in Exhibit 14, **allowance for loan losses** is a balance sheet account; it is a contra asset account to loans. (It is analogous to an account common for non-financial institutions, allowance for bad debts, which is a contra asset account to accounts receivable.) **Provision for loan losses** is an income statement expense account that increases the amount of the allowance for loan losses. Actual loan losses (i.e., charge-offs—net of recoveries) reduce the amount of the allowance for loan losses.

The allowance for loan losses matters greatly to understanding loan quality, because total loans minus the allowance for loan losses represents the expected value of the loans. A bank's balance sheet will typically show the total amount of loans, the amount of allowance for loan losses, and the net amount. Importantly, the allowance for loan losses is discretionary by its very nature. Underestimating the allowance for loan losses would overstate the amounts reported for assets and net income. Almost every bank will disclose allowances for loan losses among its most critical accounting estimates.

To effectively assess the adequacy of the allowance for loan losses, an analyst can examine measures that involve less management discretion. Net charge-offs of loans are less discretionary indicators of loan quality than the allowance for loan losses but have the disadvantage of being a confirming event: The loan has already turned out to be a non-performing asset. Another disadvantage is that net charge-offs can be used in good times to pack away earnings to be brought into earnings later through recoveries of charge-offs. Non-performing loans are another measure that can help in assessing adequacy of the allowance for loan losses. Non-performing (i.e., non-accrual) loans are loans that are not currently paying their contractual amounts due, making them a more objective measure of the quality of loans in the portfolio.

Three ratios are helpful in assessing the quality of the allowance for loan losses:

- The ratio of the allowance for loan losses to non-performing loans
- The ratio of the allowance for loan losses to net loan charge-offs
- The ratio of the provision for loan losses to net loan charge-offs

In each ratio, a discretionary measure (such as the allowance for loan losses or provision for loan losses) is compared to a more objective measure.[29] In the case of Citigroup, the loans and the allowance for loan losses are stratified between consumer loans and corporate loans. Because the types of loan customers differ greatly, the analysis of each should be performed separately. Exhibit 17 shows the variables required to compute the ratios for the last five years, selected from the management discussion and analysis of the relevant 10-Ks, and the resulting ratios.

---

[29] For more discussion on the analysis of the allowance of loan loss reserves, see Stephen G. Ryan, *Financial Instruments and Institutions: Accounting and Disclosure Rules* (Hoboken, NJ: Wiley, 2002): 100–105.

Analyzing a Bank: Example of CAMELS Approach

Exhibit 17: Citigroup's Loan Loss Analysis Data at 31 December

(In millions of dollars)	2016	2015	2014	2013	2012
Data for Calculating Allowance for Loan Loss Ratios					
Allowance for loan losses:					
Consumer	$9,358	$9,835	$13,547	$16,974	$22,585
Corporate	$2,702	$2,791	$2,447	$2,674	$2,870
Provision for loan losses:					
Consumer	$6,323	$6,228	$6,695	$7,587	$10,312
Corporate	$426	$880	$133	$17	$146
Charge-offs:					
Consumer	$7,644	$8,692	$10,650	$12,400	$16,365
Corporate	$578	$349	$458	$369	$640
Recoveries:					
Consumer	$1,594	$1,634	$1,975	$2,138	$2,357
Corporate	$67	$105	$160	$168	$417
Net charge-offs:					
Consumer	$6,050	$7,058	$8,675	$10,262	$14,008
Corporate	$511	$244	$298	$201	$223
Non-accrual loans:					
Consumer	$3,158	$3,658	$5,905	$7,045	$9,136
Corporate	$2,421	$1,596	$1,202	$1,958	$2,394
Allowance for Loan Loss Ratios					
Allowance for loan losses to non-accrual loans:					
Consumer	2.96	2.69	2.29	2.41	2.47
Corporate	1.12	1.75	2.04	1.37	1.20
Allowance for loan losses to net loan charge-offs:					
Consumer	1.55	1.39	1.56	1.65	1.61
Corporate	5.29	11.44	8.21	13.30	12.87
Provision for loan losses to net loan charge-offs:					
Consumer	1.05	0.88	0.77	0.74	0.74
Corporate	0.83	3.61	0.45	0.08	0.65

Observations on the allowance for loan losses to non-accrual loans, which are loans that have experienced some non-payment from borrowers:

- For the consumer loans, the 2016 ratio of 2.96 is the highest level in the last five years, and this ratio has been increasing in the last two years. It indicates that the allowance (a discretionary amount) is increasing faster than the actual non-accrual loans, lending confidence to analysts that the allowance is being built in advance of loans turning out poorly.

- For the corporate loans, the 2016 ratio of 1.12 is less definitive. It might be expected that the ratio would be more volatile than for the consumer business because the corporate lending business is not homogeneous, and specific credits and their failures could cause spikes in the ratio. Still, the allowance has declined in each of the last three years, and in 2016, it is at its lowest point in five years. This arouses concern that the allowance for loan losses may be a thin layer of protection against future losses.

Observations on the allowance for loan losses to net loan charge-offs:

- For the consumer loans, the 2016 ratio of 1.55 shows improvement from 2015 and indicates that there is a cushion between the allowance and the net loan charge-offs that has remained fairly constant over the last five years.
- For the corporate loans, the 2016 ratio of 5.29 shows an ample cushion between the allowance and the net loan charge-offs, although it declined greatly from 2015 and is much lower than at any time in the last five years.

Observations on the provision for loan losses to net loan charge-offs:

- The provision for loan losses is the amount added to the allowance each year, and one should expect that the provision correlates to the amount of net loan charge-offs.
- For the consumer loans, the 2016 ratio is the first ratio in five years where the provision exceeded the net loan charge-offs, and although it had been lower in the previous four years, the proportion of the provision to charge-offs had been increasing in the last three years. This indicates that the bank had become more conservative in its provisioning.
- For the corporate loans, the 2016 ratio significantly decreased from the previous year, and the ratio has been less than 1.0 in four of the last five years. This indicates that the provision for corporate loans has trailed the actual net charge-off experience. The large addition in 2015 gives the appearance of an urgent "catch-up" adjustment.

In summary, Citigroup's asset quality at the end of 2016 was mixed. The policies for investments appear to be fairly conservative, but the age of some of the investments with unrealized losses indicates a possible denial of impairment. With regard to loan quality, the ratio analysis of the allowance for loan losses suggests that the consumer loans appear to be well reserved, but the same ratio analysis for the corporate loans does not generate the same degree of comfort. A rating of 2.5—near the midpoint of the rating scale—could be assigned to the asset quality based on the mixed signals from the evidence.

Management Capabilities

External investors can observe only circumstantial evidence of management's quality. Some circumstantial evidence can be found through a review of the proxy statement.

Observations based on a review of Citigroup's 2016 proxy:

- Citigroup aims for two-thirds board representation of independent members, whereas the New York Stock Exchange requires only a majority of independent members.
- Citigroup has a separate CEO and chairman, often viewed as a good governance practice that avoids conflicts of interest. The positions have been separate since 2009.
- Citigroup's Risk Management Committee met frequently in 2016—14 times—providing evidence of attention to one of the most critical parts of a banking operation. Furthermore, the Risk Management Committee created a subcommittee in 2016 to provide oversight of data governance, data quality, and data integrity, and the subcommittee met seven times in 2016.

Although these are good practices, they do not constitute evidence of strong management capabilities. Rather, they provide evidence that an environment exists where strong management quality is permitted to flourish.

With a company as large as Citigroup, it is difficult to avoid related-party transactions. For example, BlackRock and Vanguard beneficially owned 5% or more of the outstanding shares of Citigroup's common stock as of 31 December 2016; during 2016, the company's subsidiaries provided ordinary course lending, trading, and other financial services to BlackRock and Vanguard. The proxy states that the transactions were on an arm's-length basis and contain customary terms that are substantially the terms of comparable transactions with unrelated third parties. Other related-party transactions exist and are discussed in the 10-K, but they are routine for a company of this size.

In terms of operational risk, evidence of the board's influence on management can be found in the unqualified opinion of Citigroup's auditor on the effectiveness of the system of internal controls. This is evidence of a minimally satisfactory environment in which a management should operate and not a clear signal of management competence. A qualified (or negative) opinion on the effectiveness of internal controls would be especially concerning for an investor.

In summary, although the board may be solidly constructed and appears to exert adequate control over the managers, the net performance of the company also speaks to the quality of management and directors. The asset quality, discussed above, was not overwhelmingly positive and detracts from the overall view of management quality. A rating of 2 could be assigned to management capabilities.

Earnings

Earnings ideally should be of high quality, and an indication of high-quality earnings is sustainability. Earnings are more sustainable if they are not dependent on the possibly opportunistic fine-tuning of discretionary estimates and not reliant on either non-recurring items or volatile sources of revenues.

As discussed above, allowance for loan losses and provisions for loan losses are estimated amounts that allow for management discretion. The provision for loan losses can have profound effects on the profitability of a bank in any single year and over long periods of time. Exhibit 18 shows the five-year change in Citigroup's pretax income through 2016 and the corresponding change in the consolidated total provisions for credit (i.e., loan loss reserves plus provisions for policyholder benefits and claims and unfunded lending commitments) drawn from the five-year selected financial data from the 2016 and 2015 10-Ks.

Exhibit 18: Historical Pretax Income and Total Provisions for Credit Losses

(In millions of dollars)	5-Year Net Change:	2016	2015	2014	2013	2012	2011
Pretax income		$21,477	$24,826	$14,701	$19,802	$8,165	$15,096
Change in pretax income	$6,381	($3,349)	$10,125	($5,101)	$11,637	($6,931)	—
Total provisions for credit losses		$6,982	$7,913	$7,467	$8,514	$11,329	$12,359
Change in total provisions for credit losses	($5,377)	($931)	$446	($1,047)	($2,815)	($1,030)	—

(In millions of dollars)	5-Year Net Change:	2016	2015	2014	2013	2012	2011
Net difference	$1,004						

Observations on the provisions for credit losses:

- 2013 was the only year in which pretax income increased from the previous year while the total provisions for credit losses decreased. The $2.815 billion decrease in the credit loss provisions drove 24% of the increase.
- In 2016, 2014, and 2012, the pretax income declined from the previous year. The declines would have been more severe if they had not been buffered by decreases in the total provisions for credit losses in each year.
- Over the five-year span, the change in the total credit loss provisions contributed to improving the pretax earnings in four of the years. The only exception was 2015, when the total provisions increased only negligibly compared to the size of the decreases in the other years.
- On a longer-term basis, the five-year net change in the total provisions accounted for 84% of the net change in pretax income—an indication that not much profit growth happened elsewhere.

Another indicator of sustainability is the degree to which trading income is part of a bank's revenue stream. Trading income tends to be volatile and not necessarily sustainable. Higher-quality income would be net interest income and fee-based income: These provide sustainable, returning streams of income. An analyst should examine the composition of a bank's revenue stream to determine whether it is growing and to identify the drivers of growth or decline. The five-year summary of Citigroup's revenue stream, drawn from the five-year selected financial data from the 2016 and 2015 10-Ks, is shown in Exhibit 19.

Exhibit 19: Five-Year Summary of Composition of Citigroup's Revenue

(In millions of dollars)	2016	2015	2014	2013	2012
Net interest revenue	$45,104	$46,630	$47,993	$46,793	$46,686
Principal transactions (trading income)	7,585	6,008	6,698	7,302	4,980
All other non-interest revenue	17,186	23,716	22,528	22,629	17,864
Revenues, net of interest expense	$69,875	$76,354	$77,219	$76,724	$69,530
Percent attributable to trading income	10.9%	7.9%	8.7%	9.5%	7.2%
Percent of total:					
Net interest revenue	64.5%	61.1%	62.2%	61.0%	67.1%
All other non-interest revenue	24.6%	31.1%	29.2%	29.5%	25.7%

Observations on revenue composition:

- 2016 total revenues are almost unchanged from 2012 levels.
- At 10.9% of total revenues in 2016, trading income has been trending upward as a proportion of revenues in the last five years. Instead of increasing its sustainable, non-volatile revenues, Citigroup's principal transactions/trading income is moving in the opposite direction—increasing in absolute dollars and in relative importance.

Analyzing a Bank: Example of CAMELS Approach

- In 2016, all other non-interest revenue is at its lowest representative level since 2012.
- The net interest revenue proportion improved in 2016 but is still lower than it was in 2012.

A bank's net interest revenue results from the management of interest earned on loans and other interest-bearing assets and the management of interest paid on deposits and other interest-bearing liabilities. Thus, net interest revenue earned on average interest-bearing assets minus interest expense paid on average interest-bearing liabilities. Banks may create value through maturity transformation: They can borrow money on shorter terms than the terms for lending to customers. Although this can create value by lending for long terms at a higher rate than their short-term funding costs, it can also destroy value if the markets for short-term funding experience a dislocation or the yield curve unexpectedly inverts. Therefore, a bank's risk management practices, including its diversification practices, are integral to the maturity transformation process.

Analyzing the net interest revenue can provide an investor with a view of a bank management's activity and effectiveness in this area. To continue the example with Citigroup, the next two exhibits show the average balances (average volume column) for Citigroup's balance sheet accounts. Exhibit 20 shows Citigroup's average assets, as well as interest revenue and average interest rate earned on those assets. Exhibit 21 shows the company's average liabilities, the interest expense and average interest cost of those liabilities, and its equity accounts. It also includes the company's net interest revenue and net interest margin at the bottom.

Exhibit 20: Citigroup's Average Balances and Interest Rates—Assets

In millions of dollars, except rates	Average Volume 2016	2015	2014	Interest Revenue 2016	2015	2014	% Average Rate 2016	2015	2014
Assets									
Deposits with banks	**$131,925**	$133,853	$161,741	**$971**	$727	$959	**0.74%**	0.54%	0.59%
Federal funds sold and securities borrowed or purchased under agreements to resell									
In US offices	**$147,734**	$150,340	$153,703	**$1,483**	$1,215	$1,034	**1.00%**	0.81%	0.67%
In offices outside the United States	**85,142**	84,013	101,184	**1,060**	1,301	1,332	**1.24**	1.55	1.32
Total	**$232,876**	$234,353	$254,887	**$2,543**	$2,516	$2,366	**1.09%**	1.07%	0.93%
Trading account assets									
In US offices	**$103,610**	$113,475	$113,716	**$3,791**	$3,945	$3,471	**3.66%**	3.48%	3.05%
In offices outside the United States	**94,603**	96,333	113,563	**2,095**	2,140	2,540	**2.21**	2.22	2.24
Total	**$198,213**	$209,808	$227,279	**$5,886**	$6,085	$6,011	**2.97%**	2.90%	2.64%
Investments									
In US offices									
Taxable	**$225,764**	$214,683	$188,909	**$3,980**	$3,812	$3,285	**1.76%**	1.78%	1.74%
Exempt from US income tax	**19,079**	20,034	20,383	**693**	443	626	**3.63**	2.21	3.07
In offices outside the United States	**106,159**	102,374	113,182	**3,157**	3,071	3,627	**2.97**	3.00	3.20
Total	**$351,002**	$337,091	$322,474	**$7,830**	$7,326	$7,538	**2.23%**	2.17%	2.34%
Loans (net of unearned income)									
In US offices	**$360,957**	$354,434	$361,773	**$24,240**	$25,082	$26,076	**6.72%**	7.08%	7.21%

In millions of dollars, except rates	Average Volume 2016	Average Volume 2015	Average Volume 2014	Interest Revenue 2016	Interest Revenue 2015	Interest Revenue 2014	% Average Rate 2016	% Average Rate 2015	% Average Rate 2014
In offices outside the United States	262,715	273,064	296,666	15,578	15,465	18,723	5.93	5.66	6.31
Total	$623,672	$627,498	$658,439	$39,818	$40,547	$44,799	6.38%	6.46%	6.80%
Other interest-earning assets	$56,398	$63,209	$48,954	$1,029	$1,839	$507	1.82%	2.91%	1.04%
Total interest-earning assets	$1,594,086	$1,605,812	$1,673,774	$58,077	$59,040	$62,180	3.64%	3.68%	3.71%
Non-interest-earning assets	$214,642	$218,025	$223,141						
Total assets	$1,808,728	$1,823,837	$1,896,915						

Observations from Citigroup's average assets table:

- The overall average interest rate earned declined slightly in 2016, from 3.68% to 3.64%. One reason is due to changes occurring within the loans, which are the single largest category of assets. Citigroup sold its OneMain Financial subsidiary at the end of 2015, which was engaged in US consumer installment lending and is a high-yielding loan business. That disposal pressured the interest income earned from US offices, decreasing the earned interest rate from 7.08% in 2015 to 6.72% in 2016.

- Average loans in US offices increased to $360,957 million in 2016 from $354,434 million in 2015, despite the OneMain disposal, because of the mid-2016 acquisition of Costco's credit card portfolio, which was insufficient to offset the OneMain interest income.

- Average loans in offices outside the United States decreased to $262,715 million in 2016 from $273,064 million in 2015, partly because Citigroup disposed of its retail banking and credit cards businesses in Japan in the fourth quarter of 2015.

- Although Citigroup realized better interest income from its trading account assets in 2016, earning 2.97% compared to 2.90% in 2015, it allocated less capital to trading and earned less absolute interest income from the trading account assets.

- Despite lower capital committed to deposits with banks ($131,925 million in 2016 compared to $133,853 million in 2015), the higher realized average interest rate increased Citigroup's overall interest income. The same is true for its tax-exempt investments in US offices.

Exhibit 21: Citigroup's Average Balances and Interest Rates—Liabilities, Equity, and Net Interest Revenue

In millions of dollars, except rates	Average Volume 2016	Average Volume 2015	Average Volume 2014	Interest Expense 2016	Interest Expense 2015	Interest Expense 2014	% Average Rate 2016	% Average Rate 2015	% Average Rate 2014
Liabilities									
Deposits in US offices	$288,817	$273,135	$292,062	$1,630	$1,291	$1,432	0.56%	0.47%	0.49%
In offices outside the United States	429,608	425,086	465,135	3,670	3,761	4,260	0.85	0.88	0.92
Total	$718,425	$698,221	$757,197	$5,300	$5,052	$5,692	0.74%	0.72%	0.75%
Federal funds purchased and securities loaned or sold under agreements to purchase									

Analyzing a Bank: Example of CAMELS Approach

In millions of dollars, except rates	Average Volume 2016	Average Volume 2015	Average Volume 2014	Interest Expense 2016	Interest Expense 2015	Interest Expense 2014	% Average Rate 2016	% Average Rate 2015	% Average Rate 2014
In US offices	$100,472	$108,320	$102,672	$1,024	$614	$657	1.02%	0.57%	0.64%
In offices outside the United States	57,588	66,130	88,080	888	998	1,238	1.54	1.51	1.41
Total	$158,060	$174,450	$190,752	$1,912	$1,612	$1,895	1.21%	0.92%	0.99%
Trading account liabilities									
In US offices	$29,481	$24,711	$29,263	$242	$107	$74	0.82%	0.43%	0.25%
In offices outside the United States	44,669	45,252	47,904	168	110	94	0.38	0.24	0.20
Total	$74,150	$69,963	$77,167	$410	$217	$168	0.55%	0.31%	0.22%
Short-term borrowings									
In US offices	$61,015	$64,973	$77,967	$202	$224	$161	0.33%	0.34%	0.21%
In offices outside the United States	19,184	50,803	40,282	275	299	419	1.43	0.59	1.04
Total	$80,199	$115,776	$118,249	$477	$523	$580	0.59%	0.45%	0.49%
Long-term debt									
In US offices	$175,342	$182,347	$191,364	$4,179	$4,308	$5,093	2.38%	2.36%	2.66%
In offices outside the United States	6,426	7,642	7,346	233	209	262	3.63	2.73	3.57
Total	$181,768	$189,989	$198,710	$4,412	$4,517	$5,355	2.43%	2.38%	2.69%
Total interest-bearing liabilities	$1,212,602	$1,248,399	$1,342,075	$12,511	$11,921	$13,690	1.03%	0.95%	1.02%
Demand deposits									
In US offices	$38,120	$26,144	$26,227						
Other non-interest-bearing liabilities	328,822	330,104	316,061						
Total liabilities	$1,579,544	$1,604,647	$1,684,363						
Citigroup stockholders' equity	$228,065	$217,875	$210,863						
Non-controlling interest	1,119	1,315	1,689						
Total equity	$229,184	$219,190	$212,552						
Total liabilities and stockholders' equity	$1,808,728	$1,823,837	$1,896,915						

Net interest revenue as a percentage of average interest-earning assets	Total Average Interest-Earning Assets			Net Interest Revenue			Net Interest Margin		
In US offices	$859,311	$923,309	$953,394	$27,929	$28,495	$27,496	3.25%	3.09%	2.88%
In offices outside the United States	734,775	682,503	720,380	17,637	18,624	20,994	2.40	2.73	2.91
Total	$1,594,086	$1,605,812	$1,673,774	$45,566	$47,119	$48,490	2.86%	2.93%	2.90%

Observations from Exhibit 21:

- Citigroup's cost of funding its assets increased in every category of liability in 2016. That attribute was even more pronounced in offices outside the United States, with the exception of deposit liabilities.

- This difference between US and non-US asset and liability performance extends to the net interest margin, net interest revenue as a percentage of average interest-earning assets, shown at the bottom of the table. Although the net interest margin improved to 3.25% in 2016 from 3.09% in 2015 for assets in US offices, it declined significantly for assets in offices outside the United States, from 2.73% in 2015 to 2.40% in 2016. The net interest margin in offices outside the United States has been declining consistently since 2014, when the US dollar began strengthening. Citigroup has been experiencing negative foreign currency translation impacts since then.

- An investor might exercise increased caution when observing management's future actions in making foreign investments. These results do not provide assurance that all capital is well allocated overseas or that currency risk is adequately managed. The lower returns might also be due to macroeconomic factors, such as lower yield curves (and even negative rates) overseas, creating fewer profitable opportunities. An investor should factor those possibilities into his consideration.

Analyzing the net interest revenue resulting from average interest-bearing asset and liability balances can be useful for analyzing what happened within a bank for a given period but not necessarily useful for projecting future earnings. The interest earned or paid on an average balance for a given period may have no bearing on what a bank may actually earn or pay in the next period. End-of-period balances of balance sheet components and their associated interest rates may make a better starting point for projecting future earnings than the average balance information.

In summary, the quality of Citigroup's earnings is not exceedingly high. The fact that the decreases in the provision for loan losses has driven 84% of the pretax earnings increases over the last five years does nothing to relieve quality concerns, nor does the increase in trading income over the last five years instill more confidence in the earnings quality. The analysis of the net interest revenue shows declining net interest margin over the last three years, largely attributable to the non-US offices. A rating of 3 could be justified for earnings quality.

A BRIEF OVERVIEW OF ACCOUNTING FOR DERIVATIVES

Accounting rules for derivatives are extensive. The following points are a very brief summary of this complex topic and are generally applicable to both IFRS and US GAAP.

- At inception, many derivatives contracts do not give rise to an asset or liability on the balance sheet or to a gain or loss on the income statement. For example, an interest rate swap contract can involve the exchange of future cash flows with equivalent present value. Thus, at inception, the only accounting record required for every derivatives contract is a disclosure of the notional amount of the contract. This disclosure appears in the notes to the financial statements.

- Measurement of the mark-to-market value of a derivatives contract creates an asset or liability and subsequently increases or decreases the value of the asset or liability.

- Changes in the value of the asset or liability are recorded either as part of profit and loss on the income statement or as part of comprehensive income, depending on the classification.

- Derivative instruments can be classified as a hedge of a cash flow or a hedge of a net investment in a foreign subsidiary. Classification of a derivatives contract as a hedge requires substantiating its correlation

Analyzing a Bank: Example of CAMELS Approach

> with the risk being hedged. If a derivatives contract is classified as one of these two types of hedges, changes in its value are recorded as part of other comprehensive income and will be recognized in net income over the life of the hedged transaction.
>
> - If such a derivatives contract fails classification as a hedge and is instead a free-standing derivative instrument or if the hedge is classified as a third type, a hedge of a fair value, then changes in its fair value are reported as income or expense in the income statement at each reporting period. The immediate recognition of a gain or loss in earnings, instead of reporting it in other comprehensive income, can lead to unexpected volatility of earnings and missed earnings targets. Depending on the nature of the derivative transaction, a secondary effect of a contract's failure to qualify as a hedge may also require additional posting of collateral or cash.

Liquidity Position

A bank's liquidity is an extremely important matter for its own well-being in times of financial stress. Given the interdependence of banks, through such transactions as interbank deposits and acting as counterparties in derivative transactions, a bank's liquidity also matters for the well-being of other banks—and possibly an entire economy.

Capital alone is not sufficient to assure liquidity; there must be enough capital available in cash or near-cash for the meeting of obligations. The Basel III Regulatory Framework introduced two liquidity standards to provide assurance that capital would be adequately liquid for meeting obligations under stressful conditions.

The first is the Liquidity Coverage Ratio, which is the minimum percentage of a bank's expected cash outflows to be held in highly liquid assets. Expected net cash outflows are the bank's anticipated 30-day liquidity needs in a stress scenario, and the highly liquid assets include only those of high quality and immediately convertible into cash. Expected net cash outflows are calculated by applying prescribed outflow factors to various liability categories, with any available offsets by inflows from assets maturing within the 30-day stress period. Additionally, banks must include an add-on amount to account for possible maturity mismatches between contractual cash outflows and inflows during the 30-day period to arrive at total net outflows. The minimum LCR threshold is 100%; anything less would indicate an inability to meet the liquidity needs. Exhibit 22 shows the components of Citigroup's LCR at 31 December 2016, 30 September 2016, and 31 December 2015.

Exhibit 22: Citigroup's Liquidity Coverage Ratio

(In billions of dollars)	31 Dec. 2016	30 Sep. 2016	31 Dec. 2015
High-quality liquid assets	$403.7	$403.8	$389.2
Net outflows	332.5	335.3	344.4
HQLA in excess of net outflows	$71.2	$68.5	$44.8
Liquidity Coverage Ratio	121%	120%	113%

Observations from the Liquidity Coverage Ratio:

- Citigroup's Liquidity Coverage Ratio has improved in the last two years.

- Citigroup's 2016 LCR indicates it can withstand cash outflows that are 21% higher than its 30-day liquidity needs in a stress scenario or, equivalently, it can withstand a stress level volume of cash outflows for 36.3 days (121% times 30 days). Either way, the LCR indicates adequate liquidity even in the absence of any (likely) remedial management steps in an actual stress event.

The second Basel III liquidity standard is the Net Stable Funding Ratio: a minimum percentage of required stable funding that must be sourced from available stable funding. Required stable funding depends on the composition and maturity of a bank's asset base; available stable funding is a function of the composition and maturity of a bank's funding sources (capital and liabilities). The Net Stable Funding Ratio is a kind of inverted Liquidity Coverage Ratio. Where the Liquidity Coverage Ratio evaluates short-term liquidity, the Net Stable Funding Ratio is a measure of the available stable funding to cover funding of longer-term, less liquid assets, such as loans. Highly liquid assets do not enter the calculation of the Net Stable Funding Ratio. As with the Liquidity Coverage Ratio, a ratio of 100% is the minimum acceptable threshold.

The Net Stable Funding Ratio is not yet a required Basel III standard as of the end of 2016; final rules are expected in 2017. Still, a rough calculation may be made, without the various weightings for components of both available and required stable funding that will be part of the final rules. Exhibit 23 shows one possible calculation of a Net Stable Funding Ratio, based on Citigroup's consolidated balance sheet amounts at 31 December 2016, 30 September 2016, and 31 December 2015. The calculation divides the estimated, unweighted amount of available stable funding by the estimated required amount of stable funding.

Exhibit 23: Citigroup's Net Stable Funding Ratio

(In billions of dollars)	31 Dec. 2016	30 Sep. 2016	31 Dec. 2015
Available stable funding:			
Total deposits	$929.4	$940.3	$907.9
Long-term debt	206.2	209.1	201.3
Common equity	205.9	212.3	205.1
Total available stable funding	$1,341.5	$1,361.6	$1,314.3
Required stable funding:			
Total investments	$353.3	$354.9	$343.0
Total loans, net	612.3	626.0	605.0
Goodwill	21.7	22.5	22.3
Intangible assets (other than MSRs)	5.1	5.4	3.7
Mortgage servicing rights (MSRs)	1.6	1.3	1.8
Other assets	128.0	116.5	133.7
Total required stable funding	$1,122.0	$1,126.6	$1,109.5
Net Stable Funding Ratio	120%	121%	118%

Observations on the approximated Net Stable Funding Ratio:

- Citigroup's Net Stable Funding Ratio, as calculated, has stayed relatively stable since the end of 2015, and the available stable funding is well above the minimum required funding needed.

In summary, Citigroup's liquidity position is very good, based on its Liquidity Coverage and Net Stable Funding Ratios. A rating of 1 is justifiable based on the results of the two ratios.

Sensitivity to Market Risk

Bank assets and liabilities are constantly subject to market risk, which impacts their earnings performance and liquidity. Analysts need to understand how adverse changes in interest rates, exchange rates, and other market factors can affect a bank's earnings and balance sheet.

Required disclosures in banks' financial statements make it possible to assess various sensitivities. The value at risk disclosure is helpful for assessing a bank's exposure to market factors. VaR statistics can be effective indicators of trends in intra-company risk taking; because of differences in calculation assumptions across companies, VaR is not as useful for assessing risk-taking activities between different companies.

Using a 99% confidence level, Citigroup estimates the value at risk of a potential decline in the value of a position or a portfolio under normal market conditions for an assumed single-day holding period. Citigroup uses a Monte Carlo simulation VaR model to capture material risk sensitivities of various asset classes/risk types. Citigroup's VaR includes positions that are measured at fair value but excludes investment securities classified as AFS or HTM. Exhibit 24 is an excerpt from Citigroup's 2016 VaR disclosure.

Exhibit 24: Citigroup Year-End and Average Trading VaR and Trading and Credit Portfolio VaR

(In millions of dollars)	12/31/16	2016 Average	12/31/15	2015 Average
Interest rate	$37	$35	$37	$44
Credit spread	63	62	56	69
Covariance adjustment [1]	(17)	(28)	(25)	(26)
Fully diversified interest rate and credit spread	$83	$69	$68	$87
Foreign exchange	32	24	27	34
Equity	13	14	17	17
Commodity	27	21	17	19
Covariance adjustment [1]	(70)	(58)	(53)	(65)
Total trading VaR—all market risk factors, including general and specific risk (excluding credit portfolios) [2]	$85	$70	$76	$92
Specific risk-only component [3]	$3	$7	$11	$6
Total trading VaR—general market risk factors only (excluding credit portfolios) [2]	$82	$63	$65	$86
Incremental impact of the credit portfolio [4]	$20	$22	$22	$25
Total trading and credit portfolio VaR	$105	$92	$98	$117
VaR Effects on Earnings & Capital:				
Total trading and credit portfolio VAR	$105	$92	$98	$117
Net income from continuing operations	$15,033		$17,386	

(In millions of dollars)	12/31/16	2016 Average	12/31/15	2015 Average
Common equity	$205,867		$205,139	
Total VaR as % of:				
Net income from continuing operations	0.7%	0.6%	0.6%	0.7%
Common equity	0.1%	0.0%	0.0%	0.1%

Notes:

1. Covariance adjustment reflects the fact that the risks within each and across risk types are not perfectly correlated and, consequently, the total VaR on a given day will be lower than the sum of the VARs relating to each individual risk type.
2. The total trading VaR includes mark-to-market and certain fair value option trading positions except for certain hedges. Available-for-sale and accrual exposures are not included.
3. The specific risk-only component represents the level of equity and fixed income issuer-specific risk embedded in VAR.
4. The credit portfolio is composed of mark-to-market positions associated with non-trading business units.

Observations from the VaR table:

- Citigroup's average trading VaR declined in 2016 to $70 million from $92 million in the previous year, mainly owing to changes in interest rate exposures from mark-to-market hedging activity.
- Average trading and credit portfolio VaR also declined in 2016 to $92 million from $117 million in the previous year.
- Although total trading and credit portfolio VaR increased at year end 2016 to $105 million, compared to $98 million at year end 2015, the magnitude of this worst-case single-day VaR is still less than 1% of net income from continuing operations in both years, on either an end-of-period basis (0.7%) or an average basis (0.6%). The magnitude is even more minor compared to equity, representing 0.1% on the end-of-period basis and less than 0.1% on average.
- Importantly, Citigroup's VaR is a single-day measure of market shocks that can affect a company. Market dislocations can linger for days, weeks, and even longer. Although VaR is useful for measuring the effects of very short-term shocks, it does not address the effects of longer-term market impacts.

Another useful disclosure in Citigroup's 10-K focuses on the estimated sensitivity of Citigroup's capital ratios to numerator changes of $100 million in Common Equity Tier 1 Capital, Tier 1 Capital, and Total Capital and changes of $1 billion in risk-weighted assets at the end of 2016. These sensitivities consider only a single change to either a component of capital or risk-weighted assets; an event affecting more than one factor at a time may have a far greater impact than Citigroup's estimate. Exhibit 25 shows an excerpt of the sensitivity table, along with the actual ratios calculated at the end of 2016.

Analyzing a Bank: Example of CAMELS Approach

Exhibit 25: Citigroup Capital Ratio Estimated Sensitivities at 31 December 2016

(In basis points)	Common Equity Tier 1 Capital Ratio — Impact of $100 Million Change in Common Equity Tier 1 Capital	Common Equity Tier 1 Capital Ratio — Impact of $1 Billion Change in Risk-Weighted Assets	Tier 1 Capital Ratio — Impact of $100 Million Change in Tier 1 Capital	Tier 1 Capital Ratio — Impact of $1 Billion Change in Risk-Weighted Assets	Total Capital Ratio — Impact of $100 Million Change in Total Capital	Total Capital Ratio — Impact of $1 Billion Change in Risk-Weighted Assets
Citigroup						
Advanced Approach	0.90	1.20	0.90	1.30	0.90	1.50
Standardized Approach	0.90	1.30	0.90	1.40	0.90	1.70
Actual capital ratio	14.35%	14.35%	15.29%	15.29%	17.33%	17.33%
Minimum capital ratio	4.50%	4.50%	6.00%	6.00%	8.00%	8.00%

From Citigroup's description of its risk-based capital ratios, p. 33 of 2016 10-K: "Total risk-weighted assets under the Advanced Approaches, which are primarily models based, include credit, market, and operational risk-weighted assets. Conversely, the Standardized Approach excludes operational risk-weighted assets and generally applies prescribed supervisory risk weights to broad categories of credit risk exposures. As a result, credit risk-weighted assets calculated under the Advanced Approaches are more risk sensitive than those calculated under the Standardized Approach. Market risk-weighted assets are derived on a generally consistent basis under both approaches."

Observations from the capital ratio sensitivity table:

- Regardless of the calculation (advanced or standardized approach), the effect of a $100 million change in capital or a $1 billion change in risk-weighted assets is practically nil compared to the actual capital ratios calculated at year end.
- At the same time, these are static measures of sensitivity and adjust for only one impact at a time.

In summary, Citigroup's sensitivity to market impacts appears to be controlled and provides circumstantial evidence of effective risk management. Based on the evidence, Citigroup could be justifiably rated at 1 for its management of sensitivities.

Overall CAMELS Assessment

After each CAMELS component has been analyzed and rated, the overall CAMELS assessment can be completed. One approach to consolidating CAMELS components on an entity basis would be to simply add all the components' ratings. A bank earning the best CAMELS rating, a rating of 1, for each component would have a total score of 6, and a bank that received the worst ratings would have a composite CAMELS score of 30. To translate the score into the corresponding composite CAMELS rating, the score could be divided by 6. This approach arrives at an arithmetic mean rating as the composite rating for the bank. Note that if each component receives the same rating, the weighting of the components is irrelevant. The arithmetic mean approach, however, fails to take into account the fact that some components of the CAMELS approach are more important to some analysts than others, as discussed in Section

3. Depending on the focus of the analysis, the analyst-weighted composite CAMELS score and rating could be quite different from the unweighted score and arithmetic mean of the ratings.

Exhibit 26 presents the calculation of Citigroup's overall CAMELS score from the point of view of an equity analyst who places twice as much value on asset quality and earnings than on the other CAMELS components.

Exhibit 26: Citigroup Overall CAMELS Score

	Rating	Weighting	Weighted Rating
Capital adequacy	1.0	1	1.00
Asset quality	2.5	2	5.00
Management	2.0	1	2.00
Earnings	3.0	2	6.00
Liquidity	1.0	1	1.00
Sensitivity	1.0	1	1.00
Total score	**10.5**	**8**	**16.00**
Converted to CAMELS rating (score divided by 6)	1.75		2.00

Note that without the weighting, which helps the analyst quantify his or her priorities, Citigroup has an overall CAMELS rating of 1.75—not perfect, but indicating a bank that is generally showing strong performance and risk management. Once the ratings are weighted, however, the composite score is 2.00 (16/8 = 2.00). The weighted score indicates a slightly higher degree of flaws that management may need to address.

5   ANALYZING PROPERTY AND CASUALTY INSURANCE COMPANIES

☐ describe key ratios and other factors to consider in analyzing an insurance company

Insurance companies provide protection against adverse events. Insurance companies earn revenues from **premiums** (amounts paid by the purchaser of insurance products) and from investment income earned on the **float** (amounts collected as premium and not yet paid out as benefits). Insurance companies are typically categorized as property and casualty (P&C) or life and health (L&H). The products of the two types of insurance companies differ in contract duration and variability of claims.[30] P&C insurers' policies are usually short term, and the final cost will usually be known within a year of occurrence of an insured event, whereas L&H insurers' policies are usually longer term. P&C insurers' claims are more variable and "lumpier" because they arise from accidents and other unpredictable events, whereas L&H insurers' claims are more predictable because they correlate closely with relatively stable actuarially based mortality rates when applied to large populations.

---
30 Refer to the Insurance Information Institute's website: www.iii.org.

Analyzing Property and Casualty Insurance Companies

For both types of insurance companies, important areas for analysis include business profile, earnings characteristics, investment returns, liquidity, and capitalization. In addition, for P&C companies, analysis of reserves and the combined ratio, an indicator of overall underwriting profitability, are important.

Some countries, including, for example, the United States, require insurance companies to prepare financial reports according to statutory accounting rules, which differ from US GAAP and IFRS, and have a greater focus on solvency.[31] This section discusses analysis based on US GAAP and IFRS financial reports. A discussion of P&C insurers is followed by a discussion of L&H insurers.

Property and Casualty Insurance Companies

Property and casualty (P&C) insurers provide risk management services to their insured parties. For the price of an insurance premium, they protect the insured parties against losses many times greater than the premiums paid. Premiums are collected at the outset of the insurance contract, creating a float period between their receipt and the time of any payout to the insured party for losses. During the float period, the insurance company will invest the premiums, providing another income stream apart from the underwriting results. In addition to being risk managers, insurance companies also act as investment companies.

Exhibit 27 displays the revenue composition for Travelers Companies, Inc. The net investment income is the second-highest revenue source, after premiums earned, and is significant relative to total revenues.

Exhibit 27: Travelers Companies, Inc., Revenues Composition

(For the year ended 31 December, in millions)	2016		2015		2014	
Premiums	$24,534	88.8%	$23,874	89.0%	$23,713	87.3%
Net investment income	2,302	8.3%	2,379	8.9%	2,787	10.3%
Fee income	458	1.7%	460	1.7%	450	1.7%
Net realized investment gains	68	0.2%	3	0.0%	79	0.3%
Other revenues	263	1.0%	99	0.4%	145	0.5%
Total revenues	$27,625	100.0%	$26,815	100.0%	$27,174	100.0%

Property and casualty insurers try to minimize their payouts to insured parties by exercising care in the underwriting process and charging an adequate price for the risk that they will bear. They may try to diversify the risks they accept by not concentrating excessively on one kind of policy, market, or customer type. They may also diversify their risk by transferring policies, in whole or in part, to reinsurers. Reinsurers deal only with risks insured by other insurers; they do not originate primary policies.

Property and casualty insurance companies differ from life insurance companies in that the length of their duty to perform is comparatively short. Policies are often offered on an annual basis, and the event being covered is often known with certainty

---

[31] In the United States, the National Association of Insurance Commissioners (NAIC) has developed a system of analytical tools (i.e., ratios and guideline values) for solvency monitoring, known as the NAIC Insurance Regulatory Information System (IRIS). Ratios in IRIS are based on statutory accounting reports.

during the policy period—fire or weather events, for example. Insured events can also take much longer to emerge: For instance, environmental harm occurring during the policy period may not be obvious until well after the expiration of the policy period.

Operations: Products and Distribution

Property insurance policies protect against loss or damage to property—buildings, automobiles, environmental damage, and other tangible objects of value. The events causing loss or damage vary and determine the kind of policy in force. Events may be attributed to accidents, fire, theft, or catastrophe. Casualty insurance, sometimes called *liability insurance*, protects against a legal liability related to an insured event. Casualty insurance covers the liability to a third party, such as passengers, employees, or bystanders. A single insured event may contain both property and casualty losses: For instance, an automobile accident may result in both the loss of the automobile and injury to passengers. Such policies may be referred to as *multiple peril policies*.

Property and casualty insurance may be considered as personal lines or commercial lines, depending on the customer; some products may be sold in both lines. Types of property and casualty insurance include automobile property and liability policies (an example of both personal and commercial lines selling the same product), homeowners' insurance, workers' compensation, marine insurance, and reinsurance.

There are two methods of distributing insurance: direct writing and agency writing. Direct writers of insurance have their own sales and marketing staff. Direct writers also may sell insurance policies via the internet; through direct response channels, such as mail; and through groups with a shared interest or bond, such as membership in a profession. Agency writers use independent agents, exclusive agents, and insurance brokers to sell policies.

Earnings Characteristics

In the macro view, the property and casualty insurance business is cyclical. It is a price-sensitive business, with many competitors unafraid to cut prices to obtain market share. According to A.M. Best, a US insurance rating agency, there are approximately 1,200 property and casualty groups in the United States, comprising approximately 2,650 property and casualty companies. Of those groups, the top 150 accounted for approximately 92% of the consolidated industry's total net written premiums in 2015. Once the price cutting drives out profitability, creating a "soft" pricing market for insurance premiums, the insurers reach an uncomfortably depleted level of capital. Competition lessens and underwriting standards tighten, creating a "hard" pricing market. Consequently, premiums rise and the insurers return to more reasonable levels of profitability. The increase in profitability once again attracts more entrants into the market, and the cycle repeats.

In the micro view, there are operating cost considerations that affect insurer profitability apart from the "softness" or "hardness" of the insurance market, depending on the method of distribution. Direct writers have higher fixed costs because of the in-house nature of their distribution method: The sales and marketing staff are salaried employees. Agency writers do not have this fixed cost; instead, the commissions paid to agents and brokers are a variable cost.

The underwriting cycle is driven largely by the expenses of the participants. When the industry's combined ratio—the total insurance expenses divided by the net premiums earned—is low, it indicates a hard insurance market, attracting new entrants who cut prices and push the cycle downward. The effect can be seen in the denominator of the combined ratio: The lower prices for premiums decreases the total net premiums earned, and the combined ratio increases, indicating a soft market. Competitors leave the market, either because they want to forgo unprofitable underwriting or because of their own failure.

Analyzing Property and Casualty Insurance Companies

For a single insurance company, a combined ratio higher than 100% indicates an underwriting loss. In the United States, Statutory Accounting Practices define the combined ratio as the sum of two ratios, using statutory financial statements: an underwriting loss ratio and an expense ratio. The underwriting loss ratio—losses [= claims paid plus (ending loss reserves minus beginning loss reserves)] divided by net premiums earned—is an indicator of the quality of a company's underwriting activities. Underwriting activities include decisions on whether to accept an application for insurance coverage and decisions on the premiums charged for any coverage extended. The expense ratio (underwriting expenses, including sales commissions and related employee expenses, divided by net premiums written) is an indicator of the efficiency of a company's operations in acquiring and managing underwriting business. For financial disclosures, companies sometimes report modified versions of the combined ratio. For example, the combined ratio reported by Travelers calculates the expense ratio with net earned premiums in the denominator, which is consistent with US GAAP.[32] Other companies may make different presentations.

P&C insurers' investment income is not as volatile as their operating income, because the investments are relatively low-return, low-risk holdings, as we will discuss in the next section.

One critical expense for property and casualty insurers results from the management of their loss reserves. Proper estimation of liabilities is essential to the pricing of policies. Underestimation of loss reserves may lead to undercharging for risks assumed. Development of the loss reserves is based on historical information, yet the process also incorporates estimates about future losses. It is a material account that is subject to management discretion, and its improper estimation can have consequences for the property and casualty insurer. If the loss reserves and the annual adjustments to them are too optimistic, the pricing of the insurance policies may be insufficient for the risk being borne by the insurer and insolvency may ensue. Another problematic attribute of the loss reserves is the fact that the longer the insurer's obligation runs, the more difficult it can be to estimate the loss reserve properly. For example, insurance policies covering asbestos liabilities written long before courts began awarding more generous payouts have been problematic for insurers. Their current experience is far different from what they expected when they issued the policies, and the rapid growth in the award sizes made it difficult to properly estimate the associated loss reserves.

Exhibit 28 shows the roll-forward schedule of activity in Travelers Companies' loss reserve balances, drawn from the insurance claims footnote in its 2016 financial statements. It provides a high-level view of the way the components affect the balance sheet and the income statement and offers insights into the way a property and casualty insurance company manages its assumed risks. The roll-forward activity is denominated in terms of the reserves, net of reinsurance recoverables expected to reduce Travelers' ultimate liability. The beginning and ending balances are shown at their gross amounts, reduced by the reinsurance recoverables to arrive at the net reserves.

Exhibit 28: Travelers Companies, Inc., Loss Reserve Balances and Activity

(At and for the year ended 31 December, in millions)	2016	2015	2014
Gross claims and claim adjustment expense reserves at beginning of year	$48,272	$49,824	$50,865
Less reinsurance recoverables on unpaid losses	(8,449)	(8,788)	(9,280)
Net reserves at beginning of year	39,823	41,036	41,585

---

[32] The Travelers Companies, Inc., Form 10-K for the year ended 31 December 2016 (p. 36).

(At and for the year ended 31 December, in millions)	2016	2015	2014
Estimated claims and claim adjustment expenses for claims arising in the current year	15,675	14,471	14,688
Estimated decrease in claims and claim adjustment expenses for claims arising in prior years	(680)	(817)	(885)
Total increases	14,995	13,654	13,803
Claims and claim adjustment expense payments for claims arising in:			
Current year	(6,220)	(5,725)	(5,895)
Prior years	(8,576)	(8,749)	(8,171)
Total payments	(14,796)	(14,474)	(14,066)
Acquisition	—	2	—
Unrealized foreign exchange gain	(74)	(395)	(286)
Net reserves at end of year	39,948	39,823	41,036
Plus reinsurance recoverables on unpaid losses	7,981	8,449	8,788
Gross claims and claim adjustment expense reserves at end of year	$47,929	$48,272	$49,824
Reinsurance at end of year:			
Reinsurance recoverables on unpaid losses	$7,981	$8,449	$8,788
Gross claims and claim adjustment expense reserves at end of year	$47,929	$48,272	$49,824
Percentage of claims and claim adjustment expense reserves covered by reinsurance	16.7%	17.5%	17.6%
Revisions' effect on income before income taxes:			
Downward revisions of claims and claim adjustment expenses for claims arising in prior years	$680	$817	$885
Income before income taxes	$4,053	$4,740	$5,089
Percentage of contributions of downward revisions to income before income taxes	16.8%	17.2%	17.4%

Observations from Exhibit 28:

- The 2016 claims paid of $6,220 million is 39.7% of the estimated claims and claim adjustments of $15,675 million, indicating that a major part of Travelers Companies' liability exposure is fairly short term. The two prior years show a similar exposure term.
- The company employs significant levels of reinsurance to control its risk exposure. In reinsurance, one insurance company transfers, or cedes, a portion of its risk to another insurer (the "reinsurer") for a premium. The ceding company expects to recover its losses from the reinsurer. As the table shows, Travelers has been ceding between 16.7% and 17.6% of its gross loss reserves to reinsurers.
- The total increases in loss reserves, net of decreases in claims and claim adjustment expenses for prior years' claims, affect the income statement more than any other expense. In 2016, the $14,995 million of total increases in loss reserves represented 63.6% of the $23,572 million of total claims and expenses in the income statement (which is not presented here because of space limitations).

Analyzing Property and Casualty Insurance Companies

- The company decreased its prior years' estimates of claims by $680 million in 2016, $817 million in 2015, and $885 million in 2014. Downward revisions indicate that a company is estimating its initial recognized reserves conservatively, but aggressive revisions may also be a tool for manipulating earnings. Travelers Companies' downward revisions may appear minor in comparison to the total increases, but they have a profound effect on income before taxes. This effect is shown in the bottom of the exhibit: Downward revisions of prior years' estimates contributed 16.8% to income before income taxes in 2016, 17.2% in 2015, and 17.4% in 2014.

Depending on the ratios used, the ratios of insurers' profitability may distinguish between net premiums written and net premiums earned. Net premiums written are an insurer's direct premiums written, net of any such premiums ceded to other insurers. Premiums are usually billed in advance—for example, twice per year—and they are earned over the period of coverage provided by the insurance policy. Only the net premiums written that are earned over a relevant accounting period—for example, quarterly—are considered to be the net premiums earned.

Useful ratios in analyzing property and casualty insurance companies' profitability include the following:

- *Loss and loss adjustment expense ratio = (Loss expense + Loss adjustment expense)/Net premiums earned.* This ratio indicates the degree of success an underwriter has achieved in estimating the risks insured. The lower the ratio, the greater the success.

- *Underwriting expense ratio = Underwriting expense/Net premiums written.* This ratio measures the efficiency of money spent in obtaining new premiums. A lower ratio indicates higher success.

- *Combined ratio = Loss and loss adjustment expense ratio + Underwriting expense ratio.* This ratio indicates the overall efficiency of an underwriting operation. A combined ratio of less than 100 is considered efficient.

- *Dividends to policyholders (shareholders) ratio = Dividends to policyholders (shareholders)/Net premiums earned.* This ratio is a measure of liquidity, in that it relates the cash outflow of dividends to the premiums earned in the same period.

- *Combined ratio after dividends = Combined ratio + Dividends to policyholders (shareholders) ratio.* This ratio is a stricter measure of efficiency than the ordinary combined ratio, in that it takes into account the cash satisfaction of policyholders or shareholders after consideration of the total underwriting efforts. Dividends are discretionary cash outlays, and factoring them into the combined ratio presents a fuller description of total cash requirements.[33]

Exhibit 29 displays the calculation of these ratios for a group of property and casualty insurers based on their 2016 financial reports. Notice the wide variation in the results. Markel Corp. performed the best (combined ratio of 89%), and Hartford Financial Services Group performed relatively poorly (combined ratio of 131%). The high loss and loss adjustment expense ratio (82.2%) and underwriting expense ratio (48.8%) suggest its underwriting business requires additional management attention. A review of the three ratios related to operations shows that Travelers ranks as the median with respect to loss and loss adjustment expense ratio and below median for underwriting expense and combined ratios. This finding indicates that Travelers'

---

[33] "Annual Report on the Insurance Industry," Federal Insurance Office, US Department of the Treasury (September 2015), available at www.treasury.gov.

operations are in the better-performing half of this group. After taking into account the dividend distribution policy in the combined ratio after dividends to policyholders (shareholders), Travelers' overall performance remains in the better-performing half of the group.

Exhibit 29: 2016 Ratios Calculated for Selected Property and Casualty Insurers

($ millions)	Travelers Companies	Hartford Financial Services Group	W. R. Berkley Corp.	CNA Financial Corp.	Markel Corp.
Loss and loss adjustment expense ratio:					
Loss expense and loss adjustment expense	$15,070	$11,351	$3,846	$5,270	$2,051
Net premiums earned	$24,534	$13,811	$6,293	$6,924	$3,866
Loss and loss adjustment expense ratio	**61.4%**	**82.2%**	**61.1%**	**76.1%**	**53.1%**
Underwriting expense ratio:					
Underwriting expense	$8,139	$5,156	$2,396	$2,787	$1,437
Net premiums written	$24,958	$10,568	$6,424	$6,988	$4,001
Underwriting expense ratio	**32.6%**	**48.8%**	**37.3%**	**39.9%**	**35.9%**
Combined ratio:					
Loss and loss adjustment expense ratio	61.4%	82.2%	61.1%	76.1%	53.0%
Underwriting expense ratio	32.6%	48.8%	37.3%	39.9%	35.9%
Combined ratio	**94.0%**	**131.0%**	**98.4%**	**116.0%**	**89.0%**
Dividends to policyholders (shareholders) ratio:					
Dividends to policyholders (shareholders)	$757	$334	$184	$813	$0
Net premiums earned	$24,534	$13,811	$6,293	$6,924	$3,866
Dividends to policyholders (shareholders) ratio	**3.1%**	**2.4%**	**2.9%**	**11.7%**	**0.0%**
Combined ratio after dividends:					
Combined ratio	94.0%	131.0%	98.4%	116.0%	89.0%
Dividends to policyholders (shareholders) ratio	3.1%	2.4%	2.9%	11.7%	0.0%
Combined ratio after dividends	**97.1%**	**133.4%**	**101.3%**	**127.7%**	**89.0%**

Investment Returns

Property and casualty insurance companies face much uncertainty in the risks they insure, and their business is enormously competitive when insurance pricing moves into its "hard" stage. To counteract the environment of uncertainty, property and casualty insurers conservatively invest the collected premiums. They typically favor steady-return, low-risk assets, while shunning low-liquidity investments.

An illustration is found in Exhibit 30, which is the investment portion of the assets shown in the Travelers Companies' 2016 balance sheet. Investments represent 70% of total assets in 2016 and 2015. In both years, approximately 86% of the total investment portfolio is composed of fixed-maturity investments, and nearly another 7% of investments are short-term securities, which can be considered proxies for cash. Equity securities are only 1% of investments in both years, and real estate is also a very minor component of investments in both years.

Exhibit 30: The Travelers Companies, Inc., Portfolio Composition, 2016 and 2015

At 31 December ($ millions)	2016		2015	
Fixed maturities, available for sale, at fair value (amortized cost $59,650 and $58,878)	$60,515	85.9%	$60,658	86.1%
Equity securities, available for sale, at fair value (cost $504 and $528)	732	1.0%	705	1.0%
Real estate investments	928	1.3%	989	1.4%
Short-term securities	4,865	6.9%	4,671	6.6%
Other investments	3,448	4.9%	3,447	4.9%
Total investments	$70,488	100.0%	$70,470	100.0%

As with any kind of company, the concentrations of assets merit attention. When considering the investments of a property and casualty insurer, the concentration of investments by type, maturity, credit quality, industry, or geographic location or within single issuers should be evaluated.

Investment performance can be estimated by dividing total investment income by invested assets (cash and investments). This metric can also be calculated on two different bases, by using investment income with and without unrealized capital gains, thus showing the relative importance of unrealized capital gains to the total investment income.

Given that property and casualty insurance companies stand ready to meet obligations for policy payouts, liquidity is a priority in the selection of assets. It will be addressed further in the following section.

Liquidity

The uncertainty of the payouts involved in the property and casualty business requires a high degree of liquidity so loss obligations can be met. Because the investments are typically low-risk, steady-return types of financial instruments, their nature is typically liquid. An analysis of the portfolio investments should take into account overall quality of the investments and the ease with which the investments can be converted into cash without affecting their value.

Evidence of the investment liquidity can be found by examining their status in the hierarchy of fair value reporting. Level 1 reported values are based on readily available prices for securities traded in liquid markets and thus indicate the most liquid of securities. Level 2 reported values are based on less liquid conditions: Prices for such securities are not available from a liquid market and may be inferred from similar securities trading in an active market. Thus, these securities are likely to be less liquid than those reported as Level 1 securities. Finally, Level 3 reported values are based on models and assumptions because there is no active market for the securities, implying illiquidity.

Exhibit 31 shows the fair value hierarchy for investment securities held by the Travelers Companies at 31 December 2016.

Exhibit 31: The Travelers Companies, Inc., Portfolio Composition by Fair Value Hierarchy

(at 31 December 2016, in millions)	Total	Level 1	Level 2	Level 3

Fixed maturities:

(at 31 December 2016, in millions)	Total	Level 1	Level 2	Level 3
US Treasury securities and obligations of US government and government agencies and authorities	$2,035	$2,035	$0	$0
Obligations of states, municipalities, and political subdivisions	31,910	—	31,898	12
Debt securities issued by foreign governments	1,662	—	1,662	—
Mortgage-backed securities, collateralized mortgage obligations, and pass-through securities obligations	1,708	—	1,704	4
All other corporate bonds	23,107	—	22,939	168
Redeemable preferred stock	93	3	90	—
Total fixed maturities	$60,515	$2,038	$58,293	$184
% of security class	*100.0%*	*3.4%*	*96.3%*	*0.3%*
Equity securities:				
Public common stock	$603	$603	$0	$0
Non-redeemable preferred stock	129	51	78	—
Total equity securities	$732	$654	$78	$0
% of security class	*100.0%*	*89.3%*	*10.7%*	*0.0%*

Travelers has very little of its portfolio invested in Level 1 assets—only 4.4% [($2,038 + $654)/($60,515 + $732) = 4.4%] on a combined fixed-income securities and equity securities basis. The majority is classified as Level 2 assets, implying less liquidity than Level 1, yet not implying illiquidity. The fair value footnote from the 10-K provides some assurance that the Level 2 assets are not illiquid (underline added by authors):

> The Company utilized a pricing service to estimate fair value measurements for approximately 98% of its fixed maturities at both December 31, 2016 and 2015. The pricing service utilizes market quotations for fixed maturity securities that have quoted prices in active markets. Since fixed maturities other than US Treasury securities generally do not trade on a daily basis, the pricing service prepares estimates of fair value measurements for these securities using its proprietary pricing applications, which include available relevant market information, benchmark curves, benchmarking of like securities, sector groupings and matrix pricing.
>
> Additionally, the pricing service uses an Option Adjusted Spread model to develop prepayment and interest rate scenarios. The pricing service evaluates each asset class based on relevant market information, relevant credit information, perceived market movements and sector news. The market inputs utilized in the pricing evaluation, listed in the approximate order of priority, include: benchmark yields, reported trades, broker/dealer quotes, issuer spreads, two-sided markets, benchmark securities, bids, offers, reference data, and industry and economic events. The extent of the use of each market input depends on the asset class and the market conditions. Depending on the security, the priority of the use of inputs may change or some market inputs may not be relevant. For some securities, additional inputs may be necessary.

The information does not provide an investor with absolute assurance of constant liquidity for the investments; instead, it provides persuasive evidence that the reported values are fair. The fact that the pricing service considers market information relating to liquidity (reported trades, broker/dealer quotes, issuer spreads, two-sided markets) in developing its price estimates increases an investor's confidence that the recognized values would reflect the prices Travelers might achieve if it liquidated the securities at year end 2016.

Capitalization

Unlike the banking sector, where international risk-based capital standards have existed since 1988, as of mid-2016, no such global standard exists for the insurance sector (although the IAIS is in the process of developing a risk-based global insurance capital standard).[34] The standard is expected to include a target minimum capital adequacy ratio. The ratio will be calculated as the amount of qualifying capital divided by the amount of risk-based capital required.

Although no risk-based global insurance capital standard exists, capital standards do exist in various jurisdictions. For example, in Europe, the EU adopted the "Solvency II regime" in 2014, which (among other provisions) establishes minimum capital requirements such that if an insurer falls below the requirements, the supervisory entity in the relevant country will be required to intervene.[35] In the United States, the NAIC risk-based capital requirements, begun in the 1990s, establish a minimum amount of capital an insurer must have, based on its size and risk profile.[36] Under the NAIC regime, the formula for minimum risk-based capital for P&C insurers takes into account asset risk, credit risk, underwriting risk, and other relevant risks.

ANALYZING LIFE AND HEALTH INSURANCE COMPANIES

6

☐ describe key ratios and other factors to consider in analyzing an insurance company

Insurance companies provide protection against adverse events. Insurance companies earn revenues from **premiums** (amounts paid by the purchaser of insurance products) and from investment income earned on the **float** (amounts collected as premium and not yet paid out as benefits). Insurance companies are typically categorized as property and casualty (P&C) or life and health (L&H). The products of the two types of insurance companies differ in contract duration and variability of claims. P&C insurers' policies are usually short term, and the final cost will usually be known within a year of occurrence of an insured event, whereas L&H insurers' policies are usually longer term. P&C insurers' claims are more variable and "lumpier" because they arise from accidents and other unpredictable events, whereas L&H insurers' claims are more predictable because they correlate closely with relatively stable actuarially based mortality rates when applied to large populations.

For both types of insurance companies, important areas for analysis include business profile, earnings characteristics, investment returns, liquidity, and capitalization. In addition, for P&C companies, analysis of reserves and the combined ratio, an indicator of overall underwriting profitability, are important.

---

34 See https://www.iaisweb.org/page/supervisory-material/insurance-capital-standard.
35 See http://europa.eu/rapid/press-release_MEMO-15-3120_en.htm.
36 See www.naic.org/cipr_topics/topic_risk_based_capital.htm.

Some countries, including, for example, the United States, require insurance companies to prepare financial reports according to statutory accounting rules, which differ from US GAAP and IFRS, and have a greater focus on solvency. This section discusses analysis based on US GAAP and IFRS financial reports. A discussion of P&C insurers is followed by a discussion of L&H insurers.

Life and Health Insurance Companies

Life and health insurance companies generate revenue from collecting premiums by selling life and health insurance policies—and for many firms, by providing investment products and services. Investment income is the other primary source of revenues.

Operations: Products and Distribution

The types of life insurance products vary widely, with some solely providing a benefit upon the death of the insured and others providing a savings vehicle. In the simplest types of life insurance, a premium is paid for coverage and when the insured dies, the beneficiary receives payment. For example, a term life policy provides a benefit if the insured dies within the fixed term of the contract but expires without value if the insured is still living at the end of the term. In other types of life insurance, the policy both provides a benefit upon the death of the insured and serves as a savings vehicle. Life insurance companies may also offer such investment products as annuities, with fixed payments or variable payments linked to market returns.

Health-related insurance products vary primarily by the type of coverage. Some products cover specific medical expenses and treatments, and others provide income payments if the policyholder is injured or becomes ill.

L&H companies sell their products either directly to consumers via electronic media or through agents. The agents may be either employees of the company, exclusive agents, or independent agents. Distribution via independent agents is more expensive for the insurance company but offers the benefits of minimizing fixed costs and increasing flexibility to pursue growth opportunities.[37]

It is helpful to understand the source of a company's revenue and any changes over time. Diversification reduces risks. L&H companies can be diversified across revenue sources, product offerings, geographic coverage, distribution channels, and investment assets.

EXAMPLE 7

Revenue Diversification

Exhibit 32 and Exhibit 33 present selected income statement information for Aegon N.V. and MetLife, Inc., respectively.

Exhibit 32: Selected Consolidated Income Statement Information: Aegon N.V.

(In EUR millions)	2016	2015	2014	2013	2012
Amounts based upon IFRS					
Premium income	23,453	22,925	19,864	19,939	19,049
Investment income	7,788	8,525	8,148	7,909	8,413

---

37 D. Nissim, "Analysis and Valuation of Insurance Companies," Columbia Business School Center for Excellence in Accounting and Security Analysis (November 2010).

Analyzing Life and Health Insurance Companies

(In EUR millions)	2016	2015	2014	2013	2012
Fees, commissions, other	2,414	2,452	2,145	1,957	1,865
Total revenues	33,655	33,902	30,157	29,805	29,327

Exhibit 33: Selected Income Statement Information: MetLife, Inc.

Years Ended 31 December	2016	2015	2014	2013	2012
(In $ millions)					
Premiums	$39,153	$38,545	$39,067	$37,674	$37,975
Investment income, including derivatives gains	13,358	19,916	22,273	19,154	19,713
Universal life and investment-type product policy fees, and other	10,965	11,490	11,976	11,371	10,462
Total revenues	$63,476	$69,951	$73,316	$68,199	$68,150

Notes: To create comparability in this illustration, the above exhibit combines certain line items from MetLife's income statement. The company's audited financial statements should be used for purposes other than this example.

Aegon N.V. Data in Exhibit 32

As percentage of total revenues	2016	2015	2014	2013	2012
Premium income	69.7%	67.6%	65.9%	66.9%	65.0%
Investment income	23.1%	25.1%	27.0%	26.5%	28.7%
Fees, commissions, other	7.2%	7.2%	7.1%	6.6%	6.4%

YOY percent change	2016	2015	2014	2013
Premium income	2.3%	15.4%	−0.4%	4.7%
Investment income	−8.6%	4.6%	3.0%	−6.0%
Fees, commissions, other	−1.5%	14.3%	9.6%	4.9%

MetLife, Inc., Data in Exhibit 33

As percentage of total revenues	2016	2015	2014	2013	2012
Premiums	61.7%	55.1%	53.3%	55.2%	55.7%
Investment income, including derivatives gains	21.0%	28.5%	30.4%	28.1%	28.9%
Universal life and investment-type product policy fees, and other	17.3%	16.4%	16.3%	16.7%	15.4%

YOY percent change					
Premiums		1.6%	−1.3%	3.7%	−0.8%

As percentage of total revenues	2016	2015	2014	2013	2012
Investment income, including derivatives gains	−32.9%	−10.6%	16.3%	−2.8%	
Universal life and investment-type product policy fees, and other	−4.6%	−4.1%	5.3%	8.7%	

1. Based on the data for 2016 in Exhibit 32 and Exhibit 33, compare the companies' diversification across revenue sources.

Solution:

MetLife appears to have greater diversification across revenue sources because it generates only about 62% of total revenues from premiums, compared to nearly 70% for Aegon. It should be noted that premium income can be a more stable source of revenue, and thus greater diversification of revenues should be considered along with potentially greater variability in revenues.

2. Based on the data in Exhibit 32 and Exhibit 33, describe the trends in each company's diversification across revenue sources, with specific reference to premium income.

Solution:

For both companies, the percentage of total revenues earned from premiums is greater in 2016 than in any of the previous four years. For Aegon, the increase in the proportion of revenue from premiums resulted in part from significant growth in premium income (15.4% in 2015) as well as a decline in investment income (−8.6%) in 2016. For MetLife, the increase in the proportion of revenue from premiums resulted primarily from the decline in investment income in 2015 and 2016 (−10.6% and −32.9%, respectively).

Earnings Characteristics

The major components of L&H insurers' expenses are for benefit payments to policyholders under life insurance, other types of insurance policies, annuity contracts, and other types of contracts. Some types of insurance products that accumulate a cash value include provisions for the policyholder to cancel the contract before its contractual maturity and receive the accumulated cash value. Such early cancellation is known as a contract surrender. Contract surrenders may result in additional expenses for L&H insurers.

Similar to P&C insurers, L&H insures' earnings reflect a number of accounting items that require a significant amount of judgement and estimates. L&H companies must estimate future policyholder benefits and claims based on actuarial assumptions (e.g., about life expectancy). The amounts expensed in a given period are affected by both policyholder benefits actually paid and interest on the estimated liability for future policyholder benefit. As another example of the importance of estimates, L&H companies capitalize the costs of acquiring new and renewal insurance business, which are then amortized on the basis of actual and expected future profits from that business. Another area where accounting judgement can significantly affect L&H companies' earnings—securities valuation—is discussed below in the section on investment returns.

Some general profitability measures can be applied to L&H companies, such as, for example, return on assets (ROA), return on equity (ROE), growth and volatility of capital, and book value per share. Other common profitability measures include pre- and post-tax operating margin (operating profit as a percentage of total revenues) and pre- and post-tax operating return on assets and return on equity.[38] However, most analysis goes beyond these general measures because of the complexity of L&H companies' earnings. Given the possibility of operational distortion and the importance of accounting estimates to L&H companies' reported earnings, a variety of earnings metrics specific to the insurance sector are helpful in providing a good understanding of performance. For example, the profitability ratios used by A.M. Best include (1) total benefits paid as a percentage of net premiums written and deposits and (2) commissions and expenses incurred as a percentage of net premiums written and deposits.[39]

Exhibit 34 shows return on average equity and pretax operating return on average equity for the US L&H sector and MetLife, Inc. In 2011, MetLife had a higher return on average equity than the industry average and a similar pretax operating return on average equity. After 2011, MetLife has not performed as well as the industry on these two measures. Further investigation into causes of the differences between MetLife and the industry and into the reason why the pretax operating return on average equity and return on average equity were similar for MetLife in 2014 and 2015 is needed.

Exhibit 34: Return on Equity—US L&H Sector and MetLife, Inc.

	2011	2012	2013	2014	2015	2016
US L&H Sector Return on Average Equity	4.70%	12.60%	12.90%	11.00%	11.20%	na*
US L&H Sector Pretax Operating Return on Average Equity	9.10%	18.70%	19.10%	14.30%	15.10%	na
MetLife, Inc., Return on Average Equity (Source: 10-K)	12.20%	2.00%	5.40%	9.40%	7.50%	1.00%
MetLife, Inc., Pretax Operating Return on Average Equity (Calculated)	9.00%	9.30%	9.90%	9.80%	7.80%	7.50%

* not available
Source for Sector Data: "Annual Report on the Insurance Industry," Federal Insurance Office (September 2016).

L&H companies' earnings can also be distorted by the accounting treatment of certain items. For example, mismatches between the valuation approach for assets and liabilities can introduce distortion when interest rate changes occur. In some cases, significant distortions to reported earnings have occurred because companies' assets

---

[38] "Annual Report on the Insurance Industry," Federal Insurance Office, US Department of the Treasury (September 2016), available at www.treasury.gov.
[39] A.M. Best is a widely known rating agency for insurance companies. "Best's Credit Rating Methodology: Global Life and Non-Life Insurance Edition" (28 April 2016) is available at www3.ambest.com/ambv/ratingmethodology/openpdf.aspx?ubcr=1&ri=1011.

Investment Returns

Investment returns are an important source of income for L&H companies. Key aspects in evaluating L&H companies' investment activities include diversification, investment performance, and interest rate risk. Liquidity of the portfolio is also relevant for L&H companies and is discussed in the following section.

Investment diversification begins with an assessment of allocation across asset classes and an evaluation of how the allocation corresponds to the insurer's liabilities to policyholders. Compared to P&C companies, L&H companies' relative predictability of claims generally allows them to more often seek the higher returns offered by riskier investments. However, higher-yielding assets, such as equity or real estate investments, experience greater fluctuations in valuation than investments in debt. The insurance industry has also faced investment return challenges from the low-interest rate environment of the last 10 years. It has been harder to earn an adequate risk-adjusted return on financial assets because the low interest rates have limited the available opportunities. Overall, asset concentrations by type, maturity, low credit quality, industry, or geographic location or within single issuers can be a concern, particularly to rating agencies.[41]

Investment performance of L&H companies, as with any investment portfolio's performance, can be measured broadly as the amount of investment income divided by the amount of invested assets (cash and investments). The measure can use investment income plus realized gains (losses) with and without unrealized capital gains (losses). In addition, a common metric for evaluating interest rate risk of L&H companies is the comparison of the duration of the company's assets with the duration of its liabilities.

EXAMPLE 8

Investment Portfolio

Exhibit 35 presents information on the investment portfolio of AIA Group. AIA's portfolio of financial investments constitutes 82% of its total assets (and 84% including investment properties).

Exhibit 35: AIA Group Limited Investment Portfolio

	30-Nov-16 US$m	30-Nov-16 % Total	30-Nov-15 US$m	30-Nov-15 % Total
Loans and deposits	7,062	4.6%	7,211	5.1%
Debt securities	113,618	73.3%	104,640	73.3%
Equity securities	30,211	19.5%	27,159	19.0%
Derivative financial instruments	107	0.1%	73	0.1%
Total financial investments	150,998	97.5%	139,083	97.4%

---

40 See, for example, Alistair Gray, "MetLife Loss Raises Accounting 'Noise' Concerns," *Financial Times* (16 February 2017).
41 Standard & Poor's, "Standard & Poor's Insurance Ratings Criteria: Life Edition" (2004): www.lifecriteria.standardandpoors.com. Note that Standard & Poor's makes ongoing updates to its ratings criteria.

Analyzing Life and Health Insurance Companies

	30-Nov-16		30-Nov-15	
	US$m	% Total	US$m	% Total
Investment property	3,910	2.5%	3,659	2.6%
Total	154,908	100.0%	142,742	100.0%

AIA Group Limited Investment Income

	30-Nov-16
Investment Returns	US$m
Interest income	$5,290
Dividend income	654
Rental income	140
Investment income	6,084
Gains and losses	1,471
Total investment return	$7,555

Of the $1,471 million in gains and losses, approximately $127 million was related to debt securities.

1. Based on the information in Exhibit 35, describe AIA's investment allocation in 2016 and changes from the prior year.

Solution:

The portfolio, which is mainly invested in debt securities, shows a very small shift from loans and deposits to equity securities in 2016.

2. Based on the information in Exhibit 35, estimate the return on average fixed-income assets. (For the purposes of this question, consider loans and deposits and debt securities as a single class of assets—namely, fixed-income assets.)

Solution:

The return (in $ millions) can be estimated as Investment income on fixed-income securities divided by Average investment in fixed-income securities.

The Investment income on fixed-income securities equals Interest income plus Gains on debt securities = $5,290 + $127 = $5,417.
The average amounts invested in loans and deposits and debt securities was [($7,062 + $113,618) + ($7,211 +$104,640)]/2 = $232,531/2 = $116,265.5. Therefore, the estimated return on the fixed-income investments was 4.7% (calculated as $5,417/$116,265.5).

Liquidity

An L&H company's requirements for liquidity are driven by its liabilities to creditors and, primarily, its liabilities to policyholders, including both benefits and policy surrenders. Historically, liquidity was less important to life insurers because of the long-term nature of traditional life insurance products; however, liquidity has become more important to life insurers as new products have been introduced.[42] An L&H company's sources of liquidity include its operating cash flow and the liquidity of its investment assets. An analysis of liquidity includes a review of the overall liquidity of the investment portfolio. Such investments as non-investment-grade bonds and equity real estate are typically less liquid than investment-grade fixed-income investments.[43]

In general, liquidity measures compare the amount of the company's more liquid assets, such as cash and marketable securities, to the amount of its near-term liabilities. Other liquidity measures—for example, the liquidity model used by Standard & Poor's—compare the amount of the company's assets (individually adjusted for assumptions about ready convertibility to cash) with the amount of the company's obligations (individually adjusted for assumptions about potential for withdrawals).[44] The adjusted amounts are calculated under both normal market conditions and stress. The typical "current ratio" is not directly applicable to L&H companies because their balance sheets often do not include the classifications "current" and "non-current."

Capitalization

As noted with P&C insurers, L&H companies are not guided by a global risk-based capital standard. Various jurisdictions do, however, have standards specifying the amount of capital an insurer must have based on its risk profile. If an insurer's capital falls below the minimum requirement, generally, a supervisory authority intervenes.

Differences between the P&C and L&H businesses are reflected in differences in the risk-based capital requirement. For example, because L&H claims are considered more predictable than those of P&C insurers, L&H insurers do not need as high an equity cushion and can have lower capital requirements.[45] Another difference between the factors considered in establishing minimum capital requirements for L&H companies is that many life insurance products create material exposure to interest rate risk. Accordingly, the calculation of risk-based capital for an L&H company incorporates interest rate risk.[46]

SUMMARY

- Financial institutions' systemic importance results in heavy regulation of their activities.
- Systemic risk refers to the risk of impairment in some part of the financial system that then has the potential to spread throughout other parts of the financial system and thereby to negatively affect the entire economy.
- The Basel Committee, a standing committee of the Bank for International Settlements, includes representatives from central banks and bank supervisors from around the world.
- The Basel Committee's international regulatory framework for banks includes minimum capital requirements, minimum liquidity requirements, and stable funding requirements.

---

42 "Insurance Regulatory Information Systems (IRIS) Manual: IRIS Ratios Manual for Property/Casualty, Life/Accident & Health, and Fraternal—2016 Edition," National Association of Insurance Commissioners (2016): www.naic.org/prod_serv/UIR-ZB-16_UIR_2016.pdf.
43 Standard & Poor's Liquidity Model for US and Canadian Life Insurers.
44 "Annual Report on the Insurance Industry," Federal Insurance Office, US Department of the Treasury (September 2016).
45 Nissim, "Analysis and Valuation of Insurance Companies."
46 See www.naic.org/cipr_topics/topic_risk_based_capital.htm.

Analyzing Life and Health Insurance Companies

- Among the international organizations that focus on financial stability are the Financial Stability Board, the International Association of Insurance Supervisors, the International Association of Deposit Insurers, and the International Organization of Securities Commissions.
- Another distinctive feature of financial institutions (compared to manufacturing or merchandising companies) is that their productive assets are predominantly financial assets, such as loans and securities, creating greater direct exposures to a variety of risks, such as credit risk, liquidity risk, market risk, and interest rate risk. In general, the values of their assets are relatively close to fair market values.
- A widely used approach to analyzing a bank, CAMELS, considers a bank's **C**apital adequacy, **A**sset quality, **M**anagement capabilities, **E**arnings sufficiency, **L**iquidity position, and **S**ensitivity to market risk.
- "**C**apital adequacy," described in terms of the proportion of the bank's assets that is funded with capital, indicates that a bank has enough capital to absorb potential losses without severely damaging its financial position.
- "**A**sset quality" includes the concept of quality of the bank's assets—credit quality and diversification—and the concept of overall sound risk management.
- "**M**anagement capabilities" refers to the bank management's ability to identify and exploit appropriate business opportunities and to simultaneously manage associated risks.
- "**E**arnings" refers to the bank's return on capital relative to cost of capital and also includes the concept of earnings quality.
- "**L**iquidity" refers to the amount of liquid assets held by the bank relative to its near-term expected cash flows. Under Basel III, liquidity also refers to the stability of the bank's funding sources.
- "**S**ensitivity to market risk" pertains to how adverse changes in markets (including interest rate, exchange rate, equity, and commodity markets) could affect the bank's earnings and capital position.
- In addition to the CAMELS components, important attributes deserving analysts' attention include government support, the banking entity's mission, corporate culture and competitive environment, off-balance-sheet items, segment information, currency exposure, and risk disclosures.
- Insurance companies are typically categorized as property and casualty (P&C) or life and health (L&H).
- Insurance companies earn revenues from premiums (amounts paid by the purchaser of insurance products) and from investment income earned on the float (amounts collected as premiums and not yet paid out as benefits).
- P&C insurers' policies are usually short term, and the final cost will usually be known within a year of a covered event, whereas L&H insurers' policies are usually longer term. P&C insurers' claims are more variable, whereas L&H insurers' claims are more predictable.
- For both types of insurance companies, important areas for analysis include business profile, earnings characteristics, investment returns, liquidity, and capitalization. In addition, analysis of P&C companies' profitability includes analysis of loss reserves and the combined ratio.

PRACTICE PROBLEMS

The following information relates to questions 1-7

Viktoria Smith is a recently hired junior analyst at Aries Investments. Smith and her supervisor, Ingrid Johansson, meet to discuss some of the firm's investments in banks and insurance companies.

Johansson asks Smith to explain why the evaluation of banks is different from the evaluation of non-financial companies. Smith tells Johansson the following:

Statement 1   As intermediaries, banks are more likely to be systemically important than non-financial companies.

Statement 2   The assets of banks mostly consist of deposits, which are exposed to different risks than the tangible assets of non-financial companies.

Smith and Johansson also discuss key aspects of financial regulations, particularly the framework of Basel III. Johansson tells Smith:

"Basel III specifies the minimum percentage of its risk-weighted assets that a bank must fund with equity. This requirement of Basel III prevents a bank from assuming so much financial leverage that it is unable to withstand loan losses or asset write-downs."

Johansson tells Smith that she uses the CAMELS approach to evaluate banks, even though it has some limitations. To evaluate P&C insurance companies, Johansson tells Smith that she places emphasis on the efficiency of spending on obtaining new premiums. Johansson and Smith discuss differences between P&C and L&H insurance companies. Smith notes the following differences:

Difference 1:   L&H insurers' claims are more predictable than P&C insurers' claims.

Difference 2:   P&C insurers' policies are usually short term, whereas L&H insurers' policies are usually longer term.

Difference 3:   Relative to L&H insurers, P&C insurers often have lower capital requirements and can also seek higher returns offered by riskier investments.

Johansson asks Smith to review key performance ratios for three P&C insurers in which Aries is invested. The ratios are presented in Exhibit 1.

Exhibit 1: Key Performance Ratios for Selected P&C Insurers

	Insurer A	Insurer B	Insurer C
Loss and loss adjustment expense ratio	68.8%	65.9%	64.1%
Underwriting expense ratio	33.7%	37.8%	32.9%

Practice Problems

	Insurer A	Insurer B	Insurer C
Combined ratio	102.5%	103.7%	97.0%

Johansson also asks Smith to review key performance ratios for ABC Bank, a bank in which Aries is invested. The ratios are presented in Exhibit 2.

Exhibit 2: Key Performance Ratios for ABC Bank*

	2017	2016	2015
Common equity Tier 1 capital ratio	10.7%	11.5%	12.1%
Tier 1 capital ratio	11.5%	12.6%	13.4%
Total capital ratio	14.9%	14.8%	14.9%
Liquidity coverage ratio	123.6%	121.4%	119.1%
Net stable funding ratio	114.9%	113.2%	112.7%
Total trading VaR (all market risk factors)	$11	$13	$15
Total trading and credit portfolio VaR	$15	$18	$21

Note: VaR amounts are in millions and are based on a 99% confidence interval and a single-day holding period.

1. Which of Smith's statements regarding banks is correct?

    A. Only Statement 1

    B. Only Statement 2

    C. Both Statement 1 and Statement 2

2. The aspect of the Basel III framework that Johansson describes to Smith relates to minimum:

    A. capital requirements.

    B. liquidity requirements.

    C. amounts of stable funding requirements.

3. One limitation of the approach used by Johansson to evaluate banks is that it fails to address a bank's:

    A. sensitivity to market risk.

    B. management capabilities.

    C. competitive environment.

4. The best indicator of the operations of a P&C insurance company emphasized by Johansson when evaluating P&C insurance companies is the:

    A. combined ratio.

    B. underwriting loss ratio.

    C. underwriting expense ratio.

5. Which of the differences between P&C insurers and L&H insurers noted by Smith is *incorrect*?
   A. Difference 1
   B. Difference 2
   C. Difference 3

6. Based on Exhibit 1, Smith should conclude that the insurer with the most efficient underwriting operation is:
   A. Insurer A.
   B. Insurer B.
   C. Insurer C.

7. Based on Exhibit 2, Smith and Johansson should conclude that over the past three years, ABC Bank's:
   A. liquidity position has declined.
   B. capital adequacy has improved.
   C. sensitivity to market risk has improved.

The following information relates to questions 8-13

Judith Yoo is a financial sector analyst writing an industry report. In the report, Yoo discusses the relative global systemic risk across industries, referencing Industry A (international property and casualty insurance), Industry B (credit unions), and Industry C (global commercial banks).

Part of Yoo's analysis focuses on Company XYZ, a global commercial bank, and its CAMELS rating, risk management practices, and performance. First, Yoo considers the firm's capital adequacy as measured by the key capital ratios (common equity Tier 1 capital, total Tier 1 capital, and total capital) in Exhibit 1.

Exhibit 1: Company XYZ: Excerpt from Annual Report Disclosure

At 31 December	2017	2016	2015
Regulatory capital	$m	$m	$m
Common equity Tier 1 capital	146,424	142,367	137,100
Additional Tier 1 capital	22,639	20,443	17,600
Tier 2 capital	22,456	27,564	38,200
Total regulatory capital	191,519	190,374	192,900
Risk-weighted assets (RWAs) by risk type			
Credit risk	960,763	989,639	968,600
Market risk	44,100	36,910	49,600

Practice Problems

At 31 December	2017	2016	2015
Regulatory capital	$m	$m	$m
Operational risk	293,825	256,300	224,300
Total RWAs	1,298,688	1,282,849	1,242,500

Yoo turns her attention to Company XYZ's asset quality using the information in Exhibit 2.

Exhibit 2: Company XYZ: Asset Composition

At 31 December	2017	2016	2015
	$m	$m	$m
Total liquid assets	361,164	354,056	356,255
Investments	434,256	367,158	332,461
Consumer loans	456,957	450,576	447,493
Commercial loans	499,647	452,983	403,058
Goodwill	26,693	26,529	25,705
Other assets	151,737	144,210	121,780
Total assets	1,930,454	1,795,512	1,686,752

To assess Company XYZ's risk management practices, Yoo reviews the consumer loan credit quality profile in Exhibit 3 and the loan loss analysis in Exhibit 4.

Exhibit 3: Company XYZ: Consumer Loan Profile by Credit Quality

At 31 December	2017	2016	2015
	$m	$m	$m
Strong credit quality	338,948	327,345	320,340
Good credit quality	52,649	54,515	54,050
Satisfactory credit quality	51,124	55,311	56,409
Substandard credit quality	23,696	24,893	27,525
Past due but not impaired	2,823	2,314	2,058
Impaired	8,804	9,345	10,235
Total gross amount	478,044	473,723	470,617
Impairment allowances	−5,500	−4,500	−4,000
Total	472,544	469,223	466,617

Exhibit 4: Company XYZ: Loan Loss Analysis Data

At 31 December	2017	2016	2015
	$m	$m	$m
Consumer loans			

At 31 December	2017	2016	2015
	$m	$m	$m
Allowance for loan losses	11,000	11,500	13,000
Provision for loan losses	3,000	2,000	1,300
Charge-offs	3,759	3,643	4,007
Recoveries	1,299	1,138	1,106
Net charge-offs	2,460	2,505	2,901
Commercial loans			
Allowance for loan losses	1,540	1,012	169
Provision for loan losses	1,100	442	95
Charge-offs	1,488	811	717
Recoveries	428	424	673
Net charge-offs	1,060	387	44

Finally, Yoo notes the following supplementary information from Company XYZ's annual report:

- Competition in the commercial loan space has become increasingly fierce, leading XYZ managers to pursue higher-risk strategies to increase market share.
- The net benefit plan obligation has steadily decreased during the last three years.
- Company XYZ awards above-average equity-based compensation to its top managers.

8. Which of the following industries *most likely* has the highest level of global systemic risk?

   A. Industry A

   B. Industry B

   C. Industry C

9. Based on Exhibit 1, Company XYZ's capital adequacy over the last three years, as measured by the three key capital ratios, signals conditions that are:

   A. mixed.

   B. declining.

   C. improving.

10. Based only on Exhibit 2, asset composition from 2015 to 2017 indicates:

    A. declining liquidity.

    B. increasing risk based on the proportion of total loans to total assets.

    C. decreasing risk based on the proportion of investments to total assets.

11. Based on Exhibit 3, the trend in impairment allowances is reflective of the chang-

Practice Problems

es in:

A. impaired assets.

B. strong credit quality assets.

C. past due but not impaired assets.

12. Based on Exhibit 4, a loan loss analysis for the last three years indicates that:

A. Company XYZ has become less conservative in its provisioning for consumer loans.

B. the provision for commercial loan losses has trailed the actual net charge-off experience.

C. the cushion between the allowance and the net commercial loan charge-offs has declined.

13. Which of the following supplemental factors is consistent with a favorable assessment of Company XYZ's financial outlook?

A. Competitive environment

B. Net benefit plan obligation

C. Equity-based compensation policy

The following information relates to questions 14-20

Ivan Paulinic, an analyst at a large wealth management firm, meets with his supervisor to discuss adding financial institution equity securities to client portfolios. Paulinic focuses on Vermillion Insurance (Vermillion), a property and casualty company, and Cobalt Life Insurance (Cobalt). To evaluate Vermillion further, Paulinic compiles the information presented in Exhibit 1.

Exhibit 1: Select Financial Ratios for Vermillion Insurance

Ratio	2017	2016
Loss and loss adjustment expense	59.1%	61.3%
Underwriting expense	36.3%	35.8%
Combined	95.4%	97.1%
Dividend	2.8%	2.6%

In addition to the insurance companies, Paulinic gathers data on three national banks that meet initial selection criteria but require further review. This information is shown in Exhibits 2, 3, and 4.

Exhibit 2: Select Balance Sheet Data for National Banks—Trading: Contribution to Total Revenues

Bank	2017	2013	2009	2005
N-bank	4.2%	7.0%	10.1%	8.9%
R-bank	8.3%	9.1%	17.0%	7.9%
T-bank	5.0%	5.0%	11.9%	6.8%

Focusing on N-bank and T-bank, Paulinic prepares the following data.

Exhibit 3: 2017 Select Data for N-bank and T-bank

	N-bank 2017	N-bank 2016	T-bank 2017	T-bank 2016
Average daily trading VaR ($ millions)	11.3	12.6	21.4	20.5
Annual trading revenue/average daily trading VaR	160×	134×	80×	80×

Paulinic investigates R-bank's risk management practices with respect to the use of credit derivatives to enhance earnings, following the 2008 financial crisis. Exhibit 4 displays R-bank's exposure over the last decade to credit derivatives not classified as hedges.

Exhibit 4: R-bank's Exposure to Freestanding Credit Derivatives

Credit Derivative Balances	2017	2012	2007
Notional amount ($ billions)	13.4	15.5	305.1

All of the national banks under consideration primarily make long-term loans and source a significant portion of their funding from retail deposits. Paulinic and the rest of the research team note that the central bank is unwinding a long period of monetary easing as evidenced by two recent increases in the overnight funding rate. Paulinic informs his supervisor that:

Statement 1　Given the recently reported stronger-than-anticipated macroeconomic data, there is an imminent risk that the yield curve will invert.

Statement 2　N-bank is very active in the 30-day reverse repurchase agreement market during times when the bank experiences significant increases in retail deposits.

14. Paulinic's analysis of the two insurance companies *most likely* indicates that:

    A. Cobalt has more-predictable claims than Vermillion.

    B. Cobalt has a higher capital requirement than Vermillion.

C. Vermillion's calculated risk-based capital is more sensitive than Cobalt's to interest rate risk.

15. Based only on the information in Exhibit 1, in 2017 Vermillion *most likely*:

    A. experienced a decrease in overall efficiency.

    B. improved its ability to estimate insured risks.

    C. was more efficient in obtaining new premiums.

16. Based only on Exhibit 2, which of the following statements is correct?

    A. The quality of earnings for R-bank was the highest in 2009.

    B. Relative to the other banks, N-bank has the highest quality of earnings in 2017.

    C. Trading represented a sustainable revenue source for T-bank between 2005 and 2013.

17. Based only on Exhibit 3, Paulinic should conclude that:

    A. trading activities are riskier at T-bank than N-bank.

    B. trading revenue per unit of risk has improved more at N-bank than T-bank.

    C. compared with duration, the metric used is a better measure of interest rate risk.

18. Based only on Exhibit 4, R-bank's use of credit derivatives since 2007 *most likely*:

    A. increased posted collateral.

    B. decreased the volatility of earnings from trading activities.

    C. indicates consistent correlations among the relevant risks taken.

19. Based on Statement 1, the net interest margin for the three banks' *most likely* will:

    A. decrease.

    B. remain unchanged.

    C. increase.

20. Based on Statement 2, the financial ratio *most* directly affected is the:

    A. Tier 2 capital ratio.

    B. net stable funding ratio.

    C. liquidity coverage ratio.

SOLUTIONS

1. A is correct. Banks are more likely to be systemically important than non-financial companies because, as intermediaries, they create financial linkages across all types of entities, including households, banks, corporates, and governments. The network of linkages across entities means that the failure of one bank will negatively affect other financial and non-financial entities (a phenomenon known as financial contagion). The larger the bank and the more widespread its network of linkages, the greater its potential impact on the entire financial system. The assets of banks are predominantly financial assets, such as loans and securities (not deposits, which represent most of a bank's liabilities). Compared to the tangible assets of non-financial companies, financial assets create direct exposure to a different set of risks, including credit risks, liquidity risks, market risks, and interest rate risks.

2. A is correct. Basel III specifies the minimum percentage of its risk-weighted assets that a bank must fund with equity capital. This minimum funding requirement prevents a bank from assuming so much financial leverage that it is unable to withstand loan losses or asset write-downs.

3. C is correct. The approach used by Johansson to evaluate banks, the CAMELS approach, has six components: (1) capital adequacy, (2) asset quality, (3) management capabilities, (4) earnings sufficiency, (5) liquidity position, and (6) sensitivity to market risk. While the CAMELS approach to evaluating a bank is fairly comprehensive, some attributes of a bank are not addressed by this method. One such attribute is a bank's competitive environment. A bank's competitive position relative to its peers may affect how it allocates capital and assesses risks.

4. C is correct. The underwriting expense ratio is an indicator of the efficiency of money spent on obtaining new premiums. The underwriting loss ratio is an indicator of the quality of a company's underwriting activities—the degree of success an underwriter has achieved in estimating the risks insured. The combined ratio, a measure of the overall underwriting profitability and efficiency of an underwriting operation, is the sum of these two ratios.

5. C is correct. The products of the two types of insurance companies, P&C and L&H, differ in contract duration and claim variability. P&C insurers' policies are usually short term, and the final cost will usually be known within a year of the occurrence of an insured event, while L&H insurers' policies are usually longer term. P&C insurers' claims are more variable and "lumpier" because they arise from accidents and other less predictable events, while L&H insurers' claims are more predictable because they correlate closely with relatively stable, actuarially based mortality rates applied to large populations. The relative predictability of L&H insurers' claims generally allows these companies to have lower capital requirements and to seek higher returns than P&C insurers.

6. C is correct. The combined ratio, which is the sum of the underwriting expense ratio and the loss and loss adjustment expense ratio, is a measure of the efficiency of an underwriting operation. A combined ratio of less than 100% is considered efficient; a combined ratio greater than 100% indicates an underwriting loss. Insurer C is the only insurer that has a combined ratio less than 100%.

7. C is correct. Over the past three years, there has been a downward trend in the two VaR measures—total trading VaR (all market risk factors) and total trading and credit portfolio VaR. This trend indicates an improvement in ABC Bank's

sensitivity, or a reduction in its exposure, to market risk. The two liquidity measures—the liquidity coverage ratio and the net stable funding ratio—have increased over the past three years, indicating an improvement in ABC Bank's liquidity position. Trends in the three capital adequacy measures—common equity Tier 1 capital ratio, Tier 1 capital ratio, and total capital ratio—indicate a decline in ABC Bank's capital adequacy. While the total capital ratio has remained fairly constant over the past three years, the common equity Tier 1 capital ratio and the Tier 1 capital ratio have declined. This trend suggests that ABC Bank has moved toward using more Tier 2 capital and less Tier 1 capital, indicating an overall decline in capital adequacy.

8. C is correct. Industry C, representing global commercial banks, most likely has the highest level of global systemic risk because global commercial banks have the highest proportion of cross-border business. Unlike banks, the overall insurance market (of which Industry A is a subset) has a smaller proportion of cross-border business, and insurance companies' foreign branches are generally required to hold assets in a jurisdiction that are adequate to cover the related policy liabilities in that jurisdiction. As an international property and casualty (P&C) insurer, Company A provides protection against adverse events related to autos, homes, or commercial activities; many of these events have local, rather than international, impact. Industry B, credit unions, most likely has the lowest level of global systemic risk. Credit unions are depository institutions that function like banks and offer many of the same services, but they are owned by their members rather than being publicly traded as many banks are.

9. A is correct. Company XYZ's key capital adequacy ratios show mixed conditions. The ratios are calculated as follows:

$$\text{Common Equity Tier 1 Capital Ratio} = \frac{\text{Total Common Equity Tier 1 Capital}}{\text{Total Risk-Weighted Assets}}$$

$$2015 \text{ Common Equity Tier 1 Capital Ratio} = \frac{137,100}{1,242,500} = 11.0\%$$

$$2016 \text{ Common Equity Tier 1 Capital Ratio} = \frac{142,367}{1,282,849} = 11.1\%$$

$$2017 \text{ Common Equity Tier 1 Capital Ratio} = \frac{146,424}{1,298,688} = 11.3\%$$

$$\text{Tier 1 Ratio} = \frac{\text{Common Equity Tier 1 Capital} + \text{Additional Tier 1 Capital}}{\text{Total Risk-Weighted Assets}}$$

$$2015 \text{ Tier 1 Ratio} = \frac{137,100 + 17,600}{1,242,500} = 12.5\%$$

$$2016 \text{ Tier 1 Ratio} = \frac{142,367 + 20,443}{1,282,849} = 12.7\%$$

$$2017 \text{ Tier 1 Ratio} = \frac{146,424 + 22,639}{1,298,688} = 13.0\%$$

$$\text{Total Capital Ratio} = \frac{\text{Total Capital}}{\text{Total Risk-Weighted Assets}}$$

$$2015 \text{ Total Capital Ratio} = \frac{192,900}{1,242,500} = 15.5\%$$

$$2016 \text{ Total Capital Ratio} = \frac{190,374}{1,282,849} = 14.8\%$$

$$2017 \text{ Total Capital Ratio} = \frac{191,519}{1,298,688} = 14.7\%$$

	2017	2016	2015
Common equity Tier 1 capital ratio	11.3%	11.1%	11.0%
Tier 1 capital ratio	13.0%	12.7%	12.5%
Total capital ratio	14.7%	14.8%	15.5%

The common equity Tier 1 capital ratio and the Tier 1 capital ratio both strengthened from 2015 to 2017, but the total capital ratio weakened during that same period, signaling mixed conditions.

10. A is correct. Company XYZ's liquid assets as a percentage of total assets declined each year since 2015, indicating declining liquidity.

	2017 $m	2017 % of Total Assets	2016 $m	2016 % of Total Assets	2015 $m	2015 % of Total Assets
Total liquid assets	361,164	18.7%	354,056	19.7%	356,255	21.1%
Investments	434,256	22.5%	367,158	20.4%	332,461	19.7%
Loans						
Consumer loans	456,957		450,576		447,493	
Commercial loans	499,647		452,983		403,058	
Total loans	956,604	49.6%	903,559	50.3%	850,551	50.4%
Goodwill	26,693	1.4%	26,529	1.5%	25,705	1.5%
Other assets	151,737	7.9%	144,210	8.0%	121,780	7.2%
Total assets	1,930,454	100%	1,795,512	100%	1,686,752	100%

11. C is correct. Impairment allowances have increased proportionately to the increases in the amount of past due but not impaired assets, which may be in anticipation of these past due assets becoming impaired. Impaired assets have decreased each year while strong credit quality assets have increased each year, which suggests lowering impairment allowances as a result of improving credit quality of these financial instruments.

At 31 December	2017 $m	2016 $m	2015 $m
Strong credit quality	338,948	327,345	320,340
Good credit quality	52,649	54,515	54,050
Satisfactory credit quality	51,124	55,311	56,409
Substandard credit quality	23,696	24,893	27,525
Past due but not impaired	2,823	2,314	2,058
Impaired	8,804	9,345	10,235
Total gross amount	478,044	473,723	470,617
Impairment allowances	−5,500	−4,500	−4,000
Total	472,544	469,223	466,617
YoY change in impaired assets	−5.8%	−8.7%	

Solutions

At 31 December	2017	2016	2015
	$m	$m	$m
YoY change in strong credit quality assets	3.5%	2.2%	
YoY change in past due but not impaired assets	22.0%	12.4%	
YoY change in impairment allowances	22.2%	12.5%	

Note: YoY = year-over-year

2015 to 2016 change in impaired assets: $\left(\frac{9{,}345}{10{,}235}\right) - 1 = -8.7\%$

2015 to 2016 change in strong credit quality assets: $\left(\frac{327{,}345}{320{,}340}\right) - 1 = 2.2\%$

2015 to 2016 change in past due but not impaired assets: $\left(\frac{2{,}314}{2{,}058}\right) - 1 = 12.4\%$

2015 to 2016 change in impairment allowances: $\left(\frac{-4{,}500}{-4{,}000}\right) - 1 = 12.5\%$

2016 to 2017 change in impaired assets: $\left(\frac{8{,}804}{9{,}345}\right) - 1 = -5.8\%$

2016 to 2017 change in strong credit quality assets: $\left(\frac{338{,}948}{327{,}345}\right) - 1 = 3.5\%$

2016 to 2017 change in past due but not impaired assets: $\left(\frac{2{,}823}{2{,}314}\right) - 1 = 22.0\%$

2016 to 2017 change in impairment allowances: $\left(\frac{-5{,}500}{-4{,}500}\right) - 1 = 22.2\%$

12. C is correct. The allowance for loan losses to net commercial loan charge-offs has been declining during the last three years, which indicates that the cushion between the allowance and the net commercial loan charge-offs has deteriorated.

2015 Consumer: $\frac{\text{Allowance for Loan Losses}}{\text{Net Loan Charge-Offs}} = \frac{13{,}000}{2{,}901} = 4.48$

2016 Consumer: $\frac{\text{Allowance for Loan Losses}}{\text{Net Loan Charge-Offs}} = \frac{11{,}500}{2{,}505} = 4.59$

2017 Consumer: $\frac{\text{Allowance for Loan Losses}}{\text{Net Loan Charge-Offs}} = \frac{11{,}000}{2{,}460} = 4.47$

2015 Commercial: $\frac{\text{Allowance for Loan Losses}}{\text{Net Loan Charge-Offs}} = \frac{169}{44} = 3.84$

2016 Commercial: $\frac{\text{Allowance for Loan Losses}}{\text{Net Loan Charge-Offs}} = \frac{1{,}012}{387} = 2.61$

2017 Commercial: $\frac{\text{Allowance for Loan Losses}}{\text{Net Loan Charge-Offs}} = \frac{1{,}540}{1{,}060} = 1.45$

2015 Consumer: $\frac{\text{Provision for Loan Losses}}{\text{Net Loan Charge-Offs}} = \frac{1{,}300}{2{,}901} = 0.45$

2016 Consumer: $\frac{\text{Provision for Loan Losses}}{\text{Net Loan Charge-Offs}} = \frac{2{,}000}{2{,}505} = 0.80$

2017 Consumer: $\frac{\text{Provision for Loan Losses}}{\text{Net Loan Charge-Offs}} = \frac{3{,}000}{2{,}460} = 1.22$

2015 Commercial: $\frac{\text{Provision for Loan Losses}}{\text{Net Loan Charge-Offs}} = \frac{95}{44} = 2.16$

2016 Commercial: $\frac{\text{Provision for Loan Losses}}{\text{Net Loan Charge-Offs}} = \frac{442}{387} = 1.14$

2017 Commercial: $\frac{\text{Provision for Loan Losses}}{\text{Net Loan Charge-Offs}} = \frac{1,100}{1,060} = 1.04$

	2017	2016	2015
	$m	$m	$m
Consumer loans			
Allowance for loan losses	11,000	11,500	13,000
Provision for loan losses	3,000	2,000	1,300
Charge-offs	3,759	3,643	4,007
Recoveries	1,299	1,138	1,106
Net charge-offs	2,460	2,505	2,901
Commercial loans			
Allowance for loan losses	1,540	1,012	169
Provision for loan losses	1,100	442	95
Charge-offs	1,488	811	717
Recoveries	428	424	673
Net charge-offs	1,060	387	44
Allowance for loan losses to net loan charge-offs: consumer	4.47	4.59	4.48
Allowance for loan losses to net loan charge-offs: commercial	1.45	2.61	3.84
Provision for loan losses to net loan charge-offs: consumer	1.22	0.80	0.45
Provision for loan losses to net loan charge-offs: commercial	1.04	1.14	2.16

13. B is correct. The net benefit plan obligation has steadily decreased during the last three years, which indicates a lower degree of risk posed by the benefit plan.

14. A is correct. Claims associated with life and health insurance companies (Cobalt) are more predicable than those for property and casualty insurance companies (Vermillion). Property and casualty insurers' claims are more variable and "lumpier" because they arise from accidents and other unpredictable events, whereas life and health insurers' claims are more predictable because they correlate closely with relatively stable actuarially based mortality rates when applied to large populations.

15. B is correct. The loss and loss adjustment expense ratio decreased from 61.3% to 59.1% between 2016 and 2017. This ratio is calculated as follows: (Loss Expense + Loss Adjustment Expense)/Net Premiums Earned. The loss and loss adjustment expense ratio indicates the degree of success an underwriter has achieved in estimating the risks insured. A lower ratio indicates greater success in estimating insured risks.

16. B is correct. The quality of earnings is directly related to the level of sustain-

able sources of income. Trading income tends to be volatile and not necessarily sustainable. Higher-quality income would be net interest income and fee-based service income. Because N-bank's 2017 trading revenue contribution is the lowest relative to other banks, its quality of earnings would be considered the best of the three banks.

17. B is correct. Trading revenue per unit of risk can be represented by the ratio of annual trading revenue to average daily trading value at risk (VaR) and represents a measure of reward-to-risk. The trading revenue per unit of risk improved at N-bank (from 134× to 160×) between 2016 and 2017, and there was no change at T-bank (80×). VaR can be used for gauging trends in intra-company risk taking.

18. B is correct. Exhibit 4 indicates that exposure to free-standing credit derivatives dramatically declined from a peak during the global financial crisis in 2008. If a derivatives contract is classified as freestanding, changes in its fair value are reported as income or expense in the income statement at each reporting period. The immediate recognition of a gain or loss in earnings, instead of reporting it in other comprehensive income, can lead to unexpected volatility of earnings and missed earnings targets. As a result, earnings volatility from the use of credit derivatives most likely decreased.

19. A is correct. A bank's net interest revenue represents the difference between interest earned on loans and other interest-bearing assets and the level of interest paid on deposits and other interest-bearing liabilities. Banks typically borrow money for shorter terms (retail deposits) and lend to customers for longer periods (mortgages and car loans). If the yield curve unexpectedly inverts, the short-term funding costs will increase and the net interest margin will most likely decrease (not remain unchanged or increase).

20. C is correct. Reverse repurchase agreements represent collateralized loans between a bank and a borrower. A reverse repo with a 30-day maturity is a highly liquid asset and thus would directly affect the liquidity coverage ratio (LCR). LCR evaluates short-term liquidity and represents the percentage of a bank's expected cash outflows in relation to highly liquid assets.

LEARNING MODULE 5

Evaluating Quality of Financial Reports

by Jack T. Ciesielski, CPA, CFA, Elaine Henry, PhD, CFA, and Thomas I. Selling, PhD, CPA.

Jack T. Ciesielski, CPA, CFA, is at R.G. Associates, Inc., former publisher of The Analyst's Accounting Observer (USA). Elaine Henry, PhD, CFA, is at Stevens Institute of Technology (USA). Thomas I. Selling, PhD, CPA, is at the Cox School of Business, Southern Methodist University (USA).

LEARNING OUTCOMES

Mastery	The candidate should be able to:
☐	demonstrate the use of a conceptual framework for assessing the quality of a company's financial reports
☐	explain potential problems that affect the quality of financial reports
☐	describe how to evaluate the quality of a company's financial reports
☐	evaluate the quality of a company's financial reports
☐	describe indicators of earnings quality
☐	describe the concept of sustainable (persistent) earnings
☐	explain mean reversion in earnings and how the accruals component of earnings affects the speed of mean reversion
☐	evaluate the earnings quality of a company
☐	evaluate the cash flow quality of a company
☐	describe indicators of balance sheet quality
☐	evaluate the balance sheet quality of a company
☐	describe indicators of cash flow quality
☐	describe sources of information about risk

INTRODUCTION

1

The ability to assess the quality of reported financial information can be a valuable skill. An analyst or investor who can recognize high-quality financial reporting can have greater confidence in analysis based on those financial reports and the resulting investment decisions. Similarly, an analyst or investor who can recognize poor financial reporting quality early—before deficiencies become widely known—is more likely to make profitable investment decisions or to reduce or even avoid losses.

An example of early recognition of an ultimate financial disaster is James Chanos's short position in Enron in November 2000 (Chanos 2002)—more than a year before Enron filed for bankruptcy protection (in December 2001). Despite Enron's high profile and reputation,[1] Chanos had a negative view of Enron based on both quantitative and qualitative factors. Chanos noted that Enron's return on capital was both lower than comparable companies' return on capital and lower than the company's own cost of capital. Qualitative factors contributing to Chanos's view included the company's aggressive revenue recognition policy, its complex and difficult-to-understand disclosures on related-party transactions, and one-time earnings-boosting gains. Later events that substantiated Chanos's perspective included sales of the company's stock by insiders and the resignation of senior executives.

Another example of early recognition of eventual financial troubles is June 2001 reports by analyst Enitan Adebonojo. These reports highlighted questionable accounting by Royal Ahold, a European food retailer. The questionable accounting included "claiming profits of acquired firms as 'organic growth,' booking capital gains from sale-and-leaseback deals as profit, and keeping billions in debt off its balance sheet."[2] In 2003, Royal Ahold announced that it had significantly overstated its profits in the prior two years. The CEO and CFO resigned, various regulators announced investigations, and Royal Ahold's market value dropped significantly.

This reading focuses on reporting quality and the interrelated attribute of results quality. *Reporting quality* pertains to the information disclosed in financial reports. High-quality reporting provides decision-useful information—information that is relevant and faithfully represents the economic reality of the company's activities during the reporting period and the company's financial condition at the end of the period. A separate, but interrelated, attribute of quality is *results* or *earnings quality*, which pertains to the earnings and cash generated by the company's actual economic activities and the resulting financial condition relative to expectations of current and future financial performance. Note that the term "earnings quality" is more commonly used in practice than "results quality," so throughout this reading, earnings quality is used broadly to encompass the quality of earnings, cash flow, and/or balance sheet items.

High-quality earnings reflect an adequate level of return on investment and are derived from activities that a company will likely be able to sustain in the future. Thus, high-quality earnings increase the value of a company more than low-quality earnings. When reported earnings are described as being high quality, it means that the company's underlying economic performance was good (i.e., value enhancing), and it also implies that the company had high reporting quality (i.e., that the information that the company calculated and disclosed was a good reflection of the economic reality).

Earnings can be termed "low quality" either because the reported information properly represents genuinely bad performance or because the reported information misrepresents economic reality. In theory, a company could have low-quality earnings while simultaneously having high reporting quality. Consider a company with low-quality earnings—for example, one whose only source of earnings in a period is a one-off settlement of a lawsuit without which the company would have reported huge losses. The company could nonetheless have high reporting quality if it calculated its results properly and provided decision-useful information. Although it is theoretically

---

[1] In October 2000, Enron was named in the top 25 on *Fortune* magazine's list of the World's Most Admired Companies.
[2] "Ahold: Europe's Enron," *The Economist*, (27 February 2003).

possible that a company could have low-quality earnings while simultaneously having high reporting quality, experiencing poor financial performance can motivate the company's management to misreport.

This reading begins in Section 2 with a description of a conceptual framework for and potential problems with financial reporting quality. This is followed in Section 3 with a discussion of how to evaluate financial reporting quality. Sections 4, 5, and 6 focus on the quality of reported earnings, cash flows, and balance sheets, respectively. Section 7 covers sources of information about risk. A summary and practice problems in the CFA Institute item set format complete the reading.

CONCEPTUAL FRAMEWORK

☐ demonstrate the use of a conceptual framework for assessing the quality of a company's financial reports

This section reviews a conceptual framework for assessing the quality of financial reports and then outlines potential problems that affect the quality of financial reports.

Conceptual Framework for Assessing the Quality of Financial Reports

As indicated in the introduction, financial reporting quality and results or earnings quality are related attributes of quality. Exhibit 1 illustrates this relationship and its implications. Low financial reporting quality can make it difficult or impossible to assess a company's results, and as a result, it is difficult to make investment and other decisions, such as lending and extending credit to the company.

Exhibit 1: Relationships between Financial Reporting Quality and Earnings Quality

		Financial Reporting Quality	
		Low	**High**
Earnings (Results) Quality	High	LOW financial reporting quality impedes assessment of earnings quality and impedes valuation.	HIGH financial reporting quality enables assessment. HIGH earnings quality increases company value.
	Low		HIGH financial reporting quality enables assessment. LOW earnings quality decreases company value.

Financial reporting quality varies across companies. Financial reports can range from those that contain relevant and faithfully representational information to those that contain information that is pure fabrication. Earnings (results) quality can range from high and sustainable to low and unsustainable. The presence of high-quality financial reporting is a necessary condition for enabling investors to evaluate results quality.

High-quality financial reporting alone is an insufficient condition to ensure the presence of high-quality results, but the existence of high-quality financial reporting allows the investor to make such an assessment.

Combining the two aspects of quality—financial reporting and earnings—the overall quality of financial reports from a user perspective can be thought of as spanning a continuum from the highest to the lowest. Exhibit 2 presents a spectrum that provides a basis for evaluating better versus poorer quality reports.

Exhibit 2: Quality Spectrum of Financial Reports

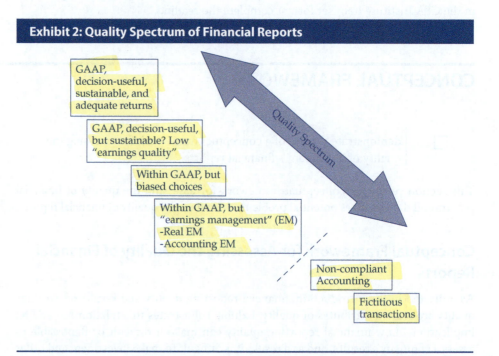

Essentially, the analyst needs to consider two basic questions:

1. Are the financial reports GAAP-compliant and decision-useful?
2. Are the results (earnings) of high quality? In other words, do they provide an adequate level of return, and are they sustainable?

These two questions provide a basic conceptual framework to assess the quality of a company's financial reports and to locate the company's financial reports along the quality spectrum. At the top of the spectrum, labeled in Exhibit 2 as "GAAP, decision-useful, sustainable, and adequate returns" are high-quality reports that provide decision-useful information about high-quality earnings. "GAAP" refers generically to the generally accepted accounting principles or the accepted accounting standards of the jurisdiction under which the company reports. Examples of GAAP are International Financial Reporting Standards (IFRS), US GAAP, and other home-country accounting standards. *Decision-useful* information embodies the characteristics of relevance and faithful representation.[3] High-quality earnings provide an *adequate level of return* on investment (i.e., a return equal to or in excess of the cost of capital) and are sustainable.

---

[3] These characteristics are from the *Conceptual Framework for Financial Reporting* (IASB 2010). The characteristics of decision-useful information are identical under IFRS and US GAAP. Relevant information is defined as information that can affect a decision and encompasses the notion of materiality. Faithful representation of economic events is complete, neutral, and free from error. The *Framework* also identifies enhancing characteristics of useful information: comparability, verifiability, timeliness, and understandability. High-quality information results when necessary trade-offs among these characteristics are made in an unbiased, skillful manner.

Sustainable indicates that the earnings are derived from activities that a company will likely be able to sustain in the future. Sustainable earnings that provide a high return on investment contribute to a higher valuation of a company and its securities.

Any deviation from the highest point on the quality spectrum can be assessed in terms of the two-question conceptual framework. For example, a company that provides GAAP-compliant, decision-useful information about low-quality earnings (they can be of low quality because they do not provide an adequate level of return and/or they are not sustainable) would appear lower on the quality spectrum. Even lower on the spectrum would be companies that provide GAAP-compliant information, which is less decision-useful because of biased choices.

Biased accounting choices result in financial reports that do not faithfully represent economic phenomena. Biased choices can be made not only in the context of reported amounts but also in the context of how information is presented. For example, companies can disclose information transparently and in a manner that facilitates analysis, or they can disclose information in a manner that aims to obscure unfavorable information and/or to emphasize favorable information.

The problem with bias in accounting choices, as with other deficiencies in financial reporting quality, is that it impedes an investor's ability to correctly assess a company's past performance, to accurately forecast future performance, and thus to appropriately value the company. Choices are deemed to be "aggressive" if they increase the company's reported performance and financial position in the current period. Aggressive choices may decrease the company's reported performance and financial position in later periods. In contrast, choices are deemed to be "conservative" if they decrease the company's reported performance and financial position in the current period. Conservative choices may increase the company's reported performance and financial position in later periods.

Another type of bias is "earnings management." An example of this bias is earnings "smoothing" to understate earnings volatility relative to the volatility if earnings were faithfully represented. Earnings volatility is decreased by understating earnings in periods when a company's operations are performing well and overstating in periods when the company's operations are struggling.

The next levels down on the spectrum mark a departure from GAAP. Financial reports that depart from GAAP can generally be considered low quality; they are of poor financial reporting quality and cannot be relied on to assess earnings quality. The lowest-quality financial reports portray fictitious transactions or omit actual transactions; such financial reports are fabrications.

POTENTIAL PROBLEMS

☐ explain potential problems that affect the quality of financial reports

The basic choices that give rise to potential problems with quality of financial reports include reported amounts and timing of recognition and classification. Remember that even GAAP-compliant financial reports can diverge from economic reality if GAAP allows for biased choices. In addition to GAAP-compliant choices, a financial statement preparer may choose to present fraudulent reports. This choice represents a divergence from GAAP and economic reality.

Reported Amounts and Timing of Recognition

The choice of the reported amount and timing of recognition may focus on a single financial statement element (assets, liabilities, owners' equity, revenue and gains [income], or expenses and losses). However, this choice may affect other elements and more than one financial statement because financial statements are interrelated.[4] It is useful to think of the impact of accounting choices in terms of the basic accounting equation (Assets = Liabilities + Equity). This equation can be restated as Assets − Liabilities = Equity, which is also equivalent to Net Assets = Equity. Choices related to income statement elements will affect the balance sheet through equity, and if equity is affected, then another balance sheet element(s) has to be affected or the balance sheet will not balance.

Following are some examples of choices—accounting choices that comply with GAAP, accounting choices that depart from GAAP, and operating choices—and their effects in the current period:

- Aggressive, premature, and fictitious revenue recognition results in overstated income and thus overstated equity. Assets, usually accounts receivable, are also overstated.
- Conservative revenue recognition, such as deferred recognition of revenue, results in understated net income, understated equity, and understated assets.
- Omission and delayed recognition of expenses results in understated expenses and overstated income, overstated equity, overstated assets, and/or understated liabilities. An understatement of bad debt expense results in overstated accounts receivable. Understated depreciation or amortization expense results in the overstatement of the related long-lived asset. Understated interest, taxes, or other expenses result in the understatement of the related liability: accrued interest payable, taxes payable, or other payable.
- Understatement of contingent liabilities is associated with overstated equity resulting from understated expenses and overstated income or overstated other comprehensive income.
- Overstatement of financial assets and understatement of financial liabilities, reported at fair value, are associated with overstated equity resulting from overstated unrealized gains or understated unrealized losses.
- Cash flow from operations may be increased by deferring payments on payables, accelerating payments from customers, deferring purchases of inventory, and deferring other expenditures related to operations, such as maintenance and research.

Example 1 describes events and choices at Satyam Computer Services Limited, which resulted in the issuance of fraudulent reports.

---

4 Depending on management's motivation, poor-quality financial reports may either over-state or under-state results. Fraudulent financial reports almost always overstate results.

Potential Problems

> **EXAMPLE 1**
>
> ### Fictitious Reports
>
> #### Satyam Computer Services Limited
>
> Satyam Computer Services Limited, an Indian information technology company, was founded in 1987 and grew rapidly by providing business process outsourcing (BPO) on a global basis. In 2007, its CEO, Ramalinga Raju, was named "Entrepreneur of the Year" by Ernst & Young, and in 2008, the World Council for Corporate Governance recognized the company for "global excellence in corporate accountability." In 2009, the CEO submitted a letter of resignation that outlined a massive financial fraud at the company. The company's decline was so rapid and significant that it came to be referred to as "India's Enron."
>
> In late 2008, the World Bank terminated its relationship with the company after finding that Satyam gave kickbacks to bank staff and billed for services that were not provided. These initial revelations of wrongdoing had the effect of putting the company under increased scrutiny. Among other misconduct, the CEO eventually admitted that he created fictitious bank statements to inflate cash and to show interest income. The CEO also created fake salary accounts and took the money paid to those "employees." The company's head of internal auditing created fictitious customer accounts and invoices to inflate revenues.[5]
>
> The external auditors did not independently verify much of the information provided by the company. Even when bank confirmations, which were sent to them directly as opposed to indirectly through Satyam, contained significantly different balances than those reported by Satyam, they did not follow up.
>
> 1. Based on the information provided, characterize Satyam's financial reports, with reference to the quality spectrum of financial reports.
>
> ### Solution:
>
> Based on the information provided, Satyam's financial reports were of the lowest quality. They clearly are at the bottom of the quality spectrum of financial reports: reports based on fictitious information.
>
> 2. Explain each of the following misconducts with reference to the basic accounting equation:
>
>   **A.** Transactions with World Bank
>
>   **B.** Fictitious interest income
>
>   **C.** CEO's embezzlement
>
>   **D.** Fictitious revenue
>
> ### Solution:
>
> The effects on the basic accounting equation of the different acts of misconduct are as follows:
>
> **A.** Upon billing for fictitious services, the company would increase an asset, such as accounts receivable, and a revenue account, such as service revenues. The kickbacks to the customer's staff, if recorded, would increase an expense account, such as commissions paid, and increase

---

5 See Bhasin (2012) for more information.

a liability, such as commissions payable, or decrease an asset, such as cash. The net effect of this misconduct is the overstatement of income, net assets, and equity.

- B. Fictitious interest income would result in overstated income; overstated assets, such as cash and interest receivable; and overstated equity. These overstatements were hidden by falsifying revenue and cash balances.
- C. The embezzlement by creating fictitious employees would increase an expense account, such as wages and salaries, and decrease the asset, cash. The resulting understatement of income and equity was offset by a real but fraudulent decrease in cash, which was hidden by falsifying revenue and cash balances.
- D. Fictitious revenues would result in overstated revenues and income; overstated assets, such as cash and accounts receivable; and overstated equity.

3. Based on the information provided, what documents were falsified to support the misconducts listed in Question 2?

Solution:

Based on the information provided, the documents that were falsified include

- invoices to the World Bank for services that were not provided,
- bank statements,
- employee records, and
- customer accounts and invoices.

The falsified documents were intended to mislead the external auditors.

An astute reader of financial statements may have identified a potential problem at Satyam by comparing the growth in revenue with the growth in assets on its balance sheet, such as short-term and long-term trade receivables and unbilled revenue. Long-term trade receivables and unbilled revenue accounts may have raised questions. Also, there was an account separate from cash, investments in bank deposits, which may have raised questions. However, fraudulent reports that are well constructed can be very challenging to identify.

4. CLASSIFICATION

> explain potential problems that affect the quality of financial reports

Choices with respect to reported amounts and timing of recognition typically affect more than one financial element, financial statement, and financial period. Classification choices typically affect one financial statement and relate to how an item is classified within a particular financial statement. The balance sheet, the statement of comprehensive income, or the cash flow statement may be the primary focus of the choice.

With respect to the balance sheet, the concern may be to make the balance sheet ratios more attractive or to hide an issue. For example, a company may focus on accounts receivable because it wants to hide liquidity or revenue collection issues.

Classification

Choices include removing the accounts receivable from the balance sheet by selling them externally or transferring them to a controlled entity, converting them to notes receivable, or reclassifying them within the balance sheet, such as by reporting them as long-term receivables. Although these amounts remain on the balance sheet as receivables of some sort, a result of their reclassification is a lower accounts receivable balance. This could imply to investors that a collection has taken place and also might favorably skew receivables measures, such as days' sales outstanding and receivables turnover.

In the 2003 Merck Annual Report, Merck & Co. reclassified a portion of its inventory to "Other assets," a long-term asset. This reclassification affects the balance sheet and financial ratios as demonstrated in Example 2.

EXAMPLE 2

Balance Sheet Reclassifications

Merck & Co., Inc. and Subsidiaries

In the 2002 Annual Report, inventory was reported at $3,411.8 million. In the 2003 Annual Report, the 2002 inventory value was reported at $2,964.3 million and $447.5 million of inventory was included in other assets. This information was contained in Note 6 to the financial statements, reproduced in Exhibit 3.

Exhibit 3: Note 6 to Consolidated Financial Statements

6. Inventories
Inventories at December 31 consisted of:

($ in millions)	2003	2002
Finished goods	$552.5	$1,262.3
Raw materials and work in process	2,309.8	2,073.8
Supplies	90.5	75.7
Total (approximate current cost)	$2,952.8	$3,411.8
Reduction to LIFO cost	—	—
	$2,952.8	$3,411.8
Recognized as:		
Inventories	$2,554.7	$2,964.3
Other assets	398.1	447.5

Inventories valued under the LIFO method comprised approximately 51% and 39% of inventories at December 31, 2003 and 2002, respectively. Amounts recognized as Other assets consist of inventories held in preparation for product launches and not expected to be sold within one year. The reduction in finished goods is primarily attributable to the spin-off of Medco Health in 2003.

1. The reclassification of a portion of inventory to other assets will *most likely* result in the days of inventory on hand:

    A. decreasing.
    B. staying the same.
    C. increasing.

> **Solution:**
>
> A is correct. The number of days of inventory on hand calculated using the reported inventory number will most likely decrease because the amount of inventory relative to cost of goods sold will decrease.

> 2. As a result of the reclassification of a portion of inventory to other assets, the current ratio will *most likely*:
>   A. decrease.
>   B. stay the same.
>   C. increase.
>
> **Solution:**
>
> A is correct. The current ratio will decrease because current assets will decrease and current liabilities will stay the same.

From Exhibit 3, notice that the reclassification is described in the sentence, "Amounts recognized as Other assets consist of inventories held in preparation for product launches and not expected to be sold within one year." The reasoning behind the reclassification's explanation is logical: Current assets include assets to be consumed or converted into cash in a company's operating cycle, which is usually one year. The inventory items associated with product launches beyond one year are more appropriately classified as "other assets." Yet, the change in classification poses analytical problems. Inventory turnover is a key indicator of efficiency in managing inventory levels and is calculated as cost of sales divided by average inventory. Although the inventory turnover can be calculated for 2003, it cannot be calculated on a consistent basis for 2002, or any year before then, because the amount of inventory that would have been classified as "other assets" in those periods is not disclosed. An investor has to recognize that a time-series comparison of Merck's inventory turnover is going to produce an inconsistent history because of the lack of consistent information.

The classification of revenues between operating and non-operating may help the user to determine sustainability of a company's earnings, but the classification has potential for misuse by a company. The classification of revenues as being derived from core, continuing operations could mislead financial statement users into considering inflated amounts of income as being sustainable. Similarly, the classification of expenses as non-operating could mislead financial statement users into considering inflated amounts of income as being sustainable. In non-GAAP metrics reported outside of the financial statements, the classification of income-reducing items as non-recurring could also mislead financial statement users into considering inflated amounts of income as being sustainable.

Classifications that result in an item being reported in other comprehensive income rather than on the income statement can affect analysis and comparison. For example, if two otherwise identical companies classify investments differently, net income may differ because the change in value of the investments may flow through net income for one company and through other comprehensive income for the other company.

Classification issues also arise specifically with the statement of cash flows for which management may have incentives to maximize the amount of cash flows that are classified as "operating." Management may be motivated to classify activities, such as the sale of long-term assets, as operating activities rather than investing activities. Operating activities are part of the day-to-day functioning of a company, such as selling inventory or providing services. For most companies, the sale of property or other long-term assets are not operating activities, and including them in operating activities

Classification

overstates the company's ability to generate cash from its operations. Management may capitalize rather than expense operating expenditures. As a result, the outflow may be classified as an investing activity rather than an operating activity.

Exhibit 4 presents a selection of potential issues, possible actions, and warning signs of possible deviations from high-quality financial reports, some of which will be specifically discussed in later sections of this reading. The warning signs may be visible in the financial statements themselves, in the notes to the financial statements, or in ratios calculated by the analyst that are assessed over time or compared with those of peer companies. Frequently, the chosen actions bias net income upward. However, a new management or management of a company in financial difficulty may be motivated to bias current income downward to enhance future periods.

Exhibit 4: Accounting Warning Signs

Potential Issues	Possible Actions/Choices	Warning Signs

• Overstatement or non-sustainability of operating income and/or net income
  • Overstated or accelerated revenue recognition
  • Understated expenses
  • Misclassification of revenue, gains, expenses, or losses
	• Contingent sales with right of return, "channel stuffing" (the practice of inducing customers to order products they would otherwise not order or order at a later date through generous terms), "bill and hold" sales (encouraging customers to order goods and retain them on seller's premises)
	• Fictitious (fraudulent) revenue
	• Capitalizing expenditures as assets
	• Classifying non-operating income or gains as part of operations
	• Classifying ordinary expenses as non-recurring or non-operating
	• Reporting gains through net income and losses through other comprehensive income
		• Growth in revenue higher than that of industry or peers
		• Increases in discounts to and returns from customers
		• Higher growth rate in receivables than revenue
		• Large proportion of revenue in final quarter of year for a non-seasonal business
		• Cash flow from operations is much lower than operating income
		• Inconsistency over time in the items included in operating revenues and operating expenses
		• Increases in operating margin
		• Aggressive accounting assumptions, such as long, depreciable lives
		• Losses in non-operating income or other comprehensive income and gains in operating income or net income
		• Compensation largely tied to financial results

Potential Issues	Possible Actions/Choices	Warning Signs

• Misstatement of balance sheet items (may affect income statement)
  • Over- or understatement of assets
  • Over- or understatement of liabilities
  • Misclassification of assets and/or liabilities
	• Choice of models and model inputs to measure fair value
	• Classification from current to non-current
	• Over- or understating reserves and allowances
	• Understating identifiable assets and overstating goodwill
		• Models and model inputs that bias fair value measures
		• Inconsistency in model inputs when measuring fair value of assets compared with that of liabilities
		• Typical current assets, such as accounts receivable and inventory, included in non-current assets
		• Allowances and reserves that fluctuate over time or are not comparable with peers
		• High goodwill value relative to total assets
		• Use of special purpose vehicles
		• Large changes in deferred tax assets and liabilities
		• Significant off-balance-sheet liabilities

• Overstatement of cash flow from operations	• Managing activities to affect cash flow from operations • Misclassifying cash flows to positively affect cash flow from operations	• **Increase in accounts payable and decrease in accounts receivable and inventory** • Capitalized expenditures in investing activities • Sales and leaseback • Increases in bank overdrafts

5. M&A ISSUES AND DIVERGENCE FROM ECONOMIC REALITY

☐ explain potential problems that affect the quality of financial reports

Quality issues with respect to financial reports often arise in connection with mergers and acquisitions. Mergers and acquisitions provide opportunities and motivations to manage financial results. For accounting purposes, the business combination is accounted for using the acquisition method, and one company is identified as the acquirer. The financial results of the combined companies are reported on a consolidated basis.

Companies with faltering cash-generating ability may be motivated to acquire other companies to increase cash flow from operations. The acquisition will be reported in the investing cash flows if paid in cash, or not even appear on the cash flow statement if paid for with equity. The consolidated cash flow from operations will include the cash flow of the acquired company, effectively concealing the acquirer's own cash flow problems. Such an acquisition can provide a one-time boost to cash from operations that may or may not be sustainable. There are no required post-acquisition "with and without acquisitions" disclosures, making it impossible for investors to reliably assess whether or not the acquirer's cash flow problems are worsening.

A potential acquisition may create an incentive for a company to report using aggressive choices or even misreport. For example, an acquirer's managers may be motivated to make choices to increase earnings to make an acquisition on more favorable terms. Evidence indicates that acquirers making an acquisition for stock may manipulate their reported earnings prior to the acquisition to inflate the value of shares being used to pay for the acquisition (Erickson and Wang 1999). Similarly, the target company's managers may be motivated to make choices to increase earnings to secure a more favorable price for their company. As another example, the acquiring managers may try to manipulate earnings upward after an acquisition if they want to positively influence investors' opinion of the acquisition.[6]

In other cases, misreporting can be an incentive to make an acquisition. Acquisitions complicate a company's financial statements and thus can conceal previous accounting misstatements. Some evidence indicates that companies engaged in intentional misreporting (specifically, companies that were subsequently accused of accounting fraud by the US SEC) are more likely than non-misreporting companies to make an acquisition. They are also more likely to acquire a company that would reduce the comparability and consistency of their financial statements, such as by targeting companies that have less public information and less similar operations (Erickson, Heitzman, and Zhang 2012).

There are also opportunities to make choices that affect the initial consolidated balance sheet and consolidated income statements in the future. When a business combination occurs, the acquirer must measure and recognize identifiable assets acquired and liabilities assumed at their fair values as of the acquisition date. These may include assets and liabilities that the acquired company had not previously recognized as assets and liabilities in its financial statements. For example, identifiable intangible assets that the acquired company developed internally and some contingent liabilities would be recognized by the acquirer. The excess of the purchase price over the recognized value of the identified assets acquired and liabilities assumed is reported as goodwill. Unlike other long-lived assets, goodwill is not amortized; however, it is subject to impairment testing. Because goodwill is not amortized, unless appropriate impairment charges are recorded, the capitalized goodwill amount continues indefinitely.

The default accounting treatment for goodwill—no future amortization expense—provides an incentive to acquirers to understate the value of amortizable intangibles when recording an acquisition. Being a residual amount, more of the value of an acquisition will thus be classified as goodwill, with its future earnings-friendly accounting treatment. That bias may result in postponement of the recognition of an uneconomic acquisition until impairment charges on the goodwill are recorded, which may be long after the acquisition. Managements may be willing to take this chance because they may be able to convince analysts and investors that a goodwill impairment charge is a non-recurring, non-cash charge—something that many will overlook. Nevertheless, the presence of goodwill should make an investor more inquisitive about a company's record in recognizing impairments and should also motivate an investor to evaluate a company's impairment testing process for goodwill. Fair value measurement, except in the case of assets and liabilities with quoted prices in active markets for identical assets or liabilities, presents an opportunity for the acquirer's management to exercise judgment and affect reported values. For example, they could understate fair value of assets to avoid future charges to expense. Understating the fair value of assets will result in a higher goodwill amount. In the absence of impairment of goodwill, there will be no charges associated with the goodwill. Many analysts question whether reported goodwill reflects economic reality.

---

[6] Findings consistent with this possibility are presented in Bens, Goodman, and Neamtiu (2012).

Financial Reporting that Diverges from Economic Reality Despite Compliance with Accounting Rules

Certain accounting standards may give rise to financial reporting that an analyst may find less useful because he or she does not view it as reflective of economic reality. Example 3 and Example 4 illustrate these types of situations. When possible, an analyst should adjust the reported information to better reflect his or her view of economic reality. If an adjustment is not possible because the relevant data are not disclosed, an analyst can instead make a qualitative assessment of the effect.

Example 3 describes one of the earlier cases of creative consolidation accounting that raised the need for an in-depth consideration of consolidation accounting and the related issue of control. Many entities are governed by the votes of shareholders under which the majority rules. However, exceptions may exist and both US GAAP and IFRS have endeavored to create regimes under which consolidation is required when it is appropriate to depict economic substance.

EXAMPLE 3

Treatment of Variable Interest (Special Purpose) Entities

SEC enforcement action regarding the financial statements of Digilog, Inc.

In order to develop and introduce a new product, Digilog created a separate business entity, DBS, that was capitalized with $10 million of convertible debt issued to Digilog. Upon conversion, Digilog would end up owning nearly 100% of DBS. Initially, owners' equity of DBS consisted of a few thousand dollars of common stock issued to DBS's manager.

During the first two years of DBS's operations, Digilog did not consolidate DBS; it argued that DBS was controlled by its manager, who owned 100% of the outstanding common shares. Even though DBS generated substantial losses over its first two years of existence, Digilog reported interest income on its investment in the convertible debt. After two years, when DBS started to generate profits, Digilog exercised its conversion option and consolidated from that point forward.

Although DBS had been set up as an "independent" corporation, the SEC took the position that the contractual and operating relationships between the two companies were such that they should have been viewed as constituting a single enterprise for financial reporting purposes. The defendants in the enforcement action, Digilog's auditors, consented to a settlement. The settlement included the opinion by the SEC that consolidation would have provided a user of the financial statements with the most meaningful presentation in accordance with GAAP—even though no specific GAAP at that time directly addressed Digilog's "creative" accounting solution.

Eventually, after many more years of debate, and in the wake of the Enron scandal, which also involved abuse of subsequent consolidation rules, the concept of a "variable interest entity" (VIE) was created. A key aspect is control for consolidation purposes; even in the absence of voting control, consolidation is necessary if the investor has the ability to exert influence on the financial and operating policy of the entity and is exposed, or has rights, to variable returns from its investment in the entity. Although the term VIE is not employed by IFRS, its provisions are similar.

M&A Issues and Divergence from Economic Reality

1. Given the facts above and the consolidation rules for a variable interest entity, Digilog is *most likely* to try to argue that it does not need to consolidate DBS because:

   A. Digilog does not have voting control.
   B. Digilog's interest income from DBS is not variable.
   C. DBS's manager has operational and financial control.

Solution:

C is correct. Digilog is most likely to assert that operational and financial control rest with DBS's manager. However, the assertion is not likely to be accepted because the manager's investment is a few thousand dollars compared with $10 million by Digilog. Simply not having voting control is not sufficient to avoid consolidation. Digilog is exposed to variable returns because of possible losses and the convertibility option.

Example 4 considers asset impairments and restructuring charges and their implications.

EXAMPLE 4

Asset Impairments and Restructuring Charges

1. Two related topics that almost always require special consideration on the part of analysts are asset impairments and restructuring charges. Asset impairments are write-downs of assets required when circumstances indicate that the carrying amount of an asset is excessive compared with the expected future benefits.

   The term "restructuring charge" is used under IFRS to indicate a sale or termination of a line of business, closure of business locations, changes in management structure, and/or a fundamental reorganization. All of these events could also give rise to the recognition of a liability (e.g., a commitment to make employee severance payments or to make a payment to settle a lease).

   On 25 April 2013, Fuji Electric Co., Ltd, a Japanese company reporting under the GAAP of its home country, announced an impairment loss on land, buildings, structures, and leased assets employed in its "solar cell and module business" in the amount of ¥6.5 billion (Fuji Electric 2013). The entire loss was recorded in its 2012 fiscal year (ending 31 March). Assets and net income were reduced by ¥6.5 billion.

   Elan Corporation, plc, a biotechnology company headquartered in Ireland, reported US$42.4 million in restructuring and other costs incurred during fiscal year 2012 related to its decision to close a research facility in San Francisco, with the loss of around 200 jobs, and to shift much of its operations back to Ireland because of changing business conditions. Some of these costs were associated with the obligation to make current and deferred employee severance payments (Leuty 2012).[7]

---

[7] See also Elan Corporation, plc, Form 20-F, filed 12 February 2013.

> Recognizing an impairment loss and restructuring charges in a single period, although consistent with most GAAP, is *most likely* to overstate:
>
> **A.** prior periods' net incomes.
>
> **B.** current period's net income.
>
> **C.** future periods' net incomes.
>
> ## Solution:
>
> A is correct. The impairment and the restructuring were likely the result of past activities and should be taken into account when evaluating past net incomes. The current period's net income, unless the impairment or restructuring is expected to be repeated, is understated. Future period net income may be overstated if reversals occur, but such behavior is not likely. Charging the entire impairment loss and restructuring charge in the current period are examples of conservative accounting principles.

An analyst would likely consider it probable that the events giving rise to Fuji Electric's impairment loss (evidently, declining activity and future prospects for its solar business) had actually occurred over a longer period than that single year. Similarly, an analyst might view the restructuring charge at Elan as relating to previous periods.

When faced with a restructuring charge, an impairment charge, or a combination of the two, an analyst should consider whether similar events occur regularly enough such that they should be factored into estimates of permanent earnings, or whether they should be regarded as one-off items that provide little information about the future earnings of the remaining activities of the company. If it is the former, then the analyst should attempt to "normalize" earnings by essentially spreading the current restructuring/impairment charge(s) over past periods as well as the current period. If an item is truly one-off—say, the financial effects of a natural disaster—then the analyst is justified in "normalizing" earnings by excluding the item from earnings. This process will require a significant amount of judgment, best informed by knowledge of the underlying facts and circumstances.

Items that are commonly encountered by analysts include the following:

- Revisions to ongoing estimates, such as the remaining economic lives of assets, may lead an analyst to question whether an earlier change in estimate would have been more appropriate.
- Sudden increases to allowances and reserves could call into question whether the prior estimates resulted in overstatement of prior periods' earnings instead of an unbiased picture of economic reality.
- Large accruals for losses (e.g., environmental or litigation-related liabilities) suggest that prior periods' earnings may have been overstated because of the failure to accrue losses earlier.

Management may use items such as reserves and allowances to manage or smooth earnings. The application of accounting standards illustrated in Example 3 and Example 4 results in financial statements that may not reflect economic reality. Accounting standards may result in some economic assets and liabilities not being reflected in the financial statements. An example is research and development (R&D) expense. Accounting standards do not permit the capitalization of expenditures for R&D expense, yet R&D produces assets that, in turn, produce future benefits. Accounting standards prohibit R&D's capitalization because of the difficulty in assessing which expenditures will actually produce future benefits and which expenditures will produce nothing. Accounting standards may also result in some information being reported in other comprehensive income rather than through net income. For example, classifying marketable securities as "available for sale" will result in their changes in fair value being reported in other comprehensive income. Contrast that reporting result against that for marketable securities classified as "trading": Their changes in fair value are reported in net income.

No basis of accounting can be expected to recognize all of the economic assets and liabilities for an entity. Consequently, figuring out what *is not* reported can be challenging. One frequently encountered example of an unrecognized asset is a company's sales order backlog. Under most GAAP, revenue is not recognized (and an asset is not created) until services have been performed and other criteria have been met. However, in certain industries, particularly large-scale manufacturing, such as airplane manufacturing, the order backlog can be a significant unrecognized asset. When the amount of backlog is significant, it is typically discussed in the management commentary, and an analyst can use this information to adjust reported amounts and to prepare forecasts.

Another dilemma for analysts is judging whether an item presented in other comprehensive income (OCI) should be included in their analysis as net income. Examples of items presented in OCI include the following:

- unrealized holding gains and losses on certain investments in equity securities,
- unrealized holding gains (and subsequent losses) on items of property and equipment for which the "revaluation option" is elected (IFRS only),
- effects on owners' equity resulting from the translation of the foreign currency-denominated financial statements of a foreign operation to the reporting currency of the consolidated entity,
- certain changes to net pension liability or asset, and
- gains and losses on derivative financial instruments (and certain foreign currency-denominated non-derivative financial instruments) accounted for as a hedge of future cash flows.

When an analyst decides that a significant item presented in OCI should be included in net income, the analyst can adjust reported and forecasted amounts accordingly.

GENERAL STEPS OF EVALUATION 6

☐ describe how to evaluate the quality of a company's financial reports

Prior to beginning any financial analysis, an analyst should clarify the purpose and context and clearly understand the following:

- What is the purpose of the analysis? What questions will this analysis answer?
- What level of detail will be needed to accomplish this purpose?
- What data are available for the analysis?
- What are the factors or relationships that will influence the analysis?
- What are the analytical limitations, and will these limitations potentially impair the analysis?

In the context of evaluating the quality of financial reports, an analyst is attempting to answer two basic questions:

1. Are the financial reports GAAP-compliant and decision-useful?

2. Are the results (earnings) of high quality? Do they provide an adequate level of return, and are they sustainable?

General steps, which fit within the general framework just mentioned, are discussed first. Following these steps may help an analyst evaluate the quality of financial reports (answering the two basic questions). Then, quantitative tools for evaluating the quality of financial reports are discussed.

General Steps to Evaluate the Quality of Financial Reports

It is important to note that the steps presented here are meant to serve as a general guideline only. An analyst may choose to add steps, emphasize or deemphasize steps, or alter the order of the steps. Companies are unique, and variation in specific analytical projects will require specific approaches.

1. Develop an understanding of the company and its industry. Understanding the economic activities of a company provides a basis for understanding why particular accounting principles may be appropriate and why particular financial metrics matter. Understanding the accounting principles used by a company *and* its competitors provides a basis for understanding what constitutes the norm—and to assess whether a company's treatment is appropriate.

2. Learn about management. Evaluate whether the company's management has any particular incentives to misreport. Review disclosures about compensation and insider transactions, especially insiders' sales of the company's stock. Review the disclosures concerning related-party transactions.

3. Identify significant accounting areas, especially those in which management judgment or an unusual accounting rule is a significant determinant of reported financial performance.

4. Make comparisons:

    A. Compare the company's financial statements and significant disclosures in the current year's report with the financial statements and significant disclosures in the prior year's report. Are there major differences in line items or in key disclosures, such as risk disclosures, segment disclosures, classification of specific expense, or revenue items? Are the reasons for the changes apparent?

    B. Compare the company's accounting policies with those of its closest competitors. Are there significant differences? If so, what is the directional effect of the differences?

    C. Using ratio analysis, compare the company's performance with that of its closest competitors.

5. Check for warnings signs of possible issues with the quality of the financial reports. For example,

    - declining receivables turnover could suggest that some revenues are fictitious or recorded prematurely or that the allowance for doubtful accounts is insufficient;
    - declining inventory turnover could suggest obsolescence problems that should be recognized; and
    - net income greater than cash provided by operations could suggest that aggressive accrual accounting policies have shifted current expenses to later periods.

6. For firms operating in multiple segments by geography or product—particularly multinational firms—consider whether inventory, sales, and expenses have been shifted to make it appear that a company is positively exposed to a geographic region or product segment that the investment community considers to be a desirable growth area. An analyst may suspect that this shift is occurring if the segment is showing strong performance while the consolidated results remain static or worsen.
7. Use appropriate quantitative tools to assess the likelihood of misreporting.

The first six steps listed describe a qualitative approach to evaluating the quality of financial reports. In addition to the qualitative approach, quantitative tools have been developed to help in evaluating financial reports.

QUANTITATIVE TOOLS TO ASSESS THE LIKELIHOOD OF MISREPORTING

7

☐ describe how to evaluate the quality of a company's financial reports
☐ evaluate the quality of a company's financial reports

This section describes some tools for assessing the likelihood of misreporting (Step 7 above). If the likelihood of misreporting appears high, an analyst should take special care in analyzing, including qualitatively analyzing, the financial reports of the company.

Beneish Model

Messod D. Beneish and colleagues conducted studies to identify quantitative indicators of earnings manipulation and to develop a model to assess the likelihood of misreporting (Beneish 1999; Beneish, Lee, and Nichols 2013). The following is the Beneish model and its variables. After the description of each variable, an intuitive explanation of why it is included is given.

The probability of manipulation (M-score) is estimated using a probit model:[8]

M-score = −4.84 + 0.920 (DSR) + 0.528 (GMI) + 0.404 (AQI) + 0.892 (SGI) + 0.115 (DEPI) − 0.172 (SGAI) + 4.679 (Accruals) − 0.327 (LEVI)

where

M-score = Score indicating probability of earnings manipulation

DSR (days sales receivable index) = (Receivables$_t$/Sales$_t$)/(Receivables$_{t-1}$/Sales$_{t-1}$).

Changes in the relationship between receivables and sales could indicate inappropriate revenue recognition.

GMI (gross margin index) = Gross margin$_{t-1}$/Gross margin$_t$.

Deterioration in margins could predispose companies to manipulate earnings.

---

[8] Variables that are statistically significant in the empirical results of Beneish (1999) include the days sales receivable index, gross margin index, asset quality index, sales growth index, and accruals.

AQI (asset quality index) = $[1 - (PPE_t + CA_t)/TA_t]/[1 - (PPE_{t-1} + CA_{t-1})/TA_{t-1}]$, where PPE is property, plant, and equipment; CA is current assets; and TA is total assets.

Change in the percentage of assets other than in PPE and CA could indicate excessive expenditure capitalization.

SGI (sales growth index) = $Sales_t/Sales_{t-1}$.

Managing the perception of continuing growth and capital needs from actual growth could predispose companies to manipulate sales and earnings.

DEPI (depreciation index) = Depreciation rate$_{t-1}$/Depreciation rate$_t$, where Depreciation rate = Depreciation/(Depreciation + PPE).

Declining depreciation rates could indicate understated depreciation as a means of manipulating earnings.

SGAI (sales, general, and administrative expenses index) = $(SGA_t/Sales_t)/(SGA_{t-1}/Sales_{t-1})$.

An increase in fixed SGA expenses suggests decreasing administrative and marketing efficiency, which could predispose companies to manipulate earnings.

Accruals = (Income before extraordinary items[9] − Cash from operations)/Total assets.

Higher accruals can indicate earnings manipulation.

LEVI (leverage index) = Leverage$_t$/Leverage$_{t-1}$, where Leverage is calculated as the ratio of debt to assets.

Increasing leverage could predispose companies to manipulate earnings.

The *M*-score in the Beneish model is a normally distributed random variable with a mean of 0 and a standard deviation of 1.0. Consequently, the probability of earnings manipulation indicated by the model can be calculated by using the cumulative probabilities for a standard normal distribution or the NORMSDIST function in Excel. For example, *M*-scores of −1.49 and −1.78 indicate that the probability of earnings manipulation is 6.8% and 3.8%, respectively. Higher *M*-scores (i.e., less negative numbers) indicate an increased probability of earnings manipulation. The probability is given by the amount in the left side of the distribution.

The use of the *M*-score to classify companies as potential manipulators depends on the relative cost of Type I errors (incorrectly classifying a manipulator company as a non-manipulator) and Type II errors (incorrectly classifying a non-manipulator as a manipulator). The cutoff value for classification minimizes the cost of misclassification. Beneish considered that the likely relevant cutoff for investors is a probability of earnings manipulation of 3.8% (an *M*-score exceeding −1.78).[10] Example 5 shows an application of the Beneish model.

---

[9] US GAAP for fiscal periods beginning after December 15, 2015, will no longer include the concept of extraordinary items.
[10] See Beneish (1999) for an explanation and derivation of the cutoff values. Beneish et al. (2013) use an *M*-score exceeding −1.78 as the cutoff value.

Quantitative Tools to Assess the Likelihood of Misreporting

> **EXAMPLE 5**
>
> ## Application of the Beneish Model
>
> Exhibit 5 presents the variables and Beneish's *M*-Score for XYZ Corporation (a hypothetical company).
>
> ### Exhibit 5: XYZ Corporation *M*-Score
>
> | | Value of Variable | Coefficient from Beneish Model | Calculations |
> |---|---|---|---|
> | DSR | 1.300 | 0.920 | 1.196 |
> | GMI | 1.100 | 0.528 | 0.581 |
> | AQI | 0.800 | 0.404 | 0.323 |
> | SGI | 1.100 | 0.892 | 0.981 |
> | DEPI | 1.100 | 0.115 | 0.127 |
> | SGAI | 0.600 | −0.172 | −0.103 |
> | Accruals | 0.150 | 4.679 | 0.702 |
> | LEVI | 0.600 | −0.327 | −0.196 |
> | Intercept | | | −4.840 |
> | *M*-score | | | −1.231 |
> | Probability of manipulation | | | 10.93% |
>
> 1. Would the results of the Beneish model lead an analyst, using a −1.78 *M*-score as the cutoff, to flag XYZ as a likely manipulator?
>
> ### Solution:
>
> Yes, the model could be expected to lead an analyst to flag XYZ as a likely manipulator. The *M*-score is higher than the cutoff of −1.78, indicating a higher-than-acceptable probability of manipulation. For XYZ Corporation, the model estimates the probability of manipulation as 10.93%. Although the classification of companies as manipulators depends on the relative cost of Type I errors and Type II errors, the value of 10.93% greatly exceeds the cutoff of 3.8% that Beneish identified as the relevant cutoff.
>
> 2. The values of DSR, GMI, SGI, and DEPI are all greater than one. In the Beneish model, what does this indicate for each variable?
>
> ### Solution:
>
> Indications are as follows:
>
> A. The value greater than one for DSR indicates that receivables as a percentage of sales have increased; this change may be an indicator of inappropriate revenue recognition. XYZ may have shipped goods prematurely and recognized revenues belonging in later periods. Alternatively, it may be caused by customers with deteriorating credit-paying ability—still a problem for the analyst of XYZ.
>
> B. The value greater than one for GMI indicates that gross margins were higher last year; deteriorating margins could predispose companies to manipulate earnings.

> C. The value greater than one for SGI indicates positive sales growth relative to the previous year. Companies could be predisposed to manipulate earnings to manage perceptions of continuing growth and also to obtain capital needed to support growth.
>
> D. The value greater than one for DEPI indicates that the depreciation rate was higher in the prior year; a declining depreciation rate can indicate manipulated earnings.

Other Quantitative Models

Researchers have examined numerous factors that contribute to assessing the probability that a company is engaged in accounting manipulation. Variables that have been found useful for detecting misstatement include accruals quality; deferred taxes; auditor change; market-to-book value; whether the company is publicly listed and traded; growth rate differences between financial and non-financial variables, such as number of patents, employees, and products; and aspects of corporate governance and incentive compensation.[11]

Limitations of Quantitative Models

Accounting is a partial representation of economic reality. Consequently, financial models based on accounting numbers are only capable of establishing associations between variables. The underlying cause and effect can only be determined by a deeper analysis of actions themselves—perhaps through interviews, surveys, or investigations by financial regulators with enforcement powers.

An additional concern is that earnings manipulators are just as aware as analysts of the power of quantitative models to screen for possible cases of earnings manipulation. It is not surprising to learn, therefore, that Beneish et al.'s 2013 study found that the predictive power of the Beneish model is declining over time. Undoubtedly, many managers have learned to test the detectability of earnings manipulation tactics by using the model to anticipate analysts' perceptions. Thus, as useful as the Beneish model may be, the search for more powerful analytical tools continues. It is necessary for analysts to use qualitative, not just quantitative, means to assess quality.

8. EARNINGS QUALITY INDICATORS

☐ describe indicators of earnings quality

This section first discusses indicators of earnings quality and then describes how to evaluate the earnings quality of a company. Analytical tools related to identifying very poor earnings/results quality, such as quantitative approaches to assessing the probability of bankruptcy, are also discussed.

---

11 A summary of research on predicting accounting misstatement is provided in Dechow, Ge, Larson, and Sloan (2011).

Indicators of Earnings Quality

In general, the term "earnings quality" can be used to encompass earnings, cash flow, and balance sheet quality. This section, however, focuses specifically on earnings quality. High earnings quality is often considered to be evidenced by earnings that are sustainable and represent returns equal to or in excess of the company's cost of capital.[12] High-quality earnings increase the value of the company more than low-quality earnings, and the term "high-quality earnings" assumes that reporting quality is high. In contrast, low-quality earnings are insufficient to cover the company's cost of capital and/or are derived from non-recurring, one-off activities. In addition, the term "low-quality earnings" can also be used when the reported information does not provide a useful indication of the company's performance.

A variety of alternatives have been used as indicators of earnings quality: recurring earnings, earnings persistence and related measures of accruals, beating benchmarks, and after-the-fact confirmations of poor-quality earnings, such as enforcement actions and restatements.

Recurring Earnings

When using a company's current and prior earnings as an input to forecast future earnings (for example, for use in an earnings-based valuation), an analyst focuses on the earnings that are expected to recur in the future. For example, earnings from subsidiaries that have been selected for disposal, which must be separately identified as "discontinued operations," are typically excluded from forecasting models. A wide range of other types of items may be non-recurring—for example, one-off asset sales, one-off litigation settlements, or one-off tax settlements. Reported earnings that contain a high proportion of non-recurring items are less likely to be sustainable and are thus considered lower quality.

Enron, an energy distribution company and a company famous for misreporting, presented non-recurring items, among other reporting issues, in such a way that they created an illusion of a solidly performing company. Example 6 shows aspects of Enron's reporting.

EXAMPLE 6

Non-Recurring Items

Enron Corp.

Exhibit 6: Excerpts from Enron and Subsidiaries Consolidated Income Statement, Year-Ended 31 December

(In millions, except per share amounts)	2000	1999	1998
Total revenues	$100,789	$40,112	$31,260
Total costs and expenses	98,836	39,310	29,882
Operating income	$1,953	$802	$1,378
Other income and deductions			
Equity in earnings of unconsolidated equity affiliates	$87	$309	$97
Gains on sales of non-merchant assets	146	541	56
Gain on the issuance of stock by TNPC, Inc.	121	0	0

---

12 The residual income model of valuation is most closely linked to this concept of high earnings quality.

(In millions, except per share amounts)	2000	1999	1998
Interest income	212	162	88
Other income, net	−37	181	−37
Income before interest, minority interests, and income taxes	$2,482	$1,995	$1,582

1. How does the trend in Enron's operating income compare with the trend in its income after other income and deductions (i.e., Income before interest, minority interests, and income taxes)?

Solution:

Enron's operating income varied dramatically from year to year, declining from 1998 to 1999 and then more than doubling in 2000. In contrast, Enron's income before interest, minority interests, and income taxes shows a smooth, upward trend with significant increases each year. The increases were 24% and 26% for 2000 and 1999 relative to 1999 and 1998, respectively.

2. What items appear to be non-recurring as opposed to being a result of routine operations? How significant are these items?

Solution:

Items that appear to be non-recurring are gains on sales of non-merchant assets and the gain on the issuance of stock by TNPC. Although gains from sales of non-merchant assets do recur in each year, this type of activity is not a part of Enron's energy distribution operations. In addition, two other non-operating items—the amount of equity in earnings from unconsolidated subsidiaries and the amount of other income—are highly variable. Two aspects of these items are significant. First, the smooth, upward trend in Enron's income is the direct result of these items. Second, these items collectively represent a significant percentage of the company's income before interest, minority interests, and income taxes, particularly in 1999 when these items represent 52% of the total: ($309 + $541+ $181)/ $1,995 = $1,031/$1,995.

3. The Enron testimony of short seller James Chanos before US Congress referred to "a number of one-time gains that boosted Enron's earnings" as one of the items that "strengthened our conviction that the market was mispricing Enron's stock" (Chanos 2002). What does Chanos's statement indicate about how Enron's earnings information was being used in valuation?

Solution:

Chanos's statement suggests that at least some market participants were mistakenly using Enron's reported income as an input to earnings-based valuation, without adjusting for non-recurring items.

Although evaluating non-recurring items for inclusion in operating metrics is important for making appropriate historical comparisons and for developing appropriate inputs in valuation, another aspect of non-recurring items merits mention. Because classification of items as non-recurring is a subjective decision, classification decisions can provide an opportunity to inflate the amount potentially identified by a user of the income statement as repeatable earnings—those earnings expected from the company's business operations, which investors label as "recurring" or "core" earnings. In the absence of special or one-time items (such as restructuring charges, employee separation costs, goodwill impairment charges, or gains on disposals of assets), operating income is representative of these kinds of earnings. So-called classification shifting, which does not affect total net income, can inflate the amount reported as recurring or core earnings. This could be accomplished by re-classifying normal expenses to special items or by shifting operating expenses to income-decreasing discontinued operations. Anecdotal evidence of classification shifting exists (see Exhibit 7), but the evidence only emerges after the fact.[13] From an analyst's perspective, after-the-fact evidence of earnings management is not particularly useful for anticipating issues with earnings quality. Although it may not be possible to identify whether a company might be engaging in classification shifting, an analyst should nonetheless give special attention to income-decreasing special items, particularly if the company is reporting unusually high operating earnings for the period or if the classification of the item enabled the company to meet or beat forecasts for operating earnings.

Exhibit 7: Anecdotal Evidence of Classification Shifting

- Borden, a food and chemicals company: The SEC determined that the company had classified $146 million of operating expenses as part of a special item (restructuring charges) when the expenses should have been included in selling, general, and administrative expenses (Hwang 1994).

- AmeriServe Food Distribution Inc., which declared bankruptcy only four months after completing a $200 million junk bond issuance: A bankruptcy court–appointed examiner found that the company's financial statements "classified substantial operating expenses... as restructuring charges," which "masked the company's serious financial underperformance and delayed recognition by all parties of the severity of the problems faced by the company (Sherer 2000)."

- Waste Management, which, in 1998, issued the then-largest restatement in SEC history: The enforcement documentation indicates that the company had improperly inflated operating income by netting non-operating gains from the sale of investments and discontinued operations against unrelated operating expenses (SEC 2001b).

- IBM: Revised disclosures, prompted by SEC scrutiny and analysts' requests, showed that the company had classified intellectual property income as an offset to selling, general, and administrative expenses. This classification resulted in an understatement of operating expenses and thus an overstatement of core earnings by $1.5 billion and $1.7 billion in 2001 and 2000, respectively (Bulkeley 2002).

Companies understand that investors differentiate between recurring and non-recurring items. Therefore, in addition to presenting components of income on the face of the income statement, many companies voluntarily disclose additional information to facilitate the differentiation between recurring and non-recurring items. Specifically, companies may disclose both total income and so-called *pro forma*

---

[13] Archival evidence of classification shifting is presented in McVay (2006). McVay first models "expected core earnings" and then documents a relationship between reported-minus-expected core earnings and the number of special items. But in any given year, a company's management could attribute the unexpectedly high core earnings to economic improvements related to the special items; therefore, only the *ex post* evidence that unexpectedly high core earnings tend to reverse in the following year is suggestive of earnings management through classification shifting.

income (or adjusted income, also referred to as non-GAAP measures, or non-IFRS measures if IFRS is applicable) that has been adjusted to exclude non-recurring items. Disclosures of *pro forma* income must be accompanied by a reconciliation between *pro forma* income and reported income. It is important to be aware, however, that determination of whether an item is non-recurring involves judgment, and some companies' managers may be motivated to consider an item non-recurring if it improves a performance metric relevant to investors. For example, Groupon, an online discount provider, included in its original initial public offering (IPO) filing a *pro forma* (i.e., non-GAAP) measure of operating income that excluded online marketing costs. The SEC determined that the measure was misleading and subsequently required the company to eliminate that measure as reported. Overall, although voluntarily disclosed adjustments to reported income can be informative, an analyst should review the information to ensure that excluded items are truly non-recurring.[14]

9. EARNINGS PERSISTENCE AND RELATED MEASURES OF ACCRUALS

☐ describe the concept of sustainable (persistent) earnings

One property of high earnings quality is earnings persistence—that is, sustainability of earnings excluding items that are obviously non-recurring and persistence of growth in those earnings. The assumption is that, for equity valuation models involving earnings forecasts, more persistent earnings are more useful inputs. Persistence can be expressed as the coefficient on current earnings in a simple model:[15]

$$Earnings_{t+1} = \alpha + \beta_1 Earnings_t + \varepsilon$$

A higher coefficient (β_1) represents more persistent earnings.

Earnings can be viewed as being composed of a cash component and an accruals component. The accrual component arises from accounting rules that reflect revenue in the period earned and expenses in the period incurred—not at the time of cash movement. For example, a sale of goods on account results in accounting income in the period the sale is made. If the cash collection occurs in a subsequent period, the difference between reported net income and cash collected constitutes an accrual. When earnings are decomposed into a cash component and an accruals component, research has shown that the cash component is more persistent (Sloan 1996). In the following model, the coefficient on cash flow (β_1) has been shown to be higher than the coefficient on accruals (β_2), indicating that the cash flow component of earnings is more persistent:

$$Earnings_{t+1} = \alpha + \beta_1 Cash\ flow_t + \beta_2 Accruals_t + \varepsilon$$

Because of the greater persistence of the cash component, indicators of earnings quality evolved to measure the relative size of the accruals component of earnings. Earnings with a larger component of accruals would be less persistent and thus of lower quality.

An important distinction is between accruals that arise from normal transactions in the period (called "non-discretionary") and accruals that result from transactions or accounting choices outside the normal, which are possibly made with the intent

---

[14] A survey of non-GAAP earnings in the S&P 500 is presented in Ciesielski and Henry (2017). In the article, the authors provide key prescriptions in evaluating non-GAAP earnings disclosure.
[15] Descriptions of certain indicators in this section follow Dechow, Ge, and Schrand (2010).

Earnings Persistence and Related Measures of Accruals

to distort reported earnings (called "discretionary accruals"). Outlier discretionary accruals are an indicator of possibly manipulated—and thus low-quality—earnings. One common approach to identifying abnormal accruals is first to model companies' normal accruals and then to determine outliers. A company's normal accruals are modeled as a function of economic factors, such as growth in credit sales and the amount of depreciable assets. Growth in credit sales would be expected to result in accounts receivable growth, and depreciable assets would be associated with the amount of depreciation. To apply this approach, total accruals are regressed on the factors expected to give rise to normal accruals, and the residual of the regression would be considered a proxy for abnormal accruals.

This approach was pioneered by academics and subsequently adopted in practice.[16] The SEC describes its approach to modeling abnormal accruals:

> Our Accounting Quality Model extends the traditional approach [often based on the popular Jones Model or the Modified Jones Model] by allowing discretionary accrual factors to be a part of the estimation. Specifically, we take filings information across all registrants and estimate total accruals as a function of a large set of factors that are proxies for discretionary and non-discretionary components.... Discretionary accruals are calculated from the model estimates and then used to screen firms that appear to be managing earnings most aggressively. (Lewis 2012)

One simplified approach to screening for abnormal accruals is to compare the magnitude of total accruals across companies. To make a relevant comparison, the accruals would be scaled—for example, by average assets or by average net operating income. Under this approach, high amounts of accruals are an indicator of possibly manipulated and thus low-quality earnings.

A more dramatic signal of questionable earnings quality is when a company reports positive net income but negative operating cash flows. This situation is illustrated in Example 7.

EXAMPLE 7

Discrepancy between Net Income and Operating Cash Flows

Allou Health & Beauty Care, Inc.

Allou Health & Beauty Care, Inc. was a manufacturer and distributor of hair and skin care products. Exhibit 8 presents excerpts from the company's financial statements from 2000 to 2002. Following the periods reported in these statements, Allou's warehouses were destroyed by fire, for which the management was found to be responsible. Allou was subsequently shown to have fraudulently inflated the amount of its sales and inventories in those years.

---

[16] See Jones (1991) and Dechow, Sloan, and Sweeney (1995). These seminal academic papers produced the Jones Model and the Modified Jones Model.

> **Exhibit 8: Illustration of Fraudulent Reporting in which Reported Net Income Significantly Exceeded Reported Operating Cash Flow, Annual Data 10-K for Allou Health & Beauty Care, Inc., and Subsidiaries**

Years ended 31 March	2002	2001	2000
Excerpt from Income Statement			
Revenues, net	$564,151,260	$548,146,953	$421,046,773
Costs of revenue	500,890,588	482,590,356	367,963,675
Gross profit	$63,260,672	$65,556,597	$53,083,098
	⋮	⋮	⋮
Income from operations	27,276,779	28,490,063	22,256,558
	⋮	⋮	⋮
Income from continuing operations*	$6,589,658	$2,458,367	$7,043,548
Excerpt from Statement of Cash Flows			
Cash flows from operating activities:			
Net income from continuing operations	$6,589,658	$2,458,367	$7,043,548
Adjustments to reconcile net income to net cash used in operating activities:			
[Portions omitted]	⋮	⋮	⋮
Decrease (increase) in operating assets:			
Accounts receivable	(24,076,150)	(9,725,776)	(25,691,508)
Inventories	(9,074,118)	(12,644,519)	(40,834,355)
Net cash used in operating activities	$(17,397,230)	$(34,195,838)	$(27,137,652)

* The difference between income from operations and income from continuing operations included deductions for interest expense and provision for income taxes in each year and for a $5,642,678 loss on impairment of investments in 2001.

Referring to Exhibit 8, answer the following questions:

1. Based on the income statement data, evaluate Allou's performance over the period shown.

Solution:

Based on the income statement, the following aspects of Allou's performance are notable. Revenues grew in each of the past three years, albeit more slowly in the latest year shown. The company's gross margin declined somewhat over the past three years but has been fairly stable. Similarly, the company's operating margin declined somewhat over the past three years but has been fairly stable at around 5%. The company's income from continuing operations was sharply lower in 2001 as a result of an impairment loss. The company showed positive net income in each year. Overall, the company showed positive net income in each year, and its performance appears to be reasonably stable based on the income statement data.

Note: Gross margin is gross profit divided by revenues. For example, for 2002, $63,260,672 divided by $564,151,260 is 11.2%. The ratios for 2001 and 2000 are 12.0% and 12.6%, respectively.

Operating margin is income from operations divided by revenues. For example, for 2002, $27,276,779 divided by $564,151,260 is 4.8%. The ratios for 2001 and 2000 are 5.2% and 5.3%, respectively.

2. Compare Allou's income from continuing operations and cash flows from operating activities.

Solution:

Allou reported positive income from continuing operations but negative cash from operating activities in each of the three years shown. Persistent negative cash from operating activities is not sustainable for a going concern.

3. Interpret the amounts shown as adjustments to reconcile income from continuing operations to net cash used in operating activities.

Solution:

The excerpt from Allou's Statement of Cash Flows shows that accounts receivable and inventories increased each year. This increase can account for most of the difference between the company's income from continuing operations and net cash used in operating activities. The company seems to be accumulating inventory and not collecting on its receivables.

Note: The statement of cash flows, prepared using the indirect method, adjusts net income to derive cash from operating activities. An increase in current assets is subtracted from the net income number to derive the cash from operating activities.

Similar to Allou, the quarterly data for Enron shown in Exhibit 9 shows positive net income but negative cash from operating activities in quarters that were subsequently shown to have been misreported.

Exhibit 9

Quarterly Data 10-Q: Enron and Subsidiaries

Three months ended 31 March ($ millions)	2001	2000
Net income	425	338
Net cash used in operating activities	(464)	(457)

Annual Data 10-K: Enron and Subsidiaries

Year ended 31 December ($ millions)	2000	1999	1998
Net income	979	893	703

Year ended 31 December ($ millions)	2000	1999	1998
Net cash provided by operating activities	4,779	1,228	1,640

An analyst might also question why net cash provided by operating activities was more than double that of net income in 1998, almost 50% greater than net income in 1999, and almost five times net income in 2000.

Although sizable accruals (roughly, net income minus operating cash flow) can indicate possibly manipulated and thus low-quality earnings, it is not necessarily the case that fraudulently reporting companies will have such a profile. For example, as shown in Exhibit 9, Enron's annual operating cash flows exceeded net income in all three years during which fraudulent financial reporting was subsequently revealed. Some of the fraudulent transactions undertaken by Enron were specifically aimed at generating operating cash flow. It is advisable for investors to explore and understand why the differences exist. The company's ability to generate cash from operations ultimately affects investment and financing within the company.

Similarly, as shown in Exhibit 10, WorldCom showed cash from operating activities in excess of net income in each of the three years shown, although the company was subsequently found to have issued fraudulent reports. WorldCom's most significant fraudulent reporting was improperly capitalizing (instead of expensing) certain costs. Because capital expenditures are shown as investing cash outflows rather than operating cash outflows, the company's fraudulent reporting had the impact of inflating operating cash flows.

Exhibit 10: Example of Fraudulent Reporting in which Reported Net Income Did Not Significantly Exceed Reported Operating Cash Flow, WorldCom Inc. and Subsidiaries ($ millions)

For the years ended 31 December	1999	2000	2001
Net income (loss)	$4,013	$4,153	$1,501
Net cash provided by operating activities	11,005	7,666	7,994

In summary, although accrual measures (i.e., differences between net income and operating cash flows) can serve as indicators of earnings quality, they cannot be used in isolation or applied mechanically. WorldCom shows how comparing cash-basis measures, such as cash provided by operating activities, with net income may provide a false sense of confidence about net income. Net income is calculated using subjective estimates, such as expected life of long-term assets, that can be easily manipulated. In each year shown in Exhibit 10, the cash provided by operations exceeded net income (earnings), suggesting that the earnings were of high quality; an analyst looking at this without considering the investing activities would have felt a false sense of security in the reported net income.

10 MEAN REVERSION IN EARNINGS

☐ explain mean reversion in earnings and how the accruals component of earnings affects the speed of mean reversion

Mean Reversion in Earnings

A key analyst responsibility is to forecast earnings for the purpose of valuation in making investment decisions. The accuracy and credibility of earnings forecasts should increase when a company's earnings stream possesses a high degree of persistence. As already discussed, earnings can be viewed as being composed of a cash flow element plus an accruals element. Sustainable, persistent earnings are driven by the cash flow element of earnings, whereas the accruals element adds information about the company's performance. At the same time, the accruals component can detract from the stability and persistence of earnings because of the estimation process involved in calculating them.

Academic research has shown empirically what we already know intuitively: Nothing lasts forever. Extreme levels of earnings, both high and low, tend to revert to normal levels over time. This phenomenon is known as "mean reversion in earnings" and is a natural attribute of competitive markets. A company experiencing poor earnings performance will shut down or minimize its losing operations and replace inferior managers with ones capable of executing an improved strategy, resulting in improved earnings. At the other extreme, a company experiencing abnormally high profits will attract competition unless the barriers to entry are insurmountable. New competitors may reduce their prices to gain a foothold in an existing company's markets, thereby reducing the existing company's profits over time. Whether a company is experiencing abnormally high or low earnings, the net effect over time is that a return to the mean should be anticipated.

Nissim and Penman (2001) demonstrated that the mean reversion principle exists across a wide variety of accounting-based measures. In a time-series study encompassing companies listed on the New York Stock Exchange and the American Stock Exchange between 1963 and 1999, they tracked such measures as residual income, residual operating income, return on common equity, return on net operating assets, growth in common equity, core sales profit margins, and others. Beginning with data from 1964, they sorted the companies into 10 equal portfolios based on their ranking for a given measure and tracked the median values in each portfolio in each of the next five-year periods. At the end of each fifth year, the portfolios were re-sorted. The process was extended through 1994, yielding means of portfolio medians over seven rankings. The findings were similar across the metrics, showing a clear reversion to the mean over time.

For example, looking at the pattern for return on net operating assets (RNOA),[17] they found that the range of observed RNOAs was between 35% and –5% at the start of the observations but had compressed to a range of 22% to 7% by the end of the study. Their work illustrates the point that extremely strong or weak performance cannot be sustained forever. They also found that the RNOAs of the portfolios that were not outliers in either direction in Year 1—outperformance or underperformance—did not stray over time, staying constant or nearly so over the entire observation period.

The lesson for analysts is clear: One cannot simply extrapolate either very high or very low earnings into the future and expect to construct useful forecasts. In order to be useful, analysts' forecasts need to take into account normalized earnings over the relevant valuation time frame. As discussed, earnings are the sum of cash flows and accruals, and they will be more sustainable and persistent when the cash flow component dominates earnings. If earnings have a significant accruals component, it may hasten the earnings' reversion to the mean, even more so when the accrual elements are outliers relative to the normal amount of accruals in a company's earnings. In constructing their forecasts of future earnings, analysts need to develop a realistic cash flow model and realistic estimates of accruals as well.

---

17 Nissim and Penman define return on net operating assets as Operating income$_t$/Net operating assets$_{t-1}$. Net operating assets are operating assets (those assets used in operations) net of operating liabilities (those generated by operations).

Beating Benchmarks

Announcements of earnings that meet or exceed benchmarks, such as analysts' consensus forecasts, typically result in share price increases. However, meeting or beating benchmarks is not necessarily an indicator of high-quality earnings. In fact, exactly meeting or only narrowly beating benchmarks has been proposed as an indicator of earnings manipulation and thus low-quality earnings. Academic research has documented a statistically large clustering slightly above zero of actual benchmark differences, and this clustering has been interpreted by some as evidence of earnings management.[18] There is, however, disagreement about whether exactly meeting or only narrowly beating is an indicator of earnings manipulation.[19] Nonetheless, a company that consistently reports earnings that exactly meet or only narrowly beat benchmarks can raise questions about its earnings quality.

External Indicators of Poor-Quality Earnings

Two external indicators of poor-quality earnings are enforcement actions by regulatory authorities and restatements of previously issued financial statements. From an analyst's perspective, recognizing poor earnings quality is generally more valuable if it can be done before deficiencies become widely known and confirmed. Therefore, the external indicators of poor earnings quality are relatively less useful to an analyst. Nonetheless, even though it might be better to recognize poor earnings quality early, an analyst should be alert to external indicators and be prepared to re-evaluate decisions.

11 REVENUE RECOGNITION CASE: SUNBEAM CORPORATION

☐ evaluate the earnings quality of a company

The aim of analyzing earnings is to understand the persistence and sustainability of earnings. If earnings do not represent the financial realities faced by a company, then any forecast of earnings based on flawed reporting will also be flawed. Choices and estimates abound in financial reporting; and with those choices and estimates, the temptations for managers to improve their companies' performance by creative accounting are enormous. All too often, companies that appear to be extraordinary performers turn out to be quite ordinary or worse once their choice of accounting methods, including fraudulent choices, is uncovered by a regulator.

To avoid repeating the mistakes of the past, it may be helpful for analysts to learn how managers have used accounting techniques to enhance their companies' reported performance. Some cases provide useful lessons. In a study of 227 enforcement cases brought between 1997 and 2002, the SEC found that the most common accounting misrepresentation occurred in the area of revenue recognition (SEC 2003). Revenue is the largest single figure on the income statement and arguably the most important. Its sheer size and its effect on earnings, along with discretion in revenue recognition policies, have made it the most likely account to be intentionally misstated. For those reasons, investors should always thoroughly and skeptically analyze revenues. Too often, however, the chief concerns of analysts center on the quantitative aspects of

---

18 See Brown and Caylor (2005); Burgstahler and Dichev (1997); and Degeorge, Patel, and Zeckhauser (1999).
19 See Dechow, Richardson, and Tuna (2003).

revenues. They may ponder the growth of revenues and whether growth came from acquisitions or organically, but they rarely focus on the quality of revenues in the same way. A focus on the quality of revenues, including specifically on how it was generated, will serve analysts well. For example, was it generated by offering discounts or through bill-and-hold sales?

Revenue Recognition Case: Sunbeam Corporation

Premature/Fraudulent Revenue Recognition

Sunbeam Corporation was a consumer goods company focused on the production and sale of household appliances and outdoor products. In the mid- to late 1990s, it appeared that its new CEO, "Chainsaw Al" Dunlap, had engineered a turnaround at Sunbeam. He claimed to have done this through cutting costs and increasing revenues. The reality was different. Had more analysts performed basic but rigorous analysis of the financial statements in the earlier phases of Sunbeam's misreporting, they might have been more skeptical of the results produced by Chainsaw Al. Sunbeam engaged in numerous sales transactions that inflated revenues. Among them were the following:

- Sunbeam included one-time disposals of product lines in sales for the first quarter of 1997 without indicating that such non-recurring sales were included in revenues.
- At the end of the first quarter of 1997 (March), Sunbeam booked revenue and income from a sale of barbecue grills to a wholesaler. The wholesaler held the merchandise over the quarter's end without accepting ownership risks. The wholesaler could return the goods if it desired, and Sunbeam would pick up the cost of shipment both ways. All of the grills were returned to Sunbeam in the third quarter of 1997.
- Sunbeam induced customers to order more goods than they would normally through offers of discounts and other incentives. Often, the customers also had return rights on their purchases. This induced ordering had the effect of inflating current results by pulling future sales into the present. This practice is sometimes referred to as "channel stuffing." This policy was not disclosed by Sunbeam, which routinely made use of channel-stuffing practices at the end of 1997 and the beginning of 1998.
- Sunbeam engaged in bill-and-hold revenue practices. In a bill-and-hold transaction, revenue is recognized when the invoice is issued while the goods remain on the premises of the seller. These are unusual transactions, and the accounting requirements for them are very strict: The buyer must request such treatment, have a genuine business purpose for the request, and must accept ownership risks. Other criteria for justifying the use of this revenue recognition practice include the seller's past experience with bill-and-hold transactions, in which buyers took possession of the goods and the transactions were not reversed.

There was no real business purpose to the channel stuffing and bill-and-hold transactions at Sunbeam other than for the seller to accelerate revenue and for the buyers to take advantage of such eagerness without any risks on their part. In the words of the SEC, "these transactions were little more than projected orders disguised as sales" (SEC 2001a). Sunbeam did not make such transactions clear to analysts, and many of its disclosures from the fourth quarter of 1996 to the middle of 1998 were inadequate. Still, its methods of inflating revenue left indicators in the financial statements that should have alerted analysts to the low quality of its earnings and revenue reporting.

If customers are induced into buying goods they do not yet need through favorable payment terms or given substantial leeway in returning such goods to the seller, days' sales outstanding (DSO) may increase and returns may also increase. Furthermore, increases in revenue may exceed past increases and the increases of the industry and/or peers. Problems with and changes in collection, expressed through accounts receivable metrics, can give an analyst clues about the aggressiveness of the seller in making sales targets. Exhibit 11 contains relevant annual data on Sunbeam's sales and receivables from 1995 (before the misreporting occurred) through 1997 (when earnings management reached its peak level in the fourth quarter).

Exhibit 11: Information on Sunbeam's Sales and Receivables, 1995–1997

($ millions)	1995	1996	1997
Total revenue	$1,016.9	$984.2	$1,168.2
Change from prior year	—	-3.2%	18.7%
Gross accounts receivable	$216.2	$213.4	$295.6
Change from prior year	—	-1.3%	38.5%
Receivables/revenue	21.3%	21.7%	25.3%
Change in receivables/revenue	0.7%	0.4%	3.6%
Days' sales outstanding	77.6	79.1	92.4
Accounts receivable turnover	4.7	4.6	4.0

Source: Based on information in original company 10-K filings.

What can an analyst learn from the information in Exhibit 11?

- Although revenues dipped 3.2% in 1996, the year the misreporting began, they increased significantly in 1997 as Sunbeam's various revenue "enhancement" programs were implemented. The important factor to notice—the one that should have given an analyst insight into the quality of the revenues—is the simultaneous, and much greater, increase in the accounts receivable balance. Receivables increasing faster than revenues suggests that a company may be pulling future sales into current periods by offering favorable discounts or generous return policies. As it turned out, Sunbeam offered all of these inducements.

- The percentage relationship of receivables to revenue is another way of looking at the relationship between sales and the time it takes a company to collect cash from its customers. An increasing percentage of receivables to revenues means that a lesser percentage of sales has been collected. The decrease in collection on sales may indicate that customers' abilities to repay have deteriorated. It may also indicate that the seller created period-end sales by shipping goods that were not wanted by customers; the shipment would produce documentation, which serves as evidence of a sale. Receivables and revenue would increase by the same absolute amount, which would increase the percentage of receivables to revenue. Customers would return the goods to the seller in the following accounting period. The same thing would happen in the event of totally fictitious revenues. Revenues from a non-existent customer would simultaneously increase receivables by the same amount. An increase in the relationship between revenue and receivables provides analysts with a clue that collections on sales have declined or that there is a possible issue with revenue recognition.

- The number of days sales outstanding [Accounts receivable/(Revenues/365)] increased each year, indicating that the receivables were not being paid on a timely basis—or even that the revenues may not have been genuine in the first place. DSO figures increasing over time indicate that there are problems, either with collection or revenue recognition. The accounts receivable turnover (365/DSO) tells the same story in a different way: It is the number of times the receivables converted into cash each year, and the figure decreased each year. A trend of slower cash collections, as exhibited by Sunbeam, shows increasingly inefficient cash collections at best and should alert an analyst to the possibility of questionable sales or revenue recognition practices.

- The accounts receivable showed poor quality. In 1997, it increased 38.5% over the previous year, while revenues gained 18.7%. The simple fact that receivables growth greatly outstripped the revenue growth suggests receivables collection problems. Furthermore, analysts who paid attention to the notes might have found even more tiles to fit into the mosaic of accounting manipulations. According to a note in the 10-K titled "Accounts Receivable Securitization Facility," in December 1997 Sunbeam had entered into an arrangement for the sale of accounts receivable. The note said that "At December 28, 1997, the Company had received approximately $59 million from the sale of trade accounts receivable." Those receivables were not included in the year-end accounts receivable balance. As the *pro forma* column in Exhibit 12 shows, the accounts receivable would have shown an increase of 66.1% instead of 38.5%; the percentage of receivables to sales would have ballooned to 30.4%, and the days' sales outstanding would have been an attention-getting 110.8 days. Had this receivables sale not occurred, and the receivables been that large, perhaps analysts would have noticed a problem sooner. Careful attention to the notes might have alerted them to how this transaction improved the appearance of the financial statements and ratios.

Exhibit 12: Information on Sunbeam's Sales and Receivables, 1995–1997, and *Pro Forma* Information, 1997

($ millions)	1995	1996	1997	1997 *Pro Forma*
Total revenue	$1,016.9	$984.2	$1,168.2	*$1,168.2*
Change from prior year	—	−3.2%	18.7%	*18.7%*
Gross accounts receivable	$216.2	$213.4	$295.6	*$354.6*
Change from prior year	—	−1.3%	38.5%	*66.1%*
Receivables/revenue	21.3%	21.7%	25.3%	*30.4%*
Change in receivables/revenue	0.7%	0.4%	3.6%	*8.7%*
Days' sales outstanding	77.7	79.2	92.3	*110.8*

($ millions)	1995	1996	1997	1997 *Pro Forma*
Accounts receivable turnover	4.7	4.6	4.0	3.2

Source: Based on information in original company 10-K filings.

Analysts observing the trend in days' sales outstanding would have been rightly suspicious of Sunbeam's revenue recognition practices, even if they were observing the days' sales outstanding simply in terms of Sunbeam's own history. If they took the analysis slightly further, they would have been even more suspicious. Exhibit 13 compares Sunbeam's DSO and accounts receivable turnover with those of an industry median based on the numbers from a group of other consumer products companies—Harman International, Jarden, Leggett & Platt, Mohawk Industries, Newell Rubbermaid, and Tupperware Brands.

Exhibit 13: Comparison of Sunbeam and Industry Median, 1995–1997

Sunbeam	1995	1996	1997
Days sales outstanding	77.7	79.2	92.3
Accounts receivable turnover	4.7	4.6	4.0
Industry median			
Days sales outstanding	44.6	46.7	50.4
Accounts receivable turnover	8.2	7.8	7.3
Sunbeam's underperformance relative to median			
Days sales outstanding	33.0	32.5	41.9
Accounts receivable turnover	(3.5)	(3.2)	(3.3)

Source: Based on information in company 10-K filings.

There was yet another clue that should have aroused suspicion in the analyst community. In the December 1997 annual report, the revenue recognition note had been expanded from the previous year's note:

> The Company recognizes revenues from product sales principally at the time of shipment to customers. *In limited circumstances, at the customer's request the Company may sell seasonal product on a bill and hold basis provided that the goods are completed, packaged and ready for shipment, such goods are segregated and the risks of ownership and legal title have passed to the customer. **The amount of such bill and hold sales at December 29, 1997 was approximately 3% of consolidated revenues.*** [Italics and emphasis added.]

Not only did Sunbeam hint at the fact that its revenue recognition policies included a method that was of questionable quality, a clue was dropped as to the degree to which it affected operations. That 3% figure may seem small, but the disclosure should have aroused suspicion in the mind of a thorough analyst. As shown in Exhibit 14, working through the numbers with some reasonable assumptions about the gross profit on the sales (28.3%) and the applicable tax rate (35%), an analyst would have seen that the bill-and-hold sales were significant to the bottom line.

Exhibit 14: Effect of Sunbeam's Bill-and-Hold Sales on Net Income ($ millions)

1997 revenue	$1,168.18
Bill-and-hold sales from note	3.0%
Bill-and-hold sales in 1997	$35.05
Gross profit margin	28.3%
Gross profit contribution	$9.92
After-tax earnings contribution	$6.45
Total earnings from continuing operations	$109.42
Earnings attributable to bill-and-hold sales	5.9%

An analyst questioning the genuineness of bill-and-hold sales and performing a simple test of the degree of exposure to their effects might have been disturbed to estimate that nearly 6% of net income depended on such transactions. This knowledge might have dissuaded an analyst from a favorable view of Sunbeam.

REVENUE RECOGNITION CASE: MICROSTRATEGY, INC.   12

☐ evaluate the earnings quality of a company

Multiple-Element Contracts

MicroStrategy, Inc. was a fast-growing software and information services company that went public in 1998. After going public, the company engaged in more complex revenue transactions than it had previously. Its revenue stream increasingly involved less outright sales of software and began tilting more to transactions containing multiple deliverables, including obligations to provide services.

Product revenue is usually recognized immediately, depending on the delivery terms and acceptance by customers, whereas service revenue is recognized as the services are provided. The relevant accounting standards for multiple-deliverable arrangements at the time permitted recognition of revenue on a software delivery only if the software sale could be separated from the service portion of the contract and only if the service revenues were in fact accounted for separately.

Analysts studying MicroStrategy's financial statements should have understood the effects of such accounting conventions on the company's revenues. MicroStrategy's revenue recognition policy in the accounting policies note of its 1998 10-K stated that the standards' requirements were, in fact, its practice:

> Revenue from product licensing arrangements is generally recognized after execution of a licensing agreement and shipment of the product, provided that no significant Company obligations remain and the resulting receivable is deemed collectible by management… Services revenue, which includes training and consulting, is recognized at the time the service is performed. The Company defers and recognizes maintenance revenue ratably over the terms of the contract period, ranging from 12 to 36 months. (p. 49)

MicroStrategy took advantage of the ambiguity present in such arrangements, however, to mischaracterize service revenues and recognize them earlier than they should have as part of the software sale. For example, in the fourth quarter of 1998, MicroStrategy entered into a $4.5 million transaction with a customer for software licenses and a broad array of consulting services. Most of the software licenses acquired by the customer were intended to be used in applications that MicroStrategy would develop in the future, yet the company recognized all of the $4.5 million as software revenue (SEC 2000).

Similarly, in the fourth quarter of 1999, MicroStrategy entered into a multiple-deliverable arrangement with another customer that included the provision for extensive services. Again, the company improperly allocated the elements of the contract, skewing them toward an earlier-recognized software element and improperly recognizing $14.1 million of product revenue in the quarter, which was material.

How could analysts have recognized this pattern of behavior? Without in-depth knowledge of the contracts, it is not possible to approve or disapprove of the revenue allocation with certainty. The company still left a trail that could have aroused the suspicion of analysts, had they been familiar with MicroStrategy's stated revenue recognition policy.

Exhibit 15 shows the mix of revenues for 1996, 1997, and 1998 based on the income statement in MicroStrategy's 1998 10-K:

Exhibit 15: MicroStrategy's Mix of Licenses and Support Revenues, 1996–1998 ($ millions)

	1996	1997	1998
Licenses	$15,873	$36,601	$72,721
Support	6,730	16,956	33,709
Total	$22,603	$53,557	$106,430
Licenses	70.2%	68.3%	68.3%
Support	29.8	31.7	31.7
Total	100.0%	100.0%	100.0%

Between 1996 and 1997, the proportion of support revenues to total revenues increased slightly. It flattened out in 1998, which was the first year known to have mischaracterization between the support revenues and the software revenues. With perfect hindsight, had the $4.5 million of consulting services not been recognized at all, overall revenues would have been $101.930 million and support revenues would have been 33.1% of the total revenues. What could have alerted analysts that something was amiss, if they could not examine actual contracts?

Looking at the quarterly mix of revenues might have aroused analyst suspicions. Exhibit 16 shows the peculiar ebb and flow of revenues attributable to support services revenues.

Exhibit 16: MicroStrategy's Revenue Mix by Quarters, 1Q1998–4Q1999

Quarter	Licenses	Support
1Q98	71.8%	28.2%

Revenue Recognition Case: MicroStrategy, Inc.

Quarter	Licenses	Support
2Q98	68.3	31.7
3Q98	62.7	37.3
4Q98	70.7	29.3
1Q99	64.6	35.4
2Q99	68.1	31.9
3Q99	70.1	29.9
4Q99	73.2	26.8

The support services revenue climbed in the first three quarters of 1998 and dropped sharply in the fourth quarter—the one in which the company characterized the $4.5 million of revenues that should have been deferred as software license revenue. Subsequently, the proportion rose again and then continued a downward trend, most sharply in the fourth quarter of 1999 when the company again mischaracterized $14.1 million of revenue as software license revenue.

There is no logical reason that the proportion of revenues from licensing and support services should vary significantly from quarter to quarter. The changes should arouse suspicions and generate questions to ask management. Management's answers, and the soundness of the logic embedded in them, might have made investors more comfortable or more skeptical.

If an analyst knows that a company has a policy of recognizing revenues for contracts with elements of multiple-deliverable arrangements—something apparent from a study of the accounting policy note—then the analyst should consider the risk that misallocation of revenue can occur. Observing trends and investigating deviations from observed trends become important habits for an analyst to practice in order to isolate exceptions. Although a study of revenue trends may not pinpoint a manipulated revenue transaction, it should be sufficient to raise doubts about the propriety of the accounting for transactions.

Enhancing the recognition of revenue is a way for managers to increase earnings, yet it can leave indicators that can be detected by analysts vigilant enough to look for them. Exhibit 17 provides a summary of how to assess the quality of revenues.

Exhibit 17: Summary: Looking for Quality in Revenues

Start with the basics

The first step should be to fully understand the revenue recognition policies as stated in the most recent annual report. Without context for the way revenue is recognized, an analyst will not understand the risks involved in the proper reporting of revenue. For instance, analysts should determine the following:

- What are the shipping terms?
- What rights of return does a customer have: limited or extensive?
- Do rebates affect revenues, and if so, how are they accounted for? What estimates are involved?
- Are there multiple deliverables to customers for one arrangement? If so, is revenue deferred until some elements are delivered late in the contract? If there are multiple deliverables, do deferred revenues appear on the balance sheet?

Age matters

A study of DSO can reveal much about their quality. Receivables do not improve with age. Analysts should seek reasons for exceptions appearing when they

- Compare the trend in DSOs or receivables turnover over a relevant time frame.
- Compare the DSO of one company with the DSOs of similar competitors over similar time frames.

Is it cash or accrual?

A high percentage of accounts receivable to revenues might mean nothing, but it might also mean that channel-stuffing has taken place, portending high future returns of inventory or decreased demand for product in the future. Analysts should

- Compare the percentage of accounts receivable to revenues over a relevant time frame.
- Compare the company's percentage of accounts receivable to revenues with that of competitors or industry measures over similar time frames.

Compare with the real world when possible

If a company reports non-financial data on a routine basis, try relating revenues to those data to determine whether trends in the revenue make sense. Examples include

- Airlines reporting extensive information about miles flown and capacity, enabling an analyst to relate increases in revenues to an increase in miles flown or capacity.
- Retailers reporting square footage used and number of stores open.
- Companies across all industries reporting employee head counts.

As always, analysts should compare any relevant revenue-per-unit measure with that of relevant competitors or industry measures.

Revenue trends and composition

Trend analysis, over time and in comparison with competitors, can prompt analysts to ask questions of managers, or it can simply evoke discomfort with the overall revenue quality. Some relationships to examine include

- The relationships between the kinds of revenue recognized. For example, how much is attributable to product sales or licenses, and how much is attributable to services? Have the relationships changed over time, and if so, why?
- The relationship between overall revenue and accounts receivable. Do changes in overall revenues make sense when compared with changes in accounts receivable?

Relationships

Does the company transact business with entities owned by senior officers or shareholders? This is a particularly sensitive area if the manager/shareholder-owned entities are private and there are revenues recognized from the private entity by a publicly owned company; it could be a dumping ground for obsolete or damaged inventory while inflating revenues.

Overstating revenues is not the only way to enhance earnings; according to the SEC study of enforcement cases brought between 1997 and 2002, the next most common financial misreporting was improper expense recognition (SEC 2003). Improper expense recognition typically involves understating expenses and has the same overstating effects on earnings as improper revenue recognition. Understating expenses also leaves indicators in the financial statements for the vigilant analyst to find and assess.

COST CAPITALIZATION CASE: WORLDCOM CORP.

☐ evaluate the earnings quality of a company

Property/Capital Expenditures Analysis

WorldCom was a major global communications company, providing phone and internet services to both the business and consumer markets. It became a major player in the 1990s, largely through acquisitions. To keep delivering the earnings expected by analysts, the company engaged in the improper capitalization of operating expenses known as "line costs." These costs were fees paid by WorldCom to third-party telecommunications network providers for the right to use their networks, and the proper accounting treatment for them is to classify them as an operating expense. This improper treatment began in 1999 and continued through the first quarter of 2002. The company declared bankruptcy in July 2002; restatements of financial reports ensued.

The company was audited by Arthur Andersen, who had access to the company's records. According to the findings of the special committee that headed the investigation of the failure (Beresford, Katzenbach, and Rogers 2003), Arthur Andersen failed to identify the misclassification of line costs, among other things, because

> Andersen concluded—mistakenly in this case—that, year after year, the risk of fraud was minimal and thus it never devised sufficient auditing procedures to address this risk. Although it conducted a controls-based audit—relying on WorldCom's internal controls—it failed to recognize the nature and extent of senior management's top-side adjustments through reserve reversals with little or no support, highly questionable revenue items, and entries capitalizing line costs. Andersen did not conduct tests to corroborate the information it received in many areas. It assumed incorrectly that the absence of variances in the financial statements and schedules—in a highly volatile business environment—indicated there was no cause for heightened scrutiny. Andersen conducted only very limited auditing procedures in many areas where we found accounting irregularities. Even so, Andersen still had several chances to uncover problems we identify in this Report. (p. 230–231)

If auditors failed to detect fraud, could analysts really be expected to do better? Analysts may not have been able to pinpoint what was going on at WorldCom, all the way down to the under-reported line costs, but if they had focused on the company's balance sheet, they certainly could have been suspicious that all was not right. If they were looking for out-of-line relationships between accounts—something that the auditors would be expected to do—they might have uncovered questionable relationships that, if unsatisfactorily explained, should have led them to shun securities issued by WorldCom.

For an operating expense to be under-reported, an offsetting increase in the balance of another account must exist. A simple scan of an annual time-series common-size balance sheet, such as is shown in Exhibit 18, might identify the possibility that capitalization is being used to avoid expense recognition. An analyst might not have known that line costs were being under-reported, but simply looking at the time series in Exhibit 18 would have shown that something unusual was going on in gross property, plant, and equipment. The fraud began in 1999, and gross property, plant, and equipment had been 30% and 31% of total assets, respectively, in the two prior years. In 1999, property, plant, and equipment became a much more significant 37% of total assets and increased to 45% in 2000 and 47% in 2001. The company had not changed strategy or anything else to justify such an increase.

Exhibit 18: Common Size Asset Portion of Balance Sheet for WorldCom, 1997–2001

	1997	1998	1999	2000	2001
Cash and equivalents	0%	2%	1%	1%	1%
Net receivables	5	6	6	7	5
Inventories	0	0	0	0	0
Other current assets	2	4	4	2	2
Total current assets	7%	12%	11%	10%	8%
Gross property, plant, and equipment	*30%*	*31%*	*37%*	*45%*	*47%*
Accumulated depreciation	3%	2%	5%	7%	9%
Net property, plant, and equipment	27%	29%	32%	38%	38%
Equity investments	NA	NA	NA	NA	1
Other investments	0	0	0	2	1
Intangibles	61	54	52	47	49
Other assets	5	5	5	3	3
Total Assets	100%	100%	100%	100%	100%

Note: NA is not available.
Source: Based on information from Standard & Poor's Research Insight database.

A curious analyst in 1999 might not have *specifically* determined that line costs were being understated, but the buildup of costs in property, plant, and equipment should have at least made the analyst suspicious that expenses were under-reported somewhere in the income statement.

Capitalizing costs is not the only possible way of understating expenses. Exhibit 19 provides a summary of how to assess the quality of expense recognition, including some things to consider.

Exhibit 19: Summary: Looking for Quality in Expense Recognition

Start with the basics

The first step should be to fully understand the cost capitalization policies as stated in the most recent annual report. Without context for the costs stored on the balance sheet, analysts will not be able to comprehend practice exceptions they may encounter. Examples of policies that should be understood include the following:

- What costs are capitalized in inventory? How is obsolescence accounted for? Are there reserves established for obsolescence that might be artificially raised or lowered?

- What are the depreciation policies, including depreciable lives? How do they compare with competitors' policies? Have they changed from prior years?

Trend analysis

Trend analysis, over time and in comparison with competitors, can lead to questions the analyst can ask managers, or it can simply evoke discomfort with overall earnings quality because of issues with expenses. Some relationships to examine include the following:

- Each quarter, non-current asset accounts should be examined for quarter-to-quarter and year-to-year changes to see whether there are any unusual increases in costs. If present, they might indicate that improper capitalization of costs has occurred.

- Profit margins—gross and operating—are often observed by analysts in the examination of quarterly earnings. They are not often related to changes in the balance sheet, but they should be. If unusual build-ups of non-current assets have occurred and the profit margins are improving or staying constant, it could mean that improper cost capitalization is taking place. Recall WorldCom and its improper capitalization of "line costs": Profitability was maintained by capitalizing costs that should have been expensed. Also, the overall industry environment should be considered: Are margins stable while balance sheet accounts are growing and the industry is slumping?

- Turnover ratio for total assets; property, plant, and equipment; and other assets should be computed (with revenues divided by the asset classification). Does a trend in the ratios indicate a slowing in turnover? Decreasing revenues might mean that the assets are used to make a product with declining demand and portend future asset write-downs. Steady or rising revenues and decreasing turnover might indicate improper cost capitalization.

- Compute the depreciation (or amortization) expense compared to the relevant asset base. Is it decreasing or increasing over time without a good reason? How does it compare with that of competitors?

- Compare the relationship of capital expenditures with gross property, plant, and equipment over time. Is the proportion of capital expenditures relative to total property, plant, and equipment increasing significantly over time? If so, it may indicate that the company is capitalizing costs more aggressively to prevent their recognition as current expenses.

Relationships

Does the company transact business with entities owned by senior officers or shareholders? This is a particularly sensitive area if the manager/shareholder-owned entities are private. Dealings between a public company and the manager-owned entity might take place at prices that are unfavorable for the public company in order to transfer wealth from the public company to the manager-owned entity. Such inappropriate transfers of wealth can also occur through excessive compensation, direct loans, or guarantees. These practices are often referred to as "tunneling" (Johnson, LaPorta, Shleifer, and Lopez-de-Silanes 2000).

In some cases, sham dealings between the manager-owned entity and the public company might be falsely reported to improve reported profits of the public company and thus enrich the managers whose compensation is performance based. In a different type of transaction, the manager-owned entity could transfer resources to the public company to ensure its economic viability and thus preserve the option to misappropriate or to participate in profits in the future. These practices are often referred to as "propping" (Friedman, Johnson, and Mitton 2003).

Assessing earnings quality should be an established practice for all analysts. Earnings quality should not automatically be accepted as "high quality" until accounting problems emerge and it is too late. Analysts should consider the quality of earnings before assigning value to the growth in earnings. In many cases, high reported earnings growth, which turned out to be fraudulent, preceded bankruptcy.

14 BANKRUPTCY PREDICTION MODELS

- [ ] evaluate the earnings quality of a company
- [ ] evaluate the cash flow quality of a company
- [ ] describe indicators of balance sheet quality
- [ ] evaluate the balance sheet quality of a company

Bankruptcy prediction models address more than just the quality of a company's earnings and include aspects of cash flow and the balance sheet as well.[20] Various approaches have been used to quantify the likelihood that a company will default on its debt and/or declare bankruptcy.

Altman Model

A well-known and early model to assess the probability of bankruptcy is the Altman model (Altman 1968). The model is built on research that used ratio analysis to identify likely failures. An important contribution of the Altman model is that it provided a way to incorporate numerous financial ratios into a single model to predict bankruptcy. The model overcame a limitation of viewing ratios independently (e.g., viewing a company with poor profitability and/or solvency position as potentially bankrupt without considering the company's strong liquidity position).

---

[20] Recall that the term "earnings quality" is used broadly to encompass the quality of earnings, cash flow, and/or balance sheet items.

Using discriminant analysis, Altman developed a model to discriminate between two groups: bankrupt and non-bankrupt companies. Altman's Z-score is calculated as follows:

Z-score = 1.2 (Net working capital/Total assets) + 1.4 (Retained earnings/Total assets) + 3.3 (EBIT/Total assets) + 0.6 (Market value of equity/Book value of liabilities) + 1.0 (Sales/Total assets)

The ratios in the model reflect liquidity, profitability, leverage, and activity. The first ratio—net working capital/total assets—is a measure of short-term liquidity risk. The second ratio—retained earnings/total assets—reflects accumulated profitability and relative age because retained earnings accumulate over time. The third ratio—EBIT (earnings before interest and taxes)/total assets, which is a variant of return on assets (ROA)—measures profitability. The fourth ratio—market value of equity/book value of liabilities—is a form of leverage ratio; it is expressed as equity/debt, so a higher number indicates greater solvency. The fifth ratio—sales/total assets—indicates the company's ability to generate sales and is an activity ratio.

Note that Altman's discriminant function shown in his original article (1968) was

$$Z\text{-score} = 0.012 X_1 + 0.014 X_2 + 0.033 X_3 + 0.006 X_4 + 0.999 X_5$$

with each of the X variables corresponding to the ratios just described. Altman (2000) explains that "due to the original computer format arrangement, variables X_1 through X_4 must be calculated as absolute percentage values. For instance, the company whose net working capital to total assets (X_1) is 10% should be included as 10.0% and not 0.10. Only variable X_5 (sales to total assets) should be expressed in a different manner: that is, a S/TA [sales/total assets] ratio of 200 percent should be included as 2.0" (p. 14). For this reason, the Z-score model is often expressed as shown in the first equation of this section.

The interpretation of the score is that a higher Z-score is better. In Altman's application of the model to a sample of manufacturing companies that had experienced losses, scores of less than 1.81 indicated a high probability of bankruptcy, scores greater than 3.00 indicated a low probability of bankruptcy, and scores between 1.81 and 3.00 were not clear indicators.

Developments in Bankruptcy Prediction Models

Subsequent research addressed various shortcomings in the Altman prediction model. One shortcoming is the single-period, static nature of the Altman model; it uses only one set of financial measures, taken at a single point in time. Shumway (2001) addressed this shortcoming by using a hazard model, which incorporates all available years of data to calculate each company's bankruptcy risk at each point in time.

Another shortcoming of the Altman model (and other accounting-based bankruptcy prediction models) is that financial statements measure past performance and incorporate the going-concern assumption. The reported values on a company's balance sheet assume that the company is a going concern rather than one that might be failing. An alternative is to use market-based bankruptcy prediction models. For example, market-based prediction models building on Merton's concept of equity as a call option on the company's assets infer the default probability from the company's equity value, amount of debt, equity returns, and equity volatility (Kealhofer 2003). Credit default swap data and corporate bond data can also be used to derive default probabilities. Other research indicates that the most effective bankruptcy prediction models include both accounting-based data and market-based data as predictor variables. For example, Bharath and Shumway (2008) model default probability based on

15. CASH FLOW QUALITY

- describe indicators of cash flow quality
- evaluate the cash flow quality of a company

Cash flow statements are free of some of the discretion embedded in the financial statements based on accrual accounting. As a result, analysts may place a great deal of importance and reliance on the cash flow statement. However, there are opportunities for management to affect the cash flow statement.

Indicators of Cash Flow Quality

Operating cash flow (OCF) is the cash flow component that is generally most important for assessing a company's performance and valuing a company or its securities. Therefore, discussions of cash flow quality typically focus on OCF.

Similar to the term "earnings quality," when reported cash flows are described as being of high quality, it means that the company's underlying economic performance was good (i.e., value enhancing) and it also implies that the company had high reporting quality (i.e., that the information calculated and disclosed by the company was a reasonable reflection of economic reality). Cash flow can be described as "low quality" either because the reported information correctly represents bad economic performance (poor results quality) or because the reported information misrepresents economic reality (poor reporting quality).

From an economic perspective, the corporate life cycle and industry profile affect cash flow and must be considered when analyzing the statement of cash flows. For example, a start-up company might be expected to have negative operating and investing cash flows, which would be funded from borrowing or from equity issuance (i.e., financing cash flows). In contrast, an established company would typically have positive operating cash flow from which it would fund necessary investments and returns to providers of capital (i.e., dividends, share repurchases, or debt repayments—all of which are financing cash flows).

In general, for established companies, high-quality cash flow would typically have most or all of the following characteristics:

- Positive OCF
- OCF derived from sustainable sources
- OCF adequate to cover capital expenditures, dividends, and debt repayments
- OCF with relatively low volatility (relative to industry participants)

As always, high quality requires not only high results quality, as in the previous list, but also high reporting quality. The reported cash flows should be relevant and faithfully represent the economic reality of the company's activities. For example, classifying a financing inflow as an operating inflow would misrepresent the economic reality.

Cash Flow Quality

From the perspective of cash flow reporting quality, OCF is generally viewed as being less easily manipulated than operating or net income. Large differences between earnings and OCF or increases in such differences can be an indication of earnings manipulation. The statement of cash flows can be used to highlight areas of potential earnings manipulation.

Even though OCF is viewed as being less subject to manipulation than earnings, the importance of OCF may create incentives for managers to manipulate the amounts reported. Therefore, quality issues with cash flow reporting can exist. One issue that arises with regard to cash flow reporting quality is timing. For example, by selling receivables to a third party and/or by delaying paying its payables, a company can boost OCF. An increase in such activities would be reflected as a decrease in the company's days' sales outstanding and an increase in the company's days of payables. Thus, an analyst can potentially detect management choices to decrease current assets or increase current liabilities, choices that will increase OCF, by looking at asset utilization (activity) ratios, changes in balance sheet accounts, and disclosures in notes to the financial statements. Another issue that arises with regard to cash flow reporting quality is related to classification of cash flows: Management may try to shift positive cash flow items from investing or financing activities to operating activities to inflate operating cash flows.

Evaluating Cash Flow Quality

Because OCF is viewed as being less subject to manipulation than earnings, the statement of cash flows can be used to identify areas of potential earnings manipulation. The financial fraud at Satyam Computer Services, an Indian information technology company, was described earlier in this reading. In that case, the use of a computer model based on accruals may have failed to detect the fraud. A *New York Times* article (Kahn 2009) provides anecdotal evidence:

> In September, [an analyst] used a computer model to examine India's 500 largest public companies for signs of accounting manipulation. He found that more than 20 percent of them were potentially engaged in aggressive accounting, but Satyam was not on the list. This is because the automated screens that analysts … use to pick up signs of fraud begin by searching for large discrepancies between reported earnings and cash flow. In Satyam's case, the cash seemed to keep pace with profits.

In other words, a computer model that screened for companies with operating cash flow persistently lower than earnings would not have identified Satyam as a potential problem because its reported operating cash flow was relatively close to reported profits.

It may be helpful to examine pertinent indicators using a more qualitative approach. Exhibit 20 presents an excerpt from the statement of cash flows for Satyam for the quarter ended 30 June 2008.

Exhibit 20: Excerpt from Satyam's IFRS Consolidated Interim Cash Flow Statement (All amounts $ millions except per share data and as otherwise stated.)

	Quarter ended 30 June 2008 (unaudited)	Quarter ended 30 June 2007 (unaudited)	Year ended 31 March 2008 (audited)
Profit before income tax	143.1	107.1	474.3

	Quarter ended 30 June 2008 (unaudited)	Quarter ended 30 June 2007 (unaudited)	Year ended 31 March 2008 (audited)
Adjustments for			
Share-based payment expense	4.3	5.9	23.0
Financial costs	1.3	0.8	7.0
Finance income	(16.2)	(16.4)	(67.4)
Depreciation and amortisation	11.5	9.3	40.3
(Gain)/loss on sale of premises and equipment	0.1	0.1	0.6
Changes in value of preference shares designated at fair value through profit or loss	0.0	0.0	(1.6)
Gain/(loss) on foreign exchange forward and option contracts	53.0	(21.1)	(7.4)
Share of (profits)/losses of joint ventures, net of taxes	(0.1)	0.0	(0.1)
	197.0	85.7	468.7
Movements in working capital			
— Trade and other receivables	(81.4)	(64.9)	(184.3)
— Unbilled revenue	(23.5)	(6.0)	(39.9)
— Trade and other payables	34.1	2.2	48.8
— Unearned revenue	5.8	2.4	11.4
— Other liabilities	(6.3)	30.3	61.2
— Retirement benefit obligations	3.7	1.3	17.8
Cash generated from operations	129.4	51.0	383.7
Income taxes paid	−3.8	−9.8	−49.4
Net cash provided by operating activities	125.6	41.2	334.3

Source: Based on information from Satyam's Form 6-K, filed 25 July 2008.

One item of note on this statement of cash flows is the $53 million non-cash item labeled "Gain/(loss) on foreign exchange forward and options contracts" (i.e., derivative instruments) in the quarter ended 30 June 2008. The item appears to be shown as a gain based on the labeling; however, it would not be correct to add back a gain in this calculation of operating cash flow because it is already included in profit before tax. When the company was asked about this item in the quarterly conference call with analysts, no answer was readily available. Instead, the company's manager said that he would "get back to" the questioner. The fact that the company's senior executives could not explain the reason for an item that represented almost 40% of the total pre-tax profit for the quarter ($53/$143.1 = 37%) is clearly a signal of potential problems. Refer to Exhibit 21 for an excerpt from the conference call.

Cash Flow Quality

> **Exhibit 21: Excerpt from Conference Call regarding Quarterly Results of Satyam, 18 July 2008**
>
> | | |
> |---|---|
> | George Price, analyst at Stifel Nicolaus: | One question which is on the cash flow statement. You had a—you had $53 million in unrealized gain on derivative financial instruments in the quarter and it's a line item that just, on quick check, I don't think we've seen in past quarters. Can you comment on exactly what that is? … On the comparison periods, there were more modest losses. What drove that large benefit? How should we think about timing of cash flow maybe over the next couple quarters? Any one-time issues like that? |
> | Srinivas Vadlamani: | I—can you repeat that, please? |
> | George Price: | Srinivas, there's was a $53 million unrealized gain in the cash flow statement, and I'm just wondering if you could explain that in a little bit more detail…. The magnitude is a little surprising. |
> | Srinivas Vadlamani: | No, let me—let me check on that. I'll get back to you. |

Another item of note on the statement of cash flows is the steady growth in receivables. Analysts examine a company's ratios, such as days' sales outstanding. Exhibit 22 presents selected annual data for Satyam. The large jump in days' sales outstanding from 2006 to 2007 could cause concern. Furthermore, the management commentary in the company's Form 20-F indicated that "Net accounts receivable… increased… primarily as a result of an increase in our revenues and increase in collection period." An increase in the collection period of receivables raises questions about the creditworthiness of the company's customers, about the efficiency of the company's collection efforts, and about the quality of the revenue recognized.

> **Exhibit 22: Selected Annual Data on Accounts Receivable for Satyam, 2005–2008**
>
> | ($ millions) | 2008 | 2007 | 2006 | 2005 |
> |---|---|---|---|---|
> | Total revenue | $2,138.1 | $1,461.4 | $1,096.3 | $793.6 |
> | *% Change from previous year* | 46.3% | 33.3% | 38.1% | |
> | | | | | |
> | Gross accounts receivable | $539.1 | $386.9 | $238.1 | $178.3 |
> | *% Change from previous year* | 39.3% | 62.5% | 33.5% | |
> | | | | | |
> | Allowance for doubtful debts | $31.0 | $22.8 | $19.1 | $17.5 |
> | *% Change from previous year* | 36.0% | 19.4% | 9.1% | |
> | | | | | |
> | **Gross receivables/revenue** | 25.21% | 26.47% | 21.72% | 22.47% |
> | *Change in receivables/revenue* | −4.8% | 21.9% | −3.3% | |
> | | | | | |
> | Days' sales outstanding | 92.0 | 96.6 | 79.3 | 82.0 |
> | Accounts receivable turnover | 4.0 | 3.8 | 4.6 | 4.5 |
>
> *Source:* Based on data from Satyam's 20-F filings.

A signal of problems related to cash, which would not have appeared on the statement of cash flows, was the purported use of the company's cash. Satyam reported increasing amounts invested in current accounts. On a conference call excerpted in Exhibit 23, an analyst asked for a specific reason why such large amounts would be held in non-interest-bearing accounts. Instead of providing a reason, the company officer instead stated that the amounts would be transferred to higher-earning accounts soon.

Exhibit 23: Excerpt from Conference Call regarding Quarterly Results for Satyam, 17 October 2008

Kawaljeet Saluja, analyst at Kotak Institutional Equities:	Hi, my questions are for Srinivas. Srinivas, any specific reason why you have $500m parked in current accounts which are not [gaining] any interest?
Srinivas Vadlamani:	No, that is basically—as on the quarter ending, but there is a statement to that [inaudible] to the deposit accounts. We have [inaudible] deposits now.
Kawaljeet Saluja:	But, Srinivas, if I look at the deposit accounts for the last four quarters, that number has remained absolutely flat. And most of the incremental cash that is parked in current accounts and this is not something which is this quarter changed. Would you highlight some of the reasons for it?
Srinivas Vadlamani:	No, basically, what will happen is these amounts will be basically in different countries. And then we will be bringing them to India based on the need. So we will be—basically, some of them are in overnight deposits and all that. So, now we have placing them into normal current deposits. So, next quarter onwards, we will see that as part of the deposits.

In Satyam CEO's January 2009 letter of resignation, he confessed that "the Balance Sheet carries as of September 30, 2008 [i]nflated (non-existent) cash and bank balances of Rs. 5,040 crore[21] (as against Rs. 5,361 crore reflected in the books)...."[22] In other words, of the amount shown as cash on the company's balance sheet, more than 90% was non-existent. It is suggested that some of the cash balances had existed but had been "siphoned off to a web of companies controlled by Mr. Raju and his family." (Kahn 2009)

Overall, the Satyam example illustrates how the statement of cash flows can suggest potential areas of misreporting. In Satyam's case, two items that raised questions were a large non-cash gain on derivatives and an increase in days' sales outstanding. Potential areas of misreporting can then be investigated by reference to the company's other financial reports. The following example illustrates how the statement of cash flows can highlight earnings manipulation and also illustrates how the cash flow information corresponds to information gleaned from analysis of the company's earnings.

Example 8 covers the application of cash flow evaluation to determine quality of earnings.

---

21 Crore is used in India to denote 10,000,000.
22 From Mr. B. Ramalinga Raju's resignation letter attached to Form 6-K that was filed with the SEC on 7 January 2009.

Cash Flow Quality

EXAMPLE 8

Sunbeam Statement of Cash Flows

As noted in the previous section, Sunbeam engaged in various improper accounting practices. Refer to the excerpt from Sunbeam's statement of cash flows in Exhibit 24 to answer the following questions:

Exhibit 24: Excerpt from Sunbeam's Consolidated Statement of Cash Flows, 1995–1997 ($ thousands)

Fiscal Years Ended	28 Dec. 1997	29 Dec. 1996	31 Dec. 1995
Operating Activities:			
Net earnings (loss)	109,415	(228,262)	50,511
Adjustments to reconcile net earnings (loss) to net cash provided by (used in) operating activities:			
Depreciation and amortization	38,577	47,429	44,174
Restructuring, impairment, and other costs	—	154,869	—
Other non-cash special charges	—	128,800	—
Loss on sale of discontinued operations, net of taxes	13,713	32,430	—
Deferred income taxes	57,783	(77,828)	25,146
Increase (decrease) in cash from changes in working capital:			
Receivables, net	(84,576)	(13,829)	(4,499)
Inventories	(100,810)	(11,651)	(4,874)
Account payable	(1,585)	14,735	9,245
Restructuring accrual	(43,378)	—	—
Prepaid expenses and other current assets and liabilities	(9,004)	2,737	(8,821)
Income taxes payable	52,844	(21,942)	(18,452)
Payment of other long-term and non-operating liabilities	(14,682)	(27,089)	(21,719)
Other, net	(26,546)	13,764	10,805
Net cash provided by (used in) operating activities	(8,249)	14,163	81,516

Note: The reason that an increase in sales is shown as a negative number on the statement of cash flows prepared using the indirect method is to reverse any sales reported in income for which cash has not yet been received.

1. One of the ways that Sunbeam misreported its financial statements was improperly inflating and subsequently reversing restructuring charges. How do these items appear on the statement of cash flows?

Solution:

Sunbeam's statement of cash flows is prepared using the indirect method (i.e., the operating section shows a reconciliation between reported net income and operating cash flow). This reconciliation highlights that the amount of non-cash charges recorded in 1996 for restructuring, impairment, and other costs totaled about $284 million ($154.869 million + $128.8 million). In the following year, the reversal of the restructuring accrual was $43 million. By inflating and subsequently reversing restructuring charges, the company's income would misleadingly portray significant improvements in performance following the arrival of its new CEO in mid-1996.

2. Another aspect of Sunbeam's misreporting was improper revenue recognition. What items on the statement of cash flow would primarily be affected by that practice?

Solution:

The items on the statement of cash flows that would primarily be affected by improper revenue recognition include net income, receivables, and inventories. Net income and receivables would be overstated. The statement of cash flows, in which an increase in receivables is shown as a negative number, highlights the continued growth of receivables. In addition, Sunbeam's practice of recording sales that lacked economic substance—because the purchaser held the goods over the end of an accounting period but subsequently returned all the goods—is highlighted in the substantial increase in inventory in 1997.

An issue that arises with regard to cash flow reporting quality is classification shifting: shifting positive cash flow items from investing or financing to inflate operating cash flows. A shift in classification does not change the total amount of cash flow, but it can affect investors' evaluation of a company's cash flows and investors' expectations for future cash flows.

Flexibility in classification exists within accounting standards. For example, IFRS permits companies to classify interest paid either as operating or as financing. IFRS also permits companies to classify interest and dividends received as operating or as investing. In contrast, US GAAP requires that interest paid, interest received, and dividends received all be classified as operating cash flows. Thus, an analyst comparing an IFRS-reporting company to a US GAAP-reporting company would want to ensure comparable classification of interest and dividends and would adjust the reported amounts, if necessary. In addition, an analyst examining an IFRS-reporting company should be alert to any year-to-year changes in classification of interest and dividends. For example, consider an IFRS-reporting company that changed its classification of interest paid from operating to financing. All else equal, the company's operating cash flow would appear higher than the prior period even if no other activities occurred in the period.

As another example of the flexibility permitted by accounting standards, cash flows from non-trading securities are classified as investing cash flows, whereas cash flows from trading securities are typically classified as operating cash flows. However, each company decides what constitutes trading and non-trading activities, depending on how it manages its securities holdings. This discretion creates an opportunity for managers to shift cash flows from one classification to another.

Example 9 illustrates a shift of cash flows from investing to operating.

EXAMPLE 9

Classification of Cash Flows

Nautica Enterprises[23]

An excerpt from the statement of cash flows from the fiscal 2000 annual report of Nautica Enterprises, an apparel manufacturer, is shown as Exhibit 25. An excerpt from the statement of cash flows from the company's fiscal 2001 annual report is shown in Exhibit 26. Use these two excerpts to answer the questions below.

---

23 Example adapted from Mulford and Comiskey (2005).

Cash Flow Quality

Exhibit 25: Excerpt from Nautica Enterprises' Consolidated Statement of Cash Flow from Annual Report, filed 27 May 2000 (amounts in thousands)

	Year ended 4 March 2000
Cash flows from operating activities	
Net earnings	$46,163
Adjustments to reconcile net earnings to net cash provided by operating activities, net of assets and liabilities acquired	
Minority interest in net loss of consolidated subsidiary	—
Deferred income taxes	(1,035)
Depreciation and amortization	17,072
Provision for bad debts	1,424
Changes in operating assets and liabilities	
Accounts receivable	(6,562)
Inventories	(3,667)
Prepaid expenses and other current assets	(20)
Other assets	(2,686)
Accounts payable: trade	(548)
Accrued expenses and other current liabilities	9,086
Income taxes payable	3,458
Net cash provided by operating activities	62,685
Cash flows from investing activities	
Purchase of property, plant, and equipment	(33,289)
Acquisitions, net of cash acquired	—
Sale (purchase) of short-term investments	21,116
Payments to register trademark	(277)
Net cash used in investing activities	(12,450)

Exhibit 26: Excerpt from Nautica Enterprises' Consolidated Statements of Cash Flows from Annual Report, filed 29 May 2001 (amounts in thousands)

	Year Ended 3 March 2001	Year Ended 4 March 2000
Cash flows from operating activities		
Net earnings	46,103	46,163
Adjustments to reconcile net earnings to net cash provided by operating activities, net of assets and liabilities acquired		
Minority interest in net loss of consolidated subsidiary	—	—
Deferred income taxes	(2,478)	(1,035)

	Year Ended 3 March 2001	Year Ended 4 March 2000
Depreciation and amortization	22,968	17,072
Provision for bad debts	1,451	1,424
Changes in operating assets and liabilities		
Short-term investments	28,445	21,116
Accounts receivable	(17,935)	(768)
Inventories	(24,142)	(3,667)
Prepaid expenses and other current assets	(2,024)	(20)
Other assets	(36)	(2,686)
Accounts payable: trade	14,833	(548)
Accrued expenses and other current liabilities	7,054	3,292
Income taxes payable	3,779	3,458
Net cash provided by operating activities	78,018	83,801
Cash flows from investing activities		
Purchase of property, plant, and equipment	(41,712)	(33,289)
Acquisitions, net of cash acquired	—	—
Purchase of short-term investments	—	—
Payments to register trademark	(199)	(277)
Net cash used in investing activities	(41,911)	(33,566)

1. What amount does Nautica report as operating cash flow for the year ended 4 March 2000 in Exhibit 25? What amount does Nautica report as operating cash flow for the same year in Exhibit 26?

Solution:

In Exhibit 25, Nautica reports operating cash flow for the year ended 4 March 2000 of $62,685 thousand. In Exhibit 26, Nautica reports operating cash flow for the same year of $83,801 thousand.

2. Exhibit 25 shows that the company had investing cash flows of $21,116 thousand from the sale of short-term investments for the year ended 4 March 2000. Where does this amount appear in Exhibit 26?

Solution:

The $21,116 thousand (i.e., the difference between the amounts of operating cash flow reported in Exhibit 25 and Exhibit 26) that appears in Exhibit 25 as investing cash flows from the sale of short-term investments for the year ended 4 March 2000 has been reclassified. In Exhibit 26, this amount appears under changes in operating assets and liabilities (i.e., as a component of operating cash flow).

Balance Sheet Quality 343

> 3. As actually reported (Exhibit 26), how did the company's operating cash flow for fiscal year 2001 compare with that for 2000? If Nautica had not changed the classification of its short-term investing activities, how would the company's operating cash flows for fiscal year 2001 have compared with that for 2000?
>
> **Solution:**
>
> As reported in Exhibit 26, the company's cash flows declined by 7% from fiscal year 2000 to fiscal year 2001 (= 78,018/83,801 − 1 = −7%). If Nautica had not changed the classification of its short-term investing activities, the company's operating cash flows for fiscal year 2001 would have been $49,573 thousand (=78,018 − 28,445), and would have shown a decline of 21% from fiscal year 2000 to fiscal year 2001 (= 49,573/62,685 − 1 = −21%).

An analyst could have identified Nautica's classification shift by comparing the statement of cash flows for 2000 in the fiscal year 2000 annual report with the statement in the fiscal year 2001 annual report. In general, comparisons of period-to-period reports issued by a company can be useful in assessing financial reporting quality. If a company restates prior years' financial statements (because of an error), recasts prior years' financial statements (because of a change in accounting policy), omits some information that was previously voluntarily disclosed, or adds some item, such as a new risk disclosure that was not previously disclosed, an analyst should aim to understand the reasons for the changes.

BALANCE SHEET QUALITY

16

☐ describe indicators of balance sheet quality
☐ evaluate the balance sheet quality of a company

With regard to the balance sheet, high financial *reporting* quality is indicated by completeness, unbiased measurement, and clear presentation. High financial *results* quality (i.e., a strong balance sheet) is indicated by an optimal amount of leverage, adequate liquidity, and economically successful asset allocation. Balance sheet strength is assessed using ratio analysis, including common-size financial statements, which is covered by the financial statement analysis readings. There are no absolute values for ratio analysis that indicate adequate financial strength; such analysis must be undertaken in the context of a firm's earnings and cash flow outlook, coupled with an understanding of the environment in which the firm operates. In this section, the focus is on high financial reporting quality.

An important aspect of financial reporting quality for the balance sheet is *completeness*. Significant amounts of off-balance-sheet obligations could be a concern for an analyst because exclusion of these obligations could understate the company's leverage. One common source of off-balance-sheet obligation is purchase contracts, which may be structured as take-or-pay contracts. Analysts typically adjust reported financial statement information by constructively capitalizing, where material, purchase obligations. Constructive capitalization means that the analyst estimates the amount of the obligation as the present value of future purchase obligation payments and then adds the amount of the obligation to the company's reported assets and liabilities.

The use of unconsolidated joint ventures or equity-method investees may reflect off-balance-sheet liabilities. In addition, certain profitability ratios (return on sales, also called "net profit margin") may be overstated because the parent company's consolidated financial statements include its share of the investee's profits but not its share of the investee's sales. If disclosures are adequate, an analyst can adjust the reported amounts to better reflect the combined amounts of sales, assets, and liabilities. A company operating with numerous or material unconsolidated subsidiaries for which ownership levels approach 50% could be a warning sign of accounting issues. Understanding why a company structures its operations in such a manner—industry practice or need for strategic alliances in certain businesses or geographies—can allay concerns.

Another important aspect of financial reporting quality for the balance sheet is *unbiased measurement*. Unbiased measurement is particularly important for assets and liabilities for which valuation is subjective. The following list presents several examples:

- As previously discussed, understatement of impairment charges for inventory; plant, property, and equipment; or other assets not only results in overstated profits on the income statement but also results in overstatement of the assets on the balance sheet. A company with substantial amounts of reported goodwill but with a market value of equity less than the book value of shareholders' equity may indicate that appropriate goodwill impairments have not been taken.

- Similarly, understatement of valuation allowance for deferred tax assets would understate tax expenses and overstate the value of the assets on the balance sheet. (Overstatement would have the opposite effect.) Significant, unexplainable variations in the valuation account can signal biased measurement.

- A company's investments in the debt or equity securities of another company would ideally be based on observable market data. For some investments, no observable market data exist and the valuation must be based solely on management estimates. The balance sheet of a company with a substantial portion of its assets valued using non-observable inputs likely warrants closer scrutiny.

- A company's pension liabilities require various estimates, such as the discount rate at which future obligations are present valued. If pension obligations exist, the level and changes for the discount rate should be examined.

Example 10 shows a company with overstated goodwill.

EXAMPLE 10

Goodwill

Sealed Air Corporation

1. In August 2012, a *Wall Street Journal* article listed six companies that were carrying more goodwill on their balance sheets than the companies' market values (Thurm 2012). At the top of the list was Sealed Air Corporation, a company operating in the packaging and containers industry. Exhibit 27 presents an excerpt from the company's income statement for the following year, and Exhibit 28 presents an excerpt from the company's balance sheet.

Balance Sheet Quality

Exhibit 27: Sealed Air Corporation and Subsidiaries Consolidated Statements of Operations ($ millions, except per share amounts)

Year ended 31 December	2012	2011	2010
Net sales	$7,648.1	$5,550.9	$4,490.1
Cost of sales	5,103.8	3,950.6	3,237.3
Gross profit	2,544.3	1,600.3	1,252.8
Marketing, administrative, and development expenses	1,785.2	1,014.4	699.0
Amortization expense of intangible assets acquired	134.0	39.5	11.2
Impairment of goodwill and other intangible assets	1,892.3	—	—
Costs related to the acquisition and integration of Diversey	7.4	64.8	—
Restructuring and other charges	142.5	52.2	7.6
Operating (loss) profit	(1,417.1)	429.4	535.0
Interest expense	(384.7)	(216.6)	(161.6)
Loss on debt redemption	(36.9)	—	(38.5)
Impairment of equity method investment	(23.5)	—	—
Foreign currency exchange (losses) gains related to Venezuelan subsidiaries	(0.4)	(0.3)	5.5
Net gains on sale (other-than-temporary impairment) of available-for-sale securities	—	—	5.9
Other expense, net	(9.4)	(14.5)	(2.9)
(Loss) earnings from continuing operations before income tax provision	(1,872.0)	198.0	343.4
Income tax (benefit) provision	(261.9)	59.5	87.5
Net (loss) earnings from continuing operations	(1,610.1)	138.5	255.9
Net earnings from discontinued operations	20.9	10.6	—
Net gain on sale of discontinued operations	178.9	—	—
Net (loss) earnings available to common stockholders	$(1,410.3)	$149.1	$255.9

Exhibit 28: Excerpt from Sealed Air Corporation and Subsidiaries Consolidated Balance Sheets ($ millions, except share data)

Year Ended 31 December	2012	2011
ASSETS		
Current assets		
Cash and cash equivalents	$679.6	$703.6
Receivables, net of allowance for doubtful accounts of $25.9 in 2012 and $16.2 in 2011	1,326.0	1,314.2
Inventories	736.4	777.5
Deferred tax assets	393.0	156.2
Assets held for sale	—	279.0
Prepaid expenses and other current assets	87.4	119.7
Total current assets	$3,222.4	$3,350.2
Property and equipment, net	$1,212.8	$1,269.2
Goodwill	3,191.4	4,209.6
Intangible assets, net	1,139.7	2,035.7
Non-current deferred tax assets	255.8	112.3

Year Ended 31 December	2012	2011
ASSETS		
Other assets, net	415.1	455.0
Total assets	$9,437.2	$11,432.0

1. Sealed Air Corporation's financial statements indicate that the number of common shares issued and outstanding in 2011 was 192,062,185. The price per share of Sealed Air Corporation's common stock was around $18 per share in December 2011 and around $14 in August 2012; the *Wall Street Journal* article (Thurm 2012) was written in 2012. What was the company's market value?
2. How did the amount of goodwill as of 31 December 2011 compare with the company's market value?
3. Why did the *Wall Street Journal* article state that goodwill in excess of the company's market value is "a potential clue to future write-offs"?
4. Based on the information in Exhibit 28, does the *Wall Street Journal* article statement appear to be correct?

Solution to 1:

Sealed Air Corporation's market cap was about $3,457 million (= 192,062,185 shares × $18 per share) in December 2011 and around $2,689 million (= 192,062,185 shares × $14 per share) when the *Wall Street Journal* article was written in August 2012.

Solution to 2:

The amount of goodwill on Sealed Air Corporation's balance sheet as of 31 December 2011 was $4,209.6 million. The amount of goodwill exceeded the company's market value. (Also note that goodwill and other intangible assets represented about 55% of Sealed Air Corporation's total assets as of 31 December 2011.)

Solution to 3:

If the market capitalization exactly equaled the reported amount of goodwill, the value implicitly assigned to all the company's other assets would equal zero. In this case, because the market capitalization is less than the reported amount of goodwill, the value implicitly attributed to all the company's other assets is less than zero. This suggests that the amount of goodwill on the balance sheet is overvalued, so a future write-off is likely.

Solution to 4:

Yes, based on the information in Exhibit 28, the *Wall Street Journal* article statement appears correct. In the fiscal year ending 31 December 2012 after the article, Sealed Air Corporation recorded impairment of goodwill and other intangible assets of $1,892.3 million.

Finally, *clear presentation* is also important for financial reporting quality for the balance sheet. Although accounting standards specify many aspects of what appears on the balance sheet, companies have discretion, for example, in determining which line items should be shown separately and which should be aggregated into a single total. For items shown as a single total, an analyst can usually consult the notes for information about the components. For example, in consulting the inventory note, an analyst may learn that inventory is carried on a last-in, first-out basis and that, consequently, in an inflationary environment, the inventory is carried on the balance sheet at a cost that is significantly lower than its current cost. This information would provide the analyst with comfort that the inventory is unlikely to be overstated.

SOURCES OF INFORMATION ABOUT RISK — 17

☐ describe sources of information about risk

A company's financial statements can provide useful indicators of financial, operating, or other risk. For example, high leverage ratios (or, similarly, low coverage ratios) derived from financial statement data can signal financial risk. As described in a previous section, analytical models that incorporate various financial data can signal bankruptcy risk, and others can predict reporting risks (i.e., the risk of a company misreporting). Operating risks can be indicated by financial data, such as highly variable operating cash flows or negative trends in profit margins. Additional information about risk can be obtained from sources other than the financial statements.

An audit opinion(s) covering financial statements (and internal controls over financial reporting, where required) can provide some information about reporting risk. However, the content of an audit opinion is unlikely to be a timely source of information about risk. A related item that is potentially a signal of problems (and thus potentially represents information about risk) is a discretionary change in auditor. For example, Allou Health & Beauty Care, discussed in Example 7, had a different auditor for 2000, 2001, and 2002.

The notes are an integral part of the financial statements. They typically contain information that is useful in understanding a company's risk. Beyond the information about risk that can be derived from a company's financial statements and notes, various other disclosures can provide information about financial, operating, reporting, or other risks. An important source of information is the management commentary, which provides management's assessment of the important risks faced by the company. Although risk-related disclosures in the management commentary sometimes overlap with disclosures contained in the financial statement notes or elsewhere in regulatory filings, the commentary should reveal the management perspective, and its content often differs from the note disclosures.

Other required disclosures that are specific to an event, such as capital raising, non-timely filing of financial reports, management changes, or mergers and acquisitions, can provide important information relevant to assessing risk. Finally, the financial press, including online media, if used judiciously, can be a useful source of information about risk.

Limited Usefulness of Auditor's Opinion as a Source of Information about Risk

An auditor's opinion is unlikely to be an analyst's first source of information about a company's risk.[24] For financial statements, a clean audit opinion states that the financial statements present the information fairly and in conformity with the relevant

---

[24] Regulators globally are considering changes to increase the usefulness of audit reports. For example, the Financial Reporting Council in the UK requires auditors to include more information in their reports on risks identified during the audit and on how the concept of materiality was applied.

accounting principles. For internal controls, a clean audit opinion states that the company maintained effective internal controls over financial reporting. A negative or going-concern audit opinion on financial statements or a report indicating an internal control weakness would clearly be a warning sign for an analyst. However, an audit opinion relates to historical information and would, therefore, typically not provide information on a timely enough basis to be a useful source of information about risk.

For example, Eastman Kodak Company filed for bankruptcy on 19 January 2012. The audit opinion for fiscal 2011 (dated 28 February 2012) is shown in Exhibit 29. The opinion is identical to the company's audit opinion for the prior fiscal year except for two differences: (1) the years have been updated, and (2) the paragraph highlighted in bold has been added. The added paragraph states that the financial statements were prepared under the "going-concern" assumption; the company has subsequently declared bankruptcy, which raises doubt about the company's ability to continue as a going concern; and the financial statements have not been adjusted to reflect the bankruptcy. An analyst would have learned about Eastman Kodak's bankruptcy on 19 January, so the audit opinion is not useful as a source of that information. In addition, the audit opinion addresses financial statements that had not been adjusted to reflect the bankruptcy, which would limit usefulness to an analyst.

Exhibit 29: Post-Bankruptcy Audit Opinion for Eastman Kodak

Report of Independent Registered Public Accounting Firm

To the Board of Directors and Shareholders of Eastman Kodak Company:
In our opinion, the consolidated financial statements listed in the index appearing under Item 15(a)(1) present fairly, in all material respects, the financial position of Eastman Kodak Company and its subsidiaries at December 31, 2011 and 2010, and the results of their operations and their cash flows for each of the three years in the period ended December 31, 2011 in conformity with accounting principles generally accepted in the United States of America. In addition, in our opinion, the financial statement schedule listed in the index appearing under Item 15(a)(2) presents fairly, in all material respects, the information set forth therein when read in conjunction with the related consolidated financial statements. Also in our opinion, the Company maintained, in all material respects, effective internal control over financial reporting as of December 31, 2011, based on criteria established in *Internal Control - Integrated Framework* issued by the Committee of Sponsoring Organizations of the Treadway Commission (COSO). The Company's management is responsible for these financial statements and financial statement schedule, for maintaining effective internal control over financial reporting and for its assessment of the effectiveness of internal control over financial reporting, included in Management's Report on Internal Control over Financial Reporting appearing under Item 9A. Our responsibility is to express opinions on these financial statements, on the financial statement schedule, and on the Company's internal control over financial reporting based on our integrated audits. We conducted our audits in accordance with the standards of the Public Company Accounting Oversight Board (United States). Those standards require that we plan and perform the audits to obtain reasonable assurance about whether the financial statements are free of material misstatement and whether effective internal control over financial reporting was maintained in all material respects. Our audits of the financial statements included examining, on a test basis, evidence supporting the amounts and disclosures in the financial statements, assessing the accounting principles used and significant estimates made by management, and evaluating the overall financial statement presentation. Our audit of internal control over financial reporting included obtaining an understanding of internal control over financial reporting, assessing the

risk that a material weakness exists, and testing and evaluating the design and operating effectiveness of internal control based on the assessed risk. Our audits also included performing such other procedures as we considered necessary in the circumstances. We believe that our audits provide a reasonable basis for our opinions.

The accompanying financial statements have been prepared assuming that the Company will continue as a going concern. As more fully discussed in Note 1 to the financial statements, on January 19, 2012, the Company and its US subsidiaries filed voluntary petitions for relief under chapter 11 of the United States Bankruptcy Code. Uncertainties inherent in the bankruptcy process raise substantial doubt about the Company's ability to continue as a going concern. Management's plans in regard to these matters are also described in Note 1. The accompanying financial statements do not include any adjustments that might result from the outcome of this uncertainty.

A company's internal control over financial reporting is a process designed to provide reasonable assurance regarding the reliability of financial reporting and the preparation of financial statements for external purposes in accordance with generally accepted accounting principles. A company's internal control over financial reporting includes those policies and procedures that (i) pertain to the maintenance of records that, in reasonable detail, accurately and fairly reflect the transactions and dispositions of the assets of the company; (ii) provide reasonable assurance that transactions are recorded as necessary to permit preparation of financial statements in accordance with generally accepted accounting principles, and that receipts and expenditures of the company are being made only in accordance with authorizations of management and directors of the company; and (iii) provide reasonable assurance regarding prevention or timely detection of unauthorized acquisition, use, or disposition of the company's assets that could have a material effect on the financial statements.

Because of its inherent limitations, internal control over financial reporting may not prevent or detect misstatements. Also, projections of any evaluation of effectiveness to future periods are subject to the risk that controls may become inadequate because of changes in conditions, or that the degree of compliance with the policies or procedures may deteriorate.

/s/ PricewaterhouseCoopers LLP

PricewaterhouseCoopers LLP
Rochester, New York
February 28, 2012
Note: Bold-face type is added for emphasis.

In the case of Kodak, an analyst would not have obtained very useful information about risk from the auditor's report. Other sources of information—financial and market data—would have provided clear and timely indications of the company's financial difficulty.

Groupon provides another example of the timing of availability of information about risk in external auditors' reports. Exhibit 30 presents a timeline of events related to the company's material weakness in internal controls. Note that no negative external auditor opinion appeared before or during the time frame in which the weakness existed. No external opinion was required for the first annual filing, and the weakness had been remedied by the second annual filing.

> **Exhibit 30: Material Weaknesses in Internal Controls at Groupon**
>
> *November 2011:* The company goes public (initial public offering)
>
> *March 2012:* The company revises financial results and discloses that management concluded there was a "material weakness" in internal controls over financial reporting, as of 31 December. Shares fall 17%. (Because of an exemption for newly public companies, no external auditor opinion on the effectiveness of internal controls was required.)
>
> *May 2012:* In its first-quarter filing, the company discloses that it is "taking steps" to correct the weaknesses but cannot provide assurance that internal controls will be considered effective by the end of the year.
>
> *August 2012:* Second-quarter filing includes a disclosure similar to that in first-quarter filing.
>
> *November 2012:* Third-quarter filing includes a disclosure similar to that in first-quarter filing.
>
> *February 2013:* Full-year filing indicates that the company "concluded that we have remediated the previously identified material weakness as of December 31, 2012." (As required for public companies, the filing includes Groupon's first external auditor opinion on the effectiveness of internal controls. The company received a clean opinion.)

In the case of Groupon, an analyst would not have obtained any useful information from the auditor's report. Other data would have given more useful indicators of the company's reporting difficulties. For example, the company was required to change its revenue recognition policy and to restate the amount of revenue reported in its IPO filing—clearly a sign of reporting difficulties. Another item of information providing a signal of likely reporting difficulties was the company's extensive number of acquisitions and explosive growth. Groupon's reported revenues for 2009 were more than 300 times the amount of 2008 reported revenues, and 2010 reported revenues were 23 times larger than 2009 revenues. As described in an August 2011 accounting blog (Catanach and Ketz 2011):

> It is absolutely ludicrous to think that Groupon is anywhere close to having an effective set of internal controls over financial reporting having done 17 acquisitions in a little over a year. When a company expands to 45 countries, grows merchants from 212 to 78,466, and expands its employee base from 37 to 9,625 in only two years, there is little doubt that internal controls are not working somewhere.

The growth data, particularly coupled with disclosures in the IPO filing about management inexperience, are a warning sign of potential reporting risks. These reporting risks were observable many months before the company disclosed its internal control weakness, and the control weaknesses did not appear in an audit opinion.

Although the content of an audit opinion is unlikely to provide timely information about risk, a change in the auditor—and especially multiple changes in the auditor—can signal possible reporting problems. For example, one of the largest feeder funds for Bernie Madoff (the perpetrator of a multi-billion-dollar Ponzi scheme) had three different auditors for the three years from 2004 to 2006, a fact highlighted in testimony as a huge warning sign indicating "auditor shopping."[25] Similarly, the use of an auditor whose capabilities seem inadequate for the complexity of the company can

---

25 From the testimony of Harry Markopolos, CFA, given before the US House of Representatives Committee on Financial Services, 4 February 2009.

indicate risk. For example, the accounting/auditing firm that audited Madoff's $50 billion operation consisted of three people (two principals and a secretary). The small size of the auditing firm relative to the size of Madoff's operations should have caused serious concern for any potential investor. In general, it is important to understand the relationship between the auditor and the firm. Any questions about the auditor's independence would be a cause for concern—for example, if the auditor and company management are particularly close or if the company represents a substantial portion of the auditing firm's revenue.

RISK-RELATED DISCLOSURES IN THE NOTES

☐ describe sources of information about risk

The notes, an integral part of the financial statements, typically contain information that is useful in understanding a company's risk. For example, both IFRS and US GAAP require specific disclosures about risks related to contingent obligations, pension and post-employment benefits, and financial instrument risks.

Disclosures about contingent obligations include a description of the obligation, estimated amounts, timing of required payments, and related uncertainties.[26] Exhibit 31 shows excerpts from two of Royal Dutch Shell's financial statement notes disclosing information about provisions and contingencies. The year-to-year changes in management's estimated costs for items such as future decommissioning and restoration could have implications for risk evaluation. The disclosure also emphasizes the uncertain timing and amounts.

Exhibit 31: Disclosures about Contingent Obligations, Excerpt from Royal Dutch Shell's Note 19 and Note 25

Decommissioning and Other Provisions

	Current		Non-Current		Total	
	31 Dec 2012	31 Dec 2011	31 Dec 2012	31 Dec 2011	31 Dec 2012	31 Dec 2011
Decommissioning and restoration	1,356	894	14,715	13,072	16,071	13,966
Environmental	366	357	1,032	1,078	1,398	1,435
Redundancy	228	406	275	297	503	703
Litigation	390	256	307	330	697	586
Other	881	1,195	1,106	854	1,987	2,049

---

26 Contingent losses are recognized (i.e., reported on the financial statements) when it is probable the loss will occur and the amount can be reasonably estimated. Contingencies are disclosed (but not recognized) when the occurrence of a loss is less than probable but greater than remote and/or the amount cannot be reliably estimated. The concepts are similar under IFRS and US GAAP despite differences in terminology. IFRS makes a distinction between "provisions," which are recognized as liabilities because they meet the definition of a liability, and "contingent liabilities," which are disclosed but not recognized.

	Current		Non-Current		Total	
	31 Dec 2012	31 Dec 2011	31 Dec 2012	31 Dec 2011	31 Dec 2012	31 Dec 2011
Total	3,221	3,108	17,435	15,631	20,656	18,739

The timing and amounts settled in respect of these provisions are uncertain and dependent on various factors that are not always within management's control. Additional provisions are stated net of reversals of provisions recognised in previous periods.

Of the decommissioning and restoration provision at December 31, 2012, an estimated $4,666 million is expected to be utilised within one to five years, $3,483 million within six to ten years, and the remainder in later periods.

Reviews of estimated decommissioning and restoration costs are carried out annually, which in 2012 resulted in an increase of $1,586 million ...

Legal Proceedings and Other Contingencies

Groundwater contamination

Shell Oil Company (including subsidiaries and affiliates, referred to collectively as SOC), along with numerous other defendants, has been sued by public and quasi-public water purveyors, as well as governmental entities. The plaintiffs allege responsibility for groundwater contamination caused by releases of gasoline containing oxygenate additives. Most of these suits assert various theories of liability, including product liability, and seek to recover actual damages, including clean-up costs. Some assert claims for punitive damages. Fewer than 10 of these cases remain. On the basis of court rulings in SOC's favour in certain cases claiming damages from threats of contamination, the claims asserted in remaining matters, and Shell's track record with regard to amounts paid to resolve varying claims, the management of Shell currently does not believe that the outcome of the remaining oxygenate-related litigation pending, as at December 31, 2012, will have a material impact on Shell.

Nigerian claims

Shell subsidiaries and associates operating in Nigeria are parties to various environmental and contractual disputes. These disputes are at different stages in litigation, including at the appellate stage, where judgments have been rendered against Shell. If taken at face value, the aggregate amount of these judgments could be seen as material. The management of Shell, however, believes that these matters will ultimately be resolved in a manner favourable to Shell. While no assurance can be provided as to the ultimate outcome of any litigation, these matters are not expected to have a material effect on Shell.

Other

In the ordinary course of business, Shell subsidiaries are subject to a number of other loss contingencies arising from litigation and claims brought by governmental and private parties. The operations and earnings of Shell subsidiaries continue, from time to time, to be affected to varying degrees by political, legislative, fiscal and regulatory developments, including those relating to the protection of the environment and indigenous groups, in the countries in which they operate. The industries in which Shell subsidiaries are engaged are also subject to physical risks of various types. The nature and frequency of these developments and events, as well as their effect on future operations and earnings, are unpredictable.

Risk-Related Disclosures in the Notes

Disclosures about pensions and post-employment benefits include information relevant to actuarial risks that could result in actual benefits differing from the reported obligations based on estimated benefits or investment risks that could result in actual assets differing from reported amounts based on estimates.

Disclosures about financial instruments include information about risks, such as credit risk, liquidity risk, and market risks that arise from the company's financial instruments, and how they have been managed.

EXAMPLE 11

Use of Disclosures

Use the excerpts from Royal Dutch Shell's note disclosing information about financial instruments in Exhibit 32 to answer the following questions:

Exhibit 32: Disclosures about Financial Instruments, Excerpt from Royal Dutch Shell's Note 21

21 Financial Instruments and Other Derivative Contracts

A – Risks

In the normal course of business, financial instruments of various kinds are used for the purposes of managing exposure to interest rate, currency and commodity price movements.

....

Interest rate risk

Most debt is raised from central borrowing programmes. Interest rate swaps and currency swaps have been entered into to effectively convert most centrally issued debt to floating rate linked to dollar Libor (London Inter-Bank Offer Rate), reflecting Shell's policy to have debt principally denominated in dollars and to maintain a largely floating interest rate exposure profile. Consequently, Shell is exposed predominantly to dollar Libor interest rate movements. The financing of most subsidiaries is also structured on a floating-rate basis and, except in special cases, further interest rate risk management is discouraged.

On the basis of the floating rate net debt position at December 31, 2012, and assuming other factors (principally foreign exchange rates and commodity prices) remained constant and that no further interest rate management action were taken, an increase in interest rates of 1% would decrease pre-tax income by $27 million (2011: $146 million).

Foreign exchange risk

Many of the markets in which Shell operates are priced, directly or indirectly, in dollars. As a result, the functional currency of most Upstream companies and those with significant cross-border business is the dollar. For Downstream companies, the local currency is typically the functional currency. Consequently, Shell is exposed to varying levels of foreign exchange risk when it enters into transactions that are not denominated in the companies' functional currencies, when foreign currency monetary assets and liabilities are translated at the reporting date and as a result of holding net investments in operations that are not dollar-functional. The main currencies to which Shell is exposed are sterling, the Canadian dollar, euro and Australian dollar. Each company has treasury policies in place that are designed to measure and manage its foreign exchange exposures by reference to its functional currency.

Exchange rate gains and losses arise in the normal course of business from the recognition of receivables and payables and other monetary items in currencies other than individual companies' functional currency. Currency exchange risk may also arise in connection with capital expenditure. For major projects, an assessment is made at the final investment decision stage whether to hedge any resulting exposure.

Hedging of net investments in foreign operations or of income that arises in foreign operations that are non-dollar functional is not undertaken.

Assuming other factors (principally interest rates and commodity prices) remained constant and that no further foreign exchange risk management action were taken, a 10% appreciation against the dollar at December 31 of the main currencies to which Shell is exposed would have the following pre-tax effects:

$ millions	Increase (decrease) in income 2012	2011	Increase in net assets 2012	2011
10% appreciation against the dollar of:				
Sterling	(185)	(58)	1,214	1,042
Canadian dollar	131	(360)	1,384	1,364
Euro	30	458	1,883	1,768
Australian dollar	246	153	142	120

The above sensitivity information is calculated by reference to carrying amounts of assets and liabilities at December 31 only. The pre-tax effect on income arises in connection with monetary balances denominated in currencies other than the relevant entity's functional currency; the pre-tax effect on net assets arises principally from the translation of assets and liabilities of entities that are not dollar-functional.

1. Does Shell appear to take a centralized or decentralized approach to managing interest rate risk?

Solution:

Shell appears to take a centralized approach to managing interest rate risk based on its statements that most debt is raised centrally and that interest rate swaps and currency swaps have been used to convert most interest rate exposure to dollar market reference rate (MRR). In addition, Shell states that apart from structuring subsidiary financing on a floating-rate basis, it discourages subsidiary's further interest rate risk management.

> 2. For the year ended 31 December 2012, Shell reported pre-tax income of $50,289 million. How significant is Shell's exposure to a 1% increase in interest rates?
>
> **Solution:**
>
> For the year ended 31 December 2012, Shell's exposure to a 1% increase in interest rates is relatively insignificant. An increase in interest rates of 1% would decrease pre-tax income by $27 million, which is less than 0.1% of Shell's 2012 reported pre-tax income of $50,289 million.
>
> 3. For the year ended 31 December 2012, what would be the impact on Shell's pre-tax income of a 10% appreciation of the Australian dollar against the US dollar?
>
> **Solution:**
>
> The impact on Shell's pre-tax income of a 10% appreciation of the Australian dollar against the US dollar would be an increase of $246 million, which is about 0.5% of Shell's 2012 reported pre-tax income of $50,289 million.
>
> These disclosures, along with expectations about future market conditions, can help an analyst assess whether the company's exposures to interest rate risk and foreign exchange risks pose a significant threat to the company's future performance.

MANAGEMENT COMMENTARY, OTHER REQUIRED DISCLOSURES, AND THE FINANCIAL PRESS

19

☐ describe sources of information about risk

The IFRS Practice Statement, *Management Commentary*, issued in December 2010, is a non-binding framework for commentary related to financial statements prepared in accordance with IFRS. One purpose of the commentary is to help users of the financial reports in understanding the company's risk exposures, approach to managing risks, and effectiveness of risk management. The practice statement includes five elements that should be contained in the commentary: (1) nature of the business; (2) objectives and strategies; (3) resources, risks, and relationships; (4) results and prospects; and (5) performance measures and indicators. The section on risks can be particularly useful (IFRS 2010).

> Management should disclose its principal strategic, commercial, operational, and financial risks, which are those that may significantly affect the entity's strategies and progress of the entity's value. The description of the principal risks facing the entity should cover both exposures to negative consequences and potential opportunities.... The principal risks and uncertainties can constitute either a significant external or internal risk to the entity. (p. 13)

Public US companies are required to include an MD&A as Item 7 of Form 10-K. The MD&A disclosures include information about (1) liquidity, (2) capital resources, (3) results of operations, (4) off-balance-sheet arrangements, and (5) contractual arrangements. Information about off-balance-sheet arrangements and contractual arrangements can enable an analyst to anticipate future impact on cash flow. Companies are required to present quantitative and qualitative information about the company's exposure to market risks as Item 7A of the 10-K. This disclosure should enable analysts to understand the impact of fluctuations in interest rates, foreign exchange, and commodity prices.[27]

The IFRS Practice Statement states specifically that companies should present only the principal risks and not list all possible risks and uncertainties. Similarly, the SEC Division of Corporation Finance's internal reference document, *Financial Reporting Manual*, states, "MD&A should not consist of generic or boilerplate disclosure. Rather, it should reflect the facts and circumstances specific to each individual registrant" (p. 296). In practice, disclosures do not always reflect the intent. One challenge faced by analysts is identifying important risks and distinguishing between risks that are generic and thus relevant to all companies and risks that are more specific to an individual company.

This challenge is illustrated by an excerpt from the "Key Risks and Uncertainties" section of Autonomy Corporation's 2010 Annual Report, its last annual report before it was acquired by Hewlett-Packard Company (HP) for $11.1 billion in 2011.[28] As shown in Exhibit 33, Autonomy's risk disclosures contain many items that are arguably generic, such as the inability to maintain the competitive value of its technology, loss of key executives, and continued unfavorable economic conditions. These types of risks would be faced by any technology company. This significant amount of generic commentary (two pages) could potentially distract a reader whose aim was to identify the specific and important risks faced by the company.

Exhibit 33: Autonomy Corporation, Key Risks and Uncertainties

Risk	Description	Impact/Sensitivity	Mitigation/Comment
Technology	Business depends on our core technology, and our strategy concentrates on developing and marketing software based on our proprietary technology.	Since substantially all of revenues derive from licensing our core technology, if unable to maintain and enhance the competitive value of our core technology, our business will be adversely affected.	Continue to invest heavily in research and development to maintain competitive advantage. Monitor market to maintain competitiveness. Apply core technology to new and additional vertical market applications.
Competition	Technology which significantly competes with our technology.	Could render our products out of date and could result in rapid loss of market share.	Invest heavily in new product development to ensure that we have products at various stages of the product life cycle.

---

27 Although not part of the MD&A, disclosures about risk factors relevant to the company's securities are also required as Item 1A of Form 10-K.

28 HP subsequently took a multi-billion-dollar write-down on its investment, which it attributed to misreporting by Autonomy Corporation, stating that "the majority of this impairment charge is linked to serious accounting improprieties, disclosure failures and outright misrepresentations at Autonomy Corporation plc that occurred prior to HP's acquisition of Autonomy and the associated impact of those improprieties, failures and misrepresentations on the expected future financial performance of the Autonomy business over the long-term" (HP earnings announcement, 20 November 2012). Of course, HP's due diligence prior to purchasing the company would have gone far beyond the published financial reports; HP would have had access to all of the company's internal reporting as well.

Risk	Description	Impact/Sensitivity	Mitigation/Comment
Variability and visibility	There may be fluctuations in results due to quarterly reporting, and variability in results due to late-in-the-quarter purchasing cycles common in the software industry.	Although quarter-to-quarter results may not be meaningful due to the short periods, negative sentiment may arise based on interpretation of results. Due to late purchasing cycles common in the software industry, variability in closure rates could become exaggerated resulting in a negative effect on operations.	Close management of sales pipelines on a quarterly basis to improve visibility in results expectations. Close monitoring of macro and micro economic conditions to understand variability in closure rates. Annual and quarterly target setting to enable results achievement.
Margins	Expenditures increasing without a commensurate increase in revenues, and rapid changes in market conditions.	If increased expenses are not accompanied by increased revenues, we could experience decreased margins or operating losses.	Close monitoring by management of revenue and cost forecasts. Adjustment to expenditures in the event of anticipated revenue shortfalls.
Average selling prices	The average selling prices of our products could decrease rapidly.	May negatively impact revenues and gross margins.	Monitor market prices on an ongoing basis. Pricing responsibility at a senior level of management for deviations from standard.
Market conditions	The continuation of unfavourable economic and market conditions.	Could result in a rapid deterioration of operating results.	Regular monitoring of economic conditions. Adjustments to costs and product offerings to anticipate and match market conditions.
Resellers	Our ability to expand sales through indirect sellers and our general reliance on sales of our products by third parties.	Inability to recruit and retain resellers who can successfully penetrate their markets could adversely affect our business.	Invest in training resources for resellers. Close monitoring of reseller sales cycles. Investment in direct sales channel.
Management	The continued service of our executive directors.	The loss of any key member of management may affect the leadership of the company.	Establish succession plan. Maintain effective management training programme. Attract and retain senior personnel.
Hiring	The hiring and retention of qualified personnel.	Without the appropriate quality and quantity of skills throughout the organisation, it would be difficult to execute the business plans and grow.	Use of external recruiters and internal bonuses. Rigorous talent management plans and reviews. Provide competitive compensation packages. Ensure that work is challenging and rewarding.
Product errors	Errors or defects in our products.	Could negatively affect our revenues and the market acceptance of our products and increase our costs.	Invest in quality control programmes. Monitor integrity and effectiveness of software. Solicit and act on customer feedback.
Acquisitions	Problems encountered in connection with potential acquisitions.	We may not successfully overcome problems in connection with potential acquisitions, which could lead to a deterioration in our results.	Carefully evaluate transactions. Conduct thorough due diligence on all targets. Carefully plan for post-acquisition integration.
IP infringement	Claims by others that we infringe on their intellectual property rights.	If our technology infringed on other parties' intellectual property rights, we could be exposed to costs and injunctive relief.	Monitor market developments closely to identify potential violations of our patents, and by the company, and take action where necessary. Maintain a significant number of patents to support our business and protect competitive advantage.

Risk	Description	Impact/Sensitivity	Mitigation/Comment
Growth	Our ability to effectively manage our growth.	Expansion places demands on management, engineering, support, operations, legal, accounting, sales and marketing personnel, and other resources. Failure to manage effectively will impact business and financial results	Recruitment and retention of key personnel. Investment in corporate infrastructure, including support, operations, legal, and accounting personnel. Focus on internal controls.
International risks	Additional operational and financial risks as we continue to expand our international operations.	Exposure to movements in exchange rates and lack of familiarity with local laws could lead to infractions.	Pricing of contracts in US dollars to the extent possible to minimise exchange risk. Retention of local staff and local advisors, reporting to headquarters, to manage risk.
Security breaches	Any breach of our security measures and unauthorised access to a customer's or our data.	Could result in significant legal liability and negative publicity.	Establish and maintain strict security standards. Test security standards on a regular basis.

Source: Section from Autonomy Corporation's 2010 Annual Report.

Other Required Disclosures

Other required disclosures that are specific to an event, such as capital raising, non-timely filing of financial reports, management changes, or mergers and acquisitions, can provide important information relevant to assessing risk. In the United States, public companies would report such events to the SEC in a Form 8-K (and NT—"notification of inability to timely file"—when appropriate). Delays in filing are often the result of accounting difficulties. Such accounting difficulties could be internal disagreement on an accounting principle or estimate, the lack of adequate financial staff, or the discovery of an accounting fraud that requires further examination. In general, an NT filing is highly likely to signal problems with financial reporting quality.

For public companies in Europe, the Committee of European Securities Regulators (CESR)[29] has published guidance concerning the types of inside information that must be disclosed on an ad hoc basis to the market. Examples of such information include changes in control; changes in management and supervisory boards; mergers, splits, and spinoffs; legal disputes; and new licenses, patents, and registered trademarks. Companies use the disclosure mechanisms specified by their relevant national authorities to make such disclosures. For example, in the United Kingdom, a company would release an announcement to the market via an approved regulatory information service.

In these cases, an examination of the information announced would be necessary to determine whether reporting quality would be affected. For example, an announcement of the sudden resignation of a company's most senior financial officer or external auditor would clearly be a warning sign of potential problems with financial reporting quality. As another example, an announcement of a legal dispute related to one of the company's important assets or products would warrant attention because it could negatively affect the company's future earnings. Announcements of mergers and acquisitions, although they might indicate future positive developments for the company, could also indicate changes in the company's risk profile, particularly during the transaction.

---

29 CESR has been replaced by the European Securities and Markets Authority (ESMA).

Financial Press as a Source of Information about Risk

The financial press can be a useful source of information about risk when, for example, a financial reporter uncovers financial reporting issues that had not previously been recognized. For example, a *Wall Street Journal* financial reporter, Jonathan Weil (2000), was one of the first people to identify problems with the accounting at Enron (and other companies that were using "gain-on-sale" accounting, an aggressive policy allowing immediate revenue recognition on long-term contracts). Indeed, the well-known investor James (Jim) Chanos cites an article by Weil as the catalyst of his investigation of Enron (Chanos 2002).

It is important to emphasize that even if an initial idea comes from a news article, further investigation is essential—first, by using definitive sources (i.e., regulatory filings) to confirm any accounting and financial disclosures and, second, by seeking supporting information from other sources, where available. For example, although a financial press article was the initial source of information for Chanos, the first step in his research was to analyze Enron's annual SEC filings (Form 10-K and 10-Q). In addition, Chanos obtained information about insider stock sales, the company's business strategy and tactics, and stock analysts' perspectives.

It is also important—and likely will become increasingly important as electronic media via the internet expands—to consider the source of any particular news article. Information reported by a well-known financial news provider is more likely to be factual than information from less-established sources. Similarly, stories or blogs written by financial journalists are more likely to be unbiased than those written by individuals with a related service or product to sell.

SUMMARY

Assessing the quality of financial reports—both reporting quality and results quality—is an important analytical skill.

- The quality of financial reporting can be thought of as spanning a continuum from the highest quality to the lowest.
- Potential problems that affect the quality of financial reporting broadly include revenue and expense recognition on the income statement; classification on the statement of cash flows; and the recognition, classification, and measurement of assets and liabilities on the balance sheet.
- Typical steps involved in evaluating financial reporting quality include an understanding of the company's business and industry in which the company is operating; comparison of the financial statements in the current period and the previous period to identify any significant differences in line items; an evaluation of the company's accounting policies, especially any unusual revenue and expense recognition compared with those of other companies in the same industry; financial ratio analysis; examination of the statement of cash flows with particular focus on differences between net income and operating cash flows; perusal of risk disclosures; and review of management compensation and insider transactions.
- High-quality earnings increase the value of the company more than low-quality earnings, and the term "high-quality earnings" assumes that reporting quality is high.

- Low-quality earnings are insufficient to cover the company's cost of capital and/or are derived from non-recurring, one-off activities. In addition, the term "low-quality earnings" can be used when the reported information does not provide a useful indication of the company's performance.
- Various alternatives have been used as indicators of earnings quality: recurring earnings, earnings persistence and related measures of accruals, beating benchmarks, and after-the-fact confirmations of poor-quality earnings, such as enforcement actions and restatements.
- Earnings that have a significant accrual component are less persistent and thus may revert to the mean more quickly.
- A company that consistently reports earnings that exactly meet or only narrowly beat benchmarks can raise questions about its earnings quality.
- Cases of accounting malfeasance have commonly involved issues with revenue recognition, such as premature recognition of revenues or the recognition of fraudulent revenues.
- Cases of accounting malfeasance have involved misrepresentation of expenditures as assets rather than as expenses or misrepresentation of the timing or amount of expenses.
- Bankruptcy prediction models, used in assessing financial results quality, quantify the likelihood that a company will default on its debt and/or declare bankruptcy.
- Similar to the term "earnings quality," when reported cash flows are described as being high quality, it means that the company's underlying economic performance was satisfactory in terms of increasing the value of the firm, and it also implies that the company had high reporting quality (i.e., that the information calculated and disclosed by the company was a good reflection of economic reality). Cash flow can be described as "low quality" either because the reported information properly represents genuinely bad economic performance or because the reported information misrepresents economic reality.
- For the balance sheet, high financial *reporting* quality is indicated by completeness, unbiased measurement, and clear presentation.
- A balance sheet with significant amounts of off-balance-sheet debt would lack the completeness aspect of financial reporting quality.
- Unbiased measurement is a particularly important aspect of financial reporting quality for assets and liabilities for which valuation is subjective.
- A company's financial statements can provide useful indicators of financial or operating risk.
- The management commentary (also referred to as the management discussion and analysis, or MD&A) can give users of the financial statements information that is helpful in assessing the company's risk exposures and approaches to managing risk.
- Required disclosures regarding, for example, changes in senior management or inability to make a timely filing of required financial reports can be a warning sign of problems with financial reporting quality.
- The financial press can be a useful source of information about risk when, for example, a financial reporter uncovers financial reporting issues that had not previously been recognized. An analyst should undertake additional investigation of any issue identified.

REFERENCES

Altman, Edward I. 1968. "Financial Ratios, Discriminant Analysis and the Prediction of Corporate Bankruptcy." Journal of Finance, vol. 23, no. 4 (September):589–609. 10.1111/j.1540-6261.1968.tb00843.x

Altman, Edward I. 2000. "Predicting Financial Distress of Companies: Revisiting the Z-Score and Zeta° Models." Working paper (July).

Beneish, Messod D. 1999. "The Detection of Earnings Manipulation." Financial Analysts Journal, vol. 55, no. 5 (September/October):24–36. 10.2469/faj.v55.n5.2296

Beneish, Messod D., Charles M.C. Lee, D. Craig Nichols. 2013. "Earnings Manipulation and Expected Returns." Financial Analysts Journal, vol. 69, no. 2 (March/April):57–82. 10.2469/faj.v69.n2.1

Bens, Daniel A., Theodore H. Goodman, Monica Neamtiu. 2012. "Does Investment-Related Pressure Lead to Misreporting? An Analysis of Reporting Following M&A Transactions." Accounting Review, vol. 87, no. 3 (May):839–865. 10.2308/accr-10210

Beresford, Dennis R., Nicholas deB. Katzenbach, C.B. Rogers. 2003. "Report of Investigation by the Special Investigative Committee of the Board of Directors of WorldCom, Inc." (31 March): www.sec.gov/Archives/edgar/data/723527/000093176303001862/dex991.htm.

Bharath, Sreedhar T., Tyler Shumway. 2008. "Forecasting Default with the Merton Distance to Default Model." Review of Financial Studies, vol. 21, no. 3 (May):1339–1369. 10.1093/rfs/hhn044

Bhasin, Madan. 2012. "Corporate Accounting Frauds: A Case Study of Satyam Computers Limited." International Journal of Contemporary Business Studies, vol. 3, no. 10 (October):16–42.

Brown, Lawrence D., Marcus L. Caylor. 2005. "A Temporal Analysis of Quarterly Earnings Thresholds: Propensities and Valuation Consequences." Accounting Review, vol. 80, no. 2 (April):423–440. 10.2308/accr.2005.80.2.423

Bulkeley, W. 2002. "Questioning the Books: IBM Annual Report Shows Stronger Core Earnings." Wall Street Journal (12 March).

Burgstahler, D., Ilia Dichev. 1997. "Earnings Management to Avoid Earnings Decreases and Losses." Journal of Accounting and Economics, vol. 24, no. 1 (December):99–126. 10.1016/S0165-4101(97)00017-7

Catanach, Anthony H., J. Edward Ketz. 2011. "Trust No One, Particularly Not Groupon's Accountants," Grumpy Old Accountants (August): http://blogs.smeal.psu.edu/grumpyoldaccountants.

Chanos, James. 2002. "Anyone Could Have Seen Enron Coming: Prepared Witness Testimony Given Feb. 6, 2002 to the House Committee on Energy and Commerce," Wall $treet Week with FORTUNE (http://www.pbs.org/wsw/opinion/chanostestimony.html).

Ciesielski, Jack T., Elaine Henry. 2017. "Accounting's Tower of Babel: Key Considerations in Assessing Non-GAAP Earnings." Financial Analysts Journal, vol. 73, no. 2:34–50.

Dechow, Patricia M., Richard G. Sloan, Amy P. Sweeney. 1995. "Detecting Earnings Management." Accounting Review, vol. 70, no. 2 (April):193–225.

Dechow, Patricia M., Scott A. Richardson, Irem Tuna. 2003. "Why Are Earnings Kinky? An Examination of the Earnings Management Explanation." Review of Accounting Studies, vol. 8, no. 2–3 (June):355–384. 10.1023/A:1024481916719

Dechow, Patricia M., Weili Ge, Catherine Schrand. 2010. "Understanding Earnings Quality: A Review of the Proxies, Their Determinants and Their Consequences." Journal of Accounting and Economics, vol. 50, no. 2–3 (December):344–401. 10.1016/j.jacceco.2010.09.001

Dechow, Patricia, Seili Ge, Chad Larson, Richard Sloan. 2011. "Predicting Material Accounting Misstatements." Contemporary Accounting Research, vol. 28, no. 1 (Spring):17–82. 10.1111/j.1911-3846.2010.01041.x

Degeorge, François, Jayendu Patel, Richard Zeckhauser. 1999. "Earnings Management to Exceed Thresholds." Journal of Business, vol. 72, no. 1 (January):1–33. 10.1086/209601

Erickson, Merle, Shiing-wu Wang. 1999. "Earnings Management by Acquiring Firms in Stock for Stock Mergers." Journal of Accounting and Economics, vol. 27, no. 2 (April):149–176. 10.1016/S0165-4101(99)00008-7

Erickson, M., S. Heitzman, X.F. Zhang. 2012. "The Effect of Financial Misreporting on Corporate Mergers and Acquisitions." Working paper.

Friedman, Eric, Simon Johnson, Todd Mitton. 2003. "Propping and Tunneling." Journal of Comparative Economics, vol. 31, no. 4 (December):732–750. 10.1016/j.jce.2003.08.004

Hwang, S.L. 1994. "Borden to Reverse, Reclassify 40% of 1992 Charge." Wall Street Journal (22 March).

IASB2010. Conceptual Framework for Financial Reporting 2010. International Accounting Standards Board (September).

IFRS2010. Management Commentary, A Framework for Presentation. IFRS Practice Statement (December).

Johnson, S., R. LaPorta, A. Shleifer, F. Lopez-de-Silanes. 2000. "Tunneling." American Economic Review, vol. 90, no. 2 (May):22–27. 10.1257/aer.90.2.22

Jones, Jennifer J. 1991. "Earnings Management during Import Relief Investigations." Journal of Accounting Research, vol. 29, no. 2 (Autumn):193–228. 10.2307/2491047

Kahn, Jeremy. 2009. "In India, Clues Unfold to a Fraud's Framework." New York Times (26 January).

Kealhofer, Stephen. 2003. "Quantifying Credit Risk I: Default Prediction." Financial Analysts Journal, vol. 59, no. 1 (January/February):30–44. 10.2469/faj.v59.n1.2501

Leuty, Ron. 2012. "Elan Will Shutter South S.F. Center as It Shifts R&D to New Company." San Francisco Business Times (5 October 2012): www.bizjournals.com/sanfrancisco/blog/biotech/2012/09/elan-neotope-onclave-alzheimers.html?page=all.

Lewis, Craig M. 2012. "Risk Modeling at the SEC: The Accounting Quality Model," Speech given at the Financial Executives International Committee on Finance and Information Technology (13 December): www.sec.gov/news/speech/2012/spch121312cml.htm.

McVay, Sarah E. 2006. "Earnings Management Using Classification Shifting: An Examination of Core Earnings and Special Items." Accounting Review, vol. 81, no. 3 (May):501–532. 10.2308/accr.2006.81.3.501

Mulford, Charles W., Eugene E. Comiskey. 2005. Creative Cash Flow Reporting: Uncovering Sustainable Financial Performance. Hoboken, NJ: John Wiley & Sons.

Nissim, Doron, Stephen H. Penman. 2001. "Ratio Analysis and Equity Valuation: From Research to Practice." Review of Accounting Studies, vol. 6, no. 1 (March):109–154. 10.1023/A:1011338221623

SEC2000. "Accounting and Auditing Enforcement, Release No. 1350." US Securities and Exchange Commission (14 December): www.sec.gov/litigation/admin/34-43724.htm.

SEC2001a "Accounting and Auditing Enforcement, Release No. 1393." US Securities and Exchange Commission (15 May): www.sec.gov/litigation/admin/33-7976.htm.

SEC2001b. "Accounting and Auditing Enforcement, Release No. 1405." US Securities and Exchange Commission (19 June): www.sec.gov/litigation/admin/34-44444.htm.

SEC2003. "Report Pursuant to Section 704 of the Sarbanes-Oxley Act of 2002" US Securities and Exchange Commission (24 January): www.sec.gov/news/studies/sox704report.pdf.

Sherer, P. 2000. "AmeriServe Examination Finds Financial Woes." Wall Street Journal (3 July).

Shumway, Tyler. 2001. "Forecasting Bankruptcy More Accurately: A Simple Hazard Model." Journal of Business, vol. 74, no. 1 (January):101–124. 10.1086/209665

Sloan, Richard G. 1996. "Do Stock Prices Fully Reflect Information in Accruals and Cash Flows about Future Earnings?" Accounting Review, vol. 71, no. 3 (July):289–315.

Thurm, Scott. 2012. "Buyers Beware: The Goodwill Games." Wall Street Journal (12 August).

Weil, Jonathan. 2000. "Energy Traders Cite Gains, But Some Math is Missing," Wall Street Journal (20 September).

PRACTICE PROBLEMS

The following information relates to questions 1-7

Ioana Matei is a senior portfolio manager for an international wealth management firm. She directs research analyst Teresa Pereira to investigate the earnings quality of Miland Communications and Globales, Inc.

Pereira first reviews industry data and the financial reports of Miland Communications for the past few years. Pereira then makes the following three statements about Miland:

Statement 1	Miland shortened the depreciable lives for capital assets.
Statement 2	Revenue growth has been higher than that of industry peers.
Statement 3	Discounts to customers and returns from customers have decreased.

Pereira also observes that Miland has experienced increasing inventory turnover, increasing receivables turnover, and net income greater than cash flow from operations. She estimates the following regression model to assess Miland's earnings persistence:

$$\text{Earnings}_{t+1} = \alpha + \beta_1 \text{Cash flow}_t + \beta_2 \text{Accruals}_t + \varepsilon$$

Pereira and Matei discuss quantitative models such as the Beneish model, used to assess the likelihood of misreporting. Pereira makes the following two statements to Matei:

Statement 1	An advantage of using quantitative models is that they can determine cause and effect between model variables.
Statement 2	A disadvantage of using quantitative models is that their predictive power declines over time because many managers have learned to test the detectability of manipulation tactics by using the model.

Pereira concludes her investigation of Miland by examining the company's reported pre-tax income of $5.4 billion last year. This amount includes $1.2 billion of acquisition and divestiture-related expenses, $0.5 billion of restructuring expenses, and $1.1 billion of other non-operating expenses. Pereira determines that the acquisition and divestiture-related expenses as well as restructuring expenses are non-recurring expenses, but other expenses are recurring expenses.

Matei then asks Pereira to review last year's financial statements for Globales, Inc. and assess the effect of two possible misstatements. Upon doing so, Pereira judges that Globales improperly recognized EUR50 million of revenue and improperly capitalized EUR100 million of its cost of revenue. She then estimates the effect of these two misstatements on net income, assuming a tax rate of 25%.

Pereira compares Globales, Inc.'s financial statements with those of an industry competitor. Both firms have similar, above-average returns on equity (ROE), although Globales has a higher cash flow component of earnings. Pereira applies the mean reversion principle in her forecasts of the two firms' future ROE.

1. Which of Pereira's statements describes an accounting warning sign of potential

overstatement or non-sustainability of operating and/or net income?

- **A.** Statement 1
- **B.** Statement 2
- **C.** Statement 3

2. Which of Pereira's statements about Miland Communications is *most likely* a warning sign of potential earnings manipulation?
   - **A.** The trend in inventory turnover
   - **B.** The trend in receivables turnover
   - **C.** The amount of net income relative to cash flow from operations

3. Based on the regression model used by Pereira, earnings persistence for Miland would be highest if:
   - **A.** β_1 is less than 0.
   - **B.** β_1 is greater than β_2.
   - **C.** β_2 is greater than β_1.

4. Which of Pereira's statements regarding the use of quantitative models to assess the likelihood of misreporting is correct?
   - **A.** Only Statement 4
   - **B.** Only Statement 5
   - **C.** Both Statement 4 and Statement 5

5. Based on Pereira's determination of recurring and non-recurring expenses for Miland, the company's recurring or core pre-tax earnings last year is *closest* to:
   - **A.** $4.3 billion.
   - **B.** $4.8 billion.
   - **C.** $7.1 billion.

6. After adjusting the Globales, Inc. income statement for the two possible misstatements, the decline in net income is *closest* to:
   - **A.** EUR37.5 million.
   - **B.** EUR112.5 million.
   - **C.** EUR150.0 million.

7. Pereira should forecast that the ROE for Globales is likely to decline:
   - **A.** more slowly than that of the industry competitor.
   - **B.** at the same rate as the industry competitor.
   - **C.** more rapidly than that of the industry competitor.

Practice Problems

The following information relates to questions 8–14

Emmitt Dodd is a portfolio manager for Upsilon Advisers. Dodd meets with Sonya Webster, the firm's analyst responsible for the machinery industry, to discuss three established companies: BIG Industrial, Construction Supply, and Dynamic Production. Webster provides Dodd with research notes for each company that reflect trends during the last three years:

BIG Industrial:

Note 1	Operating income has been much lower than operating cash flow (OCF).
Note 2	Accounts payable has increased, while accounts receivable and inventory have substantially decreased.
Note 3	Although OCF was positive, it was just sufficient to cover capital expenditures, dividends, and debt repayments.

Construction Supply:

Note 1	Operating margins have been relatively constant.
Note 2	The growth rate in revenue has exceeded the growth rate in receivables.
Note 3	OCF was stable and positive, close to its reported net income, and just sufficient to cover capital expenditures, dividends, and debt repayments.

Dynamic Production:

Note 1	OCF has been more volatile than that of other industry participants.
Note 2	OCF has fallen short of covering capital expenditures, dividends, and debt repayments.

Dodd asks Webster about the use of quantitative tools to assess the likelihood of misreporting. Webster tells Dodd she uses the Beneish model, and she presents the estimated *M*-scores for each company in Exhibit 1.

Exhibit 1: Beneish Model *M*-scores

Company	2017	2016	Change in *M*-score
BIG Industrial	−1.54	−1.82	0.28
Construction Supply	−2.60	−2.51	−0.09
Dynamic Production	−1.86	−1.12	−0.74

Webster tells Dodd that Dynamic Production was required to restate its 2016 financial statements as a result of its attempt to inflate sales revenue. Customers of Dynamic Production were encouraged to take excess product in 2016, and they were then allowed to return purchases in the subsequent period, without penalty. Webster's industry analysis leads her to believe that innovations have caused some of the BIG Industrial's inventory to become obsolete. Webster expresses concern to Dodd that although the notes to the financial statements for BIG Industrial are informative about its inventory cost methods, its inventory is overstated.

The BIG Industrial income statement reflects a profitable 49% unconsolidated equity investment. Webster calculates the return on sales of BIG Industrial based on the reported income statement. Dodd notes that industry peers consolidate similar investments. Dodd asks Webster to use a comparable method of calculating the return on sales for BIG Industrial.

8. Which of Webster's notes about BIG Industrial provides an accounting warning sign of a potential reporting problem?

    A. Only Note 1

    B. Only Note 2

    C. Both Note 1 and Note 2

9. Do either of Webster's Notes 4 or 5 about Construction Supply describe an accounting warning sign of potential overstatement or non-sustainability of operating income?

    A. No

    B. Yes, Note 4 provides a warning sign

    C. Yes, Note 5 provides a warning sign

10. Based on Webster's research notes, which company would *most likely* be described as having high-quality cash flow?

    A. BIG Industrial

    B. Construction Supply

    C. Dynamic Production

11. Based on the Beneish model results for 2017 in Exhibit 1, which company has the highest probability of being an earnings manipulator?

    A. BIG Industrial

    B. Construction Supply

    C. Dynamic Production

12. Based on the information related to its restatement, Dynamic Production reported poor operating cash flow quality in 2016 by understating:

    A. inventories.

    B. net income.

    C. trade receivables.

13. Webster's concern about BIG Industrial's inventory suggests poor reporting qual-

Practice Problems

ity, *most likely* resulting from a lack of:

A. completeness.

B. clear presentation.

C. unbiased measurement.

14. In response to Dodd's request, Webster's recalculated return on sales will *most likely*:

A. decrease.

B. remain the same.

C. increase.

The following information relates to questions 15-18

Mike Martinez is an equity analyst who has been asked to analyze Stellar, Inc. by his supervisor, Dominic Anderson. Stellar exhibited strong earnings growth last year; however, Anderson is skeptical about the sustainability of the company's earnings. He wants Martinez to focus on Stellar's financial reporting quality and earnings quality.

After conducting a thorough review of the company's financial statements, Martinez concludes the following:

Conclusion 1 — Although Stellar's financial statements adhere to generally accepted accounting principles (GAAP), Stellar understates earnings in periods when the company is performing well and overstates earnings in periods when the company is struggling.

Conclusion 2 — Stellar most likely understated the value of amortizable intangibles when recording the acquisition of Solar, Inc. last year. No goodwill impairment charges have been taken since the acquisition.

Conclusion 3 — Over time, the accruals component of Stellar's earnings is large relative to the cash component.

Conclusion 4 — Stellar reported an unusually sharp decline in accounts receivable in the current year, and an increase in long-term trade receivables.

15. Based on Martinez's conclusions, Stellar's financial statements are *best* categorized as:

A. non-GAAP compliant.

B. GAAP compliant, but with earnings management.

C. GAAP compliant and decision useful, with sustainable and adequate returns.

16. Based on Conclusion 2, after the acquisition of Solar, Stellar's earnings are *most likely*:

    A. understated.

    B. fairly stated.

    C. overstated.

17. In his follow-up analysis relating to Conclusion 3, Martinez should focus on Stellar's:

    A. total accruals.

    B. discretionary accruals.

    C. non-discretionary accruals.

18. What will be the impact on Stellar in the current year if Martinez's belief in Conclusion 4 is correct? Compared with the previous year, Stellar's:

    A. current ratio will increase.

    B. days sales outstanding (DSO) will decrease.

    C. accounts receivable turnover will decrease.

SOLUTIONS

1. B is correct. Higher growth in revenue than that of industry peers is an accounting warning sign of potential overstatement or non-sustainability of operating income. Shortening the depreciable lives of capital assets is a conservative change and not a warning sign. An increase (not a decrease) in discounts and returns would be a warning sign.

2. C is correct. Net income being greater than cash flow from operations is a warning sign that the firm may be using aggressive accrual accounting policies that shift current expenses to future periods. Decreasing, not increasing, inventory turnover could suggest inventory obsolescence problems that should be recognized. Decreasing, not increasing, receivables turnover could suggest that some revenues are fictitious or recorded prematurely or that the allowance for doubtful accounts is insufficient.

3. B is correct. When earnings are decomposed into a cash component and an accruals component, research has shown that the cash component is more persistent. A beta coefficient (β_1) on the cash flow variable that is larger than the beta coefficient (β_2) on the accruals variable indicates that the cash flow component of earnings is more persistent than the accruals component. This result provides evidence of earnings persistence.

4. B is correct. Earnings manipulators have learned to test the detectability of earnings manipulation tactics by using the model to anticipate analysts' perceptions. They can reduce their likelihood of detection; therefore, Statement 5 is correct. As a result, the predictive power of the Beneish model can decline over time. An additional limitation of using quantitative models is that they cannot determine cause and effect between model variables. Quantitative models establish only associations between variables, and Statement 4 is incorrect.

    A is incorrect because quantitative models cannot determine cause and effect between model variables. They are capable only of establishing associations between variables. Therefore, Statement 4 is incorrect.

5. C is correct. Recurring or core pre-tax earnings would be $7.1 billion, which is the company's reported pre-tax income of $5.4 billion plus the $1.2 billion of non-recurring (i.e., one-time) acquisitions and divestiture expenses plus the $0.5 billion of non-recurring restructuring expenses.

6. B is correct. The correction of the revenue misstatement would result in lower revenue by EUR50 million, and the correction of the cost of revenue misstatement would result in higher cost of revenue by EUR100 million. The result is a reduction in pre-tax income of EUR150 million. Applying a tax rate of 25%, the reduction in net income would be 150 × (1 − 0.25) = EUR112.5 million.

7. A is correct. Based on the principle of mean reversion, the high ROE for both firms should revert towards the mean. Globales has a higher cash flow component to its return than the peer firm, however, so its high return on common equity should persist longer than that of the peer firm. The peer firm has a higher accruals component, so it is likely to revert more quickly.

8. B is correct. Only Note 2 provides a warning sign. The combination of increases in accounts payable with substantial decreases in accounts receivable and inventory are an accounting warning sign that management may be overstating cash flow from operations. Note 1 does not necessarily provide a warning sign.

Operating income being greater than operating cash flow is a warning sign of a potential reporting problem. In this case, however, BIG Industrial's operating income is lower than its operating cash flow.

9. A is correct. Neither Note 4 nor Note 5 provides an accounting warning sign of potential overstatement or non-sustainability of operating income.

Increases in operating margins can be a warning sign of potential overstatement or non-sustainability of operating and/or net income. In this case, however, operating margins for Construction Supply have been relatively constant during the last three years.

A growth rate in receivables exceeding the growth rate in revenue is an accounting warning sign of potential overstatement or non-sustainability of operating income. In this case, however, Construction Supply's revenue growth exceeds the growth rate in receivables.

10. B is correct. High-quality OCF means the performance is of high reporting quality and also of high results quality. For established companies, high-quality operating cash flow would typically be positive; be derived from sustainable sources; be adequate to cover capital expenditures, dividends, and debt repayments; and have relatively low volatility compared with industry peers. Construction Supply reported positive OCF during each of the last three years. The OCF appears to be derived from sustainable sources, because it compares closely with reported net income. Finally, OCF was adequate to cover capital expenditures, dividends, and debt repayments. Although the OCF for BIG Industrial has been positive and just sufficient to cover capital expenditures, dividends, and debt repayments, the increases in accounts payable and substantial decreases in accounts receivable and inventory during the last three years are an accounting warning sign that management may be overstating cash flow from operations. For Dynamic Production, OCF has been more volatile than other industry participants, and it has fallen short of covering capital expenditures, dividends, and debt repayments for the last three years. Both of these conditions are warning signs for Dynamic Production.

11. A is correct. Higher *M*-scores indicate an increased probability of earnings manipulation. The company with the highest *M*-score in 2017 is BIG Industrial, with an *M*-score of −1.54. Construction Supply has the lowest *M*-score at −2.60, and Dynamic Production also has a lower *M*-score at −1.86. The *M*-score for BIG Industrial is above the relevant cutoff of −1.78.

12. A is correct. The items primarily affected by improper revenue recognition include net income, receivables, and inventories. When revenues are overstated, net income and receivables will be overstated and inventories will be understated.

13. C is correct. Webster is concerned that innovations have made some of BIG Industrial's inventory obsolete. This scenario suggests impairment charges for inventory may be understated and that the inventory balance does not reflect unbiased measurement.

14. A is correct. The use of unconsolidated joint ventures or equity-method investees may reflect an overstated return on sales ratio, because the parent company's consolidated financial statements include its share of the investee's profits but not its share of the investee's sales. An analyst can adjust the reported amounts to better reflect the combined amounts of sales. Reported net income divided by the combined amount of sales will result in a decrease in the net profit margin.

15. B is correct. Stellar's financial statements are GAAP compliant (Conclusion 1) but cannot be relied upon to assess earnings quality. There is evidence of earnings

Solutions

management: understating and overstating earnings depending upon the results of the period (Conclusion 1), understated amortizable intangibles (Conclusion 2), and a high accruals component in the company's earnings (Conclusion 3).

16. C is correct. Martinez believes that Stellar most likely understated the value of amortizable intangibles when recording the acquisition of a rival company last year. Impairment charges have not been taken since the acquisition (Conclusion 2). Consequently, the company's earnings are likely to be overstated because amortization expense is understated. This understatement has not been offset by an impairment charge.

17. B is correct. Martinez concluded that the accruals component of Stellar's earnings was large relative to the cash component (Conclusion 3). Earnings with a larger component of accruals are typically less persistent and of lower quality. An important distinction is between accruals that arise from normal transactions in the period (called non-discretionary) and accruals that result from transactions or accounting choices outside the normal (called discretionary accruals). The discretionary accruals are possibly made with the intent to distort reported earnings. Outlier discretionary accruals are an indicator of possibly manipulated—and thus low quality earnings. Thus, Martinez is primarily focused on discretionary accruals, particularly outlier discretionary accruals (referred to as abnormal accruals).

18. B is correct. Because accounts receivable will be lower than reported in the past, Stellar's DSO [Accounts receivable/(Revenues/365)] will decrease. Stellar's accounts receivable turnover (365/days' sales outstanding) will increase with the lower DSO, giving the false impression of a faster turnover. The company's current ratio will decrease (current assets will decrease with no change in current liabilities).

LEARNING MODULE 6

Integration of Financial Statement Analysis Techniques

by Jack T. Ciesielski, CPA, CFA.

Jack T. Ciesielski, CPA, CFA, is at R.G. Associates, Inc., former publisher of The Analyst's Accounting Observer (USA).

LEARNING OUTCOMES

Mastery	The candidate should be able to:
☐	demonstrate the use of a framework for the analysis of financial statements, given a particular problem, question, or purpose (e.g., valuing equity based on comparables, critiquing a credit rating, obtaining a comprehensive picture of financial leverage, evaluating the perspectives given in management's discussion of financial results)
☐	identify financial reporting choices and biases that affect the quality and comparability of companies' financial statements and explain how such biases may affect financial decisions
☐	evaluate the quality of a company's financial data and recommend appropriate adjustments to improve quality and comparability with similar companies, including adjustments for differences in accounting standards, methods, and assumptions
☐	evaluate how a given change in accounting standards, methods, or assumptions affects financial statements and ratios
☐	analyze and interpret how balance sheet modifications, earnings normalization, and cash flow statement related modifications affect a company's financial statements, financial ratios, and overall financial condition

The Financial Statement Modeling learning module should also appear in the Financial Statement Analysis topic area, not in the Corporate Issuers topic area. We regret the error in its placement in the print curriculum. It has been placed correctly in the candidate learning ecosystem online.

1 INTRODUCTION

☐ demonstrate the use of a framework for the analysis of financial statements, given a particular problem, question, or purpose (e.g., valuing equity based on comparables, critiquing a credit rating, obtaining a comprehensive picture of financial leverage, evaluating the perspectives given in management's discussion of financial results)

It is important to keep in mind that financial analysis is a means to an end and not the end itself. Rather than try to apply every possible technique and tool to every situation, it is essential for the investor to consider and identify the proper type of analysis to apply in a given situation.

The primary reason for performing financial analysis is to help in making an economic decision. Before making such decisions as whether to lend to a particular long-term borrower or to invest a large sum in a common stock, venture capital vehicle, or private equity candidate, an investor or financial decision-maker wants to make sure that the probability of a successful outcome is on his or her side. Rather than leave outcomes to chance, a financial decision-maker should use financial analysis to identify and make more visible potential favorable and unfavorable outcomes.

The purpose of this reading is to provide examples of the effective use of financial analysis in decision making. The framework for the analysis is shown in Exhibit 1. The case study follows the basic framework shown in Exhibit 1.

Exhibit 1: A Financial Statement Analysis Framework

Phase	Sources of Information	Examples of Output
1. Define the purpose and context of the analysis.	<ul><li>The nature of the analyst's function, such as evaluating an equity or debt investment or issuing a credit rating</li><li>Communication with client or supervisor on needs and concerns</li><li>Institutional guidelines related to developing specific work product</li></ul>	<ul><li>Statement of the purpose or objective of the analysis</li><li>A list (written or unwritten) of specific questions to be answered by the analysis</li><li>Nature and content of report to be provided</li><li>Timetable and budgeted resources for completion</li></ul>
2. Collect input data.	<ul><li>Financial statements, other financial data, questionnaires, and industry/economic data</li><li>Discussions with management, suppliers, customers, and competitors</li><li>Company site visits (e.g., to production facilities or retail stores)</li></ul>	<ul><li>Organized financial statements</li><li>Financial data tables</li><li>Completed questionnaires, if applicable</li></ul>
3. Process input data, as required, into analytically useful data.	<ul><li>Data from the previous phase</li></ul>	<ul><li>Adjusted financial statements</li><li>Common-size statements</li><li>Ratios and graphs</li><li>Forecasts</li></ul>
4. Analyze/interpret the data.	<ul><li>Input data and processed data</li></ul>	<ul><li>Analytical results</li></ul>

Phase	Sources of Information	Examples of Output
5. Develop and communicate conclusions and recommendations (e.g., with an analysis report).	• Analytical results and previous reports • Institutional guidelines for published reports	• Analytical report answering questions posed in Phase 1 • Recommendation regarding the purpose of the analysis, such as whether to make an investment or grant credit
6. Follow-up.	• Information gathered by periodically repeating above steps, as necessary, to determine whether changes to holdings or recommendations are necessary	• Updated reports and recommendations

CASE STUDY 1

☐ demonstrate the use of a framework for the analysis of financial statements, given a particular problem, question, or purpose (e.g., valuing equity based on comparables, critiquing a credit rating, obtaining a comprehensive picture of financial leverage, evaluating the perspectives given in management's discussion of financial results)

The portfolio manager for the food sector of a large public employee pension fund wants to take a long-term equity position in a publicly traded food company and has become interested in Nestlé S.A., a global company. In its 2014 annual report, Nestlé's management outlined its long-term objectives for organic growth, margin and earnings per share improvement, and capital efficiency. The management report indicated the following general strategic direction: "Our ambition is not just to be the leader but the industry reference for Nutrition, Health and Wellness. In recent years we have built on the strong foundations of our unrivalled food and beverage portfolio, exploring the benefits of nutrition's therapeutic role with Nestlé Health Science." Nestlé's stated objectives, including expansion of the company's mission into "nutrition's therapeutic role," captured the portfolio manager's attention: She became intrigued with Nestlé as an investment possibility. She asks an analyst to evaluate Nestlé for consideration as a large core holding. Before investing in the company, the portfolio manager has several concerns that she has conveyed to the analyst:

- What are Nestlé's sources of earnings growth? How sustainable is Nestlé's performance? Do the company's reported earnings represent its economic reality? And if Nestlé's performance is fairly reported, will it be sustainable for an extended period, such as 5 to 10 years, while the pension fund has the common stock as a core holding?
- In determining the quality of earnings over a long-term time frame, the portfolio manager wants to understand the relationship of earnings to cash flow.
- Having started out in the investment business as a lending officer, the portfolio manager wants to know how well Nestlé's balance sheet takes into account the company's full rights and obligations. She wants to know whether the capital structure of the company can support future operations and strategic plans. Even if the investor is primarily concerned with

the earnings potential of a possible investee, the balance sheet matters. For example, if asset write-downs or new legal liabilities decrease a company's financial position, it is difficult for a company to sustain profitability if it has to repair its balance sheet. Worse still for an investor: If "repairing the balance sheet" means the issuance of dilutive stock, it can be even more costly to existing investors.

The analyst develops a plan of analysis to address the portfolio manager's concerns by following the framework presented in Exhibit 1. Phases 3 and 4 will be the focus of most of the work.

Phase 1: Define a Purpose for the Analysis

The analyst states the purpose and context of the analysis as identifying the factors that have driven the company's financial success and assessing their sustainability. He also states the need to identify and understand the risks that may affect the sustainability of returns.

Phase 2: Collect Input Data

The analyst finds that Nestlé has an extensive collection of financial statements on its website. After gathering several years of annual reports, he is ready to begin processing the data.

3 PHASES 3 AND 4: DUPONT ANALYSIS

- [ ] demonstrate the use of a framework for the analysis of financial statements, given a particular problem, question, or purpose (e.g., valuing equity based on comparables, critiquing a credit rating, obtaining a comprehensive picture of financial leverage, evaluating the perspectives given in management's discussion of financial results)
- [ ] identify financial reporting choices and biases that affect the quality and comparability of companies' financial statements and explain how such biases may affect financial decisions
- [ ] evaluate the quality of a company's financial data and recommend appropriate adjustments to improve quality and comparability with similar companies, including adjustments for differences in accounting standards, methods, and assumptions

Phase 3: Process Data and Phase 4: Analyze/Interpret the Processed Data

The analyst intends to accomplish his purpose stated in Phase 1 through a series of financial analyses, including

- a DuPont analysis;[1]
- an analysis of the composition of Nestlé's asset base;
- an analysis of Nestlé's capital structure;
- a study of the company's segments and the allocation of capital among them;
- an examination of the company's accruals in reporting as they affect earnings quality;
- a study of the company's cash flows and their adequacy for the company's continued operations and strategies; and
- a decomposition and analysis of the company's valuation.

While processing the input data consistent with the needs of these analyses, the analyst plans to simultaneously interpret and analyze the resulting data. In his view, Phases 3 and 4 of the framework are best considered jointly.

DuPont Analysis

The analyst decides to start the assessment of Nestlé with a DuPont analysis. The investment is expected to be in the company's common stock, and ultimately, the DuPont analysis separates the components affecting the return on common equity. Furthermore, the disaggregation of return on equity (ROE) components leads to more trails to follow in assessing the drivers of Nestlé's performance. The analyst also intends to investigate the quality of the earnings and underlying cash flows, as well as to understand the common shareholders' standing in the Nestlé capital structure.

One basic premise underlying all research and analysis is to constantly look beneath the level of information presented—to constantly search for meaningful insights through disaggregation of the presented information, whether it is a single line on a financial statement or within segments of an entire entity. This constant reduction of information into smaller components can reveal a company's earnings drivers; it can also highlight weaker operations being concealed by stronger ones in the aggregate. That premise of "seeking granularity" underlies DuPont analysis: By isolating the different components of ROE, it helps the analyst discover a company's strengths and allows the analyst to assess their sustainability.[2] Seeking granularity also helps the analyst find potential operational flaws and provides an opening for dialogue with management about possible problems.

The analyst begins to process the data gathered in Phase 2 in order to assemble the information required for the DuPont analysis. Exhibit 2 shows the last three years of income statements for Nestlé; Exhibit 3 shows the last four years of Nestlé balance sheets.

From his study of the income statement, the analyst notes that Nestlé has a significant amount of "income from associates and joint ventures" (hereafter referred to in the text as income from associates) in all three years. In 2014, this income amounted

---

1 A reminder to the reader: This case study is an example, and starting the financial statement analysis with a DuPont analysis is not a mandate. Alternatively, another analyst might be more interested in the trends of various income and expense categories than in the sources of returns on shareholder equity as a financial statement analysis starting point. This analyst might have preferred starting with a time-series common-size income statement. The starting point depends on the perspective of the individual analyst.
2 ROE can be decomposed in a variety of ways:ROE = Return on assets × Leverage ROE = Net profit margin × Asset turnover × LeverageROE = EBIT margin × Tax burden × Interest burden × Asset turnover × Leverage

to CHF8,003 million, or 53.7%, of Nestlé's net income (referred to by Nestlé as "profit for the year"). The income from associates[3] is a pure net income figure, presented after taxes and with no related revenue in the income statement. Much of the income from associates relates to Nestlé's 23.4% stock ownership of L'Oréal, a cosmetics company.

In 2014, L'Oréal affected the amount of income from associates in a variety of ways. In 2014, Nestlé reduced its L'Oréal ownership by selling 48.5 million shares of its holding back to L'Oréal. In return, Nestlé gained full ownership of Galderma, a joint venture it had with L'Oréal. The partial disposal of L'Oréal shares resulted in a net gain of CHF4,569 million. Income from associates included a revaluation gain of CHF2,817 million from the increase in ownership of Galderma. Nestlé had owned 50% of Galderma, with L'Oréal holding the other 50%. When Nestlé bought the remaining ownership from L'Oréal, its original 50% ownership position was revalued at current fair value, which was based on the price paid. As of July 2014, Galderma became an affiliated company that was fully consolidated. Because of its L'Oréal stock ownership, Nestlé recognizes a share of L'Oréal's net income.

The share of results at other companies that Nestlé included in income from associates was CHF828 million in 2014.

The analyst wants to decompose the company's financial results as much as possible in order to identify any problem operations or to find hidden opportunities. Including the net investments and returns of associates with the full reported value of Nestlé's own assets and income would introduce noise into the analytical signals produced by the DuPont analysis. Unlike the "pure Nestlé" operations and resources, the returns earned by associates are not under the direct control of Nestlé's management. To avoid making incorrect inferences about the profitability of Nestlé's operations, the analyst wants to remove the effects of the investments in associates from the balance sheet and income statement. Otherwise, such DuPont analysis components as net profit margin and total asset turnover would combine the impact of pure Nestlé operations with that of the operations of associated companies: Conclusions about Nestlé-only business would be flawed because they would be based on commingled information.

Exhibit 2: Nestlé S.A. Income Statements, 2014–2012 (CHF millions)

	2014	2013	2012 (restated)[d]
Sales	91,612	92,158	89,721
Other revenue	253	215	210
Cost of goods sold	(47,553)	(48,111)	(47,500)
Distribution expenses	(8,217)	(8,156)	(8,017)
Marketing and administration expenses	(19,651)	(19,711)	(19,041)
Research and development costs	(1,628)	(1,503)	(1,413)
Other trading income	110	120	141
Other trading expenses[a]	(907)	(965)	(637)
Trading operating profit[b]	14,019	14,047	13,464
Other operating income	154	616	146
Other operating expenses[c]	(3,268)	(1,595)	(222)
Operating profit (EBIT)	10,905	13,068	13,388
Financial income	135	219	120

---

[3] Associates are companies in which Nestlé has the power to exercise significant influence but does not exercise control. Associates and joint ventures are accounted for by the equity method.

Phases 3 and 4: DuPont Analysis

	2014	2013	2012 (restated)[d]
Financial expense	(772)	(850)	(825)
Profit before taxes, associates, and joint ventures (EBT)	**10,268**	**12,437**	**12,683**
Taxes	(3,367)	(3,256)	(3,259)
Income from associates and joint ventures	8,003	1,264	1,253
Profit for the year	**14,904**	**10,445**	**10,677**
of which attributable to non-controlling interests	448	430	449
of which attributable to shareholders of the parent (net profit)	14,456	10,015	10,228
Earnings per share			
Basic earnings per share	4.54	3.14	3.21
Diluted earnings per share	4.52	3.13	3.20

Excerpted information from notes to the financial statements:	2014	2013	2012 (restated)
[a] Other trading expenses include:			
Restructuring costs	(257)	(274)	(88)
Impairment of PP&E	(136)	(109)	(74)
Impairment of intangible assets (other than goodwill)	(23)	(34)	—
Litigation and onerous contracts	(411)	(380)	(369)
Unusual charges contained within operating profit	(827)	(797)	(531)
[b] Expenses allocated by function:			
Depreciation of PP&E	(2,782)	(2,867)	(2,655)
Amortisation of intangible assets	(276)	(301)	(394)
	(3,058)	(3,168)	(3,049)
[c] Other operating expenses include:			
Impairment of goodwill	(1,908)	(114)	(14)

[d] *The 2012 information came from the 2013 Annual Report; 2012 comparatives were restated by Nestlé following the implementation of IFRS 11 and IAS 19 revised, as described in Note 22.*

Exhibit 3: Nestlé S.A. Balance Sheets, 2014–2011 (CHF millions)

	2014	2013	2012 (restated)[a]	2011 (revised)[b]
Assets				
Current assets				
Cash and cash equivalents	7,448	6,415	5,713	4,769
Short-term investments	1,433	638	3,583	3,013
Inventories	9,172	8,382	8,939	9,095
Trade and other receivables	13,459	12,206	13,048	12,991
Prepayments and accrued income	565	762	821	879
Derivative assets	400	230	576	722
Current income tax assets	908	1,151	972	1,053

	2014	2013	2012 (restated)[a]	2011 (revised)[b]
Assets held for sale	576	282	368	16
Total current assets	**33,961**	**30,066**	**34,020**	**32,538**
Non-current assets				
Property, plant, and equipment (PP&E)	28,421	26,895	26,576	23,460
Goodwill	34,557	31,039	32,688	28,613
Intangible assets	19,800	12,673	13,018	8,785
Investments in associates and joint ventures	8,649	12,315	11,586	10,317
Financial assets	5,493	4,550	4,979	7,153
Employee benefits assets	383	537	84	127
Current income tax assets	128	124	27	39
Deferred tax assets	2,058	2,243	2,899	2,408
Total non-current assets	**99,489**	**90,376**	**91,857**	**80,902**
Total assets	**133,450**	**120,442**	**125,877**	**113,440**
Liabilities and equity				
Current liabilities				
Financial debt	8,810	11,380	18,408	15,945
Trade and other payables	17,437	16,072	14,627	13,544
Accruals and deferred income	3,759	3,185	3,078	2,780
Provisions	695	523	452	575
Derivative liabilities	757	381	423	632
Current income tax liabilities	1,264	1,276	1,608	1,379
Liabilities directly associated with assets held for sale	173	100	1	—
Total current liabilities	**32,895**	**32,917**	**38,597**	**34,855**
Non-current liabilities				
Financial debt	12,396	10,363	9,008	6,165
Employee benefits liabilities	8,081	6,279	8,360	6,912
Provisions	3,161	2,714	2,827	3,079
Deferred tax liabilities	3,191	2,643	2,240	1,974
Other payables	1,842	1,387	2,181	2,113
Total non-current liabilities	**28,671**	**23,386**	**24,616**	**20,243**
Total liabilities	**61,566**	**56,303**	**63,213**	**55,098**
Equity				
Share capital	322	322	322	330
Treasury shares	(3,918)	(2,196)	(2,078)	(6,722)
Translation reserve	(17,255)	(20,811)	(17,924)	(16,927)
Retained earnings and other reserves	90,981	85,260	80,687	80,184
Total equity attributable to shareholders of the parent	**70,130**	**62,575**	**61,007**	**56,865**
Non-controlling interests	1,754	1,564	1,657	1,477
Total equity	**71,884**	**64,139**	**62,664**	**58,342**
Total liabilities and equity	**133,450**	**120,442**	**125,877**	**113,440**

[a] *The 2012 information came from the 2013 Annual Report; 2012 comparatives were restated by Nestlé following the implementation of IFRS 11 and IAS 19 revised, as described in Note 22.*
[b] *The analyst revised the 2011 balance sheet from that reported in the 2012 Consolidated Financial*

Phases 3 and 4: DuPont Analysis

Statements of the Nestlé Group.

To keep the DuPont analysis as logically consistent as possible throughout all the periods of study, the analyst revises the 2011 balance sheet (from that reported in the 2012 Consolidated Financial Statements of the Nestlé Group) for the effects of implementing IFRS 11 and IAS 19 revised. He identifies the 1 January 2012 adjustments from the 2013 financial statements and revises the 31 December 2011 year-end balances accordingly. The analyst's revisions to the as-reported 2011 balance sheet are shown in Exhibit 4.

Exhibit 4: Modifications to 2011 Balance Sheet (CHF millions)

	2011 (as reported)	Effects of IAS 19 (1)	Effects of IFRS 11 (2)	2011 (revised)
Assets				
Current assets				
Cash and cash equivalents	4,938	—	(169)	4,769
Short-term investments	3,050	—	(37)	3,013
Inventories	9,255	—	(160)	9,095
Trade and other receivables	13,340	—	(349)	12,991
Prepayments and accrued income	900	—	(21)	879
Derivative assets	731	—	(9)	722
Current income tax assets	1,094	—	(41)	1,053
Assets held for sale	16	—	—	16
Total current assets	33,324	—	(786)	32,538
Non-current assets				
Property, plant, and equipment	23,971	—	(511)	23,460
Goodwill	29,008	—	(395)	28,613
Intangible assets	9,356	—	(571)	8,785
Investments in associates and joint ventures	8,629	—	1,688	10,317
Financial assets	7,161	—	(8)	7,153
Employee benefits assets	127	—	—	127
Current income tax assets	39	—	—	39
Deferred tax assets	2,476	(5)	(63)	2,408
Total non-current assets	80,767	(5)	140	80,902
Total assets	114,091	(5)	(646)	113,440
Liabilities and equity				
Current liabilities				
Financial debt	16,100	—	(155)	15,945
Trade and other payables	13,584	—	(40)	13,544
Accruals and deferred income	2,909	—	(129)	2,780
Provisions	576	—	(1)	575
Derivative liabilities	646	—	(14)	632
Current income tax liabilities	1,417	—	(38)	1,379
Liabilities directly associated with assets held for sale	—	—	—	—
Total current liabilities	35,232	—	(377)	34,855
Non-current liabilities				

	2011 (as reported)	Effects of IAS 19 (1)	Effects of IFRS 11 (2)	2011 (revised)
Financial debt	6,207	—	(42)	6,165
Employee benefits liabilities	7,105	(91)	(102)	6,912
Provisions	3,094	—	(15)	3,079
Deferred tax liabilities	2,060	18	(104)	1,974
Other payables	2,119	—	(6)	2,113
Total non-current liabilities	20,585	(73)	(269)	20,243
Total liabilities	55,817	(73)	(646)	55,098
Equity				
Share capital	330	—	—	330
Treasury shares	(6,722)	—	—	(6,722)
Translation reserve	(16,927)	—	—	(16,927)
Retained earnings and other reserves	80,116	68	—	80,184
Total equity attributable to shareholders of the parent	56,797	68	—	56,865
Non-controlling interests	1,477	—	—	1,477
Total equity	58,274	68	—	58,342
Total liabilities and equity	114,091	(5)	(646)	113,440

(1) IAS 19 Revised 2011—Employee Benefits was implemented in 2013, with comparative restatement made to 1 January 2012. This standard revised the calculation of benefit plan obligations. The 1 January 2012 adjustments were imposed on the 31 December 2011 balance sheet by the analyst, taken from Note 22 (Restatements and adjustments of 2012 comparatives) of the 2013 Annual Report.

(2) IFRS 11—Joint Arrangements was implemented in 2013, with comparative restatement made to 1 January 2012. Nestlé had used proportional consolidation for two of its joint arrangements (Cereal Partners Worldwide and Galderma), and the standard required that they be accounted for using the equity method of investments. The 1 January 2012 adjustments were imposed on the 31 December 2011 balance sheet by the analyst, taken from Note 22 (Restatements and adjustments of 2012 comparatives) of the 2013 Annual Report.

4. PHASES 3 AND 4: DUPONT DECOMPOSITION

☐ demonstrate the use of a framework for the analysis of financial statements, given a particular problem, question, or purpose (e.g., valuing equity based on comparables, critiquing a credit rating, obtaining a comprehensive picture of financial leverage, evaluating the perspectives given in management's discussion of financial results)

☐ evaluate the quality of a company's financial data and recommend appropriate adjustments to improve quality and comparability with similar companies, including adjustments for differences in accounting standards, methods, and assumptions

The analyst considers what information he needs for a DuPont analysis. He extracts the data shown in Exhibit 5 from Exhibits 2 and 3:

Phases 3 and 4: DuPont Decomposition

Exhibit 5: Data Needed for DuPont Analysis (CHF millions)

	2014	2013	2012	2011
Income Statement Data:				
Sales	91,612	92,158	89,721	
Operating profit (EBIT)	10,905	13,068	13,388	
Profit before taxes, associates, and joint ventures (EBT)	10,268	12,437	12,683	
Profit for the year	14,904	10,445	10,677	
Income from associates and joint ventures	8,003	1,264	1,253	
Profit, excluding associates and joint ventures	6,901	9,181	9,424	
Balance Sheet Data:				
Total assets	133,450	120,442	125,877	113,440
Investments in associates and joint ventures	8,649	12,315	11,586	10,317
Total assets, excluding associates and joint ventures	124,801	108,127	114,291	103,123
Total equity	71,884	64,139	62,664	58,342
Investments in associates and joint ventures	8,649	12,315	11,586	10,317
Total equity, excluding associates and joint ventures	63,235	51,824	51,078	48,025

The five-way decomposition of ROE is expanded to isolate the effects of the investment in associates in Nestlé's asset base and earnings. The necessary modifications to the reported financial data to isolate these effects are shown in Exhibit 5. Subtracting income from associates from the net income (profit for the year) gives the profits generated by Nestlé's own asset base. Subtracting the amount of investment in associates from total assets results in a figure that more closely represents Nestlé's own asset base. With this information, the analyst can assess the profitability and returns of the largest and most relevant part of the entire Nestlé entity: the core Nestlé company.

Exhibit 6 shows the results of expanding the DuPont analysis. The net profit margin component and the asset turnover component require adjustments to remove the impact of the associates on the return on assets. To adjust the net profit margin component, the analyst subtracts the associates' income from the net income and divides the result by sales. For 2014, the Nestlé-only net profit margin was 7.53% (= Profit excluding income from associates/Sales = 6,901/91,612). To adjust the asset turnover, the analyst subtracts the investment in associates from total assets to arrive at the assets used by the core Nestlé company. Sales divided by the average of the beginning and ending assets (excluding investment in associates) gives the Nestlé-only asset turnover. For 2014, the Nestlé-only asset turnover was 0.787 {= 91,612/[(108,127 + 124,801)/2] = 91,612/116,464}. Including the investment in associates in total assets, the asset turnover was 0.722 {= 91,612/[(120,442 + 133,450)/2] = 91,612/126,946}. The difference between the asset turnover based on unadjusted financial statement amounts and the Nestlé-only asset turnover gives the effect on total asset turnover of the investment in associates: a decrease of 0.065 in 2014.

The net profit margin can be decomposed into three components: EBIT margin × Tax burden × Interest burden. The tax and interest burdens indicate what is left for the company after the effects of taxes and interest, respectively. To adjust the tax burden component, the analyst divides profit (excluding income from associates) by profit before taxes and income from associates (EBT). For 2014, the tax burden was

67.21% (= 6,901/10,268). The interest burden is calculated by dividing the profit before taxes, associates, and joint ventures (EBT) by operating profit (EBIT). For 2014, the interest burden was 94.16% (= 10,268/10,905). The EBIT margin is earnings before interest and taxes (operating profit) divided by revenue (sales). For 2014, the EBIT margin was 11.90% (= 10,905/91,612).

Multiplying the three components together yields the Nestlé-only net profit margin. In 2014, the Nestlé-only net profit margin was 7.53% (= 67.21% × 94.16% × 11.90%). Calculating the net profit margin without excluding income from associates gives 16.27% (= Net income/ Revenue = Profit for the year/Sales = 14,904/91,612), which is not representative of the Nestlé-only operations. Dividing the net profit margin by the net profit margin *without* the associates' income (16.27%/7.53% = 216.07%) quantifies the magnifying effect of the associates' income on Nestlé's own margins. The "Nestlé-only" entity earned 7.53% on every sale, but including the associates' income in net profit increases the net profit margins by 116.07% [(100.00% + 116.07%) × 7.53% = 16.27%]. A 16.27% level of profitability is not representative of what Nestlé's core operations can generate.

Exhibit 6: Expanded DuPont Analysis

	2014	2013	2012
Tax burden (excl. associates)	67.21%	73.82%	74.30%
× Interest burden	94.16%	95.17%	94.73%
× EBIT margin	11.90%	14.18%	14.92%
= Net profit margin (excl. associates)	7.53%	9.96%	10.50%
× Associates' effect on net profit margin	216.07%	113.76%	113.33%
= Net profit margin	**16.27%**	**11.33%**	**11.90%**
Total asset turnover (excl. associates)	0.787	0.829	0.825
Effect of associates' investments on turnover	(0.065)	(0.081)	(0.075)
× Total asset turnover	**0.722**	**0.748**	**0.750**
= Return on assets	11.75%	8.47%	8.93%
× Leverage	**1.87**	**1.94**	**1.98**
= Return on equity (ROE)	**21.97%**	**16.44%**	**17.67%**
Traditional ROE calculation (CHF millions):			
Net income	14,904	10,445	10,677
÷ Average total equity	68,012	63,402	60,503
= ROE	**21.91%**	**16.47%**	**17.65%**

Note: Differences in ROE calculations because of rounding.

PHASES 3 AND 4: ADJUSTING FOR UNUSUAL CHARGES

5

☐ demonstrate the use of a framework for the analysis of financial statements, given a particular problem, question, or purpose (e.g., valuing equity based on comparables, critiquing a credit rating, obtaining a comprehensive picture of financial leverage, evaluating the perspectives given in management's discussion of financial results)

☐ evaluate the quality of a company's financial data and recommend appropriate adjustments to improve quality and comparability with similar companies, including adjustments for differences in accounting standards, methods, and assumptions

☐ evaluate how a given change in accounting standards, methods, or assumptions affects financial statements and ratios

☐ analyze and interpret how balance sheet modifications, earnings normalization, and cash flow statement related modifications affect a company's financial statements, financial ratios, and overall financial condition

In 2012 and 2013, the net profit margin (including income from associates) was fairly stable at 11.90% and 11.33%, respectively. But it increased significantly in 2014—to 16.27%—as a result of the increase in income from associates attributable to the L'Oréal disposal and Galderma revaluation. The analyst, however, is interested in the ongoing operations of Nestlé, unaffected by such non-repeating types of gains. The net profit margin excluding income from associates shows a disturbing trend: It decreased each year in the 2012–2014 period. This finding prompts the analyst to try to identify a reason for the declining profitability of the Nestlé-only business. Searching the income statements and notes in the annual reports, he notices that Nestlé has recorded goodwill impairments over the period under study, with a particularly large one, CHF1,908 million, occurring in 2014. This impairment was related to Nestlé's acquisitions of ice cream and pizza businesses in the United States. He also notices that Nestlé has recorded provisions each year for restructuring activities, environmental liabilities, litigation reserves, and other activities. To see how much these events affected the Nestlé-only profitability, he constructs the table shown in Exhibit 7. He calls these events "unusual charges" for convenience of presentation.

Exhibit 7: Profitability Adjusted for Provisions and Impairment Charges (CHF millions)

	2014	2013	2012
Sales	91,612	92,158	89,721
Profit excluding income from associates (from Exhibit 5)	6,901	9,181	9,424
Impairment of goodwill	1,908	114	14
Total provisions for restructuring, environmental, litigation, and other (not tax-affected: assumed non-taxable in year of recognition)	920	862	618

	2014	2013	2012
Profit adjusted for unusual charges	9,729	10,157	10,056
Net profit margin: excl. associates, with all unusual charges incl.	7.53%	9.96%	10.50%
Net profit margin: excluding associates and unusual charges	10.62%	11.02%	11.21%
Profit margin consumed by unusual charges	3.09%	1.06%	0.71%

The analyst notices that the adjusted profits and the adjusted profit margins were more stable over the three-year period than the profits and profit margins excluding associates. However, the adjusted profits and profit margins and the profits and profit margins excluding associates decreased over the same period. Although the provisions and impairment charges potentially explain the significant decrease in the Nestlé-only profit margins, in particular from 2013 to 2014, the analyst decides *not* to adjust the remaining DuPont analysis to exclude these charges. They involve decisions by management, they recur regularly, and they affect the returns to shareholders. In assessing the company's prospects, he believes that these charges are important variables that should not to be ignored.

Returning to the DuPont analysis, he now realizes the significance of the associates' earnings to the entire Nestlé entity. The margin is greater in each year if the associates' earnings are included in net profit as opposed to looking at Nestlé alone. Consistently, the company's profit margins are smaller without the boost from associates' earnings. Asset turnover is consistently lower when assets include the investment in associates.

The adjustments thus far have isolated the operational aspects of Nestlé's performance and the assets that produced them from non-Nestlé operations. The financial leverage ratio has not been adjusted by the analyst in similar fashion to profit margin and asset turnover. The profit margin and asset turnover components of the DuPont analysis are relatively easy to consider when including or excluding associates: Both the Nestlé assets and the non-Nestlé assets produce a certain pre-tax return. Isolating those assets and their respective returns from each other makes it possible to see the contributions of each to the aggregate performance. It might be tempting to likewise adjust the financial leverage ratio by subtracting the investment in associates from total assets and equity, but the financial leverage component need not be adjusted. The analyst assumes that there will be no change in the Nestlé capital structure and that a similar blend of debt and equity in the company's capital structure finances the investment in associates' assets and the Nestlé-only assets.

From Exhibit 6, multiplying the three conventionally calculated components of ROE (net profit margin, total asset turnover, and leverage) yields the ROE when the effect of associates is included (top row of Exhibit 8). The ROE exhibits an overall increasing trend when examined without adjusting for investment in associates. The analyst wants to compare the ROE for Nestlé alone with the ROE including associates. Calculating the ROE on a Nestlé-only basis is done by multiplying the net profit margin excluding associates by the total asset turnover excluding associates by the financial leverage. For 2014, the Nestlé-only ROE was 11.08% (7.53% × 0.787 × 1.87 = 11.08%).

Exhibit 8 shows the ROE including and excluding the effects of associates. The difference between the two sets of ROE figures reveals the amount of ROE contribution from the associates. The trend in the ROE including associates, which shows a significant increase in 2014, is largely the result of the gains in 2014 from the transactions involving the investments in associates (exchange of L'Oréal shares for complete ownership of Galderma). Nestlé only shows a different trend: decreasing in each of the last two years.

Phases 3 and 4: Adjusting for unusual charges

Exhibit 8: ROE Performance Due to Investment in Associates

	2014 (%)	2013 (%)	2012 (%)
ROE including associates	21.97	16.44	17.67
Less Nestlé-only ROE	11.08	16.02	17.15
Associates' contribution to ROE	10.89	0.42	0.52

The analyst is particularly troubled by the sharp drop-off in the Nestlé-only ROE in 2014. He knows that there was an unusually large goodwill impairment charge in 2014, which may explain the sudden decrease. To see the role played by such unusual charges in the ROE trend, he reworks the Nestlé-only ROE figures on the basis of revised net profit margins (excluding associates and unusual charges) as shown in Exhibit 7. For 2014, the Nestlé-only ROE was 15.63% (10.62% × 0.787 × 1.87 = 15.63%). The results are shown in Exhibit 8.

Exhibit 9: Nestlé-Only ROE, with Unusual Charges Removed from Pre-tax Margins

	2014	2013	2012
Nestlé-only ROE	15.63%	17.73%	18.31%

Absent the unusual charges, the magnitude of the Nestlé-only ROE improved significantly in all three years, but the trend remained on a downward slope. This trend is a genuine concern to the analyst; the investment in associates might provide incremental returns, but he believes the biggest part of the entire entity should be the most significant driver of returns.

Underscoring the significance of the investment in associates—and the deterioration of the Nestlé-only business—is the increasing spread between the as-reported and the Nestlé-only net profit margins in a with- and without-associates comparison (Exhibit 10). The profit margins include all the previously identified unusual charges because the analyst believes that they should not be excluded. They are real costs of doing business and seem to recur; they were actually incurred by the managers, who should be accountable for their stewardship of the shareholders' resources.

Exhibit 10: Net Profit Margin Spread

	2014	2013	2012
Consolidated net profit margin based on as-reported figures	16.27%	11.33%	11.90%
Nestlé-only profit margin	7.53%	9.96%	10.50%
Spread	8.74%	1.37%	1.40%

The analyst decides to focus on learning more about the drivers of Nestlé-only growth and revenues. He makes a note to himself to investigate the valuation aspects of the investment holdings later.

6 PHASES 3 AND 4: ASSET BASE COMPOSITION

☐ demonstrate the use of a framework for the analysis of financial statements, given a particular problem, question, or purpose (e.g., valuing equity based on comparables, critiquing a credit rating, obtaining a comprehensive picture of financial leverage, evaluating the perspectives given in management's discussion of financial results)

Asset Base Composition

The analyst examines the composition of the balance sheet over time, as shown in Exhibit 11.

Exhibit 11: Asset Composition as a Percentage of Total Assets

	2014 (%)	2013 (%)	2012 (%)	2011 (%)
Cash and equivalents	5.6	5.3	4.5	4.2
Short-term investments	1.1	0.5	2.8	2.7
Inventories	6.9	7.0	7.1	8.0
Trade and other receivables	10.1	10.1	10.4	11.5
Other current	1.8	2.0	2.2	2.4
Total current	**25.5**	**24.9**	**27.0**	**28.8**
Property, plant, and equipment, net	21.3	22.3	21.1	20.7
Goodwill	25.9	25.8	26.0	25.2
Intangible assets	14.8	10.5	10.3	7.7
Other non-current	12.5	16.4	15.6	17.7
Total	**100.0**	**99.9***	**100.0**	**100.1***

Does not add to 100% because of rounding.

Although he expected significant investments in current assets, inventory, and physical plant assets—given that Nestlé is a food manufacturer and marketer—he is surprised to see so much investment in intangible assets, indicating that Nestlé's success may depend, in part, on successful acquisitions. Apparently, the company has been actively acquiring companies in the last four years. Goodwill and intangible assets, hallmarks of a growth-by-acquisition strategy, composed 40.7% of total assets in 2014; at the end of 2011, they amounted to 32.9% of total assets. The investing section of the statement of cash flows (Exhibit 12) shows that there have been acquisitions.

Exhibit 12: Nestlé Investing Activities, 2012–2014 (CHF millions)

	Total	2014	2013	2012
Capital expenditure	(14,115)	(3,914)	(4,928)	(5,273)
Expenditure on intangible assets	(1,236)	(509)	(402)	(325)

	Total	2014	2013	2012
Acquisition of businesses	(13,223)	(1,986)	(321)	(10,916)
Disposal of businesses	884	321	421	142
Investments (net of divestments) in associates and joint ventures	3,851	3,958	(28)	(79)
Outflows from non-current treasury investments	(573)	(137)	(244)	(192)
Inflows from non-current treasury investments	4,460	255	2,644	1,561
Inflows/(outflows) from short-term treasury investments	115	(962)	400	677
Other investing activities	668	(98)	852	(86)
Cash flow from investing activities	(19,169)	(3,072)	(1,606)	(14,491)
Acquisitions' percentage of total investing activities	69.0%	64.6%	20.0%	75.3%

Except for a slowdown in acquisitions in 2013, Nestlé had been very active in devoting resources to acquisitions. For the full three-year span, 69.0% of the cash expenditures for investing activities were devoted to acquisitions. The largest single acquisition occurred in 2012, when Nestlé acquired the nutritional business of Wyeth for CHF10,846 million; this acquisition was 74.8% (= 10,846/14,491) of the cash used for investing activities in 2012.

PHASES 3 AND 4: CAPITAL STRUCTURE ANALYSIS

☐ demonstrate the use of a framework for the analysis of financial statements, given a particular problem, question, or purpose (e.g., valuing equity based on comparables, critiquing a credit rating, obtaining a comprehensive picture of financial leverage, evaluating the perspectives given in management's discussion of financial results)

Capital Structure Analysis

From the DuPont analysis, the analyst understands that Nestlé's overall financial leverage was rather stable over the last three years, which does not completely satisfy the analyst's curiosity regarding Nestlé's financing strategies. He knows that one shortcoming of financial leverage as a capital structure metric is that it says nothing about the nature, or riskiness, of the different financing instruments used by a company. For example, the financial burden imposed by bond debt is more onerous and bears more consequences in the event of default than do employee benefit plan obligations.

He decides to investigate Nestlé's capital structure more deeply by constructing a chart on a common-size basis, shown in Exhibit 13. The DuPont analysis indicated that the company's financial leverage remained within a narrow range over the last three years, from a low of 1.87 to a high of 1.98. A look at Exhibit 13, however, shows that Nestlé has been making its capital structure financially riskier over the last four years. Not only is the proportion of equity financing decreasing—from 74.2% in 2011 to 71.5% in 2014—but long-term financial liabilities have become a significantly greater part of the capital mix, increasing to 12.3% in 2014 from 7.8% in 2011. The "other long-term liabilities" (primarily employee benefit plan obligations and provisions) decreased from 17.9% in 2011 to 16.2% in 2014.

Exhibit 13: Percentages of Long-Term Capital Structure

	2014	2013	2012	2011
Long-term financial liabilities	12.3	11.8	10.3	7.8
Other long-term liabilities	16.2	14.9	17.9	17.9
Total equity	71.5	73.3	71.8	74.2
Total long-term capital	100.0	100.0	100.0	99.9*

Does not add to 100% because of rounding.

Given the increased leverage in the long-term capital structure, the analyst wonders whether there have also been changes in the company's working capital accounts. He decides to examine Nestlé's liquidity situation. From the financial statements in Exhibits 2 and 3, he constructs the table shown in Exhibit 14.

Exhibit 14: Nestlé Working Capital Accounts and Ratios, 2011–2014

	2014	2013	2012	2011
Current ratio	1.03	0.91	0.88	0.93
Quick ratio	0.68	0.59	0.58	0.60
Defensive interval ratio*	106.6	91.9	110.0	110.5
Days sales outstanding (DSO)	51.1	50.0	53.0	54.7
Days on hand of inventory (DOH)	67.4	65.7	69.3	70.4
Number of days payables	(126.5)	(117.8)	(108.6)	(105.3)
Cash conversion cycle	(8.0)	(2.1)	13.7	19.8

From Exhibit 2, for 2014: Daily cash expenditure = Expenses – Non-cash items = [Cost of goods sold + Distribution expenses + Marketing and administration expenses + R&D expenses – (Depreciation of PP&E + Amortisation of intangible assets) + Net trading expenses – (Impairment of PP&E and intangible assets) + (Net other operating expenses – Impairment of goodwill) + Net financial expenses]/365 = [47,553 + 8,217 + 19,651 + 1,628 – 3,058 + 797 – 159 + (3,114 – 1,908) + 637]/365 = 209.5. The defensive interval ratio is 22,340/209.5 = 106.6.

The analyst notices that the current and quick ratios improved slightly in 2014, after three years of relative stability. He also notices that the defensive interval ratio improved in 2014 after a significant decrease in 2013 from its prior levels. The improvements were modest; given the increase in long-term leverage, he was expecting more of a liquidity cushion in the working capital accounts. He found the cushion in that the speed of cash generation has been increasing: Since 2011, days' sales outstanding has decreased, as has days on hand of inventory, and the number of days payables has increased. In fact, the management of the working capital accounts has changed so much that Nestlé now has a negative eight days for its cash conversion cycle, mostly attributable to its steadily increasing delay in paying its vendors. In effect, Nestlé has been generating cash from its working capital accounts eight days before applying the cash to accounts payable.

PHASES 3 AND 4: EARNINGS AND CAPITAL

☐ demonstrate the use of a framework for the analysis of financial statements, given a particular problem, question, or purpose (e.g., valuing equity based on comparables, critiquing a credit rating, obtaining a comprehensive picture of financial leverage, evaluating the perspectives given in management's discussion of financial results)

☐ evaluate how a given change in accounting standards, methods, or assumptions affects financial statements and ratios

Segment Analysis and Capital Allocation

The DuPont analysis showed the declining profitability of Nestlé in its core operations, leading the analyst to subsequently learn more about the composition of the assets and to study the company's financing. He knows that asset turnover has been slowing at Nestlé and that the company has been looking to acquisitions for growth. But he still wonders about the health of the different businesses under the Nestlé umbrella and how effectively management has allocated capital to them. DuPont analysis does not provide answers to these kinds of questions, and he knows there is more information in the financial statements that might shed light on how management allocates capital internally as opposed to making acquisitions.

To understand any geopolitical investment risks, as well as the economies in which Nestlé operates, the analyst wants to know which geographic areas are of the greatest importance to the company. One issue the analyst identifies is that Nestlé reports segment information by management responsibility and geographic area (hereafter referred to as "segment"), not by segments based exclusively on geographic areas. From the segment information in Exhibit 15, he notes that the sales and operating profit of the European segment decreased in absolute terms and as a percentage of total business in 2014 compared with 2012. The decrease in profits has been consistent over the period. The sales of the Americas segment have also become a smaller contributor to the whole company's revenue base in the same period and, like the European segment, have decreased slightly since 2012. The Americas operating profit has decreased consistently since 2012, and like the European segment, the Americas contribution to total operating profit in 2014 is a smaller proportion than in 2012. The Asia, Oceania, and Africa segment repeated the pattern: lower sales and operating profit, with a decrease in both measures in each of the two years following 2012. The smallest segment, Nestlé Waters, was not a true geographic segment. It showed minor growth in revenues and operating profit between 2012 and 2014 and contributed essentially the same proportion of sales and operating profit in 2014 as it did in 2012. Nestlé Nutrition grew significantly during the period: It contributed 10.5% of revenues in 2014 (only 8.8% in 2012), and its operating profit contributed 14.2% of revenues in 2014 compared with 11.2% in 2012. The analyst remembers that Nestlé acquired the Wyeth Nutritionals business in 2012, which would explain the solid growth. "Other businesses," which is a collectively large group of disparate businesses, also increased in importance between 2012 and 2014, accounting for 15.2% of sales in 2014 (13.2% in 2012) and 18.9% of operating profit (15.3% in 2012). Both measures (sales and operating profit) grew in 2014, and the analyst attributes that growth to Nestlé's gaining full control of Galderma in 2014.

Exhibit 15: Sales and EBIT by Segment (CHF millions)

Sales	2014 Amount	2014 % Total	2013 Amount	2013 % Total	2012 Amount	2012 % Total	Y-o-Y % Change 2014	Y-o-Y % Change 2013
Europe	15,175	16.6	15,567	16.9	15,388	17.2	−2.5	1.2
Americas	27,277	29.8	28,358	30.8	28,613	31.9	−3.8	−0.9
Asia, Oceania, and Africa	18,272	19.9	18,851	20.5	18,875	21.0	−3.1	−0.1
Nestlé Waters	7,390	8.1	7,257	7.9	7,174	8.0	1.8	1.2
Nestlé Nutrition	9,614	10.5	9,826	10.7	7,858	8.8	−2.2	25.0
Other businesses[a]	13,884	15.2	12,299	13.3	11,813	13.2	12.9	4.1
	91,612	100.0	92,158	100.0	89,721	100.0		

Trading operating profit	2014 Amount	2014 % Total	2013 Amount	2013 % Total	2012 Amount	2012 % Total	Y-o-Y % Change 2014	Y-o-Y % Change 2013
Europe	2,327	16.6	2,331	16.6	2,363	17.6	−0.2	−1.4
Americas	5,117	36.5	5,162	36.7	5,346	39.7	−0.9	−3.4
Asia, Oceania, and Africa	3,408	24.3	3,562	25.4	3,579	26.6	−4.3	−0.5
Nestlé Waters	714	5.1	665	4.7	640	4.8	7.4	3.9
Nestlé Nutrition	1,997	14.2	1,961	14.0	1,509	11.2	1.8	30.0
Other businesses[a]	2,654	18.9	2,175	15.5	2,064	15.3	22.0	5.4
Unallocated items	(2,198)	−15.7	(1,809)	−12.9	(2,037)	−15.1	21.5	−11.2
	14,019	100.0	14,047	100.0	13,464	100.0		

[a] Group mainly includes Nespresso, Nestlé Professional, Nestlé Health Science, and Nestlé Skin Health.

For several reasons, the analyst is somewhat frustrated by the segment information presented by Nestlé. He would like to look at trends over more than just three years, but the change in accounting principles in 2013 (for IFRS 11) was not carried back in the segment information prior to 2012. That accounting change eliminated the proportional consolidation method of accounting for joint ventures and made the 2011 segment information non-comparable with the figures presented for 2012 and later. The earlier amounts included proportional amounts of sales and operating profits for the segments, and a comparison with later years would be flawed.

Another problem with the segment information is that it is not defined by category with fully geographic information or product information. The analyst notes that three geographically classified segments accounted for 66.3% of revenues in 2014 and 70.1% in 2012; the operating profit for the same three segments amounted to 77.4% in 2014 and 83.9% in 2012. Thus, these segments are declining in importance to Nestlé as a whole, whereas Nestlé Waters and Other businesses are increasing in size and importance. Yet, it would seem likely that both of these segments have geographically different operations as well, which are not being accounted for in the other three geographic segments. These segments are growing in relevance, and more information about them would be useful. For instance, the Other businesses segment includes a coffee product line, professional products, health care products, and skin care products. Together, they amount to almost 19% of operating profit, yet they seem unlikely to have similar distribution channels, profitability levels, and growth potential.

PHASES 3 AND 4: CASH FLOW AND CAPITAL

- [ ] demonstrate the use of a framework for the analysis of financial statements, given a particular problem, question, or purpose (e.g., valuing equity based on comparables, critiquing a credit rating, obtaining a comprehensive picture of financial leverage, evaluating the perspectives given in management's discussion of financial results)
- [ ] analyze and interpret how balance sheet modifications, earnings normalization, and cash flow statement related modifications affect a company's financial statements, financial ratios, and overall financial condition

The segment information is presented on the basis that management uses to make decisions. The analyst moves on with his segment analysis and evaluation of capital allocation, gathering the segment information shown in Exhibit 16 regarding Nestlé's capital expenditures and assets.

Exhibit 16: Asset and Capital Expenditure Segment Information (CHF millions)

	Assets*			Capital Expenditures		
	2014	2013	2012	2014	2013	2012
Europe	11,308	11,779	11,804	747	964	1,019
Americas	20,915	21,243	22,485	1,039	1,019	1,073
Asia, Oceania, and Africa	15,095	14,165	14,329	697	1,280	1,564
Nestlé Waters	6,202	6,046	6,369	308	377	407
Nestlé Nutrition	24,448	22,517	24,279	363	430	426
Other businesses[a]	21,345	9,564	9,081	573	642	550
	99,313	85,314	88,347	3,727	4,712	5,039

* Assets do not equal total assets on the balance sheet because of inter-segment assets and non-segment assets.
[a] *Group mainly includes Nespresso, Nestlé Professional, Nestlé Health Science, and Nestlé Skin Health.*

Using the information from Exhibit 14 to calculate EBIT margins, as well as the information about the asset and capital expenditure distribution from Exhibit 16, the analyst constructs the table in Exhibit 17, ranking by descending order of EBIT profitability in 2014.

Exhibit 17: EBIT Margin, Asset, and Capital Expenditure Proportions by Segment

	EBIT Margin %			% of Total Assets			% of Total Capital Expenditures		
	2014	2013	2012	2014	2013	2012	2014	2013	2012
Nestlé Nutrition	20.77	19.96	19.20	24.6	26.4	27.5	9.7	9.1	8.5
Other businesses[a]	19.12	17.68	17.47	21.5	11.2	10.3	15.4	13.6	10.9
Americas	18.76	18.20	18.68	21.1	24.9	25.5	27.9	21.6	21.3
Asia, Oceania, and Africa	18.65	18.90	18.96	15.2	16.6	16.2	18.7	27.2	31.0
Europe	15.33	14.97	15.36	11.4	13.8	13.4	20.0	20.5	20.2
Nestlé Waters	9.66	9.16	8.92	6.2	7.1	7.2	8.3	8.0	8.1
				100.0	100.0	100.1*	100.0	100.0	100.0

*Does not add to 100% because of rounding.
[a] Group mainly includes Nespresso, Nestlé Professional, Nestlé Health Science, and Nestlé Skin Health.

Although the segmentation is not purely geographic, the analyst can still make some judgments about the allocation of capital. On the premise that the largest investments in assets require a similar proportion of capital expenditures, he calculates ratios of the capital expenditure proportion to the total asset proportion for the last three years and compares them with the current EBIT profitability ranking. The resulting table is shown in Exhibit 18.

Exhibit 18: Ratio of Capital Expenditure Percentage to Total Asset Percentage Ranked by EBIT Margin

	EBIT Margin %	Ratio of Total Capital Expenditure % to Total Asset %		
	2014	2014	2013	2012
Nestlé Nutrition	20.77	0.39	0.34	0.31
Other businesses[a]	19.12	0.72	**1.21**	**1.06**
Americas	18.76	**1.32**	0.87	0.84
Asia, Oceania, and Africa	18.65	**1.23**	**1.64**	**1.91**
Europe	15.33	**1.75**	**1.49**	**1.51**
Nestlé Waters	9.66	**1.34**	**1.13**	**1.13**

[a] Group mainly includes Nespresso, Nestlé Professional, Nestlé Health Science, and Nestlé Skin Health.

A ratio of 1 indicates that the segment's proportion of capital expenditures is the same as its proportion of total assets. A ratio of *less than* 1 indicates that the segment is being allocated a lesser proportion of capital expenditures than its proportion of total assets; if a trend develops, the segment will become less significant over time. A ratio of *greater than* 1 indicates the company is growing the segment; the segment is receiving a "growth allocation" of capital spending. Comparing the ratio with the EBIT margin percentage gives the analyst an idea of whether the company is investing its capital in the most profitable segments. (In Exhibit 18, the ratios greater than 1 are bolded for ease of viewing.)

Equipped with these premises, the analyst is puzzled by the capital allocation taking place within Nestlé. The most profitable segment is Nestlé Nutrition, but over the last three years, it has received the lowest proportion of capital expenditures. The company has invested in the nutrition segment by acquisition, such as the Wyeth Nutritionals business in 2012. One would expect that a more substantial operation would require more capital expenditures on maintenance. The capital expenditures for the nutrition segment have increased only nominally since 2012.

The Other businesses segment is the next most profitable segment in EBIT margin terms. The analyst has difficulty understanding just why the profit margins are high in this segment because of the variety of businesses it contains. It appears that the company's managers are allocating capital to it in a significant way. Although it did not receive a "growth allocation" of capital expenditures in 2014, it received a growth allocation in the previous two years. The Americas segment and the Asia, Oceania, and Africa segment have similar EBIT margins, which are in the same range as those of the Nestlé Nutrition and Other businesses segments. Given their profitability levels and substantial operations, the analyst is encouraged to see that they are receiving "growth allocations" of capital spending.

Less encouraging, however, is the past and continuing significant allocation of capital spending to the European segment. Even more questionable is the high proportional allocation of capital spending to the Nestlé Waters segment, which has had the lowest profit margins. The analyst is uncomfortable with growth investments in such a low-return business but notes that the absolute levels of capital expenditures are the lowest of all the segments in each year.

In a worst-case scenario, if the company were to continue making growth allocations of capital toward the lowest-margined businesses, such as Europe and Nestlé Waters, the overall Nestlé-only returns might be affected negatively. As a result, Nestlé might become more dependent on its investment in associates to sustain performance.

The analyst knows that accrual performance measures, such as EBIT, can produce results that do not indicate an entity's ability to generate cash flow, and he wonders whether this limitation has any effect on Nestlé management's capital allocation decisions. He also knows that at the segment level, cash flow information is not publicly available. He decides to at least approximate cash flow by adding depreciation expense to operating profit and then relate the approximated cash flow to the average total assets of each segment. This approach provides an approximation of cash return relative to the continued investment in a particular segment.

The analyst combines the segment operating profit from Exhibit 14 and the segment depreciation and amortisation in Exhibit 19 to estimate the segment cash generation shown in Exhibit 19. Because he wants to eliminate the effects of any investment peaks or valleys, he also averages the total assets for each segment in Exhibit 19. The average total assets in 2012 include the 2011 total assets that were prepared on a pre–IFRS 11 basis, for which no adjustment is available. The analyst is aware of the irreconcilable difference but believes that the averaging of the two years' amounts will help dilute the difference. He notes that if any resulting measures based on 2011 data points appear to be outliers, he will dismiss them.

Exhibit 19: Segment Depreciation and Amortisation, Segment Cash Generation, and Average Assets (CHF millions)

	Depreciation and Amortisation			Segment Cash Generation			Average Total Assets*		
	2014	2013	2012	2014	2013	2012	2014	2013	2012
Europe	473	517	533	2,800	2,848	2,896	11,544	11,792	11,683
Americas	681	769	899	5,798	5,931	6,245	21,079	21,864	22,783
Asia, Oceania, and Africa	510	520	553	3,918	4,082	4,132	14,630	14,247	14,068
Nestlé Waters	403	442	491	1,117	1,107	1,131	6,124	6,208	6,486
Nestlé Nutrition	330	337	176	2,327	2,298	1,685	23,483	23,398	18,564
Other businesses[a]	525	437	295	3,179	2,612	2,359	15,455	9,323	10,009

* Average of total assets at beginning and end of the year.
[a] Group mainly includes Nespresso, Nestlé Professional, Nestlé Health Science, and Nestlé Skin Health.

In Exhibit 20, the analyst computes each segment's cash operating return on total assets and compares the results with the 2014 ranking of capital expenditures (Exhibit 18) as well as the EBIT margins. They are ranked in descending order of the ratio of capital expenditure percentage to percentage of total assets. The lighter shading indicates the highest EBIT margin and cash return on assets for each year, and the darker shading indicates the lowest EBIT margin and cash return on assets for each year.

Exhibit 20: Segment Cash Operating Return on Assets

	2014		Segment Cash Return on Average Total Assets		
	Capex %/ Asset %	EBIT %	2014 (%)	2013 (%)	2012 (%)
Europe	1.75	15.3	24.3	24.2	24.8
Nestlé Waters	1.34	9.7	18.2	17.8	17.4
Americas	1.32	18.8	27.5	27.1	27.4
Asia, Oceania, and Africa	1.23	18.7	26.8	28.7	29.4
Other businesses[a]	0.72	19.1	20.6	28.0	23.6
Nestlé Nutrition	0.39	20.8	9.9	9.8	9.1

[a] Group mainly includes Nespresso, Nestlé Professional, Nestlé Health Science, and Nestlé Skin Health.

PHASES 3 & 4: SEGMENT ANALYSIS BY PRODUCT GROUP

> ☐ demonstrate the use of a framework for the analysis of financial statements, given a particular problem, question, or purpose (e.g., valuing equity based on comparables, critiquing a credit rating, obtaining a comprehensive picture of financial leverage, evaluating the perspectives given in management's discussion of financial results)

The analyst is surprised to see that the Nestlé Nutrition segment, which has the highest EBIT profit margin, consistently has the lowest cash return on total assets. When he looks at the segments with respect to EBIT margins, he is disappointed with the allocation of capital spending to Nestlé Nutrition, thinking that it is too low. When he looks at it using the cash return on total assets measure, the low allocation of spending makes much more sense. He is pleased to see that the segments with the highest cash return on total assets each year—the Americas and the Asia, Oceania, and Africa segments—are receiving growth allocations of capital spending. He is also encouraged that the European segment, though a poor performer with respect to EBIT margin, has cash returns on total assets that are competitive with the other segments and far ahead of Nestlé Waters and Nestlé Nutrition. Even Nestlé Waters, which had not appeared very attractive with respect to EBIT margin, is generating strong cash returns on total assets. The exercise restores the analyst's confidence that management is allocating capital in a rational manner. It makes sense to him that if management makes capital budgeting decisions on a cash flow basis, they should be evaluated on a cash flow basis also.

He decides to look at Nestlé's capital allocation process from a product group standpoint. The sales and EBIT information is shown in Exhibit 21. From the table, he notes that the Nutrition and Health Science product group is the only one with significant growth in either sales or EBIT, and that is the segment in which the company has been making its acquisitions in the last few years. He also notes that the EBIT margin for the Nutrition and Health Science product group has increased in each of the last two years, and although it is among the highest over the last three years, the Powdered and Liquid Beverages product group has consistently shown higher EBIT margins. The Powdered and Liquid Beverages product group EBIT margins far exceed the lowest-ranking EBIT margins of the Water product group.

Exhibit 21: Sales and EBIT Segment Information by Product Group (CHF millions)

	2014	% Total	2013	% Total	2012	% Total	Year-to-Year % Change 2014	2013
Sales								
Powdered and Liquid Beverages	20,302	22.2	20,495	22.2	20,248	22.6	−0.9	1.2
Water	6,875	7.5	6,773	7.3	6,747	7.5	1.5	0.4
Milk Products and Ice Cream	16,743	18.3	17,357	18.8	17,344	19.3	−3.5	0.1

	2014	% Total	2013	% Total	2012	% Total	Year-to-Year % Change 2014	2013
Sales								
Nutrition and Health Science	13,046	14.2	11,840	12.8	9,737	10.9	10.2	21.6
Prepared Dishes and Cooking Aids	13,538	14.8	14,171	15.4	14,394	16.0	−4.5	−1.5
Confectionery	9,769	10.7	10,283	11.2	10,441	11.6	−5.0	−1.5
Pet Care	11,339	12.4	11,239	12.2	10,810	12.0	0.9	4.0
	91,612	100.0	92,158	100.0	89,721	100.0		
EBIT								
Powdered and Liquid Beverages	4,685	33.4	4,649	33.1	4,445	33.0	0.8	4.6
Water	710	5.1	678	4.8	636	4.7	4.7	6.6
Milk Products and Ice Cream	2,701	19.3	2,632	18.7	2,704	20.1	2.6	−2.7
Nutrition and Health Science	2,723	19.4	2,228	15.9	1,778	13.2	22.2	25.3
Prepared Dishes and Cooking Aids	1,808	12.9	1,876	13.4	2,029	15.1	−3.6	−7.5
Confectionery	1,344	9.6	1,630	11.6	1,765	13.1	−17.5	−7.6
Pet Care	2,246	16.0	2,163	15.4	2,144	15.9	3.8	0.9
Unallocated items	(2,198)	−15.7	(1,809)	−12.9	(2,037)	−15.1	21.5	−11.2
	14,019	100.0	14,047	100.0	13,464	100.0		

EBIT margin	2014	2013	2012
Powdered and Liquid Beverages	23.1%	22.7%	22.0%
Water	10.3%	10.0%	9.4%
Milk Products and Ice Cream	16.1%	15.2%	15.6%
Nutrition and Health Science	20.9%	18.8%	18.3%
Prepared Dishes and Cooking Aids	13.4%	13.2%	14.1%
Confectionery	13.8%	15.9%	16.9%
Pet Care	19.8%	19.2%	19.8%
Total	15.3%	15.2%	15.0%

Unfortunately for purposes of his analysis, Nestlé does not provide capital expenditure information by product group. Compared with the segment analysis he performed, the analyst's scope is more limited in examining product groups. All that can be done is to look at the return on assets with respect to EBIT rather than on a cash-generated basis. Nevertheless, the analyst decides to work with all the available information. To further examine capital allocation decisions, he gathers the asset information by product group from the financial statements, as shown in Exhibit 22. The reported

Phases 3 & 4: Segment Analysis by Product Group

total assets differ by segment and product group presentation because Nestlé reports its assets on an *average* basis for product groups and on a *year-end* basis for segments. A significant amount of assets is unallocated to segments, but there is no unallocated amount by product group. He calculates the EBIT return on assets as EBIT divided by average assets and determines the proportion of total average assets devoted to each product group. The highest EBIT percentage, EBIT return on assets, and percentage of total assets each year are lightly shaded, and the lowest are shaded darker.

Exhibit 22: Asset Segment Information by Product Group (CHF millions)

	Average Assets 2014	Average Assets 2013	Average Assets 2012	EBIT % 2014	EBIT Return on Assets 2014	EBIT Return on Assets 2013	EBIT Return on Assets 2012	% Total Assets 2014	% Total Assets 2013	% Total Assets 2012
Powdered and Liquid Beverages	11,599	11,044	10,844	23.1%	40.4%	42.1%	41.0%	11.6%	11.5%	12.4%
Water	5,928	6,209	6,442	10.3%	12.0%	10.9%	9.9%	6.0%	6.4%	7.4%
Milk Products and Ice Cream	14,387	14,805	14,995	16.1%	18.8%	17.8%	18.0%	14.4%	15.4%	17.1%
Nutrition and Health Science	32,245	28,699	19,469	20.9%	8.4%	7.8%	9.1%	32.4%	29.8%	22.2%
Prepared Dishes and Cooking Aids	13,220	13,289	13,479	13.4%	13.7%	14.1%	15.1%	13.3%	13.8%	15.4%
Confectionery	7,860	8,190	8,343	13.8%	17.1%	19.9%	21.2%	7.9%	8.5%	9.5%
Pet Care	14,344	14,064	13,996	19.8%	15.7%	15.4%	15.3%	14.4%	14.6%	16.0%
	99,583	96,300	87,568	15.3%	14.1%	14.6%	15.4%	100.0%	100.0%	100.0%

The analyst uses this information to make some important observations:

- The Nutrition and Health Science product group—which the company has been investing in over the last several years—has the lowest EBIT return on assets in each of the last three years and makes up the greatest portion of total assets.
- The EBIT return on assets for the Nutrition and Health Science product group is even lower than that of the Water product group, which has the lowest EBIT margin.
- The Nutrition and Health Science product group's EBIT return on assets is well below the total company's EBIT return on assets (8.4% versus 14.1% in 2014, 7.8% versus 14.6% in 2013, and 9.1% versus 15.4% in 2012).
- The Nutrition and Health Science product group drags down the overall return in each year as it becomes a bigger part of the whole.
- The EBIT return on assets is highest for the Powdered and Liquid Beverages product group, possibly because it might not need much in the way of assets or capital spending: It is one of the lesser components of total assets. Furthermore, it has the highest EBIT margin of all the product groups. Given the high EBIT margin, the high EBIT return on assets, and the low dedication of total assets, the analyst wonders whether the company is allocating capital among its product offerings effectively. It would make sense to devote as many resources as possible to where returns are best.
- He also wonders about management's capital allocation skills regarding acquisitions. The EBIT return on assets in the Nutrition and Health Science product group is weak, and the company has been making acquisitions in

that group. He finds it troubling that Nestlé took a goodwill impairment charge of CHF1,908 million in 2014—something directly related to management's skill in making past acquisitions.

11. PHASES 3 & 4: ACCRUALS AND EARNINGS QUALITY

☐ demonstrate the use of a framework for the analysis of financial statements, given a particular problem, question, or purpose (e.g., valuing equity based on comparables, critiquing a credit rating, obtaining a comprehensive picture of financial leverage, evaluating the perspectives given in management's discussion of financial results)

☐ identify financial reporting choices and biases that affect the quality and comparability of companies' financial statements and explain how such biases may affect financial decisions

☐ evaluate the quality of a company's financial data and recommend appropriate adjustments to improve quality and comparability with similar companies, including adjustments for differences in accounting standards, methods, and assumptions

At this point, the information reviewed by the analyst has not increased his enthusiasm for Nestlé's operating and capital allocation prowess. He considers a worst-case possibility: Could the company try to make up for weak operating performance by manipulating accounting inputs? He makes it a point to understand whether accruals play a role in the company's performance.

He decides to examine the balance-sheet-based accruals and the cash-flow-based accruals over the last few years. From the Nestlé financial statements, he assembles the information and intermediate calculations shown in Exhibit 23.

Exhibit 23: Selected Information from Balance Sheet and Statement of Cash Flows (CHF millions)

	2014	2013	2012	2011
Balance Sheet Accrual Info:				
Total assets	133,450	120,442	125,877	113,440
Cash and short-term investments	8,881	7,053	9,296	7,782
Operating assets (A)	124,569	113,389	116,581	105,658
Total liabilities	61,566	56,303	63,213	55,098
Long-term debt	12,396	10,363	9,008	6,165
Debt in current liabilities	8,810	11,380	18,408	15,945
Operating liabilities (B)	40,360	34,560	35,797	32,988
Net operating assets (NOA) [(A) − (B)]	84,209	78,829	80,784	72,670
Balance-sheet-based aggregate accruals (year-to-year change in NOA)	5,380	(1,955)	8,114	6,218
Average NOA	81,519	79,807	76,727	69,561
Statement of Cash Flows Accrual Info:				

Phases 3 & 4: Accruals and Earnings Quality

	2014	2013	2012	2011
Profit from continuing operations	14,904	10,445	10,677	
Operating cash flow	(14,700)	(14,992)	(15,668)	
Investing cash flow	3,072	1,606	14,491	
Cash-flow-based aggregate accruals	3,276	(2,941)	9,500	

The analyst calculates the balance-sheet-based and cash-flow-based accruals ratios, which are measures of financial reporting quality.[4] The ratios are calculated as follows:

Balance sheet accruals ratio for time t
= $(NOA_t - NOA_{t-1})/[(NOA_t + NOA_{t-1})/2]$, and

Cash flow accruals ratio for time $t = [NI_t - (CFO_t + CFI_t)]/[(NOA_t + NOA_{t-1})/2]$,

where NI is net income, CFO is cash flow from operations, and CFI is cash flow from investing.

The accruals ratios for the last three years are shown in Exhibit 24.

Exhibit 24: Accruals Ratios (CHF millions)

	2014	2013	2012
Balance-sheet-based aggregate accruals (year-to-year change in NOA)	5,380	(1,955)	8,114
Divided by: Average NOA	81,519	79,807	76,727
Balance-sheet-based accruals ratio	6.6%	−2.4%	10.6%
Cash-flow-based aggregate accruals	3,276	(2,941)	9,500
Divided by: Average NOA	81,519	79,807	76,727
Cash-flow-based accruals ratio	4.0%	−3.7%	12.4%

The analyst notes that the absolute level of accruals on the balance sheet is minor relative to the size of the operating assets, on either an ending balance basis or an average basis. Similarly, the fluctuation in the balance-sheet-based accruals ratio is low. The analyst would have been more concerned if the absolute levels of the accruals ratio were high; even more worrisome would have been if they were consistently trending higher. That was not the case. The cash-flow-based accruals ratio exhibits a similar pattern. For the most recent two years, both ratios are lower than in 2012 and indicate that accruals are not a large factor in the financial results. The analyst still decides to examine the quality of Nestlé's cash flow and its relationship to net income.

---

4 If you are interested in subcomponents of accrual activity, simply focus on the relevant line item from the balance sheet. For example, looking at the change in net receivables over a fiscal period deflated by average NOA will give you a sense of the magnitude of accrued revenue attributable to net credit sales.

12. PHASES 3 & 4: CASH FLOW RELATIONSHIPS

☐ demonstrate the use of a framework for the analysis of financial statements, given a particular problem, question, or purpose (e.g., valuing equity based on comparables, critiquing a credit rating, obtaining a comprehensive picture of financial leverage, evaluating the perspectives given in management's discussion of financial results)

☐ analyze and interpret how balance sheet modifications, earnings normalization, and cash flow statement related modifications affect a company's financial statements, financial ratios, and overall financial condition

He begins his analysis with the compilation of Nestlé's statements of cash flows shown in Exhibit 25.

Exhibit 25: Nestlé's Statement of Cash Flows, 2012–2014 (CHF millions)

	2014	2013	2012
Operating activities			
Operating profit	10,905	13,068	13,388
Non-cash items of income and expense	6,323	4,352	3,217
Cash flow before changes in operating assets and liabilities	17,228	17,420	16,605
Decrease/(increase) in working capital	(114)	1,360	2,015
Variation of other operating assets and liabilities	85	(574)	(95)
Cash generated from operations	17,199	18,206	18,525
Net cash flows from treasury activities	(356)	(351)	(324)
Taxes paid	(2,859)	(3,520)	(3,118)
Dividends and interest from associates and joint ventures	716	657	585
Operating cash flow	**14,700**	**14,992**	**15,668**
Investing activities			
Capital expenditure	(3,914)	(4,928)	(5,273)
Expenditure on intangible assets	(509)	(402)	(325)
Acquisition of businesses	(1,986)	(321)	(10,916)
Disposal of businesses	321	421	142
Investments (net of divestments) in associates and joint ventures	3,958	(28)	(79)
Outflows from non-current treasury investments	(137)	(244)	(192)
Inflows from non-current treasury investments	255	2,644	1,561
Inflows/(outflows) from short-term treasury investments	(962)	400	677
Other investing activities	(98)	852	(86)
Cash flow from investing activities	**(3,072)**	**(1,606)**	**(14,491)**
Financing activities			
Dividends paid to shareholders of the parent	(6,863)	(6,552)	(6,213)
Dividends paid to non-controlling interests	(356)	(328)	(204)
Acquisition (net of disposal) of non-controlling interests	(49)	(337)	(165)

Phases 3 & 4: Cash Flow Relationships

	2014	2013	2012
Purchase of treasury shares	(1,721)	(481)	(532)
Sale of treasury shares	104	60	1,199
Inflows from bonds and other non-current financial debt	2,202	3,814	5,226
Outflows from bonds and other non-current financial debt	(1,969)	(2,271)	(1,650)
Inflows/(outflows) from current financial debt	(1,985)	(6,063)	2,325
Cash flow from financing activities	**(10,637)**	**(12,158)**	**(14)**
Currency retranslations	42	(526)	(219)
Increase/(decrease) in cash and cash equivalents	**1,033**	**702**	**944**
Cash and cash equivalents at beginning of year	**6,415**	**5,713**	**4,769**
Cash and cash equivalents at end of year	**7,448**	**6,415**	**5,713**

The analyst's most pressing concerns include the following: Are Nestlé's operating earnings backed by cash flow? Are the accrual measures telling the whole story? Are the operating earnings the result of accounting choices? To convince himself of the representativeness of the Nestlé earnings, he first compares the cash generated by operations with the operating profit as shown in Exhibit 26. The amounts in Exhibit 26 are found in the cash flow statements in Exhibit 25.

Exhibit 26: Operating Cash Flow to Operating Profit, 2012–2014 (CHF millions)

	2014	2013	2012
Cash generated from operations	17,199	18,206	18,525
Operating profit	10,905	13,068	13,388
Cash generated from operations/Operating profit	1.58	1.39	1.38

The cash generated from operations is comparable to accrual basis operating income *but on a cash flow basis*. If the cash flow generated by operations was significantly or consistently less than operating profit, one would have reason to be suspicious about the quality of the operating profit. The analyst is encouraged by the fact that the cash generated from operations substantially exceeded the operating profit in each of the last three years.

Knowing that Nestlé has made a number of acquisitions, the analyst decides to examine the relationship between operating cash flow and total assets. *Cash flow* is a measure of the operational success of the company's investment projects: Successful investments generate cash rather than absorbing it. *Total assets* reflect the sum total of management's resource allocations over time. Cash generated by total assets indicates the kind of cash return that is generated by all investments. The relationship is shown in Exhibit 27.

Exhibit 27: Ratio of Operating Cash Flow to Total Assets, 2012–2014 (CHF millions)

	2014	2013	2012
Cash generated from operations	17,199	18,206	18,525

	2014	2013	2012
Average total assets	126,946	123,160	119,659
Cash return on total assets	13.5%	14.8%	15.5%

Again, the analyst finds himself concerned about the effectiveness of management's asset allocation decisions. Although the 13.5% cash return on total assets is a high return on investment, the trend is declining. The analyst thinks back to the 2014 goodwill impairment and the poor EBIT return on assets in the Nutrition and Health Science product group, in which acquisitions have been occurring lately.

Given the negative trend in asset returns, the analyst looks at Nestlé's liquidity and funding ability relative to cash flow. He decides to compare cash flow with reinvestment, debt, and debt-servicing capacity, as shown in Exhibit 28.

The analyst sees that reinvestment needs have been covered by cash flow by a factor of 3.89 in 2014, 3.42 in 2013, and 3.31 in 2012. Even better, the trend is improving.

He also sees that based on the relationship of cash flow to total debt, the company is not highly leveraged, with cash generated from operations at 78.3% of total debt at the end of 2014. The ratio is high enough to indicate that additional borrowing could be arranged should an investment opportunity arise. Furthermore, the analyst notes that Nestlé has the capacity to pay off its debt in approximately two years even while maintaining its current reinvestment policy [21,963/(17,199 − 4,423)].

Finally, the cash flow interest coverage ratio indicates more than satisfactory financial strength in the current year, with cash flow 33.2 times the interest paid. Like the ratio of cash flow to total debt, it indicates that the company has sufficient financial capacity to add more debt if there is an investment opportunity.

Exhibit 28: Ratio of Operating Cash Flow to Reinvestment, Debt, and Debt-Servicing Capacity, 2012–2014 (CHF millions)

	2014	2013	2012
*Cash flow to reinvestment:**			
Cash generated from operations	17,199	18,206	18,525
Capital expenditures	3,914	4,928	5,273
Expenditure on intangible assets	509	402	325
Total reinvestment spending	4,423	5,330	5,598
Ratio of cash flow to reinvestment	**3.89**	**3.42**	**3.31**
Cash flow to total debt:			
Cash generated from operations	17,199	18,206	18,525
Current debt (short-term financial liabilities)	8,810	11,380	18,408
Current derivative liabilities	757	381	423
Long-term debt (long-term financial liabilities)	12,396	10,363	9,008
Total debt	21,963	22,124	27,839
Ratio of cash flow to total debt	**78.3%**	**82.3%**	**66.5%**
Cash flow interest coverage:			
Cash generated from operations	17,199	18,206	18,525
Cash interest paid	518	505	559
Cash flow interest coverage	**33.2**	**36.1**	**33.1**

*Information is from Exhibit 25.

PHASES 3 & 4: DECOMPOSITION AND ANALYSIS OF THE COMPANY'S VALUATION

☐ demonstrate the use of a framework for the analysis of financial statements, given a particular problem, question, or purpose (e.g., valuing equity based on comparables, critiquing a credit rating, obtaining a comprehensive picture of financial leverage, evaluating the perspectives given in management's discussion of financial results)

☐ evaluate the quality of a company's financial data and recommend appropriate adjustments to improve quality and comparability with similar companies, including adjustments for differences in accounting standards, methods, and assumptions

At this point, the analyst believes he has obtained sufficient information about the company's sources of earnings and returns on shareholders' equity, its capital structure, the results of its capital allocation decisions, and its earnings quality. Before he makes his report to the portfolio manager, he wants to study the company's market valuation. During his reading of the annual reports, he noted that Nestlé has a significant equity position (23.4%) in L'Oréal (Paris exchange: OR), a French cosmetics company. L'Oréal is accounted for in the financial statements as an investment in associates because Nestlé's ownership position does not give it control. Although L'Oréal contributes to the earnings of Nestlé as a whole, it is also valued separately in the public markets, and its discrete valuations may be very different from its embedded Nestlé valuation. To determine the value that the market places solely on Nestlé operations, the analyst first removes the value of the L'Oréal holding from the Nestlé market value, as shown in Exhibit 29.

Exhibit 29: Nestlé Market Value without L'Oréal as of 31 December 2014 (Currency in millions, except share prices)

L'Oréal value:

31 Dec 2014 share price	€139.30
Shares held by Nestlé (millions)	129.881
L'Oréal holding value	€18,092
31 Dec CHF/EUR rate	1.202
L'Oréal holding value	CHF21,747

Nestlé market value, with and without L'Oréal:

Nestlé 29 Dec 2014 share price	CHF72.95
Shares outstanding (millions)	3,168.400
Nestlé market capitalization	CHF231,135
Value of L'Oréal holding	(21,747)
Implied value of Nestlé operations	CHF209,388

Pro rata market value:

L'Oréal	9.4%

Nestlé	90.6%
	100.0%

The value of the L'Oréal holding is slightly less than 10% of the value of Nestlé's market capitalization. The analyst now wants to remove the earnings of L'Oréal from the earnings of the combined entity (Exhibit 30) to make a price-to-earnings comparison for Nestlé earnings alone. For L'Oréal, this comparison is simple: Nestlé discloses in its annual report that L'Oréal has contributed CHF934 million to current year earnings. After isolating the different earnings sources, the analyst prepares the table shown in Exhibit 31, which compares the different market values and price-to-earnings ratios.

Exhibit 30: Calculation of Nestlé Earnings without L'Oréal as of 31 December 2014 (CHF millions)

Calculation of Nestlé standalone earnings:	2014
Nestlé consolidated earnings	14,904
Less: L'Oréal earnings	(934)
Nestlé standalone earnings	13,970
Less: Non-controlling interests	(448)
Nestlé standalone earnings to shareholders	13,522

At the time of the analysis (early 2015), Nestlé's common stock traded at a price-to-earnings multiple of 16.0 based on its year-end market value of CHF231,135 million and trailing earnings (attributable to controlling interests) of CHF14,456 million: a discount of 20% to the price-to-earnings multiple of 19.9 for the S&P 500 Index at year-end 2014. Once the earnings and available market value of the L'Oréal holding are taken out of the price-to-earnings valuation, the shares of the "Nestlé-only" company are selling at a slightly higher discount: At 15.5 times earnings, the discount to the overall market's price-to-earnings multiple was a steeper 22%. At first, the analyst is surprised by Nestlé's discount to the market multiple, given that the company has consistently demonstrated meaningful cash flows and earnings and possesses low financial leverage. He considers whether the discount might be attributable to Nestlé's slipping core profitability. The analyst concludes that Nestlé shares may be discounted by the market because investors may be developing a skeptical attitude toward the company.

Exhibit 31: Comparison of Decomposed Nestlé Earnings and Price-to-Earnings Ratios

Earnings (CHF millions)	Market Value	Earnings (Group Shareholder Level)	Respective Price-to-Earnings Ratios
L'Oréal	21,747	934	23.3
Implied Nestlé-only	209,388	13,522	15.5

Earnings (CHF millions)	Market Value	Earnings (Group Shareholder Level)	Respective Price-to-Earnings Ratios
Actual earnings available to Nestlé parent company shareholders	231,135	14,456	16.0

Recap (%):	Market Value	Earnings
L'Oréal	9.4	6.5
Implied Nestlé-only	90.6	93.5
	100.0	100.0

At this point, the analyst believes that he has processed and analyzed the data sufficiently to pull together his findings and make his report to the portfolio manager.

PHASES 5 AND 6: CONCLUSIONS AND FOLLOW-UP

☐ demonstrate the use of a framework for the analysis of financial statements, given a particular problem, question, or purpose (e.g., valuing equity based on comparables, critiquing a credit rating, obtaining a comprehensive picture of financial leverage, evaluating the perspectives given in management's discussion of financial results)

Phase 5: Develop and Communicate Conclusions and Recommendations (e.g., with an Analysis Report)

As a result of the analyses performed, the analyst has gathered sufficient evidence regarding many of Nestlé's operational and financial characteristics and believes he is able to address the concerns initially expressed by the portfolio manager. Summary points he will cover in his report are divided into two classes: support for an investment in Nestlé shares and causes for concern.

Support for an Investment in Nestlé Shares

- Nestlé has the financial stability to fund growth in its existing operations and carry out its growth-by-acquisition strategy. The company's current liquidity and cash flows are more than adequate for future operating and investment purposes. The company has low leverage, and the capital structure is capable of supporting future operations and strategic plans.
- The operating cash flows have consistently exceeded the operating earnings. The ratio of operating cash to operating profit has been consistently favorable, providing confidence in the quality of the earnings. Measures comparing cash flow with reinvestment, debt, and debt-servicing capacity indicate strength in financial capacity.

- Decomposing earnings into Nestlé-only and L'Oréal and considering the respective price-to-earnings ratios, it appears that the implied Nestlé-only portion is undervalued. The implied Nestlé-only portion has a far lower price-to-earnings ratio than L'Oréal or the market. This finding should be considered an opportunity, given Nestlé's demonstrated cash flows and low financial leverage.

Causes for Concern

- Although Nestlé has significant, world-class brands and global reach, its core business has deteriorated in profitability in the last several years, as shown by the decomposition of the ROE. Even when taking into account the unusual items affecting profit margins, core operations still show decreases in profitability.
- The negative trend also shows in the cash returns on total assets. They have decreased each year since 2012.
- The acquisition activities in the Nutrition and Health Science product group do not appear to build on the company's traditional strengths. They do not seem to provide a remedy for the deterioration in the core profitability.
- The company's priorities in the allocation of capital in making acquisitions are of some concern. Although the Nutrition and Health Science product group and the Nestlé Nutrition segment show excellent EBIT margins, they rank very low in return on assets. This finding raises the question of whether management is overpaying for acquired companies.
- The company's write-down of goodwill from earlier acquisitions may signal ineffective allocation of capital. It is troubling that Nestlé has taken write-downs on previous acquisitions while actively making new ones.

The analyst concludes that Nestlé is not clearly a good investment opportunity *at this time* and recommends waiting to see whether a further discount makes it more attractive or the operations improve.

Phase 6: Follow-up

The portfolio manager is surprised by the analyst's findings and recommendations. The portfolio manager is convinced that the purchase of shares is justified because of the discount and because, in her opinion, Nestlé is experiencing only temporary issues. She commits the pension fund to a cautious, less-than-core investment holding of Nestlé common stock. The size of the holding is less than originally anticipated because, despite her enthusiasm for the company, the portfolio manager is troubled by the analyst's observations about the resource allocation within the company. She wants him to continually re-evaluate the holding. Unproductive capital spending may be a trigger for eliminating the holding. The analyst is asked to update his findings in the initial research report at each reporting period, emphasizing the quality measures expressed by the accruals tests and the cash flow support of earnings, with particular regard to return on assets.

Phases 5 and 6: Conclusions and Follow-up

SUMMARY

The case study demonstrates the use of a financial analysis framework in investment decision making. Although each analysis undertaken may have a different focus, purpose, and context that result in the application of different techniques and tools, the case demonstrates the use of a common financial statement analysis framework. The analyst starts with a global, summarized view of a company and its attributes and digs below the surface of the financial statements to find economic truths that are not apparent from a superficial review. In the case of Nestlé, the analyst applied disaggregation techniques to review the company's performance in terms of ROE and then successively examined the drivers of ROE in increasing detail to evaluate management's skills in capital allocation.

An economic decision is reached, which is consistent with the primary reason for performing financial analysis: to facilitate an economic decision.

PRACTICE PROBLEMS

Quentin Abay, CFA, is an analyst for a private equity firm interested in purchasing Bickchip Enterprises, a conglomerate. His first task is to determine the trends in ROE and the main drivers of the trends using DuPont analysis. To do so he gathers the data in Exhibit 1.

Exhibit 1: Selected Financial Data for Bickchip Enterprises (€ Thousands)

	2020	2019	2018
Revenue	72,448	66,487	55,781
Earnings before interest and tax	6,270	4,710	3,609
Earnings before tax	5,101	4,114	3,168
Net income	4,038	3,345	2,576
Asset turnover	0.79	0.76	0.68
Assets/Equity	3.09	3.38	3.43

After conducting the DuPont analysis, Abay believes that his firm could increase the ROE without operational changes. Further, Abay thinks that ROE could improve if the company divested segments that were generating the lowest returns on capital employed (total assets less non-interest-bearing liabilities). Segment EBIT margins in 2020 were 11 percent for Automation Equipment, 5 percent for Power and Industrial, and 8 percent for Medical Equipment. Other relevant segment information is presented in Exhibit 2.

Exhibit 2: Segment Data for Bickchip Enterprises (€ Thousands)

	Capital Employed			Capital Expenditures (Excluding Acquisitions)		
Operating Segments	2020	2019	2018	2020	2019	2018
Automation Equipment	10,705	6,384	5,647	700	743	616
Power and Industrial	15,805	13,195	12,100	900	849	634
Medical Equipment	22,870	22,985	22,587	908	824	749
	49,380	42,564	40,334	2,508	2,416	1,999

Abay is also concerned with earnings quality, so he intends to calculate Bickchip's cash-flow-based accruals ratio and the ratio of operating cash flow before interest and taxes to operating income. To do so, he prepares the information in Exhibit 3.

Exhibit 3: Earnings Quality Data for Bickchip Enterprises (€ Thousands)

	2020	2019	2018
Net income	4,038	3,345	2,576

Practice Problems

	2020	2019	2018
Net cash flow provided by (used in) operating activity[a]	9,822	5,003	3,198
Net cash flow provided by (used in) investing activity	(10,068)	(4,315)	(5,052)
Net cash flow provided by (used in) financing activity[b]	(5,792)	1,540	(2,241)
Average net operating assets	43,192	45,373	40,421
[a] includes cash paid for taxes of:	(1,930)	(1,191)	(1,093)
[b] includes cash paid for interest of:	(1,169)	(596)	(441)

1. Over the three-year period presented in Exhibit 1, Bickchip's return on equity is *best* described as:

    A. stable.

    B. trending lower.

    C. trending higher.

2. Based on the DuPont analysis, Abay's belief regarding ROE is *most likely* based on:

    A. leverage.

    B. profit margins.

    C. asset turnover.

3. Based on Abay's criteria, the business segment *best* suited for divestiture is:

    A. medical equipment.

    B. power and industrial.

    C. automation equipment.

4. Bickchip's cash-flow-based accruals ratio in 2020 is *closest* to:

    A. 9.9%.

    B. 13.4%.

    C. 23.3%.

5. The cash-flow-based accruals ratios from 2018 to 2020 indicate:

    A. improving earnings quality.

    B. deteriorating earnings quality.

    C. no change in earnings quality.

6. The ratio of operating cash flow before interest and taxes to operating income for Bickchip for 2020 is *closest* to:

    A. 1.6.

B. 1.9.

C. 2.1.

7. Based on the ratios for operating cash flow before interest and taxes to operating income, Abay should conclude that:

   A. Bickchip's earnings are backed by cash flow.

   B. Bickchip's earnings are not backed by cash flow.

   C. Abay can draw no conclusion due to the changes in the ratios over time.

SOLUTIONS

1. C is correct. The ROE has been trending higher. ROE can be calculated by multiplying (net profit margin) × (asset turnover) × (financial leverage). Net profit margin is net income/sales. In 2018 the net profit margin was 2,576/55,781 = 4.6% and the ROE = 4.6% × 0.68 × 3.43 = 10.8%. Using the same method, ROE was 12.9 percent in 2019 and 13.6 percent in 2020.

2. A is correct. The DuPont analysis shows that profit margins and asset turnover have both increased over the last three years, but leverage has declined. The reduction in leverage offsets a portion of the improvement in profitability and turnover. Thus, ROE would have been higher if leverage had not decreased.

3. B is correct. The Power and Industrial segment has the lowest EBIT margins but uses about 31 percent of the capital employed. Further, Power and Industrial's proportion of the capital expenditures has increased from 32 percent to 36 percent over the three years. Its capital intensity only looked to get worse, as the segment's percentage of total capital expenditures was higher than its percentage of total capital in each of the three years. If Abay is considering divesting segments that do not earn sufficient returns on capital employed, this segment is most suitable.

4. A is correct. The cash-flow-based accruals ratio = [NI − (CFO + CFI)]/(Average NOA) = [4,038 − (9,822 − 10,068)]/43,192 = 9.9%.

5. A is correct. The cash-flow-based accruals ratio falls from 11.0 percent in 2018 to 5.9 percent in 2019, and then rises to 9.9 percent in 2020. However, the change over the three-year period is a net modest decline, indicating a slight improvement in earnings quality.

6. B is correct. Net cash flow provided by (used in) operating activity has to be adjusted for interest and taxes, as necessary, in order to be comparable to operating income (EBIT). Bickchip, reporting under IFRS, chose to classify interest expense as a financing cash flow so the only necessary adjustment is for taxes. The operating cash flow before interest and taxes = 9,822 + 1,930 = 11,752. Dividing this by EBIT of 6,270 yields 1.9.

7. A is correct. Operating cash flow before interest and taxes to operating income rises steadily (not erratically) from 1.2 to 1.3 to 1.9. The ratios over 1.0 and the trend indicate that earnings are supported by cash flow.

Glossary

Abnormal earnings See *residual income*.

Abnormal return The amount by which a security's actual return differs from its expected return, given the security's risk and the market's return.

Absolute convergence The idea that developing countries, regardless of their particular characteristics, will eventually catch up with the developed countries and match them in per capita output.

Absolute valuation model A model that specifies an asset's intrinsic value.

Absolute version of PPP An extension of the law of one price whereby the prices of goods and services will not differ internationally once exchange rates are considered.

Accounting estimates Estimates used in calculating the value of assets or liabilities and in the amount of revenue and expense to allocate to a period. Examples of accounting estimates include, among others, the useful lives of depreciable assets, the salvage value of depreciable assets, product returns, warranty costs, and the amount of uncollectible receivables.

Accumulated benefit obligation The actuarial present value of benefits (whether vested or non-vested) attributed, generally by the pension benefit formula, to employee service rendered before a specified date and based on employee service and compensation (if applicable) before that date. The accumulated benefit obligation differs from the projected benefit obligation in that it includes no assumption about future compensation levels.

Accuracy The percentage of correctly predicted classes out of total predictions. It is an overall performance metric in classification problems.

Acquisition When one company, the acquirer, purchases from the seller most or all of another company's (the target) shares to gain control of either an entire company, a segment of another company, or a specific group of assets in exchange for cash, stock, or the assumption of liabilities, alone or in combination. Once an acquisition is complete, the acquirer and target merge into a single entity and consolidate management, operations, and resources.

Activation function A functional part of a neural network's node that transforms the total net input received into the final output of the node. The activation function operates like a light dimmer switch that decreases or increases the strength of the input.

Active factor risk The contribution to active risk squared resulting from the portfolio's different-than-benchmark exposures relative to factors specified in the risk model.

Active return The return on a portfolio minus the return on the portfolio's benchmark.

Active risk The standard deviation of active returns.

Active risk squared The variance of active returns; active risk raised to the second power.

Active share A measure of how similar a portfolio is to its benchmark. A manager who precisely replicates the benchmark will have an active share of zero; a manager with no holdings in common with the benchmark will have an active share of one.

Active specific risk The contribution to active risk squared resulting from the portfolio's active weights on individual assets as those weights interact with assets' residual risk.

Adjusted funds from operations (AFFO) Funds from operations adjusted to remove any non-cash rent reported under straight-line rent accounting and to subtract maintenance-type capital expenditures and leasing costs, including leasing agents' commissions and tenants' improvement allowances.

Adjusted present value As an approach to valuing a company, the sum of the value of the company, assuming no use of debt, and the net present value of any effects of debt on company value.

Adjusted R^2 Goodness-of-fit measure that adjusts the coefficient of determination, R^2, for the number of independent variables in the model.

Administrative regulations or administrative law Rules issued by government agencies or other regulators.

Advanced set An arrangement in which the reference interest rate is set at the time the money is deposited.

Advanced settled An arrangement in which a forward rate agreement (FRA) expires and settles at the same time, at the FRA expiration date.

Agency issues Conflicts of interest that arise when the agent in an agency relationship has goals and incentives that differ from the principal to whom the agent owes a fiduciary duty. Also called *agency problems* or *principal–agent problems*.

Agglomerative clustering A bottom-up hierarchical clustering method that begins with each observation being treated as its own cluster. The algorithm finds the two closest clusters, based on some measure of distance (similarity), and combines them into one new larger cluster. This process is repeated iteratively until all observations are clumped into a single large cluster.

Akaike's information criterion (AIC) A statistic used to compare sets of independent variables for explaining a dependent variable. It is preferred for finding the model that is best suited for prediction.

Allowance for loan losses A balance sheet account; it is a contra asset account to loans.

Alpha The return on an asset in excess of the asset's required rate of return; the risk-adjusted return.

American Depositary Receipt A negotiable certificate issued by a depositary bank that represents ownership in a non-US company's deposited equity (i.e., equity held in custody by the depositary bank in the company's home market).

Analysis of variance (ANOVA) The analysis that breaks the total variability of a dataset (such as observations on the dependent variable in a regression) into components representing different sources of variation.

Application programming interface (API) A set of well-defined methods of communication between various software components and typically used for accessing external data.

Arbitrage 1) The simultaneous purchase of an undervalued asset or portfolio and sale of an overvalued but equivalent asset or portfolio, in order to obtain a riskless profit on the price differential. Taking advantage of a market inefficiency in a risk-free manner. 2) The condition in a financial market in which equivalent assets or combinations of assets sell for two different prices, creating an opportunity to profit at no risk with no commitment of money. In a well-functioning financial market, few arbitrage opportunities are possible. 3) A risk-free operation that earns an expected positive net profit but requires no net investment of money.

Arbitrage-free models Term structure models that project future interest rate paths that emanate from the existing term structure. Resulting prices are based on a no-arbitrage condition.

Arbitrage-free valuation An approach to valuation that determines security values consistent with the absence of any opportunity to earn riskless profits without any net investment of money.

Arbitrage opportunity An opportunity to conduct an arbitrage; an opportunity to earn an expected positive net profit without risk and with no net investment of money.

Arbitrage portfolio The portfolio that exploits an arbitrage opportunity.

Ask price The price at which a trader will sell a specified quantity of a security. Also called *ask*, *offer price*, or *offer*.

Asset-based approach Approach that values a private company based on the values of the underlying assets of the entity less the value of any related liabilities.

Asset-based valuation An approach to valuing natural resource companies that estimates company value on the basis of the market value of the natural resources the company controls.

At market contract When a forward contract is established, the forward price is negotiated so that the market value of the forward contract on the initiation date is zero.

Authorized participants (APs) A special group of institutional investors who are authorized by the ETF issuer to participate in the creation/redemption process. APs are large broker/dealers, often market makers.

Autocorrelations The correlations of a time series with its own past values.

Autoregressive model (AR) A time series regressed on its own past values in which the independent variable is a lagged value of the dependent variable.

Backtesting The process that approximates the real-life investment process, using historical data, to assess whether an investment strategy would have produced desirable results.

Backward propagation The process of adjusting weights in a neural network, to reduce total error of the network, by moving backward through the network's layers.

Backwardation A condition in the futures markets in which the spot price exceeds the futures price, the forward curve is downward sloping, and the convenience yield is high.

Bag-of-words (BOW) A collection of a distinct set of tokens from all the texts in a sample dataset. BOW does not capture the position or sequence of words present in the text.

Balance sheet restructuring Altering the composition of the balance sheet by either shifting the asset composition, changing the capital structure, or both.

Bankruptcy A declaration provided for by a country's laws that typically involves the establishment of a legal procedure that forces creditors to defer their claims.

Barbell portfolio Fixed-income portfolio that combines short and long maturities.

Base error Model error due to randomness in the data.

Basic earnings per share (EPS) Net earnings available to common shareholders (i.e., net income minus preferred dividends) divided by the weighted average number of common shares outstanding during the period.

Basis The difference between the spot price and the futures price. As the maturity date of the futures contract nears, the basis converges toward zero.

Basis trade A trade based on the pricing of credit in the bond market versus the price of the same credit in the CDS market. To execute a basis trade, go long the "underpriced" credit and short the "overpriced" credit. A profit is realized as the implied credit prices converge.

Bearish flattening Term structure shift in which short-term bond yields rise more than long-term bond yields, resulting in a flatter yield curve.

Benchmark value of the multiple In using the method of comparables, the value of a price multiple for the comparison asset; when we have comparison assets (a group), the mean or median value of the multiple for the group of assets.

Best ask The offer to sell with the lowest ask price. Also called *best offer* or *inside ask*.

Best bid The highest bid in the market.

Best offer The lowest offer (ask price) in the market.

Bias error Describes the degree to which a model fits the training data. Algorithms with erroneous assumptions produce high bias error with poor approximation, causing underfitting and high in-sample error.

Bid price In a price quotation, the price at which the party making the quotation is willing to buy a specified quantity of an asset or security.

Bid–ask spread The ask price minus the bid price.

Bill-and-hold basis Sales on a bill-and-hold basis involve selling products but not delivering those products until a later date.

Blockage factor An illiquidity discount that occurs when an investor sells a large amount of stock relative to its trading volume (assuming it is not large enough to constitute a controlling ownership).

Bond indenture A legal contract specifying the terms of a bond issue.

Bond risk premium The expected excess return of a default-free long-term bond less that of an equivalent short-term bond.

Bond yield plus risk premium (BYPRP) approach An estimate of the cost of common equity that is produced by summing the before-tax cost of debt and a risk premium that captures the additional yield on a company's stock relative to its bonds.

Bonus issue of shares A type of dividend in which a company distributes additional shares of its common stock to shareholders instead of cash.

Book value The net amount shown for an asset or liability on the balance sheet; book value may also refer to the company's excess of total assets over total liabilities. Also called *carrying value*.

Book value of equity Shareholders' equity (total assets minus total liabilities) minus the value of preferred stock; common shareholders' equity.

Book value per share The amount of book value (also called carrying value) of common equity per share of common stock, calculated by dividing the book value of shareholders' equity by the number of shares of common stock outstanding.

Bootstrap aggregating (or bagging) A technique whereby the original training dataset is used to generate n new training datasets or bags of data. Each new bag of data is generated by random sampling with replacement from the initial training set.

Bootstrapping The use of a forward substitution process to determine zero-coupon rates by using the par yields and solving for the zero-coupon rates one by one, from the shortest to longest maturities.

Bottom-up approach With respect to forecasting, an approach that usually begins at the level of the individual company or a unit within the company.

Breakup value The value derived using a sum-of-the-parts valuation.

Breusch–Godfrey (BG) test A test used to detect autocorrelated residuals up to a predesignated order of the lagged residuals.

Breusch–Pagan (BP) test A test for the presence of heteroskedasticity in a regression.

Bullet portfolio A fixed-income portfolio concentrated in a single maturity.

Bullish flattening Term structure change in which the yield curve flattens in response to a greater decline in long-term rates than short-term rates.

Bullish steepening Term structure change in which short-term rates fall by more than long-term yields, resulting in a steeper term structure.

Buy-side analysts Analysts who work for investment management firms, trusts, bank trust departments, and similar institutions.

Buyback A transaction in which a company buys back its own shares. Unlike stock dividends and stock splits, share repurchases use corporate cash.

CDS spread A periodic premium paid by the buyer to the seller that serves as a return over a market reference rate required to protect against credit risk.

Callable bond A bond containing an embedded call option that gives the issuer the right to buy the bond back from the investor at specified prices on pre-determined dates.

Canceled shares Shares that were issued, subsequently repurchased by the company, and then retired (cannot be reissued).

Capital asset pricing model (CAPM) A single factor model such that excess returns on a stock are a function of the returns on a market index.

Capital charge The company's total cost of capital in money terms.

Capital deepening An increase in the capital-to-labor ratio.

Capitalization of earnings method In the context of private company valuation, a valuation model based on an assumption of a constant growth rate of free cash flow to the firm or a constant growth rate of free cash flow to equity.

Capitalization rate The divisor in the expression for the value of perpetuity. In the context of real estate, it is the divisor in the direct capitalization method of estimating value. The cap rate equals net operating income divided by value.

Capitalized cash flow method In the context of private company valuation, a valuation model based on an assumption of a constant growth rate of free cash flow to the firm or a constant growth rate of free cash flow to equity. Also called *capitalized cash flow model*.

Capitalized income method In the context of private company valuation, a valuation model based on an assumption of a constant growth rate of free cash flow to the firm or a constant growth rate of free cash flow to equity.

Capped floater Floating-rate bond with a cap provision that prevents the coupon rate from increasing above a specified maximum rate. It protects the issuer against rising interest rates.

Carry arbitrage model A no-arbitrage approach in which the underlying instrument is either bought or sold along with an opposite position in a forward contract.

Carry benefits Benefits that arise from owning certain underlyings; for example, dividends, foreign interest, and bond coupon payments.

Carry costs Costs that arise from owning certain underlyings. They are generally a function of the physical characteristics of the underlying asset and also the interest forgone on the funds tied up in the asset.

Cash available for distribution See *adjusted funds from operations*.

Cash-generating unit The smallest identifiable group of assets that generates cash inflows that are largely independent of the cash inflows of other assets or groups of assets.

Cash settlement A procedure used in certain derivative transactions that specifies that the long and short parties settle the derivative's difference in value between them by making a cash payment.

Catalyst An event or piece of information that causes the marketplace to re-evaluate the prospects of a company.

Ceiling analysis A systematic process of evaluating different components in the pipeline of model building. It helps to understand what part of the pipeline can potentially improve in performance by further tuning.

Centroid The center of a cluster formed using the k-means clustering algorithm.

Chain rule of forecasting A forecasting process in which the next period's value as predicted by the forecasting equation is substituted into the right-hand side of the equation to give a predicted value two periods ahead.

Cheapest-to-deliver The debt instrument that can be purchased and delivered at the lowest cost yet has the same seniority as the reference obligation.

Classification and regression tree A supervised machine learning technique that can be applied to predict either a categorical target variable, producing a classification tree, or a continuous target variable, producing a regression tree. CART is commonly applied to binary classification or regression.

Clean surplus relation The relationship between earnings, dividends, and book value in which ending book value is equal to the beginning book value plus earnings less dividends, apart from ownership transactions.

Club convergence The idea that only rich and middle-income countries sharing a set of favorable attributes (i.e., are members of the "club") will converge to the income level of the richest countries.

Cluster A subset of observations from a dataset such that all the observations within the same cluster are deemed "similar."

Clustering The sorting of observations into groups (clusters) such that observations in the same cluster are more similar to each other than they are to observations in other clusters.

Cobb–Douglas production function A function of the form $Y = K^{\alpha} L^{1-\alpha}$ relating output (Y) to labor (L) and capital (K) inputs.

Coefficient of determination The percentage of the variation of the dependent variable that is explained by the independent variables. Also referred to as the R-squared or R^2.

Cointegrated Describes two time series that have a long-term financial or economic relationship such that they do not diverge from each other without bound in the long run.

Collateral return The component of the total return on a commodity futures position attributable to the yield for the bonds or cash used to maintain the futures position. Also called *collateral yield*.

Collection frequency (CF) The number of times a given word appears in the whole corpus (i.e., collection of sentences) divided by the total number of words in the corpus.

Commercial real estate properties Income-producing real estate properties; properties purchased with the intent to let, lease, or rent (in other words, produce income).

Commodity swap A type of swap involving the exchange of payments over multiple dates as determined by specified reference prices or indexes relating to commodities.

Company fundamental factors Factors related to the company's internal performance, such as factors relating to earnings growth, earnings variability, earnings momentum, and financial leverage.

Company share-related factors Valuation measures and other factors related to share price or the trading characteristics of the shares, such as earnings yield, dividend yield, and book-to-market value.

Comparables Assets used as benchmarks when applying the method of comparables to value an asset. Also called *comps*, *guideline assets*, or *guideline companies*.

Compiled financial statements Financial statements that are not accompanied by an auditor's opinion letter.

Complexity A term referring to the number of features, parameters, or branches in a model and to whether the model is linear or non-linear (non-linear is more complex).

Composite variable A variable that combines two or more variables that are statistically strongly related to each other.

Comprehensive income All changes in equity other than contributions by, and distributions to, owners; income under clean surplus accounting; includes all changes in equity during a period except those resulting from investments by owners and distributions to owners. Comprehensive income equals net income plus other comprehensive income.

Comps Assets used as benchmarks when applying the method of comparables to value an asset.

Concentrated ownership Ownership structure consisting of an individual shareholder or a group (controlling shareholders) with the ability to exercise control over the corporation.

Conditional convergence The idea that convergence of per capita income is conditional on the countries having the same savings rate, population growth rate, and production function.

Conditional heteroskedasticity A condition in which the variance of residuals of a regression are correlated with the value of the independent variables.

Conditional VaR (CVaR) The weighted average of all loss outcomes in the statistical (i.e., return) distribution that exceed the VaR loss. Thus, CVaR is a more comprehensive measure of tail loss than VaR is. Sometimes referred to as the *expected tail loss* or *expected shortfall*.

Confirmation bias A belief perseverance bias in which people tend to look for and notice what confirms their beliefs, to ignore or undervalue what contradicts their beliefs, and to misinterpret information as support for their beliefs.

Confusion matrix A grid used for error analysis in classification problems, it presents values for four evaluation metrics including true positive (TP), false positive (FP), true negative (TN), and false negative (FN).

Conglomerate discount When an issuer is trading at a valuation lower than the sum of its parts, which is generally the result of diseconomies of scale or scope or the result of the capital markets having overlooked the business and its prospects.

Constant dividend payout ratio policy A policy in which a constant percentage of net income is paid out in dividends.

Constant returns to scale The condition that if all inputs into the production process are increased by a given percentage, then output rises by that same percentage.

Contango A condition in the futures markets in which the spot price is lower than the futures price, the forward curve is upward sloping, and there is little or no convenience yield.

Contingent consideration Potential future payments to the seller that are contingent on the achievement of certain agreed-on occurrences.

Continuing earnings Earnings excluding nonrecurring components. Also referred to as *core earnings*, *persistent earnings*, or *underlying earnings*.

Continuing residual income Residual income after the forecast horizon.

Continuing value The analyst's estimate of a stock's value at a particular point in the future.

Control premium An increment or premium to value associated with a controlling ownership interest in a company.

Convergence The tendency for differences in output per capita across countries to diminish over time. In technical analysis, the term describes the case when an indicator moves in the same manner as the security being analyzed.

Conversion period For a convertible bond, the period during which bondholders have the right to convert their bonds into shares.

Conversion price For a convertible bond, the price per share at which the bond can be converted into shares.

Conversion rate (or ratio) For a convertible bond, the number of shares of common stock that a bondholder receives from converting the bond into shares.

Conversion value For a convertible bond, the value of the bond if it is converted at the market price of the shares. Also called *parity value*.

Convertible bond Bond that gives the bondholder the right to exchange the bond for a specified number of common shares in the issuing company.

Convexity A measure of how interest rate sensitivity changes with a change in interest rates.

Cook's distance A metric for identifying influential data points. Also known as Cook's D (D_i).

Core earnings Earnings excluding nonrecurring components. Also referred to as *continuing earnings*, *persistent earnings*, or *underlying earnings*.

Core real estate investment style Investing in high-quality, well-leased, core property types with low leverage (no more than 30% of asset value) in the largest markets with strong, diversified economies. It is a conservative strategy designed to avoid real estate–specific risks, including leasing, development, and speculation in favor of steady returns. Hotel properties are excluded from the core categories because of the higher cash flow volatility resulting from single-night leases and the greater importance of property operations, brand, and marketing.

Corpus A collection of text data in any form, including list, matrix, or data table forms.

Cost approach An approach that values a private company based on the values of the underlying assets of the entity less the value of any related liabilities. In the context of real estate, this approach estimates the value of a property based on what it would cost to buy the land and construct a new property on the site that has the same utility or functionality as the property being appraised.

Cost of carry model A model that relates the forward price of an asset to the spot price by considering the cost of carry (also referred to as future-spot parity model).

Cost of debt The required return on debt financing to a company, such as when it issues a bond, takes out a bank loan, or leases an asset through a finance lease.

Cost of equity The return required by equity investors to compensate for both the time value of money and the risk. Also referred to as the required rate of return on common stock or the required return on equity.

Cost restructuring Actions to reduce costs by improving operational efficiency and profitability, often to raise margins to a historical level or to those of comparable industry peers.

Country risk premium (CRP) The additional return required by investors to compensate for the risk associated with investing in a foreign country relative to the investor's domestic market.

Country risk rating (CRR) The rating of a country based on many risk factors, including economic prosperity, political risk, and ESG risk.

Covariance stationary Describes a time series when its expected value and variance are constant and finite in all periods and when its covariance with itself for a fixed number of periods in the past or future is constant and finite in all periods.

Covered bonds A senior debt obligation of a financial institution that gives recourse to the originator/issuer and a predetermined underlying collateral pool.

Covered interest rate parity The relationship among the spot exchange rate, the forward exchange rate, and the interest rates in two currencies that ensures that the return on a hedged (i.e., covered) foreign risk-free investment is the same as the return on a domestic risk-free investment. Also called *interest rate parity*.

Cox-Ingersoll-Ross model A general equilibrium term structure model that assumes interest rates are mean reverting and interest rate volatility is directly related to the level of interest rates.

Creation basket The list of securities (and share amounts) the authorized participant (AP) must deliver to the ETF manager in exchange for ETF shares. The creation basket is published each business day.

Creation units Large blocks of ETF shares transacted between the authorized participant (AP) and the ETF manager that are usually but not always equal to 50,000 shares of the ETF.

Creation/redemption The process in which ETF shares are created or redeemed by authorized participants transacting with the ETF issuer.

Credit correlation The correlation of credit (or default) risks of the underlying single-name CDS contained in an index CDS.

Credit curve The credit spreads for a range of maturities of a company's debt.

Credit default swap A derivative contract between two parties in which the buyer makes a series of cash payments to the seller and receives a promise of compensation for credit losses resulting from the default.

Credit derivative A derivative instrument in which the underlying is a measure of the credit quality of a borrower.

Credit event An event that defines a payout in a credit derivative. Events are usually defined as bankruptcy, failure to pay an obligation, or an involuntary debt restructuring.

Credit protection buyer One party to a credit default swap; the buyer makes a series of cash payments to the seller and receives a promise of compensation for credit losses resulting from the default.

Credit protection seller One party to a credit default swap; the seller makes a promise to pay compensation for credit losses resulting from the default.

Credit risk The risk of loss caused by a counterparty's or debtor's failure to make a promised payment. Also called *default risk*.

Credit spread The compensation for the risk inherent in a company's debt security.

Credit valuation adjustment The value of the credit risk of a bond in present value terms.

Cross-validation A technique for estimating out-of-sample error directly by determining the error in validation samples.

Cumulative preferred stock Preferred stock that requires that the dividends be paid in full to preferred stock owners for any missed dividends prior to any payment of dividends to common stock owners.

Current exchange rate For accounting purposes, the spot exchange rate on the balance sheet date.

Current rate method Approach to translating foreign currency financial statements for consolidation in which all assets and liabilities are translated at the current exchange rate. The current rate method is the prevalent method of translation.

Curvature One of the three factors (the other two are level and steepness) that empirically explain most of the changes in the shape of the yield curve. A shock to the curvature factor affects mid-maturity interest rates, resulting in the term structure becoming either more or less hump-shaped.

Curve trade Buying a CDS of one maturity and selling a CDS on the same reference entity with a different maturity.

Customer concentration risk The risk associated with sales dependent on a few customers.

Cyclical businesses Businesses with high sensitivity to business- or industry-cycle influences.

Data preparation (cleansing) The process of examining, identifying, and mitigating (i.e., cleansing) errors in raw data.

Data snooping The practice of determining a model by extensive searching through a dataset for statistically significant patterns.

Data wrangling (preprocessing) This task performs transformations and critical processing steps on cleansed data to make the data ready for ML model training (i.e., preprocessing), and includes dealing with outliers, extracting useful variables from existing data points, and scaling the data.

Deep learning Machine learning using neural networks with many hidden layers.

Deep neural networks Neural networks with many hidden layers—at least 2 but potentially more than 20—that have proven successful across a wide range of artificial intelligence applications.

Default risk See *credit risk*.

Defined benefit pension plans Plans in which the company promises to pay a certain annual amount (defined benefit) to the employee after retirement. The company bears the investment risk of the plan assets.

Defined contribution pension plans Individual accounts to which an employee and typically the employer makes contributions during their working years and expect to draw on the accumulated funds at retirement. The employee bears the investment and inflation risk of the plan assets.

Delay costs Implicit trading costs that arise from the inability to complete desired trades immediately. Also called *slippage*.

Delta The relationship between the option price and the underlying price, which reflects the sensitivity of the price of the option to changes in the price of the underlying. Delta is a good approximation of how an option price will change for a small change in the stock.

Dendrogram A type of tree diagram used for visualizing a hierarchical cluster analysis; it highlights the hierarchical relationships among the clusters.

Depository Trust and Clearinghouse Corporation A US-headquartered entity providing post-trade clearing, settlement, and information services.

Diluted earnings per share (Diluted EPS) Net income, minus preferred dividends, divided by the weighted average number of common shares outstanding considering all dilutive securities (e.g., convertible debt and options); the EPS that would result if all dilutive securities were converted into common shares.

Dilution A reduction in proportional ownership interest as a result of the issuance of new shares.

Dimension reduction A set of techniques for reducing the number of features in a dataset while retaining variation across observations to preserve the information contained in that variation.

Diminishing marginal productivity When each additional unit of an input, keeping the other inputs unchanged, increases output by a smaller increment.

Direct capitalization method In the context of real estate, this method estimates the value of an income-producing property based on the level and quality of its net operating income.

Discount To reduce the value of a future payment in allowance for how far away it is in time; to calculate the present value of some future amount. Also, the amount by which an instrument is priced below its face value.

Discount factor The price equivalent of a zero rate. Also may be stated as the present value of a currency unit on a future date.

Discount for lack of control An amount or percentage deducted from the pro rata share of 100% of the value of an equity interest in a business to reflect the absence of some or all of the powers of control.

Discount for lack of marketability An amount of percentage deducted from the value of an ownership interest to reflect the relative absence of marketability.

Discount function Discount factors for the range of all possible maturities. The spot curve can be derived from the discount function and vice versa.

Discounted abnormal earnings model A model of stock valuation that views intrinsic value of stock as the sum of book value per share plus the present value of the stock's expected future residual income per share.

Discounted cash flow (DCF) method Income approach that values an asset based on estimates of future cash flows discounted to present value by using a discount rate reflective of the risks associated with the cash flows. In the context of real estate, this method estimates the value of an income-producing property based on discounting future projected cash flows.

Discounted cash flow method Income approach that values an asset based on estimates of future cash flows discounted to present value by using a discount rate reflective of the risks associated with the cash flows. In the context of real estate, this method estimates the value of an income-producing property based on discounting future projected cash flows.

Discounted cash flow model A model of intrinsic value that views the value of an asset as the present value of the asset's expected future cash flows.

Dispersed ownership Ownership structure consisting of many shareholders, none of which has the ability to individually exercise control over the corporation.

Divestiture When a seller sells a company, segment of a company, or group of assets to an acquirer. Once complete, control of the target is transferred to the acquirer.

Dividend A distribution paid to shareholders based on the number of shares owned.

Dividend coverage ratio The ratio of net income to dividends.

Dividend discount model (DDM) A present value model of stock value that views the intrinsic value of a stock as present value of the stock's expected future dividends.

Dividend discount model (DDM) The model of the value of stock that is the present value of all future dividends, discounted at the required return on equity.

Dividend displacement of earnings The concept that dividends paid now displace earnings in all future periods.

Dividend imputation tax system A taxation system that effectively assures corporate profits distributed as dividends are taxed just once and at the shareholder's tax rate.

Dividend index point A measure of the quantity of dividends attributable to a particular index.

Dividend payout ratio The ratio of cash dividends paid to earnings for a period.

Dividend policy The strategy a company follows with regard to the amount and timing of dividend payments.

Dividend rate The annualized amount of the most recent dividend.

Dividend recapitalization Restructuring the mix of debt and equity, typically shifting the capital structure from equity to debt through debt-financed share repurchases. The objective is to reduce the issuer's weighted average cost of capital by replacing expensive equity with cheaper debt by purchasing equity from shareholders using newly issued debt.

Dividend yield Annual dividends per share divided by share price.

Divisive clustering A top-down hierarchical clustering method that starts with all observations belonging to a single large cluster. The observations are then divided into two clusters based on some measure of distance (similarity). The algorithm then progressively partitions the intermediate clusters into smaller ones until each cluster contains only one observation.

Document frequency (DF) The number of documents (texts) that contain a particular token divided by the total number of documents. It is the simplest feature selection method and often performs well when many thousands of tokens are present.

Document term matrix (DTM) A matrix where each row belongs to a document (or text file), and each column represents a token (or term). The number of rows is equal to the number of documents (or text files) in a sample text dataset. The number of columns is equal to the number of tokens from the BOW built using all the documents in the sample dataset. The cells typically contain the counts of the number of times a token is present in each document.

Dominance An arbitrage opportunity when a financial asset with a risk-free payoff in the future must have a positive price today.

Double taxation system Corporate earnings are taxed twice when paid out as dividends. First, corporate pretax earnings are taxed regardless of whether they will be distributed as dividends or retained at the corporate level. Second, dividends are taxed again at the individual shareholder level.

Downstream A transaction between two related companies, an investor company (or a parent company) and an associate company (or a subsidiary) such that the investor company records a profit on its income statement. An example is a sale of inventory by the investor company to the associate or by a parent to a subsidiary company.

Dual-class shares Shares that grant one share class superior or even sole voting rights, whereas the other share class has inferior or no voting rights.

Due diligence Investigation and analysis in support of an investment action, decision, or recommendation.

Dummy variable An independent variable that takes on a value of either 1 or 0, depending on a specified condition. Also known as an *indicator variable*.

Duration A measure of the approximate sensitivity of a security to a change in interest rates (i.e., a measure of interest rate risk).

Durbin–Watson (DW) test A test for the presence of first-order serial correlation.

Dutch disease A situation in which currency appreciation driven by strong export demand for resources makes other segments of the economy (particularly manufacturing) globally uncompetitive.

ESG integration An ESG investment approach that focuses on systematic consideration of material ESG factors in asset allocation, security selection, and portfolio construction decisions for the purpose of achieving the product's stated investment objectives. Used interchangeably with **ESG investing**.

Earnings surprise The portion of a company's earnings that is unanticipated by investors and, according to the efficient market hypothesis, merits a price adjustment.

Earnings yield EPS divided by price; the reciprocal of the P/E.

Economic profit Equal to accounting profit less the implicit opportunity costs not included in total accounting costs; the difference between total revenue (TR) and total cost (TC). Also called *abnormal profit* or *supernormal profit*.

Economic sectors Large industry groupings.

Economic value added (EVA®) A commercial implementation of the residual income concept; the computation of EVA® is the net operating profit after taxes minus the cost of capital, where these inputs are adjusted for a number of items.

Economies of scale A situation in which average costs per unit of good or service produced fall as volume rises. In reference to mergers, the savings achieved through the consolidation of operations and elimination of duplicate resources.

Edwards–Bell–Ohlson model A model of stock valuation that views intrinsic value of stock as the sum of book value per share plus the present value of the stock's expected future residual income per share.

Effective convexity A *curve convexity* statistic that measures the secondary effect of a change in a benchmark yield curve on a bond's price.

Effective duration Sensitivity of the bond's price to a 100 bps parallel shift of the benchmark yield curve, assuming no change in the bond's credit spread.

Effective spread Two times the difference between the execution price and the midpoint of the market quote at the time an order is entered.

Eigenvalue A measure that gives the proportion of total variance in the initial dataset that is explained by each eigenvector.

Eigenvector A vector that defines new mutually uncorrelated composite variables that are linear combinations of the original features.

Embedded options Contingency provisions found in a bond's indenture or offering circular representing rights that enable their holders to take advantage of interest rate movements. They can be exercised by the issuer, by the bondholder, or automatically depending on the course of interest rates.

Ensemble learning A technique of combining the predictions from a collection of models to achieve a more accurate prediction.

Ensemble method The method of combining multiple learning algorithms, as in ensemble learning.

Enterprise value Total company value (the market value of debt, common equity, and preferred equity) minus the value of cash and investments.

Enterprise value multiple A valuation multiple that relates the total market value of all sources of a company's capital (net of cash) to a measure of fundamental value for the entire company (such as a pre-interest earnings measure).

Equity charge The estimated cost of equity capital in money terms.

Equity investment A company purchasing another company's equity but less than 50% of its shares. The two companies maintain their independence, but the investor company has investment exposure to the investee and, in some cases depending on the size of the investment, can have representation on the investee's board of directors to influence operations.

Equity REITs REITs that own, operate, and/or selectively develop income-producing real estate.

Equity risk premium (ERP) Compensation for bearing market risk.

Equity swap A swap transaction in which at least one cash flow is tied to the return on an equity portfolio position, often an equity index.

Error autocorrelations The autocorrelations of the error term.

***Ex ante* tracking error** A measure of the degree to which the performance of a given investment portfolio might be expected to deviate from its benchmark; also known as *relative VaR*.

***Ex ante* version of PPP** The hypothesis that expected changes in the spot exchange rate are equal to expected differences in national inflation rates. An extension of relative purchasing power parity to expected future changes in the exchange rate.

Ex-dividend Trading ex-dividend refers to shares that no longer carry the right to the next dividend payment.

Ex-dividend date The first date that a share trades without (i.e., "ex") the right to receive the declared dividend for the period.

Excess earnings method Income approach that estimates the value of all intangible assets of the business by capitalizing future earnings in excess of the estimated return requirements associated with working capital and fixed assets.

Exercise date The date when employees actually exercise stock options and convert them to stock.

Exercise value The value of an option if it were exercised. Also sometimes called *intrinsic value*.

Expanded CAPM An adaptation of the CAPM that adds to the CAPM a premium for small size and company-specific risk.

Expectations approach A procedure for obtaining the value of an option derived from discounting at the risk-free rate its expected future payoff based on risk neutral probabilities.

Expected exposure The projected amount of money an investor could lose if an event of default occurs, before factoring in possible recovery.

Expected shortfall The average loss conditional on exceeding the VaR cutoff; sometimes referred to as *conditional VaR* or *expected tail loss*.

Expected tail loss See *expected shortfall*.

Exploratory data analysis (EDA) The preliminary step in data exploration, where graphs, charts, and other visualizations (heat maps and word clouds) as well as quantitative methods (descriptive statistics and central tendency measures) are used to observe and summarize data.

Exposure to foreign exchange risk The risk of a change in value of an asset or liability denominated in a foreign currency due to a change in exchange rates.

Extendible bond Bond with an embedded option that gives the bondholder the right to keep the bond for a number of years after maturity, possibly with a different coupon.

Extra dividend A dividend paid by a company that does not pay dividends on a regular schedule, or a dividend that supplements regular cash dividends with an extra payment.

F1 score The harmonic mean of precision and recall. F1 score is a more appropriate overall performance metric (than accuracy) when there is unequal class distribution in the dataset and it is necessary to measure the equilibrium of precision and recall.

FX carry trade An investment strategy that involves taking long positions in high-yield currencies and short positions in low-yield currencies.

Factor A common or underlying element with which several variables are correlated.

Factor betas An asset's sensitivity to a particular factor; a measure of the response of return to each unit of increase in a factor, holding all other factors constant.

Factor portfolio See *pure factor portfolio*.

Factor price The expected return in excess of the risk-free rate for a portfolio with a sensitivity of 1 to one factor and a sensitivity of 0 to all other factors.

Factor risk premium The expected return in excess of the risk-free rate for a portfolio with a sensitivity of 1 to one factor and a sensitivity of 0 to all other factors. Also called *factor price*.

Factor risk premiums The expected return in excess of the risk-free rate for a portfolio with a sensitivity of 1 to one factor and a sensitivity of 0 to all other factors. Also called factor price.

Failure to pay When a borrower does not make a scheduled payment of principal or interest on any outstanding obligations after a grace period.

Fair market value The price, expressed in terms of cash equivalents, at which a property (asset) would change hands between a hypothetical willing and able buyer and a hypothetical willing and able seller, acting at "arm's length" in an open and unrestricted market, when neither is under compulsion to buy or sell and when both have reasonable knowledge of the relevant facts. Fair market value is most often used in a tax reporting context in the United States.

Fair value The amount at which an asset could be exchanged, or a liability settled, between knowledgeable, willing parties in an arm's-length transaction; the price that would be received to sell an asset or paid to transfer a liability in an orderly transaction between market participants.

Fama–French models Factor models that explain the drivers of returns related to three, four, or five factors.

Feature engineering A process of creating new features by changing or transforming existing features.

Feature selection A process whereby only pertinent features from the dataset are selected for model training. Selecting fewer features decreases model complexity and training time.

Features The independent variables (X's) in a labeled dataset.

Finance (or capital) lease A lease that is viewed as a financing arrangement.

Financial contagion A situation in which financial shocks spread from their place of origin to other locales. In essence, a faltering economy infects other, healthier economies.

Financial leverage The use of fixed sources of capital, such as debt, relative to sources without fixed costs, such as equity.

Financial transaction A purchase involving a buyer having essentially no material synergies with the target (e.g., the purchase of a private company by a company in an unrelated industry or by a private equity firm would typically be a financial transaction).

First-differencing A transformation that subtracts the value of the time series in period $t - 1$ from its value in period t.

First-order serial correlation The correlation of residuals with residuals adjacent in time.

Fitting curve A curve which shows in- and out-of-sample error rates (E_{in} and E_{out}) on the y-axis plotted against model complexity on the x-axis.

Fixed price tender offer Offer made by a company to repurchase a specific number of shares at a fixed price that is typically at a premium to the current market price.

Fixed-rate perpetual preferred stock Nonconvertible, non-callable preferred stock that has a fixed dividend rate and no maturity date.

Flight to quality During times of market stress, investors sell higher-risk asset classes such as stocks and commodities in favor of default-risk-free government bonds.

Float Amounts collected as premium and not yet paid out as benefits.

Floored floater Floating-rate bond with a floor provision that prevents the coupon rate from decreasing below a specified minimum rate. It protects the investor against declining interest rates.

Flotation cost Fees charged to companies by investment bankers and other costs associated with raising new capital.

Forced conversion For a convertible bond, when the issuer calls the bond and forces bondholders to convert their bonds into shares, which typically happens when the underlying share price increases above the conversion price.

Foreign currency transactions Transactions that are denominated in a currency other than a company's functional currency.

Forward curve A series of forward rates, each having the same time frame.

Forward dividend yield A dividend yield based on the anticipated dividend during the next 12 months.

Forward-looking estimates Estimates based on current and expectations. Also referred to as ex ante estimates.

Forward P/E A P/E calculated on the basis of a forecast of EPS; a stock's current price divided by next year's expected earnings.

Forward price Represents the price agreed upon in a forward contract to be exchanged at the contract's maturity date, T. This price is shown in equations as $F_0(T)$.

Forward pricing model The model that describes the valuation of forward contracts.

Forward propagation The process of adjusting weights in a neural network, to reduce total error of the network, by moving forward through the network's layers.

Forward rate An interest rate determined today for a loan that will be initiated in a future period.

Forward rate agreement An over-the-counter forward contract in which the underlying is an interest rate on a deposit. A forward rate agreement (FRA) calls for one party to make a fixed interest payment and the other to make an interest payment at a rate to be determined at contract expiration.

Forward rate model The forward pricing model expressed in terms of spot and forward interest rates.

Forward rate parity The proposition that the forward exchange rate is an unbiased predictor of the future spot exchange rate.

Forward value The monetary value of an existing forward contract.

Franchising An owner of an asset and associated intellectual property divests the asset and licenses intellectual property to a third-party operator (franchisee) in exchange for royalties. Franchisees operate under the constraints of a franchise agreement.

Franking credit A tax credit received by shareholders for the taxes that a corporation paid on its distributed earnings.

Free cash flow method Income approach that values an asset based on estimates of future cash flows discounted to present value by using a discount rate reflective of the risks associated with the cash flows.

Free cash flow to equity The cash flow available to a company's common shareholders after all operating expenses, interest, and principal payments have been made and necessary investments in working and fixed capital have been made.

Free cash flow to equity model A model of stock valuation that views a stock's intrinsic value as the present value of expected future free cash flows to equity.

Free cash flow to the firm The cash flow available to the company's suppliers of capital after all operating expenses (including taxes) have been paid and necessary investments in working and fixed capital have been made.

Free cash flow to the firm model A model of stock valuation that views the value of a firm as the present value of expected future free cash flows to the firm.

Frequency analysis The process of quantifying how important tokens are in a sentence and in the corpus as a whole. It helps in filtering unnecessary tokens (or features).

Functional currency The currency of the primary economic environment in which an entity operates.

Fundamental factor models A multifactor model in which the factors are attributes of stocks or companies that are important in explaining cross-sectional differences in stock prices.

Fundamentals Economic characteristics of a business, such as profitability, financial strength, and risk.

Funds available for distribution (FAD) See *adjusted funds from operations*.

Funds from operations (FFO) Net income (computed in accordance with generally accepted accounting principles) *plus* (1) gains and losses from sales of properties and (2) depreciation and amortization.

Futures price The pre-agreed price at which a futures contract buyer (seller) agrees to pay (receive) for the underlying at the maturity date of the futures contract.

Futures value The monetary value of an existing futures contract.

Gamma A numerical measure of how sensitive an option's delta (the sensitivity of the derivative's price) is to a change in the value of the underlying.

General linear F-test A test statistic used to assess the goodness of fit for an entire regression model, so it tests all independent variables in the model.

Generalize When a model retains its explanatory power when predicting out-of-sample (i.e., using new data).

Global CAPM (GCAPM) A single-factor model with a global index representing the single factor.

Going-concern assumption The assumption that the business will maintain its business activities into the foreseeable future.

Going-concern value A business's value under a going-concern assumption.

Goodwill An intangible asset that represents the excess of the purchase price of an acquired company over the value of the net identifiable assets acquired.

Gordon growth model A DDM that assumes dividends grow at a constant rate into the future.

Grant date The day that stock options are granted to employees.

Green bond Bonds in which the proceeds are designated by issuers to fund a specific project or portfolio of projects that have environmental or climate benefits.

Greenmail The purchase of the accumulated shares of a hostile investor by a company that is targeted for takeover by that investor, usually at a substantial premium over market price.

Greenwashing The risk that a green bond's proceeds are not actually used for a beneficial environmental or climate-related project.

Grid search A method of systematically training a model by using various combinations of hyperparameter values, cross validating each model, and determining which combination of hyperparameter values ensures the best model performance.

Gross domestic product The market value of all final goods and services produced within the economy during a given period (output definition) or, equivalently, the aggregate income earned by all households, all companies, and the government within the economy during a given period (income definition).

Gross lease A lease under which the tenant pays a gross rent to the landlord, who is responsible for all operating costs, utilities, maintenance expenses, and real estate taxes relating to the property.

Ground truth The known outcome (i.e., target variable) of each observation in a labelled dataset.

Growth accounting equation The production function written in the form of growth rates. For the basic Cobb–Douglas production function, it states that the growth rate of output equals the rate of technological change plus α multiplied by the growth rate of capital plus (1 – α) multiplied by the growth rate of labor.

Growth capital expenditures Capital expenditures needed for expansion.

Guideline assets Assets used as benchmarks when applying the method of comparables to value an asset.

Guideline companies Assets used as benchmarks when applying the method of comparables to value an asset.

Guideline public companies Public-company comparables for the company being valued.

Guideline public company method A variation of the market approach; establishes a value estimate based on the observed multiples from trading activity in the shares of public companies viewed as reasonably comparable to the subject private company.

Guideline transactions method A variation of the market approach; establishes a value estimate based on pricing multiples derived from the acquisition of control of entire public or private companies that were acquired.

Harmonic mean A type of weighted mean computed as the reciprocal of the arithmetic average of the reciprocals.

Hazard rate The probability that an event will occur, given that it has not already occurred.

Hedonic index Unlike a repeat-sales index, a hedonic index does not require repeat sales of the same property. It requires only one sale. The way it controls for the fact that different properties are selling each quarter is to include variables in the regression that control for differences in the characteristics of the property, such as size, age, quality of construction, and location.

Heteroskedastic When the variance of the residuals differs across observations in a regression.

Heteroskedasticity The property of having a nonconstant variance; refers to an error term with the property that its variance differs across observations.

Hierarchical clustering An iterative unsupervised learning procedure used for building a hierarchy of clusters.

High-leverage point An observation of an independent variable that has an extreme value and is potentially influential.

Highest and best use The concept that the best use of a vacant site is the use that would result in the highest value for the land. Presumably, the developer that could earn the highest risk-adjusted profit based on time, effort, construction and development cost, leasing, and exit value would be the one to pay the highest price for the land.

Historical exchange rates For accounting purposes, the exchange rates that existed when the assets and liabilities were initially recorded.

Historical scenario analysis A technique for exploring the performance and risk of investment strategies in different structural regimes.

Historical simulation A simulation method that uses past return data and a random number generator that picks observations from the historical series to simulate an asset's future returns.

Historical simulation method The application of historical price changes to the current portfolio.

Historical stress testing The process that tests how investment strategies would perform under some of the most negative (i.e., adverse) combinations of events and scenarios.

Ho–Lee model The first arbitrage-free term structure model. The model is calibrated to market data and uses a binomial lattice approach to generate a distribution of possible future interest rates.

Holdout samples Data samples that are not used to train a model.

Homoskedasticity The property of having a constant variance; refers to an error term that is constant across observations.

Horizontal ownership Companies with mutual business interests (e.g., key customers or suppliers) that have cross-holding share arrangements with each other.

Human capital An implied asset; the net present value of an investor's future expected labor income weighted by the probability of surviving to each future age. Also called *net employment capital*.

Hybrid approach With respect to forecasting, an approach that combines elements of both top-down and bottom-up analyses.

Hyperparameter A parameter whose value must be set by the researcher before learning begins.

iNAVs "Indicated" net asset values are intraday "fair value" estimates of an ETF share based on its creation basket.

ISDA Master Agreement A standard or "master" agreement published by the International Swaps and Derivatives Association. The master agreement establishes the terms for each party involved in the transaction.

I-spreads Shortened form of "interpolated spreads" and a reference to a linearly interpolated yield.

Idiosyncratic risk premium (IRP) The additional return required for bearing company-specific risks.

Illiquidity discount A reduction or discount to value that reflects the lack of depth of trading or liquidity in that asset's market.

Impairment Diminishment in value as a result of carrying (book) value exceeding fair value and/or recoverable value.

Impairment of capital rule A legal restriction that dividends cannot exceed retained earnings.

Implementation shortfall (IS) The difference between the return for a notional or paper portfolio, where all transactions are assumed to take place at the manager's decision price, and the portfolio's actual return, which reflects realized transactions, including all fees and costs.

Implied volatility The standard deviation that causes an option pricing model to give the current option price.

In-sample forecast errors The residuals from a fitted time-series model within the sample period used to fit the model.

Income approach A valuation approach that values an asset as the present discounted value of the income expected from it. In the context of real estate, this approach estimates the value of a property based on an expected rate of return. The estimated value is the present value of the expected future income from the property, including proceeds from resale at the end of a typical investment holding period.

Incremental borrowing rate (IBR) The rate of interest that the lessee would have to pay to borrow using a collateralized loan over the same term as a lease.

Incremental VaR (IVaR) A measure of the incremental effect of an asset on the VaR of a portfolio by measuring the difference between the portfolio's VaR while including a specified asset and the portfolio's VaR with that asset eliminated.

Indenture A written contract between a lender and borrower that specifies the terms of the loan, such as interest rate, interest payment schedule, or maturity.

Independent board directors Directors with no material relationship with the company with regard to employment, ownership, or remuneration.

Independent regulators Regulators recognized and granted authority by a government body or agency. They are not government agencies per se and typically do not rely on government funding.

Index CDS A type of credit default swap that involves a combination of borrowers.

Industry risk premium (IP) The additional return that is required to bear industry-specific risk.

Industry shocks Unexpected changes to an industry from regulations or the legal environment, technology, or changes in the growth rate of the industry.

Industry structure An industry's underlying economic and technical characteristics.

Influence plot A visual that shows, for all observations, studentized residuals on the y-axis, leverage on the x-axis, and Cook's D as circles whose size is proportional to the degree of influence of the given observation.

Influential observation An observation in a statistical analysis whose inclusion may significantly alter regression results.

Information gain A metric which quantifies the amount of information that the feature holds about the response. Information gain can be regarded as a form of non-linear correlation between Y and X.

Information ratio (IR) Mean active return divided by active risk; or alpha divided by the standard deviation of diversifiable risk.

Informational frictions Forces that restrict availability, quality, and/or flow of information and its use.

Inside ask See *best ask*.

Inside bid See *best bid*.

Inside spread The spread between the best bid price and the best ask price. Also called the *market bid-ask spread*, *inside bid-ask spread*, or *market spread*.

Insiders Corporate managers and board directors who are also shareholders of a company.

Intangible assets Assets without a physical form, such as patents and trademarks.

Inter-temporal rate of substitution The ratio of the marginal utility of consumption s periods in the future (the numerator) to the marginal utility of consumption today (the denominator).

Interaction term A term that combines two or more variables and represents their joint influence on the dependent variable.

Intercept dummy An indicator variable that allows a single regression model to estimate two lines of best fit, each with differing intercepts, depending on whether the dummy takes a value of 1 or 0.

Interest rate risk The risk that interest rates will rise and therefore the market value of current portfolio holdings will fall so that their current yields to maturity then match comparable instruments in the marketplace.

Interlocking directorates Corporate structure in which individuals serve on the board of directors of multiple corporations.

International CAPM (ICAPM) A two-factor model with a global index and a wealth-weighted currency index.

International Fisher effect The proposition that nominal interest rate differentials across currencies are determined by expected inflation differentials.

Intrinsic value The amount gained (per unit) by an option buyer if an option is exercised at any given point in time. May be referred to as the exercise value of the option.

Inverse price ratio The reciprocal of a price multiple—for example, in the case of a P/E, the "earnings yield" E/P (where P is share price and E is earnings per share).

Investment value The value to a specific buyer, taking account of potential synergies based on the investor's requirements and expectations.

Joint test of hypotheses The test of hypotheses that specify values for two or more independent variables in the hypotheses.

Joint venture Two or more companies form and control a new, separate company to achieve a business objective. Each participant contributes assets, employees, know-how, or other resources to the joint venture company. The participants maintain their independence otherwise and continue to do business apart from the joint venture, but they share in the joint venture's profits or losses.

Judicial law Interpretations of courts.

Justified price multiple The estimated fair value of the price multiple, usually based on forecasted fundamentals or comparables.

Justified (fundamental) P/E The price-to-earnings ratio that is fair, warranted, or justified on the basis of forecasted fundamentals.

***K*-fold cross-validation** A technique in which data (excluding test sample and fresh data) are shuffled randomly and then are divided into k equal sub-samples, with $k - 1$ samples used as training samples and one sample, the kth, used as a validation sample.

***K*-means** A clustering algorithm that repeatedly partitions observations into a fixed number, k, of non-overlapping clusters.

***K*-nearest neighbor** A supervised learning technique that classifies a new observation by finding similarities ("nearness") between this new observation and the existing data.

Kalotay–Williams–Fabozzi (KWF) model An arbitrage-free term structure model that describes the dynamics of the log of the short rate and assumes constant drift, no mean reversion, and constant volatility.

Key rate durations Sensitivity of a bond's price to changes in specific maturities on the benchmark yield curve. Also called *partial durations*.

***k*th-order autocorrelation** The correlation between observations in a time series separated by *k* periods.

LASSO Least absolute shrinkage and selection operator is a type of penalized regression which involves minimizing the sum of the absolute values of the regression coefficients. LASSO can also be used for regularization in neural networks.

Labeled dataset A dataset that contains matched sets of observed inputs or features (*X*'s) and the associated output or target (*Y*).

Labor force Everyone of working age (ages 16 to 64) who either is employed or is available for work but not working.

Labor force participation rate The percentage of the working age population that is in the labor force.

Labor productivity The quantity of goods and services (real GDP) that a worker can produce in one hour of work.

Labor productivity growth accounting equation States that potential GDP growth equals the growth rate of the labor input plus the growth rate of labor productivity.

Lack of marketability discount An extra return to investors to compensate for lack of a public market or lack of marketability.

Latency The elapsed time between the occurrence of an event and a subsequent action that depends on that event.

Law of one price A principle that states that if two investments have the same or equivalent future cash flows regardless of what will happen in the future, then these two investments should have the same current price.

Leading dividend yield Forecasted dividends per share over the next year divided by current stock price.

Leading P/E A P/E calculated on the basis of a forecast of EPS; a stock's current price divided by next year's expected earnings.

Learning curve A curve that plots the accuracy rate (= 1 − error rate) in the validation or test samples (i.e., out-of-sample) against the amount of data in the training sample, which is thus useful for describing under- and overfitting as a function of bias and variance errors.

Learning rate A parameter that affects the magnitude of adjustments in the weights in a neural network.

Level One of the three factors (the other two are steepness and curvature) that empirically explain most yield curve shape changes. A shock to the level factor changes the yield for all maturities by an almost identical amount.

Leverage A measure for identifying a potentially influential high-leverage point.

Leveraged buyout (LBO) An acquirer (typically an investment fund specializing in LBOs) uses a significant amount of debt to finance the acquisition of a target and then pursues restructuring actions, with the goal of exiting the target with a sale or public listing.

Libor–OIS spread The difference between Libor and the overnight indexed swap rate.

Likelihood ratio (LR) test A method to assess the fit of logistic regression models and is based on the log-likelihood metric that describes the model's fit to the data.

Limit order book The book or list of limit orders to buy and sell that pertains to a security.

Linear classifier A binary classifier that makes its classification decision based on a linear combination of the features of each data point.

Linear trend A trend in which the dependent variable changes at a constant rate with time.

Liquidating dividend A dividend that is a return of capital rather than a distribution from earnings or retained earnings.

Liquidation value The value of a company if the company were dissolved and its assets sold individually.

Liquidity preference theory A term structure theory that asserts liquidity premiums exist to compensate investors for the added interest rate risk they face when lending long term.

Liquidity premium An extra return that compensates investors for the risk of loss relative to an investment's fair value if the investment needs to be converted to cash quickly.

Local currency The currency of the country where a company is located.

Local expectations theory A term structure theory that contends the return for all bonds over short periods is the risk-free rate.

Log-linear model With reference to time-series models, a model in which the growth rate of the time series as a function of time is constant.

Log odds The natural log of the odds of an event or characteristic happening. Also known as the *logit function*.

Logistic regression (logit) A regression in which the dependent variable uses a logistic transformation of the event probability.

Logistic transformation The log of the probability of an occurrence of an event or characteristic divided by the probability of the event or characteristic not occurring.

Long/short credit trade A credit protection seller with respect to one entity combined with a credit protection buyer with respect to another entity.

Look-ahead bias A bias caused by using information that was unavailable on the test date.

Lookback period The time period used to gather a historical data set.

Loss given default The amount that will be lost if a default occurs.

Macroeconomic factor model A multifactor model in which the factors are surprises in macroeconomic variables that significantly explain equity returns.

Macroeconomic factors Factors related to the economy, such as the inflation rate, industrial production, or economic sector membership.

Maintenance capital expenditures Capital expenditures needed to maintain operations at the current level.

Majority shareholders Shareholders that own more than 50% of a corporation's shares.

Majority-vote classifier A classifier that assigns to a new data point the predicted label with the most votes (i.e., occurrences).

Marginal VaR (MVaR) A measure of the effect of a small change in a position size on portfolio VaR.

Market approach Valuation approach that values an asset based on pricing multiples from sales of assets viewed as similar to the subject asset.

Market conditions Interest rates, inflation rates, and other economic characteristics that comprise the macroeconomic environment.

Market conversion premium per share For a convertible bond, the difference between the market conversion price and the underlying share price, which allows investors to identify the premium or discount payable when buying a convertible bond rather than the underlying common stock.

Market conversion premium ratio For a convertible bond, the market conversion premium per share expressed as a percentage of the current market price of the shares.

Market efficiency A finance perspective on capital markets that deals with the relationship of price to intrinsic value. The traditional efficient markets formulation asserts that an asset's price is the best available estimate of its intrinsic value. The rational efficient markets formulation asserts that investors should expect to be rewarded for the costs of information gathering and analysis by higher gross returns.

Market fragmentation Trading the same instrument in multiple venues.

Market impact The effect of the trade on transaction prices. Also called *price impact*.

Market model A regression model with the return on a stock as the dependent variable and the returns on a market index as the independent variable.

Market value of invested capital The market value of debt and equity.

Mature growth rate The earnings growth rate in a company's mature phase; an earnings growth rate that can be sustained long term.

Maximum drawdown The worst cumulative loss ever sustained by an asset or portfolio. More specifically, maximum drawdown is the difference between an asset's or a portfolio's maximum cumulative return and its subsequent lowest cumulative return.

Maximum likelihood estimation (MLE) A method that estimates values for the intercept and slope coefficients in a logistic regression that make the data in the regression sample most likely.

Mean reversion The tendency of a time series to fall when its level is above its mean and rise when its level is below its mean; a mean-reverting time series tends to return to its long-term mean.

Metadata Data that describes and gives information about other data.

Method based on forecasted fundamentals An approach to using price multiples that relates a price multiple to forecasts of fundamentals through a discounted cash flow model.

Method of comparables An approach to valuation that involves using a price multiple to evaluate whether an asset is relatively fairly valued, relatively undervalued, or relatively overvalued when compared to a benchmark value of the multiple.

Midquote price The average, or midpoint, of the prevailing bid and ask prices.

Minority interest The proportion of the ownership of a subsidiary not held by the parent (controlling) company.

Minority shareholders Particular shareholders or a block of shareholders holding a small proportion of a company's outstanding shares, resulting in a limited ability to exercise control in voting activities.

Mispricing Any departure of the market price of an asset from the asset's estimated intrinsic value.

Model specification The set of independent variables included in a model and the model's functional form.

Molodovsky effect The observation that P/Es tend to be high on depressed EPS at the bottom of a business cycle and tend to be low on unusually high EPS at the top of a business cycle.

Momentum indicators Valuation indicators that relate either price or a fundamental (such as earnings) to the time series of their own past values (or in some cases to their expected value).

Monetary assets and liabilities Assets and liabilities with value equal to the amount of currency contracted for, a fixed amount of currency. Examples are cash, accounts receivable, accounts payable, bonds payable, and mortgages payable. Inventory is not a monetary asset. Most liabilities are monetary.

Monetary/non-monetary method Approach to translating foreign currency financial statements for consolidation in which monetary assets and liabilities are translated at the current exchange rate. Non-monetary assets and liabilities are translated at historical exchange rates (the exchange rates that existed when the assets and liabilities were acquired).

Monetizing Unwinding a position to either capture a gain or realize a loss.

Monte Carlo simulation A technique that uses the inverse transformation method for converting a randomly generated uniformly distributed number into a simulated value of a random variable of a desired distribution. Each key decision variable in a Monte Carlo simulation requires an assumed statistical distribution; this assumption facilitates incorporating non-normality, fat tails, and tail dependence as well as solving high-dimensionality problems.

Mortgage A loan with real estate serving as collateral for the loan.

Multicollinearity When two or more independent variables are highly correlated with one another or are approximately linearly related.

Multiple linear regression Modeling and estimation method that uses two or more independent variables to describe the variation of the dependent variable. Also referred to as *multiple regression*.

Mutual information Measures how much information is contributed by a token to a class of texts. MI will be 0 if the token's distribution in all text classes is the same. MI approaches 1 as the token in any one class tends to occur more often in only that particular class of text.

N-grams A representation of word sequences. The length of a sequence varies from 1 to n. When one word is used, it is a unigram; a two-word sequence is a bigram; and a 3-word sequence is a trigram; and so on.

n-Period moving average The average of the current and immediately prior $n - 1$ values of a time series.

NTM P/E Next 12-month P/E: current market price divided by an estimated next 12-month EPS.

Naked credit default swap A position where the owner of the CDS does not have a position in the underlying credit.

Name entity recognition An algorithm that analyzes individual tokens and their surrounding semantics while referring to its dictionary to tag an object class to the token.

Negative serial correlation A situation in which residuals are negatively related to other residuals.

Nested models Models in which one regression model has a subset of the independent variables of another regression model.

Net asset balance sheet exposure When assets translated at the current exchange rate are greater in amount than liabilities translated at the current exchange rate. Assets exposed to translation gains or losses exceed the exposed liabilities.

Net asset value per share (NAVPS) Net asset value divided by the number of shares outstanding.

Net lease A lease under which the tenant pays a net rent to the landlord and an additional amount based on the tenant's pro rata share of the operating costs, utilities, maintenance expenses, and real estate taxes relating to the property.

Net liability balance sheet exposure When liabilities translated at the current exchange rate are greater assets translated at the current exchange rate. Liabilities exposed to translation gains or losses exceed the exposed assets.

Net operating income (NOI) Gross rental revenue minus operating costs but before deducting depreciation, corporate overhead, and interest expense. In the context of real estate, a measure of the income from the property after deducting operating expenses for such items as property taxes, insurance, maintenance, utilities, repairs, and insurance but before deducting any costs associated with financing and before deducting federal income taxes. It is similar to EBITDA in a financial reporting context.

Net regulatory burden The private costs of regulation less the private benefits of regulation.

Network externalities The impact that users of a good, a service, or a technology have on other users of that product; it can be positive (e.g., a critical mass of users makes a product more useful) or negative (e.g., congestion makes the product less useful).

Neural networks Computer programs based on how our own brains learn and process information.

No-arbitrage approach A procedure for obtaining the value of an option based on the creation of a portfolio that replicates the payoffs of the option and deriving the option value from the value of the replicating portfolio.

No-growth company A company without positive expected net present value projects.

No-growth value per share The value per share of a no-growth company, equal to the expected level amount of earnings divided by the stock's required rate of return.

Non-cash rent An amount equal to the difference between the average contractual rent over a lease term (the straight-line rent) and the cash rent actually paid during a period. This figure is one of the deductions made from FFO to calculate AFFO.

Non-convergence trap A situation in which a country remains relatively poor, or even falls further behind, because it fails to implement necessary institutional reforms and/or adopt leading technologies.

Non-monetary assets and liabilities Assets and liabilities that are not monetary assets and liabilities. Non-monetary assets include inventory, fixed assets, and intangibles, and non-monetary liabilities include deferred revenue.

Non-renewable resources Finite resources that are depleted once they are consumed; oil and coal are examples.

Non-residential properties Commercial real estate properties other than multi-family properties, farmland, and timberland.

Nonearning assets Cash and investments (specifically cash, cash equivalents, and short-term investments).

Normal EPS The EPS that a business could achieve currently under mid-cyclical conditions. Also called *normalized EPS*.

Normal Q-Q plot A visual used to compare the distribution of the residuals from a regression to a theoretical normal distribution.

Normalized EPS The EPS that a business could achieve currently under mid-cyclical conditions. Also called *normal EPS*.

Normalized earnings The expected level of mid-cycle earnings for a company in the absence of any unusual or temporary factors that affect profitability (either positively or negatively).

Normalized P/E P/E based on normalized EPS data.

Notional amount The amount of protection being purchased in a CDS.

Off-the-run A series of securities or indexes that were issued/created prior to the most recently issued/created series.

Offshoring Refers to relocating operations from one country to another, mainly to reduce costs through lower labor costs or to achieve economies of scale through centralization, but still maintaining operations within the corporation.

Omitted variable bias Bias resulting from the omission of an important independent variable from a regression model.

On-the-run The most recently issued and most actively traded sovereign securities.

One hot encoding The process by which categorical variables are converted into binary form (0 or 1) for machine reading. It is one of the most common methods for handling categorical features in text data.

One-sided durations Effective durations when interest rates go up or down, which are better at capturing the interest rate sensitivity of bonds with embedded options that do not react symmetrically to positive and negative changes in interest rates of the same magnitude.

One-tier board Board structure consisting of a single board of directors, composed of executive (internal) and non-executive (external) directors.

Opportunity cost Reflects the foregone opportunity of investing in a different asset. It is typically denoted by the risk-free rate of interest, r.

Option-adjusted spread (OAS) Constant spread that, when added to all the one-period forward rates on the interest rate tree, makes the arbitrage-free value of the bond equal to its market price.

Orderly liquidation value The estimated gross amount of money that could be realized from the liquidation sale of an asset or assets, given a reasonable amount of time to find a purchaser or purchasers.

Other comprehensive income Items of comprehensive income that are not reported on the income statement; comprehensive income minus net income.

Other post-employment benefits Promises by the company to pay benefits in the future, such as life insurance premiums and all or part of health care insurance for its retirees.

Out-of-sample forecast errors The differences between actual and predicted values of time series outside the sample period used to fit the model.

Outlier An observation that has an extreme value of the dependent variable and is potentially influential.

Outsourcing Shifting internal business services to a subcontractor that can offer services at lower costs by scaling to serve many clients.

Overfitting Situation in which the model has too many independent variables relative to the number of observations in the sample, such that the coefficients on the independent variables represent noise rather than relationships with the dependent variable.

Overnight indexed swap (OIS) rate An interest rate swap in which the periodic floating rate of the swap equals the geometric average of a daily unsecured overnight rate (or overnight index rate).

PEG ratio The P/E-to-growth ratio, calculated as the stock's P/E divided by the expected earnings growth rate.

Pairs trading An approach to trading that uses pairs of closely related stocks, buying the relatively undervalued stock and selling short the relatively overvalued stock.

Par curve A sequence of yields-to-maturity such that each bond is priced at par value. The bonds are assumed to have the same currency, credit risk, liquidity, tax status, and annual yields stated for the same periodicity.

Par swap A swap in which the fixed rate is set so that no money is exchanged at contract initiation.

Parametric method A method of estimating VaR that uses the historical mean, standard deviation, and correlation of security price movements to estimate the portfolio VaR. Generally assumes a normal distribution but can be adapted to non-normal distributions with the addition of skewness and kurtosis. Sometimes called the *variance–covariance method* or the *analytical method*.

Partial regression coefficient Coefficient that describes the effect of a one-unit change in the independent variable on the dependent variable, holding all other independent variables constant. Also known as *partial slope coefficient*.

Parts of speech An algorithm that uses language structure and dictionaries to tag every token in the text with a corresponding part of speech (i.e., noun, verb, adjective, proper noun, etc.).

Payout amount The loss given default times the notional.

Payout policy The principles by which a company distributes cash to common shareholders by means of cash dividends and/or share repurchases.

Payouts Cash dividends and the value of shares repurchased in any given year.

Penalized regression A regression that includes a constraint such that the regression coefficients are chosen to minimize the sum of squared residuals *plus* a penalty term that increases in size with the number of included features.

Pension obligation The present value of future benefits earned by employees for service provided to date.

Perfect capital markets Markets in which, by assumption, there are no taxes, transaction costs, or bankruptcy costs and in which all investors have equal ("symmetric") information.

Perpetuity A perpetual annuity, or a set of never-ending level sequential cash flows, with the first cash flow occurring one period from now.

Persistent earnings Earnings excluding nonrecurring components. Also referred to as *core earnings*, *continuing earnings*, or *underlying earnings*.

Physical settlement Involves actual delivery of the debt instrument in exchange for a payment by the credit protection seller of the notional amount of the contract.

Point-in-time data Data consisting of the exact information available to market participants as of a given point in time. Point-in-time data is used to address look-ahead bias.

Portfolio balance approach A theory of exchange rate determination that emphasizes the portfolio investment decisions of global investors and the requirement that global investors willingly hold all outstanding securities denominated in each currency at prevailing prices and exchange rates.

Positive serial correlation A situation in which residuals are positively related to other residuals.

Potential GDP The maximum amount of output an economy can sustainably produce without inducing an increase in the inflation rate. The output level that corresponds to full employment with consistent wage and price expectations.

Precision In error analysis for classification problems it is ratio of correctly predicted positive classes to all predicted positive classes. Precision is useful in situations where the cost of false positives (FP), or Type I error, is high.

Preferred habitat theory A term structure theory that contends that investors have maturity preferences and require yield incentives before they will buy bonds outside of their preferred maturities.

Premise of value The status of a company in the sense of whether it is assumed to be a going concern or not.

Premium leg The series of payments the credit protection buyer promises to make to the credit protection seller.

Premiums Amounts paid by the purchaser of insurance products.

Present value model A model of intrinsic value that views the value of an asset as the present value of the asset's expected future cash flows.

Present value of growth opportunities The difference between the actual value per share and the no-growth value per share. Also called *value of growth*.

Presentation currency The currency in which financial statement amounts are presented.

Price improvement When trade execution prices are better than quoted prices.

Price momentum A valuation indicator based on past price movement.

Price multiples The ratio of a stock's market price to some measure of value per share.

Price-to-earnings ratio (P/E) The ratio of share price to earnings per share.

Priced risk Risk for which investors demand compensation for bearing (e.g., equity risk, company-specific factors, macroeconomic factors).

Principal components analysis (PCA) An unsupervised ML technique used to transform highly correlated features of data into a few main, uncorrelated composite variables.

Principle of no arbitrage In well-functioning markets, prices will adjust until there are no arbitrage opportunities.

Prior transaction method A variation of the market approach; considers actual transactions in the stock of the subject private company.

Private market value The value derived using a sum-of-the-parts valuation.

Pro forma financial statements Financial statements that include the effect of a corporate restructuring.

Probability of default The likelihood that a borrower defaults or fails to meet its obligation to make full and timely payments of principal and interest.

Probability of survival The probability that a bond issuer will meet its contractual obligations on schedule.

Procedural law The body of law that focuses on the protection and enforcement of the substantive laws.

Projection error The vertical (perpendicular) distance between a data point and a given principal component.

Prospective P/E A P/E calculated on the basis of a forecast of EPS; a stock's current price divided by next year's expected earnings.

Protection leg The contingent payment that the credit protection seller may have to make to the credit protection buyer.

Protection period Period during which a bond's issuer cannot call the bond.

Provision for loan losses An income statement expense account that increases the amount of the allowance for loan losses.

Prudential supervision Regulation and monitoring of the safety and soundness of financial institutions to promote financial stability, reduce system-wide risks, and protect customers of financial institutions.

Pruning A regularization technique used in CART to reduce the size of the classification or regression tree—by pruning, or removing, sections of the tree that provide little classifying power.

Purchasing power gain A gain in value caused by changes in price levels. Monetary liabilities experience purchasing power gains during periods of inflation.

Purchasing power loss A loss in value caused by changes in price levels. Monetary assets experience purchasing power loss during periods of inflation.

Purchasing power parity (PPP) The idea that exchange rates move to equalize the purchasing power of different currencies.

Pure expectations theory A term structure theory that contends the forward rate is an unbiased predictor of the future spot rate. Also called the *unbiased expectations theory*.

Pure factor portfolio A portfolio with sensitivity of 1 to the factor in question and a sensitivity of 0 to all other factors.

Putable bond Bond that includes an embedded put option, which gives the bondholder the right to put back the bonds to the issuer prior to maturity, typically when interest rates have risen and higher-yielding bonds are available.

Qualitative dependent variable A dependent variable that is discrete (binary). Also known as a *categorical dependent variable*.

Quality of earnings analysis The investigation of issues relating to the accuracy of reported accounting results as reflections of economic performance. Quality of earnings analysis is broadly understood to include not only earnings management but also balance sheet management.

Random forest classifier A collection of a large number of decision trees trained via a bagging method.

Random walk A time series in which the value of the series in one period is the value of the series in the previous period plus an unpredictable random error.

Rate implicit in the lease (RIIL) The discount rate that equates the present value of the lease payment with the fair value of the leased asset, considering also the lessor's direct costs and the present value of the leased asset's residual value.

Rational efficient markets formulation See *market efficiency*.

Readme files Text files provided with raw data that contain information related to a data file. They are useful for understanding the data and how they can be interpreted correctly.

Real estate investment trusts (REITs) Tax-advantaged entities (companies or trusts) that own, operate, and—to a limited extent—develop income-producing real estate property.

Real estate operating companies (REOCs) Regular taxable real estate ownership companies that operate in the real estate industry in countries that do not have a tax-advantaged REIT regime in place or that are engage in real estate activities of a kind and to an extent that do not fit in their country's REIT framework.

Real interest rate parity The proposition that real interest rates will converge to the same level across different markets.

Real options Options that relate to investment decisions such as the option to time the start of a project, the option to adjust its scale, or the option to abandon a project that has begun.

Rebalance return A return from rebalancing the component weights of an index.

Recall Also known as *sensitivity*, in error analysis for classification problems it is the ratio of correctly predicted positive classes to all actual positive classes. Recall is useful in situations where the cost of false negatives (FN), or Type II error, is high.

Recency bias The behavioral tendency to place more relevance on recent events.

Reconstitution When dealers recombine appropriate individual zero-coupon securities and reproduce an underlying coupon Treasury.

Recovery rate The percentage of the loss recovered.

Redemption basket The list of securities (and share amounts) the authorized participant (AP) receives when it redeems ETF shares back to the ETF manager. The redemption basket is published each business day.

Reference entity The borrower (debt issuer) covered by a single-name CDS.

Reference obligation A particular debt instrument issued by the borrower that is the designated instrument being covered.

Regime With reference to a time series, the underlying model generating the times series.

Regular expression (regex) A series of texts that contains characters in a particular order. Regex is used to search for patterns of interest in a given text.

Regularization A term that describes methods for reducing statistical variability in high-dimensional data estimation problems.

Regulatory arbitrage Entities identify and use some aspect of regulations that allows them to exploit differences in economic substance and regulatory interpretation or in foreign and domestic regulatory regimes to their (the entities') advantage.

Regulatory burden The costs of regulation for the regulated entity.

Regulatory capture Theory that regulation often arises to enhance the interests of the regulated.

Regulatory competition Regulators may compete to provide a regulatory environment designed to attract certain entities.

Reinforcement learning Machine learning in which a computer learns from interacting with itself or data generated by the same algorithm.

Relative-strength indicators Valuation indicators that compare a stock's performance during a period either to its own past performance or to the performance of some group of stocks.

Relative VaR See *ex ante tracking error*.

Relative valuation models A model that specifies an asset's value relative to the value of another asset.

Relative version of PPP The hypothesis that changes in (nominal) exchange rates over time are equal to national inflation rate differentials.

Renewable resources Resources that can be replenished, such as a forest.

Rental price of capital The cost per unit of time to rent a unit of capital.

Reorganization A court-supervised restructuring process available in some jurisdictions for companies facing insolvency from burdensome debt levels. A bankruptcy court assumes control of the company and oversees an orderly negotiation process between the company and its creditors for asset sales, conversion of debt to equity, refinancing, and so on.

Repeat sales index As the name implies, this type of index relies on repeat sales of the same property. In general, the idea supporting this type of index is that because it is the same property that sold twice, the change in value between the two sale dates indicates how market conditions have changed over time.

Replacement cost In the context of real estate, the value of a building assuming it was built today using current construction costs and standards.

Reporting unit For financial reporting under US GAAP, an operating segment or one level below an operating segment (referred to as a component).

Required rate of return on equity The minimum rate of return required by an investor to invest in an asset, given the asset's riskiness. Also known as the required return on equity.

Residential properties Properties that provide housing for individuals or families. Single-family properties may be owner-occupied or rental properties, whereas multi-family properties are rental properties even if the owner or manager occupies one of the units.

Residual autocorrelations The sample autocorrelations of the residuals.

Residual income Earnings for a given period, minus a deduction for common shareholders' opportunity cost in generating the earnings. Also called *economic profit* or *abnormal earnings*.

Residual income method Income approach that estimates the value of all intangible assets of the business by capitalizing future earnings in excess of the estimated return requirements associated with working capital and fixed assets.

Residual income model (RIM) A model of stock valuation that views intrinsic value of stock as the sum of book value per share plus the present value of the stock's expected future residual income per share. Also called *discounted abnormal earnings model* or *Edwards–Bell–Ohlson model*.

Restricted model A regression model with a subset of the complete set of independent variables.

Restructuring Reorganizing the capital structure of a firm.

Return on invested capital A measure of the profitability of a company relative to the amount of capital invested by the equity- and debtholders.

Reverse carry arbitrage A strategy involving the short sale of the underlying and an offsetting opposite position in the derivative.

Reverse stock split A reduction in the number of shares outstanding with a corresponding increase in share price, but no change to the company's underlying fundamentals.

Reverse stress testing A risk management approach in which the user identifies key risk exposures in the portfolio and subjects those exposures to extreme market movements.

Reviewed financial statements A type of non-audited financial statements; typically provide an opinion letter with representations and assurances by the reviewing accountant that are less than those in audited financial statements.

Rho The change in a given derivative instrument for a given small change in the risk-free interest rate, holding everything else constant. Rho measures the sensitivity of the option to the risk-free interest rate.

Risk-based models Models of the return on equity that identify risk factors or drivers and sensitivities of the return to these factors.

Risk budgeting The establishment of objectives for individuals, groups, or divisions of an organization that takes into account the allocation of an acceptable level of risk.

Risk decomposition The process of converting a set of holdings in a portfolio into a set of exposures to risk factors.

Risk factors Variables or characteristics with which individual asset returns are correlated. Sometimes referred to simply as *factors*.

Risk-free rate The minimum rate of return expected on a security that has no default risk.

Risk parity A portfolio allocation scheme that weights stocks or factors based on an equal risk contribution.

Robust standard errors Method for correcting residuals for conditional heteroskedasticity. Also known as *heteroskedasticity-consistent standard errors* or *White-corrected standard errors*.

Roll When an investor moves its investment position from an older series to the most current series.

Roll return The component of the return on a commodity futures contract attributable to rolling long futures positions forward through time. Also called *roll yield*.

Rolling down the yield curve A maturity trading strategy that involves buying bonds with a maturity longer than the intended investment horizon. Also called *riding the yield curve*.

Rolling windows A backtesting method that uses a rolling-window (or walk-forward) framework, rebalances the portfolio after each period, and then tracks performance over time. As new information arrives each period, the investment manager optimizes (revises and tunes) the model and readjusts stock positions.

Root mean squared error (RMSE) The square root of the average squared forecast error; used to compare the out-of-sample forecasting performance of forecasting models.

Sale-leaseback A situation in which a company sells the building it owns and occupies to a real estate investor and the company then signs a long-term lease with the buyer to continue to occupy the building. At the end of the lease, use of the property reverts to the landlord.

Sales comparison approach In the context of real estate, this approach estimates value based on what similar or comparable properties (comparables) transacted for in the current market.

Sales risk The uncertainty regarding the price and number of units sold of a company's products.

Scaled earnings surprise Unexpected earnings divided by the standard deviation of analysts' earnings forecasts.

Scaling The process of adjusting the range of a feature by shifting and changing the scale of the data. Two of the most common ways of scaling are normalization and standardization.

Scatterplot matrix A visualization technique that shows the scatterplots between different sets of variables, often with the histogram for each variable on the diagonal. Also referred to as a *pairs plot*.

Scenario analysis A technique for exploring the performance and risk of investment strategies in different structural regimes.

Schwarz's Bayesian information criterion (BIC or SBC) A statistic used to compare sets of independent variables for explaining a dependent variable. It is preferred for finding the model with the best goodness of fit.

Scree plots A plot that shows the proportion of total variance in the data explained by each principal component.

Screening The application of a set of criteria to reduce a set of potential investments to a smaller set having certain desired characteristics.

Seasonality A characteristic of a time series in which the data experience regular and predictable periodic changes; for example, fan sales are highest during the summer months.

Secured overnight financing rate (SOFR) A daily volume-weighted index of rates on qualified cash borrowings collateralized by US Treasuries that is expected to replace Libor as a floating reference rate for swaps.

Security selection risk See *active specific risk*.

Segmented markets theory A term structure theory that contends yields are solely a function of the supply and demand for funds of a particular maturity.

Self-regulating organizations (SROs) Self-regulating bodies that are given recognition and authority, including enforcement power, by a government body or agency.

Self-regulatory bodies Private, non-governmental organizations that both represent and regulate their members. Some self-regulating organizations are also independent regulators.

Sell-side analysts Analysts who work at brokerages.

Sensitivity analysis Analysis that shows the range of possible outcomes as specific assumptions are changed.

Sentence length The number of characters, including spaces, in a sentence.

Serial correlation A condition found most often in time series in which residuals are correlated across observations. Also known as *autocorrelation*.

Serial-correlation consistent standard errors Method for correcting serial correlation. Also known as *serial correlation and heteroskedasticity adjusted standard errors*, *Newey–West standard errors*, and *robust standard errors*.

Service period For employee stock options, usually the period between the grant date and the vesting date.

Settled in arrears An arrangement in which the interest payment is made (i.e., settlement occurs) at the maturity of the underlying instrument.

Settlement The closing date at which the counterparties of a derivative contract exchange payment for the underlying as required by the contract.

Shadow banking Lending by financial institutions that are not regulated as banks.

Shaping risk The sensitivity of a bond's price to the changing shape of the yield curve.

Share repurchase A transaction in which a company buys back its own shares. Unlike stock dividends and stock splits, share repurchases use corporate cash.

Shareholder activism Strategies used by shareholders to attempt to compel a company to act in a desired manner.

Shareholders' equity Total assets minus total liabilities.

Simulation A technique for exploring how a target variable (e.g. portfolio returns) would perform in a hypothetical environment specified by the user, rather than a historical setting.

Single-name CDS Credit default swap on one specific borrower.

Sinking fund bond A bond that requires the issuer to set aside funds over time to retire the bond issue, thus reducing credit risk.

Size premium (SP) Additional return compensation for bearing the additional risk associated with smaller companies.

Slope dummy An indicator variable that allows a single regression model to estimate two lines of best fit, each with differing slopes, depending on whether the dummy takes a value of 1 or 0.

Soft margin classification An adaptation in the support vector machine algorithm which adds a penalty to the objective function for observations in the training set that are misclassified.

Sovereign yield spread The spread between the yield on a foreign country's sovereign bond and a similar-maturity domestic sovereign bond.

Special dividend A dividend paid by a company that does not pay dividends on a regular schedule, or a dividend that supplements regular cash dividends with an extra payment.

Specific-company risk premium (SCRP) Additional return required by investors for bearing non-diversifiable company-specific risk.

Spin off When a company separates a distinct part of its business into a new, independent company. The term is used to describe both the transaction and the separated component, while the company that conducts the transaction and formerly owned the spin off is known as the parent.

Split-rate tax system In reference to corporate taxes, a split-rate system taxes earnings to be distributed as dividends at a different rate than earnings to be retained. Corporate profits distributed as dividends are taxed at a lower rate than those retained in the business.

Spot curve A sequence of yields-to-maturity on zero-coupon bonds. Sometimes called *zero* or *strip curve* (because coupon payments are "stripped" off the bonds).

Spot price The current price of an asset or security. For commodities, the current price to deliver a physical commodity to a specific location or purchase and transport it away from a designated location.

Spot rate The interest rate that is determined today for a risk-free, single-unit payment at a specified future date.

Spot yield curve The term structure of spot rates for loans made today.

Stabilized NOI In the context of real estate, the expected NOI when a renovation is complete.

Stable dividend policy A policy in which regular dividends are paid that reflect long-run expected earnings. In contrast to a constant dividend payout ratio policy, a stable dividend policy does not reflect short-term volatility in earnings.

Standardized beta With reference to fundamental factor models, the value of the attribute for an asset minus the average value of the attribute across all stocks, divided by the standard deviation of the attribute across all stocks.

Standardized unexpected earnings Unexpected earnings per share divided by the standard deviation of unexpected earnings per share over a specified prior time period.

Statistical factor model A multifactor model in which statistical methods are applied to a set of historical returns to determine portfolios that best explain either historical return covariances or variances.

Statutes Laws enacted by legislative bodies.

Glossary

Steady-state rate of growth The constant growth rate of output (or output per capita) that can or will be sustained indefinitely once it is reached. Key ratios, such as the capital–output ratio, are constant on the steady-state growth path.

Steepness The difference between long-term and short-term yields that constitutes one of the three factors (the other two are level and curvature) that empirically explain most of the changes in the shape of the yield curve.

Stock dividend A type of dividend in which a company distributes additional shares of its common stock to shareholders instead of cash.

Stop-loss limit Constraint used in risk management that requires a reduction in the size of a portfolio, or its complete liquidation, when a loss of a particular size occurs in a specified period.

Straight bond An underlying option-free bond with a specified issuer, issue date, maturity date, principal amount and repayment structure, coupon rate and payment structure, and currency denomination.

Straight debt Debt with no embedded options.

Straight-line rent The average annual rent under a multi-year lease agreement that contains contractual increases in rent during the life of the lease.

Straight-line rent adjustment See *non-cash rent*.

Straight voting A shareholder voting process in which shareholders receive one vote for each share owned.

Stranded assets Assets that are obsolete or not economically viable.

Strategic transaction A purchase involving a buyer that would benefit from certain synergies associated with owning the target firm.

Stress tests A risk management technique that assesses the portfolio's response to extreme market movements.

Stripping A dealer's ability to separate a bond's individual cash flows and trade them as zero-coupon securities.

Studentized residual A *t*-distributed statistic that is used to detect outliers.

Substantive law The body of law that focuses on the rights and responsibilities of entities and relationships among entities.

Succession event A change of corporate structure of the reference entity, such as through a merger, a divestiture, a spinoff, or any similar action, in which ultimate responsibility for the debt in question is unclear.

Sum-of-the-parts valuation A valuation that sums the estimated values of each of a company's businesses as if each business were an independent going concern.

Summation operator A functional part of a neural network's node that multiplies each input value received by a weight and sums the weighted values to form the total net input, which is then passed to the activation function.

Supernormal growth Above-average or abnormally high growth rate in earnings per share.

Supervised learning A machine learning approach that makes use of labeled training data.

Support vector machine A linear classifier that determines the hyperplane that optimally separates the observations into two sets of data points.

Survivorship bias The exclusion of poorly performing or defunct companies from an index or database, biasing the index or database toward financially healthy companies.

Sustainable growth rate The rate of dividend (and earnings) growth that can be sustained over time for a given level of return on equity, keeping the capital structure constant and without issuing additional common stock.

Swap curve The term structure of swap rates.

Swap rate The fixed rate to be paid by the fixed-rate payer specified in a swap contract.

Swap rate curve The term structure of swap rates.

Swap spread The difference between the fixed rate on an interest rate swap and the rate on a Treasury note with equivalent maturity; it reflects the general level of credit risk in the market.

Synergies The combination of two companies being more valuable than the sum of the parts. Generally, synergies take the form of lower costs ("cost synergies") or increased revenues ("revenue synergies") through combinations that generate lower costs or higher revenues, respectively.

Systematic risk Risk that affects the entire market or economy; it cannot be avoided and is inherent in the overall market. Systematic risk is also known as non-diversifiable or market risk.

Systemic risk Refers to risks supervisory authorities believe are likely to have broad impact across the financial market infrastructure and affect a wide swath of market participants.

TED spread A measure of perceived credit risk determined as the difference between Libor and the T-bill yield of matching maturity.

Tail risk The risk that losses in extreme events could be greater than would be expected for a portfolio of assets with a normal distribution.

Takeover premium The amount by which the per-share takeover price exceeds the unaffected price expressed as a percentage of the unaffected price. It reflects the amount shareholders require to relinquish their control of the company to the acquirer.

Tangible assets Identifiable, physical assets such as property, plant, and equipment.

Tangible book value per share Common shareholders' equity minus intangible assets reported on the balance sheet, divided by the number of shares outstanding.

Target In machine learning, the dependent variable (*Y*) in a labeled dataset; the company in a merger or acquisition that is being acquired.

Target capital structure A company's chosen proportions of debt and equity.

Target payout ratio A strategic corporate goal representing the long-term proportion of earnings that the company intends to distribute to shareholders as dividends.

Taxable REIT subsidiaries Subsidiaries that pay income taxes on earnings from non-REIT-qualifying activities like merchant development or third-party property management.

Technical indicators Momentum indicators based on price.

Temporal method A variation of the monetary/non-monetary translation method that requires not only monetary assets and liabilities, but also non-monetary assets and liabilities that are measured at their current value on the balance sheet date to be translated at the current exchange rate. Assets and liabilities are translated at rates consistent with the timing of their measurement value. This method is typically used when the functional currency is other than the local currency.

Term frequency (TF) Ratio of the number of times a given token occurs in all the texts in the dataset to the total number of tokens in the dataset.

Term premium The additional return required by lenders to invest in a bond to maturity net of the expected return from continually reinvesting at the short-term rate over that same time horizon.

Terminal price multiples The price multiple for a stock assumed to hold at a stated future time.

Terminal share price The share price at a particular point in the future.

Terminal value of the stock The analyst's estimate of a stock's value at a particular point in the future. Also called *continuing value of the stock*.

Test sample A data sample that is used to test a model's ability to predict well on new data.

Theta The change in a derivative instrument for a given small change in calendar time, holding everything else constant. Specifically, the theta calculation assumes nothing changes except calendar time. Theta also reflects the rate at which an option's time value decays.

Time series A set of observations on a variable's outcomes in different time periods.

Tobin's q The ratio of the market value of debt and equity to the replacement cost of total assets.

Token The equivalent of a word (or sometimes a character).

Tokenization The process of representing ownership rights to physical assets on a blockchain or distributed ledger.

Top-down approach With respect to forecasting, an approach that usually begins at the level of the overall economy. Forecasts are then made at more narrowly defined levels, such as sector, industry, and market for a specific product.

Total factor productivity (TFP) A multiplicative scale factor that reflects the general level of productivity or technology in the economy. Changes in total factor productivity generate proportional changes in output for any input combination.

Total invested capital The sum of market value of common equity, book value of preferred equity, and face value of debt.

Tracking error The standard deviation of the differences between a portfolio's returns and its benchmark's returns; a synonym of *active risk*. Also called *tracking risk*.

Tracking risk The standard deviation of the differences between a portfolio's returns and its benchmarks returns. Also called *tracking error*.

Trailing dividend yield The reciprocal of current market price divided by the most recent annualized dividend.

Trailing P/E A stock's current market price divided by the most recent four quarters of EPS (or the most recent two semi-annual periods for companies that report interim data semi-annually). Also called *current P/E*.

Training sample A data sample that is used to train a model.

Tranche CDS A type of credit default swap that covers a combination of borrowers but only up to pre-specified levels of losses.

Transaction exposure The risk of a change in value between the transaction date and the settlement date of an asset of liability denominated in a foreign currency.

Treasury shares/stock Shares that were issued and subsequently repurchased by the company.

Trend A long-term pattern of movement in a particular direction.

Triangular arbitrage An arbitrage transaction involving three currencies that attempts to exploit inconsistencies among pairwise exchange rates.

Trimming Also called truncation, it is the process of removing extreme values and outliers from a dataset.

Triple-net leases Leases that require each tenant to pay its share of the following three operating expenses: common area maintenance and repair expenses; property taxes; and building insurance costs. Also known as *NNN leases*.

Two-tier board Board structure consisting of a supervisory board that oversees a management board.

Unbiased expectations theory A term structure theory that contends the forward rate is an unbiased predictor of the future spot rate. Also called the *pure expectations theory*.

Unconditional heteroskedasticity When heteroskedasticity of the error variance is not correlated with the regression's independent variables.

Uncovered interest rate parity The proposition that the expected return on an uncovered (i.e., unhedged) foreign currency (risk-free) investment should equal the return on a comparable domestic currency investment.

Underlying earnings Earnings excluding nonrecurring components. Also referred to as *continuing earnings*, *core earnings*, or *persistent earnings*.

Unexpected earnings The difference between reported EPS and expected EPS. Also referred to as an *earnings surprise*.

Unit root A time series that is not covariance stationary is said to have a unit root.

Unrestricted model A regression model with the complete set of independent variables.

Unsupervised learning A machine learning approach that does not make use of labeled training data.

Upfront payment The difference between the credit spread and the standard rate paid by the protection buyer if the standard rate is insufficient to compensate the protection seller. Also called *upfront premium*.

Upfront premium See *upfront payment*.

Upstream A transaction between two related companies, an investor company (or a parent company) and an associate company (or a subsidiary company) such that the associate company records a profit on its income statement. An example is a sale of inventory by the associate to the investor company or by a subsidiary to a parent company.

Validation sample A data sample that is used to validate and tune a model.

Valuation The process of determining the value of an asset or service either on the basis of variables perceived to be related to future investment returns or on the basis of comparisons with closely similar assets.

Value additivity An arbitrage opportunity when the value of the whole equals the sum of the values of the parts.

Value at risk (VaR) The minimum loss that would be expected a certain percentage of the time over a certain period of time given the assumed market conditions.

Value of growth The difference between the actual value per share and the no-growth value per share.

Variance error Describes how much a model's results change in response to new data from validation and test samples. Unstable models pick up noise and produce high variance error, causing overfitting and high out-of-sample error.

Variance inflation factor (VIF) A statistic that quantifies the degree of multicollinearity in a model.

Glossary

Vasicek model A partial equilibrium term structure model that assumes interest rates are mean reverting and interest rate volatility is constant.

Vega The change in a given derivative instrument for a given small change in volatility, holding everything else constant. A sensitivity measure for options that reflects the effect of volatility.

Venture capital investors Private equity investors in development-stage companies.

Vertical ownership Ownership structure in which a company or group that has a controlling interest in two or more holding companies, which in turn have controlling interests in various operating companies.

Vested benefit obligation The actuarial present value of vested benefits.

Vesting date The date that employees can first exercise stock options.

Visibility The extent to which a company's operations are predictable with substantial confidence.

Voting caps Legal restrictions on the voting rights of large share positions.

Web spidering (scraping or crawling) programs Programs that extract raw content from a source, typically web pages.

Weighted average cost of capital (WACC) A weighted average of the after-tax required rates of return on a company's common stock, preferred stock, and long-term debt, where the weights are the fraction of each source of financing in the company's target capital structure.

Weighted harmonic mean See *harmonic mean*.

Winsorization The process of replacing extreme values and outliers in a dataset with the maximum (for large value outliers) and minimum (for small value outliers) values of data points that are not outliers.

Write-down A reduction in the value of an asset as stated in the balance sheet.

Yield curve factor model A model or a description of yield curve movements that can be considered realistic when compared with historical data.

Zero A bond that does not pay a coupon but is priced at a discount and pays its full face value at maturity.

Zero-coupon bond A bond that does not pay interest during its life. It is issued at a discount to par value and redeemed at par. Also called *pure discount bond*.